Lecture Notes in Computer Science   16194

Founding Editors

Gerhard Goos
Juris Hartmanis

Editorial Board Members

Elisa Bertino, USA
Wen Gao, China

Bernhard Steffen, Germany
Moti Yung, USA

Formal Methods

Subline of Lecture Notes in Computer Science

Subline Series Editors

Ana Cavalcanti, *University of York, UK*

Marie-Claude Gaudel, *Université de Paris-Sud, France*

Subline Advisory Board

Manfred Broy, *TU Munich, Germany*

Annabelle McIver, *Macquarie University, Sydney, NSW, Australia*

Peter Müller, *ETH Zurich, Switzerland*

Erik de Vink, *Eindhoven University of Technology, The Netherlands*

Pamela Zave, *AT& T Laboratories Research, Bedminster, NJ, USA*

More information about this series at https://link.springer.com/bookseries/558

Ferruccio Damiani · Marie Farrell
Editors

Integrated Formal Methods

20th International Conference, iFM 2025
Paris, France, November 19–21, 2025
Proceedings

Editors
Ferruccio Damiani Ⓟ
Università degli Studi di Torino
Turin, Italy

Marie Farrell Ⓟ
The University of Manchester
Manchester, UK

ISSN 0302-9743   ISSN 1611-3349   (electronic)
Lecture Notes in Computer Science
ISBN 978-3-032-10793-0   ISBN 978-3-032-10794-7   (eBook)
https://doi.org/10.1007/978-3-032-10794-7

Preface

This volume contains the papers presented at the 20th International Conference on integrated Formal Methods (iFM 2025), held at Inria Paris Center, France, during November 17–21, 2025.

In recent decades, we have witnessed a proliferation of approaches that integrate several modelling, verification and simulation techniques, facilitating more versatile and efficient analysis of software-intensive systems. These approaches provide powerful support for the analysis of different functional and non-functional properties of the systems, complex interaction of components of different natures as well as validation of diverse aspects of system behaviour. The iFM conference series is a forum for discussing recent research advances in the development of integrated approaches to formal modelling and analysis. The conference covers all aspects of the design of integrated techniques, including language design, verification and validation, automated tool support and the use of such techniques in software engineering practice.

The iFM 2025 conference solicited high-quality papers reporting research results and/or experience reports related to the overall theme of formal methods integration. The conference interleaved various disciplines in formal methods, including deductive verification, model checking, reachability analysis, model-based testing, synthesis, timing and stochastic modelling, cyber-physical systems, autonomous systems, security and blockchain. There were two submission categories for iFM 2025:

1. Regular research papers presenting original scientific research results, tools, their foundation and evaluations, and applications of formal methods, including rigorous evaluations and case studies.
2. Short papers describing any work in the area of formal methods, including work-in-progress and preliminary results that are sufficiently interesting for the iFM community.

Regular research paper submissions were restricted to 16 pages, and short papers to 6 pages, excluding the bibliography and appendices. Two additional pages were granted for accepted papers, for revising and finalizing the camera-ready contributions included in these proceedings.

The Program Committee (PC) received a total of 69 paper submissions from authors in 29 different countries: 65 regular papers and 4 short papers. Each submission was rigorously reviewed by at least three PC members, who further relied on subreviewers. All submissions were reviewed using a single-blind reviewing process. Based on the review reports, the PC had a thorough discussion on each paper. As a result, the PC decided to accept 24 papers, out of which there were 23 regular research papers and 1 short paper. This corresponds to an overall acceptance rate of 34.8%. Each accepted paper at iFM 2025 had either all positive reviews or a "championing" PC member who argued in favor of accepting the paper.

To improve and reward reproducibility and to give more visibility and credit to the efforts of tool developers in our community, authors of accepted papers at iFM 2025 were invited to submit possible artifacts associated with their papers for evaluation. An artifact might consist of a tool, models, proofs or other data required for validation of the results of the paper. Artifact submission was voluntary at iFM 2025 and the result of the artifact evaluation did not alter the respective paper's acceptance decision.

The Artifact Evaluation Committee (AEC) was tasked with reviewing the submitted artifacts, based on their availability, ease of use and, most importantly, whether the results presented in the corresponding paper could be accurately reproduced. In total, artifacts of 15 accepted papers at iFM 2025 were submitted to artifact evaluation and each submission successfully passed artifact evaluation. In addition to an availability badge, each of the 15 artifacts received either a functional or a (functional and) reusable badge. As a result, at iFM 2025 we awarded 30 artifact badges, using the EAPLS artifact badging. Papers with artifacts that were successfully evaluated by the AEC include the awarded badges on their first page in these proceedings.

We were proud to award the **Distinguished Reviewer Award** to Timothy Bourke (Inria) for their very careful analysis of papers and proactive investment in the reviewing and selection process.

The PC also shortlisted three papers as **candidates for the Best Paper Award**. These papers are (in no specific order):

- "When Separation Arithmetic Is Enough", co-authored by Jean-Christophe Filliatre, Andrei Paskevich and Olivier Danvy.
- "Quick Theory Exploration for Algebraic Data Types via Program Transformations", co-authored by Gidon Ernst and Grigory Fedyukovich.
- "Security of the Lightning Network: Model Checking a Stepwise Refinement with TLA+", co-authored by Matthias Grundmann and Hannes Hartenstein.

The decision on the iFM 2025 best paper award was taken during the iFM 2025 conference, by taking into account also the presentation of the paper at the conference.

The iFM 2025 conference featured **keynotes** by

- **Paula Herber**: "Integrated Formal Methods for the Verification of Cyber-Physical and Autonomous Systems",
- **Marieke Huismann**: "Bug-Free Software: A Realisable Dream? (and How VerCors Will Help…)", and
- **Stephan Merz**: "The TLA$^+$ Framework: From High-Level Specifications to Distributed Programs".

iFM 2025 also hosted the iFM Doctoral Symposium 2025, providing PhD students with a forum to present early results and to receive constructive feedback and mentoring. Further, the International Workshop on Formal Methods for Autonomous Systems was organized as an affiliated event of iFM 2025.

We would like to thank everyone who helped to make iFM 2025 successful. A huge thanks goes to our

- **authors** for submitting or presenting their work at iFM 2025,
- **invited speakers** who kindly agreed to give keynote talks during the conference,

- **PC members** and **additional reviewers** for providing detailed reports on papers they reviewed and actively engaging in the PC discussions,
- **artifact evaluation committee chairs Roberto Casadei** (Università di Bologna, Italy) and **Daniela Kaufmann** (TU Wien, Austria),
- **AEC members** for their timely reviews during artifact evaluation,
- **steering committee** and, in particular, former PC chairs for valuable advice,
- **PhD Symposium Chairs Wolfgang Ahrendt** (Chalmers University of Technology, Sweden) and **Rosemary Monahan** (Maynooth University, Ireland), as well as all members of the **PhD Symposium Program Committee**,
- **Publicity Chair Giorgio Audrito** (Università degli Studi di Torino, Italy),
- **student volunteers** for their assistance throughout the conference, and
- last but not least: special thanks to our **General Chair Caterina Urban** (Inria & ENS — PSL, France) for her valiant effort to make iFM 2025 a wonderful event in Paris.

We acknowledge the financial support provided by Springer, Inria and École Normale Supérieure. We are grateful for the institutional support iFM 2025 received from The University of Manchester, Università degli Studi di Torino, Università di Bologna and TU Wien. We are also grateful for the invaluable support provided by the EasyChair developers.

November 2025

Ferruccio Damiani
Marie Farrell

Organization

Program Committee Chairs

Ferruccio Damiani · Università degli Studi di Torino, Italy
Marie Farrell · The University of Manchester, UK

Program Committee

Wolfgang Ahrendt · Chalmers University of Technology, Sweden
Timothy Bourke · Inria Paris & ENS — Université PSL, France
Giovanna Broccia · ISTI-CNR, Italy
Carlos E. Budde · Technical University of Denmark, Denmark
Ivana Černá · Masaryk University, Czech Republic
Alessandro Cimatti · Fondazione Bruno Kessler, Italy
John Derrick · University of Sheffield, UK
Jyotirmoy V. Deshmukh · University of Southern California, USA
Brijesh Dongol · University of Surrey, UK
Claire Dross · AdaCore, France
Jérôme Feret · Inria Paris & ENS — Université PSL, France
Simon Foster · University of York, UK
Carlo A. Furia · Università della Svizzera Italiana, Switzerland
Klaus Havelund · Jet Propulsion Laboratory, California Institute of Technology, USA
Paula Herber · University of Münster, Germany
Heber Herencia-Zapana · Collins Aerospace, USA
Marieke Huisman · University of Twente, Netherlands
Inigo Incer · University of Michigan, USA
Fuyuki Ishikawa · National Institute of Informatics, Japan
Xiaoqing Jin · Apple, USA
Einar Broch Johnsen · University of Oslo, Norway
Sebastian Junges · Radboud University, Netherlands
Joseph Kiniry · Galois Inc., USA
Nikolai Kosmatov · Thales Research & Technology, France
Thierry Lecomte · ClearSy, France
Michael Leuschel · University of Düsseldorf, Germany
Edoardo Manino · The University of Manchester, UK
Anastasia Mavridou · KBR, Inc./NASA Ames Research Center, USA

Dominique Méry	Université de Lorraine, France
Stephan Merz	Inria Nancy, France
Rosemary Monahan	Maynooth University, Ireland
Mariano Moscato	AMA, Inc./NASA Langley Research Center, USA
Mohammad Reza Mousavi	King's College London, UK
Luca Paolini	Università degli Studi di Torino, Italy
Violet Ka I Pun	Western Norway University of Applied Sciences, Norway
Juliane Päßler	University of Oslo, Norway
Luciana Rebelo	Gran Sasso Science Institute, Italy
Giles Reger	Amazon Web Services and The University of Manchester, UK
Peter Riviere	Japan Advanced Institute of Science and Technology, Japan
David Šafránek	Masaryk University, Czech Republic
Gerhard Schellhorn	Universität Augsburg, Germany
Silvia Lizeth Tapia Tarifa	University of Oslo, Norway
Maurice H. ter Beek	ISTI-CNR, Italy
Mattias Ulbrich	Karlsruhe Institute of Technology, Germany
Petra van den Bos	University of Twente, Netherlands
Heike Wehrheim	University of Oldenburg, Germany
Anton Wijs	Eindhoven University of Technology, Netherlands
Burkhart Wolff	Université Paris-Saclay, France
Naijun Zhan	Peking University, China

Artifact Evaluation Committee Chairs

Roberto Casadei	Università di Bologna, Italy
Daniela Kaufmann	TU Wien, Austria

Artifact Evaluation Committee

Gianluca Aguzzi	Università di Bologna, Italy
Lorenzo Bacchiani	Università di Bologna, Italy
Chen Chen	Hong Kong University of Science and Technology (Guangzhou), China
Leyi Cui	Columbia University, USA
Oyendrila Dobe	Amazon Web Services, USA
Sona Ghahremani	Hasso Plattner Institute, Germany
Yuanjun Gong	University of Trento, Italy

Thomas Hader	TU Wien, Austria
Marton Hajdu	TU Wien, Austria
Clemens Hofstadler	Johannes Kepler University Linz, Austria
Guangyu Hu	Hong Kong University of Science and Technology, China
Ondrej Huvar	Masaryk University, Czech Republic
Åsmund Kløvstad	University of Oslo, Norway
Yonghui Liu	Monash University, Australia
Ondrej Kuzlik	Masaryk University, Czech Republic
Nils Lommen	RWTH Aachen University, Germany
Karthik Nukala	SRI International, USA
Lukas Panneke	Carl von Ossietzky University Oldenburg, Germany
Sara Pettinari	Gran Sasso Science Institute, Italy
Neea Rusch	Augusta University, USA
Pedro Saccomani	Universidade Federal de Minas Gerais, Brazil
Giordano Scarso	Università di Torino, Italy
Florian Sextl	TU Wien, Austria
Arijit Shaw	Chennai Mathematical Institute, India
Riccardo Sieve	University of Oslo, Norway
Amrita Suresh	University of Oxford, UK
Mark van Wijk	University of Twente, Netherlands

Additional Reviewers

Jie An
Giorgio Audrito
Alessio Baldazzi
Franco Barbanera
Christopher Brix
Ugo de' Liguoro
Jana Dražanová
Martin Fabian
Shenghua Feng
David Geleßus
Eduard Kamburjan
Ekkart Kindler
Michael Kirsten
Jonas Klamroth
Peter Lammich
Caroline Lemke
Delphine Longuet
Guy McCusker

Robert Mensing
Andrzej Murawski
Jan Obdrzalek
Andrea Pferscher
Jessica Piccioni
José Proença
Jose Ignacio Requeno
Cedric Richter
Lorenzo Rossi
Jonas Schiffl
Nicolas Schnepf
Nicola Thoben
Franck Vedrine
Fabian Vu
Hao Wu
Hengjun Zhao
Margherita Zorzi

Invited Talks

Integrated Formal Methods for the Verification of Cyber-Physical and Autonomous Systems

Paula Herber

University of Münster, Germany

Cyber-physical systems pose significant challenges for formal methods, due to their inherent heterogeneity and interaction with a physical environment. In addition, we see a tremendous increase in the use of learning to make autonomous decisions in dynamic environments, and an increasing demand to cope with uncertainties and unforeseen events. These developments call for the development of new theories and tools, but also for the integration of existing formal methods. In this talk, I will summarize some of our recent efforts towards developing methods for the integration of formal methods to support reusable specification and scalable verification of cyber-physical and autonomous systems.

Bug-free Software: A Realisable Dream? (and How VerCors Will Help...)

Marieke Huisman

University of Twente, Netherlands

Software is everywhere, and (almost) everything we do relies on software. But can we actually rely on software? Software bugs are just as old as software, and frequently cause major disruptions, such as the recent CrowdStrike's outage due to a software update.

I will argue that it should be possible to improve this situation by developing program verification tools that can be used efficiently to provide guarantees about programs in different programming languages, and for a wide range of properties. I will outline how we work towards this dream with the VerCors team. In particular, I will discuss some of the recent developments around VerCors, and I will sketch the ideas I have for the future development of VerCors.

The TLA$^+$ Framework: From High-Level Specifications to Distributed Programs

Stephan Merz

University of Lorraine, CNRS, Inria, LORIA, Nancy, France

TLA$^+$ [4] is a formalism for precisely describing algorithms. It combines a language of mathematical set theory for describing the data on which an algorithm operates with a temporal logic for expressing the behavior of the algorithm as a state machine, augmented by fairness and liveness assumptions. The formal verification of properties, including the refinement of an algorithm by another TLA+ specification written at a lower level of abstraction, is supported by model checkers [3, 5] as well as a proof assistant [2]. Recent work has explored how a distributed program can be validated against the TLA$^+$ specification of the algorithm the program is supposed to implement by collecting traces of program executions and then checking if these traces are allowed by the specification [1]. This presentation will give an overview of the TLA+ framework, highlighting the complementary use of the different verification techniques for increasing the confidence one may have in the correctness of a system.

References

1. Cirstea, H., Kuppe, M.A., Loillier, B., Merz, S.: Validating traces of distributed programs against TLA$^+$ specifications. In: Madeira, A., Knapp, A. (eds.) Software Engineering and Formal Methods. SEFM 2024. LNCS, vol. 15280, pp. 126–143. Springer, Cham (2024). https://doi.org/10.1007/978-3-031-77382-2_8
2. Cousineau, D., Doligez, D., Lamport, L., Merz, S., Ricketts, D., Vanzetto, H.: TLA$^+$ proofs. In: Giannakopoulou, D., Méry, D. (eds.) FM 2012: Formal Methods. LNCS, vol. 7436, pp. 147–154. Springer, Heidelberg (2012). https://doi.org/10.1007/978-3-642-32759-9_14
3. Konnov, I., Kukovec, J., Tran, T.H.: TLA$^+$ model checking made symbolic. In: Proceedings of the ACM Programming Languages, vol. 3 (OOPSLA) (2019)
4. Lamport, L.: Specifying Systems. Addison-Wesley, Boston (2002)
5. Yu, Y., Manolios, P., Lamport, L.: Model checking TLA$^+$ specifications. In: Pierre, L., Kropf, T. (eds.) Correct Hardware Design and Verification Methods. CHARME 1999. LNCS, vol. 1703, pp. 54–66. Springer, Heidelberg (1999). https://doi.org/10.1007/3-540-48153-2_6

Contents

Model-Based Testing and Synthesis

Timing and Stochastic Modelling

Deductive Verification

Unfolding Iterators: Specification and Verification of Higher-Order Iterators in OCaml

Ion Chirica[(✉)] and Mário Pereira

NOVA LINCS, Nova School of Science and Technology, Lisbon, Portugal
`i.chirica@campus.fct.unl.pt`

Abstract. Albeit being a central notion of every programming language, formally and modularly reasoning about iteration proves itself to be a non-trivial feat, especially in the context of higher-order iteration. In this paper, we present a generic approach to the specification and deductive verification of higher-order iterators, written in the OCaml language. Our methodology is established on the basis of two building blocks: first, the usage of the Gospel specification language to describe the general behaviour of any iteration schema; second, the usage of the Cameleer framework to deductively verify that every iteration client is correct with respect to its logical specification. To validate our approach we develop a set of verified case studies, ranging from classic list iterators to graph algorithms implemented in the widely used OCamlGraph library.

1 Introduction

Iteration plays a crucial role in every programming language. It comes in various shapes, be it through loops, recursive functions or even higher-order iterators. The usage of an iteration process is normally associated with the need to repeat a computation, *e.g.*, process every element in a data structure. Nonetheless, despite our extensive experience with the use of iteration, implementing and ensuring that an iterative algorithm is exempt from errors remains a non-trivial task.

Testing is a very popular approach to analyze a given program. It is a simple and fast methodology that can be easily incorporated into traditional development cycles. However, tests are rarely exhaustive and for that reason, their correctness guarantees are as limited as their coverage. If we wish to give the highest assurance of program correctness, we quickly turn to formal methods [19]. This field uses mathematical principles to reason about program correctness. In particular, we focus on *deductive software verification* [12], which translates correctness properties into logical implications to be proven by a computer. This technique is also known as *formal software proving.*

In this work we tackle the problem of formally verifying programs that employ higher-order iterators. The iteration patterns defined within the class of higher-

F. Damiani and M. Farrell (Eds.): iFM 2025, LNCS 16194, pp. 3–22, 2026.
https://doi.org/10.1007/978-3-032-10794-7_1

order iterators are common and well established that we believe a *generic* specification should be able to formally capture its behaviour. Our purpose is to establish a *quasi*-automatic verification methodology, in a way that we avoid the cumbersome effort of conducting such reasoning in a proof assistant. The programs of interest are written in OCaml, a language of the ML family, where iteration is naturally expressed using higher-order functions. While OCaml allows combining a functional programming style with imperative mechanisms, notably memory updates, this turns out to be a challenge for deductive verification tools. To address these challenges, we present (1) a generic way to specify high-order iterators where we capture, in first-order logic, essential patterns that any iterator should adopt; (2) a proof methodology based on translating a higher-order iterator into an equivalent program in first-order, using the notion of cursor, *i.e.*, a step-by-step iterator. Our approach is implemented as a set of extensions to the specification language Gospel [6] and Cameleer [21], a deductive verification tool for OCaml programs. All the examples are available in an online artifact [7]. In this paper, we adopt a literate programming style of listing presentation. Readers can ignore the surrounding text and consider reassembling the excerpt presented.

Structure of the Paper. Sections 2 and 3 overview the background on reasoning about iteration and the tools used; Sect. 4 sets forth the running example used throughout the paper; Sect. 5 demonstrates how generic cursors can be used in WhyML, both in logic and regular code; Sects. 6 to 8 showcase our methodology for specifying higher-order iterators, how they are translated in WhyML and how they cope with mutability; Sect. 9 materializes our work with case studies: higher-order iterations over sequences, trees and graphs; Sects. 10 and 11 wrap up with related work and avenues for future work.

2   Reasoning About Iteration

The effort to formally reason about iteration is not novel, having been explored through loop invariants [17] and verification condition generation [11]. More recently, Filliâtre and Pereira [16] proposed a modular approach using two predicates per iterator: `permitted` (for values produced during iteration) and `completed` (for termination), and a ghost sequence of visited elements [13]. Exemplifying, when iterating over a sequence s, the `permitted` predicate ensures that any sequence of visited elements v must be a valid prefix of s, formally:

$$\texttt{permitted}(v, s) \triangleq ||v|| \leqslant ||s|| \land \forall i.0 \leqslant i \leqslant ||v|| \implies v[i] = s[i]$$

On the other hand, the `complete` predicate simply states that the iteration is finished when the length of the visited sequence v equals the length ($|| \cdot ||$) of s, formally captured with:

$$\texttt{complete}(v, s) \triangleq ||v|| = ||s||$$

Based on these two predicates, we are able to capture any kind of iteration, be it over a collection or enumeration of results of an algorithm, be it finite and deterministic or infinite and non-deterministic [16].

3   Specification and Verification of OCaml Programs

Gospel (Generic OCaml Specification Language) is a behavioural specification language for OCaml interfaces [6]. It is a contract-based, strongly typed language with formal semantics defined in terms of a translation into Separation Logic [23]. The main goal of Gospel is to provide a concise and accessible specification language for OCaml interfaces, which can be used for various purposes. However, there is a strong emphasis on verification, using tools that translate Gospel-annotated OCaml into languages understandable by automated theorem provers. Gospel specifications are added as comments beginning with @, (*@ ... *), at the end of the function definition.

Conversely, Cameleer is a tool for deductive verification of OCaml programs, conceived with proof automation in mind [21]. This tool takes Gospel, additionally supporting implementation specifications, annotated OCaml code and translates it to an equivalent WhyML [14] program, which can be verified using automated provers like CVC5, Alt-Ergo, or Z3, or interactive ones such as Rocq and Isabelle.

4   Motivating Example

To motivate our approach and tool choices, we consider summing a finite, deterministic sequence of integers using two classic patterns: recursion and loops. Later, we revisit this example using cursors and higher-order iterators.

From a recursive perspective, the function sums elements from upper to lower, using get to access elements (whose complexity we ignore in the context of this example). Termination is ensured by making upper the decreasing argument and bounding both lower and upper within s. We ensure that the result matches the mathematical sum over that range. This is implemented in OCaml and specified in Gospel, as follows:

```
let rec sum_recursive s lower upper =                    Gospel + OCaml
  if upper ≤ lower then 0
  else (get s (upper - 1)) + sum_recursive s lower (upper - 1)
(*@ r = sum_recursive s lower upper
    variant upper
    requires 0 ≤ lower ≤ upper ≤ ||s||
    ensures r = ∑_{i=lower}^{upper} s[i]*)
```

Using a loop, this can be solved by introducing two mutable variables, index to get the *n-th* element of a sequence, and acc the accumulator of the sum. In this loop, we iterate over the length of s and successively add its elements:

```
let sum_loop s =                                                OCaml
  let index = ref 0 and acc = ref 0 in
  while !index < (length s) do
```

The loop specification first states that the termination measure is given by a decrease in the to-be visited elements, followed by the invariant: `index` is contained within the limits of the sequence and the contents of `acc` holds the current sum of the elements on `s`, up until `!index`. Formally expressed as follows:

```
(*@ variant ||s|| - !index                                  Gospel + OCaml
      invariant 0 ≤ !index ≤ ||s|| ∧ !acc = ∑ᵢ₌₀^!index s[i] *)
  acc := !acc + (get s !index);
  index := !index + 1;
done;
!acc
```

Finally, the specification of `sum_loop` is given by the post-condition that the result, `r`, of calling this function equals the logical definition of a sum:

```
(*@ r = sum_loop s                                          Gospel + OCaml
      ensures r = ∑ᵢ₌₀^||s|| s[i]*)
```

The specification we present here is a very high-level one, however, there is a definition within Gospel's Standard Library for the summation operator. When fed to Cameleer, the above specifications and OCaml implementations, will be translated into a WhyML program for which Why3 generates a total of 9 Verification Conditions (VCs): 4 for the recursive definition and 5 for the loop based one, all of them quickly dispatched by the Alt-Ergo SMT solver.

5   Revisiting Modular Specification for First Order Iteration

In this section we present a refinement of the existing WhyML cursor specification. This refinement is a key part of our translation schemas (c.f. Sect. 7), where we resort to Why3's module system to achieve a generic specification for cursors.

Cursors are defined using two functions, `has_next()` and `next()`, testing whether the iteration has completed, and returning the next element in the iteration, respectively. Building on the ideas of Filliâtre and Pereira [16], we propose an extension to their cursors in WhyML. This extension embeds the predicates `permitted` and `complete` within the type of a `cursor` and resorts to type invariants to provide stronger specification to this type, as follows:

```
type cursor α = abstract {                                        WhyML
  mutable visited   : seq α;
          permitted : seq α → bool;
          complete  : seq α → bool;
} invariant { permitted visited }
```

The sequence of visited elements, the first field, holds the sequence of polymorphic elements `visited`, and the other two are predicates, parameterized with a polymorphic sequence of elements. By embedding these predicates within the `cursor` type, we generalize the iteration to any collection. Additionally, this allows us to decorate this type definition with a type invariant, stating that: at any point before a function call, possibly invalidated in between, but fully restored by the function's exit, the sequence of visited elements is `permitted`. This type is `abstract`, that is, its fields are visible in the specification while being opaque in the implementation.

This refinement of a cursor and the functions `next` and `has_next` are fully generic, irrespective of which iteration we desire to express. Notwithstanding, we lack a function that creates a cursor, `create`. Fundamentally, this function differs from cursor to cursor, and thus unable to be generic. For that reason, the definition of this function is delegated to the cursor client, allowing for iterations over diverse data structures or the specification of custom iteration patterns.

Coming back to our recurring theme of iterations over sequences, we can finish the definition of such a cursor by instantiating its fields, like so:

```
val create (s: seq α) : (c : cursor α)                          WhyML
  ensures { result.visited   = empty }
  ensures { result.permitted = (fun v → ||v|| ⩽ ||s|| ∧
                                 ∀ i. 0 ⩽ i < ||v|| → v[i] = s[i]) }
  ensures { result.complete  = (fun v → ||v|| = ||s||) }
```

The first post-condition is natural, at creation we ensure a cursor with an empty sequence of visited elements. Afterwards, we give body to the predicates `permitted`, with the definition of v being a prefix of the collection to be iterated, and the `complete` given by the comparison of both lengths. The direct conclusion is that by instantiating the predicate pair at the cursor creation, we claim the same result as the work of Filliâtre and Pereira [16].

Having defined a cursor over sequences, let us now present how a client uses this construct to sum all the elements of a sequence of integers:

```
let sum_cursor (s: int seq) : int                               WhyML
Ⓐ    ensures { result = sum (fun i → s[i]) 0 (length s) } =
  let acc = ref 0 in
  let c = create s in
Ⓑ  while has_next c do
     variant { ||s|| - ||c.visited|| }
Ⓒ    invariant { !acc = sum (fun i → c.visited[i]) 0 ||c.visited|| }
Ⓓ    let x = next c in
   acc := !acc + x;
  done;
  !acc
```

Its specification can be understood in the following way: in Ⓐ we ensure that the result is equal to the mathematical sum[1] of all the elements of s; from

---

[1] The function `sum f l u`, defined as the sum $\sum_{i=l}^{u} f(i)$, is included in the Why3 Standard Library. https://www.why3.org/stdlib/int.html.

Ⓑ to Ⓒ we find the test of termination, the loop variant and invariant, given by the accumulator being the sum of all the visited elements; finally, in Ⓓ we produce an element, x, and the subsequently update to the accumulator with the sum of acc and x.

By calling Why3 on sum_cursor and the presented specification, we end up with 6 VCs, three of them concerned with the loop invariants, two with the preconditions of the next and has_next and the last with the post-condition of sum_cursor. All are fully dispatched by Alt-Ergo.

6   Higher-Order Iteration Specification

Computing the sum of all elements in a sequence naturally aligns with a well-known higher-order iteration pattern: a so called fold function. This is ubiquitous in mainstream languages such as OCaml, Haskell, or Scala. In this section, we formalize such a computation by considering a parameterized OCaml module, Sequences, which captures the essence of this higher-order abstraction.

This module is parameterized by another module S, which specifies a polymorphic sequence type seq[2] and two higher-order functions: fold and iter. The function fold takes three arguments: a binary function of type $\alpha \to \beta \to \alpha$, an initial accumulator value of type α, and a sequence of type β seq, producing a value of type α. It also provides a iter function, which applies a function of type $\alpha \to$ unit to each element of a given sequence, solely for its side effects.

In the Sequences module, we define sum_fold, which computes the sum of a sequence using fold, with the binary operator (+) as the consumer function and initial value 0. We also define stack_of_seq, which builds a stack from a sequence using iter, where the consumer function pushes elements onto the stack in-place. The definition of iter and implementation of stack_of_seq are specified in Sect. 8 where we highlight how to cope with mutability.

```ocaml
module Sequences (S : sig                                      OCaml
    type α seq
    val fold : (α → β → α) → α → β seq → α
    val iter : (α → unit) → α seq → unit (* Refer to Section 8 *)
  end) = struct
    let sum_fold (s : int S.seq) = S.fold (fun acc x → acc + x) 0 s

    let stack_of_seq (s: int S.seq) = (* Refer to Section 8 *)
      let stack = Stack.create () in
      S.iter (fun x → Stack.push x stack) s; stack
  end
```

In the previous section, we presented a generic approach to iteration through the use of cursors, focusing exclusively on the definition of the create function. We observe that iteration is a two-fold task: first, abstracting what it means to

---

[2] This type denotes a sequence: an ordered collection of elements where repetitions are permitted, *e.g.*, lists or arrays. It should not be mistaken with OCaml's Seq.seq type.

iterate over an arbitrary collection; and second, defining the concrete semantics of the iteration process itself. The former is captured by an OCaml interface, the module S, via the definition of the `fold` function, while the latter is tied to the implementation, here the `Sequences` module, specifically when `fold` is called.

In the remaining of this section, we demonstrate how such constructs can be formally specified using Gospel. We then present our extensions to the language, together with their translation into WhyML via Cameleer. Our focus lies in providing specification support for the most commonly used iteration patterns, namely `iter`, `fold`, `filter`, and `map`. Furthermore, we argue that supporting `fold` alone would be theoretically sufficient, as the remaining patterns can be viewed as degenerate forms of the fold abstraction.

6.1   Interface Specification

Considering the previous example, let us now show how to define an iteration over a sequence in Gospel, using `permitted` and `complete` as new keywords. A function specification begins by introducing arbitrary, user-chosen names for the result `r` and the arguments `func`, `acc`, and `col`:

```
val fold: (α → β → α) → α → β seq → α          Gospel + OCaml
(*@ r = fold func acc col
```

Our extensions to the language begin by specifying which iteration pattern we wish to define, and dealing with a fold, we indicate this using the new keyword:

```
folds                                          Extended Gospel
```

After that, we instantiate the predicates `permitted` and `complete`, both of which take the sequence of visited elements as an argument. To refer to the collection being iterated over within these predicates, one utilizes the keyword `collection`:

```
~permitted:(fun v → ||v|| ≤ ||collection|| ∧          Extended Gospel
            ∀ i. 0 ≤ i < ||v|| → v[i] = (collection)[i])
~complete:(fun v → ||v|| = ||collection||)
```

At this point, we have to be explicit about some typing information: the type of the structure we are iterating over, `structure`, the type of elements that the cursor produces, `elt`, and as auxiliary information, what is the name of the accumulator in the header of the specification: *Extended Gospel*

```
with structure = (β seq), elt = β, accumulator = acc *)
```

The reader may have noticed that, although an argument of `fold`, we make no mention of the consumer function, `func`. Part of turning a higher-order iterator into a first-order cursor client is to delay, acknowledging, its existence until it has been instantiated. In fact, our specification of `fold` abstracts away three fundamental aspects of the consumer function: (1) the only side-effects performed by the higher-order iteration are those of the consumer function; (2) the only exceptions, potentially, raised by the higher-order iteration are those raised by the consumer function; (3) we state the consumer function re-establishes the user-supplied invariant, step-by-step, for each new enumerated element.

6.2   Implementation Specification

Having defined a generic cursor interface, we now specify its behaviour. This is possible only through `fold` in the implementation. Recall the function `sum_fold`:

```
let sum_fold (s: S.seq) = S.fold (fun a x → a + x) 0 s          OCaml
```

This function employs the higher-order iterator `fold`, whose implementation remains opaque to the user. While they cannot see how the iteration proceeds, they expect the consumer function to be applied to every element of `s`, starting with the accumulator 0. By hiding the iteration details in logic, we require only that the user specifies the essentials. The user starts by first stating the expected iteration pattern; since we are dealing with a fold, we begin with the keyword:

```
(*@ folds                                    Extended Gospel
```

Next, and in no particular order, they indicate the collection being iterated over:

```
    ~collection:s                            Extended Gospel
```

The termination measure, in the case of finite and deterministic enumerations, follows a pattern: the number of to-be-visited elements converging to zero:

```
    ~convergence:(fun c v → ||c|| - ||v||)           Extended Gospel
```

And lastly, the iteration invariant:

```
    ~inv:(fun a v → a = sum (fun i → v[i]) 0 ||v||) *)   Extended Gospel
```

This new syntax may have introduced a lot of new ideas at once. Let us make them clear. As we have also seen in the interface, we have to identify what iteration pattern we wish to express, through the keyword `folds`, which establishes what first-order client schema to generate during translation. All the other parametric fields are Gospel logical terms. Note how the parameter `convergence` takes two arguments, the collection that is being iterated and the sequence of visited elements. The `inv`, in the case of a fold, which introduced the notion of an accumulator, is also parameterized with two arguments, the current value of the accumulator and the sequence of visited elements.

7   Translation-Based Approach to Iteration Verification

In this section we present our extensions to Cameleer through translation schemas. Though we implemented four schemas, one for each iteration pattern, for presentation purposes, we only focus on `fold`. Once again, we argue that the other patterns (`iter`, `filter`, and `map`) are degenerate cases of `fold`. Specifically, `iter` corresponds to a `fold` where the accumulator has type `unit`, and `map` can be expressed as a `fold` that builds a new collection by applying a function to each element and adding the result. Likewise, `filter` can be implemented as a `fold` that adds elements to the new collection only if they satisfy a predicate.

7.1 Translating Iteration Declarations

The first translation schema is concerned with a higher-order function declaration. These declarations can be found in OCaml interface files or as arguments of a functor. The general specification form for a fold is the following:

```
val fold: (α → β → α) → α → β t → α        Extended Gospel + OCaml
(*@ r = fold func acc col
    folds ~permitted:(fun v → term_p) ~complete:(fun v → term_c)
    with structure = τ_s, elt = τ_e, accumulator = acc *)
```

As we have seen, `permitted` and `complete` are defined using Gospel logical terms. The types `structure` and `elt` are also part of the specification, and the `accumulator` is identified by its name in the header.

We can translate such a specification into creating a cursor. In Cameleer, this replaces the original function declaration with a `scope`, *i.e.*, a WhyML namespace [15]. The translation schema follows the general shape:

```
scope Fold                                                    WhyML
  use seq.Seq
  clone export cursor.CursorLib
  val create (collection: τ_s) : cursor τ_e
    ensures { result.visited = empty }
    ensures { result.permitted = (fun v → term_p) }
    ensures { result.complete  = (fun v → term_c) }
end
```

In the scope, we clone the `CursorLib` module, containing the developments from Sect. 5. It exposes the generics of a cursor, and defines the `create` function by extracting and translating the types, τ_s and τ_e, and terms, $term_p$ and $term_c$.

7.2 Translating an Iteration Client

When it comes to iteration clients, we extend Cameleer to translate the specification below into a first-order iteration using a cursor:

```
fold (fun a e → ...) col x0                          Extended Gospel + OCaml
(*@ folds ~inv: (fun a v → term_i) ~collection: term_c'
    ~convergence: (fun c v → term_v) *)
```

Our translation schema starts by initializing the accumulator, `acc`, with the value of x_0. We then follow by creating a cursor over the collection $term_{c'}$:

```
let acc = ref x0 in                                          WhyML
let cursor = Fold.create term_c' in
```

Here we find the while-loop, conditioned by the `has_next` function. Note that if this loop ends, then when it does, the predicate `complete` holds:

```
while Fold.has_next cursor do                                    WhyML
```

The variant of the loop is $term_v$, where we apply $term_{c'}$, the collection that is being iterated, and the sequence of visited elements. On the other hand, the invariant is $term_i$, where we apply the accumulator and the visited sequence:

```
variant { (fun c v → term_v) term_c' cursor.visited }          WhyML
invariant { (fun a v → term_i) !acc cursor.visited }
```

We produce the next element in the iteration and store it in x, followed by the application of the consumer function to the accumulator and x:

```
let x = Fold.next cursor in                                      WhyML
acc := (fun a e → ...) !acc x;
done;
```

Alas, we return the contents of the `accumulator`:

```
!acc                                                             WhyML
```

This concludes our translation schema, which makes higher-order specifications amenable to automated verification by translating them into a first-order form.

8   Coping with Mutability

We have promised that our methodology is also capable of capturing iterations where the consumer function performs side-effects, *e.g.*, writing to a reference. Let us present an example of a function that produces a stack from a sequence. This function employs the `iter` higher-order iterator to traverse a sequence and systematically push elements to the stack, modifying the stack in-place. Recalling the `iter` function, we decorate it with a specification in the following way:

```
val iter: (α → unit) → α seq → unit            Extended Gospel + OCaml
(*@ r = iter func col
  iters ~permitted:(fun v → ||v|| ≤ ||collection|| ∧
                   ∀ i. 0 ≤ i < ||v|| → v[i] = (collection)[i])
        ~complete:(fun v → ||v|| = ||collection||)
  with structure = (α seq), elt = α *)
```

This specification is very similar to that of `fold`, with the primary differences being the use of the `iters` keyword and the absence of an explicit accumulator. This is expected, as both iterators operate over the same data structure and in the same direction, resulting in identical definitions for `permitted` and `complete`.

Consider the `stack_of_seq` function: it begins by creating an empty stack, modeled logically as a list, and then uses `iter` to traverse the sequence s, pushing each element onto the stack. Once iteration completes, the stack is returned.

```
let stack_of_seq s =                                    Extended Gospel + OCaml
   let stack = Stack.create () in
   S.iter (fun x → Stack.push x stack) s
   (*@ iters ~inv:(fun v → reverse stack = s[..||v||])
       ~collection:s ~convergence:(fun c v → ||c|| - ||v||) *); stack
 (*@ r = stack_of_seq s
     ensures reverse r = s *)
```

The invariant states that the reverse of the stack, reflecting insertion order, equals the visited prefix, s[..i] is the prefix of s until i. The variant is the decreasing number of elements left to visit. The postcondition follows from termination: once has_next returns false, it ensures that complete holds. By the invariant, the accumulator then contains the full reverse of s. Despite the side effects, after applying our translation, Alt-Ergo discharges the VCs in roughly 3 s.

9   Case Study: OCamlGraph

In this section, we present our main case study, proving the correctness of modules taken from OCamlGraph, a generic library with a wide range of graph structures and algorithms [8]. Widely used across OPAM packages, it relies on higher-order iterators, making it a suitable candidate to validate our methodology. A particular module within OCamlGraph we aim to prove correct is the module Oper[3]. This module provides common operations such as the intersection and union of two graphs, and the complement and mirror of a graph.

9.1   Logical Model of a Graph

The mathematical definition of a graph is through sets, and for our purposes these will be finite. It is modeled using a domain, the set of vertices that make up a graph, and a function that takes a vertex and returns a set of vertices, these will be the successors of a vertex. In other words, the set of edges in the graph.

The module Oper takes as an argument another module, G, that represents our graph. The module Oper starts by defining the type of a vertex and a graph:

```
module Oper (G : sig                                           OCaml
   type vt (* arbitrary vertex type *)
   type gt (* arbitrary graph type *)
```

The type graph is annotated with a logical model. It is made up of a domain dom and the map suc. Additionally, we give this type an invariant stating that the graph's domain is closed under the map suc, and for every element that is not in the domain, its set of successors is empty.

---

[3] https://github.com/backtracking/ocamlgraph/blob/master/src/oper.ml.

14   I. Chirica and M. Pereira

```
(*@ model dom: vt fset                                          Gospel
    model suc: vt → vt fset
    invariant (∀ v1, v2. v1 ∈ dom ∧ v2 ∈ (suc v1) → v2 ∈ dom) ∧
              (∀ v1. ¬(v1 ∈ dom) → (suc v1) == ∅) *)
```

A logical model is an uninvasive way to decorate a type with properties that are accessible only in specification and, subsequently, in verification. For starters, we take the OCamlGraph definition of an empty graph. Its specification is given with respect to the logical model: this is a graph with no vertices nor edges:

```
val empty : unit → gt                                    Gospel + OCaml
(*@ g = empty ()
    ensures g.dom = ∅ ∧ g.suc = (fun _ → ∅) *)
```

Additionally, we provide a specification to a function that copies a graph, copy. Its role will become clear later. It is specified as such:

```
val copy: gt → gt                                        Gospel + OCaml
(*@ g' = copy g
    ensures g.dom = g'.dom ∧ ∀ v. g.suc v = g'.suc v *)
```

The OCamlGraph library defines two essential graph descriptions, they can be either *persistent* where modifications return a fresh graph, or *imperative* where modifications are done in-place. For the former, an implementation of copy is the identity function, while for the latter, we would need to hard copy the graph.

Iterations are only as interesting as the structure they target. While an empty graph is still a graph, iterating over it amounts to traversing an empty set. To address this, we should also be able to add vertices and edges. Accordingly, we define two functions, `add_vertex` and `add_edge`, and specify them with respect to the logical model of the argument and resulting graphs. The first function, `add_vertex`, extends a graph's domain with a new vertex while leaving the successor map unchanged. In other words, it registers the vertex without adding edges: existing successors stay the same, and the new vertex starts with none. Formally, we specify this in Gospel as follows:

```
val add_vertex : gt → vt → gt                            Gospel + OCaml
(*@ g' = add_vertex g v
    ensures g'.dom = add v (g.dom) ∧ ∀ v. g'.suc v = g.suc v *)
```

The second function, `add_edge`, adds an edge from v to v'. The domain stays the same, and only v's successors are updated to include v', leaving all other vertices unchanged. Formally, we specify this in Gospel as follows:

```
val add_edge : gt → vt → vt → gt                         Gospel + OCaml
(*@ g' = add_edge g v v'
    ensures g'.dom = g.dom ∧ g'.suc = g.suc[v ← add v' (g.suc v)] *)
```

These functions cover the necessary ground to build graphs, expanding its domain set or set of successor. We make use of these functions in subsequent sections.

9.2   Higher-Order Iterators over Graphs

We have covered how to build graphs, but we are yet to mention how to iterate over one. The module `Oper` makes use of two functions, `fold_vertex` and `fold_succ`, to iterate over graphs, more precisely, over finite sets. The former is defined as:

```
val fold_vertex : (vt → α → α) → gt → α → α                    OCaml
```

In order to produce elements, the visited set has to be a subset ($\subseteq$) of the graph's domain; and have to be all pair-wise distinct. The iteration is complete when we have visited all the elements in the graph's domain. From the function's arguments we conclude that we are iterating over a graph and producing vertices.

```
(*@ r = fold_vertex func graph acc                        Extended Gospel
    folds ~complete:(fun v → v = collection.dom)
          ~permitted:(fun v → v ⊆ collection.dom ∧ distinct v)
    with structure = gt, elt = vt, accumulator = acc *)
```

The second function that iterates a graph is `fold_succ`, taking as an argument a graph and a vertex, while iterating over its successors. Its signature is as follows:

```
val fold_succ : (gt → α → α) → α → gt → vt → α                 OCaml
```

This iteration is also over sets, with the structure of iteration being a pair (`gt`, `vt`), as it does not make much sense to iterate over a vertex without a graph nor over successors of which we do not know their origin. Both `permitted` and `complete` are in regard to the successors of `s` in `g`. This iteration produces vertices.

```
(*@ r = fold_succ func acc pair                          Extended Gospel
    folds ~complete:(fun v → let (g, s) = collection in ||v|| = ||g.suc s||)
          ~permitted:(fun v → let (g, s) = collection in
                              v ⊆ (g.suc s) ∧ distinct v)
    with structure = (gt * vt), elt = vt, accumulator = acc *)
```

We are less precise in the `complete` predicate: we only say that they have to be equal in their cardinality ($||\cdot||$) but not in the enumeration of their elements. This is also correct, from classical set theory follows that if a set `s1` is a subset of `s2` and their cardinality is the same, then they are the same set.

9.3   Union

The union of two graphs, `g1` and `g2`, produces a new graph that combines their vertex sets and successor functions. This is done by iterating over each vertex `s` in `g1` and adding `s` and its successors to a copy of `g2`, used as an accumulator. The result satisfies the postcondition of representing the full union of both graphs.

```
let union g1 g2 =                                   Extended Gospel + OCaml
  fold_vertex
    (fun g v →
```

```
        fold_succ (fun e g → add_edge g v e) (add_vertex g v) g1 v
          (*@ folds ~inv:(union_inner g1 g2 v) ~collection:(g1,v)
              ~convergence:(fun (g, s) v → ||g.suc s|| - ||v||) *)) g1 (copy g2)
      (*@ folds ~inv:(union_outer g1 g2) ~collection:g1
          ~convergence:(fun g v → ||g.dom|| - ||v||) *)
  (*@ gr = union g1 g2
      ensures gr.dom = g1.dom ∪ g2.dom
      ensures ∀ src. (gr.suc src) = (g1.suc src) ∪ (g2.suc src) *)
```

Since we are dealing with two higher-order iterators, each requires an invariant. The outer one, `union_outer`, applies to `fold_vertex`. It states that the accumulator's domain is the union of g2's domain and the visited vertices of g1; for visited vertices v, their successors in `acc` are the union from g1 and g2; and for unvisited vertices, successors match those in g2. As the information automatically applied during translation is insufficient, we manually partially apply the graphs to both invariants, and additionally the vertex being iterated to the innermost.

```
  (*@ predicate union_outer (g1 g2: gt)                          Gospel
      (* outer iteration *)  (visited: vt seq) (acc: gt) =
      (acc.dom = visited ∪ g2.dom)
    ∧ (∀ v. v ∈ visited → acc.suc v = (g1.suc v) ∪ (g2.suc v))
    ∧ (∀ v. v ∈ (acc.dom \ visited) → acc.suc v = g2.suc v) *)
```

The inner invariant, `union_inner`, is more subtle. We begin by stating that the accumulator graph's domain is the union of the visited vertices and that of g2:

```
  (*@ predicate union_inner (g1 g2: gt) (src: vt)               Gospel
      (* inner iteration *)  (visited': vt seq) (acc': gt)
      (* outer iteration *)  (visited: vt seq) (acc: gt)  =
      (acc'.dom = visited ∪ g2.dom)
```

Successors of unvisited vertices are still those from g2:
```
    ∧ (∀ v. v ∈ (acc'.dom \ visited) → acc'.suc v = g2.suc v)
```

For visited vertices other than the one currently being processed, its successors in the accumulator are the union from both graphs:
```
    ∧ (∀ v. v ∈ visited ∧ v ≠ src → acc'.suc v = (g1.suc v) ∪ (g2.suc v))
```

Finally, the current vertex `src` accumulates successors incrementally:
```
    ∧ (acc'.suc src = visited' ∪ (g2.suc src)) *)
```

Note that we did not use the outer accumulator, since `acc'` is already an updated version of `acc`. After translation, Alt-Ergo dispatches the generated VCs of `union`.

9.4   Intersection

The intersection of two graphs g1 and g2 is a new graph containing only the vertices and successors present in both. As in the previous example, we use the same iteration scheme, but here we start from an empty graph. We iterate over the vertices of **g1**, keeping those also in **g2**, and then over their successors in **g1**, adding an edge only if the successor is also in **g2**.

```
let intersect g1 g2 =                            Extended Gospel + OCaml
  fold_vertex
    (fun g v →
      if mem_vertex g2 v then
        fold_succ
          (fun e g → if mem_edge g2 v e then add_edge g v e else g)
          (add_vertex g v) g1 v
      (*@ folds ~inv:(intersect_inner g1 g2 v) ~collection:(g1, v)
          ~convergence:(fun (g, s) v → ||g.suc s|| - ||v||) *)
      else g) g1 (empty())
(*@ folds ~inv:(intersect_outer g1 g2) ~collection:g1
    ~convergence:(fun g v → ||g.dom|| - ||v||) *)
```

This function returns a new graph g where its domain is the intersection of the domains of **g1** and **g2**, and their successors sets:

```
(*@ g = intersect g1 g2                                          Gospel
    ensures g.dom = g1.dom ∩ g2.dom
    ensures ∀ v. g.suc v = (g1.suc v) ∩ (g2.suc v) *)
```

The outer invariant is relatively simple. We state that the accumulator graph has a domain which is the result of the intersection of the set of visited vertices with the domain of **g2**. And for every visited vertex, its successor set in **acc** is the intersection of the respective sets in **g1** and **g2**:

```
(*@ predicate intersect_outer (g1 g2: gt)                        Gospel
        (* outer iteration *) (visited: vt seq) (acc: gt)    =
    (acc.dom = visited ∩ g2.dom)
  ∧ (∀ v. v ∈ visited → acc.suc v = (g1.suc v) ∩ (g2.suc v)) *)
```

The inner invariant starts by preserving the first statement of the outer invariant, followed by a partial preservation of the second statement up until **src**, as we have not finished the iteration of **src**, which unables us to say anything about its successors. This is sustained by the last statement, the successor set of **src** in the accumulator is the intersection of the set of visited successors and the respective set in **g2**:

```
(*@ predicate intersect_inner (g1 g2: gt) (src: vt)              Gospel
        (* inner iteration *) (visited': vt seq) (acc': gt)
        (* outer iteration *) (visited: vt seq) (_acc: gt)    =
    (acc'.dom = visited ∩ g2.dom)
  ∧ (∀ v. v ≠ src → v ∈ visited → acc'.suc v = (g1.suc v) ∩ (g2.suc v))
  ∧ (acc'.suc src = visited' ∩ (g2.suc src)) *)
```

As in the previous case of **union**, we have not used the outer accumulator. Once more, after translation, Alt-Ergo is quick to dispatch all the generated VCs.

9.5 Summary of Verified Case Studies

In this section we summarize a collection of case studies, and Table 1 summarizes some statistics. The examples defined with an `iter` all have side-effects. We note that the user never had to reason about the generated WhyML code, and all the verification conditions were automatically dispatched. The case-studies and extensions to the tools are available in an online artifact [7].

Table 1. Summary of verified iteration case studies.

Iteration client	# VCs	LoC / LoS	Time (s)	Iteration	Effects
Sequences	18	10 / 12			
sum_seq	6	1 / 2	10.45	fold	-
stack_of_seq	1	3 / 2	3.01	iter	✓
queue_of_seq	1	3 / 2	1.13	iter	✓
gt_seq	8	1 / 2	16.01	filter	-
counter_filter_seq	1	1 / 2	0.32	filter	✓
counter_map_seq	1	1 / 2	0.29	map	✓
Graphs	275	124 / 286			
intersect	13	12 / 15	3.13	fold + fold	-
union	11[†]	4 / 17	4.40	fold + fold	-
complement	12	8 / 23	5.80	fold + fold	-
mirror	6	5 / 8	2.51	fold	-
copy_vertices	1	1 / 2	1.64	fold	-
check_path	71	44 / 103	47.79	iter	✓
check_path[†]	161	50 / 118	105.07	-	✓
Binary trees	14	5 / 6			
sum_tree	5	1 / 2	10.51	fold	-
height_tree	1	1 / 2	1.02	fold	-
gt_tree	8	3 / 2	37.05	iter	✓

Sequences. The `sum_seq` function generates more VCs than others in the module, due to `split_vc` and `in_line` goals introduced by a Why3 strategy. Yet, examples with a single VC suggest this splitting was unnecessary. Although `queue_of_seq` and `stack_of_seq` are similar, the latter's specification includes a sequence reversal, adding a slight overhead to proof replay. The `gt_seq` function counts elements above a threshold by filtering and then measuring the length of the resulting sequence. Finally, `counter_filter_seq` and `counter_map_seq` are simple iterators: one filters positives, the other increments elements. Both write to a reference, but their effects are correctly identified by the consumer functions.

Graphs. All graph operations are fully automatic. The slowest among these is the complement of a graph, essentially due to its verbosity and need to keep track of the universe of vertices that have not been explored. This verbosity is observable when relating the number of lines of specification (LoS) of each case study to their proof time, which tends to grow linearly. Within the Check[4] module, we revisited a path-checking algorithm, check_path. A version of this function, proved correctly in previous work [4], check_path †, relied on manually deconstructing the iteration into a recursive function and then specifying the iteration. In contrast, our approach allows for a direct specification of the higher-order iterators, resulting in half as many VCs, thus, halving the proof time.

Binary Trees. We specified iteration over binary trees using classical structures. The permitted predicate flattens a tree into a sequence and reasoning about it as such. The sum of integers values of a tree sum_tree has similar performance as its counterpart sum_seq, though facing similar challenges. For computing tree height, we used a different higher-order iterator, fold_level, which proceeds level by level, akin to breadth-first search. Its permitted predicate ensures that each position i of the visited sequence holds all elements at level i. The height then follows directly from this specification. Alternatively, in gt_tree, we used an iter to count elements exceeding a threshold. The impact in performance is clearly noticeable, this can be partially due to either the fact that we are flatting the tree into a sequence or using an iterator with effects.

In any case, we note that the number of lines of specification (LoS) tends to exceed the number of lines of code (LoC). This is not surprising, as the specification effort is generally greater than the implementation. To count the number of total VCs, we use the command why3 session info <session>, where a session is a case study. Regarding the ratio LoS and LoC, we used ocamlwc to count commented lines and lines of OCaml code. The benchmarks were conducted on a machine with a i5-2520M 2-cores @ 3.2 GHz; 12 Gb RAM; 64-bit Linux Kernel 6.9.5. The proof replay times are results of 5 executions of Why3's replay command, using hyperfine with 3 warm-up executions.

10 Related Work

Recently, several works have been published addressing the formal verification of higher-order iterators. Like our approach, these works are based on a specification methodology that exploit the pair of predicates permitted and complete. However, the works described below differ from our presentation primarily in their target language (none use OCaml) and the verification toolchain employed.

Regarding the Rust programming language, we find the works of Denis and Jourdan [9], as well as the work by Bílý et al. [3]. The former use the permitted and complete predicates to formally verify higher-order iterators using the Creusot tool [10]. The latter adopt the same underlying methodology but carry out the verification process in Prusti [1], a tool that translates Rust programs into the Viper verification language [20]. Unlike traditional functional languages, Rust does not provide a type for anonymous functions. It is up to the user to decide, in each case, the appropriate kind of closure to use: Fn, FnMut, or FnOnce, that is, by ownership, mutable reference, or immutable

---

[4] https://github.com/backtracking/ocamlgraph/blob/master/src/path.ml.

reference. This decision has a direct impact on the verbosity of the resulting specification. In OCaml, and in our approach in particular, we support any consumer function, regardless of its nature, without affecting the generated specification.

Additionally, Pottier's work [22] represents a significant application of the `permitted/complete` methodology outside the scope of an automatic verification platform. In this work, the author uses the CFML [5] tool to formally verify the implementation of a hash table from the OCaml standard library, as well as the iterators provided for this data structure. The proofs are carried out entirely in Rocq, which demands a high level of proof effort and human interaction, especially when compared to our approach using Cameleer.

11   Conclusions and Future Work

We developed an extension to Gospel focused on the specification of higher-order iterators. We developed, as well, an extension to Cameleer that can translate these specifications into regular WhyML code that can, in turn, be deductively verified using Why3. Additionally, we devised a collection of case studies that showcase how one might use our work to verify higher-order iterator clients, through the `permitted` and `complete` predicates. We tackled the verification of realistic OCaml code, as taken from the OCamlGraph library, which shows that our methodology scales-up well in practice. In summary, we presented a simple, generic and modular specification to capture higher-order iteration. This specifications abstracts away how the iteration is implemented, focusing only on the important logical elements of an iteration: the `permitted/complete` relations and a user-supplied invariant. We now follow with possible lines of future work.

Generic specification for patterns. Our generic iteration specification captures patterns that any client or iterator must follow, regardless of their concrete implementation. This specification would introduce a concept similar to *typeclasses* [25] or *traits* [24] in Gospel, as it would only be necessary to describe the general abstractions and provide concrete instances for each specific use.

Relational equivalence. The correctness of our translation schemas is based on an informal argument that a higher-order iterator can be converted in a cursor that plays the iteration part. One possible extension to our methodology could be to generate a skeleton of a proof, for example, in Rocq that captures such equivalence. It would be natural to resort to binary logic, *e.g.*, Relational Hoare Logic [2], allowing us to reason about the equivalence of two OCaml programs.

Verification of Iteration Implementations. While we focused on specifying higher-order iterators and translating them into cursor-based definitions and clients, we have yet to verify existing implementations against these specifications. In that regard, we propose verifying that higher-order function implementations conform to their `permitted/complete` based specifications, likely requiring formal proofs in interactive frameworks like CFML or Iris [18].

Acknowledgments. We thank the anonymous reviewers for their constructive feedback. This work is supported by UID/04516/NOVA Laboratory for Computer Science and Informatics (NOVA LINCS) with the financial support of FCT.IP and partially financed by Agence Nationale de la Recherche (ANR) project ANR-22-CE48-0013-01 (GOSPEL).

References

1. Astrauskas, V., Müller, P., Poli, F., Summers, A.J.: Leveraging rust types for modular specification and verification. Proc. ACM Program. Lang. **3**(OOPSLA), 147:1–147:30 (2019). https://doi.org/10.1145/3360573

2. Benton, N.: Simple relational correctness proofs for static analyses and program transformations. SIGPLAN Not. **39**(1), 14–25 (2004). https://doi.org/10.1145/982962.964003

3. Bílý, A., Hansen, J., Müller, P., Summers, A.J.: Compositional reasoning for side-effectful iterators and iterator adapters (2022). https://arxiv.org/abs/2210.09857

4. Castanho, D., Pereira, M.: Auto-active verification of graph algorithms, written in OCaml (2022). https://arxiv.org/abs/2207.09854

5. Charguéraud, A.: Characteristic formulae for the verification of imperative programs. SIGPLAN Not. **46**(9), 418–430 (2011). https://doi.org/10.1145/2034574.2034828

6. Charguéraud, A., Filliâtre, J., Lourenço, C., Pereira, M.: GOSPEL — Providing OCaml with a Formal Specification Language. In: Formal Methods - The Next 30 Years - Third World Congress. LNCS, vol. 11800, pp. 484–501. Springer (2019), https://doi.org/10.1007/978-3-030-30942-8_29

7. Chirica, I., Pereira, M.: Unfolding iterators: specification and verification of higher-order iterators. OCaml (2025). https://doi.org/10.5281/zenodo.16930341

8. Conchon, S., Filliâtre, J., Signoles, J.: Designing a generic graph library using ML Functors. In: Morazán, M.T. (ed.) Proceedings of the Eighth Symposium on Trends in Functional Programming, TFP 2007, New York City, New York, USA. Trends in Functional Programming, vol. 8, pp. 124–140. Intellect (2007)

9. Denis, X., Jourdan, J.H.: Specifying and verifying higher-order rust iterators. In: Sankaranarayanan, S., Sharygina, N. (eds.) Tools and Algorithms for the Construction and Analysis of Systems (TACAS). LNCS, vol. 13994, pp. 93–110. ETAPS, Springer, Paris, France (2023). https://doi.org/10.1007/978-3-031-30820-8_9

10. Denis, X., Jourdan, J., Marché, C.: Creusot: a foundry for the deductive verification of rust programs. In: Riesco, A., Zhang, M. (eds.) Formal Methods and Software Engineering - 23rd International Conference on Formal Engineering Methods, ICFEM 2022, Madrid, Spain, 24-27 October 2022, Proceedings. LNCS, vol. 13478, pp. 90–105. Springer (2022). https://doi.org/10.1007/978-3-031-17244-1_6

11. Dijkstra, E.W.: A Discipline of Programming, 1st edn. Prentice Hall PTR, USA (1997)

12. Filliâtre, J.C.: Deductive software verification. Int. J. Softw. Tools Technol. Transfer (STTT) **13**(5), 397–403 (2011). https://doi.org/10.1007/s10009-011-0211-0

13. Filliâtre, J.-C., Gondelman, L., Paskevich, A.: The spirit of ghost code. Formal Methods Syst. Des. **48**(3), 152–174 (2016). https://doi.org/10.1007/s10703-016-0243-x

14. Filliâtre, J.C., Paskevich, A.: Why3: where programs meet provers. In: Proceedings of the 22nd European Conference on Programming Languages and Systems, pp. 125–128. ESOP 2013, Springer-Verlag, Berlin, Heidelberg (2013). https://doi.org/10.1007/978-3-642-37036-6_8

15. Filliâtre, J.C., Paskevich, A.: Abstraction and genericity in Why3. In: ISoLA 2021 - 9th International Symposium On Leveraging Applications of Formal Methods, Verification and Validation, vol. 12476. Rhodes, Greece (2021). https://doi.org/10.1007/978-3-030-61362-4_7

16. Filliâtre, J.-C., Pereira, M.: A modular way to reason about iteration. In: Rayadurgam, S., Tkachuk, O. (eds.) NFM 2016. LNCS, vol. 9690, pp. 322–336. Springer, Cham (2016). https://doi.org/10.1007/978-3-319-40648-0_24

17. Hoare, C.A.R.: An axiomatic basis for computer programming. Commun. ACM **12**(10), 576–580 (1969). https://doi.org/10.1145/363235.363259

18. Jung, R., Krebbers, R., Jourdan, J.H., Bizjak, A., Birkedal, L., Dreyer, D.: Iris from the ground up: a modular foundation for higher-order concurrent separation logic. J. Funct. Program. **28**(e20) (2018). https://doi.org/10.1017/S0956796818000151

19. Monin, J.: Understanding Formal Methods. Springer (2003). http://www.springer.com/computer/swe/book/978-1-85233-247-1

20. Müller, P., Schwerhoff, M., Summers, A.: Viper: a verification infrastructure for permission-based reasoning, pp. 104–125 (2017). https://doi.org/10.3233/978-1-61499-810-5-104

21. Pereira, M., Ravara, A.: **Cameleer**: a deductive verification tool for OCaml. In: Silva, A., Leino, K.R.M. (eds.) CAV 2021. LNCS, vol. 12760, pp. 677–689. Springer, Cham (2021). https://doi.org/10.1007/978-3-030-81688-9_31

22. Pottier, F.: Verifying a hash table and its iterators in higher-order separation logic. In: Proceedings of the 6th ACM SIGPLAN Conference on Certified Programs and Proofs, pp. 3–16. CPP 2017, Association for Computing Machinery, New York, NY, USA (2017). https://doi.org/10.1145/3018610.3018624

23. Reynolds, J.: Separation logic: a logic for shared mutable data structures. In: Proceedings 17th Annual IEEE Symposium on Logic in Computer Science, pp. 55–74 (2002). https://doi.org/10.1109/LICS.2002.1029817

24. Schärli, N., Ducasse, S., Nierstrasz, O., Black, A.P.: Traits: composable units of behaviour. In: Cardelli, L. (ed.) ECOOP 2003. LNCS, vol. 2743, pp. 248–274. Springer, Heidelberg (2003). https://doi.org/10.1007/978-3-540-45070-2_12

25. Sozeau, M., Oury, N.: First-class type classes. In: Mohamed, O.A., Muñoz, C., Tahar, S. (eds.) TPHOLs 2008. LNCS, vol. 5170, pp. 278–293. Springer, Heidelberg (2008). https://doi.org/10.1007/978-3-540-71067-7_23

When Separation Arithmetic is Enough

Jean-Christophe Filliâtre[1]([✉]), Andrei Paskevich[1], and Olivier Danvy[2]

[1] Université Paris-Saclay, CNRS, ENS Paris-Saclay, Inria,
Laboratoire Méthodes Formelles, Gif-sur-Yvette 91190, France
`jean-christophe.filliatre@cnrs.fr`,
`andrei.paskevich@universite-paris-saclay.fr`
[2] School of Computing, National University of Singapore, Singapore, Singapore
`danvy@acm.org`

Abstract. In the practice of deductive program verification, it is desirable to make proofs as automated as possible. Today, the best tools for that are SMT solvers, which are able to handle both first-order logic and linear arithmetic. However, SMT solvers are not well suited for inductive reasoning, which is often needed to deal with recursive data structures such as linked lists or trees. In this paper, we propose a technique for specifying and proving imperative programs manipulating pointer-based recursive data structures, which stays within reach of first-order provers. The idea is to map a recursive structure onto a flat integer-indexed sequence, in such a way that separation and frame properties can be expressed using only simple arithmetic relations. We illustrate this approach with two examples: an original variant of list reversal and Morris's algorithm for constant-space traversal of a binary tree.

1 Introduction

Program verification, and deductive verification specifically, benefits enormously from proof automation, as provided by SMT solvers and their powerful combination of first-order logic and linear arithmetic. Today we get fully automated proofs for programs which would in the past require copious amounts of interactive reasoning.

Yet automated provers are far from a silver bullet. They are highly sensitive to the size and shape of their tasks, so that adding a new premise or even slightly reformulating the existing ones may cause a solver to no more being able to prove a goal that was easily proved before. They struggle with tasks that require lots of premise instantiation, especially when combined with interpreted theories like arithmetic. And, finally, they are not made for inductive reasoning.

This last limitation is especially felt when we verify pointer-based data structures like lists or trees, where well-formedness and other important properties are most naturally introduced with recursive definitions. Here we find ourselves between two seemingly conflicting principles:

This research was supported by the Décysif project funded by the Île-de-France region and by the French government in the context of "Plan France 2030".

F. Damiani and M. Farrell (Eds.): iFM 2025, LNCS 16194, pp. 23–37, 2026.
https://doi.org/10.1007/978-3-032-10794-7_2

The good specification is the one that is easy to understand.

The good invariant is the one that is easy to verify.

For our specification to be clear and convincing for those who will read it later, we would want to stay with recursive definitions. For our invariants to be within reach of SMT solvers, we would rather switch to a non-recursive formulation.

In this paper, we introduce an approach that allows us to reconcile, in certain cases, these two principles, achieving mostly automated proofs for pointer-based data structures. The key idea is to organize the elements of the manipulated data structure into a flat integer-indexed sequence, where the separation and frame properties can be expressed as simple linear inequalities, the comfort zone of SMT solvers. This sequence is only used for the intermediate stages of the proof, where it is created, as a ghost object, from the original recursive specification. The soundness of this translation is relatively easy to verify. Indeed, it amounts to a simple conversion between two mathematical models of the same data structure, done entirely in ghost code and without any modification of the actual program memory.

In what follows, we introduce and illustrate our approach through a series of examples. We chose OCaml as the implementation language, as this is the language that Why3 [9], our verification tool of choice, is based upon, making it easier for the reader to link the specification to the implementation. However, the same ideas can be applied when verifying code written in a language without algebraic data types and/or with actual pointers, like C. Source code and proofs are available at https://doi.org/10.5281/zenodo.17225346.

We start with the classic list reversal on linked lists (Sect. 2) as a way to introduce all necessary notions through an easy and well-known case. We then consider a variant of list reversal, where instead of reversing the "next" pointers, we rearrange the values in the list cells (Sect. 3). This program runs in constant space by reversing and then restoring the "next" pointers, using the list structure itself to temporarily store information. Our next example in Sect. 4 is the in-order traversal of a binary tree in constant space using Morris's algorithm [16]. Like in the previous example, Morris's algorithm temporarily mutates a data structure in order to avoid memory allocation. Finally, we cite in Sect. 5 the second challenge of the 9th VerifyThis verification competition [1]—an algorithm converting a doubly-linked list into a binary tree—which was the original inspiration for the present work. We conclude with a brief survey of related work and a discussion of the scope and limitations of the proposed method.

2 Warm Up: Classic List Reversal

To introduce our approach, let us revisit the classic list reversal. An OCaml type for mutable linked lists can be defined as follows:

```
type lst =
  | Nil
  | Cons of { mutable car: elt; mutable cdr: lst }
```

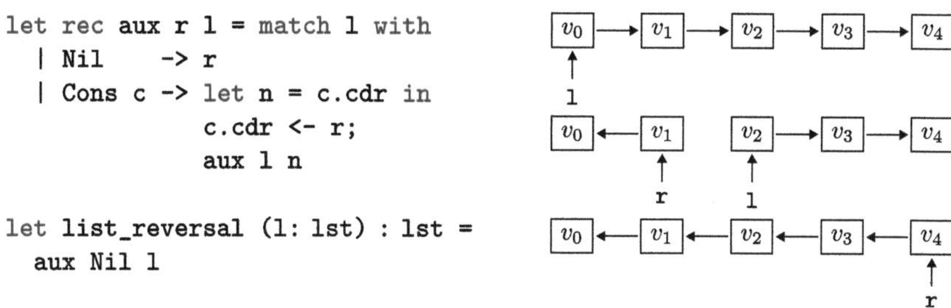

```
let rec aux r l = match l with
  | Nil     -> r
  | Cons c -> let n = c.cdr in
              c.cdr <- r;
              aux l n

let list_reversal (l: lst) : lst =
  aux Nil l
```

Fig. 1. Classic List Reversal.

This type is compiled in a natural and efficient way: a list is either the empty list `Nil`, implemented as a scalar, or a pointer to a heap-allocated `Cons` block with two mutable fields `car` and `cdr`. For simplicity, we consider here monomorphic lists that carry values of some fixed type `elt`.

The following diagram represents a list of five elements stored in a variable `l`. We make a slight abstraction, by showing only `car` values and representing `cdr` pointers as horizontal arrows.

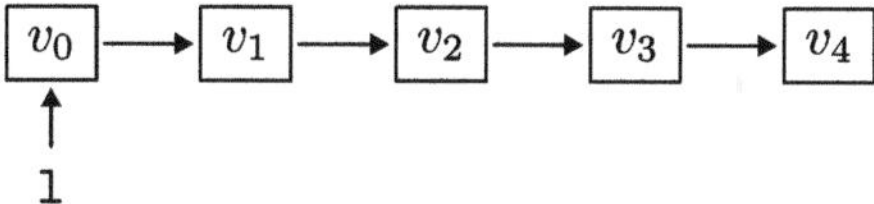

Figure 1 shows OCaml code for a function `list_reversal` that takes a list argument, performs in-place reversal, and returns the reversed list. The input list may be empty, in which case the output is also the empty list. When the input list is not empty, the returned value is the head of the reversed list, which is the last cell of the input list.

The heart of the algorithm is a recursive function `aux` with two list parameters `r` and `l`. The list `r` is the head of the already reversed prefix of the input, and the list `l` is the head of the still-to-be-reversed suffix of the input. The pictures on the right illustrate the initial state (when `aux` is called with `r` equal to `Nil`), an intermediate state, and the final state (when `l` is `Nil` and `r` is returned).

To verify the code in Fig. 1, we introduce a Why3 model of OCaml lists as follows. An abstract Why3 type `lst` models the values of OCaml lists, with a constant `nil` representing the empty list[1]. The program memory is modeled using Burstall's component-as-array principle [5]: a mutable `lst`-indexed map for each field of the data structure:

```
type mem = { mutable mcar: lst -> elt;
             mutable mcdr: lst -> lst }
```

The main idea of our "separation arithmetic" approach is to map the recursive structure of a list onto a ghost sequence of elements of type `lst`. This

---

[1] As `lst` is not a sum type in the Why3 model, we cannot reuse the `Nil` constructor.

sequence complements the unstructured heap model and provides the necessary support to describe intermediate structures and shapes that appear during the program execution. For the five element list from Fig. 1, this looks as follows:

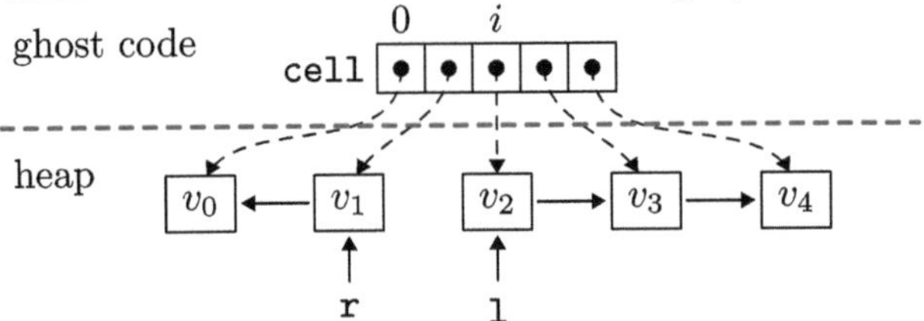

On the bottom side, we have the OCaml heap and the five list cells. On the top side, we have a ghost sequence `cell` that contains, in order, the list elements. This way, the specification and the proof may conveniently use sequence indices to refer to list elements and list segments. For instance, a ghost variable i can be used to track the list cell pointed to by the program variable `l`. Then we can state that `r` is the list comprising the cells from $i - 1$ to 0, and similarly that `l` is the list comprising the cells from i to the end of `cell`.

We introduce a new Why3 type `list_shape` for this ghost sequence. It is composed of an integer-indexed function and a length:

```
type list_shape = { cell : int -> lst; size : int }
```

We equip this type with several invariants, which state that the sequence elements are non-nil and pairwise distinct:

```
invariant { 0 <= size }
invariant { forall i. 0 <= i <  size -> cell[i] <> nil }
invariant { forall i. 0 <= i <  size ->
            forall j. 0 <= j <= size -> i <> j -> cell[i] <> cell[j] }
```

Note that the index j in the last invariant goes up to `size` inclusive. In this way, `cell[size]` serves as a sentinel, which can be `nil`, for a Nil-terminated list, or non-nil, for a segment of a larger list. This is not required for the classic list reversal, but will prove handy for the algorithm in the next section.

We can now introduce predicates that relate a given list shape to the contents of the heap. One such predicate states that a list segment from p to q is composed of the list shape cells from `lo` to `hi` inclusive:

```
predicate listLR (ls: list_shape) (m: mem) (p: lst) (lo hi: int) (q: lst) =
  0 <= lo <= hi <= ls.size /\ p = ls.cell[lo] /\ q = ls.cell[hi] /\
  forall i. lo <= i < hi -> m.mcdr[ls.cell[i]] = ls.cell[i+1]
```

Notice how the rightmost element q is stated to be equal to the sequence element at the index hi. In a similar fashion, we define a predicate that describes a reversed list segment. This time we consider the sequence elements from right to left: from, but not including, the index k and down to 0.

```
predicate listRL (ls: list_shape) (m: mem) (p: lst) (k: int) =
  (k = 0 /\ p = nil) \/
  (0 < k <= ls.size /\ p = ls.cell[k-1] /\ m.mcdr[ls.cell[0]] = nil /\
    forall i. 0 < i < k -> m.mcdr[ls.cell[i]] = ls.cell[i-1])
```

This predicate is more complex than the previous one, because the invariants of `list_shape` do not require `cell[-1]` to be `nil`.

Lastly, we introduce a frame predicate stating that memory is not modified outside of the list shape:

```
predicate frame (ls: list_shape) (m1 m2: mem) =
  forall p. (forall i. 0 <= i < ls.size -> p <> ls.cell[i]) ->
    m1.mcar[p] = m2.mcar[p] && m1.mcdr[p] = m2.mcdr[p]
```

Here, the condition `forall i. 0 <= i < ls.size -> p <> ls.cell[i]` means that pointer `p` does not occur anywhere in the list shape `ls`. The `frame` predicate appears in the postcondition of `list_reversal`, where it is applied to the pre-state and the post-state of the program memory, ensuring that all memory changes during the reversal could only have happened inside the list shape.

The key point here is that the definitions of these predicates are not recursive. Instead, they are all defined using universal quantifiers and linear arithmetic.

Taking a list shape and the current position as ghost parameters, the contract of the `aux` function is rather straightforward:

```
let rec aux (ghost ls: list_shape) (ghost i: int) (r l: lst) : lst
  requires { listLR ls mem l i ls.size nil }
  requires { listRL ls mem r i }
  variant  { ls.size - i }
  writes   { mem.mcdr }
  ensures  { listRL ls mem result ls.size  }
  ensures  { frame  ls mem (old mem) }
```

Here, `mem` is a global variable that represents the current state of the heap. The preconditions relate `l` and `r` to the list shape using the ghost index `i`. The initial and final states are nicely captured by $i = 0$ and $i = \text{ls.size}$, respectively. The `writes` clause states that only `cdr` fields have been modified. The postconditions express the reversal and frame properties. Finally, the termination of `aux` is justified by the variant `ls.size - i`. The verification condition is easily discharged by SMT solvers (e.g., Z3 proves it in a fraction of a second). The main function `list_reversal`, which is merely a call to function `aux`, is also readily verified:

```
let list_reversal (ghost ls: list_shape) (p: lst) : (r: lst)
  requires { listLR ls mem p 0 ls.size nil }
  writes   { mem.mcdr }
  ensures  { listRL ls mem r ls.size }
  ensures  { frame  ls mem (old mem) }
= aux (ghost ls) (ghost 0) nil p
```

To complete the verification, we must link our easy-to-prove shape-based invariant to a final, easy-to-understand specification. To do that, we must first build a suitable list shape and prove the corresponding instance of `listLR`. We can do this with a ghost function, as follows:

```
let ghost shape_of_list (p q: lst) : (ls: list_shape)
  requires { linked_list mem p q }
  ensures  { listLR ls mem p 0 ls.size q }
```

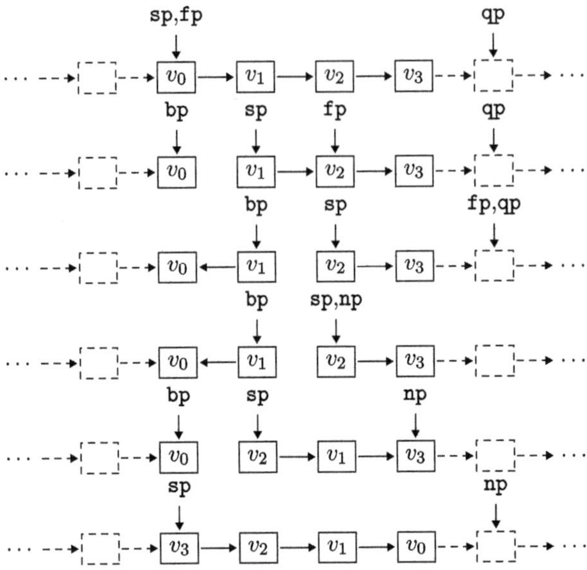

Fig. 2. Reversing values in constant space.

The precondition posits that the heap contains a list segment going from p to q. We intentionally do not provide a definition for the `linked_list` predicate in the paper. Indeed, it can be defined in any number of ways: recursively or as an inductive predicate, or as an existence of a particular mathematical model mapped to the program memory, maybe even as an existence of a suitable `list_shape`. In our implementation, we opted for a traditional recursive definition.

In the following sections, we omit the discussion of this translation between two specification styles, and concentrate on the internal proof-oriented specification.

3   Reversing Values in Constant Space

To demonstrate the benefits of our approach on a more complex example, we introduce a variant of the classic list reversal where the list is reversed by swapping the contents of the `car` fields instead of reversing the direction of the `cdr` fields. To run in constant space, the algorithm proceeds as follows. First, it uses the Tortoise and Hare algorithm (TH for short) [13, ex. 6, p. 7] [7] to reach the middle of the list, while simultaneously performing the *list reversal* of the first half. Second, it simultaneously traverses the two halves of the list, swapping the contents of the `car` fields and restoring the `cdr` fields of the first half.

```
1   let rec back_again bp sp np = match bp, np with
2     | Cons bc, Cons nc ->
3         let tmp = bc.car in bc.car <- nc.car; nc.car <- tmp;
4         let nbp = bc.cdr in bc.cdr <- sp;
5         back_again nbp bp nc.cdr
6     | _ -> ()
7
8   let rec tortoise_hare bp sp fp qp = match sp, fp with
9     | _ when fp == qp ->
10        back_again bp sp sp
11    | Cons sc, Cons {cdr = nfp} when nfp == qp ->
12        back_again bp sp sc.cdr
13    | Cons sc, Cons {cdr = Cons {cdr = nfp}} ->
14        let nsp = sc.cdr in sc.cdr <- bp;
15        tortoise_hare sp nsp nfp qp
16
17  let value_reverse (sp: lst) (qp: lst) : unit =
18    tortoise_hare Nil sp sp qp
```

Fig. 3. Reversing values in constant space.

Figure 2 illustrates the algorithm on a 4-element list. In the picture, qp stands
for the terminator of the list, which can be either Nil or—if we want to reverse
the values inside a list segment—the first cell after the end of the segment. The
TH algorithm traverses the list at speed 1 (the tortoise) and 2 (the hare), using
two pointers sp (slow pointer) and fp (fast pointer), respectively. With four
elements in the list, the fast pointer reaches qp in two steps (third line). At this
point, the slow pointer sp is at the first element of the second half, while the
reversed first half is accessible via the "back pointer" bp, which lingers one step
behind sp. Now we start the second part of the algorithm. We traverse the first
half with bp and the second half with np. We swap the values at bp and np, we
restore the next pointer of bp (line 5), and we move bp and np further in the
lists. Note how sp is maintained so that we can restore the first half of the list.

An OCaml implementation of the algorithm is given in Fig. 3. Function
tortoise_hare implements the first part of the algorithm (TH + list reversal).
Lines 9–10 handle lists with an even number of elements (as in our example), and
lines 11–12 handle lists with odd length. In the latter case, we have sp pointing
at the middle element and np pointing at the head of the second half:

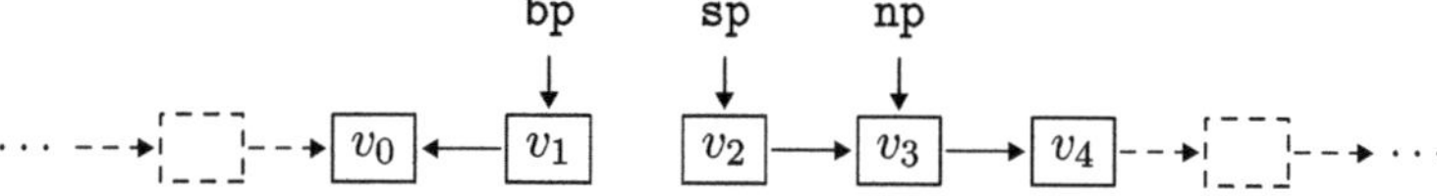

Function back_again implements the second part (swaps + list reversal).
Note that all recursive calls in the two functions are tail calls, which are opti-
mized by the OCaml compiler, ensuring that the program runs in constant space.
Alternatively, the same algorithm can be easily implemented with loops.

```
let rec warp p (N q) =
  if q.right == E then (q.right <- p; true ) else
  if q.right == p then (q.right <- E; false) else
  warp p q.right

let rec morris visit (N {left; dat; right} as p) =
  if left != E && warp p left then
    morris visit left
  else (
    visit dat;
    if right != E then morris visit right )

let traversal (visit: elt -> unit) (p: tree) : unit =
  if p != E then morris visit p
```

Fig. 4. Morris's algorithm.

To verify the three functions from Fig. 3, we reuse the `list_shape` type and the predicates from the previous section. For instance, the main function is given the following contract:

```
let value_reverse (ghost ls: list_shape) (sp qp: lst) : unit
  requires { listLR ls mem sp 0 ls.size qp }
  ensures  { forall i. 0 <= i < ls.size ->
          mem.mcar[ls.cell[i]] = old mem.mcar[ls.cell[ls.size-1-i]]
       /\ mem.mcdr[ls.cell[i]] = old mem.mcdr[ls.cell[i]] }
  ensures  { frame ls mem (old mem) }
```

Auxiliary functions `back_again` and `tortoise_hare` are specified in a similar way, with another ghost integer parameter to relate the pointer parameters to the sequence, as we did for the classic list reversal. Again, the verification using SMT solvers is straightforward, without need for user assistance of any kind.

4   Binary Tree Traversal Using Morris's Algorithm

Let us now go from linked lists to binary trees. Mutable binary trees can be defined in OCaml as follows:

```
type tree =
  | E
  | N of { mutable left: tree; mutable dat: elt; mutable right: tree }
```

As before, we consider that tree nodes carry values of some fixed type `elt`.

Morris's algorithm accomplishes in-order tree traversal in constant space by adding, temporarily, backward edges that cycle from the final rightmost node of each left subtree to the parent node of that subtree. An OCaml implementation of the algorithm is given in Fig. 4. It takes as parameters the binary tree to traverse and the visitor function. This function should be applied, in order, to each element stored in the tree: first, the elements from the left subtree, then the parent node, and then the elements from the right subtree.

When the main function, `morris`, is applied to a non-empty node p, it checks whether the left subtree L is empty. If it is, then p can be visited right away, and the traversal continues down the right subtree. If L is non-empty, `morris` calls an auxiliary function `warp` which descends to the rightmost node of L; this node would be the final node in the in-order traversal of L. If, during the descent, `warp` reaches an empty right subtree, then it adds an edge from that node to p, creating a cycle, and returns `true` to inform `morris` that L is now "warped". If, however, `warp` reaches p, this means that L has already been warped, and we actually just finished traversing it. In this case, `warp` removes the backward edge and returns `false`, so that `morris` does not go through L for the second time.

Notice that all recursive function calls in the program are tail calls, leading to a fixed stack size during execution. Alternatively, the same algorithm can be implemented using nested loops.

In order to verify Morris's algorithm, we project, once again, the recursive structure of a tree onto a flat ghost sequence. We do it in the expected order of the traversal: the elements of a left subtree appear in the sequence before the parent node and the elements of the right subtree. In addition to the sequence itself, we want to store the structural relations between the elements of the sequence. Specifically, for each tree node in the sequence we want to know the positions of its left and right children, as well as the positions of its leftmost and rightmost descendants. This leads us to the following Why3 type:

```
type tree_shape = {
  cell : int -> tree;  (* tree nodes *)
  lchd : int -> int;   (* left child *)
  rchd : int -> int;   (* right child *)
  lmdt : int -> int;   (* leftmost descendant *)
  rmdt : int -> int;   (* rightmost descendant *)
  size : int }
```

We only store non-empty tree nodes in the sequence. When a node at index i has an empty left subtree, we put i in the `lchd` and `lmdt` fields. When a node at index i has an empty right subtree, we put i in the `rchd` and `rmdt` fields. Here is an example of a tree shape for a six-node tree:

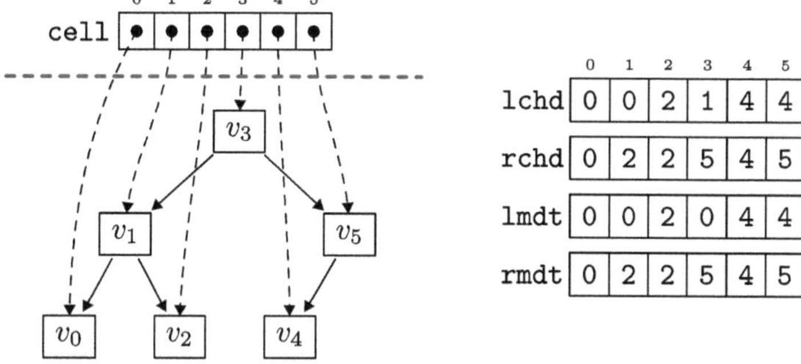

	0	1	2	3	4	5
lchd	0	0	2	1	4	4
rchd	0	2	2	5	4	5
lmdt	0	0	2	0	4	4
rmdt	0	2	2	5	4	5

The `tree_shape` type is equipped with a number of invariants:

```
invariant { 0 <= size }
invariant { forall i. 0 <= i < size -> cell[i] <> empty }
invariant { forall i. 0 <= i < size ->
            forall j. 0 <= j < size -> i <> j -> cell[i] <> cell[j] }
invariant { forall i. 0 <= i < size ->
  (0 <= lmdt[i] = lmdt[lchd[i]] <= lchd[i] <= i) /\
  (i <= rchd[i] <= rmdt[rchd[i]] = rmdt[i] < size) }
invariant { forall i. 0 <= i < size ->
  (if lchd[i] = i then lmdt[i] = i else rmdt[lchd[i]] = i-1) /\
  (if rchd[i] = i then rmdt[i] = i else lmdt[rchd[i]] = i+1) }
```

The first three invariants state that cells are non-empty and pairwise distinct. These are identical to the invariants for `list_shape` in Sect. 2. We use a constant symbol `empty` to represent the empty tree E, similarly to `nil` standing for the empty list in the Why3 model. The fourth invariant states that cells are listed according to the in-order traversal. The last invariant states that there are no spurious cells: if a node i has a left subtree, then the rightmost descendant of that tree appears right before i in the sequence, and similarly for the right subtree.

The next ingredients are the heap model and the predicates that relate a tree shape to the contents of the heap:

```
type mem = { mutable mleft:  tree -> tree;
             mutable mdat:   tree -> elt;
             mutable mright: tree -> tree }

predicate wf_lhs (t: tree_shape) (m: mem) (lo hi: int) =
  forall i. 0 <= lo <= i < hi <= t.size ->
  (t.lmdt[i] = t.lchd[i] = i /\ m.mleft[t.cell[i]] = empty) \/
  (t.lchd[i] <= t.rmdt[t.lchd[i]] = i-1 /\
                        m.mleft[t.cell[i]] = t.cell[t.lchd[i]])

predicate wf_rhs (t: tree_shape) (m: mem) (lo hi: int) =
  forall i. 0 <= lo <= i < hi <= t.size ->
  (i = t.rchd[i] = t.rmdt[i] /\ m.mright[t.cell[i]] = empty) \/
  (i+1 = t.lmdt[t.rchd[i]] <= t.rchd[i] /\
                        m.mright[t.cell[i]] = t.cell[t.rchd[i]])
```

These predicates state, separately for the left-hand side and the right-hand side, the well-formedness of a tree object stored in memory, by showing that the pointer structure is reflected by the given tree shape. Once again, we can define them without recursion, using only universal quantifiers and linear arithmetic.

Using these predicates, we can write the specification of `traversal`:

```
let traversal (ghost t: tree_shape) (ghost k: int) (p: loc) : unit
  requires { trace.length = 0 }
  requires { 0 <= k <= t.size }
  requires { if t.size = 0 then p = empty
             else k < t.size /\ t.cell[k] = p /\
                  t.lmdt[k] = 0 /\ t.rmdt[k] = t.size-1 }
```

```
requires { wf_lhs t mem 0 t.size }
requires { wf_rhs t mem 0 t.size }
writes   { mem.mright, trace }
ensures  { forall q. mem.mright q = old mem.mright q }
ensures  { trace.length = t.size }
ensures  { forall i. 0 <= i < t.size -> trace[i] = t.cell[i] }
```

The tree shape and the index of the root node in the sequence are passed as ghost arguments. Instead of a `visit` function parameter, we store visited nodes in a global mutable sequence, called `trace`. The last two postconditions state that the final trace coincides with the node sequence in the shape. The `writes` clause says that only the right child pointers and the trace sequence are modified, and the first postcondition states that all right child pointers at the end of `traversal` are restored to their initial values.

The predicates above are suitable for the initial and the final state of the algorithm. However, we also need to describe the intermediate states, where some left subtrees in the tree are warped and cycle back to their respective parent nodes. This is expressed by the following `warped_rhs` predicate:

```
predicate warped_rhs (t: tree_shape) (m: mem) (lo hi: int) =
  forall i. 0 <= lo <= i < hi <= t.size ->
  (i = t.rchd[i] = t.rmdt[i] /\ (
    ((i < t.size-1 /\ t.lmdt[i+1] <= lo /\
                                m.mright[t.cell[i]] = t.cell[i+1]) \/
     (i < t.size-1 /\ lo < t.lmdt[i+1] /\ m.mright[t.cell[i]] = empty) \/
     (i = t.size-1 /\ m.mright[t.cell[i]] = empty))) \/
  (i+1 = t.lmdt[t.rchd[i]] <= t.rchd[i] /\
                                m.mright[t.cell[i]] = t.cell[t.rchd[i]])
```

This extends the `wf_rhs` predicate by saying that a node at the index i whose right child is empty according to the tree shape (`i = t.rchd[i] = t.rmdt[i]`), may nonetheless have the `right` field pointing to the next node in the sequence: `m.mright[t.cell[i]] = t.cell[i+1]`. The node `t.cell[i+1]` is thus the parent of a warped left subtree, whose rightmost node is `t.cell[i]`. Moreover, only those left subtrees that contain index lo are warped: `t.lmdt[i+1] <= lo <= i`. In the precondition of `morris`, we set lo to the index of the current node p.

In order to verify `morris` and `warp`, we need an intermediate lemma that states that for any two subtrees, either one is contained in the other, or they are disjoint and there is at least one tree node between them in the in-order traversal. This lemma is proved separately, using a lemma-function.

We also provide a ghost function that computes a suitable tree shape from a traditional recursive description of a binary tree in the heap.

5   Bonus Example: VerifyThis 2021

The approach presented in this paper originates from a Why3 solution to the second challenge from the VerifyThis 2021 verification competition [10]. The task

was to verify an algorithm converting doubly linked lists into binary trees. We
start with a list containing a sequence of values $v_0, v_1, \ldots$:

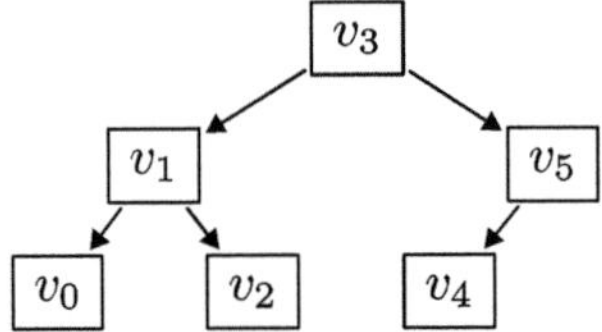

Each cell contains a pointer `prev` towards the previous cell (or `null` for the
first cell) and a pointer `next` towards the next cell (or `null` for the last cell).
The algorithm rearranges the `prev` and `next` pointers, creating a binary tree,
where `prev` points to the left subtree and `next` to the right subtree.

The order of elements is preserved, meaning that an in-order traversal of the
final tree enumerates the values $v_0, v_1, \ldots$ in the same order as in the initial list.
This way, sorted lists become binary search trees. Furthermore, the result tree
is balanced. The core of the algorithm is a recursive function that converts the
list prefix of a given length and returns the root node of the resulting tree and
the first non-consumed list cell.

In order to specify and verify the algorithm, we can again resort to separation
arithmetic. As for the list reversal, we introduce a ghost sequence `s` of list cells:

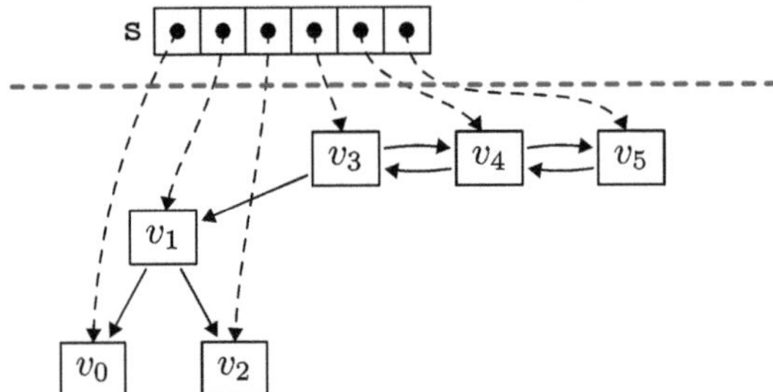

Based on this sequence, we define a predicate `dll s p lo hi` which states
that `p` is the first cell of a doubly-linked list formed by the cells in `s` between
the indices `lo` and `hi`. We also define a predicate `tree s p lo hi` which states
that `p` is the root of a binary tree formed, in order, by the cells in `s` between the
indices `lo` and `hi`. Similarly to other well-formedness predicates in this paper,
the `dll` predicate is non-recursive, which allows SMT solvers to easily discharge
frame-related proof obligations. A full Why3 proof of the program is available
online [10].

6   Related Work

The classic list reversal via pointer reversal is the introductory example in
Reynolds's seminal paper introducing Separation Logic [18][2]. Since then, it has

---

[2] And long before that, it was a proof example in the aforementioned 1972 paper by
Burstall introducing the component-as-array principle [5].

been reused as an example in most flavors and implementations of separation logic. The proof is based on a recursively-defined predicate *list ℓ p* that states the existence in the heap of a list ℓ starting at pointer p. The definition of such a predicate looks like

$$list \; \varepsilon \; p \; \overset{\text{def}}{=} \; p = null$$
$$list \; (v \cdot \ell) \; p \; \overset{\text{def}}{=} \; \exists q. \; p \mapsto (v, q) \star list \; \ell \; q$$

where $\star$ denotes the separating conjunction, meaning that the head cell of the list is disjoint from the cells composing its tail. This is similar to the third invariant on our type `list_shape` (see page 4), where we state that all cells are pairwise distinct. However, the proofs in separation logic require a great deal of user interaction, via lemmas and manual opening/closing of the recursive definition above. This is particularly true in incarnations of separation logic within proof assistants, for instance in Coq [6, chapter 3] or Isabelle [20, section 5]. Even when separation logic tools are based on SMT solvers, such as Jacobs's VeriFast [12], reasoning on mutable lists still requires a serious amount of user interaction; see for instance the `doubly_linked_list.c` example in VeriFast sources.

Blanchard et al. [2] describe the verification with Frama-C/WP of the C implementation of linked lists that is part of the operating system Contiki. For the purpose of specification, an inductive predicate relates C linked lists with an algebraic list data type, in a way similar to that of the *list* predicate above. Some lemmas then require proofs by induction, unsurprisingly; those are out of reach of SMT solvers, and performed with the Rocq Prover. Section 5 of the paper compares this approach to a previous verification effort using ghost arrays, which would be closer to our work. Their conclusion leans towards ghost lists rather than ghost arrays, but mostly for technical reasons. Indeed, Frama-C does not ensure by default the separation of program data and ghost data, which incurs extra annotations and proof obligations. It is worth pointing out that both verification approaches, either with ghost lists or with ghost arrays, require some lemmas and assertions to be discharged interactively within the Rocq Prover.

The idea of using local invariants based on universal quantification rather than recursive definitions is not new, and is folklore in program verification [8]. Examples include reachability predicates (e.g., paths in graphs) and structural properties (e.g., a binary tree is a heap). The contribution of this work is using them to express separation properties.

Schorr-Waite graph marking algorithm [19] is another instance of pointer reversal algorithm, which actually predates Morris's algorithm. Morris himself tackled the verification of the algorithm with a pen-and-paper proof [17]. Later it was turned into a formal verification by Bornat [3] and then became a classic in mechanized verification [4,11,14,15]. Even if Morris's algorithm may seem to be a simple instance of Schorr-Waite algorithm, the two are quite different, as Schorr-Waite requires extra space within nodes to store information needed by the algorithm, whereas Morris's algorithm only uses the existing left and right pointers. For our approach, Schorr-Waite presents an additional challenge since the traversal sequence is not apparent in the initial graph. In order to construct an appropriate shape structure, we would have to simulate the same traversal in ghost code, before starting the actual computation, which would then handle the elements of the graph exactly as they are arranged in the shape.

7   Conclusion

Above, we described a method of verifying imperative programs which manipulate pointer-based recursive data structures. This technique eschews recursive specifications and relies instead on flat integer-indexed sequences to provide a logical model of the data structure. Then separation and frame properties that arise during the proof can be stated using simple arithmetic and discharged automatically by an SMT solver. Such sequences can be derived from a traditional recursively-defined model via auxiliary ghost functions, allowing us to preserve the user-facing specification and to use separation arithmetic only for proof.

To take advantage of this approach, one has to come up with a suitable flat model for the manipulated data structure. We expect this to be straightforward for lists and trees, as demonstrated by the examples in the paper. The task is more difficult for dags and graphs, where multiple paths can lead to the same cell. Our next challenge, therefore, is to show how to apply separation arithmetic in these cases, starting with the classical Schorr-Waite algorithm.

References

1. The VerifyThis program verification competition (2011). https://www.pm.inf.ethz.ch/research/verifythis.html
2. Blanchard, A., Kosmatov, N., Loulergue, F.: Logic against ghosts: comparison of two proof approaches for a list module. In: Proceedings of the 34th ACM/SIGAPP Symposium On Applied Computing (SAC 2019), pp. 2186–2195. ACM (2019)
3. Bornat, R.: Proving pointer programs in Hoare logic. In: Backhouse, R., Oliveira, J.N. (eds.) Mathematics of Program Construction, pp. 102–126. Springer, Berlin, Heidelberg (2000). https://doi.org/10.1007/10722010_8
4. Bubel, R.: The Schorr-Waite algorithm. Verification of Object-Oriented Software. The KeY Approach, pp. 569–587 (2007)
5. Burstall, R.M.: Some techniques for proving correctness of programs which alter data structures. Mach. Intell. **7**(3), 23–50 (1972)
6. Charguéraud, A.: Separation Logic Foundations, Software Foundations, vol. 6. Electronic textbook (2025). https://softwarefoundations.cis.upenn.edu
7. Danvy, O.: The tortoise and the hare algorithm for finite lists, compositionally. ACM Trans. Program. Lang. Syst. **45**(1) (2023). https://doi.org/10.1145/3564619
8. Filliâtre, J.C.: Simpler proofs with decentralized invariants. J. Logical Algebraic Methods Program. **121** (2021). https://doi.org/10.1016/j.jlamp.2021.100645, https://usr.lmf.cnrs.fr/~jcf/spdi/
9. Filliâtre, J.C., Paskevich, A.: Why3 — where programs meet provers. In: Felleisen, M., Gardner, P. (eds.) Proceedings of the 22nd European Symposium on Programming. vol. 7792, pp. 125–128 (2013)

10. Filliâtre, J.C., Paskevich, A.: Solution for Challenge 2 of the 9th VerifyThis program verification competition (2021). https://toccata.gitlabpages.inria.fr/toccata/gallery/verifythis_2021_dll_to_bst.en.html
11. Hubert, T., Marché, C.: A case study of C source code verification: the Schorr-Waite algorithm. In: Third IEEE International Conference on Software Engineering and Formal Methods (SEFM 2005), pp. 190–199 (2005). https://doi.org/10.1109/SEFM.2005.1
12. Jacobs, B., Smans, J., Philippaerts, P., Vogels, F., Penninckx, W., Piessens, F.: VeriFast: a powerful, sound, predictable, fast verifier for C and Java. In: Bobaru, M., Havelund, K., Holzmann, G.J., Joshi, R. (eds.) NFM 2011. LNCS, vol. 6617, pp. 41–55. Springer, Heidelberg (2011). https://doi.org/10.1007/978-3-642-20398-5_4
13. Knuth, D.E.: The Art of Computer Programming, volume 2 (3rd ed.): Seminumerical Algorithms. Addison-Wesley Longman Publishing Co., Inc. (1997). https://doi.org/10.5555/270146
14. Leino, K.R.M.: Dafny: an automatic program verifier for functional correctness. In: Clarke, E.M., Voronkov, A. (eds.) LPAR 2010. LNCS (LNAI), vol. 6355, pp. 348–370. Springer, Heidelberg (2010). https://doi.org/10.1007/978-3-642-17511-4_20
15. Mehta, F., Nipkow, T.: Proving pointer programs in higher-order logic. In: Baader, F. (ed.) CADE 2003. LNCS (LNAI), vol. 2741, pp. 121–135. Springer, Heidelberg (2003). https://doi.org/10.1007/978-3-540-45085-6_10
16. Morris, J.M.: Traversing binary trees simply and cheaply. Inf. Process. Lett. 9(5), 197–200 (1979). http://dblp.uni-trier.de/db/journals/ipl/ipl9.html#Morris79a
17. Morris, J.M.: A proof of the Schorr-Waite algorithm. In: Broy, M., Schmidt, G. (eds) Theoretical Foundations of Programming Methodology: Lecture Notes of an International Summer School, directed by FL Bauer, EW Dijkstra and CAR Hoare, pp. 43–51. Springer (1982). https://doi.org/10.1007/978-94-009-7893-5_5
18. Reynolds, J.C.: Separation logic: a logic for shared mutable data structures. In: Proceedings of the 17th Annual IEEE Symposium on Logic in Computer Science, p. 55–74. LICS 2002, IEEE Computer Society, USA (2002)
19. Schorr, H., Waite, W.M.: An efficient machine-independent procedure for garbage collection in various list structures. Commun. ACM 10(8), 501–506 (1967). https://doi.org/10.1145/363534.363554
20. Weber, T.: Towards mechanized program verification with separation logic. In: Marcinkowski, J., Tarlecki, A. (eds.) Comput. Sci. Logic, pp. 250–264. Springer, Berlin Heidelberg, Berlin, Heidelberg (2004). https://doi.org/10.1007/978-3-540-30124-0_21

Verified Implementation of Associative Containers with Iterators Using Threaded Red-Black Trees

Jorge Blázquez[(✉)], Manuel Montenegro, and Clara Segura

Universidad Complutense de Madrid, Madrid, Spain
{jorblazq,mmontene,clsegura}@ucm.es

Abstract. We address the verification of abstract data types (ADTs) implementing associative containers like maps and sets with fine-grained specifications for iterators, which allow for multiple readers and writers in client code. Our verified implementations are written in the verification-aware programming language Dafny. In this paper we introduce new methodological contributions in verifying heap-allocated data structures, such as separation between heap-based components and functional behavior, and fine-grained control of verification proofs. Additionally, we have implemented a library of associative containers in Dafny, including a verified implementation of threaded red-black trees with iterators. These contributions aim to reduce proof complexity in order to improve verification times, while maintaining proper encapsulation.

Keywords: Program verification · Red-black trees · Dafny · Iterators · Heap-allocated data structures

1 Introduction

The development and adoption of computer-aided verification platforms has seen significant growth in the last decade, mostly driven by the latest advances in formal verification techniques and the increasing need for reliability in safety-critical software. Among the wide spectrum of verification tools, ranging from fully automatic approaches [21,32] to interactive tools [3,25], there is a number of *auto-active* tools [18], which combine user-provided proof annotations with automatic proof search, the latter usually supported by SMT solvers [24].

In this paper we focus on verifying programs that make use of a mutable heap, which is the most common scenario in mainstream object-oriented languages. In particular, we address the verification of abstract data types (ADTs) that implement associative containers—maps and sets—with fine-grained specifications for iterators. Such specifications state, for example, how the modification of a container affects the iterators that are currently traversing it (in particular, which of these iterators remain valid in order to traverse and/or modify the container), and enable verification of algorithms that involve multiple readers and writers on

F. Damiani and M. Farrell (Eds.): iFM 2025, LNCS 16194, pp. 38–58, 2026.
https://doi.org/10.1007/978-3-032-10794-7_3

the same ADT[1]. Specifications and implementations are written in Dafny [18], a programming language and verification platform that allows programmers to specify the expected behavior of their programs (via preconditions and postconditions) and checks, with the help of user-provided annotations, that the program satisfies its specification. Regarding heap management, Dafny relies on *dynamic frames* [14]. For each method, the programmer has to specify a frame expression (`modifies` clause) that denotes the set of memory locations that might be modified during the execution of the method. Analogously, the programmer also specifies, for each pure function, another frame expression (`reads` clause) that denotes the set of memory locations which the returned value might depend on.

One of the challenges in verifying heap-allocated ADTs via dynamic frames consists in properly specifying the side-effects of a method while preserving the modularity of the ADT. A common approach involves specifying, for each ADT, its *footprint*, which is the set of memory locations owned by the ADT's representation. From the implementer's point-of-view, the ADT's internal state depends on the footprint, and their methods may modify only the footprint locations and/or extend the footprint only with freshly allocated cells. From the client's point-of-view, each ADT has a footprint, but its concrete definition is hidden. The client is made responsible for proving that the footprints of different ADTs do not intersect with each other.

In previous work [5] we introduced some methodological guidelines and applied them to the verification of linear data types (lists, stacks and queues). However, there are some scalability issues when verifying programs that make use of several ADTs. Firstly, if a program applies a sequence of operations to a given ADT, the corresponding heap effects are accumulated, and the set of verification conditions that involve ADTs' footprints and their interplay become unwieldy. This implies, as we shall see in Sect. 3.3, that a large amount of verification time is devoted to reasoning about footprints rather than proving the essential functional properties relative to ADTs' abstract models. Secondly, fine-grained iterator specifications are usually given by complex first-order formulas involving universal quantifiers [5]. For example, removing an element from a linked list invalidates *every* iterator pointing to that element, but *any other* iterator remains valid. Regardless of whether such a fine-grained specification is useful to a client in a specific context or not, it is still present in verification conditions, and it might slow down the verification process. Slow verification times are a nuisance when working with an auto-active verifier, as it prevents the programmer from receiving immediate feedback on the correctness of their program.

The aim of our research is to introduce some methodological contributions in the verification of heap-allocated data structures with iterators. In this case, we focus on associative containers (maps and sets). These contributions are directed towards three specific aspects of program verification involving ADTs:

---

[1] In this work, this means that several readers and writers may coexist over the same data structure at a given time; it does not imply concurrent access by threads.

- *Specification of associative containers.* We provide a specification of sets and maps with iterators traversing them. We structure this specification in two levels: an abstract level, devoted solely to the ADTs' corresponding models, and a concrete level, which also includes fine-grained specifications regarding iterator invalidation. We make a distinction between *ordered containers* (i.e., those in which elements are traversed in ascending order) and *unordered containers* (i.e., those in which elements are traversed in an unspecified order).
- *Verification of client code,* that is, code that makes use of these specifications. Our methodological contributions in this area include greater control of visibility in specifications which allows a client to selectively reveal their postconditions, and a distinction between heap-validity and model-validity properties which applies to both client code and ADT implementation. These guidelines result in significant speed-ups in verification of methods that involve several ADTs with iterators.
- *Implementation of associative containers.* We introduce a novel verified implementation of *threaded red-black trees*[2] which conforms to the fine-grained specification introduced previously. In order to obtain shorter verification times, we have two complementary implementations of a data structure: an auxiliary pure functional implementation, in which properties involving the ADT's model are proved, and a heap-based implementation, which is proved to mirror the functional one and is the one meant to be used by client code.

Most of these contributions are oriented towards reducing proof complexity and enhancing the interaction between the user and the auto-active verifier, while maintaining proper encapsulation. The verified source code is available online[3]. The execution times reported in Secs. 3 and 4 are reproducible through a separate artifact [6].

In the rest of this section we shall introduce the main concepts involved in ADT verification. In Sect. 2 we give a specification of maps and sets, and the iterators that traverse them. In Sect. 3 we explain our methodological contributions when verifying client code (i.e., code that uses ADTs), whereas Sect. 4 is devoted to the internal implementation of our ADTs by means of threaded red-black trees. In these two sections we assess the impact of these contributions on verification times. Finally, Sect. 5 concludes.

1.1 Preliminaries on ADT Verification in Dafny

A module in Dafny comprises, on the one hand, definitions of *ghost*[4] *functions* and *predicates*, which we use for specification and verification, and on the other hand, *classes* and *methods* (as in OOP) typically employed for implementations. Readers interested in further details about the Dafny language may refer to

---

[2] Here, *threaded trees* denote trees with threaded pointers (i.e., links to traversal successors and predecessors), rather than concurrency-oriented data structures.

[3] https://github.com/jorge-jbs/adt-verification-dafny/tree/IFM25.

[4] A function or field is ghost if it is used only for specification and verification purposes, but it does not play any role at runtime (i.e., no code is generated for it).

[19] and [20]. Throughout this paper we use classes to implement ADTs. We assume that each class provides three *ghost* functions defining common concepts in verification: model, footprint, and representation invariant [5,17].

- The *model* is the underlying mathematical entity represented by the ADT. In the context of containers, models are usually given by Dafny's built-in immutable types (`seq`, `set`, `map`, etc.). For instance, the model of the `UnorderedSet` class (introduced in the following sections) is an immutable `set`. For every ADT, we assume the existence of a ghost function `Model` (also named *abstraction function*) that returns its model. All ADT's public operations are specified in terms of the model.
- The *footprint* is the set of memory locations owned by the ADT. We assume that there is a ghost function `Repr` that returns this set. Each method in the ADT specifies that the objects contained within `Repr` may mutate, and that the set `Repr` may grow only with freshly allocated objects.
- The *representation invariant* is given by a ghost predicate `Valid`. Each method's specification states that `Valid` holds before and after executing the method.

In order to make verification easier, the implementation of an ADT may contain, besides a footprint, a more structured representation of this set: the *spine* [5]. For example, the spine of a linked list is a *sequence* of references to its nodes in the same order as they are linked, so that the representation invariant can be expressed more easily. Note that the spine is always private to the ADT. From a client's point-of-view, a footprint is still an unstructured set of locations.

For those containers that provide support for iterators, we assume that each iterator provides a `Valid` ghost predicate that tells whether the iterator is still valid (i.e., can still be used to traverse the container), and a `Parent` ghost function that returns the container the iterator is associated with. Analogously, for every container we assume a ghost function `Iterators` which returns the set of iterators that have been created for that container, regardless on whether they are still valid or not. We assume that for every container `c` and iterator `it` in `c.Iterators()` it holds that `it.Parent() == c`.

In order to improve verification performance in Dafny, we fine-tune certain aspects of automatic proof search using `twostate` `opaque` definitions, and `reveal` statements. In general, a function depends on the current heap state, and its definition is expanded wherever the function is applied. However, a `twostate` function may also reference the `old` heap state, which corresponds to the state at the beginning of a method's execution. Additionally, declaring a function as `opaque` prevents its definition from being expanded automatically; instead, it must be explicitly revealed using a `reveal` statement. This mechanism gives the programmer greater control over the proof context.

2   Specification of Associative Containers

In this section we use Dafny *traits* [1] to define specification templates of associative containers with iterators. In particular, we present specification of both

42   J. Blázquez et al.

unordered and ordered versions of sets and maps. Since they are very similar we explain sets in more detail. These traits can be extended to specify new traits with finer-grained details about iterators behavior or to define verified implementations. We use opaque two-state predicates to define method postconditions and ghost functions. In Sect. 3 we show examples that involve these containers and evaluate the impact of using this kind of predicates in verification times.

```
 1    trait UnorderedSetIterator { ...
 2      ghost predicate HasPeek?()
 3
 4      ghost function Peek?(): K
 5        requires HasPeek?()
 6        ensures PeekSpec(Peek?())
 7
 8      opaque ghost predicate PeekSpec(p: K)
 9        requires HasPeek?()
10      { p ∈ Parent().Model() ∧ p ∉ Before() }
11
12      ghost function Before(): set⟨K⟩
13        requires HasPeek?()
14        ensures BeforeSpec(Before())
15
16      opaque ghost predicate BeforeSpec(before: set⟨K⟩)
17        requires HasPeek?()
18      { before ⊂ Parent().Model() }
19
20      ghost function Traversed(): set⟨K⟩ // Total version of Before()
21      { if HasPeek?() then Before() else Parent().Model() }
22    }
```

Fig. 1. Specification functions in `UnorderedSetIterator`.

2.1 Unordered Types

Traits `UnorderedSet` and `UnorderedSetIterator` specify sets that can be traversed in no specific order using iterators. In Fig. 1 we show some ghost predicates and functions used to specify their methods[5]. Each iterator either points to an element of the set which has not been traversed yet, or it does not point to any element because there are no elements left to traverse with such iterator, and in that case we will call it a *past-the-end* iterator. The model of an unordered set is a Dafny `set` (Fig. 2, line 2) and the model of an iterator is given by a ghost predicate `HasPeek?` (Fig. 1, line 2) which distinguishes between past-the-end iterators and those pointing to elements; a ghost function `Peek?` (Fig. 1, line 4) which returns the current element in case it points to one; and a ghost function `Before` (Fig. 1, line 12) which returns the elements of the set which have been already traversed by the iterator if it points to an element of the set.

In Figs. 2 and 3 we show the specification of some methods of unordered sets and of iterators on them. Abstract set operations include the standard methods `Empty`, `Size`, `Contains`, `Add` (Fig. 2, line 4) and `Remove`, and also the following ones that involve iterators:

---

[5] Boilerplate code concerning memory allocation, freshness and validity is omitted.

```
 1   trait UnorderedSet { ...
 2     ghost function Model(): set<K>
 3
 4     method Add(x: K)
 5       ensures AddModel(x)
 6
 7     opaque twostate predicate AddModel(x: K)
 8     { Model() = old(Model()) ∪ {x} }
 9
10     method Find(x: K) returns (it: UnorderedSetIterator)
11       ensures fresh(it) ∧ it.Valid() ∧ it.Parent() = this
12       ensures Iterators() ⊇ {it} ∪ old(Iterators())
13       ensures FindModel(x, it)
14       ensures SameIterators()
15
16     opaque twostate predicate FindModel(x: K, new it: UnorderedSetIterator) {
17     { Model() = old(Model()) ∧ it.HasPeek?() = (x in old(Model())) ∧ (it.HasPeek?() ⟹ it.Peek?() = x) }
18
19     opaque twostate predicate SameIterators() {
20     { ∀it ←old(Iterators()) | old(it.Valid()) • it.Valid() ∧ SameIteratorModel(it) }
21
22     opaque twostate predicate SameIteratorModel(it: UnorderedSetIterator)
23       requires it in old(Iterators())
24       requires old(it.Valid())
25       requires it.Valid()
26     { it.HasPeek?() = old(it.HasPeek?())
27       ∧ (it.HasPeek?() ⟹ it.Peek?() = old(it.Peek?()) ∧ it.Before() = old(it.Before()))
28     }
29   }
```

Fig. 2. Specification of methods `Find` and `Add` in `UnorderedSet`.

- **First** to create a new iterator that has not traversed any elements yet;
- **Find** (Fig. 2, line 10), which given an element returns either an iterator pointing to this element if it belongs to the set, or a past-the-end iterator otherwise;
- **Erase**, which removes an element of the set pointed to by an iterator and returns a new iterator which either points to one of the not yet traversed elements if there are left, or it is past-the-end otherwise.

Abstract iterator operators include methods `HasPeek` to check whether there are elements left to traverse, `Peek` (Fig. 3, line 2) to return the pointed element, and `Next` (Fig. 3, line 13) to continue traversing with the current iterator. After executing a method that may modify the model, e.g. `Add`, there is no guarantee about the validity of the iterators pointing to the set, and we say that they become invalid. However, after executing a method that does not modify the model, e.g. `Find`, we can guarantee the validity of those iterators pointing to the set that were already valid before the execution, and also that their model remains unchanged. This property is expressed by the predicate `SameIterators` (Fig. 2, line 19). Notice that this predicate also allows the allocation of new iterators. It also holds after executing some iterator methods, such as `Peek`. Method `Next` however uses predicate `NextIterators` (Fig. 3, line 22) to express that all iterators pointing to the parent but itself remain unchanged.

We have defined similar traits, called `UnorderedMap` and `UnorderedMapIterator`, for the specification of maps with iterators where keys behave as an unordered set and each key has an associated value which can be retrieved using method `At`. In this case, method `Peek` returns a pair with the key and the value.

```
1   trait UnorderedSetIterator { . . .
2     method Peek() returns (p: K)
3       requires HasPeek?()
4       ensures HasPeek?()
5       ensures PeekModel(p)
6       ensures Parent().SameIterators()
7
8     opaque twostate predicate PeekModel(p: K)
9       requires old(HasPeek?())
10      requires HasPeek?()
11    { Parent().Model() = old(Parent().Model()) ∧ Before() = old(Before()) ∧ p = Peek?() = old(Peek?()) }
12
13    method Next()
14      requires HasPeek?()
15      ensures NextModel()
16      ensures NextIterators()
17
18    opaque twostate predicate NextModel()
19      requires old(HasPeek?())
20    { Parent().Model() = old(Parent().Model()) ∧ Traversed() = {old(Peek?())} ∪ old(Before()) }
21
22    opaque twostate predicate NextIterators() {
23    { ∀it ←old(Parent().Iterators()) | old(it.Valid()) • it.Valid()
24                                    ∧ (it ≠this ⟹ Parent().SameIteratorModel(it)) }
25  }
```

Fig. 3. Specification of methods `Peek` and `Next` in `UnorderedSetIterator`.

```
1   trait TreeSet extends OrderedSet { . . .
2     method Add(k: K)
3       ensures AddModel(k)
4       ensures AddIterators(k)
5
6     opaque twostate predicate AddIterators(x: K)
7     { ∀it ←old(Iterators()) | old(it.Valid()) • it.Valid() ∧ AddIteratorModel(it, x) }
8
9     opaque twostate predicate AddIteratorModel(it: UnorderedSetIterator, k: K)
10    { it.HasPeek?() = old(it.HasPeek?())
11      ∧ (it.HasPeek?() ⟹ it.Peek?() = old(it.Peek?()))
12      ∧ if k in old(Model()) ∨ (it.HasPeek?() ∧ it.Peek?() < k) then
13            it.Traversed() = old(it.Traversed())
14        else
15            it.Traversed() = old(it.Traversed()) ∪ {k} }
16  }
```

Fig. 4. Refined iterator invalidation policy of `Add` in `TreeSet`.

2.2   Ordered Types

In order to specify ordered sets and their corresponding iterators we define the traits `OrderedSetIterator` and `OrderedSet`, that extend their unordered counterparts. The elements can be traversed in increasing order using iterators. For that reason the specification of `Peek` is refined by adding to the postcondition the predicate `PeekOrderSpec`, which guarantees the ordered traversal:

```
1   opaque ghost predicate PeekOrderSpec(p: K)
2     requires HasPeek?()
3   { (∀ x ←Before() • x < p) ∧ (∀ x ←Parent().Model() − Before() • p ≤ x) }
```

This property uniquely determines the current element from `HasPeek?` and `Before`. Elements can be traversed in ascending order by means of `First` and `Next`, but also in descending order by means of other methods, `Last` and `Prev`.

In ordered sets, iterator invalidation happens as in unordered sets when any method modifies the set. However, trait `TreeSet` shown in Fig. 4, refines trait `OrderedSet` by adding a new iterator invalidation policy:

- In any method, valid past-the-end iterators remain valid and unchanged.
- If we add an existing element or remove a non-existing one, all iterators remain valid and unchanged.
- If we `Add` a new element k to the set, valid iterators remain valid and they still point to the element they were pointing before the method execution. So in order to respect the specification of `Peek?`, all iterators pointing to elements bigger than k will add k to `Traversed`.
- Analogously, if we `Remove` (or `Erase`) an existing element k, all iterators but those pointing to k remain valid, and those that point to elements greater than k will delete k from `Traversed`.

We have defined similar traits, `OrderedMap` and `TreeMap` to specify maps with iterator specifications similar to those of `OrderedSet` and `TreeSet`, respectively. We have implemented `TreeSet` using `TreeMap` [7], and `TreeMap` using threaded red-black trees in Sect. 4.

3   Client Code Verification Methodology

In this section we introduce a methodology for verifying user code in a systematic and efficient way by means of several examples. We propose the following components, which are explained in more detail below:

1. Separately define properties concerning heap-validity, model behaviour and iterator invalidation.
2. Encapsulate the loop invariant into an opaque ghost predicate.
3. Define a separate method for the loop body and use the invariant predicate to specify it.

The first element of the methodology is to modularize the verification process by dividing it into three parts: validity and termination properties, set model properties and iterator invalidation properties. Validity properties include the representation invariant and footprint disjointness. These are essential properties without which we cannot prove any other property so it is convenient to prove them first. For this purpose, we will provide opaque ghost definitions to express the different kinds of properties, e.g. `Valid2` for validity and `LoopBound` for termination. The modularization eases reasoning and reduces verification time in larger examples.

The second component of the methodology consists of defining the loop invariant as an opaque ghost predicate that depends on the variables involved in the loop. As predicates are opaque, the programmer of client code must now explicitly prove that the invariant holds before loop execution, that it is maintained by the loop, and that the postconditions follow from the invariant when

```
1    method Contained(s1: UnorderedSet, s2: UnorderedSet) returns (b: bool)
2      requires Valid2(s1, s2)
3      ensures Valid2(s1, s2) ∧ ContainedModel(s1, s2, b)
4    {
5      b := true; var it1 := s1.First(); var it1HasPeek := it1.HasPeek();
6
7      assert ContainedInvariant(s1, it1, s2, b) by {
8        reveal ContainedInvariant();
9        reveal s1.FirstModel(), it1.HasPeekModel();
10     }
11     while it1HasPeek ∧ b
12       decreases LoopBound(s1, it1, b)
13       invariant Valid2(s1, s2) ∧ ValidIt(s1, it1)
14       invariant it1HasPeek = it1.HasPeek?()
15       invariant ContainedInvariant(s1, it1, s2, b)
16     {
17       ghost var initialLoopBound := LoopBound(s1, it1, b);
18
19       var p := it1.Peek();
20       b := s2.Contains(p);
21       it1.Next(); it1HasPeek := it1.HasPeek();
22
23       assert LoopBound(s1, it1, b) < initialLoopBound by { /* reveal */ }
24       assert ContainedInvariant(s1, it1, s2, b) by { /* reveal */ }
25     }
26     assert ContainedModel(s1, s2, b) by { /* reveal */ }
27   }
```

Fig. 5. Method that checks whether a set is contained in another set.

the loop ends. They also have to prove that the loop bound decreases after each loop iteration. Although it seems that the user is repeating in detail all the verification conditions of a loop, all these proofs can be systematically achieved by revealing the involved predicates themselves and the postconditions of the methods invoked in the initialization of variables and the loop body, as explained in the `Contained` method in Sect. 3.1.

The third element of the methodology is extracting the loop body in a method `LoopBody`, whose parameters and results include all the variables involved in the loop, and whose specification, both precondition and postcondition, must include the invariant. This is shown in method `Pairs` in Sect. 3.2.

We have also applied the methodology to examples which require higher verification times such as the `Intersection` method [7], which computes the intersection of two ordered sets by means of two iterators that traverse both sets in increasing order. In Sect. 3.3, we assess the impact of the alternative ADT specifications and the methodology we propose for the client code.

3.1   Abstract Sets Examples

Method `Contained`, see Fig. 5, checks whether an unordered set `s1` is contained in another unordered set `s2` by traversing `s1` with an iterator `it1` and invoking method `Contains` for each of its elements on `s2`.

In this example the validity properties are expressed by means of the predicates `Valid2(s1,s2)`, that guarantees that `s1` and `s2` are valid and disjoint; and `ValidIt(s1, it1)`, that guarantees that `it1` is a valid iterator on `s1`.

```
1    method Pairs(s: TreeSet, W: int)
2    {
3      var itl := s.First(); var itg := s.Last();
4      var b := CheckLoopCondition(s,itl,itg);
5      while b
6        decreases LoopBound(s,itl,itg)
7        invariant b = LoopCondition(s,itl,itg)
8      { itl, itg, b := LoopBody(s, old(s.Model()), itl, itg,W); }
9    }
10
11   opaque ghost predicate LoopCondition(s: TreeSet, itl, itg: OrderedSetIterator)
12   { itl.HasPeek?() ∧ itg.HasPeek?() ∧ itl.Peek?() < itg.Peek?() }
13
14   opaque ghost function LoopBound(s: TreeSet, it: OrderedSetIterator): nat
15   { if LoopCondition(s,itl,itg) then |itg.Traversed()| − |itl.Traversed()| else 0 }
16
17   method LoopBody(s: TreeSet, ghost sModel: set<K>, itl, itg: OrderedSetIterator, W: int)
18        returns (newitl, newitg: OrderedSetIterator, b: bool)
19     requires LoopCondition(s,itl,itg)
20     ensures b = LoopCondition(s,newitl,newitg)
21     ensures LoopBound(s, newitl, newitg) < old(LoopBound(s, itl,itg))
22   {
23      var itlPeek := itl.Peek(); var itgPeek := itg.Peek();
24      if itlPeek + itgPeek ≤ W
25      { newitl, newitg := MakePair(s, itl, itg); }
26      else
27      { itg.Prev(); newitl := itl; newitg := itg; }
28      b := CheckLoopCondition(s, newitl, newitg);
29   }
30
31   method MakePair(s: TreeSet, itl, itg: OrderedSetIterator) returns (newitl, newitg: OrderedSetIterator)
32     ensures s.Valid() ∧ ValidIt(s, itl) ∧ ValidIt(s, itg)
33   {
34      newitl := s.Erase(itl); newitg := itg.Copy(); newitg.Prev();
35      var newitlPeek := newitl.Peek(); var itgPeek := itg.Peek();
36      if newitlPeek = itgPeek // Iterators are about to cross, last pair to erase
37         { newitl := s.Erase(itg); }
38      else
39         { var _ := s.Erase(itg); }
40   }
```

Fig. 6. Maximum number of pairs example.

The properties concerning the model are defined in predicates `ContainedModel` and `ContainedInvariant`. Both guarantee that the model of each set does not change. Additionally, `ContainedModel` describes the result of the method, i.e. `b == (s1.Model() <= s2.Model())`, while `ContainedInvariant` describes the fact that `it1` is traversing `s1` and that `b` registers whether the traversed elements belong to `s2`, i.e. `it1.Traversed() <= s1.Model() && b == (it1.Traversed() <= s2.Model())`. In order to prove termination we define function `LoopBound` as `|s1.Model()| - |it1.Traversed()| + (if b then 1 else 0)`. Regarding iterator invalidation, we have proved that the iterators remain valid (`s1.SameIterators() && s2.SameIterators()`), but we do not show the proof details in Fig. 5.

3.2   Fine-Grained Iterator Invalidation Policy

Method `Pairs`, shown in Fig. 6, receives a natural number `W` and a set `s` of natural numbers. It is a greedy algorithm that maximizes the number of (disjoint) pairs of values from s whose sum is smaller or equal than W. The values that match are removed from s. We use two iterators, itl and itg, to traverse and modify the set s simultaneously in ascending and descending order. Method `CheckLoopCondition` (not shown) checks whether the iterators cross. In that case all the values have already been traversed and the loop ends.

Table 1. Verification time of examples with different methodologies

Example	Methodology	Time	RU
Contained	OpaqueSpec	28.6 s (20.3 s)	53M (39M)
	TransparentSpec.Opaque	18.2 s (12.5 s)	36M (27M)
	TransparentSpec.Transparent	10.7 s (11.8 s)	22M (25M)
	TransparentSpec.Plain	**3.35 s** (6.84 s)	**7M** (15M)
Pairs	OpaqueSpec	85.6 s (23.4 s)	163M (41M)
	TransparentSpec.Opaque	69.1 s (24.1 s)	101M (44M)
	TransparentSpec.Transparent	**48 s** (21.6 s)	**68M** (39M)
	TransparentSpec.Plain	142 s (56.8 s)	222M (101M)
Intersection	OpaqueSpec	**35.6 s** (16.7 s)	**51M** (23M)
	TransparentSpec.Opaque	36.7 s (17.8 s)	54M (30M)
	TransparentSpec.Transparent	48.9 s (23.9 s)	73M (42M)
	TransparentSpec.Plain	9640 s (8590 s)	N/A (N/A)

Method `LoopBody` takes care of each loop iteration: If the sum of the smallest and the highest values, pointed respectively by itl and itg, sum less than W both elements are removed from the set using method `MakePair`. Otherwise, the highest value stays in the set, so the iterator itg proceeds to the next highest value. The smallest value still could be matched with another one, so itl remains in the same place. As an example, if W = 13 and s = {1,3,10,11,12,15}, the values in pairs (1,12) and (3,10) are removed, so s becomes {11, 15} after the method execution.

Method `MakePair` removes elements pointed by itl and itg. It removes first the value pointed by itl (using method `Erase`) and then newitl will point (if there is any) to the next element. Before removing the value pointed by itg, a copy newitg (obtained with method `Copy`) must be moved towards the previous value (using method `Prev`) in order to be able to continue the descending traversal. In case the iterators are about to cross (case newitlPeek == itgPeek), then this is the last pair to be removed, and iterator newitl finally points past itg. This happens in the example when removing values 3 and 10. After removing value 3, newitl is pointing to 10. Then newitg points to past-the-beginning and value 10 is removed, but newitl points to 11. This is essential because an invariant of the algorithm is that both iterators are valid. The refined iterator invalidation policy of `TreeSet` guarantees that after erasing values in `MakePair` using two iterators, both of them still remain valid and can continue the traversal.

3.3   Evaluation

In Table 1 we compare the verification times[6] for each of the three examples mentioned in this section to assess the impact of each methodological decision introduced in this paper. Since verification times can be unpredictable due to the verifier's internal use of nondeterminism, we enabled a Dafny feature (`measure-complexity` [20]) that reruns each test case multiple times applying semantic-preserving code changes designed to expose these nondeterministic behaviors. The results shown in the figure are the average of 20 executions but we observe a high coefficient of variation, greater than 15% on every test case.

With respect to the ADTs specification we consider the methodology described in Sect. 2 (`OpaqueSpec`) and another one in which the postconditions of the methods are not hidden in opaque predicates (`TransparentSpec`). The client code of the examples that use `OpaqueSpec` follows the methodology explained previously in this section. As for `TransparentSpec`, each example has been implemented using three different client-code approaches: (i) The one described in this section (`TransparentSpec.Opaque`); (ii) a modular version with the same code structure as `Opaque` but where auxiliary definitions are not opaque (`TransparentSpec.Transparent`); and (iii) a version where all the client code is inlined into one method and no auxiliary definitions are added to aid in verification (`TransparentSpec.Plain`).

The most significant improvement in verification times can be found in the `Intersection` method, the most complex example of the three, which enjoys a 271x improvement by using all of the methodological techniques we propose. Additionally, `Pairs`, a slightly simpler example, still shows the benefits of modularization, but both `OpaqueSpec` and `TransparentSpec.Opaque` perform worse than `TransparentSpec.Transparent`. On the other hand, `Contained` takes longer to verify as we introduce the methodological concepts explained in this paper. We attribute this to the fact that `Contained` is a simple example compared to the rest, and Dafny performs better in such an example when it is presented with all the assertions at once. All in all, we observe a considerable reduction in verification times when we modularize the code of moderate to highly complex examples. Hiding definitions by making them opaque also improves verification time in complex examples, although not to the extent that modularization does. We consider that the increased verification time in smaller examples is still manageable, while the verification time of a bigger example without our contributions, such as the `Intersection` example with `TransparentSpec.Plain`, requires up to 2 h 40 min of verification time on average. Moreover, its standard deviation is 1 h.

In Table 1 we have added in parenthesis the verification times devoted to prove representation invariants and footprint disjointness. They show that a significant amount of time is devoted only to prove heap properties. This has

---

[6] All code has been evaluated with an Intel Core i7-6560U processor and 16GB of RAM using Dafny version 4.10.0. We show resource unit (RU) count, a measure provided by the underlying SMT solver, Z3, that is independent of hardware configuration.

a big impact on the interactivity with Dafny, since these properties have to be proved before those regarding the model.

4   ADT Implementation and Verification Methodology

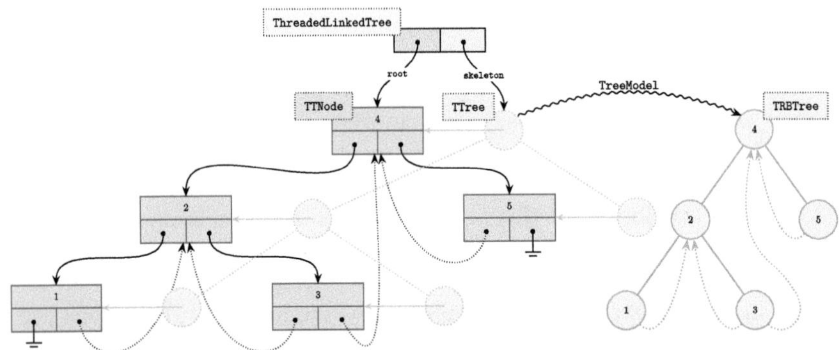

Fig. 7. Tree nodes in memory (red), ghost skeleton (blue) and tree model (green) (Color figure online)

```
1   class ThreadedLinkedTree {
2     var root: TTNode?
3     ghost var skeleton: TTree
4
5     ghost predicate Valid()
6     { ValidRec(root, skeleton) ∧ Threaded(Empty, skeleton, Empty) }
7
8     ghost function Model(): TRBTree { TreeModel(skeleton) }
9   }
10
11  class TTNode {
12    const key: K; var value: V;
13    var color: Color;
14    var isThreadLeft: bool; var left: TTNode?;
15    var isThreadRight: bool; var right: TTNode?;
16  }
```

Fig. 8. The tree alongside its skeleton in the `ThreadedLinkedTree` class

In this section we explore the implementation and verification of the associative containers specified in Sect. 2. We focus on maps, since sets have been implemented [7] using an instance of abstract type `TreeMap`, which is a map whose keys are the elements of the set and the associated values are irrelevant. Regarding maps, our implementation `TreeMapImpl` is based on threaded red-black trees. In particular, we combine left-leaning red-black trees, as described by Sedgewick

[30], with the standard threaded tree representation [15]. We omit the implementation and verification of iterators and the `Remove` method since they follow the same principles as the ones we describe in this section, but they are included in the repository mentioned in Sect. 1.

In order to ease reasoning and improve verification times we consider the following elements, illustrated in Fig. 7 and explained in more detail below:

- The threaded red-black tree of nodes stored in memory (Fig. 7 in red), used to implement the map. It involves classes `ThreadedLinkedTree` and `TTNode`, defined in Fig. 8.
- The skeleton of nodes, which is a ghost functional tree (Fig. 7 in blue) storing pointers to the nodes, used to facilitate reasoning about validity properties, in a similar way to the spine of a list in [5]. It is a ghost field of the implemented class and it involves the type `TTree`, defined in Fig. 9.
- A purely functional threaded red-black tree (Fig. 7 in green) which is the model of the implementation in the same way as an immutable sequence is the model of a list. It involves the type `TRBTree`, defined in Fig. 10.

The nodes of the tree that are stored in memory are defined in the `TTNode` class of Fig. 8. The field `isThreadLeft` determines whether the `left` field constitutes a child or a link (called *thread*) to the previous node in the inorder traversal of the tree. Its symmetric counterpart is `isThreadRight`.

To reason about the shape of the tree in memory we define the type `TTree` to represent the skeleton of nodes, shown in Fig. 9. There we define predicates `ValidRec` and `ValidChild` that mutually recurse on the skeleton to enforce that there are no loops between nodes, and also `Threaded` to enforce that threads are linked according to an inorder traversal. Both of them are used in class `ThreadedLinkedTree` to define the representation invariant (Fig. 8, line 5).

The functional model of `ThreadedLinkedTree` is defined by the `TRBTree` type of Fig. 10. The invariants of red-black trees (`RedBlackTree`), as well as the increasing order of the keys (`SearchTree`), are defined and proved only on the functional model. Since our tree implementation is aimed at implementing associative data structures, we define function `toMap` that transforms the tree into the model of the ADT (i.e., a map). We prove the map-related properties exclusively on the functional model in a completely independent way from the heap implementation. We also define the functional behavior of iterators based on the `TRBTree` type. Since iteration depends on the threads between nodes, we model these threads functionally by storing the key of the pointed node within the `Thread` constructor, rather than the node itself, as `TRBTree` is a fully functional datatype.

The verification of the implementation comprises three elements: (1) the functional behavior, (2) the imperative implementation and (3) the integration between the previous elements. For example, in Fig. 11 we define the functional behavior (first element) of method `Add` by means of the recursive function `AddTRBT` which adds or modifies an entry in a `TRBTree`. It calls `RestoreTRBT`, a function that reestablishes the red-black invariants by performing various operations on the tree depending on its state. The invariant preservation proof, contained inside the `AddInv` lemma and associated lemmas not shown in the figure, performs a case

```
1    type TTree = t: TTreeOrThread | t.Empty? ∨ t.Node?
2    datatype TTreeOrThread = Empty | Thread(thread: TTNode)
3      | Node(left: TTreeOrThread, root: TTNode, right: TTreeOrThread)
4    type Pointer = t: TTreeOrThread | t.Empty? ∨ t.Thread?
5
6    ghost function nodes(t: TTreeOrThread): set⟨TTNode⟩ { /* every node in t */ }
7
8    ghost predicate ValidChild(node: TTNode?, sk: TTreeOrThread, isThread: bool) {
9      match sk
10     case Thread(n) ⇒ isThread ∧ node = n
11     case _ ⇒ ¬isThread ∧ ValidRec(node, sk)
12   }
13
14   ghost predicate ValidRec(node: TTNode?, sk: TTree) {
15     match sk
16     case Empty ⇒ node = null
17     case Node(l, x, r) ⇒
18         x = node ∧ x ∉ nodes(l) ∧ x ∉ nodes(r) ∧ nodes(l) ∩ nodes(r) = {}
19       ∧ ValidChild(node.left, l, node.isThreadLeft) ∧ ValidChild(node.right, r, node.isThreadRight)
20   }
21
22   ghost predicate ThreadedL(prev: Pointer, t: TTreeOrThread, next: Pointer) {
23     match t
24     case Empty ⇒ prev.Empty?
25     case Thread(k) ⇒ prev.Thread? ∧ prev.thread = k
26     case Node(l, x, r) ⇒ ThreadedL(prev, l, Thread(x)) ∧ ThreadedR(Thread(x), r, next)
27   }
28
29   ghost predicate Threaded(prev: Pointer, t: TTree, next: Pointer) {
30     t.Node? ⟹ ThreadedL(prev, t.left, Thread(t.root))
31             ∧ ThreadedR(Thread(t.root), t.right, next) /*dual to ThreadedL*/
32   }
```

Fig. 9. Ghost skeleton (`TTree`) and memory representation invariants.

by case analysis to conclude that the invariant is preserved after every execution path. The proof is relieved of directly proving any property of the imperative implementation, therefore making it much easier to write and to maintain. However, its result is carried over to the imperative implementation thanks to the connection between the functional model and the imperative implementation made by `TreeModel`. We also prove that the entry is added to the model of the ADT in lemma `AddMap`.

In Fig. 12 we show the imperative implementation (second element), method `AddImpl`, which follows the same algorithm as the functional implementation. We only need to prove that `Valid` is maintained and that the manipulations on the tree are equivalent to those of `AddTRBT` (line 6).

In Fig. 13 we implement and verify method `Add` in `ThreadedLinkedTree`, by simply calling `AddImpl` and using `AddInv` to prove that the invariants are maintained (third element). Finally, we can implement the `TreeMap` ADT mentioned in Sect. 2 as a wrapper of `ThreadedLinkedTree`.

We have evaluated the verification time improvements of applying the methodology described in this section by comparing it against another version where we do not have a functional model of the tree to verify its properties separately. Instead, we proved heap properties and the properties of the ADT's model simultaneously. The results are shown in Table 2 and display a 4.05x

```
1   type TRBTree = t: TRBTreeOrThread | t.Empty? ∨ t.Node?
2   datatype TRBTreeOrThread = Empty | Thread(thread: K)
3     | Node(left: TRBTreeOrThread, key: K, value: V, right: TRBTreeOrThread, color: Color)
4   type TRBPointer = t: TRBTreeOrThread | t.Empty? ∨ t.Thread?
5
6   ghost function TreeModel(sk: TTreeOrThread): TRBTreeOrThread {
7     match sk
8     case Empty ⇒ Empty
9     case Thread(n) ⇒ Thread(n.key)
10    case Node(l, n, r) ⇒ Node(TreeModel(l), n.key, n.value, TreeModel(r), n.color)
11  }
12
13  ghost predicate SearchTree(t: TRBTreeOrThread) { /* ...*/ }
14  ghost predicate RedBlackTree(t: TRBTreeOrThread) { /* ...*/ }
15
16  ghost function toMap(t: TRBTreeOrThread): map⟨K, V⟩ {
17    match t
18    case Empty | Thread(_) ⇒ map[ ]
19    case Node(l, k, v, r, c) ⇒ toMap(l) + map[k := v] + toMap(r)
20  }
```

Fig. 10. Functional model (`TRBTree`) and red-black trees invariant

```
1   ghost function AddTRBT(prev: TRBPointer, t: TRBTreeOrThread, next: TRBPointer, k': K, v': V): TRBTree {
2     match t
3     case Empty | Thread(_) ⇒ Node(prev, k', v', next, Red)
4     case Node(l, k, v, r, c) ⇒
5       if k < k' then RestoreTRBT(Node(l, k, v, AddTRBT(Thread(k), r, next, k', v'), c))
6       else if k' < k then /* symmetric to left recursion */
7       else Node(l, k, v', r, c)
8   }
9
10  ghost function RestoreTRBT(t: TRBTree): TRBTree
11    requires t.Node?
12  {
13    var t' := if isRed(t.right) then RotateLeftTRBT(t) else t;
14    var t'' := if isRed(t'.left) ∧ isRed(t'.left.left) then RotateRightTRBT(t') else t';
15    if isRed(t''.left) ∧ isRed(t''.right) then FlipColorsTRBT(t'') else t''
16  }
17
18  lemma AddInv(prev: TRBPointer, t: TRBTreeOrThread, next: TRBPointer, k: K, v: V)
19    requires SearchTree(t) ∧ RedBlackTree(t)
20    requires ¬(isRed(t) ∧ isRed(t.left))
21    ensures isBlack(t) ∧ isRed(RestoreTRBT(t)) ⟹ ¬isRed(RestoreTRBT(t).left)
22    ensures keys(t) + {k} = keys(Add(prev, t, next, k, v))
23    ensures k ∈ keys(t) ⟹ keys(t) = keys(Add(prev, t, next, k, v))
24    ensures SearchTree(Add(prev, t, next, k, v))
25    ensures RedBlackTree(Add(prev, t, next, k, v))
26    ensures BlackHeight(t) = BlackHeight(Add(prev, t, next, k, v))
27
28  lemma AddMap(prev: TRBPointer, t: TRBTreeOrThread, next: TRBPointer, k: K, v: V)
29    ensures toMap(Add(prev, t, next, k, v)) = toMap(t)[k := v]
```

Fig. 11. Definition of `Add` on `TRBTree` and red-black invariant preservation lemma

improvement in the total verification time. Most importantly, the methodology
we propose enjoys greater interactivity by being more modular, since each definition is smaller and faster to verify individually. Modularity comes at a small
line-count cost given that, in our case, the number of lines of code is increased
by 1.2x.

5   Related Work and Conclusions

Verification of ADTs is a well-studied topic in the area of automated verification. The work of Polikarpova et al. [27,31] is one of the most comprehensive container libraries and it provides associative containers. The interplay between iterators and their parent containers is modeled by semantic collaboration [28]. A difference is that a collection is unaware of the types of iterators traversing it, while in our library each collection has its own type of iterator. This allows us to have fine-grained invalidation policies that are specific to the container.

Regarding iterators, Filliâtre et al. [12] introduce an abstract specification together with some verified implementations in Why3. In their work, iterators are not necessarily tied to the traversal of a data structure; however, when they are, they become invalidated whenever the underlying structure is modified. A similar notion of iterators has also been studied in the context of Rust [8], allowing side-effectful computations during traversal. In this case, Rust's type system forbids modifications to a data structure while it is being traversed. The problem of verifying non-interference between iterators has been addressed with several techniques, which include versioning [9], separation logic [16], typestates [4] and use of coroutines [13]. There, invalidation policies consist in preventing simultaneous traversal and modifications, or in invalidating all iterators whenever the ADT's model changes. A more refined approach is that of Malecha et al. [22] based on separation logic and fractional permissions, which allows for multiple readers and a single writer. Our approach allows multiple readers and writers, as shown in Section 3.2.

Regarding red-black trees, there are machine-checked implementations based on term algebras [23] and permission-based separation logic [2], the latter of which allows one writer or several readers on the same tree. Also based on separation logic, Schellhorn et al. [29] introduce a verified implementation of red-black trees in KIV [11]. As in our approach, there is a high-level functional implementation, in which properties are proved, and a heap-based implementation that is mapped to the former. A variant of red-black trees has already been verified in Dafny [26] but only in its functional segment, akin to the tree model we use to verify red-black properties. None of these implementations are threaded neither provide support for iterators.

We have developed a verification methodology that lets implementors and users verify their code in a systematic and interactive way. We build upon our previous work [5], but we extend it to better accommodate the increased complexity of associative containers. Notably, verification of client code becomes very slow when several structures and iterators on them are involved because pairwise disjointness has to be guaranteed after each method execution. Modularizing client code and defining all the ghost predicates and functions as opaque leads to a substantial reduction in verification time; however, this improvement incurs a cost. The programmer is required to write additional code and perform extra manual steps, notably the insertion of `reveal` statements. Nonetheless, much of this supplementary code is boilerplate, and a future objective is to automate its generation.

```
1   method AddImpl(prev: Pointer, node: TTNode?, isThread: bool, next: Pointer,
2                  ghost sk: TTreeOrThread, k: K, v: V)
3       returns (newNode: TTNode, ghost newSk: TTree)
4     requires ValidChild(node, sk, isThread) ∧ Threaded(prev, sk, next)
5     ensures ValidRec(newNode, newSk) ∧ Threaded(prev, newSk, next)
6     ensures TreeModel(newSk) = AddTRBT(TreeModel(prev), old(TreeModel(sk)), TreeModel(next), k, v)
7   {
8     if node = null ∨ isThread {
9       newNode := new TTNode(prev, k, v, next, Red);
10      newSk := Node(/* ...*/, newNode, /* ...*/);
11    } else {
12      if k = node.key {
13        node.value := v; newNode := node; newSk := sk;
14      } else if node.key < k {
15        node.right, newSkRight := AddImpl(node, node.right, node.isThreadRight, next, sk.right, k, v);
16        node.isThreadRight := false;
17        newSk := Node(sk.left, node, newSkRight);
18        newNode, newSk := RestoreImpl(prev, newNode, next, newSk);
19      } else { /* ...symmetric to right recursion... */ }
20    }
21  }
```

Fig. 12. `AddImpl` resembles functional behaviour and preserves memory invariant.

```
1   class ThreadedLinkedTree { ...
2     method Add(k: K, v: V)
3       requires Valid() ∧ SearchTree(Model()) ∧ RedBlackTree(Model())
4       ensures Valid() ∧ SearchTree(Model()) ∧ RedBlackTree(Model())
5       ensures Model() = AddTRBT(Empty, old(Model()), Empty, k, v).(color := Black)
6     {
7       AddInv(Empty, TreeModel(skeleton), Empty, k, v);
8       root, skeleton := AddImpl(null, root, false, null, skeleton, k, v);
9       root.color := Black;
10    }
11  }
```

Fig. 13. Implementation of `Add` in `ThreadedLinkedTree` using `AddImpl`.

Table 2. Plain versus modular version verification times and resource units (RU)

	Plain (time)	Plain (RU)	Modular (time)	Modular (RU)
Definitions & misc.	**17.3 s**	3.87M	20.1 s (0.86x)	**2.27M** (1.70x)
FlipColors	**5.74 s**	2.66M	6.79 s (0.84x)	**1.32M** (2.02x)
RotateLeft	43.4 s	16.1M	**8.93 s** (4.87x)	**4.03M** (3.99x)
RotateRight	56.1 s	25.3M	**9.16 s** (6.12x)	**4.79M** (5.28x)
Restore	96.5 s	68.1M	**8.11 s** (11.9x)	**4.21M** (16.2x)
Insert	111 s	83.4M	**28.5 s** (3.91x)	**29.5M** (2.83x)
Total	330 s	199M	**81.7 s** (4.05x)	**46.1M** (4.33x)

Separation logic imposes the disjointness of address locations by defining
primitive operators on the logic. The approach we follow, however, is to explicitly
declare that the footprints of different instances of our ADTs are disjoint. We
leave as future work studying how to adapt our approach to separation logic,
and whether it improves the verification time or the complexity of our proofs.

The ADTs defined in this work are, at the moment, fixed to contain keys of type `int`, since Dafny does not support bounded polymorphism. To overcome this limitation every definition would need to take the ordering relation as an extra argument and require the ordering properties. We leave as future work making our ADTs parametric on the type of keys and its order relation. Besides this, alternative implementations of these ADTs are subject of future work (e.g., trees with parent pointers or B-trees [10]) where the methodological considerations introduced in this paper would still be appliable.

Acknowledgments. Work partially supported by the Spanish AEI project ProCode-UCM (PID2019-108528RB-C22) and joint public call (Comunidad de Madrid and UCM) for proposals for projects led by early-career PhD holders (PR17/24-31913).

References

1. Ahmadi, R., Leino, K.R.M., Nummenmaa, J.: Automatic verification of Dafny programs with traits. In: Proceedings of the 17th Workshop on Formal Techniques for Java-like Programs. FTfJP 2015. Association for Computing Machinery, New York (2015)
2. Armborst, L., Huisman, M.: Permission-based verification of red-black trees and their merging. In: IEEE/ACM Formal Methods in Software Engineering (FormaliSE), pp. 111–123 (2021)
3. Bertot, Y., Castéran, P.: Interactive Theorem Proving and Program Development. Coq'Art: The Calculus of Inductive Constructions. Texts in Theoretical Computer Science. Springer (2004)
4. Bierhoff, K.: Iterator specification with Typestates. In: SAVCBS 2006, pp. 79–82. ACM (2006)
5. Blázquez, J., Montenegro, M., Segura, C.: Verification of mutable linear data structures and iterator-based algorithms in Dafny. J. Log. Algebraic Methods Program. **134**, 100875 (2023)
6. Blázquez, J., Montenegro, M., Segura, C.: Artifact for "Verified implementation of associative containers with iterators using threaded red-black trees" (2025). https://doi.org/10.5281/zenodo.16883686
7. Blázquez, J., Montenegro, M., Segura, C.: Verified implementation of associative containers with iterators using threaded red-black trees (Technical report - Additional examples) (2025). https://doi.org/10.5281/zenodo.17199658
8. Bílý, A., Hansen, J., Müller, P., Summers, A.J.: Compositional reasoning for side-effectful iterators and iterator adapters (2022). https://arxiv.org/abs/2210.09857
9. Cok, D.R.: Specifying Java iterators with JML and Esc/Java2. In: SAVCBS 2006, pp. 71–74. ACM (2006)
10. Cormen, T., Leiserson, C., Rivest, R., Stein, C.: Introduction to Algorithms, 4th edn. MIT Press (2022). https://books.google.es/books?id=HOJyzgEACAAJ
11. Ernst, G., Pfähler, J., et al.: KIV: overview and VerifyThis competition. Int. J. Softw. Tools Technol. Transf. **17**(6), 677–694 (2015)
12. Filliâtre, J.-C., Pereira, M.: A modular way to reason about iteration. In: Rayadurgam, S., Tkachuk, O. (eds.) NFM 2016. LNCS, vol. 9690, pp. 322–336. Springer, Cham (2016). https://doi.org/10.1007/978-3-319-40648-0_24

13. Jacobs, B., Piessens, F., Schulte, W.: VC generation for functional behavior and non-interference of iterators. In: Specification and Verification of Component-Based Systems, SAVCBS 2006, pp. 67–70. ACM (2006)
14. Kassios, I.T.: The dynamic frames theory. Formal Aspects Comput. **23**, 267–288 (2011)
15. Knuth, D.: The Art of Computer Programming: Fundamental Algorithms, Volume 1. Pearson Education (1997)
16. Krishnaswami, N.R.: Reasoning about iterators with separation logic. In: SAVCBS 2006, pp. 83–86. ACM (2006)
17. Leino, K.R.M.: Specification and verification of object-oriented software. In: Engineering Methods and Tools for Software Safety and Security, pp. 231–266. IOS Press (2009)
18. Leino, K.R.M.: Dafny: an automatic program verifier for functional correctness. In: Clarke, E.M., Voronkov, A. (eds.) LPAR 2010. LNCS (LNAI), vol. 6355, pp. 348–370. Springer, Heidelberg (2010). https://doi.org/10.1007/978-3-642-17511-4_20
19. Leino, K.R.M.: Program Proofs. The MIT Press (2023)
20. Leino, K.R.M., Ford, R.L., Cok, D.R.: Dafny Reference Manual. The Dafny-Lang community (2025). https://dafny.org/dafny/DafnyRef/DafnyRef.html. Accessed 16 Sept 2025
21. Li, Z., Wang, J., Sun, M., Lui, J.C.: Mirchecker: detecting bugs in rust programs via static analysis. In: CCS 2021, pp. 2183–2196. ACM (2021)
22. Malecha, G., Morrisett, G.: Mechanized verification with sharing. In: Cavalcanti, A., Deharbe, D., Gaudel, M.-C., Woodcock, J. (eds.) ICTAC 2010. LNCS, vol. 6255, pp. 245–259. Springer, Heidelberg (2010). https://doi.org/10.1007/978-3-642-14808-8_17
23. Manna, Z., Sipma, H.B., Zhang, T.: Verifying balanced trees. In: Artemov, S.N., Nerode, A. (eds.) LFCS 2007. LNCS, vol. 4514, pp. 363–378. Springer, Heidelberg (2007). https://doi.org/10.1007/978-3-540-72734-7_26
24. de Moura, L., Bjørner, N.: Z3: an efficient SMT solver. In: Ramakrishnan, C.R., Rehof, J. (eds.) TACAS 2008. LNCS, vol. 4963, pp. 337–340. Springer, Heidelberg (2008). https://doi.org/10.1007/978-3-540-78800-3_24
25. Moura, L., Ullrich, S.: The lean 4 theorem prover and programming language. In: Platzer, A., Sutcliffe, G. (eds.) CADE 2021. LNCS (LNAI), vol. 12699, pp. 625–635. Springer, Cham (2021). https://doi.org/10.1007/978-3-030-79876-5_37
26. Peña, R.: An assertional proof of red-black trees using dafny. J. Autom. Reason. **64**(4), 767–791 (2020)
27. Polikarpova, N., Tschannen, J., Furia, C.A.: A fully verified container library. Formal Aspects Comput. **30**(5), 495–523 (2018)
28. Polikarpova, N., Tschannen, J., Furia, C.A., Meyer, B.: Flexible invariants through semantic collaboration. In: Jones, C., Pihlajasaari, P., Sun, J. (eds.) FM 2014. LNCS, vol. 8442, pp. 514–530. Springer, Cham (2014). https://doi.org/10.1007/978-3-319-06410-9_35
29. Schellhorn, G., Bodenmüller, S., Bitterlich, M., Reif, W.: Separating separation logic – modular verification of red-black trees. In: VSTTE 2023, pp. 129–147. Springer (2023)
30. Sedgewick, R., Wayne, K.: Algorithms, 4th edn. Addison-Wesley (2011)

31. Tschannen, J., Furia, C.A., Nordio, M., Polikarpova, N.: AutoProof: auto-active functional verification of object-oriented programs. In: Baier, C., Tinelli, C. (eds.) TACAS 2015. LNCS, vol. 9035, pp. 566–580. Springer, Heidelberg (2015). https://doi.org/10.1007/978-3-662-46681-0_53
32. VanHattum, A., Schwartz-Narbonne, D., Chong, N., Sampson, A.: Verifying dynamic trait objects in Rust. In: ICSE-SEIP, pp. 321–330. ACM (2022)

Formal Verification of Legal Contracts: A Translation-Based Approach

Reiner Hähnle[1], Cosimo Laneve[2], and Adele Veschetti[1(✉)]

[1] Department of Computer Science, TU Darmstadt, Darmstadt, Germany
`{reiner.haehnle,adele.veschetti}@tu-darmstadt.de`
[2] DISI, University of Bologna, Bologna, Italy
`cosimo.laneve@unibo.it`

Abstract. *Stipula* is a domain-specific programming language designed to model legal contracts with enforceable properties, especially those involving asset transfers and obligations. This paper presents a methodology to formally verify the correctness of Stipula contracts through translation into Java code annotated with Java Modeling Language specifications. As a verification backend, the deductive verification tool KeY is used. Both, the translation and the verification of partial and total correctness for a large subset of *Stipula* contracts, those with disjoint cycles, is fully automatic. Our work demonstrates that a general-purpose deductive verification tool can be used successfully in a translation approach.

Keywords: Formal Verification · Stipula Language · Translation-based Verification · Deductive Verification

1   Introduction

As the legal domain continues its digital transformation, the demand for precise, machine-verifiable representations of legal contracts becomes increasingly important. Traditional legal texts, written in natural language, are inherently ambiguous and prone to misinterpretation, making them challenging to process, analyze, or verify by automated means. To address this issue, several projects are being developed for defining programming languages to write legal contracts, *e.g.* [17–19,21]. Although these projects introduce a precise syntax for legal contracts and provide graphical tools to associate normative elements with code, they pay limited attention to the verification of correctness. Yet, this aspect is crucial in legal contexts, where ambiguities or unintended behavior during execution can lead to significant legal and financial repercussions. Despite advances in the formal verification of legal contracts, formal reasoning is rare in practice due to tool complexity.

To overcome this lack of automatic verification techniques, in 2021, we designed *Stipula* [7,8,16], a new domain-specific language with few concise and intelligible primitives that have a precise correspondence with the distinctive

F. Damiani and M. Farrell (Eds.): iFM 2025, LNCS 16194, pp. 59–78, 2026.
https://doi.org/10.1007/978-3-032-10794-7_4

elements of legal contracts. The language has a formal operational semantics, so that the behavior is fully specified and amenable to automatic verification. Its current tool chain [9] contains a runtime environment, a type checker, a graphical IDE, and an analyzer verifying the reachability of clauses [10,15].

In this paper, we advance the automatic verification of *Stipula* contracts by introducing a systematic approach for verifying contracts through translation into a general-purpose deductive verification tool. Specifically, we translate *Stipula* contracts into Java programs annotated with JML (Java Modeling Language) specifications, and we employ the KeY verification system [3,5] as a backend. We define translation patterns and principles that preserve the semantics of core *Stipula* constructs—such as asset transfers, functions, and events—within the program logic supported by KeY. Our approach admits both manual and automated translation, and it accommodates a variety of contract types, including those with cyclic behavior and partial asset transfers.

It is by no means evident that a translation-based approach to verification will succeed. For deductive verification tools such as KeY to operate in a fully automated mode, the availability of sufficiently precise specification annotations is crucial. In the general case, such specifications need to be provided manually, which renders deductive verification inherently interactive and, consequently, costly. In the case of *Stipula*, every smart contract is associated with a well-defined automaton: the states represent control points of the contract, while the transitions correspond to its clauses, such as functions or events. This automaton-based representation makes the contract's behavior explicit and provides a natural foundation for reasoning about possible execution paths. Moreover, when the automaton of a contract satisfies the structural property of *disjoint cycles* – that is, cycles that do not share any states – it becomes possible to automatically synthesize suitable JML annotations, including guarantees and loop invariants. This synthesis step significantly reduces the annotation burden and paves the way for a high degree of automation in the verification process, thus demonstrating the potential of the translation-based approach in practice.

Nonetheless, there are limitations that affect full generality. Time-dependent behavior must be scheduled symbolically and evaluated statically. Our technique handles this by using symbolic boolean variables representing the time constraint. The event is then translated into a conditional guarded by the symbolic variable that KeY evaluates by exploring both possibilities: one where the event occurs and one where it does not. More complex forms of time management, such as dynamically registered events during loops or asynchronous behavior, are outside the current scope. Similarly, non-deterministic behavior, such as contracts where multiple transitions may be enabled concurrently, is not yet supported: our translation assumes that guards deterministically select a unique transition. These aspects pose challenges for extending the approach beyond the verified fragment we currently target.

The paper is structured as follows. Section 2 introduces the *Stipula* language and its execution semantics; an illustrative example highlights how obligations, permissions, and events are expressed in *Stipula*. We also provide a short introduction to KeY. Section 3 formalizes our translation methodology from *Stipula* to Java, detailing how fields, assets, functions, events, and contract behavior are encoded in Java and specified with JML. Section 4 discusses the implementation of our translator tool and presents case studies that apply our approach to representative *Stipula* contracts, demonstrating the effectiveness of the method and discussing verification outcomes. Section 5 reviews related efforts in contract languages and formal verification. Section 6 concludes the paper and outlines directions for future work.

2   Background

To set the stage for our translation-based verification method, we briefly review the relevant background. Section 2.1 presents the *Stipula* language, emphasizing its constructs for assets, states, and timed events. Section 2.2 introduces the KeY system, which we later employ as the verification backend.

2.1   *Stipula*

```
stipula C {
     asset h̄
     field x̄
     agreement(Ā) {
         Ā₁ : x̄₁
         ···     // ⋃_{i∈1..n} Āᵢ ⊆ Ā,   ⋃_{i∈1..n} x̄ᵢ ⊆ x̄,   ⋂_{i∈1..n} x̄ᵢ = ∅
         Āₙ : x̄ₙ
     } ⇒ @Q
     F
}
```

$$
\begin{array}{lll}
\textit{Functions} & F ::= & \_ \;\mid\; \texttt{@Q A}: \texttt{f}(\overline{y})[\overline{k}]\,(E)\{\,S\;\;W\,\} \Rightarrow \texttt{@Q}'\;F \\
\textit{Prefixes} & P ::= & E \rightarrow \texttt{x} \;\mid\; E \rightarrow \texttt{A} \;\mid\; E \multimap \texttt{h},\texttt{h}' \;\mid\; E \multimap \texttt{h},\texttt{A} \\
\textit{Statements} & S ::= & \_ \;\mid\; P\,S \;\mid\; \texttt{if}\,(E)\{\,S\,\}\,\texttt{else}\,\{\,S\,\}\,S \\
\textit{Events} & W ::= & \_ \;\mid\; \texttt{now}+k \gg \texttt{@Q}\{\,S\,\} \Rightarrow \texttt{@Q}'\;W \\
\textit{Expressions} & E ::= & v \;\mid\; X \;\mid\; E\,\texttt{op}\,E \;\mid\; \texttt{uop}\,E \\
\textit{Values} & v ::= & n \;\mid\; \texttt{false} \;\mid\; \texttt{true} \;\mid\; s
\end{array}
$$

Fig. 1. Syntax of *Stipula*

A *Stipula* contract consists of a set of parties, states, assets, fields, and a set of functions and events, generically called *clauses*. The declaration of a contract is defined in Fig. 1, where C is the name of the contract, h̄ and x̄ are the *assets* and *fields*, respectively, Ā are the *parties*. The **agreement** construct declares the parties that set the initial value of the fields and the initial state of the contract.

For example, if the agreement has three parties A_1, A_2, A_3 and the contract has two fields x_1, x_2, if it declares $A_1 : x_1$ and $A_2, A_3 : x_2$ then x_1 will be set by A_1 and x_2 will be set upon agreement on the value between A_2 and A_3. When the agreement is concluded, the parties may invoke a function in F.

A *function* @Q A : $f(\overline{y})[\overline{k}]\,(E)\{\,S;\ W\,\} \Rightarrow$ @Q$'$ can be invoked by a party A if the contract is in state Q and the guard E is *true*. The names $\overline{y}$ and $\overline{k}$ are the formal parameters of f; they are kept separate because $\overline{y}$ are field values while $\overline{k}$ are asset quantities.

Function bodies are *statements* followed by *events*. The former include value transfers, asset movements, conditional logic, and field assignments. *Stipula* distinguishes between different transfer operations: field and message updates use the symbol $\rightarrow$ with the usual semantics of assignment, while asset transfers use the linear implication operator $\multimap$ to emphasize the conservation semantics. For instance, an expression like "1 $\multimap$ wallet, Seller " denotes exclusive transfer of a unit in wallet to the Seller and, *at the same time*, the wallet is decreased by 1. In contrast "code $\rightarrow$ Licensee" models non-exclusive passing of information. The operation "wallet $\multimap$ wallet, Seller " is always shortened to "wallet $\multimap$ Seller ".

Events **now** $+ k \gg$ @Q$\{\,S\,\} \Rightarrow$ @Q$'$, where k is either a natural number or a field name, define a statement S to be executed if, *after* k time units from the current execution, the contract is in the state Q. If the event is executed, the contract will transition to the state Q$'$.

We refer to article [8] for background on the design of *Stipula*, as well as its formal semantics. A comment about the model of time in *Stipula* may be useful for what follows. The model has a multiset of events to be executed; every event has a time value that is a natural number representing minutes. This number is computed when the event is created by replacing **now** with 0 in the expression **now** $+ k$ (recall that k is either a natural number or a field name). Time advances when the contract has no statements to execute and no events can be triggered. In such cases, a "tick" occurs, decrementing the time values in the multiset of events. Events with negative time values are discarded. Subsequently, any event whose initial state matches the current contract state and whose time value reaches zero may be scheduled for execution.[1]

In this paper we use the state transition models of *Stipula* contracts, called the *underlying automata*. The states of these automata are those of the *Stipula* contract. The transitions correspond to clauses and are labelled either with the function name (the party name is always omitted, for simplicity's sake we assume that function names are pairwise different) or with the event line number (*e.g.*, ev_{10} is the event at code line 10). Figure 2 shows an underlying automaton.

We illustrate *Stipula* through two representative examples that allow us to highlight crucial *Stipula* features:

***normative permissions*:** functions are enabled only for specific parties in specific states;

---

[1] The syntax of *Stipula* in [8] admits absolute time expressions like "2022/1/1:00:15"; these expressions are rewritten into terms **now** $+ k$ when the event is created.

asset safety: assets are never duplicated or lost; transfers are explicitly encoded and conditional;

timed obligations: the event construct encodes deadlines and enforces compliance without external intervention;

stateful logic: contract progress is encoded through explicit state transitions, supporting both branching and linear workflows.

Example 1 (The License Contract). Listing 1 defines a *license contract* that regulates a licensing transaction between a `Licensor` and a `Licensee`, with time-bound trial periods and the possibility to purchase or decline the license. In particular, the `Licensee` may request a trial and then decide whether to buy the license. If the `Licensee` does not purchase the license before the trial period expires, the contract terminates and the cost is automatically returned to the `Licensee`.

The contract begins with an **agreement** clause in Line 4, where both parties define the trial start time (`t_start`), its duration (`t_limit`), and the license `cost`. This mirrors the legal principle of mutual consent ("meeting of the minds"): no contract behavior is enabled until consensus is reached. Upon agreement, the first control state is `@Init` (Line 6).

```
1   stipula License {
2       asset balance, token
3       field t_start, t_limit, cost, code
4       agreement (Licensor, Licensee)(t_start, t_limit, cost) {
5           Licensor, Licensee : t_start, t_limit, cost
6       } ⇒ @Init
7       @Init Licensor: offer(x)[n] {
8           n ⊸ token
9           x ⟶ code
10          now + t_start ≫ @Prop { token ⊸ Licensor } ⇒ @End
11      } ⇒ @Prop
12      @Prop Licensee: activate()[b] (b == cost) {
13          b ⊸ balance
14          code ⟶ Licensee
15          now + t_limit ≫ @Trial {
16                  balance ⊸ Licensee
17                  token ⊸ Licensor
18                  } ⇒ @End
19      } ⇒ @Trial
20      @Trial Licensee: buy()[] {
21          balance ⊸ Licensor
22          token ⊸ Licensee
23      } ⇒ @End
24  }
```

Listing 1. The License contract in *Stipula*

The *underlying automaton* of `License` is shown in Fig. 2. In the `Init` state, the `Licensor` may invoke `offer`, transferring a `token` (representing the license)

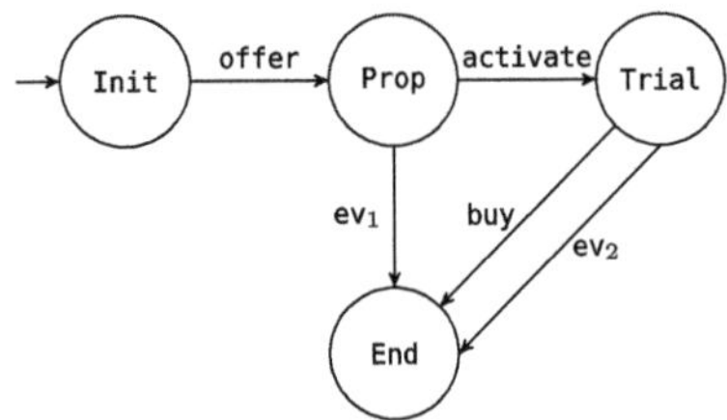

Fig. 2. Underlying automaton of the License contract

into escrow and generating a license code. A scheduled event is simultaneously registered at t_start time units in the future to reclaim the token if the Licensee fails to act within the trial start window. The contract then moves to Prop. If no function is called in this state, then time is advanced by one unit, eventually triggering the timeout at t_start. These event transitions are dynamically added to the state machine during function execution, *e.g.*, the two events in Fig. 2 are not initially present. This dynamic creation increases the expressiveness of *Stipula* [10].

In Prop, the Licensee can activate the trial by paying the cost (observe that b is an asset of the Licensee), which is transferred to the contract's balance: the contract acts as a notary for assets that are not finally disposed. Now the license code is revealed to the Licensee and another event is scheduled to handle the expiration of the trial period: if the license is not purchased before t_limit time units, the balance is refunded and the token is returned to the Licensor.

In the Trial state, the Licensee has the option to purchase the license via buy, which finalizes the transaction by transferring the balance to the Licensor and assigning the token permanently to the Licensee. In either case, the contract terminates in the End state, without retaining any asset.

Example 2 (The Deposit Contract). Listing 2 presents a *deposit contract* that models the interaction between a Farm and a Client. The Farm deposits flour, while the Client purchases and withdraws the corresponding amount at an agreed price. The contractual terms are enforced over a validity period of 365 d. The clause send allows the Farm to deposit flour into the contract's stock. In send()[h], the assignment h→Client is only an informational message to the Client about the deposited amount (h is not emptied), while the asset transfer h—∘flour increases the contract's internal balance of flour (and, at the same time, empties the asset h). Observe that the converse ordering of the instructions (h—∘flour h→Client) sends 0 to the Client as informational message. Also, no flour is transferred to the Client by send. Actual delivery occurs only with buy()[w], where (w/cost_flour)—∘flour, Client transfers flour from the contract's stock to the Client (hence w/cost_flour must not be greater than flour) and w—∘Farm represents the payment to the Farm. In this way, send supplies the stock, whereas buy withdraws from it under payment.

```
1   stipula Deposit {
2       asset flour
3       field cost_flour
4       agreement (Client, Farm)(cost_flour) {
5           Client, Farm : cost_flour
6       } ⇒ @Start
7       @Start Farm : begin()[h]{
8           h ⟶ Client
9           h ⊸ flour
10          now + 365 ≫ @RunF { flour ⊸ Farm } ⇒ @End
11          now + 365 ≫ @RunC { flour ⊸ Farm } ⇒ @End
12      } ⇒ @RunC
13      @RunF Farm : send()[h]{
14          h ⟶ Client
15          h ⊸ flour
16      } ⇒ @RunC
17      @RunC Client : buy()[w](w/cost_flour <= flour){
18          (w/cost_flour) ⊸ flour, Client
19          w ⊸ Farm
20      } ⇒ @RunF
21  }
```

Listing 2. The Deposit contract in *Stipula*

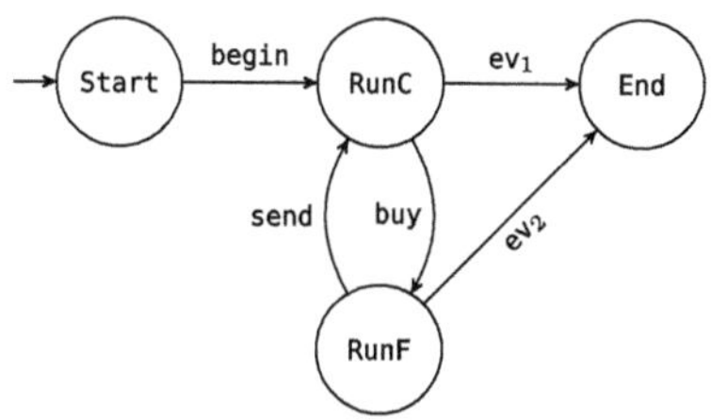

Fig. 3. Underlying automaton of the Deposit contract

Unlike the License contract, the Deposit contract has cyclic interactions: the Farm and Client can repeatedly invoke send and buy as long as the contract remains valid, as shown in the automaton in Fig. 3. This is modeled by the function send transitioning from RunF to RunC and the function buy in the reverse direction, enabling iteration until the validity period expires.

The alternation between RunF and RunC in Example 2 is by design: it ensures that each iteration of the cycle is well-formed and contributes to disjointness of cycles in the underlying automaton. Allowing the Client to buy repeatedly without intervening deposits would introduce overlapping cycles, which are outside the scope of the current automatic verification approach. Cycles increase the complexity of formal analysis [15]. In particular, this feature, combined with deadlines (the events) and permission-dependent transitions enlarge the state space and introduce subtle cross dependencies, making automated verification challenging.

Definition 1 (Cyclic Contracts and Disjoint Cycles). *A* Stipula *contract is* cyclic *if its underlying automaton has a sequence of pairwise different states* $Q_1, \ldots, Q_n$ *with transitions* $Q_i \xrightarrow{\mu_i} Q_{i+1}$ *and* $Q_n \xrightarrow{\mu_n} Q_1$ *where* μ_i *are either function names or events. The contract has* disjoint cycles *if different cycles have no state in common.*

We focus on contracts whose automata contain only disjoint cycles—a structural property that simplifies path generation and enables modular, fully automatic verification. For example, the `Deposit` contract includes a single cycle, while `License` is entirely acyclic. Disjoint cycles ensure determinism: If a state has multiple outgoing transitions, at most one of them belongs to any given cycle. This allows our tool to synthesize all execution paths statically, without ambiguity or runtime checks.

While this restriction enhances tractability, it limits generality. Contracts with overlapping cycles are currently out of scope, though we discuss possible extensions in the conclusion. The current implementation does not yet enforce that cycles are disjoint; an algorithm for checking it is presented in the extended version of the paper [13] and will be integrated in a future version.

2.2   Deductive Verification with the KeY System

The KeY system [3,5] is a deductive verification framework for Java that combines symbolic execution, invariant reasoning, and method contracts[2] on top of a calculus for an expressive program logic. The main use case of KeY is formal verification of Java programs annotated with specifications written in JML. It provides an interactive user environment, where one can construct correctness proofs of Java methods against their JML contracts. These contracts typically include preconditions (**requires**), postconditions (**ensures**), frame conditions (**assignable**), class invariants, and auxiliary annotations such as loop invariants and assertions. Given a JML-annotated Java class, KeY translates the specifications into logical proof obligations and attempts to discharge them using its symbolic execution engine. The details of the verification process are irrelevant for the purpose of this paper: KeY is used as a *black box*, the input is a JML-annotated Java file that results from translation of a *Stipula* contract. In general, KeY is used in interactive or auto-active mode, however, for all case studies discussed below, the verification is *fully automatic*.

3   Translation Approach

To enable formal verification of *Stipula* contracts, we define a systematic translation into Java code annotated with JML specifications. Java and JML are

---

[2] Not to be confused with *Stipula* contracts. In this paper, both kinds of contract are featured, but it should be obvious from the context when we mean *Stipula* contracts or Java/JML method contracts.

versatile enough to express *Stipula* in a natural manner: functions are modeled by stateful Java methods, the specific semantics of assets are modeled by suitable JML method contracts, etc.; the details are given below. Our translation preserves the semantics of *Stipula*'s normative constructs, including asset ownership, state transitions, permissions, and events, by representing them as verifiable Java/JML proof obligations.

3.1   Assets, Fields and States

We distinguish three categories of contract data: *fields*, *assets*, and the *control state*. Each is translated into corresponding elements in the target Java class, along with accompanying JML specifications to capture correctness properties.

Fields. *Stipula* contracts define mutable fields that store contract-specific state information, such as numeric counters, time stamps, or configuration parameters. These fields evolve during execution and influence both transitions and obligations. We must ensure that field updates are explicitly modeled and tracked in the translated Java code.

Definition 2 (Field Mapping). *Let $\mathcal{F}$ be the set of mutable fields declared in a Stipula contract. Each field $f \in \mathcal{F}$ is translated to a* **static** *Java field, which holds the contract state data. Changes to these fields are tracked and constrained using JML* **assignable** *clauses.*

This representation allows JML to reason about field updates and supports the specification of frame conditions through **assignable** clauses.

Assets. In *Stipula*, assets are classified automatically as *divisible* or *indivisible* to enable explicit ownership modeling and prevent asset duplication or loss. The translator infers this heuristically from usage: assets transferred with a variable quantity ("v—∘ h, h' ") are treated as divisible and represented as an `int`, while those transferred directly ("h—∘ h' ") are considered indivisible and represented as a `boolean`. To enforce exclusivity for indivisible assets, safety preconditions like "**requires** !h.token" are generated. Based on this classification, we now formally define how asset ownership is represented.

Definition 3 (Asset Ownership Representation). *Let $\mathcal{A}$ be the set of declared assets, and $\mathcal{P}$ the set of participants in a Stipula contract* C. *Each asset $a \in \mathcal{A}$ is represented by a set of Java fields:*

$$\{P.a \mid P \in \mathcal{P}\} \cup \{C.a\},$$

where each field P.a *is either of a numeric type (*`int`*) indicating the quantity of asset* a *held by party* P *or a boolean variable indicating that the party* P *owns asset* a. *The field* C.a *tracks the quantity owned by the contract itself.*

To ensure that each indivisible asset is held by exactly one owner at all times, we define an invariant that formalizes the exclusivity constraint.

Property 1 (Indivisible Asset Exclusivity). Each asset is owned by exactly one party in $\mathcal{P}$ or by the contract C at any given time. Formally, the following invariant must hold for all $a \in \mathcal{A}$: $\bigvee_{X \in \mathcal{P} \cup \{C\}} \left(X.a \wedge \bigwedge_{Y \neq X} \neg Y.a \right)$.

This invariant becomes part of the translated Java class as a static JML `invariant`, ensuring asset linearity throughout execution.

In our current encoding, exclusivity of indivisible assets is often enforced via explicit postconditions on methods. Alternatively, these properties can be stated as JML class invariants, which would provide a more uniform and modular treatment; we plan to explore this refinement in future versions of the tool.

Example 3. The asset `token` in the License contract in Sect. 2 is modeled by three Java fields: `License.token`, `Licensee.token`, and `Licensor.token`. Property 1 is ensured in JML as:

```
static invariant (License.token∧¬Licensee.token∧¬Licensor.token)
             ∨(Licensee.token∧¬License.token∧¬Licensor.token)
             ∨(Licensor.token∧¬License.token∧¬Licensee.token)
```

For divisible assets, rather than enforcing exclusivity, we ensure that the total quantity of the asset remains constant throughout the contract execution. This principle is captured by the following property, which generalizes the invariants used in examples such as currency transfers and resource tracking.

Property 2 (Divisible Asset Conservation). For each divisible asset $a \in \mathcal{A}$, declared with a fixed total quantity κ_a , the system ensures that the total amount held by all participants in $\mathcal{P}$ and the contract C remains constant:

$$\sum_{X \in \mathcal{P} \cup \{C\}} X.a = \kappa_a$$

Example 4. The `Deposit` contract provides an illustration of Property 2. In this contract, the farmer transfers an amount `h` of the divisible asset `flour` to the contract by calling the `send(h)` function. Importantly, this transfer does not create assets: the amount `h` is subtracted from the farmer's `Farm.flour` field and added to the contract's `Deposit.flour` field. This is reflected in the generated JML postcondition:

```
/*@ public normal_behavior
    ...
  @ ensures     Deposit.flour == \old(Deposit.flour) + h
  @             && Farm.flour == \old(Farm.flour) - h
  @             && Client.flour == \old(Client.flour);
    ...
  @*/
  public final static void send(int h) {
```

```
        Deposit.flour = Deposit.flour + h;
        Farm.flour = Farm.flour - h;
    }
```

Thus, the total quantity of the asset `flour` remains constant across the system, as required by the conservation property. The complete translation of the `Deposit` contract, including this method, is shown in [13].

Functions. In *Stipula*, contract behavior is defined by transitions that correspond to functions and events. Each transition is enabled under specific conditions, such as the current control state, the invoking party, and the availability of required assets. And it may update fields, transfer assets, or trigger further state changes. To reflect this logic in Java, each *Stipula* function is translated into a static Java method with a formal specification in terms of a JML contract:

- the **requires** clause specifies the initial control state, party permissions, and preconditions over asset ownership and fields;
- the **ensures** clause describes the resulting state transition, updates to fields, and asset transfers;
- the **assignable** clause enumerates the state variables that may be modified.

   Preconditions in the generated JML specifications are derived directly from *Stipula*'s guards, permissions, and asset requirements. In particular, they capture the enabling conditions for invoking a function, rather than being reconstructed backwards from the post-state.

Example 5. We illustrate the encoding of functions and states in JML with the `buy()` function in Listing 1. Observe that the invariant for asset exclusivity is implicitly present in the pre- and postcondition. Fully automatic verification of the contract in KeY, including invariant preservation, takes fractions of a second.

```
/*@ public normal_behavior
  @ requires   License.balance && License.token;
  @ ensures    Licensor.balance && !License.balance &&
  @            Licensee.token && !License.token;
  @ assignable Licensor.balance, License.balance, Licensee.token, License.token;
  @*/
public final static void buy() {
    Licensor.balance = true;
    License.balance = false;
    Licensee.token = true;
    License.token = false;
}
```

Definition 4 (Indivisible Asset Transfer Semantics). *Let $a \in \mathcal{A}$ be an indivisible asset of contract C, and $P, Q \in \mathcal{P}$. A transfer of a from P to Q is modeled by the following postcondition:*

$$\neg P.a \wedge Q.a \wedge \bigwedge_{R \in \mathcal{P} \cup \{C\} \setminus \{P,Q\}} (R.a = old(R.a))$$

where $old(\mathsf{R.a})$ *refers to the value of* $\mathsf{R.a}$ *before the transfer is executed.*

This pattern guarantees that only the ownership of P and Q changes, preserving the asset exclusivity invariant of *Stipula*. In addition, all changes are confined to the locations occurring in the **assignable** clause. If we assume Property 1 to be ensured by the exclusivity invariant, then $\mathsf{Q.a}$ alone is sufficient as postcondition. Conditional statements and field updates in a *Stipula* function body are translated directly into Java code.

3.2   Time and Events

Timed clauses in *Stipula* define transitions that become enabled only once logical time reaches a specified value. Such a transition is written as

$$\mathbf{now} + \mathsf{k} \gg @\mathsf{Q}\,\{\,\mathsf{S}\,\} \Rightarrow @\mathsf{Q}'$$

which expresses that, when time reaches $\mathbf{now} + \mathsf{k}$ and the current state is Q, the contract may execute S and move to state Q'. In the Java translation, these time-dependent transitions are not realized by manipulating a global clock. Instead, each timed event is guarded by a symbolic boolean variable representing the time constraint. For example, a transition scheduled at a future time is translated into code of the form:

```
if (ev_event1) { event1(); return; }
```

Here, ev_event1 is a symbolic guard introduced by the translator. Verification tools such as KeY handle this guard symbolically, thereby exploring both possibilities: one where the event occurs and one where it does not. Each event is mapped to a dedicated Java method, named systematically (event1(), event2(), ...), that encapsulates the corresponding body S .[3] A key point is that the symbolic guard ev_event1 does not encode the source state Q explicitly. Instead, state constraints are enforced structurally: our translator automatically generates so-called *scenario methods* (see Sect. 3.4), which represent feasible execution paths. An event method is reachable only from the correct source state along such a path. In other words, the interplay between scenario construction and method preconditions guarantees that events can fire only in the intended states.

All event methods are statically defined during translation and never generated dynamically at runtime. This strategy eliminates the need for explicit clocks or schedulers: time-dependent behavior is captured entirely through symbolic guards. As a result, temporal reasoning can be carried out using standard symbolic verification tools. Furthermore, static analyses can identify and prune unreachable event branches, improving efficiency. For instance, the technique described in [15] can be integrated into our translator, and we plan to pursue this as future work.

---

[3] Deterministic event names are assigned via an internal counter to guarantee consistency and traceability.

3.3   Cyclic Behavior and Loop Translation

When translating a *Stipula* contract whose underlying automaton exhibits disjoint cycles, each cycle is mapped to a dedicated Java **while** loop. Conceptually, the body of the loop corresponds to a single traversal of the cycle, *i.e.*, one complete execution of the contract operations contained within it. During each iteration, the loop updates both the contract's asset variables and its control-state fields to reflect the effect of the executed operations. Loop execution is not governed by explicit counters hard-coded in the program, but by symbolic scalar variables introduced during translation. These variables represent iteration bounds and loop counters, and they serve two complementary purposes:

1. *operational control*: they determine when and how many times the loop body may be executed;
2. *specification support*: they provide the basis for precise JML annotations, such as loop invariants and postconditions, that capture the intended effect of repeated executions.

This combination ensures that the generated Java code remains faithful to the original contract semantics while enabling deductive verification tools to reason soundly about all possible iterations. By structuring cycles as loops annotated with symbolic constraints, the translation bridges the gap between the automaton view of contracts and the logic-based reasoning frameworks used in verification.

Example 6. Consider the `Deposit` contract in Listing 2. The translator generates scalar parameters `h`, `w`, `h_send`, and `counter` to represent single asset transfer amounts and the number of iterations, respectively. The generated code implements the cyclic behavior as follows: For instance, one part of the invariant states that the amount of `flour` held by the contract evolves according to the sum of incoming deposits minus outgoing uses:

```
/*@ loop_invariant
  @ ... flour == \old(flour) - i * w/cost_flour + i * h_send; ...
  @*/
while (i < counter) {
  buy(w);
  send(h_send);
  i++;
}
```

Other parts of the invariant reflect the evolution of the farm and client asset fields (`Farm.flour`, `Client.flour`, etc.) and include standard loop annotations such as bounds and decreases clauses. The translator automatically generates the full invariant by analyzing how each variable changes during loop execution (see [13] for the complete form).

It is important to emphasize a limitation of our current encoding strategy. Parameters such as `w` in Example 6 are treated as symbolic constants throughout the entire execution of a loop. In other words, all iterations are analyzed under a single symbolic instantiation of the parameter. While the semantics of *Stipula* would, in principle, permit different values of w across different iterations, verifying such non-deterministic behavior would require loop invariants that quantify over sequences of iteration-dependent values. At present, verification tools such as KeY cannot discharge such invariants automatically. Supporting this more general setting remains theoretically possible by allowing user-supplied invariants and resorting to interactive proofs, but this goes beyond the scope of our fully automated approach.

We also note that the loop in Example 6 is bounded by the symbolic parameter `counter`, which provides an upper bound on the number of iterations. Our construction associates a decreasing variant, namely (`counter - i`), which enables KeY to automatically prove termination for contracts whose automata consist of disjoint cycles. For more intricate cyclic structures, where such simple variants are not available, proving termination would require richer annotations and remains an open direction for future work.

Finally, regarding correctness, the loop invariants generated by our translation suffice to establish preservation of the basic asset and state properties in the examples we studied. In general, however, automatically synthesized invariants are intentionally conservative: they guarantee soundness but may be incomplete, in the sense that they do not allow KeY to prove every conceivable postcondition. Our design philosophy prioritizes invariants that are simple, structurally derived, and always generated automatically. This choice ensures robustness and automation for typical *Stipula* contracts, while leaving open the possibility of user-supplied annotations in cases where more complex behaviors demand stronger reasoning power.

3.4 Scenario-Based Reasoning

To verify behavioral properties across complete execution paths within a *Stipula* contract, we declare *scenario methods* that represent legal sequences of contract actions. These methods model complete paths through the underlying automaton of a *Stipula* contract, from initial to final states. Each such method is annotated with a JML contract summarizing its overall effect, including field updates, asset transfers, and control state progression.

Example 7. The following scenario method models the successful completion of the contract in Listing 1. It ensures that the assets are swapped as expected. During verification, the already proven contracts of the called methods are used, the method bodies need not be inlined.

```
/*@ requires Licensor.token && Licensee.balance ;
  @ ensures  Licensee.token && Licensor.balance ;*/
public static void success() {
    offer(); activate(); buy();
}
```

When a *Stipula* contract features disjoint cycles or branching behavior that may lead to structurally distinct executions, our translator automatically generates a dedicated scenario method for each feasible path. Each scenario method corresponds to a linearized execution trace, thereby capturing one possible evolution of the *Stipula* contract. The generation process begins with a static analysis of the contract's control structure. In particular, the translator verifies that the clauses of the contract give rise to disjoint control paths. This is achieved by constructing the set of linear traces induced by the underlying automaton and checking that the cycles explored along each trace do not overlap. Once this structural property has been established, the translator can safely emit one scenario per disjoint trace, with each scenario representing a distinct and non-interfering contract behavior. This design makes contract executions explicit for automated reasoning, and isolates traces into independent scenarios to avoid combinatorial explosion.

Example 8. Consider a `Loan` contract that regulates a sequence of financial operations between a `Client` and a `Bank`.

```
@Start Bank : give_money()[w](w == amount) {
    w —o Client ;
    now + 30 >> @Pay1 {  } ⇒ @Fail
} ⇒ @Pay1


@Start Bank : withdraw()[u](u == amount * interest_rate) {
    u —o Client
    "The_Bank_withdraws" —→ Client;
} ⇒ @Withdraw
```

In particular, the `Client` and the `Bank` agree on the `amount` of the loan and the `interest_rate`. They also agree on a number of installment payments and on a conditional early withdrawal by the `Bank`. If the `Bank` exercises the early withdraw then it has to pay a penalty to the client that is equal to `amount * interest_rate`. (The complete code with three payment installments is available in [13].) This contract exhibits two disjoint execution paths: one where the `Client` proceeds through all the payment steps, and another where the `Bank` initiates an early withdrawal. The two execution paths are represented by the following two scenarios automatically generated by the translator (variables u, h, w are bound in the precondition of the JML contract of the scenario, not shown here):

```
public final static void seq1() {              public final static void seq2() {
  give_money(w);                                  withdraw(u);
  if (ev_event1) { event1(); return; }         }
  pay_installment1(h);
  if (ev_event2) { event2(); return; }
  pay_installment2(h);
  if (ev_event3) { event3(); return; }
  pay_installment3(h); }
```

4   Implementation and Evaluation

To evaluate our translation and verification method, we implemented a translator available in the online repository [14]. The tool, realized in ca. 2,000 lines of Java, uses ANTLR4 for parsing and a listener-based traversal to extract contract components such as parties, assets, fields, states, and transitions. We assess its effectiveness in this section by analyzing four representative *Stipula* contracts:

Betting: illustrating branching resolution logic based on external outcomes;
Deposit: modeling recurring resource exchanges between client and provider, with timed fallback events and cyclic asset flows;
Loan: encoding installment-based repayment with symbolic arithmetic over loan parameters and time-triggered enforcement mechanisms;
License: involving timed obligations and conditional asset transfers.

These case studies encompass the main features of *Stipula* contracts, including asset transfer, exclusive ownership, timed events, and cyclic interaction. While not fully exhaustive, this selection demonstrates that our approach handles the major constructs found in practice. Each *Stipula* contract was automatically translated using our tool chain (see [13] for the *Stipula* source and generated Java+JML code), and verified using KeY in automatic mode. No manual proof steps or user-supplied annotations were required. The reported performance results were obtained on a MacBook Pro (2023) equipped with an Apple M2 Pro processor and 16 GB of RAM.

We focus on generic contract properties that are automatically generated together with the Java+JML code and verified without user interaction. These include functional correctness, loop invariants, total termination, and symbolic handling of time-triggered transitions. Custom or domain-specific properties could be added manually as additional postconditions, but are not required for the scenarios we test. The following verification goals are considered:

P1: Functional Correctness Each scenario method satisfies the expected final state as specified by the automatically generated **ensures** clauses.
P2: Loop Termination All loops are annotated with decreasing variant terms that are sufficient to prove termination.
P3: Loop Invariant Preservation Automatically generated inductive invariants ensure that key state relationships are preserved across iterations.
P4: Time-Guard Soundness Event-triggered clauses are guarded by symbolic boolean variables (e.g., `ev_event1`), ensuring that transitions corresponding to timed clauses occur only under valid scheduling conditions.

Table 1 summarizes the successfully verified and relevant properties for each contract. Verification time reflects the duration reported by KeY when proving the main top-level scenario. Verification times for other scenarios tend to be somewhat less and the times to verify individual function and event contracts are negligible.

Table 1. Properties verified in the case studies. A dash ("$-$") denotes that no property of the corresponding category applies to the given contract.

Contract	P1	P2	P3	P4	Time
Betting	✓	–	–	✓	∼2.1 s
Deposit	✓	✓	✓	–	∼1.3 s
Loan	✓	–	–	✓	∼1.8 s
License	✓	–	–	✓	∼0.7 s

For the `Betting` contract, the outcome logic is expressed through mutually exclusive branches in its `data()` method. Verification ensures that all valid symbolic inputs result in safe asset redistribution, and that execution halts in a consistent final configuration.

In the `Deposit` contract, cyclic interactions between client and provider are translated into a **while** loop with a symbolic iteration bound (`counter`). Loop invariants preserve the consistency of transferred assets across rounds, while a variant term guarantees termination. Timed transitions are abstracted via symbolic events (e.g., `ev_event1`, `ev_event2`), which may interrupt execution early.

The `Loan` contract models installment-based repayment with time constraints. The translated code verifies that each installment is transferred correctly and only when the corresponding symbolic time guard holds. The contract's structure relates to properties **P1** and **P4**.

In the `License` contract, verification ensures that all conditional obligations and asset transfers, such as license activation or revocation, occur only under valid scheduling conditions. All possible contract outcomes are covered, based on symbolic inputs like price, deadlines, and initial ownership.

5   Related Work

The formal modeling and verification of digital contracts receives increasing attention, especially at the intersection of legal informatics, programming languages, and formal methods. Our work contributes by bridging a legal domain-specific language (*Stipula*) with a deductive verification framework (KeY) through translation into JML-annotated Java.

Legal modeling frameworks like Ergo [20], OpenLaw [21], Lexon [17], and Accord [19] embed contracts into broader systems, but they lack a precise formal semantics. *Stipula* offers an operational model with explicit permissions, assets, and timed clauses. While Catala [18] formalizes legislative logic and has a runtime environment, it does not address contract verification.

Closer to our work, prior efforts explored translation-based verification: OCL-to-Java with JML [12], and Circus-to-Java for formal reasoning [11]. Our approach applies this paradigm to legal contracts, preserving their normative and temporal semantics.

While the current *Stipula* runtime is realized by compilation to Java [9], the language is implementation-agnostic and could be compiled to blockchain smart contracts like Solidity [1] or Obsidian [2]. This path is promising, as our verification approach using KeY [3] can build on established work that already applies the system to blockchain platforms like Hyperledger Fabric [6] and Solidity via the SolidiKeY tool [4]. Using these advances would enable rigorous verification of *Stipula* contracts on decentralized infrastructures.

6   Conclusion

We presented a translation-based approach for verifying *Stipula* contracts by translating them into JML-annotated Java and applying deductive verification. This enables reasoning over normative properties—permissions, asset transfers, state transitions, and timed clauses—using an existing deductive verification tool. What we verify in this setting is the correctness of the Java/JML encoding of *Stipula*'s semantics, derived automatically from generation of scenarios, rather than an independent abstract notion of functional correctness of contracts. Allowing users to state additional derived properties directly in *Stipula* would be a natural extension, but it is beyond the scope of this work. Alternative paradigms based on state-based formalisms (e.g., statecharts or timed automata) could in principle support reasoning in temporal logics over possible behaviors. We chose a deductive setting with KeY to leverage its mature automation and direct JML support, while exploring complementary verification approaches remains a promising avenue for the future.

Our translation targets an expressive, yet analyzable, fragment of *Stipula*, with symbolic time, disjoint loops, loop-free clauses, and limited non-determinism. Within this fragment, verification is fully automatic and requires no manual annotation or interactive proof. Case studies confirm that functional and temporal behavior can be verified compositionally, suggesting that legal contracts can be verifiable by design if execution semantics is preserved.

The current approach synthesizes scenario methods by statically traversing the contract automaton. This relies on a structural restriction: all cycles must be disjoint. Future work will focus on lifting this restriction to support overlapping cycles and more general control flow. One possible direction is to introduce dynamic scheduling mechanisms, such as a *dispatch* table, that can track and trigger enabled clauses at runtime. While this would increase expressiveness, it also introduces verification challenges that may require interactive proofs or hybrid verification strategies.

Deductive tools like KeY can often produce counterexamples, which, when mapped back to the legal domain, help authors detect inconsistencies and refine their contracts. Another direction is integrating runtime or hybrid verification to support cases where full deductive reasoning is infeasible.

Acknowledgments. We thank Maximilian Scheid for his work on the implementation of the translator.

References

1. Solidity documentation: State machine common pattern. https://docs.soliditylang. org/en/v0.8.0/common-patterns.html#state-machine
2. Obsidian: A safer blockchain programming language (2018). http://obsidian-lang. com/
3. Ahrendt, W., Beckert, B., Bubel, R., Hähnle, R., Schmitt, P.H., Ulbrich, M. (eds.): Deductive Software Verification: The KeY Book, LNCS, vol. 10001. Springer, Cham (2016). https://doi.org/10.1007/978-3-319-49812-6
4. Ahrendt, W., Bubel, R.: Functional verification of smart contracts via strong data integrity. In: ISoLA (3). LNCS, vol. 12478, pp. 9–24. Springer (2020). https://doi. org/10.1007/978-3-030-61467-6_2
5. Beckert, B., Bubel, R., Drodt, D., Hähnle, R., Lanzinger, F., Pfeifer, W., Ulbrich, M., Weigl, A.: The Java verification tool KeY: A tutorial. In: Platzer, A., Rozier, K.Y., Pradella, M., Rossi, M. (eds.) Proc. 26th International Symposium on Formal Methods, Milan, Italy. LNCS, vol. 14934, pp. 597–623. Springer, Cham (2024). https://doi.org/10.1007/978-3-031-71177-0_32
6. Beckert, B., Herda, M., Kirsten, M., Schiffl, J.: Formal specification and verification of hyperledger fabric chaincode. In: 3rd Symposium on Distributed Ledger Technology (SDLT), Gold Coast, Australia, November 12, 2018, pp. 44–48. Institute for Integrated and Intelligent Systems (2018)
7. Crafa, S., Laneve, C.: Programming legal contracts - A beginners guide to stipula. In: The Logic of Software. A Tasting Menu of Formal Methods. LNCS, vol. 13360, pp. 129–146. Springer (2022).https://doi.org/10.1007/978-3-031-08166-8_7
8. Crafa, S., Laneve, C., Sartor, G., Veschetti, A.: Pacta sunt servanda: legal contracts in Stipula. Sci. Comput. Program. **225**, 102911 (2023). https://doi.org/10.1016/j. scico.2022.102911
9. Crafa, S., Laneve, C., Veschetti, A.: Stipula Prototype (2022). https://github.com/ stipula-language
10. Delzanno, G., Laneve, C., Sangnier, A., Zavattaro, G.: Decidability problems for micro-stipula. In: COORDINATION. LNCS, vol. 15731, pp. 133–152. Springer (2025). https://doi.org/10.1007/978-3-031-95589-1_7
11. Freitas, A.F., Cavalcanti, A.: Automatic translation from Circus to Java. In: Misra, J., Nipkow, T., Sekerinski, E. (eds.) Formal Methods, 14th International Symposium on Formal Methods, Hamilton, Canada. LNCS, vol. 4085, pp. 115–130. Springer (2006). https://doi.org/10.1007/11813040_9.
12. Hamie, A.: Translating the object constraint language into the Java modelling language. In: Haddad, H., Omicini, A., Wainwright, R.L., Liebrock, L.M. (eds.) Proc. of the ACM Symposium on Applied Computing (SAC), Nicosia, Cyprus, pp. 1531–1535. ACM (2004).https://doi.org/10.1145/967900.968206
13. Hähnle, R., Laneve, C., Veschetti, A.: Formal verification of legal contracts: a translation-based approach (Extended Version) (2025). https://arxiv.org/abs/ 2509.20421
14. Hähnle, R., Laneve, C., Veschetti, A.: Tool implementation prototype (2025). https://github.com/stipula-language/stipula/tree/master/Stipula-KeY-Tool
15. Laneve, C.: Reachability analysis in Micro-Stipula. In: Proceedings of the 26th International Symposium on Principles and Practice of Declarative Programming, PPDP 2024, pp. 17:1–17:12. ACM (2024). https://doi.org/10.1145/3678232. 3678247

16. Laneve, C., Parenti, A., Sartor, G.: Legal contracts amending with Stipula. In: Jongmans, S., Lopes, A. (eds.) Coordination Models and Languages, 25th IFIP WG 6.1 Intl. Conf., COORDINATION, Lisbon, Portugal. LNCS, vol. 13908, pp. 253–270. Springer, Cham (2023). https://doi.org/10.1007/978-3-031-35361-1_14
17. Lexon foundation: Lexon home page (2019). http://www.lexon.tech
18. Merigoux, D., Chataing, N., Protzenko, J.: CATALA: a programming language for the law. Proc. ACM Program. Lang. **5**(ICFP), 1–29 (2021).https://doi.org/10.1145/3473582
19. Open source contributors: the accord project (2018). https://accordproject.org
20. Roche, N., Hernandez, W., Chen, E., Siméon, J., Selman, D.: Ergo - a programming language for smart legal contracts. CoRR abs/2112.07064 (2021). https://arxiv.org/abs/2112.07064
21. Wright, A., Roon, D., ConsenSys AG: OpenLaw web site. https://www.openlaw.io (2019)

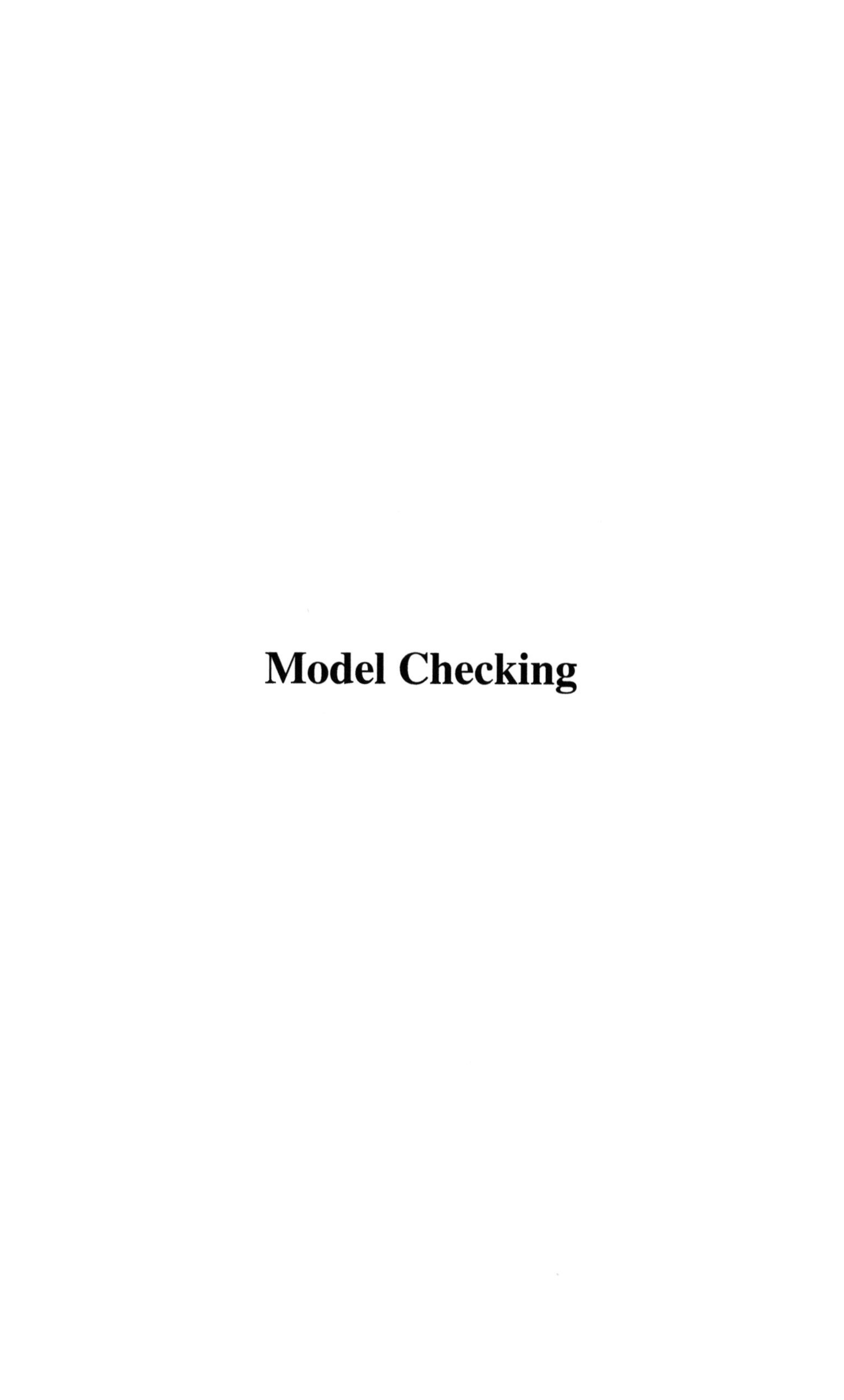

Model Checking

CTL Model Checking Partially Specified Systems

Eshita Zaman[1]([✉]) [iD], Christopher Johannsen[2] [iD], Andrew S. Miner[2] [iD],
Gianfranco Ciardo[2] [iD], and Samik Basu[2] [iD]

[1] Department of Computer Science, Utah Valley University, Orem, UT, USA
`eshita.zaman@uvu.edu`

[2] Department of Computer Science, Iowa State University, Ames, IA, USA
`{cgjohann,asminer,ciardo,sbasu}@iastate.edu`

Abstract. The behavioral specifications of a system are often partial
at early stages of development due to pending design decisions. We view
such specifications as being parameterized by these decisions and consider the problem of identifying a possible concretization, i.e., taking
a subset of these decisions, to ensure that the system conforms to the
desired requirements. We capture such a partially specified system as
a partially-labeled Kripke structure (`plKS`), where certain propositions
labeling the states of the Kripke structure correspond to pending design
decisions, thus may be *unknown*. We then reduce the verification problem to model checking different `plKS` instances, each corresponding to
a specific set of design decisions taken, inducing a semi-lattice on the
instances. Central to our solution strategy is the effective and efficient
exploration of this semi-lattice and the application of model checking
techniques to `plKS`s with 3-valued semantics of temporal properties, to
take into account unknown state labels. We also address the problem
of identifying an optimal instance of a partially-specified system that
satisfies a desired property, where the cost of design decisions drive the
optimality criterion. We use a prototype implementation of our strategy
to validate its viability on a multi-objective path planning problem.

Keywords: Partially specified systems · Design space exploration ·
3-valued logic · CTL model checking

1 Introduction

Model checking is a well-established technique to automatically verify desired
system properties by examining all possible system behaviors. Model checkers [8,
17,21] take as input a system design expressed in a high-level formalism, such as a
Petri net, and properties of interest expressed as formulas in some temporal logic,
and decide whether each property holds in the system. However, in practice,
modern software systems are frequently developed and analyzed under partial
knowledge. Whether due to incomplete specifications, evolving requirements,

F. Damiani and M. Farrell (Eds.): iFM 2025, LNCS 16194, pp. 81–98, 2026.
https://doi.org/10.1007/978-3-032-10794-7_5

unavailable components, or deferred implementation details, engineers often lack a fully defined model at design time. Yet, critical correctness properties such as safety, liveness, or access control must still be verified to ensure dependable system behavior. This challenge arises in diverse contexts, including software product lines, security auditing, runtime verification, and autonomous systems.

Driving Problem. We consider a system design where a subset of behavioral aspects is partially specified due to pending design decisions. In this context, the challenge is to decide whether there exists a combination of design decisions that results in a system design satisfying the desired properties. As there may be multiple sets of design decisions which yield the same conformance, we aim to identify an optimal set of design decisions achieving conformance based on a cost assigned to each decision. This leads to two core verification tasks: (i) feasibility analysis: determining the existence of satisfying instantiations, and (ii) optimization: identifying a cost-optimal instantiation. Design decisions may be related, as one decision may require another decision to be taken, or certain decisions may be mutually exclusive.

As a concrete example, consider the planning problem of an autonomous rover that can navigate a terrain with obstacles while collecting samples from specific locations. The rover is powered by a battery with a given capacity and each rover movement consumes battery energy. The property of interest is whether the rover can reach a specified destination, collect a specified minimal number of samples, and maintain the battery level above a certain amount of energy. Here, the minimum number of samples and battery level drive design decisions. One can develop a partial design of the rover behavior where different choices of design decisions result in different instances of the rover behavior. For instance, deciding to maintain the battery level above 5 vs. 10 units results in different rover behaviors.

Solution Strategy. We view the partial behavioral system design as a parameterized system, where the parameters capture the pending design decisions. We model such a system using Petri nets and show that the semantics of the model can be captured using *partially-labeled Kripke structures*, where the states of the Kripke structures are labeled with some propositions whose valuations are associated with the design decisions yet to be considered and are, therefore, *unknown*. Model checking such a Kripke structure against temporal properties expressed in CTL results in true, false, or unknown answers following the 3-valued logical semantics for CTL. Our objective is to identify an optimal set of changes to the valuations of unknown-propositions (true or false) so that the resulting (possibly still partially-labeled) Kripke structure satisfies the CTL property. We show that the possible changes in the valuations of unknown-propositions (corresponding to pending design decisions) induce a semi-lattice over partially-labeled Kripke structures, which forms the solution space for the problem. We present an algorithm to efficiently explore this solution space to compute the partially-labeled Kripke structure and a corresponding set of optimal design decisions that result in satisfaction of a desired property. Key to our efficient exploration is that we compute the state-space of a given partially-labeled Kripke structure (corresponding to given unknown design decisions) once and examine the property conformance corresponding to different instantiations of design decisions in the context of the generated state-space, thus avoiding repeated generation of the state-space for different configurations of design decisions.

Organization. Section 2 discusses modeling formalisms and necessary background on 3-valued model checking; Sect. 3 formalizes an interpretation of 3-valued models as design spaces and provides an algorithm to find an optimal design; Sect. 4 applies our formalism and algorithm on a case study involving an autonomous rover; Sect. 5 describes related work; Sect. 6 discusses impacts and future work.

2   Background

Petri nets (PNs) are a well-known high-level formalism to model distributed and concurrent systems. PNs can represent different classes of models such as Kripke structures, labeled transition systems, etc. [24]. Even with just a few places, a PN can represent a model with an enormous state space, which makes it an excellent choice for compactly modeling partially specified systems.

Definition 1. A Petri net $(\mathcal{P}, \mathcal{T}, \mathbf{D}^-, \mathbf{D}^+, \mu_{init})$ is a finite bipartite marked multigraph where $\mathcal{P} = \{p_1, ..., p_P\}$ and $\mathcal{T} = \{t_1, ..., t_T\}$ are disjoint sets of *places* and *transitions*; $\mathbf{D}^-, \mathbf{D}^+ \in \mathbb{N}^{\mathcal{P} \times \mathcal{T}}$ describe the cardinality of the *input* and *output* arcs; and $\mu_{init} \in \mathbb{N}^{\mathcal{P}}$ is the initial *marking* (an assignment of *tokens* to the places). If the PN is in marking μ (a vector where μ_i is the number of tokens in p_i), transition $t_j \in \mathcal{T}$ is *enabled* iff $\forall p_i \in \mathcal{P}, \mu_i \geq \mathbf{D}^-[i, j]$, in which case it may *fire*, leading to marking μ' s.t. $\forall p_i \in \mathcal{P}, \mu'_i = \mu_i - \mathbf{D}^-[i, j] + \mathbf{D}^+[i, j]$.   □

Marking μ' is *reachable* from marking μ if there is a sequence σ of (enabled) transition firings that leads from μ to μ', we write $\mu \xrightarrow{\sigma} \mu'$, or simply $\mu \xrightarrow{*} \mu'$ if the specific σ is not important. The reachability set $\mathcal{S}_{reach}$ of the PN is defined as $\mathcal{S}_{reach} = \{\mu : \mu_{init} \xrightarrow{*} \mu\}$. We consider PNs whose $\mathcal{S}_{reach}$ is finite, in which case their semantics are captured by a Kripke structure formally defined as follows.

Definition 2. A Kripke structure $M = (\mathcal{S}, \mathcal{S}_{init}, \mathcal{N}, \mathcal{A}, L)$ describes a finite set of states $\mathcal{S}$, a set of initial states $\mathcal{S}_{init} \subseteq \mathcal{S}$, a left-total next-state relation over states $\mathcal{N} \subseteq \mathcal{S} \times \mathcal{S}$, a finite set of atomic propositions $\mathcal{A}$, and a labeling function $L : \mathcal{S} \times \mathcal{A} \to \{\mathbb{T}, \mathbb{F}\}$ specifying which atomic propositions hold in each state.   □

In the above definition, the relation between a PN and its corresponding M_{KS} is $\mathcal{S} = \mathcal{S}_{reach}, \mathcal{S}_{init} = \{\mu_{init}\}, \mathcal{N} = \{(\mu, \mu') : \mu \in \mathcal{S}, \exists t \in \mathcal{T}, \mu \xrightarrow{t} \mu'\}^1$, while $\mathcal{A}$ and L are defined using comparisons of arithmetic expressions on the number of tokens in places and integer constants. For example, if $a \equiv p_2 > 3$ is an atomic proposition, then $L(\mu, a) = \mathbb{T}$ iff $\mu_2 > 3$.

---

[1] An arbitrary PN may not satisfy the requirement that $\mathcal{N}(\mu) \neq \emptyset$ for all reachable markings μ, i.e., it may have *dead* markings. This situation can be detected, so we assume it does not occur or is managed by adding a self-loop on dead markings.

2.1 Kripke Structures in 3-Valued Logic

As discussed in Sect. 1, we consider partially specified systems, which result from system specifications with pending design decisions. We incorporate such pending decisions in the PN representation of the system. If a design decision related to the enabling of a PN transition in the system is yet to be taken, then whether or not the transition can be fired remains *unknown*—concretizing such design decision (partially) concretizes the behavioral evolution of the system. In other words, the presence of pending design decisions may result in systems whose conformance to requirements is unknown and some pending design decisions may need to be concretized to ensure the conformance. The pending decisions can be viewed as propositions with unknown valuation in the Kripke structure semantics of the PN models. Consider, for instance, design decision d and proposition a labeling a Kripke structure state defined as follows:

$$a \equiv d \wedge (p_2 > 3),$$

then the valuation of a evaluates to $p_2 > 3$ when the decision is taken (d is $\mathbb{T}$) and evaluates to $\mathbb{U}$ if decision for selecting d is yet to be taken. In the above, we have followed Kleene's logical framework for 3-valued logic [20] to define the semantics of the standard logical operators $\neg$, $\wedge$, and $\vee$ on this domain:

$\neg$	
$\mathbb{T}$	$\mathbb{F}$
$\mathbb{F}$	$\mathbb{T}$
$\mathbb{U}$	$\mathbb{U}$

$\wedge$	$\mathbb{T}$	$\mathbb{F}$	$\mathbb{U}$
$\mathbb{T}$	$\mathbb{T}$	$\mathbb{F}$	$\mathbb{U}$
$\mathbb{F}$	$\mathbb{F}$	$\mathbb{F}$	$\mathbb{F}$
$\mathbb{U}$	$\mathbb{U}$	$\mathbb{F}$	$\mathbb{U}$

$\vee$	$\mathbb{T}$	$\mathbb{F}$	$\mathbb{U}$
$\mathbb{T}$	$\mathbb{T}$	$\mathbb{T}$	$\mathbb{T}$
$\mathbb{F}$	$\mathbb{T}$	$\mathbb{F}$	$\mathbb{U}$
$\mathbb{U}$	$\mathbb{T}$	$\mathbb{U}$	$\mathbb{U}$

We refer to a Kripke structure with such 3-valued labeling as a partially-labeled Kripke structure.

Definition 3. A partially-labeled Kripke structure (plKS) $M = (\mathcal{S}, \mathcal{S}_{init}, \mathcal{N}, \mathcal{A}, L)$ describes a finite set of states $\mathcal{S}$, a set of initial states $\mathcal{S}_{init} \subseteq \mathcal{S}$, a nondeterministic next-state function over states $\mathcal{N} : \mathcal{S} \times \mathcal{S}$, a finite set of atomic propositions $\mathcal{A}$, and a labeling function $L : \mathcal{S} \times \mathcal{A} \to \{\mathbb{T}, \mathbb{F}, \mathbb{U}\}$. □

Bruns and Godefroid call such structures "partial Kripke structures" [3,4], as they can be used to describe system behavior with partial specification in terms of state-labels. Similar consideration of partial behavioral specification also forms the basis for modal transition systems [15,18], used to describe system families in product lines [16,22]. Chechik et al. [6] further extend this setup by considering general multi-valued logic (with domain $\mathcal{D}$ of interpretation beyond $\{\mathbb{T}, \mathbb{F}, \mathbb{U}\}$). The key to automatic verification of Kripke structures with such logic against temporal properties is that the semantics of temporal properties implies a partition of size $|\mathcal{D}|$. We use partially labeled Kripke structure as a way to capture the high-level description of systems with pending design decisions. The following presents a brief overview of the temporal logic CTL and the semantics of CTL in the context of partially labeled Kripke structures.

$$\forall p \in \mathcal{A}, \ [\![p, M]\!] = \langle \{s : L(s,p) = \mathbb{T}\}, \{s : L(s,p) = \mathbb{F}\} \rangle$$

$$[\![\neg\varphi, M]\!] = \overline{[\![\varphi, M]\!]}$$

$$[\![\varphi_1 \wedge \varphi_2, M]\!] = [\![\varphi_1, M]\!] \cap [\![\varphi_2, M]\!]$$

$$[\![\mathbf{EX}(\varphi), M]\!] = \langle \{s : \exists \sigma_s, \sigma_s[1] \in [\![\varphi, M]\!]_{\mathbb{T}}\}, \{s : \forall \sigma_s, \sigma_s[1] \in [\![\varphi, M]\!]_{\mathbb{F}}\} \rangle$$

$$[\![\mathbf{AF}(\varphi), M]\!] = \langle \{s : \forall \sigma_s, \exists i \geq 0, \sigma_s[i] \in [\![\varphi, M]\!]_{\mathbb{T}}\}, \{s : \exists \sigma_s, \forall i \geq 0, \sigma_s[i] \in [\![\varphi, M]\!]_{\mathbb{F}}\} \rangle$$

$$[\![\mathbf{E}(\varphi_1 \, \mathbf{U} \, \varphi_2), M]\!] = \langle \{s : \exists \sigma_s, \exists i \geq 0, \sigma_s[i] \in [\![\varphi_2, M]\!]_{\mathbb{T}} \wedge \forall j < i, \sigma_s[j] \in [\![\varphi_1, M]\!]_{\mathbb{T}}\},$$
$$\{s : \forall \sigma_s, \forall i \geq 0, \sigma_s[i] \in [\![\varphi_2, M]\!]_{\mathbb{F}} \vee \exists j < i, \sigma_s[j] \in [\![\varphi_1, M]\!]_{\mathbb{F}}\} \rangle$$

Fig. 1. CTL semantics on `plKS` M. $\sigma_{s_0} = s_0 \rightarrow s_1 \rightarrow \cdots$ denotes an infinite path starting at state s_0, and $\sigma_{s_0}[i]$ the ith state in it, for $i \in \mathbb{N}$.

2.2   CTL Semantics for `plKSs`

We focus on the temporal logic CTL [9], which describes the branching behavior of a system. The syntax of a CTL formula is given by

$$\varphi \rightarrow a \mid \neg\varphi \mid \varphi \wedge \varphi \mid \mathbf{EX}(\varphi) \mid \mathbf{AF}(\varphi) \mid \mathbf{E}(\varphi \, \mathbf{U} \, \varphi),$$

where $a \in \mathcal{A}$. Informally, state s satisfies $\mathbf{EX}(\varphi)$ if it has at least one next state satisfying φ, $\mathbf{AF}(\varphi)$ if all evolutions starting from s reach some state satisfying φ, and $\mathbf{E}(\varphi_1 \, \mathbf{U} \, \varphi_2)$ if there is an evolution from s leading to a state satisfying φ_2 and all states before that satisfy φ_1. The above syntax includes an adequate set of boolean and temporal operators in the sense that other CTL operators such as AX, EF, AG, EF, and AU can be expressed using EX, AF, and EU (see [9] for details).

The semantics of CTL interpreted on a Kripke structure with 3-valued logic was presented in [5,6]; we recall the semantic function for completeness' sake. The semantics of a CTL property φ in the context of a `plKS` returns a 3-way partition of the state space $\mathcal{S}$: the set of states satisfying φ, not satisfying φ, and undetermined to satisfy φ. We represent this partition as the pair of disjoint sets $\langle \mathcal{S}_T, \mathcal{S}_F \rangle$, respectively satisfying and not satisfying φ, so that the set of states where φ is undetermined is implicitly given by $\mathcal{S} \setminus (\mathcal{S}_T \cup \mathcal{S}_F)$. The basic set operations over such a pair satisfy:

$$\overline{\langle \mathcal{S}_T, \mathcal{S}_F \rangle} = \langle \mathcal{S}_F, \mathcal{S}_T \rangle;$$
$$\langle \mathcal{S}_T, \mathcal{S}_F \rangle \cup \langle \mathcal{S}_T', \mathcal{S}_F' \rangle = \langle \mathcal{S}_T \cup \mathcal{S}_T', \mathcal{S}_F \cap \mathcal{S}_F' \rangle;$$
$$\langle \mathcal{S}_T, \mathcal{S}_F \rangle \cap \langle \mathcal{S}_T', \mathcal{S}_F' \rangle = \langle \mathcal{S}_T \cap \mathcal{S}_T', \mathcal{S}_F \cup \mathcal{S}_F' \rangle.$$

The semantic function $[\![\ ]\!]$ takes as input CTL formula φ and `plKS` M, and returns $\langle \mathcal{S}_T, \mathcal{S}_F \rangle$, where $\mathcal{S}_T$ is the set of states of M that satisfy φ and $\mathcal{S}_F$ is the set of states of M that satisfy $\neg\varphi$. Figure 1 shows the formal definition of $[\![\ ]\!]$.

For any `plKS` M and CTL formula φ, we say that $M \models \varphi$ iff each initial state satisfies φ, $M \not\models \varphi$ iff some initial state does not satisfy φ, and $M \not\models^? \varphi$ otherwise, i.e., no initial state does not satisfy φ but for at least one initial state it is not determined whether it satisfies φ.

3   Exploring Concretizations of a plKS

Now that we have a formalism to describe systems with potentially unknown properties, we move on to defining some types of analysis we can perform on such systems. In particular, we present the concept of *concretizing* unknown values (i.e., changing unknown values to true or false) to obtain a more "concrete" system. Recall that the unknown values of state propositions are induced by the design decisions yet to be taken and this allows us to interpret these systems as *design spaces*. We define an algorithm to search a design space and find a minimum-cost concretized system that satisfies some CTL formula φ.

3.1   A Semi-lattice of plKSs

Consider a plKS $M_L = (\mathcal{S}, \mathcal{S}_{init}, \mathcal{N}, \mathcal{A}, L)$ and let $\mathcal{U}_L = \{(s, a) : L(s, a) = \mathbb{U}\}$ be the set of state and atomic proposition pairs for which the labeling in M is unknown; also, let $|\mathcal{U}_L| = m$.

Labeling function L' is a *concretization* of L iff $L(s, a) = \mathbb{T} \Rightarrow L'(s, a) = \mathbb{T}$ and $L(s, a) = \mathbb{F} \Rightarrow L'(s, a) = \mathbb{F}$, implying that $\mathcal{U}_{L'} \subseteq \mathcal{U}_L$. Let $\mathcal{L}$ be the set of the 3^m possible concretizations of L. Note that $M_{L'}$ is an ordinary Kripke structure for any of the 2^m full concretizations L' of L, i.e., whenever $L' : \mathcal{S} \times \mathcal{A} \to \{\mathbb{T}, \mathbb{F}\}$.

We define the "join" binary operator $\oplus$ on $\{\mathbb{T}, \mathbb{F}, \mathbb{U}\}$ as

$$\mathbb{T} \oplus \mathbb{U} = \mathbb{U} \oplus \mathbb{T} = \mathbb{T} \oplus \mathbb{F} = \mathbb{F} \oplus \mathbb{T} = \mathbb{F} \oplus \mathbb{U} = \mathbb{U} \oplus \mathbb{F} = \mathbb{U} \oplus \mathbb{U} = \mathbb{U}$$

$$\mathbb{T} \oplus \mathbb{T} = \mathbb{T} \qquad \mathbb{F} \oplus \mathbb{F} = \mathbb{F},$$

and extend it to $\mathcal{L}$ as follows:

$$\forall L, L' \in \mathcal{L}, (s,a) \in \mathcal{S} \times \mathcal{A} : (L \oplus L')(s,a) = L(s,a) \oplus L'(s,a).$$

If we let $L \leq L' \Leftrightarrow L \oplus L' = L$, then $(\mathcal{L}, \leq, \oplus)$ is a meet-semi-lattice with least element L, so that "strictly greater" means "having $\mathbb{T}$ or $\mathbb{F}$ instead of $\mathbb{U}$ in some positions". This induces an analogous meet-semi-lattice over the set of plKSs $\{M_L : L \in \mathcal{L}\}$; see Fig. 2 for an example.

We can try to find a concretization L such that $M_L \models \varphi$ by searching the semi-lattice for such an L. If no such L exists we know that no concretization of M satisfies φ. Observe that, if there exists an L such that $M_L \not\models \varphi$, then no further concretization of L needs to be explored, as $\forall L', L \leq L' \Rightarrow M_{L'} \not\models \varphi$.

This setting provides fine concretizations of the plKS. In practice, however, a design decision likely changes many values of L from $\mathbb{U}$ to $\mathbb{T}$ or $\mathbb{F}$ at once, thus only a subset of $\mathcal{L}$ may be actually realizable. A design decision could thus map an element $L \in \mathcal{L}$ to another $L' \in \mathcal{L}$, subject to $L < L'$ (with at least one but possibly many $\mathbb{U}$ entries changed to $\mathbb{T}$ or $\mathbb{F}$). A concretization L with m unknowns can in principle be further concretized in $3^m - 1$ possible ways (the number of L' satisfying $L < L'$). We instead assume a (relatively) small set of design decisions, each of which, if applicable to concretization L, changes it into L', by changing a specific subset of $\mathbb{U}$ values of L into $\mathbb{T}$ or $\mathbb{F}$, in a fixed way.

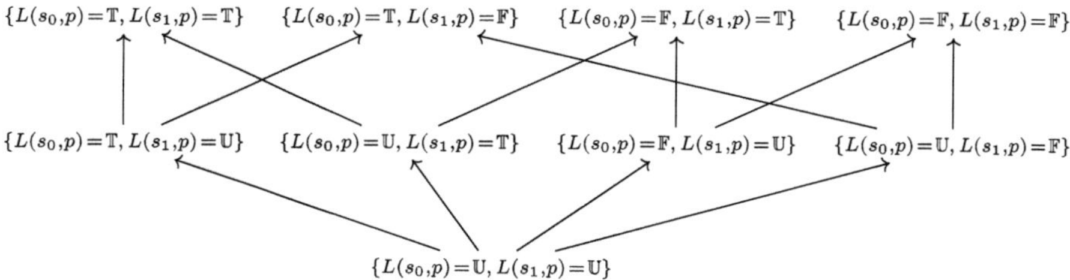

Fig. 2. A meet-semi-lattice $(\mathcal{L}, \leq, \oplus)$ with $m = 2$, $\mathcal{S} = \{s_0, s_1\}$, $\mathcal{A} = \{p\}$, and $L(s_0, p) = L(s_1, p) = \mathbb{U}$ is a directed acyclic graph whose nodes are the elements of $\mathcal{L}$ organized into $m + 1$ levels, with level m at the top and level 0 at the bottom, according to the number $n \in \{0, ..., m\}$ of $\mathbb{U}$ values that have been changed to $\mathbb{T}$ or $\mathbb{F}$.

3.2   Concretizing plKS: Exploring the Design Space

We consider plKSs where the uncertainty can stem from whether a given atomic proposition holds in a given state or whether a transition is possible between a given pair of states. In an actual design process, however, the available design decisions normally present themselves at a high level, so that taking one such design decision simultaneously concretizes many uncertain aspects in the partially-labeled Kripke structure. Thus, an underlying plKS M with m unknowns has 3^m potential concretizations, but the number of possible concretizations of the high-level model defining M is **at most** $\prod_{i=1}^{n}(1 + D_i)$, if there are n possible design decisions, and the i-th one can take one of D_i values (or remain untaken).

In the following paragraphs, we proceed with the presentation of plKSs in the context of design decisions, where a design decision corresponds to a possible concretization of the labeling function of a plKS. In other words, the labeling function of a plKS is parameterized with respect to the concretization induced by the specific design decisions.

Definition 4. A *structured concretizable* plKS is a tuple $(\mathcal{S}, \mathcal{S}_{init}, \mathcal{N}, \mathcal{A}, \mathcal{D}, L)$, where $\mathcal{S}$, $\mathcal{S}_{init}$, $\mathcal{N}$ and $\mathcal{A}$ are defined as before (see Definition 3), and

- $\mathcal{D} = \{\mathbb{T}, \mathbb{U}\}^{\{\delta_1, ..., \delta_Q\}}$ is the *design decision space*: concretization $\mathbf{d} = [d_1, ..., d_Q] \in \mathcal{D}$ indicates which design decisions have been taken, i.e., $d_h = \mathbb{T}$ iff design decision δ_h has been taken. Each decision δ_h is described by a 5-tuple $(\mathcal{U}_h, \mathcal{T}_h^-, \mathcal{F}_h^-, \mathcal{T}_h^+, \mathcal{F}_h^+)$ of subsets of $\mathcal{S} \times \mathcal{A}$, satisfying the following conditions:

$$\mathcal{T}_h^+ \cup \mathcal{F}_h^+ \subseteq \mathcal{U}_h \qquad \mathcal{T}_h^+ \cap \mathcal{F}_h^+ = \emptyset,$$

i.e., $\mathcal{T}_h^+$ and $\mathcal{F}_h^+$ are disjoint subsets of $\mathcal{U}_h$ and

$$\mathcal{T}_h^- \cap \mathcal{F}_h^- = \emptyset \qquad \mathcal{T}_h^- \cap \mathcal{U}_h = \emptyset \qquad \mathcal{F}_h^- \cap \mathcal{U}_h = \emptyset,$$

i.e., $\mathcal{T}_h^-$, $\mathcal{F}_h^-$, and $\mathcal{U}_h$ have no common elements. This 5-tuple describes when δ_h can be taken, and its effect (details are given below).

88   E. Zaman et al.

- $L : \mathcal{D} \times \mathcal{S} \times \mathcal{A} \to \{\mathbb{T}, \mathbb{F}, \mathbb{U}\}$ is a labeling function specifying whether atomic proposition a holds in state s for concretization $\mathbf{d}$. We let $L_{\mathbf{d}}(s, a)$ denote the function L with arguments $\mathbf{d} \in \mathcal{D}, s \in \mathcal{S}$ and $a \in \mathcal{A}$. $\qquad\square$

A design decision δ_h of the form $(\mathcal{U}_h, \mathcal{T}_h^-, \mathcal{F}_h^-, \mathcal{T}_h^+, \mathcal{F}_h^+)$ is *enabled*, thus can be taken, in concretization $\mathbf{d} = [d_1, ..., d_Q]$, with $d_h = \mathbb{U}$, if $\mathcal{U}_h \subseteq \{(s, a) : L_{\mathbf{d}}(s, a) = \mathbb{U}\}$, $\mathcal{T}_h^- \subseteq \{(s, a) : L_{\mathbf{d}}(s, a) = \mathbb{T}\}$, and $\mathcal{F}_h^- \subseteq \{(s, a) : L_{\mathbf{d}}(s, a) = \mathbb{F}\}$, i.e., if the labeling of each element of $\mathcal{U}_h, \mathcal{T}_h^-$, and $\mathcal{F}_h^-$ is, respectively, $\mathbb{U}, \mathbb{T}$, and $\mathbb{F}$ for concretization $\mathbf{d}$; then, $\mathcal{T}_h^+$ and $\mathcal{F}_h^+$ are the state-proposition pairs whose labeling changes from $\mathbb{U}$ to, respectively, $\mathbb{T}$ or $\mathbb{F}$ if the decision δ_h is taken in concretization $\mathbf{d}$.

The initial concretization where no design decision has been taken is then $\mathbf{d}_{init} = [\mathbb{U}, ..., \mathbb{U}] \in \mathcal{D}$. The initial mapping of states-proposition pairs to $\mathbb{T}, \mathbb{F}$ and $\mathbb{U}$ is captured by the function parameterized with $\mathbf{d}_{init}$, i.e., $L_{\mathbf{d}_{init}} = L_{orig}$, where $L_{orig}(s, a)$ is $\mathbb{T}$ if initially we know a holds in state s, is $\mathbb{F}$ if initially we know a does not hold in state s, and is $\mathbb{U}$ otherwise.

Taking enabled design decision δ_h in $\mathbf{d}$ leads to concretization $\mathbf{d}'$, equal to $\mathbf{d}$ except that d_h is $\mathbb{T}$ instead of $\mathbb{U}$, and results in the new labeling function $L_{\mathbf{d}'}$ satisfying:

$$\forall (s, a) \in \mathcal{T}_h^+, \ L_{\mathbf{d}'}(s, a) = \mathbb{T}$$
$$\forall (s, a) \in \mathcal{F}_h^+, \ L_{\mathbf{d}'}(s, a) = \mathbb{F}$$
$$\forall (s, a) \in \mathcal{S} \times \mathcal{A} \setminus (\mathcal{T}_h^+ \cup \mathcal{F}_h^+), \ L_{\mathbf{d}'}(s, a) = L_{\mathbf{d}}(s, a).$$

We can then define $\mathcal{D}_{reach} \subseteq \mathcal{D}$ as the set of concretizations reachable from the initial concretization $\mathbf{d}_{init}$ by taking any sequence of enabled design decisions. Generally, this means that $\mathbf{d}'$ could be reachable from $\mathbf{d}$ by taking a certain subset of design decisions in a particular order, while taking the same subset in a different order might not be possible. If this is undesirable or unrealistic, one can prevent it by appropriately setting the values of $\mathcal{T}_h^-, \mathcal{F}_h^-$, and $\mathcal{U}_h$ for each or some of the design decisions δ_h as these three components constrain when δ_h can be taken; in other words, having already taken a design decision δ_g may "disable" design decision δ_h. To guarantee an optimal search, it is sufficient to assume that once a design decision δ_h becomes disabled because of a previously-taken decision δ_g, it cannot become enabled due to taking yet another decision δ_l. This is implied by the fact that each design decision monotonically changes $\mathbb{U}$'s into $\mathbb{T}$'s or $\mathbb{F}$'s, but never changes $\mathbb{T}$'s or $\mathbb{F}$'s.

Given two concretizations $\mathbf{d}, \mathbf{d}' \in \mathcal{D}$, we write $\mathbf{d} \leq \mathbf{d}'$ if $\mathbf{d}'$ is *more concrete* than $\mathbf{d}$, i.e., if it is obtained from $\mathbf{d}$ by taking zero or more design decisions: $\forall h \in [1, Q], d_h = \mathbb{T} \Rightarrow d_h' = \mathbb{T}$. Note that this order on concretizations is consistent with the order on the corresponding labeling functions defined by these concretizations: for any $\mathbf{d}'$ reached from $\mathbf{d}$ by taking a sequence of design decisions, if $L_{\mathbf{d}}(s, a) \in \{\mathbb{T}, \mathbb{F}\}$, then $L_{\mathbf{d}'}(s, a) = L_{\mathbf{d}}(s, a)$, thus $L_{\mathbf{d}} \leq L_{\mathbf{d}'}$.

Proceeding further, we formulate the problem of identifying which design decisions can be taken so that (partially specified) systems conform to requirements in terms of satisfaction of temporal properties by concretizable p1KS.

Problem 1. Given a structured concretizable plKS $(\mathcal{S}, \mathcal{S}_{init}, \mathcal{N}, \mathcal{A}, \mathcal{D}, L)$ and a CTL formula φ, find $\mathbf{d} \in \mathcal{D}$ reachable from $\mathbf{d}_{init}$ such that $M = (\mathcal{S}, \mathcal{S}_{init}, \mathcal{N}, \mathcal{A}, L_{\mathbf{d}})$ satisfies φ, i.e., $M \models \varphi$. Alternatively, determine that no such $\mathbf{d}$ exists. $\square$

3.3   Assigning Cost and Finding a Minimal Cost Concretization

Assume we have a *cost function* $C : \{\delta_1, ..., \delta_Q\} \to [0, \infty)$ quantifying the cost of taking each (enabled) decision δ_h, and that the cost of taking a subset of design decisions $\mathcal{D}' \subseteq \mathcal{D}$ (in any order that allows all of them to be applied) is simply the sum of the individual cost of each design decision taken in $\mathcal{D}'$. Then, we can define the cost of a concretization $\mathbf{d} \in \mathcal{D}$ as $C(\mathbf{d}) = \sum_{h \in \{1, ..., Q \,:\, d_h = \mathbb{T}\}} C(\delta_h)$.

The optimization problem corresponding to decision Problem 1, therefore, involves identifying a $\mathbf{d} \in \mathcal{D}$ of minimal cost such that plKS M satisfies φ.

To find such a minimal cost concretization, we search the lattice of concretizations, starting from the initial one where no decisions has been taken, until we find a concretization that satisfies the target formula. We use a best-first search strategy where, at each step of the search process, the algorithm selects the most promising concretization, with the lowest cost, from a priority queue. The use of a priority queue allows the greedy search to explore the solution space in a systematic and structured manner in order of increasing cost.

Figure 5 illustrates an example design space and the order in which concretizations are considered. For each $\mathbf{d}$ in the queue, we check the property using $L_{\mathbf{d}}$. If the property evaluates to $\mathbb{T}$, then we have found a concretization with minimum cost, and we can stop the search. If the property evaluates to $\mathbb{F}$, then we do not explore further from $\mathbf{d}$, since the property will evaluate to $\mathbb{F}$ for $L_{\mathbf{d}'}$ whenever $\mathbf{d} \leq \mathbf{d}'$; in fact, $\mathbf{d}$ is a minimal set of decisions for which the property is not satisfied. However, $\mathbf{d}$ may be reachable by applying the same set of decisions in different order. One way to detect and ignore these situations is to enumerate all possible supersets of concretization $\mathbf{d}$ as $\mathbf{d}'$ and remove those from the queue to verify the property (but the time and memory to do this is exponential in the number of decisions). Alternatively, one can store a table of all the minimal concretizations already explored for which the property evaluates to $\mathbb{F}$ and, when extracting the next candidate concretization $\mathbf{d}$ from the priority queue, search if it is a (not necessarily strict) superset of an entry in the current table; only if it is not, this concretization is model-checked and, if the property evaluates to $\mathbb{U}$, each new concretization obtained from $\mathbf{d}$ by independently taking one of the enabled design decisions in $\mathbf{d}$, is added to the priority queue (this is the approach we use in our prototype).

4   Case Study

To demonstrate the feasibility of our approach, we implemented a C++ prototype in the model-checking tool SMART [7], and used it to run preliminary experiments on a multi-objective path-finding problem for an autonomous rover moving from a *start* base station to an *end* base station. Along the path, the rover collects samples present in certain locations for future analysis, while avoiding certain forbidden locations (Fig. 3):

$		⊗		*end*
		⊗		
start			$	⊗

Fig. 3. Example grid: $ is a sampling location, ⊗ is a forbidden location.

- The rover can move over an area described as an $N \times N$ grid of square cells, thus the position of the rover is given as a cell $[i, j]$, for $0 \leq i, j \leq N - 1$.
- The rover has a B_{max} kWh battery, initially fully charged, and consumes 1 kWh to move from cell $[i, j]$ to any of the four adjacent cells, $[i - 1, j]$, $[i+1, j]$, $[i, j - 1]$, or $[i, j + 1]$, subject to not exiting the grid and not entering a forbidden cell. For safety, the battery must not fall below B_{min}.
- A set $\mathcal{F} = \{f_1, ..., f_F\}$ describes F *forbidden cells*, e.g., cells to be avoided due to difficult terrain.
- A set of cells $\mathcal{G} = \{g_1, ..., g_G\}$ describes G *locations of interest* for sample collection. The rover collects a sample the first time it visits a location in $\mathcal{G}$, and must collect at least S_{min} samples.
- The rover starts in cell $[0, 0]$ and must end in cell $[N - 1, N - 1]$.

We can specify a property defining "success" using propositions to describe the position and battery level of the rover, as well as the number of samples it has collected. This property is satisfiable, if there exists a sequence of moves that realizes success.

We use S_{min} and B_{min} to define a set of design decisions for our analysis. For example, the decisions $S_{min} = s$ for $s \in \{1, 2\}$ and $B_{min} = b$ for $b \in \{1, 2, 4\}$ corresponds to a total of $Q = 2 + 3 = 5$ decisions; of course, the first two, for the value of S_{min}, are mutually exclusive (taking one of them disables the other one), as are the last three, for the value of B_{min}. Later on, we will illustrate how choosing a specific value for B_{min} ($B_{min} = 4$) can affect the labeling of a state in the model, changing it from $\mathbb{U}$ to either $\mathbb{T}$ or $\mathbb{F}$.

4.1   Petri Net Model of the Rover

The rover can successfully complete iff the initial state satisfies the CTL formula

$$\varphi \equiv \mathbf{E}\ (battery \geq B_{min})\ \mathbf{U}\ (position = [N - 1, N - 1] \wedge\ samples \geq S_{min}),$$

where B_{min} kWh is the lowest level of battery charge we are willing to accept (below that, there is an excessive risk that the rover fails to reach its destination) and S_{min} is the minimum number of samples we are willing to consider for the mission to be declared a success.

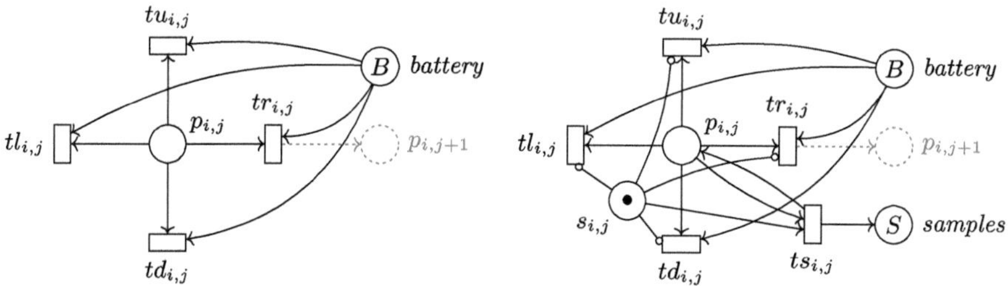

Fig. 4. Our PN model for an individual cell at a generic location (i, j). The left figure is for cells that are not sampling locations, the right figure is for cells that are sampling locations. Initially, place *battery* contains $B = B_{max}$ tokens and place *samples* contains $S = 0$ tokens (of course, places *battery* and *samples* are global, shared by all cells). For a particular (i, j), any of the transitions $tl_{i,j}$, $tu_{i,j}$, $tr_{i,j}$, or $td_{i,j}$ may be absent, if it would correspond to moving outside the grid or into a forbidden location.

Atomic propositions related to the position of the rover are specified as $position = [i, j]$, which holds whenever the rover is in cell $[i, j]$. Atomic propositions related to the battery level and the number of samples involve design decisions that correspond to choosing the thresholds B_{min} and S_{min}.

For a given battery level, atomic proposition $(battery \geq B_{min})$ is initially unknown, but becomes true or false in each state as soon as we decide a value for B_{min}. Similarly, for a given number of collected samples, atomic proposition $(samples \geq S_{min})$ is initially unknown, but becomes true or false in each state as soon as we decide a value for S_{min}.

Figure 4 shows a single (non-forbidden) cell in our PN model describing the system, depending on whether it is a sampling location (right) or not (left); the cell models are connected together in a grid. Each cell is modeled as a place $p_{i,j}$, and a token in it signifies that the rover is currently in the cell. Transitions $tl_{i,j}$, $tr_{i,j}$, $tu_{i,j}$, and $td_{i,j}$ respectively move the rover left to location $(i, j-1)$, right to location $(i, j+1)$, up to location $(i+1, j)$, or down to location $(i-1, j)$, except that no movement is possible to forbidden cells or cells outside the $N \times N$ grid. The battery level is modeled using a global place *battery*, initialized with B_{max} tokens, and a token (corresponding to 1 kWh) is removed from this place each time a cell is entered (a transition $tl_{i,j}$, $tr_{i,j}$, $tu_{i,j}$, or $td_{i,j}$ fires).

Sampling location cells have a place $s_{i,j}$, where a token signifies that a sample has not yet been collected from this location. Global place *samples* counts the number of collected samples. Transition $ts_{i,j}$ collects a sample the first time the rover reaches cell (i, j). Inhibitor arcs[2] from place $s_{i,j}$ to the movement transitions $tl_{i,j}$, $tr_{i,j}$, $tu_{i,j}$, and $td_{i,j}$ force the rover to collect a sample before moving. Collecting a sample depletes the battery by a negligible amount.

The system state at any given time can be described as (p, b, s) where p is the current position of the rover (determined by which place $p_{i,j}$ contains a token), b is the current battery level of the rover (tokens in place *battery*), and s is the sample information: which positions have been sampled (place $s_{i,j}$ is empty) and the number of collected samples (tokens in place *samples*). In this model, only the *number* of collected samples is important; the sample locations are needed only to ensure that samples are collected from different locations.

The design decisions are the different valuations of minimum battery level (B_{min}) and minimum number of samples (S_{min}). Then, taking the design decision δ_h, say, corresponding to $B_{min} = 4$, determines that, in all states with battery level ≥ 4, atomic proposition $a \equiv battery \geq B_{min}$ is true. In this case, $\delta_h = (\mathcal{U}_h, \mathcal{T}_h^-, \mathcal{F}_h^-, \mathcal{T}_h^+, \mathcal{F}_h^+)$, where

$$\mathcal{U}_h = \{((p, b, s), a)\} \qquad \text{(proposition } a \text{ is initially unknown in all states)}$$

$$\mathcal{T}_h^- = \mathcal{F}_h^- = \emptyset \qquad \text{(no other dependency affects the enabling of } \delta_h\text{)}$$

$$\mathcal{T}_h^+ = \{((p, b, s), a) \mid b \geq 4\} \text{ (proposition } a \text{ becomes true in states with } b \geq 4\text{)}$$

$$\mathcal{F}_h^+ = \{((p, b, s), a) \mid b < 4\} \text{ (proposition } b \text{ becomes false in states with } b < 4\text{)}.$$

When we take an enabled design decision δ_h (we decide a particular value for B_{min}, in this case), the labeling for a subset of state-proposition pairs in $\mathcal{U}_h$ changes to $\mathbb{T}$, if they are in $\mathcal{T}_h^+$, or $\mathbb{F}$, if they are in $\mathcal{F}_h^+$. This results in a concretization with additional $\mathbb{T}$ or $\mathbb{F}$ valuations, and these values cannot be reverted back to $\mathbb{U}$ by taking further enabled decisions, ensuring the mutual exclusion of the design decisions regarding B_{min}.

Figure 5 presents the lattice of concretizations **d** for the example grid in Fig. 3. The first two components of each node in Fig. 5 refer to $S_{min} = 1$ and $S_{min} = 2$, the number of samples collected, and the last three components refer to $B_{min} = 1$, $B_{min} = 2$, and $B_{min} = 4$, the remaining battery level. Design decisions regarding S_{min} and B_{min} are independent of each other and choices for the value of B_{min} (also for S_{min}) are mutually exclusive. For example, let the design decisions for B_{min} be represented as b_1, b_2, and b_4. One could define $enabled(b_1) \equiv \neg taken(b_2) \wedge \neg taken(b_4)$ to state that decision b_1 can only be taken if decision b_2 and decision b_4 have not been taken; $enabled(b_2)$ and $enabled(b_4)$ are defined similarly. The same reasoning applies to possible design choices for S_{min} as well. The order in which the concretization is explored is presented as annotations of the corresponding concretization in Fig. 5. It is important to remember that our objective is not to maximize the number of samples collected for a given system configuration (minimum battery level). Instead, we are looking for a set of design decisions (at least S_{min} samples will be collected maintaining

---

[2] An inhibitor arc from a place p to a transition t disables t whenever p is not empty; for a PN with a finite state space like ours, it is just "syntactic sugar", i.e., its effect could be achieved using an additional place and an ordinary input and output arc.

at least B_{min} battery) for which the property is satisfied in the system within a budget constraint. The output of our algorithm is not a path in M_{L_d} that proves the satisfaction of the property, but a set of design decisions such that by taking those decisions the system conforms to the property, implying that a path exists for which the property is satisfied (this path could then be obtained as a witness for the existential CTL property).

The optimal concretization for which the rover successfully completes the mission is $\mathbf{d} = [\mathbb{U}, \mathbb{T}, \mathbb{U}, \mathbb{U}, \mathbb{T}]$. Suppose the cost of taking the decisions is given as $C(S_{min} = 1) = 4$, $C(S_{min} = 2) = 2$, $C(B_{min} = 1) = 16$, $C(B_{min} = 2) = 8$, and $C(B_{min} = 4) = 4$. The total cost for the mission success is then $C(\mathbf{d}) = 2+4 = 6$.

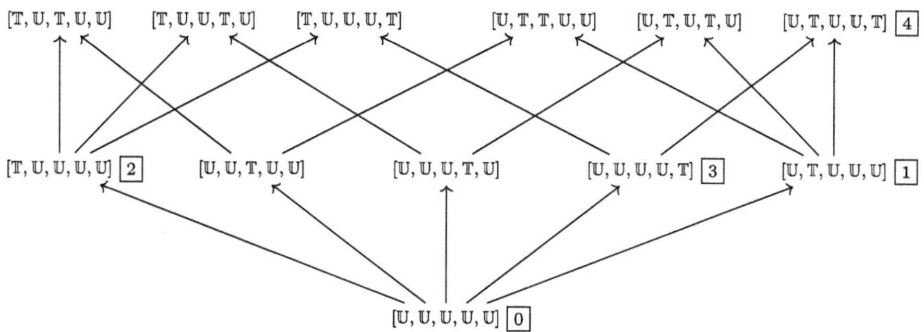

Fig. 5. Evaluation lattice of the decision vector for our example.

Table 1. Results for the autonomous rover for two combinations of N, G, F, B_{max}. The forbidden cell locations are randomly generated, and affect the number of reachable states in the model; thus we show four sample models for each combination.

Parameters				Kripke Structure			Concretizations			Solution Found		
N	G	F	B_{max}	**States**	**Edges**	**Time**	$\mathcal{D}_{srch}$	$\mathcal{D}_{rch}$	**Time**	S_{min}	B_{min}	**Cost**
15	5	5	40	31,855	105,595	4.97 s	13	36	0.46 s	4	4	341
				23,884	78,097	3.75 s	14	36	0.37 s	3	5	341
				47,270	159,877	8.29 s	11	36	0.63 s	4	5	316
				30,067	99,782	4.78 s	14	36	0.46 s	3	5	341
20	5	10	40	22,048	72,994	6.36 s	33	36	1.02 s	3	1	516
				25,418	85,169	7.39 s	29	36	1.04 s	5	1	471
				18,277	60,906	5.14 s	33	36	0.85 s	3	1	516
				26,077	88,865	7.51 s	33	36	1.21 s	3	1	516

4.2   Experimental Evaluation

Experimental Setup: We ran experiments using $N \times N$ grids, for grid sizes $N \in \{15, 20, 30, 35\}$, with different values for G (the number of sample locations), F (the number of forbidden cells), and B_{max} (the starting battery level).

We used mutually exclusive decisions to determine the values for the minimum battery level $B_{min} \in \{1, 4, 6, 8, 10\}$ and the number of samples taken $S_{min} \in \{1, 2, ..., G\}$. The costs assigned to design decisions for B_{min} are 200, 150, 100, 50, and 25 in increasing order of remaining battery level. Lowering B_{min} increases the risk of failing to complete the mission (collect sample and reach the destination), thus the cost is higher for lower values of B_{min}. Higher values for S_{min} correspond instead to higher reward from a completed mission; hence the cost is lower cost for higher valuations of S_{min}. When $S_{min} = g$, we assign a cost

$$100(G - (1 + 1/2 + \cdots + 1/g))$$

for $g \in \{1, 2, ..., G\}$ (i.e., the cost decreases approximately logarithmically with increase in the valuation of S_{min}). This captures a "law of diminishing returns": as the number of collected samples g increases, the additional value of the last collected sample grows as $O(1/g)$.

Summary of Results: Table 1 and Table 2 summarize our experimental results; for each PN, we show the size (number of states and edges) of the underlying Kripke structure, and the time required to generate the KS model; the total number of concretizations searched and the total time required to check them; and the design decisions S_{min}, and B_{min} that led to a minimum cost solution. All experiments were run on an Apple Macintosh M1 Pro laptop with 16 GB of RAM, under Ventura 13.3.1.

For Table 1, we randomly assigned F forbidden cells, and repeated the experiment multiple times for a specific choice of N, G, F, and B_{max}. For Table 2, given specific values of N and G, we ran experiments by varying F and B_{max}. In this setup, we first run experiments by assigning forbidden cells for the smallest values of F and randomly add forbidden cells for larger values of F. For instance, for $N = 20$ and $G = 10$, we start with $F = 10$, thus randomly select 10 forbidden cells; then, for $F = 20$, we use the same grid with the previously selected 10 forbidden cells and randomly add 10 more forbidden cells. Thus, the model with $N = 20$, $G = 10$, and $F = 10$ differs from the one with $N = 20$, $G = 10$, and $F = 20$ only in the location of the 10 additional forbidden cells.

The number $\mathcal{D}_{srch}$ gives an indication of how much computation time our approach would save, as compared to running a model checker on a suite of PN models with varying S_{min} and B_{min} values "hard coded" into the models: we would need to generate the Kripke structure for *every* PN, while our approach only builds it once. It took several hours for the model generation and computation times for our largest Kripke structure ($N = 35$, $F = 40$, $B_{max} = 80$). For example, consider configuration $N = 35$, $G = 15$, $F = 30$, and $B_{max} = 80$: our approach took $(22{,}874 + 2{,}367) = 25{,}241$ s (about 7 h) to explore 28 different concretizations, while verifying each PN separately for a particular set of design decisions would have instead taken $28 \times 22{,}874 + 2{,}367 = 642{,}839$ s (about 178.5 h).

The number of reachable states in the model is (loosely) upper-bounded by

$$(N^2 - F) \cdot 2^G \cdot (1 + B_{max}/2) \tag{1}$$

because the rover can potentially be in any of the non-forbidden cells, each of the G sampling locations could have been visited or not, and any cell that can be visited, will be reachable either in even- or odd-length paths from $[0,0]$. As shown in Table 1 and 2, the actual number of reachable states can be much smaller. For example, when $N = 20$, $G = 10$, $F = 20$, and $B_{max} = 40$, Eq. (1) gives a bound of 8,171,520 states, but only 87,083 states are reachable.

Table 2. Results for the autonomous rover, for various model instances.

Parameters				Kripke Structure			Concretizations			Solution Found		
N	G	F	B_{max}	**States**	**Edges**	**Time**	$\mathcal{D}_{srch}$	$\mathcal{D}_{rch}$	**Time**	S_{min}	B_{min}	**Cost**
20	10	10	40	89,687	293,159	29 s	59	66	10 s	5	1	971
		20	40	87,083	277,910	26 s	59	66	7 s	5	1	971
30	15	20	60	2,422,351	8,113,490	1600 s	83	96	529 s	7	1	1,440
		30	60	2,263,154	7,490,314	1463 s	83	96	491 s	7	1	1,440
35	15	30	80	25,939,995	89,170,887	22,874 s	28	96	2,367 s	8	5	1,253
		40	80	25,694,819	87,550,513	22,740 s	28	96	2,334 s	8	5	1,253

Complexity Analysis. The worst-case complexity of the algorithm is the number N of nodes of the semi-lattice of concretizations that need to be explored (potentially $N = 2^n$, if there are n decisions and they are all independent, possibly many fewer if some of the n decisions are mutually exclusive), times the complexity of CTL model checking for the concretization corresponding to the node (the complexity of CTL model checking is linear in the size of the Kripke structure M and in the size of the CTL formula φ, i.e., $\mathcal{O}(|M| \cdot |\varphi|)$ where $|M| = |\mathcal{S}| + |\mathcal{N}|$). If $\mathcal{D}_{search} \subseteq \mathcal{D}_{reach}$ is the set of concretizations that must be explored, model checking a CTL formula in a partially specified system M with n design decisions has a time complexity in $\mathcal{O}(|\mathcal{D}_{search}| \cdot |M| \cdot |\varphi|)$ where $|\mathcal{D}_{search}| \leq |\mathcal{D}_{reach}| \leq 2^n$.

5   Related Work

Chechik et al. [13] discussed an approach for dealing with "uncertainty" in the software development process. They define uncertainty as having multiple possible modeling choices instead of just one. These uncertainties can arise from problem-domain ambiguities, various design alternatives, or differing interpretations of requirements by multiple stakeholders. They define a partial model as the "union" of potential (low-level) model designs and verify if the property of interest is satisfied in any, all, or none of these models. Based on the result, they apply algorithms to refine the models. The key difference between their approach and ours is that they propose a bottom-up approach to find a "unified" system design that satisfies the property, while we propose a top-down approach where the input is a high-level model defining M, while the (likely quite large) set of potential designs is an output. In our approach, only a subset of these potential designs may need to be considered, as they are explored in increasing cost order. Notably, [13] does not incorporate the notion of cost in their approach to decide a particular system design.

Design Space Exploration (DSE) is a related field with techniques similar to the ones presented. Specific to Software Product Lines (SPLs), [2] uses constraint programming to perform automated SPL exploration. FORMULA [19] is a DSE tool that pre-processes then encodes an exploration query into an SMT-query via a user-defined domain-specific language. DESERT [25] is similar to FORMULA, but uses BDDs and a system hierarchy to guide their search. [23] instead uses a pseudo-Boolean encoding to optimize component-based software system designs. Importantly, none of these approaches consider temporal logic properties as system constraints.

For temporal logic-based DSE, FuseIC3 [11] modifies the IC3 algorithm to perform model checking on sets of potential models. Similarly, D^3 [12] is a pre-processing technique that prunes an input space of potential models by leveraging the structural relationships between them. As a case study, [14] investigates the design space of a NASA automated ATC using model checking and contract-based design. None of these techniques consider CTL model checking. [10] solves a similar problem by performing a model checking of "feature CTL" (fCTL). The authors annotate temporal operators with propositional formulas specifying which configurations that CTL expression must hold for. [1] also does model checking of fCTL formulas, instead using SAT-based algorithms. None of these techniques consider cost, thus optimization.

Pecheur and Raimondi [26] introduced the formalism Mixed Transition System (MTS) that combines the definition of a Kripke structure and a Labeled Transition System and proposed Action-Restricted CTL (ARCTL) to describe the behaviors of MTS. A typical reachability property in ARCTL is expressed as $E_\alpha F\varphi$: there exists a path where the action label of each edge in the path satisfies α and the path leads to a state satisfying φ. The authors presented a reduction of ARCTL model checking over MTSs to CTL model checking over KSs using a "post-projection" that pushes action labels from transitions to their target states. In contrast, our framework maintains classical CTL syntax, eliminating the need to transform formulas or extend the logic. Instead, it handles incompleteness at the model level by introducing *unknown* design decisions, and evaluates properties over sets of concretizations that extend the partial model.

6   Conclusion

We presented a formalism and algorithmic framework for verifying systems with incomplete specifications, where incompleteness arises from pending design decisions during development. These unresolved decisions are captured as atomic propositions with unknown values in a partially labeled Kripke structure. Our approach identifies concrete decisions that lead to satisfaction of CTL-specified requirements. While CTL is interpreted over Kripke structures, we use Petri nets as a high-level modeling formalism to compactly generate large state spaces and to encode how design choices concretize unknowns in the underlying structure.

Future work includes developing incremental verification strategies that exploit lattice-based relationships between labelings, with the goal of reusing results when extending partial assignments. We also plan to investigate cost-guided heuristics that not only prioritize low-cost decisions but also estimate the likelihood of those decisions leading to successful completions.

References

1. Ben-David, S., Sterin, B., Atlee, J.M., Beidu, S.: Symbolic model checking of product-line requirements using sat-based methods. In: 2015 IEEE/ACM 37th IEEE International Conference on Software Engineering, vol. 1, pp. 189–199. IEEE (2015)
2. Benavides, D., Trinidad, P., Ruiz-Cortés, A.: Automated reasoning on feature models. In: Pastor, O., Falcão e Cunha, J. (eds.) CAiSE 2005. LNCS, vol. 3520, pp. 491–503. Springer, Heidelberg (2005). https://doi.org/10.1007/11431855_34
3. Bruns, G., Godefroid, P.: Model checking partial state spaces with 3-valued temporal logics. In: Proceedings of the 11th International Conference on Computer Aided Verification, pp. 274–287. CAV 1999, Springer-Verlag, London, UK (1999). http://dl.acm.org/citation.cfm?id=647768.733795
4. Bruns, G., Godefroid, P.: Generalized model checking: Reasoning about partial state spaces. In: Concurrency Theory, pp. 168–182. CONCUR, Springer-Verlag, Heidelberg (2000). http://dl.acm.org/citation.cfm?id=646735.701611
5. Bruns, G., Godefroid, P.: Model checking with multi-valued logics. In: Díaz, J., Karhumäki, J., Lepistö, A., Sannella, D. (eds.) Automata, Languages and Programming, pp. 281–293. Springer, Berlin Heidelberg, Berlin, Heidelberg (2004). https://doi.org/10.1007/978-3-540-27836-8_26
6. Chechik, M., Devereux, B., Easterbrook, S., Gurfinkel, A.: Multi-valued symbolic model-checking 12(4) (2003). https://doi.org/10.1145/990010.990011
7. Ciardo, G., Miner, A.S., Wan, M.: Advanced features in SMART: the stochastic model checking analyzer for reliability and timing. ACM SIGMETRICS Perf. Eval. Rev. 36(4), 58–63 (2009)
8. Cimatti, A., et al.: NuSMV 2: an opensource tool for symbolic model checking. In: Brinksma, E., Larsen, K.G. (eds.) CAV 2002. LNCS, vol. 2404, pp. 359–364. Springer, Heidelberg (2002). https://doi.org/10.1007/3-540-45657-0_29
9. Clarke, E.M., Emerson, E.A.: Design and synthesis of synchronization skeletons using branching time temporal logic. In: Procedings IBM Workshop on Logics of Programs, pp. 52–71. LNCS 131, Springer (1981). https://doi.org/10.1007/bfb0025774
10. Classen, A., Heymans, P., Schobbens, P.Y., Legay, A.: Symbolic model checking of software product lines. In: Proceedings of the 33rd International Conference on Software Engineering, pp. 321–330 (2011)
11. Dureja, R., Rozier, K.Y.: FuseIC3: an algorithm for checking large design spaces. In: 2017 Formal Methods in Computer Aided Design (FMCAD), pp. 164–171. IEEE (2017)
12. Dureja, R., Rozier, K.Y.: More scalable LTL model checking via discovering design-space dependencies (D^3). In: Beyer, D., Huisman, M. (eds.) TACAS 2018. LNCS, vol. 10805, pp. 309–327. Springer, Cham (2018). https://doi.org/10.1007/978-3-319-89960-2_17

13. Famelis, M., Salay, R., Chechik, M.: Partial models: towards modeling and reasoning with uncertainty. In: 2012 34th International Conference on Software Engineering (ICSE), pp. 573–583 (2012). https://doi.org/10.1109/ICSE.2012.6227159

14. Gario, M., Cimatti, A., Mattarei, C., Tonetta, S., Rozier, K.Y.: Model checking at scale: automated air traffic control design space exploration. In: Chaudhuri, S., Farzan, A. (eds.) CAV 2016. LNCS, vol. 9780, pp. 3–22. Springer, Cham (2016). https://doi.org/10.1007/978-3-319-41540-6_1

15. Godefroid, P., Huth, M., Jagadeesan, R.: Abstraction-Based Model Checking Using Modal Transition Systems. In: Larsen, K.G., Nielsen, M. (eds.) CONCUR 2001. LNCS, vol. 2154, pp. 426–440. Springer, Heidelberg (2001). https://doi.org/10.1007/3-540-44685-0_29

16. Gruler, A., Leucker, M., Scheidemann, K.: Modeling and model checking software product lines. In: Barthe, G., de Boer, F.S. (eds.) Formal Methods for Open Object-Based Distributed Systems, pp. 113–131. Springer, Berlin Heidelberg, Berlin, Heidelberg (2008). https://doi.org/10.1007/978-3-540-68863-1_8

17. Holzmann, G.J.: The SPIN Model Checker. Addison-Wesley (2003)

18. Huth, M., Jagadeesan, R., Schmidt, D.A.: Modal transition systems: a foundation for three-valued program analysis. In: European Symposium on Programming Languages and Systems, pp. 155–169. ESOP 2001, Springer-Verlag, London, UK, UK (2001). http://dl.acm.org/citation.cfm?id=645395.651926

19. Kang, E., Jackson, E., Schulte, W.: An approach for effective design space exploration. In: Calinescu, R., Jackson, E. (eds.) Monterey Workshop 2010. LNCS, vol. 6662, pp. 33–54. Springer, Heidelberg (2011). https://doi.org/10.1007/978-3-642-21292-5_3

20. Kleene, S.C.: Introduction to Metamathematics. North Holland (1987)

21. Kwiatkowska, M., Norman, G., Parker, D.: PRISM: probabilistic symbolic model checker. In: Field, T., Harrison, P.G., Bradley, J., Harder, U. (eds.) TOOLS 2002. LNCS, vol. 2324, pp. 200–204. Springer, Heidelberg (2002). https://doi.org/10.1007/3-540-46029-2_13

22. Larsen, K.G., Nyman, U., Wasowski, A.: On Modal refinement and consistency. In: Caires, L., Vasconcelos, V.T. (eds.) CONCUR 2007. LNCS, vol. 4703, pp. 105–119. Springer, Heidelberg (2007). https://doi.org/10.1007/978-3-540-74407-8_8

23. Manolios, P., Vroon, D., Subramanian, G.: Automating component-based system assembly. In: Proceedings of the 2007 International Symposium on Software Testing and Analysis, pp. 61–72 (2007)

24. Murata, T.: Petri nets: properties, analysis and applications. Proc. IEEE **77**(4), 541–579 (1989)

25. Neema, S., Sztipanovits, J., Karsai, G., Butts, K.: Constraint-based design-space exploration and model synthesis. In: Alur, R., Lee, I. (eds.) EMSOFT 2003. LNCS, vol. 2855, pp. 290–305. Springer, Heidelberg (2003). https://doi.org/10.1007/978-3-540-45212-6_19

26. Pecheur, C., Raimondi, F.: Symbolic model checking of logics with actions. In: Edelkamp, S., Lomuscio, A. (eds.) MoChArt 2006. LNCS (LNAI), vol. 4428, pp. 113–128. Springer, Heidelberg (2007). https://doi.org/10.1007/978-3-540-74128-2_8

Extending Timed Automata with Clock Derivatives

David Cortés[1], Jean Leneutre[1], Vadim Malvone[1], James Ortiz[1,2(✉)],
and Pierre-Yves Schobbens[3]

[1] LTCI, Institut Polytechnique de Paris, Télécom Paris, Palaiseau, France
`{david.cortes,jean.leneutre,vadim.malvone,`
`james.ortizvega}@telecom-paris.fr`
[2] LACL, Université Paris Est Creteil, Creteil 94010, France
`james.ortiz-vega@u-pec.fr`
[3] NADI, University of Namur, Namur, Belgium
`pierre-yves.schobbens@unamur.be`

Abstract. The increasing complexity of safety-critical systems in domains like aerospace, robotics, and industrial control demands precise modeling and verification methods. While Timed Automata (TA) and Distributed Timed Automata (DTA) are standard formalisms for real-time systems, they assume synchronized clocks or lack the expressiveness to capture clock drift and indirect timing dependencies. To overcome these limits, we propose Timed Automata with Clock Derivatives (idTA), extending TA with rate constraints to model independent clock evolution. We also introduce DL_ν, a temporal logic over Multi-Timed Labeled Transition Systems (MLTS), capturing properties of systems with unsynchronized clocks. We show that model checking for DL_ν is EXPTIME-complete. Finally, we present MIMETIC, a model checking tool supporting idTA and DL_ν, providing a platform for analyzing clock interactions and verification of Distributed Real-time Systems (DRTS).

Keywords: Timed Automata · Reachability · Distributed Timed Systems

1 Introduction

Distributed Real-Time Systems (DRTS) are foundational to many critical applications, including traffic light coordination, avionics, telecommunication infrastructures, and medical monitoring devices. These systems consist of spatially distributed components that operate concurrently under strict timing requirements. An essential aspect of DRTS is how time is managed across components. Two primary approaches exist: *synchronous semantics* and *asynchronous semantics*. In synchronous semantics, all clocks in the system evolve at the same uniform rate, assuming perfect synchronization akin to a global Newtonian time. In contrast, asynchronous semantics allow clocks to evolve at different rates, enabling components to operate independently and adaptively. Numerous real-time formalisms

© The Author(s), under exclusive license to Springer Nature Switzerland AG 2026
F. Damiani and M. Farrell (Eds.): iFM 2025, LNCS 16194, pp. 99–119, 2026.
https://doi.org/10.1007/978-3-032-10794-7_6

have been proposed to model and verify DRTS. While Timed Automata (TA) [4] have proven effective in modeling real-time systems, they assume perfectly synchronized clocks, which is often unrealistic in distributed settings. Extensions such as Distributed Timed Automata (DTA) [18] and Timed Automata with Independent Clocks (icTA) [1], and Distributed Event Clock Automata (DECA) [23] address this by allowing clocks to evolve independently. Hybrid Automata (HA) extend TA by incorporating both discrete transitions and continuous dynamics [26]. There are also several temporal logic formalisms, such as Timed μ-calculus [14], L_ν [19], and TCTL,ch6TY01. These logics are used to specify sequential timed properties governed by timing constraints. Other logics, such as DRTL [21], APTL [30], DECTL [23], and ML_ν [22], have been developed to capture the timing properties of distributed components in DRTS.

However, these models still fall short in expressing relative rate constraints or indirect clock dependencies, a common requirement in many real-world DRTS scenarios [17,27]. To illustrate, consider two sensors, A and B, each with its own local clock x and y. Sensor A samples every $2\,$s (w.r.t. x), and B must calibrate exactly after every two samples, using only y. With no direct communication, synchrony must be maintained by enforcing $\dot{y} = \dot{x}$. This dependency is rate-based, whereas standard TA are event-driven: clocks have fixed rate 1 and guards test only their values. Hence TA cannot express state-dependent rates or integral constraints, one needs priced/weighted TA [2] or (hybrid) stopwatch automata [9] instead. This type of inter-clock rate constraint cannot be captured by either DTA, icTA or DECA. To overcome these shortcomings, we propose Timed Automata with Clock Derivatives (independent-derivative timed automata (idTA)) an expressive yet decidable extension of TA. The key innovation in idTA lies in its ability to impose rate constraints over the derivatives of clocks, allowing modelers to express relative timing requirements between components. These constraints define how quickly each clock is allowed to evolve, either in absolute terms or relative to others. Crucially, while idTA enables richer timing behavior, it does not generalize to arbitrary differential equations as in Hybrid Automata (HA). Instead, it preserves decidability by limiting rate expressions to derivative comparisons, avoiding the complexity and undecidability issues that plague full hybrid models. This balance of expressiveness and tractability allows idTA remaining compatible with symbolic verification methods such as zone-based reachability analysis. Symbolic compatibility means our operators and constraints admit finite symbolic representations and effective fixpoint computation.

To reason about properties expressed in idTA, we introduce a novel temporal logic: $DL\nu$, an extension of the timed modal logic L_ν. It adds time-bounded modalities and simple clock constraints to basic modal logic. Our $DL\nu$ captures the semantics of idTA, allowing specification of timing relationships influenced by clock derivatives. We also present MIMETIC, a prototype tool that supports symbolic verification for idTA and L_ν, allowing efficient model checking to verifying distributed systems with dynamic timing behavior.

Structure of the Paper. Section 2 covers preliminaries. Section 3 defines idTA, extending TA and DTA with rate constraints. Section 4 proves decidability of reachability. Section 5 introduces the logic DL_ν and shows its model checking is EXPTIME-complete. Section 6 discusses expressiveness, and Sect. 7 presents the MIMETIC tool. Sections 8 and 9 cover related work and conclude.

2   Background

Let $\mathbb{N}_{>0}$ and $\mathbb{N}_{\geq 0}$ denote the sets of positive and non-negative natural, $\mathbb{R}_{\geq 0}$ the non-negative reals and $\mathbb{Z}$ the integers. For sets X and Y, we use standard set operations: intersection $(X \cap Y)$, union $(X \cup Y)$, disjoint union $(X \uplus Y)$, complement $(\overline{X})$, difference $(X \backslash Y)$, empty set $(\emptyset)$, and (strict) inclusion $(X \subseteq Y, X \subset Y)$. A timed word over an alphabet Σ is a finite sequence $\theta = ((\sigma_0, t_0)(\sigma_1, t_1) \ldots (\sigma_n, t_n)) \in (\Sigma \times \mathbb{R}_{\geq 0})^*$, where timestamps are non-decreasing: $t_i \leq t_{i+1}$. A timed language $\mathcal{L}$ is any subset of $(\Sigma \times \mathbb{R}_{\geq 0})^*$.

Clock Constraints. Let X be a finite set of variables (clocks) ranging over $\mathbb{R}_{\geq 0}$. The set $\Phi^+(X)$ of clock constraints over X is given by the following grammar:

$$\phi := true \mid x \sim c \mid x - y \sim c \mid \phi_1 \wedge \phi_2$$

where $x, y \in X$, $c \in \mathbb{N}$, and $\sim \in \{<, >, \leq, \geq, =\}$. The clock constraints of the form $true$, $x \sim c$ are called *non-diagonal constraints* and those of the form $x - y \sim c$ are called *diagonal constraints*. The set of non-diagonal constraints over X is denoted by $\Phi(X)$.

Clock Invariants. Let X be a finite set of clocks. Let $\Delta(X)$ be a set of clock invariants. Clock invariants are clock constraints as follows:

$$\varphi := true \mid x < c \mid x \leq c \mid \varphi_1 \wedge \varphi_2$$

where $x, y \in X$, $c \in \mathbb{N}$. Clock invariants restrict the amount of time that can be spent in a given state without changing to the next state.

Clock Valuations. A clock valuation $\nu \in \mathbb{R}_{\geq 0}^X$ over X is a mapping $\nu : X \to \mathbb{R}_{\geq 0}$. We note ν_0 the mapping that associates 0 to each clock. For a time value $t \in \mathbb{R}_{\geq 0}$, we denote by $\nu + t$ the valuation defined by $(\nu + t)(x) = \nu(x) + t$. Given a clock subset $Y \subseteq X$, we note $\nu[Y \leftarrow 0]$ the valuation defined as follows: $\nu[Y \leftarrow 0](x) = 0$ if $x \in Y$ and $\nu[Y \leftarrow 0](x) = \nu(x)$ otherwise. Given a clock constraint $\phi \in \Phi(X)$ and a clock valuation ν, we say that ν satisfies ϕ, denoted by $\nu \models \phi$ and formally defined as follows:

$$\nu \models x \sim c \Longleftrightarrow \nu(x) \sim c$$
$$\nu \models \phi_1 \wedge \phi_2 \Longleftrightarrow \nu(x) \models \phi_1 \wedge \nu(x) \models \phi_2$$
$$\nu \models true \Longleftrightarrow true$$

Similarly, for a clock invariant $\delta \in \Delta(X)$ and a clock valuation ν, ν satisfies δ, denoted by $\nu \models \delta$.

Timed Automata. (TA) are an extension of finite automata with a set of clocks, that evolve synchronously with time and enable measuring delays [4].

Definition 1 (Timed Automata). *A TA is a tuple $\mathcal{A} = (S, s_0, \Sigma, X, \rightarrow_{ta}, I, F)$ where: S is a finite set of locations, $s_0 \in S$ is the initial location, Σ is a finite alphabet, X is a finite set of clock names, $\rightarrow_{ta} \subseteq S \times \Sigma \times \Phi(X) \times 2^X \times S$ is the finite transition relation, $I : S \rightarrow \Delta(X)$ associates to each location a clock invariant, $F \subseteq S$ is a finite set of final locations.*

For a transition $(s, a, \phi, Y, s') \in \rightarrow_{ta}$, we write $s \xrightarrow{a,\phi,Y} s'$ and call s and s' the source and target locations, ϕ the guard, a the action, Y the reset set of clocks.

Definition 2 (Semantics of TA). *The semantics of a TA $\mathcal{A}$ is given by a Timed Labeled Transition Systems $TLTS(\mathcal{A}) = (Q, Q_F, q_0, \Sigma \uplus \mathbb{R}_{\geq 0}, \rightarrow_{tlts})$ where $Q = \{(s, \nu) \in S \times \mathbb{R}_{\geq 0}^X \mid \nu \models I(s)\}$ is the set of states over $\mathcal{A}$, with initial state $q_0 = (s_0, \nu_0)$, $Q_F = \{(s_f, \nu) \in F \times \mathbb{R}_{\geq 0}^X \mid \nu \models I(s_f)\}$ is the set of final states over $\mathcal{A}$ and $\rightarrow_{tlts} \subseteq Q \times (\Sigma \uplus \mathbb{R}_{\geq 0}) \times Q$ is the transition relation defined by:*

1. *Discrete transition: $(s, \nu) \xrightarrow{a}_{tlts} (s', \nu')$, such that $s \xrightarrow{a,\phi,Y} s'$, $\nu \models \phi$, $\nu' = \nu[Y \leftarrow 0]$ and $\nu' \models I(s')$,*
2. *Delay transition: $(s, \nu) \xrightarrow{t}_{tlts} (s, \nu + t)$ for any $t \in \mathbb{R}_{\geq 0}$, such that $\nu + t \models I(s)$.*

Distributed Timed Automata (DTA), icTA, and Reachability. In [1], each process in a TA has its own clocks (DTA, icTA) that evolve synchronously within, but independently across, processes, all driven by a shared hardware clock. Clocks are globally readable but locally resettable. In contrast, [18] models interleaved execution, yielding a subclass of stopwatch automata [9]. While reachability in TA is decidable [4], region-based methods are often intractable. Convex unions of regions, or zones [7], enable more scalable analysis, as implemented in tools like UPPAAL and KRONOS.

Zone Graphs and Difference Bound Matrices (DBMs). In the analysis of TA, clock zones symbolically represent sets of valuations as convex sets defined by diagonal constraints $\phi \in \Phi^+(X)$, where a zone is given by $\mathcal{Z} = \{\nu \mid \nu \models \phi\}$. To normalize this representation, a reference clock $x_0 = 0$ is added to the clock set X. A symbolic state is a pair $(s, \mathcal{Z})$, where s is a location and $\mathcal{Z}$ a zone. The set of symbolic states and transitions forms the zone graph of a TA $\mathcal{A}$, written $ZG(\mathcal{A}) = (Q, q_0, \Sigma, T)$, where Q is the set of symbolic states, q_0 the initial one, and T the transition relation. Transition come directly from the operational semantics of TA, lifted to zones via symbolic post operators. Operations such as time elapse, resets, and intersections preserve zones [4,7]. Zones are efficiently represented using *Difference Bound Matrices* (DBMs) [7]. A DBM is a square matrix indexed by $X := X \cup \{x_0\}$, where each entry $\mathbf{d}_{i,j} = (d_{i,j}, \preceq)$ encodes the constraint $x_i - x_j \preceq d_{i,j}$ with $\preceq \in \{<, \leq\}$ and $d_{i,j} \in \mathbb{Z} \cup \{\infty, -\infty\}$. The semantics of a DBM $\mathcal{D}$ is the clock zone: $\mathcal{Z} = (x_0 = 0) \wedge \bigwedge_{0 \leq i \neq j \leq n} x_i - x_j \preceq d_{i,j}$. To improve efficiency, DBMs are canonicalized via the Floyd-Warshall algorithm [10]. Zone abstraction using $Extra_{LU}$ and $Extra_{LU}^+$ [8] keeps only bounds relevant to guards and invariants, yielding a finite zone graph and better reachability performance.

Timed Logic L_ν and Time Language. L_ν is a modal logic used to specify properties of states in a TLTS over the set of actions [19]. Formulas combine simple state predicates (e.g., constraints on clocks) with modalities over steps (time elapse and labeled actions), and a greatest fixpoint operator to express invariants/safety. We denote by $\mathcal{L}(\mathcal{A})$ the timed language of a TA $\mathcal{A}$, i.e., the set of timed words generated by accepting runs: $\mathcal{L}(\mathcal{A}) = \mathcal{L}(\text{TLTS}(\mathcal{A}))$

3 Timed Automata with Clock Derivatives

In this section, we present a derivative-based timed semantics for TA, called idTA, which incorporates clock derivatives to capture the rates of change of independent clocks. This extension enables more accurate modeling of timing behavior in distributed systems, where clocks may evolve at different rates. Our semantics offer two main advantages. First, expressiveness is significantly enhanced: while previous frameworks like [22] allowed for independent clocks, they lacked explicit rate constraints. In contrast, idTA introduces precise rate bounds (e.g., $\dot{x} \leq \dot{y}$), allowing direct and indirect timing dependencies between components. This subsumes the multi-timed semantics in [22] and enables the modeling of richer distributed behaviors. Second, idTA supports modular verification by associating rate constraints with locations, allowing local analysis of each component under its own timing constraints, simplifying reasoning in large-scale systems.

Definition 3 (Rate Constraints). *Let X be a finite set of clocks. Let $\dot{X}$ be a finite set of time clock derivatives. The set $\Psi(X)$ of rate constraints over the set of clocks X is given by the following grammar:*

$$\psi := true \mid \dot{x} \sim 1 \mid \dot{x} \sim \dot{y} \mid \psi_1 \wedge \psi_2$$

where $\dot{x}, \dot{y} \in \dot{X}$, $x, y \in X$ and $\sim \in \{<, >, \leq, \geq, =\}$. A rate constraint ψ is a conjunction of comparing two clock derivative values or a clock derivative value with a natural constant 1. A classical clock (as in TA) will be described by $\dot{x} = 1$.

The constant 1 serves as a standard reference rate, representing normal time progression as in traditional TA. By focusing on $\dot{x} = 1$, we ensure the framework remains expressive enough for key use cases like DRTS, while avoiding unnecessary complexity. Allowing general comparisons with arbitrary constants would increase the complexity of the semantics and model-checking process without necessarily providing meaningful added expressiveness for the intended applications. As previously mentioned, TA assumes perfectly synchronous clocks, which is not always feasible in DRTS, where clocks may evolve differently due to factors like temperature, humidity, pressure, or aging. To formalize the independent evolution of these local clocks, we slightly adapt the definition of rates from [1].

Definition 4 (Rates). *Let X be a finite set of clocks. A rate is a tuple $\tau = (\tau_x)_{x \in X}$ of local time functions. Each local time function τ_x maps the reference time (i.e., a global time) to the time of the clock x, i.e., $\tau_x : \mathbb{R}_{\geq 0} \to \mathbb{R}_{\geq 0}$. The functions τ_x must be continuous, strictly increasing, divergent, and satisfy $\tau_x(0) = 0$. The set of all these tuples τ is denoted by Rates. For all $x \in X$ and $t \in \mathbb{R}_{\geq 0}$, $\tau(t) = (\tau_x(t))_{x \in X}$ where $\tau_x(t)$ is a member of the tuple $\tau(t)$.*

Definition 5 (Addition to a valuation). *Let X be a finite set of clocks, a clock valuation $\nu : X \to \mathbb{R}_{\geq 0}$ and $\boldsymbol{d} \in \mathbb{R}_{\geq 0}^{X}$: the valuation $\nu + \boldsymbol{d}$ is defined by $(\nu + \boldsymbol{d})(x) = \nu(x) + \boldsymbol{d}_x$ for all $x \in X$.*

Definition 6 (Semantics of Rate Constraints). *Let X be a finite set of clocks. Given a rate constraint $\psi \in \Psi(X)$ and a tuple of functions $\tau \in$ Rates, we denote that τ satisfies ψ at time t with $(\tau, t) \models \psi$. In particular, the formal definition is as follows:*

$$(\tau, t) \models true \iff true$$

$$(\tau, t) \models \dot{x} \sim 1 \iff \tau_x \text{ is differentiable at } t \text{ and } d\tau_x/dt(t) \sim 1$$

$$(\tau, t) \models \dot{x} \sim \dot{y} \iff \tau_x \text{ is differentiable at } t \text{ and } \tau_y \text{ is differentiable at } t$$

$$\text{and } d\tau_x/dt(t) \sim d\tau_y/dt(t)$$

$$(\tau, t) \models \psi_1 \wedge \psi_2 \iff (\tau, t) \models \psi_1 \text{ and } (\tau, t) \models \psi_2$$

The semantics of our idTA is defined via an extension of the TLTS framework called MLTS [22], where each run is a sequence of action–timestamp tuples, capturing the local times of independent clocks. This enables precise modeling of distributed timing across components.

Definition 7 (Timed Automata with Clock Derivatives (idTA) *A Timed automaton with Clock Derivatives (idTA) is a tuple $\mathcal{A} = (S, s_0, \Sigma, X, \to_{idTA}, I, R, F)$ where : S is a finite set of locations, $s_0 \in S$ is the initial location, Σ is a finite alphabet, X is a finite set of clock names, $\to_{idTA} \subseteq S \times \Sigma \times \Phi(X) \times 2^X \times S$ is the finite transition relation, $I : S \to \Delta(X)$ associates to each location a clock invariant, $R : S \to \Psi(X)$ associates to each location a rate constraint, $F \subseteq S$ is a finite set of final locations.*

Definition 8 (Semantics of (idTA). *Given an idTA $\mathcal{A} = (S, s_0, \Sigma, X, \to_{idTA}, I, R, F)$ and $\tau \in$ Rates, the timed semantics of $\mathcal{A}$ is given by a MLTS over X, denoted by $MLTS(\mathcal{A}, \tau) = (Q, q_0, \Sigma, Q_F, \to_{mlts})$, where the set of states Q consists of triples composed of a location, a clock valuation and lastly the reference time: $Q = \{(s, \nu, t) \in S \times \mathbb{R}_{\geq 0}^{X} \times \mathbb{R}_{\geq 0} \mid \nu \models I(s) \text{ and } (\tau, t) \models R(s)\}$, the starting state is $q_0 = (s_0, \nu_0, 0)$, where ν_0 is the valuation that initializes all the clocks to zero, Σ is the alphabet of $\mathcal{A}$, the set of final states Q_F consists of triples $\{(s_f, \nu, t) \in F \times \mathbb{R}_{\geq 0}^{X} \times \mathbb{R}_{\geq 0} \mid \nu \models I(s_f) \text{ and } (\tau, t) \models R(s_f)\}$, and the transition relation $\to_{mlts}$ is defined by:*

1. Discrete transition: A transition (q_i, a, q_{i+1}) is denoted $q_i \xrightarrow{a}_{mlts} q_{i+1}$ where $q_i = (s_i, \nu_i, t_i)$, $q_{i+1} = (s_{i+1}, \nu_{i+1}, t_{i+1})$, $a \in \Sigma$, there exists a transition $(s_i, a, \phi, Y, s_{i+1}) \in \rightarrow_{idTA}$, such that $\nu_i \models \phi$, $\nu_{i+1} = \nu_i[Y \leftarrow 0]$, $\nu_{i+1} \models I(s_{i+1})$, $(\tau, t_{i+1}) \models R(s_{i+1})$, $t_i = t_{i+1}$ and,

2. Delay transition: A transition (q_i, d, q_i') is denoted $q_i \xrightarrow{d}_{mlts} q_i'$ where $q_i = (s_i, \nu_i, t_i)$, $q_i' = (s_i, \nu_i + d, t_{i+1})$, $d = \tau(t_{i+1}) - \tau(t_i)$ and $\forall t \in [t_i, t_{i+1}]$: $\nu_i + (\tau(t) - \tau(t_i)) \models I(s_i)$ and $(\tau, t) \models R(s_i)$.

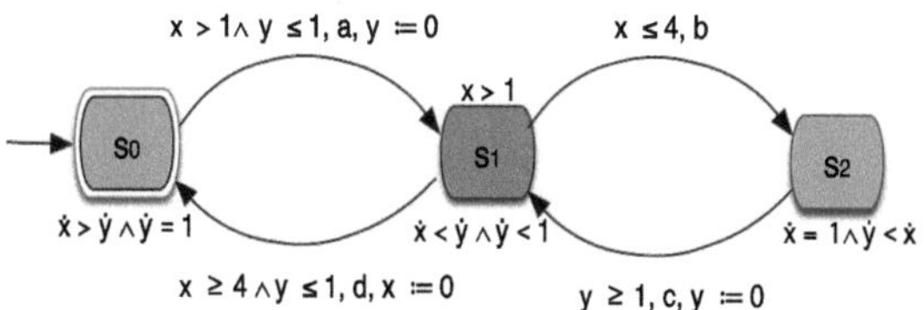

Fig. 1. A TA with Clock Derivatives (idTA) $\mathcal{A}$.

Example 1. Fig. 1 shows an idTA $\mathcal{M}$ with alphabet $\Sigma = \{a, b, c, d\}$, clocks $X = \{x, y\}$, and rate constraints in locations s_0, s_1 and s_2. The language of the automaton $\mathcal{M}$ includes all timed words where action a occurs first, followed by b, c and d with delays constrained by the rate conditions imposed in each location $(s_0 = \dot{x} > \dot{y}$ and $\dot{y} = 1)$, $(s_1 = \dot{x} < \dot{y}$ and $\dot{y} < 1)$ and $(s_2 = \dot{y} < \dot{x}$ and $\dot{x} = 1)$.

4   Decidability

In this section, we use zone-based abstraction [5] to define timed zone graphs that account for clock derivatives and to present a reachability algorithm. The algorithm is a symbolic breadth-first search (BFS) over the zone graph: from a symbolic state $(s, \mathcal{Z}$ we take all admissible time elapses at once (respecting invariants), intersect with guards, apply resets, canonicalize/abstract the resulting zones, and enqueue any new successors; the search stops when some zone intersects the target. We also show that reachability for idTA is decidable.

4.1   Clock Zones and Operations with Clock Derivatives

A symbolic state $q = (s, \mathcal{Z})$ represents all concrete states $(s', \nu) \in q$ such that $s = s'$ and $\nu \in \mathcal{Z}$, i.e., all valuations ν in zone $\mathcal{Z}$ at location s. Similarly, we write $(s, \mathcal{Z}) \subseteq (s', \mathcal{Z}')$ if $s = s'$ and $\mathcal{Z} \subseteq \mathcal{Z}'$. To define clock zones [19] over a clock set X, we use $\Phi^+(X)$, the set of diagonal constraints. In standard TA, synchronized clocks make differences meaningful, but idTA requires adapting zone operations to handle independent rates. We extend time and discrete successor/predecessor operations accordingly, while intersection, restricted projection, and resets retain their standard semantics [7,28].

Definition 9 (Semantic Operations on clock zones). *Let $\mathcal{Z}$ be a clock zone. The semantics of the time successor and time predecessor on a clock zone can be defined as:*

1. *Time successor:* $\mathcal{Z} \uparrow_\psi = \{\nu + d \mid \nu \in \mathcal{Z},\ d \in \mathbb{R}^X_{\geq 0}, \exists t, t' > 0, t \leq t',\ and\ \exists \tau \in$ *Rates*, $d = \tau(t') - \tau(t)\ and\ \exists \psi \in \Psi(X),\ (\tau, t) \models \psi\}$,
2. *Time predecessor:* $\mathcal{Z} \downarrow_\psi = \{\nu - d \mid \nu \in \mathcal{Z},\ d \in \mathbb{R}^X_{\geq 0}, \exists t, t' > 0, t \leq t',\ and\ \exists \tau \in$ *Rates*, $d = \tau(t') - \tau(t)\ and\ \exists \psi \in \Psi(X),\ (\tau, t) \models \psi\}$.

Intuitively, $\mathcal{Z} \uparrow_\psi$ collects all valuations reachable by letting time flow from $\mathcal{Z}$ along allowed rates while ψ holds, and $\mathcal{Z} \downarrow_\psi$ the valuations that could have flowed into $\mathcal{Z}$, for example, in standard TA with $\dot{x} = \dot{y} = 1$, if $\mathcal{Z}$ contains $(x = 2, y = 0)$ then $\mathcal{Z} \uparrow$ includes $(x = 5, y = 3)$ after $3\,$s, and conversely from $(x = 5, y = 3)$ we have $(x = 2, y = 0) \in \mathcal{Z} \downarrow$.

Proposition 1. *Let $\mathcal{Z}$ be a clock zone. Then $\mathcal{Z} \uparrow_\psi$, and $\mathcal{Z} \downarrow_\psi$ are also clock zones.*

Definition 10 (Discrete Successor). *Let $q = (s, \mathcal{Z})$ be a zone and $e = (s, a, \phi, Y, s') \in \to_{idTA}$ be a transition of $\mathcal{A}$, then* $\mathsf{post}(\mathcal{Z}, e) = \{\nu' \mid \exists \nu \in \mathcal{Z}, \exists \tau \in$ *Rates*, $(s, \nu) \xrightarrow{e}_{mlts(\mathcal{A}, \tau)} (s', \nu')\}$ *is the set of valuations q can reach by transition e.*

The zone $(s', \mathsf{post}(\mathcal{Z}, e))$ describes the discrete successor of the zone $(s, \mathcal{Z})$ under the transition e. The definition is similar for the discrete predecessor.

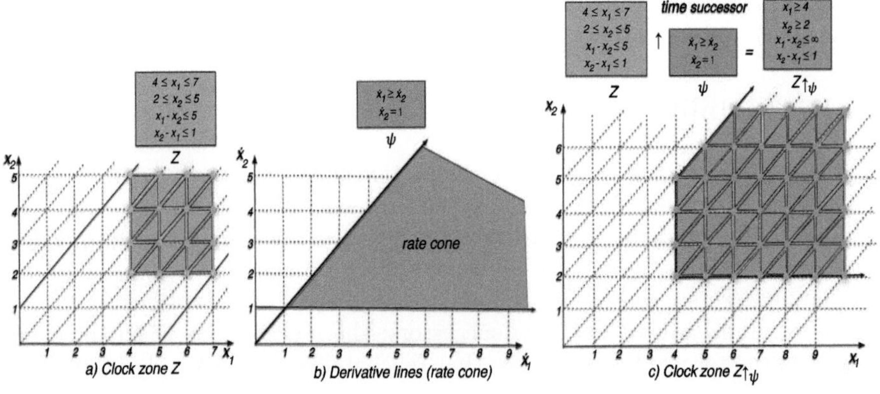

Fig. 2. a) The clock zone $\mathcal{Z}$, b) Derivative lines, c) The time successor of $\mathcal{Z}$ ($\mathcal{Z} \uparrow_\psi$).

Example 2. Consider a clock zone $\mathcal{Z} = \{(4 \leq x_1 \leq 7) \wedge (2 \leq x_2 \leq 5)\}$, rate constraint $\psi = (\dot{x}_2 = 1) \wedge (\dot{x}_1 \geq \dot{x}_2)$, and clock invariant $I = \{(x_1 \leq 6) \wedge (x_2 \geq 4)\}$. Figure 2 presents an example of $a)$ a clock zone $\mathcal{Z}$, $b)$ the derivative lines (rate cone), $c)$ the time successor of the clock zone $\mathcal{Z}$ ($\mathcal{Z} \uparrow_\psi$). The time successor of $\mathcal{Z}$ is: $\mathcal{Z} \uparrow_\psi = \{(x_1 \geq 4) \wedge (1 \leq x_2 \leq 5) \wedge (x_2 - x_1 \leq 1)\}$. Figure 3 presents an example of the intersection of the clock zone $\mathcal{Z} \uparrow_\psi$ of Fig. 2.c with the invariant $I = \{(x_1 \leq 6) \wedge (x_2 \geq 4)\}$.

4.2 Difference Bound Matrices with Clock Derivatives

We introduce Difference Bound Matrices with Clock Derivatives (DBMCs), an extension of classical DBMs [7,10], designed to capture the independent evolution of clocks by tracking differences between clock derivatives rather than clock values. Traditional DBMs assume synchronous clocks, where differences remain stable over time, but DBMCs allow for clocks advancing at variable rates, making them suitable for distributed systems. Each DBMC encodes a set of rate constraints: comparisons between two derivatives or between a derivative and the constant 1. They serve two purposes: (1) checking the consistency of rate constraints, and (2) adjusting clock differences during time successor and predecessor computations. Essentially, DBMCs extend DBMs by explicitly managing rate constraints in our idTA.

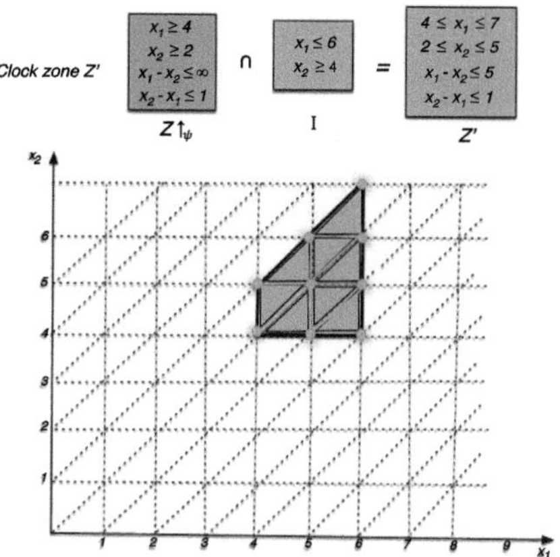

Fig. 3. The clock zone $\mathcal{Z}'$ after intersection with the invariant $I = \{x_1 \leq 6 \wedge x_2 \geq 4\}$.

Definition 11 (Difference Bound Matrix with Clock Derivatives). *A Difference Bound Matrix (DBMC) over the set of n clock derivatives $\{\dot{x}_1, \dot{x}_2, \ldots, \dot{x}_n\}$ is a $(n+1) \times (n+1)$ square matrix (arrowhead matrix) of $(\{-1, 0, 1\} \times \{<, \leq\}) \cup \{(\infty, <)\}$ with rows and columns indexed by $\{\dot{x}_0, \dot{x}_1, \dot{x}_2, \ldots, \dot{x}_n\}$. The DBMC can be represented as follows:*

$$\mathcal{E} = (e_{i,j})_{0 \leq i,j \leq n}$$

where each $e_{i,j}$ is of the form $(e_{i,j}, \preceq)$, $\preceq \in \{<, \leq\}$ and $e_{i,j} \in \{-1, 0, 1\}$ is called a bound. Formally, the semantics of DBMC $\mathcal{E}$ is the rate constraints:

$$\psi = (\dot{x}_0 = 0) \wedge \bigwedge_{0 \leq i \neq j \leq n} \dot{x}_i - \dot{x}_j \preceq e_{i,j}$$

where $\dot{x}_i$ is a clock derivative of the row i, $\dot{x}_j$ is a clock derivative of the column j and the clock $\dot{x}_0$ is always equal to 0.

Since the variable x_0 is always equal to 0, it can be used to express rate constraints that involve only a single variable (clock derivatives). The language of rate constraints only allows comparison with 1. Thus, $\mathbf{e}_{i,0} = (e_{i,0}, \preceq)$ means $\dot{x}_i \preceq e_{i,0}$ and $e_{i,0} = 1$ (or $e_{i,0} = \infty$). Similarly, $\mathbf{e}_{0,j} = (e_{0,j}, \preceq)$ means $-\dot{x}_j \preceq e_{0,j}$. Also, for each clock difference $\dot{x}_i - \dot{x}_i$, let $\mathbf{e}_{i,i} = (0, \leq)$ or for each unbounded clock difference $\dot{x}_i - \dot{x}_j$ with $i \neq j$ and $i, j \geq 1$, let $\mathbf{e}_{i,j} = (0, \leq)$ (or $e_{i,j} = \infty$). A DBMC $\mathcal{E}$ that satisfied the definition of rates, implies that $\dot{x}_i > 0$ for $0 \leq i \leq n$, thus $\mathcal{E}_{0,i}$ is at least $(0, <)$. Our DBMCs and their canonical forms are defined analogously to standard DBMs.

Example 3. Consider the following clock zone with independent local clocks:

$$\mathcal{Z} = [\![3 \leq x_1 \leq 7 \wedge x_2 \geq 0 \wedge 3 \leq x_1 - x_2 \leq 5]\!]$$

The clock zone $\mathcal{Z}$ can be represented by the matrix $\mathcal{D}$ and by canonizing it, we can get $\mathcal{D}'$:

$$\mathcal{D} = \begin{array}{c} \\ x_0 \\ x_1 \\ x_2 \end{array}
\begin{array}{c} x_0 \\ \left(\begin{matrix} (0, \leq) \\ (7, \leq) \\ (\infty, <) \end{matrix} \right. \end{array}
\begin{array}{c} x_1 \\ (-3, \leq) \\ (0, \leq) \\ (-3, \leq) \end{array}
\begin{array}{c} x_2 \\ \left. \begin{matrix} (0, \leq) \\ (5, \leq) \\ (0, \leq) \end{matrix} \right) \end{array},
\qquad
\mathcal{D}' = \begin{array}{c} \\ x_0 \\ x_1 \\ x_2 \end{array}
\begin{array}{c} x_0 \\ \left(\begin{matrix} (0, \leq) \\ (7, \leq) \\ (4, \leq) \end{matrix} \right. \end{array}
\begin{array}{c} x_1 \\ (-3, \leq) \\ (0, \leq) \\ (-3, \leq) \end{array}
\begin{array}{c} x_2 \\ \left. \begin{matrix} (0, \leq) \\ (5, \leq) \\ (0, \leq) \end{matrix} \right) \end{array}$$

We can see that $\mathcal{D}$ does not capture many implicit rate constraints. Therefore, the conjunction of the atomic rate constraints $\psi = \{\dot{x}_2 \geq 1 \wedge \dot{x}_2 \geq \dot{x}_1\}$ is represented by the matrix $\mathcal{E}$:

$$\mathcal{E} = \begin{array}{c} \\ \dot{x}_0 \\ \dot{x}_1 \\ \dot{x}_2 \end{array}
\begin{array}{c} \dot{x}_0 \\ \left(\begin{matrix} (0, \leq) \\ (\infty, <) \\ (\infty, <) \end{matrix} \right. \end{array}
\begin{array}{c} \dot{x}_1 \\ (\infty, <) \\ (0, \leq) \\ (\infty, <) \end{array}
\begin{array}{c} \dot{x}_2 \\ \left. \begin{matrix} (-1, \leq) \\ (0, \leq) \\ (0, \leq) \end{matrix} \right) \end{array}$$

The canonical form of DBMCs follows the same principles as standard DBMs, using the Floyd-Warshall shortest-path algorithm [10] to ensure consistency. In addition to computing the canonical form, we verify the satisfiability of atomic rate constraints by checking the emptiness of the corresponding derivative cone (rate line) and ensuring compatibility with the encoded constraints. Zone transformation operations, such as time successor and predecessor, must also be adapted to respect rate constraints. For example, consider a DBM $\mathcal{D}'$ representing the zone $\mathcal{Z}' = [\![3 \leq x_1 \leq 7 \wedge 0 \leq x_2 \leq 4 \wedge 3 \leq x_1 - x_2 \leq 5]\!]$ and a DBMC $\mathcal{E}$ encoding rate constraints $\psi = \{\dot{x}_2 \geq 1 \wedge \dot{x}_2 \geq \dot{x}_1\}$. The time successor operation computes $\mathcal{Z} \uparrow_\psi$, representing all reachable valuations by delays satisfying ψ. This is achieved by removing individual clock upper bounds and relaxing constraints on clock differences. Specifically, all first-column entries $\mathbf{d}_{i,0}$ ($1 \leq i \leq n$) are set to $(\infty, <)$, and diagonal entries $\mathbf{d}_{i,j}$ ($i \neq j$) are set to $(\infty, \leq)$ when $\mathbf{e}_{i,j} = (\infty, <)$. Figure 4 illustrates the representation of a clock zone $\mathcal{Z}'$ in conjunction with the rate constraints ψ for the clock zone $\mathcal{Z}' =$

$[\![3 \leq x_1 \leq 7 \wedge 0 \leq x_2 \leq 4 \wedge 3 \leq x_1 - x_2 \leq 5]\!]$ and rate constraints $\psi = \{\dot{x}_2 \geq 1 \wedge \dot{x}_2 \geq \dot{x}_1\}$. Using matrices $\mathcal{D}'$ and $\mathcal{E}$, we obtain the following matrix:

$$\mathcal{D}'' = \begin{array}{c} \\ x_0 \\ x_1 \\ x_2 \end{array} \begin{array}{ccc} x_0 & x_1 & x_2 \\ \left((0,\leq) \right. & (-3,\leq) & (0,\leq) \\ (\infty,<) & (0,\leq) & (5,\leq) \\ (\infty,<) & (\infty,<) & \left. (0,\leq) \right) \end{array}$$

We now implement two essential operations on our DBMC-based representation of clock zones, required for reachability analysis: time successor and time predecessor [7,28]. These operations extend the classical definitions from [7], but are adapted to incorporate clock derivatives, enabling precise handling of independent clock rates and derivative-based constraints.

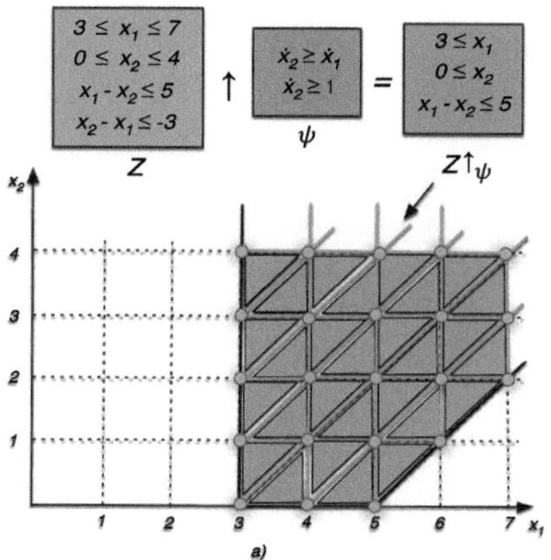

Fig. 4. A clock zone $\mathcal{Z}$.

Time Successor: A time successor operation can be computed using a canonical DBM $\mathcal{D} = (\mathbf{d}_{i,j})_{0 \leq i,j \leq n}$ and a canonical DBMC $\mathcal{E} = (\mathbf{e}_{i,j})_{0 \leq i,j \leq n}$ where the computation of the time successor operation of a DBM $\mathcal{D}'$ where $\mathcal{D}' = (\mathbf{d}'_{i,j})_{0 \leq i,j < n}$, consists first in removing from $\mathcal{D} = (\mathbf{d}_{i,j})_{0 \leq i,j \leq n}$ all the upper bounds on the values of clocks, that is, for each $0 \leq i \leq n$, $\mathbf{d}'_{i,0} = (\infty,<)$. Second, the upper bounds of the constraints on the differences between clocks are removed, which is done by replacing the entries in the diagonal clock constraints of $\mathcal{D}'$ ($\mathbf{d}'_{i,j}$ and with $i \neq j$ and $i, j \geq 1$) by $(\infty,<)$, when the entries $\mathbf{e}_{i,j} = (\infty,<)$ with $i \neq j$ and $i, j \geq 1$. The successor algorithm works as follows: it repeatedly removes the upper bounds of all individual clocks, which is done by replacing all elements in the first column of $\mathcal{D}'$ by $(\infty,<)$ and replacing the diagonal elements of $\mathcal{D}'$ ($\mathbf{d}'_{i,j}$ and with $i \neq j$ and $i, j \geq 1$) by $(\infty,<)$ when the entry $\mathbf{e}_{i,j} = (\infty,<)$ with $i \neq j$ and $i, j \geq 1$.

Time Predecessor: A time predecessor operation can be computed using a canonical DBM $\mathcal{D} = \mathcal{D} = (\mathbf{d}_{i,j})_{0 \leq i,j \leq n}$ and a canonical DBMC $\mathcal{E} = (\mathbf{e}_{i,j})_{0 \leq i,j \leq n}$

where the computation of the time predecessor operation of a DBM $\mathcal{D}'$ where $\mathcal{D}' = (\mathbf{d}'_{i,j})_{0 \leq i,j < n}$, consists first in removing from $\mathcal{D} = (\mathbf{d}_{i,j})_{0 \leq i,j \leq n}$ all the lower bounds on the values of clocks, that is, for each $1 \leq i \leq n$, $\mathbf{d}'_{0,i} = (0, \leq)$. Second, the lower bounds of the constraints on the differences between clocks are removed, which is done by replacing the entries in the diagonal clock constraints of $\mathcal{D}'$ ($\mathbf{d}'_{i,j}$ and with $i \neq j$ and $i, j \geq 1$) by $(0, <)$, when the entries $\mathbf{e}_{i,j} = (0, <)$ with $i \neq j$ and $i, j \geq 1$. The predecessor algorithm works as follows: it repeatedly removes the lower bounds of all individual clocks, which is done by replacing all elements in the first column of $\mathcal{D}'$ by $(0, <)$ and replacing the diagonal elements $\mathbf{d}'_{i,j}$ and with $i \neq j$ and $i, j \geq 1$ by $(0, <)$ when the entry $\mathbf{e}_{i,j} = (0, <)$ with $i \neq j$ and $i, j \geq 1$.

Reachability Algorithm: The Algorithm 1 constructs a finite symbolic zone graph ($\mathsf{ZG}_{Extra^+_{LU}}(\mathcal{A})$) for a given idTA $\mathcal{A}$ using a depth-first search approach. Algorithm 1 starts with the pair $q_0 = (s_0, Extra^+_{LU}(\mathcal{Z}_0))$ where s_0 is the initial location of the automaton $\mathcal{A}$, $\mathcal{Z}_0 \leftarrow [\![\bigwedge_{x \in X} x = 0]\!]$ represents the initial zone, where all clocks are set to 0 and $Extra^+_{LU}$ [6,8] (line 5) is the extrapolation abstraction technique. D and Q represents the waiting set of pairs and set of visited pairs Q such that $\mathsf{D} \subseteq \mathsf{Q}$ and a set of transitions T_{ZG} in line 6. The algorithm consists of a loop that iterates over D in line 7. At each iteration, the algorithm takes a pair $\mathcal{Z}_1$ from D and removes it from D in line 8. The algorithm enters an inner loop (lines 9–18) and for each discrete transition $e = (s, a, \phi, Y, s')$ with $\mathcal{Z} \wedge \phi \neq \emptyset$ the algorithm computes the successors of s and associates each successor with the zones $(s', Extra^+_{LU}(\mathsf{post}(\mathcal{Z}, e))) = \mathcal{Z}_2$ (lines 11–12). This result is a set of new pairs $(s, \mathcal{Z}) \in S \times \Phi^+(X)$. The transitions e with successors are stored in the set of labels E_{ZG} in line 12. In line 13, it is checked if there exists an already visited pair $(s', \mathcal{Z}_3) \in \mathsf{Q}$ such that $\mathcal{Z}_2) \subseteq \mathcal{Z}_3$. If true, the discrete transition between $(s, \mathcal{Z}_1) \xrightarrow{e}_{\mathsf{ZG}} (s', \mathcal{Z}_3)$ is stored in the set of transitions T_{ZG} (line 14). Otherwise, the discrete transition between $(s, \mathcal{Z}_1) \xrightarrow{e}_{\mathsf{ZG}} (s', \mathcal{Z}_2)$ is stored in the set of transitions T_{ZG} and the successor pair $(s', \mathcal{Z}_2)$ is stored in Q and D (lines 16–18). During the search, the algorithm also computes the delay transition by the conjunction between the time successors of the current construction zone $\mathcal{Z}_1$ $(s, Extra^+_{LU}(\mathcal{Z}_1) \uparrow)$, the invariant constraint and rate constraint of the current location s (i.e., $Extra^+_{LU}(\mathcal{Z}_1 \uparrow_{R(s)} \wedge I(s))$) in line 19. In line 20, it is checked if there exists an already visited pair $(s, \mathcal{Z}_3) \in \mathsf{Q}$ such that $\mathcal{Z}_2 \subseteq \mathcal{Z}_3$. If true, the delay transition between $(s, \mathcal{Z}_1) \xrightarrow{e}_{\mathsf{ZG}} (s, \mathcal{Z}_3)$ is stored in the set of transitions T_{ZG} (line 21). Otherwise, the delay transition between $(s, \mathcal{Z}_1) \xrightarrow{e}_{\mathsf{ZG}} (s, \mathcal{Z}_2)$ is stored in the set of transitions T_{ZG} and the successor pair $(s, \mathcal{Z}_2)$ is stored in Q and D (lines 23-26). Finally, in line 26, the algorithm returns a zone graph.

Proposition 2 (Soundness). *Let $\mathcal{A}$ be an idTA, and let $ZG(\mathcal{A})$ be the zone graph constructed by Algorithm 1. Then for every transition $(s, \mathcal{Z}_1) \xrightarrow{e}_{\mathsf{ZG}} (s', \mathcal{Z}_2)$ in the graph, and every clock valuation $\nu \in \mathcal{Z}_1$, there exists an execution in the concrete semantics of $\mathcal{A}$ starting from (s, ν) that leads to some (s', ν') with $\nu' \in \mathcal{Z}_2$.*

Algorithm 1. Reachable Zone Graph with Subsumption.
Input: An idTA $\mathcal{A}=(S, s_0, \Sigma, X, \rightarrow_{idTA}, I, R, F)$
Output: A reachable zone graph $ZG(\mathcal{A}) = (Q, q_0, (\Sigma \cup \{\epsilon\}), T_{ZG})$

1:   $// \ s \in S$ $\triangleright$ is a location of $\mathcal{A}$, $\mathcal{Z}_{1 \leq i \leq 3}$ are DBM
2:   $// \ T_{ZG}$ $\triangleright$ is a set of transitions (i.e. $\rightarrow_{ZG} = T_{ZG}$)
3:   $//$D and Q $\triangleright$ are sets of pairs in $S \times \Phi^+(X)$
4:   **function** ZG BuildZoneGraph(idTA $\mathcal{A}$)
5:      $q_0 = (s_0, Extra^+_{LU}(\mathcal{Z}_0))$ $\triangleright$ s.t for all $x \in X$ and $\nu \in \mathcal{Z}_0$, $\nu(x) = 0$
6:      Q, D $= \{q_0\}$, $T_{ZG} = \emptyset$
7:      **while** D $!= \emptyset$ **do**
8:          Choose and Remove $(s, \mathcal{Z}_1)$ from D
9:          **for all** transition $e = (s, a, \phi, Y, s')$ s.t $\mathcal{Z}_1 \wedge \phi \neq \emptyset$ **do**
10:             $//\mathcal{Z}_2$ is the successor
11:             $\mathcal{Z}_2 = Extra^+_{LU}(\mathsf{post}(\mathcal{Z}_1, e))$
12:             $E_{ZG} = E_{ZG} \cup \{e\}$
13:             **if** $\exists (s', \mathcal{Z}_3) \in Q$ s.t $\mathcal{Z}_2 \subseteq \mathcal{Z}_3$ **then**
14:                $T_{ZG} = T_{ZG} \cup \{(s, \mathcal{Z}_1) \xrightarrow{e}_{ZG} (s', \mathcal{Z}_3)\}$
15:             **else**
16:                $T_{ZG} = T_{ZG} \cup \{(s, \mathcal{Z}_1) \xrightarrow{e}_{ZG} (s', \mathcal{Z}_2)\}$
17:                Q $= Q \cup \{(s', \mathcal{Z}_2)\}$
18:                D $= D \cup \{(s', \mathcal{Z}_2)\}$
19:             $\mathcal{Z}_2 = Extra^+_{LU}((\mathcal{Z}_1 \uparrow_{R(s)} \wedge I(s)))$
20:             **if** $\exists (s, \mathcal{Z}_3) \in Q$ s.t $\mathcal{Z}_2 \subseteq \mathcal{Z}_3$ **then**
21:                $T_{ZG} = T_{ZG} \cup \{(s, \mathcal{Z}_1) \xrightarrow{\epsilon}_{ZG} (s, \mathcal{Z}_3)\}$
22:             **else**
23:                $T_{ZG} = T_{ZG} \cup \{(s, \mathcal{Z}_1) \xrightarrow{\epsilon}_{ZG} (s', \mathcal{Z}_2)\}$
24:                Q $= Q \cup \{(s, \mathcal{Z}_2)\}$
25:                D $= D \cup \{(s, \mathcal{Z}_2)\}$
26:      **return** $ZG(Q, q_0, (\Sigma \cup \{\epsilon\}), T_{ZG})$

Proposition 3 (Completeness). *Let $\mathcal{A}$ be an idTA, and let (s', ν') be a state reachable in the concrete semantics of $\mathcal{A}$ from the initial state (s_0, ν_0). Then there exists a path in the zone graph $ZG(\mathcal{A})$ from $(s_0, \mathcal{Z}_0)$ to some $(s', \mathcal{Z}')$ such that $\nu' \in \mathcal{Z}'$.*

Proposition 4 (Termination). *Let $\mathcal{A}$ be a finite idTA with clocks X. For each $x \in X$, let the maximal constant be $M(x) := \max\{c \in \mathbb{N} \mid$ a constraint of the form $x - x_0 \bowtie c$ or $x_0 - x \bowtie c$ occurs in a guard or invariant of $\mathcal{A}\}$, where x_0 is the reference clock $(x_0 = 0)$ and $\bowtie \in \{<, \leq\}$. Then Algorithm 1 terminates and computes a finite zone graph $ZG(\mathcal{A})$.*

Proposition 5 (Complexity). *Let $\mathcal{A}$ be an idTA. Then the reachability problem for $\mathcal{A}$ is PSPACE-complete.*

5   Timed Modal Logic with Clock Derivatives

In this section, we introduce DL_ν, an extension of L_ν [19] that incorporates clock derivatives. We present its syntax and semantics over executions of MLTS, and establish that the model checking problem for DL_ν is EXPTIME-complete.

Definition 12. *Let Σ be a finite alphabet, X be a finite set of clocks and Id the set of proposition identifiers. The formulas of DL_ν over Σ, X, and Id are defined by the grammar:*

$$\varphi ::= true \mid false \mid \varphi \wedge \varphi \mid \phi \mid \psi \mid [a]\varphi \mid \langle a \rangle \varphi \mid x \underline{\ in\ } \varphi \mid \exists \varphi \mid \forall \varphi \mid x - y \sim k \mid D$$

where $a \in \Sigma$, $x, y \in X$, $k = d - c$ and c, d are non-negative integers and , $\sim \in \{=, >, \geq, <, \leq\}$, $D \in \mathsf{Id}$, $\phi \in \Phi(X)$ a clock constraint, $\psi \in \Psi(X)$ a rate constraint, $[a]\varphi$, $\langle a \rangle \varphi$ are two modalities of the logic, and $\exists \varphi$ and $\forall \varphi$ are the two timed modalities.

The identifiers Id are specified within a declaration environment E, which assigns a DL_ν formula to each identifier, enabling the definition of properties with greatest fixpoints. A declaration is denoted as $D \overset{\text{def}}{=} \varphi$, meaning that $E(D) = \varphi$. We now formally define the semantics of DL_ν formulas. Let $\mathcal{A}$ be an idTA over $\tau \in \mathsf{Rates}$, with its semantics given by $\mathsf{MLTS}(\mathcal{A}, \tau) = (Q, q_0, \Sigma, Q_F, \to_{mlts})$. We interpret DL_ν formulas over extended states, where an extended state is a pair (q, μ), with $q \in Q$ representing an MLTS state and μ a valuation for the formula clocks in X. An extended state satisfies an identifier D if it belongs to the maximal fixpoint of the equation $D = E(D)$. The formal semantics of DL_ν formulas, interpreted over $\mathsf{MLTS}(\mathcal{A}, \tau)$, is defined by the satisfaction relation $\models$, which corresponds to the largest relation satisfying the implications in Definition 13.

Definition 13. *Let Σ be a finite alphabet, X be a finite set of clocks. The semantics of formulas in DL_ν is implicitly given with respect to a given MLTS inductively as follows:*

$$
\begin{aligned}
(q, \mu) &\models & true &\Leftrightarrow true \\
(q, \mu) &\models & false &\Leftrightarrow false \\
(q, \mu) &\models & \varphi_1 \wedge \varphi_2 &\Leftrightarrow (q, \mu) \models \varphi_1 \text{ and } (q, \mu) \models \varphi_2 \\
(q, \mu) &\models & \phi &\Leftrightarrow \mu \models \phi \text{ for } \phi \in \Phi(X) \\
(q, \mu) &\models & \psi &\Leftrightarrow \mu \models \psi \text{ for } \psi \in \Psi(X) \\
(q, \mu) &\models & [a]\varphi &\Leftrightarrow \forall q \xrightarrow{a}_{mlts} q', (q', \mu) \models \varphi \\
(q, \mu) &\models & \langle a \rangle \varphi &\Leftrightarrow \exists q \xrightarrow{a}_{mlts} q', (q', \mu) \models \varphi \\
(q, \mu) &\models & x \underline{\ in\ } \varphi &\Leftrightarrow (q, \mu[x \to 0]) \models \varphi \\
(q, \mu) &\models & \exists \varphi &\Leftrightarrow \exists d \in \mathbb{R}^X_{\geq 0}, \exists q' \in Q, \text{ such that } q \xrightarrow{d}_{mlts} q', \\
& & & \quad (q, \mu + d) \models \varphi \\
(q, \mu) &\models & \forall \varphi &\Leftrightarrow \forall d \in \mathbb{R}^X_{\geq 0}, \forall q' \in Q, \text{ such that } q \xrightarrow{d}_{mlts} q', \\
& & & \quad (q, \mu + d) \models \varphi \\
(q, \mu) &\models x + c \sim y + d &&\Leftrightarrow \mu(x) + c \sim \mu(y) + d \\
(q, \mu) &\models & D &\quad \text{the maximal fixpoint in } E(D)
\end{aligned}
$$

Two formulas are equivalent (i.e., $\equiv$) iff they are satisfied by the same set of extended states in every MLTS.

Definition 14. *A state q in a MLTS satisfies a formula φ, iff $(q, \mu_0) \models \varphi$ where μ_0 is the clock valuation that maps each formula clock to zero.*

Let $\mathcal{A}$ be an idTA and $\varphi \in \mathsf{DL}_\nu$, then $\mathcal{A} \models \varphi$ iff $\forall \tau \in \mathsf{Rates}$, $\mathsf{MLTS}(\mathcal{A}, \tau) \models \varphi$.

Theorem 1. *Let X be a set of clocks. Let $\mathcal{M}$ be a MLTS and q_1, q_2 be equivalent states in Q. Let μ be a clock valuation for the formula clocks in X, then the extended states (q_1, μ) and (q_2, μ) satisfy exactly the same formula in DL_ν.*

Example 4. Consider the idTA $\mathcal{M}$ described in Fig. 1. Let X be a set of clocks and $\dot{X}$ be a set of clock derivatives, where $x, y \in X$ and $\dot{x}$, $\dot{y} \in \dot{X}$. The initial state (q_0, μ_0) (i.e., $q_0 = (S_0, \nu_0)$) satisfies the following DL_ν formula φ:

$$\varphi = y \ \underline{in} \ \exists((\ 2 \geq y \geq 0 \ \wedge \ \dot{x} > \dot{y} \ \wedge \langle a \rangle \ S_1) \wedge \ (x \geq 1 \ \wedge \ \dot{y} = 1) \ \wedge \ \langle a \rangle \ S_1)$$

Intuitively, this formula means that the action a can be performed after a delay between 0 and 2, and satisfying the rate constraint $\dot{x} > \dot{y}$, for instance, 1 and the action a can be performed after a delay 1 time units, and satisfying the rate constraint $\dot{y} = 1$.

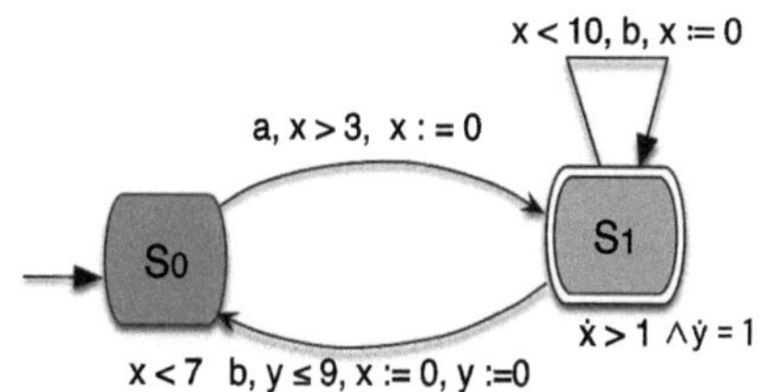

Fig. 5. A TA with clock derivatives (idTA) $\mathcal{M}$.

Example 5. Consider the idTA $\mathcal{M}$ described in Fig. 5. The state (q_1, μ_1) (i.e., $q_1 = (S_1, \nu_1)$) satisfies the following DL_ν formula φ:

$$D_{S_1} = x \ \underline{in} \ \exists(x \leq 10 \ \wedge \ \dot{x} > 1 \ \wedge \ \dot{y} = 1 \ \wedge \ \langle b \rangle \ D_{S_1}) \wedge [b] \ (x \leq 10 \ \wedge \dot{x} >$$
$$1 \wedge \dot{y} = 1 \ \wedge \ x \ \underline{in} \ D_{S_1}) \wedge \forall \ D_{S_1} \ \vee \ y \ \underline{in} \ \exists(y \leq 9 \ \wedge \ \langle b \rangle \ S_0) \ \wedge \ x \ \underline{in} \ (\langle b \rangle \ S_0)$$

Intuitively, this formula means that the action b can be performed before a delay 10 time units (self-loop) or the action b can be performed before a delay 9 time units.

Now, we consider the model checking problem of DL_ν sentences on idTA models, that is given a DL_ν formula φ and an idTA $\mathcal{A}$, in deciding whether $\mathcal{A} \models \varphi$ holds.

Theorem 2. *The model checking problem of DL_ν on idTA is EXPTIME-complete.*

6 Expressiveness of IdTA

Here, we compare the expressiveness of idTA with existing formalisms such as TA, DTA, and subclasses of Hybrid Automata (HA) [26] including Initialized Rectangular Hybrid Automata (IRHA) [13] and Linear Hybrid Automata (LHA) [3]. We define idTA as a strict extension of these models by proving language containment and separation results.

Theorem 3 (TA vs idTA and idTA vs TA).

1. *Let $\mathcal{A} = (S, s_0, \Sigma, X, \to_{TA}, I, F)$ be a TA, where all clocks evolve synchronously at a uniform rate. There exists an idTA $\mathcal{A}' = (S, s_0, \Sigma, X, \to_{idTA}, I, R, F)$ such that $\mathcal{L}(\mathcal{A}) = \mathcal{L}(\mathcal{A}')$, where $R = \{\dot{x} = 1 \mid x \in X\}$.*
2. *There exists an idTA $\mathcal{A} = (S, s_0, \Sigma, X, \to_{idTA}, I, R, F)$ such that no TA $\mathcal{B}$ exists with $\mathcal{L}(\mathcal{B}) = \mathcal{L}(\mathcal{A})$. Specifically, let $\mathcal{A}$ have two locations s_1 and s_2 with rate constraints $\dot{x} = 1$ in s_1 and $\dot{x} > 1$ in s_2. No TA with globally synchronous clocks can simulate this behavior.*

Example 6. In an asynchronous sensor network, each sensor runs on an independent local clock that may drift due to factors like battery level or signal strength. idTA captures this behavior by allowing clocks to evolve at variable rates (e.g., $\dot{x}_i > 1$) and by supporting constraints such as $\dot{x}_i \geq \dot{x}_j$ to express partial synchronization. In contrast, standard TA assumes all clocks advance uniformly, making it unsuitable for modeling such timing variability.

Theorem 4 (DTA vs idTA and idTA vs DTA).

1. *Let $Proc$ be a set of processes. Let $\mathcal{D} = (S, s_0, \Sigma, \{X_i\}_{i \in Proc}, \to_{DTA}, I, F)$ be a DTA where each process i has independent clocks X_i. There exists an idTA $\mathcal{D} = (S, s_0, \Sigma, X, \to_{idTA}, I, R, F)$ such that $\mathcal{L}(\mathcal{D}) = \mathcal{L}(\mathcal{D}')$, where R enforces the same independent evolution as in $\mathcal{D}$.*
2. *There exists an idTA $\mathcal{A} = (S, s_0, \Sigma, X, \to_{idTA}, I, R, F)$ such that no DTA $\mathcal{B}$ exists with $\mathcal{L}(\mathcal{B}) = \mathcal{L}(\mathcal{A})$. Specifically, let $\mathcal{A}$ have rate constraints $\dot{x}_1 > \dot{x}_2$. Since DTA assumes independent clocks, no DTA can enforce this dependency.*

Theorem 5 (*idTA vs HA*). *Let $\mathcal{H} = (S, s_0, \Sigma, X, \to_{HA}, I, F, F_X)$ be a HA where F_X defines arbitrary differential equations $\dot{x} = f(x, u)$. Then, there exists an HA $\mathcal{H}$ such that no idTA $\mathcal{A}$ can satisfy $\mathcal{L}(\mathcal{H}) = \mathcal{L}(\mathcal{A})$, since idTA is restricted to constraints of the form $a \leq \dot{x} \leq b$ with constant bounds.*

Proof. Since idTA only allows rate constraints of the form $\dot{x} \sim 1$ or $\dot{x} \sim \dot{y}$ with $\sim \in \{<, >, \leq, \geq, =\}$, it cannot model systems where clock derivatives depend on continuous variables. Consider a hybrid automaton where $\dot{x} = x^2$ (quadratic growth). Any equivalent idTA must encode this with a finite set of constant derivatives, which cannot fully capture the smooth, non-linear evolution of HA. This proves that idTA is strictly weaker than HA.

Theorem 6 (idTA vs IRHA). *Let $\mathcal{A}$ be an idTA, and $\mathcal{I}$ an IRHA. Then, (1) for every idTA $\mathcal{A}$, there exists an IRHA $\mathcal{I}$ such that $\mathcal{L}(\mathcal{A}) = \mathcal{L}(\mathcal{I})$. (2) There exists an IRHA $\mathcal{I}'$ such that for every idTA $\mathcal{A}$, $\mathcal{L}(\mathcal{A}) \neq \mathcal{L}(\mathcal{I}')$.*

Theorem 7 (idTA vs LHA). *Let $\mathcal{A}$ be an idTA and $\mathcal{H}$ an LHA. Then $\mathcal{L}(\mathcal{A}) \subset \mathcal{L}(\mathcal{H})$.*

Theorem 8 (IRHA vs LHA). *Let $\mathcal{I}$ be an IRHA and $\mathcal{L}$ a LHA. Then, (1) for every IRHA $\mathcal{I}$, there exists an LHA $\mathcal{L}$ such that $\mathcal{L}(\mathcal{I}) = \mathcal{L}(\mathcal{L})$. (2) there exists a LHA $\mathcal{L}'$ such that for every IRHA $\mathcal{I}$, $\mathcal{L}(\mathcal{I}) \neq \mathcal{L}(\mathcal{L}')$.*

Theorem 9. *The expressiveness hierarchy among the models satisfies the following strict inclusions: $\mathcal{L}(TA) \subset \mathcal{L}(idTA) \subset \mathcal{L}(IRHA) \subset \mathcal{L}(LHA)$.*

7   Model Checker MIMETIC

We have developed a model checking prototype called MIMETIC[1], which implements the symbolic zone-based reachability algorithm presented in this paper. The tool supports the verification of properties expressed in our extended temporal logic, DL_ν. Its architecture is modular and extensible, integrating components for parsing, symbolic analysis, and interactive property evaluation. As illustrated in Fig. 6, MIMETIC comprises several core components. The tool reads system models described in a XML-based format inspired by UPPAAL, but extended to support rate constraints over clock derivatives. Parsing is handled by an ANTLR-based engine [24], which processes both the system description and the corresponding DL_ν property to be verified. The user interface allows the user to load an XML model file, write or paste a DL_ν formula into a dedicated text box, and launch the verification process. Once complete, the tool displays the result in a human-readable format, indicating whether the property holds along with reachability statistics. MIMETIC is implemented in Java 11 and supports both command-line and graphical execution. The graphical interface provides capabilities for loading models, editing temporal formulas, visualizing the generated

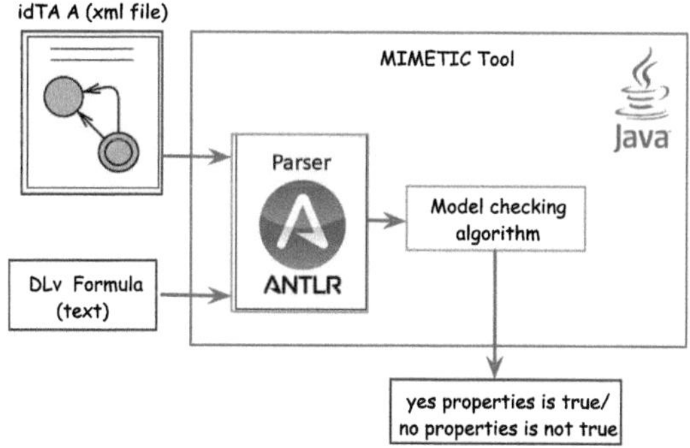

Fig. 6. MIMETIC Tool.

---

[1] MIMETIC source code and jar are available at: https://github.com/jortizve/MIMETIC/.

transition system, and viewing execution logs. For users working with UPPAAL, models can be easily adapted by introducing derivative constraints directly in the XML used by MIMETIC. As an illustrative example, the user might enter the following formula:

```
1   $$y in EE(y <= 3 &&  y >= 1 &\& <a>tt) &&  (x' >= 1 &&  <a>tt)$$
```

This formula specifies a drift-aware temporal condition, combining reachability with rate-based constraints.

8 Related Work

Several formalisms focus on handling distributed timing behaviors in DRTS. Asynchronous Distributed Timed Automata (ADTA), introduced by Krishnan [18], model independently evolving clocks for each component, reflecting the decentralized nature of distributed systems. Akshay et al. [1] examined the untimed language of DTA, while extensions such as Distributed Event Clock Automata (DECA) [23] introduced independent clocks in event-driven systems. Timed Input/Output Automata (TIOA) [16] further enhanced the modeling of distributed algorithms, particularly for applications like clock synchronization [15]. Robust extensions address uncertainties in real-time systems, such as clock drift. Puri [25] developed robust timed automata where clocks drift within bounded intervals, accommodating imprecise timing in physical systems. These extensions improve the reliability of models when precise synchronization is unattainable, making them suitable for fault-tolerant designs. Hybrid Automata (HA) [12] extend TA by incorporating both discrete transitions and continuous dynamics. Hybrid Input/Output Automata (HIOA) [20] model systems with complex behaviors, including trajectory-based state evolution. Similarly, Stopwatch Timed Automata (SWA) [3] allow clocks to be paused and resumed, enhancing expressiveness. Two important subclasses of HA are Initialized Rectangular Hybrid Automata (IRHA) [13] and Linear Hybrid Automata (LHA) [3]. IRHA restricts the dynamics of continuous variables to piecewise-constant bounds and requires variables to be reset upon entering new modes. LHA, on the other hand, allows linear dynamics and constraints over both discrete and continuous variables, with some restrictions to preserve decidability. We find that idTA subsumes many behaviors that can be expressed by IRHA, especially in scenarios where clock derivatives are constant or reset upon transitions. However, unlike IRHA, idTA do not require initialization of all variables upon mode changes, allowing for more flexible modeling of persistent timing constraints. Compared to LHA, idTA provide a subset of linear behaviors specifically, those that can be encoded by clock derivatives and guarded transitions, but without the full generality of arbitrary differential equations or affine constraints. However, several hybrid modal extensions face significant undecidability challenges, with reachability and simulation problems often being undecidable [9,15]. Despite their advancements, many existing tools, such as UPPAAL [29],

TEMPO [11], and HyTech [3], face limitations. Tools like SWA and HIOA suffer from undecidability issues, while others, such as UPPAAL, primarily support forward reachability analysis, lacking adaptability for complex distributed interactions.

9 Conclusion

In this paper, we have introduced idTA, an extension of both DTA and TA, featuring new semantics that incorporate independent clocks and rate constraints. In addition, we extended the logic $L\nu$ to support these rate constraints, resulting in the more expressive logic DL_ν. We demonstrated that the model checking problem for this logic is EXPTIME-complete, preserving decidability while increasing expressiveness. We also provided several examples illustrating how distributed real-time behaviors can be modeled using idTA and DL_ν, and we described in detail the implementation and functionalities of our model-checking algorithms. There are several promising directions for future work. One avenue is to further examine the connections between idTA and subclasses of Hybrid Automata (HA) [26], such as Linear HA or Initialized Rectangular HA. Another direction is the application of idTA and DL_ν to model and verify realistic industrial systems. We also aim to enhance our verification tool, MIMETIC, by incorporating least and greatest fixpoint operators for richer temporal reasoning.

Acknowledgments. This work has been partially supported by the French National Research Agency under the France 2030 label (Superviz ANR-22- PECY-0008). The views reflected herein do not necessarily reflect the opinion of the French government.

References

1. Akshay, S., Bollig, B., Gastin, P., Mukund, M., Narayan Kumar, K.: Distributed timed automata with independently evolving clocks. In: van Breugel, F., Chechik, M. (eds.) CONCUR 2008. LNCS, vol. 5201, pp. 82–97. Springer, Heidelberg (2008). https://doi.org/10.1007/978-3-540-85361-9_10
2. Alur, R., La Torre, S., Pappas, G.J.: Optimal paths in weighted timed automata. In: Computation and Control, pp. 49–62 (2001)
3. Alur, R., et al.: The algorithmic analysis of hybrid systems. Theor. Comput, Sci (1995)
4. Alur, R., Dill, D.L.: A theory of timed automata. Theor. Comput. Sci. **126**(2), 183–235 (1994)
5. Behrmann, G., Bouyer, P., Fleury, E., Larsen, K.G.: Static guard analysis in timed automata verification. In: Garavel, H., Hatcliff, J. (eds.) TACAS 2003. LNCS, vol. 2619, pp. 254–270. Springer, Heidelberg (2003). https://doi.org/10.1007/3-540-36577-X_18
6. Behrmann, G., Bouyer, P., Larsen, K.G., Pelánek, R.: Lower and upper bounds in zone-based abstractions of timed automata. Int. J. Softw. Tools Technol. Transfer **8**(3), 204–215 (2006)

7. Bengtsson, J., Yi, W.: Timed automata: semantics, algorithms and tools. In: Lecture Notes on Concurrency and Petri Nets (2004)

8. Bouyer, P.: Forward analysis of updatable timed automata. Formal Methods Syst. Des. **24**(3), 281–320 (2004)

9. Cassez, F., Larsen, K.: The impressive power of stopwatches. In: Palamidessi, C. (ed.) CONCUR 2000. LNCS, vol. 1877, pp. 138–152. Springer, Heidelberg (2000). https://doi.org/10.1007/3-540-44618-4_12

10. Dill, D.L.: Timing assumptions and verification of finite-state concurrent systems. In: Sifakis, J. (ed.) CAV 1989. LNCS, vol. 407, pp. 197–212. Springer, Heidelberg (1990). https://doi.org/10.1007/3-540-52148-8_17

11. Georgiou, C., Musial, P.M., Ploutarchou, C.: Tempo-toolkit: tempo to Java translation module. In: 2013 IEEE 12th International Symposium on Network Computing and Applications, Cambridge, MA, USA, 22-24 August 2013. IEEE Computer Society (2013)

12. Henzinger, T.: The theory of hybrid automata. In: Proceedings 11th Annual IEEE Symposium on Logic in Computer Science, pp. 278–292 (1996). https://doi.org/10.1109/LICS.1996.561342

13. Henzinger, T.A., Kopke, P.W., Puri, A., Varaiya, P.: What's decidable about hybrid automata? In: Proceedings of the Twenty-Seventh Annual ACM Symposium on Theory of Computing, pp. 373–382. STOC 1995, Association for Computing Machinery, New York, NY, USA (1995). https://doi.org/10.1145/225058.225162

14. Henzinger, T.A., Nicollin, X., Sifakis, J., Yovine, S.: Symbolic model checking for real-time systems. Inf. Comput. **111**(2), 193–244 (1994)

15. Kaynar, D., Lynch, N., Segala, R., Vaandrager, F.: The Theory of Timed I/O Automata. Morgan & Claypool Publishers, 2nd edn. (2010)

16. Kaynar, D.K., Lynch, N., Segala, R., Vaandrager, F.: Timed i/o automata: a mathematical framework for modeling and analyzing real-time systems. In: Proceedings of the 24th IEEE International Real-Time Systems Symposium, pp. 166–. RTSS 2003, IEEE Computer Society, Washington, DC, USA (2003)

17. Kopetz, H.: Real-Time Systems: Design Principles for Distributed Embedded Applications, 3rd edn. Springer, Cham (2022). https://doi.org/10.1007/978-3-031-11992-7. published on September 24, 2022

18. Krishnan, P.: Distributed Timed Automata. In: Workshop on Distr, Systems (1999)

19. Laroussinie, F., Larsen, K.G., Weise, C.: From timed automata to logic — and back. In: Wiedermann, J., Hájek, P. (eds.) MFCS 1995. LNCS, vol. 969, pp. 529–539. Springer, Heidelberg (1995). https://doi.org/10.1007/3-540-60246-1_158

20. Lynch, N., Segala, R., Vaandrager, F.: Hybrid i/o automata. Inf. Comput. **185**, 105–157 (2003)

21. Mall, R., Patnaik, L.: Specification and verification of timing properties of distributed real-time systems (1990)

22. Ortiz, J.J., Amrani, M., Schobbens, P.: Multi-timed bisimulation for distributed timed automata. In: NASA Formal Methods - 9th International Symposium, NFM 2017, Moffett Field, CA, USA, 16-18 May 2017, Proceedings (2017)

23. Ortiz, J., Legay, A., Schobbens, P.-Y.: Distributed event clock automata. In: Bouchou-Markhoff, B., Caron, P., Champarnaud, J.-M., Maurel, D. (eds.) CIAA 2011. LNCS, vol. 6807, pp. 250–263. Springer, Heidelberg (2011). https://doi.org/10.1007/978-3-642-22256-6_23

24. Parr, T.: The Definitive ANTLR 4 Reference, 2nd edn. Pragmatic Bookshelf, Raleigh, NC (2013)

25. Puri, A.: Dynamical properties of timed automata. Discr. Event Dyn. Syst. **10**(1), 87–113 (2000)
26. Raskin, J.: An introduction to hybrid automata. In: Handbook of Networked and Embedded Control Systems, pp. 491–518. Birkhäuser (2005)
27. Ruh, J., Steiner, W., Fohler, G.: Clock synchronization in virtualized distributed real-time systems using IEEE 802.1as and ACRN (2021). https://arxiv.org/abs/2105.03374
28. Tripakis, S., Yovine, S.: Analysis of timed systems using time-abstracting bisimulations. Formal Methods Syst. Des. **18**(1), 25–68 (2001)
29. The UPPAAL tool. http://www.uppaal.com/
30. Wang, F., Mok, A.K., Emerson, E.A.: Distributed real-time system specification and verification in aptl. ACM Trans. Softw. Eng. Methodol. **2**, 346–378 (1993)

Model Checking Buffered Durable Linearizability in CSP

Chelsea Edmonds[1], John Derrick[1], Brijesh Dongol[2(✉)], Gerhard Schellhorn[3], and Heike Wehrheim[4]

[1] University of Sheffield, Sheffield, UK
[2] University of Surrey, Guildford, UK
b.dongol@surrey.ac.uk
[3] University of Augsburg, Augsburg, Germany
[4] Carl von Ossietzky Universität Oldenburg, Oldenburg, Germany

Abstract. Non-volatile memory (NVM) is a high-performance memory technology that supports persistency (i.e., durability) of data in case of a system crash (e.g., power failure). For implementations of concurrent objects (e.g., concurrent data structures such as stacks and hash maps), NVM poses a correctness problem: can the implementation recover to a consistent state after a crash and continue execution? In this paper, we study a notion of correctness known as *buffered durable linearizability* for implementations of periodically persistent concurrent objects, and develop a refinement-based proof method for buffered durable linearizability. To support our proofs, we develop a generic abstract specification of a buffered durable linearizable object that is generated from the object's sequential specification. Our main case study is a concurrent hash map known as Dalí, which we show satisfies buffered durable linearizability. Specifically, we use FDR, a model checker based on CSP, that offers a fully automatic method for checking trace refinement.

1 Introduction

Byte-addressable *non-volatile (aka persistent) memory (NVM)* [9,28] provides resilience to system-wide crashes. Unlike DRAM, the contents of NVM survive failures (e.g., a power outage). However, how should one design concurrent objects under NVM? Correctness of persistent concurrent objects is supported by a range of new correctness conditions (see [2] for a survey), which typically combine a notion of *failure atomicity* (to support recoverability) with conditions such as *linearizability* or *strict serializability* (to support concurrency).

These correctness conditions trade-off between the strength of the guarantees and performance: stronger guarantees require more synchronisation in the

Edmonds and Derrick are supported by EPSRC grant EP/X015114/1. Dongol is supported by VeTSS and EPSRC grants EP/X037142/1, EP/X015149/1, EP/V038915/1, and EP/R025134/2. Schellhorn is supported by DFG project RE 828/26-1. Wehrheim is supported by DFG project 467386514. We also thank Joseph Izraelevitz for helpful comments on an earlier draft of this paper.

F. Damiani and M. Farrell (Eds.): iFM 2025, LNCS 16194, pp. 120–139, 2026.
https://doi.org/10.1007/978-3-032-10794-7_7

corresponding object's implementation, which decreases throughput. For persistent concurrent objects, one of the main correctness conditions is *durable linearizability* [19], which simply requires every history of method invocations and responses as well as (full-system) crashes to be linearizable [18] when the crashes are removed. This ensures that any operation that responds before a crash occurs survives the crash, while any operation that has not responded before the crash either survives in its entirety or not at all. However, this also means that every operation must be fully persisted before it returns, which induces expensive "flush" instructions that must be executed before the operation responds, reducing the performance of the concurrent object.

To address this issue, alternative correctness conditions such as *buffered durability* have been introduced [19], where some *completed* operations may be "lost" if a crash occurs. Yet, buffered durability requires preservation of a *consistent cut*, which in turn guarantees that the operations that "survive" a system-level crash form a linearizable history that is consistent with a sequential execution of the data structure's operations. This means that the number of synchronous persistency operations (as needed for durable linearizability) is reduced, resulting in higher performance. There are now several implementations of concurrent objects that exploit this idea [8,24,32], however, there has not been any proof technique to ensure correctness of buffered durable linearizability, which has previously only been defined declaratively.

In this paper, we present an approach to verifying buffered durable linearizability that builds on existing work on verifying durable concurrent data structures [10], transactional memory implementations [3,12,26,30] and transformation libraries [6]. All of these works, however, address proofs over strong correctness conditions that require operations to persist before they return. The approach involves defining an operational abstract specification whose histories are guaranteed to satisfy the required property and a proof of *refinement* of the implementation against this specification. In this paper, we develop, for the first time, a proof technique for *buffered* durable linearizability. Our approach is summarised by the following key contributions:

(1) We present a technique for developing a *canonical buffered durable linearizable abstract object* (see Fig. 1) derived from the underlying sequential object being implemented. The histories of this canonical abstract object are guaranteed to satisfy buffered durable linearizability, which allows us to prove the correctness of an implementation via a standard proof of refinement (see Theorem 1), eschewing complex reasoning about histories.

(2) We encode this abstract specification (instantiated to a hash map) in the CSP process algebra, as required by the FDR4 model checker (cf [12,22, 25]).

(3) We apply the above to our main case study, Dalí, a sophisticated buffered durable linearizable hash map whose buckets are implemented by a linked list [24]. This includes a CSP encoding of Dalí[1] and the underlying NVM

---

[1] Based off the original paper [24], as the full implementation is closed-source.

memory model. Together with **(2)** above, this enables automated trace refinement proofs using FDR4 against several parameters.

(4) Although buffered durable linearizability is, in general, not a local (aka compositional) property, we show that Dalí does in fact guarantee a form of compositionality across different buckets (see Theorem 2). Thus proving correctness of a single bucket of Dalí implies correctness of the entire hash map.

(5) Our model checking process revealed several subtle issues occurring in the original Dalí specification [24], highlighting where care must be taken during implementation to ensure buffered durable linearizability (see Sect. 5.2).

Overview and Supplementary Material. This paper is structured as follows. Sect. 2 provides some background on correctness conditions and Sect. 3 provides our generic abstract object for buffered durable linearizability. Our main case study (Dalí) is given in Sect. 4 and its refinement proof and analysis in 5. The CSP models referred to in Sect. 3, Sect. 4 and Sect. 5 are provided as a publicly available artifact [14].

2   Background

2.1   Sequential Object Specifications

Objects offer operations $op \in Op$ to clients, who invoke operations $\mathsf{inv}(op, u)$ with input $u \in Val$, then receive responses $\mathsf{res}(op, v)^2$ with return values $v \in Val$.

Definition 1. *A sequential object* $\mathbb{S}$ *is a 4-tuple* (Op, S, s_0, ρ) *where* Op *is the alphabet of operations,* S *is a set of states and* $s_0 \in S$ *is the initial state, and* $\rho : S \times Op \times Val \to 2^{S \times Val}$ *is a* transition function *generating a set of next states and output values for a given state, operation and input values.*

We often write $(s, op(u, v), s') \in \rho$ for $(s', v) \in \rho(s, op, u)$ and refer to $op(u, v)$ as an *action*.

Example 1. Dalí implements a concurrent hash map. The corresponding sequential object contains states which are mappings $\mu : K \to V$ from keys K to values V. We assume operations $Op = \{\mathsf{read}, \mathsf{update}\}$ (used to implement typical hash map operations like set and get). Values Val consist of pairs of $K \times V$, single values in V and K as well as some specific "null" value $\bot$. Initially, the map is empty, assigning $\bot$ to all keys K. The transition relation is defined as follows:

$$\rho(\mu, \mathsf{update}, \langle k, v \rangle) = \{(\mu[k \mapsto v], \bot)\} \qquad \rho(\mu, \mathsf{read}, k) = \{(\mu, \mu(k))\}$$

In this, $\mu[k \mapsto v]$ is mapping μ with value of key k set to v.

An execution of a sequential object is a sequence σ of states and actions, where $\sigma = s_0 \alpha_1 s_1 \alpha_2 s_2 \ldots s_n$ such that $(s_{i-1}, \alpha_i, s_i) \in \rho$ for all $1 \le i \le n$, and a *trace* corresponding to σ, denoted $trace(\sigma)$, is the execution σ restricted to actions.

---

^{2} We assume that every operation has exactly one input and one return value.

2.2 Histories

To formalise correctness conditions for concurrent objects (Sect. 2.3), we first define the notion of a *history*, which is a finite sequence of invocation and response events of the form $\mathsf{inv}_\tau(op, u)$ and $\mathsf{res}_\tau(op, v)$, respectively. These events represent calls to and returns from an operation op by a thread $\tau \in Tid$ of a client.

Concatenation of two histories h_1 and h_2 is written as $h_1 \cdot h_2$. For some event e and history h, we write $e \in h$ if e occurs in h. A response event *matches* an invocation event if they belong to the same thread τ and operation op. An invocation is *pending* in a history if it is not followed by a matching response. For a history h we write $h|_\tau$ for the subsequence of h consisting of events of thread τ only. A history is *sequential* if every invocation event except for possibly the last one is directly followed by a matching response, and every response is immediately preceded by its matching invocation. A history h is *well-formed* if $h|_\tau$ is sequential for every thread $\tau \in Tid$. Two histories h_1, h_2 are *equivalent*, $h_1 \equiv h_2$, if $h_1|_\tau = h_2|_\tau$ for all $\tau \in Tid$. A response event e *precedes* (or happens before) an invocation event e' in a history h, $e \prec_h e'$, if e occurs before e' in the sequence h. For example, consider the history of Example 2 below: there, we e.g. have $e \prec_h e'$ for $e = \mathsf{res}_1(\mathsf{update}, \bot)$ and $e' = \mathsf{inv}_3(\mathsf{read}, \text{"foo"})$. The ordering $\prec_h$ is also often referred to as the "real-time" order of operations in h which is to be preserved by linearizability.

A sequential object $\mathbb{S}$ naturally gives rise to (sequential) histories. For each action α of $\mathbb{S}$, the set of invocation/response pairs corresponding to α is given by $invres(\alpha) = \{\langle \mathsf{inv}_\tau(op, u), \mathsf{res}_\tau(op, v)\rangle \mid \alpha = op(u, v) \land \tau \in Tid\}$, which splits the action into a separate invocation and response event and includes an identifier for the thread executing the action. The set of histories of $\mathbb{S}$ is derived from an execution σ of $\mathbb{S}$ as follows ($tr(i)$ being the ith action of tr):

$$\{I_0 R_0 I_1 R_1 \cdots \mid \exists tr.\ tr = trace(\sigma) \land \forall i.\langle I_i, R_i\rangle \in invres(tr(i))\}$$

2.3 Correctness Conditions

Linearizability. Linearizability relates concurrent histories with corresponding legal sequential histories. To accommodate for pending operations that may have linearized, we use *extensions* of histories h which are constructed by appending response events to the end of h for zero or more (but not necessarily all) pending invocations. Then, to remove pending operations that have not linearized, we use $trunc(h)$ to denote the subsequence of h consisting of invocations and their matching responses (the *completed* operations), eliding all pending invocations.

Definition 2. *A well-formed history h is* linearizable *wrt. a sequential object $\mathbb{S}$ if there is an extension h' of h as well as a (sequential) history h_s of $\mathbb{S}$ such that* **(L1)** $trunc(h') \equiv h_s$ *and* **(L2)** $\prec_{h'} \subseteq \prec_{h_s}$.

Example 2. The history

> $\mathsf{inv}_1(\mathbf{update}\ (\text{``foo''}, 42))$ $\mathsf{inv}_2(\mathbf{update}\ (\text{``foo''},11))$ $\mathsf{res}_1(\mathbf{update}, \bot)$ $\mathsf{res}_2(\mathbf{update}, \bot)$
> $\mathsf{inv}_3(\mathbf{read}, \text{``foo''})$ $\mathsf{res}_3(\mathbf{read}, 42)$ $\mathsf{inv}_4(\mathbf{read}, \text{``foo''})$ $\mathsf{res}_4(\mathbf{read}, 11)$

is not a linearizable history of the hash map. The first two operations (**update** of thread 1 and of thread 2) are concurrent, so we could put them in any order to satisfy **L2**. However, the resulting sequential history is not a valid history of the hash map object from Example 1, as the reads of threads 3 and 4 (which are invoked after both updates are completed) return different values for key "foo".

Buffered Durable Linearizability. To extend linearizability to NVM, a number of different proposals have been made. Here, we consider *buffered durable linearizability* [19] which is the correctness condition envisaged in the design of Dalí. For buffered durable linearizability, we look at histories with *crash* events crash which model the situation in which all contents of volatile memory is lost and only persistent memory is kept (e.g., a power loss). For a history h with crash events, we let $ops(h)$ be the history restricted to non-crash events. The crash events partition a history h into *eras* of histories with no crashes. Like Izraelevitz et al. [19], we assume threads to be active in at most one era.

Buffered durable linearizability allows effects of operations within eras to not be persisted, although they have returned. However, whenever we have a persisted operation which is real-time ordered *after* other operations, these operations also need to be persisted. To capture this, we introduce the notion of consistent cut. For a history h, let h' be a subsequence of h such that h' is a well-formed history. We say that h' is a $\prec_h^+$-*consistent cut* if for all events $e_1, e_2 \in h$, if $e_2 \in h'$ and $e_1 \prec_h^+ e_2$, then $e_1 \in h'$ holds.

Definition 3. *A well-formed history* $h = h_1$ crash h_2 crash ... crash h_n *with* $n-1$ *crash events is* buffered durable linearizable *wrt. a sequential object* $\mathbb{S}$ *if there exist* $\prec_h^+$*-consistent cuts* $h'_1, \ldots, h'_{n-1}$ *of* $h_1, \ldots, h_{n-1}$, *respectively, such that for all* i, $1 \le i \le n$, *the history* $h'_1 \ldots h'_{i-1} h_i$ *is linearizable.*

Example 3. We   give   an   example   of a buffered durable linearizable history, h, of a concurrent hash map below.

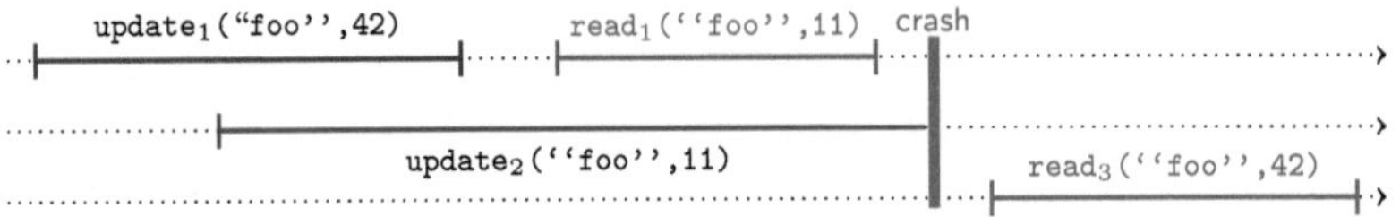

In this, bars depict invocations and responses of operations and the x-axis is time. Thus, the diagram depicts the following history h:

> $\mathsf{inv}_1(\mathbf{update}\ (\text{``foo''}, 42))$ $\mathsf{inv}_2(\mathbf{update}\ (\text{``foo''},11))$ $\mathsf{res}_1(\mathbf{update}, \bot)$ $\mathsf{inv}_1(\mathbf{read}, \text{``foo''})$
> $\mathsf{res}_1(\mathbf{read}, 11)$ crash $\mathsf{inv}_3(\mathbf{read}, \text{``foo''})$ $\mathsf{res}_3(\mathbf{read}, 42)$

Thus h is of the form h_1 crash h_2. For $i = 1$, clearly h_1 is linearizable. For $i = 2$, let $h'_1 = \mathsf{inv}_1(\mathbf{update}\ (\text{``foo''}, 42))$ $\mathsf{res}_1(\mathbf{update}, \bot)$, which is a consistent cut of h_1. It is straightforward to see that $h'_1 h_2$ is linearizable. Note that h does not satisfy the stronger condition, *durable linearizability* [19] since h, after removing the crashes, is not linearizable.

Buffered durable linearizability is not generally *local* (i.e., not compositional, see [19]): locality would ensure that buffered durable linearizability of individual objects also guarantees buffered durable linearizability of their combined usage. However, certain conditions can give rise to locality properties for specific aspects of a data structure, as we will later see in our case study (see Theorem 2).

3 An Abstract Specification of Buffered Durable Linearizability

We design an abstract specification for an arbitrary data structure which only has buffered durable linearizable histories (Sect. 3.1). Hence, any concrete implementation whose traces are a subset of this specification's traces will also be buffered durable linearizable by trace refinement. Such proofs are often performed using forward or backward simulations aided by an abstraction relation [11]. However, due to the manual nature of such proofs, we aim for an alternative automated approach using the FDR model checker [17], which has been used in prior work to check other consistency conditions [12, 22, 25, 26]. This requires a CSP encoding of our abstract specification for the data structure of interest (Sect. 3.2).

3.1 The Automaton Specification

We use an input/output automaton to define our abstract specification.

Definition 4 (IOA [23]). *An* input/output automaton (IOA) *is a labelled transition system A with a set of states $states(A)$, a set of actions $acts(A)$, a set of start states $start(A) \subseteq states(A)$, and a transition relation $trans(A) \subseteq states(A) \times acts(A) \times states(A)$. We require that $acts(A)$ is partitioned into $internal(A)$ that are hidden from the environment, and $external(A)$ representing the IOA's interactions with its environment.*

IOAs can be specified by giving the states in terms of state variables and their initial values. For every action $\alpha \in acts(A)$ we give a precondition Pre on the state s that enables a step $(s, \alpha, s') \in trans(A)$ (elided when it is equal to *true*), and specify the result state s' by assignments given under Eff. For example, our abstract specification is depicted by the IOA in Fig. 1.

An *execution of an IOA A* is a sequence $\sigma = s_0\alpha_0 s_1\alpha_1 \ldots s_n\alpha_n s_{n+1}$ of alternating states and actions, such that $s_0 \in start(A)$ and for all states s_i, $(s_i, \alpha_i, s_{i+1}) \in trans(A)$. A *trace of an IOA A* (an element of $traces(A)$) is any sequence of (external) actions obtained by projecting out the external actions of any execution of A. Proofs of linearizability are often supported by a canonical linearizable object that is obtained from a sequential object [11]. It turns out that this idea can be extended to buffered durable linearizability. Given a sequential object $\mathbb{S}$ (see Definition 1), the *canonical buffered durable linearizable automaton of* $\mathbb{S}$ (denoted $\mathbb{A}(\mathbb{S})$) is the IOA given in Fig. 1. Note that every trace of $\mathbb{A}(\mathbb{S})$ is a well-formed history.

Theorem 1. *Every trace of $\mathbb{A}(\mathbb{S})$, for a sequential object $\mathbb{S}$, is buffered durable linearizable.*

State variables

$pc : Tid \rightarrow \{notStarted, crashed, idle\} \cup$ (initially: $\forall\ \tau \in Tid$.

      $\{\mathsf{inv}(op, v), \mathsf{res}(op, v) \mid op \in Op \wedge v \in Val\}$ $pc(\tau) = notStarted)$

$vmem : S$ (initially: $vmem = s_0$)

$pmem : S$ (initially: $pmem = s_0$)

Actions ($\mathsf{inv}_\tau(\_)$, $\mathsf{res}_\tau(\_)$ and crash are external; $\mathsf{do}_\tau(\_)$ and persist are internal)

$\mathsf{inv}_\tau(op, v)$ $\mathsf{do}_\tau(op)$ $\mathsf{res}_\tau(op, o)$

Pre: $pc(\tau) \in \begin{Bmatrix} notStarted, \\ idle \end{Bmatrix}$ Pre: $pc(\tau) = \mathsf{inv}(op, v)$ Pre: $pc(\tau) = \mathsf{res}(op, o)$

                                     $(s, o) \in \rho(vmem, op, v)$ Eff: $pc(\tau) := idle$

Eff: $pc(\tau) := \mathsf{inv}(op, v)$ Eff: $pc(\tau) := \mathsf{res}(op, o)$

                                         $vmem := s$

crash   persist

Eff: $pc := \lambda\tau : Tid.\ \textbf{if}\ pc(\tau) = notStarted\ \textbf{then}\ pc(\tau)$ Eff: $pmem := vmem$

                            $\textbf{else}\ crashed$

      $vmem := pmem$

Fig. 1. A buffered durable linearizable automaton $\mathbb{A}(\mathbb{S})$ for a sequential object $\mathbb{S} = (Op, S, s_0, \rho)$

Proof. Let $h \in traces(\mathbb{A}(\mathbb{S}))$ be a history with crashes and

$$\sigma = s_{11}\alpha_{11} \ldots s_{1k_1}\mathsf{crash}s_{21} \ldots s_{2k_2}\mathsf{crash} \ldots \mathsf{crash}s_{\ell 1} \ldots s_{\ell k_\ell}$$

be its underlying execution with $\ell - 1$ crashes partitioning the execution into eras. For every era, let m_i, $1 \leq i < \ell$, be the largest index such that α_{m_i} is a persist action. If there is no persist action in an era, we let $m_i = 1$. The indices m_i determine the consistent cuts, i.e., we get h'_i to be the sequence $s_{i1} \ldots s_{im_i}$ projected onto external actions. Then all histories $h'_1 \ldots h'_{j-1}h_j$ are linearizable: we take the ordering of do actions in $s_{i1} \ldots s_{im_i}$ as the sequential order and for the extension add res events for every such do action which has no corresponding res event. $\qquad\square$

Note that $\mathbb{A}(\mathbb{S})$ depends on the states, operations and transition relation of $\mathbb{S}$. Its set of external actions are the inv and res actions as well as the crash. The internal actions are the do actions (which correspond to operations of $\mathbb{S}$) as well as the persist action, which backs up the state of $\mathbb{S}$ to NVM. Unlike $\mathbb{S}$, which only allows sequential calls, $\mathbb{A}(\mathbb{S})$ allows concurrent calls to operations of $\mathbb{S}$ (as depicted in Example 3).

3.2 The Abstract Encoding in CSP

The IOA in Fig. 1 provides a general abstract specification, which given Thm. 1, could be used as the basis for a variety of proof approaches. This section focuses on encoding an instantiation of the IOA for a specific data structure (i.e., a hash map) in the process algebra CSP, enabling our automated proof approach using the FDR model checker. CSP (the theory of *communicating sequential processes*) was first introduced to describe the *interactions* between concurrent processes [7,27]. As such, to use it to model an IOA, we must translate each aspect to *processes* that respond to different *events* communicated over various *channels*. Our final model utilises many standard aspects of CSPM[3] syntax. For example, given processes P and Q and a set of events A, we use non-deterministic external choice (P [] Q), parallel interleaving (P ||| Q), parallel composition with synchronisation on events in A (P [| A |] Q), and exceptions (P [| A |> Q) which behave like P until events in A occur, then behave like Q. Roscoe's textbook, for example, provides further details [27].

The canonical buffered durable linearizable automaton of a hash map instantiates the IOA using the states, operations, and transition relations of its sequential counterpart, as given in Example 1. We then encode this in CSP using processes and events, an overview of which is given in Listing 1.1.

```
1  -- Process for updating/reading memory state variables
2  MapOps(vmem, pmem, c, pmemc) =
3    if vmem==emptyMap then doRead?_?_.TNull -> -- doRead when empty
4      MapOps(vmem, pmem, c, pmemc)
5    else doRead?_?k?v :{mapLookupNull(vmem, k)} -> -- doRead
6      MapOps(vmem, pmem, c, pmemc)
7    [] if (c) < card(NodeID) then -- doUpdate if enough free nodes
8      doUpdate?_?k?v -> MapOps(mapUpdate(vmem,k,v), pmem, c+1, pmemc)
9    -- doUpdate does nothing if map is already full
10     else doUpdateFull?_ -> MapOps(vmem, pmem, c, pmemc))
11     [] crash -> ([] x:{pmemc..c} @ MapOps(pmem, pmem, x, x)) -- crash
12     [] persist -> MapOps(vmem, vmem, c, c) -- persist
13  -- Optimised MapOps process with fixed initial values
14  MapSpec = (dbisim(MapOps(emptyMap, emptyMap, 0, 0)))
15
16  -- Process tracking thread state (crashed, idle etc)
17  AllThreadHandler(usedThreads) = ...
18  -- Process performing external actions on thread (inv -> do -> res)
19  MapThread(me) = invRead.me?key -> doRead.me.key?value ->
20    resRead.me.value -> MapThread(me)
21    [] invUpdate.me?key?value -> ...
22  -- Many threads may run in parallel
23  AllMapThreads = getUsedThreads?ts -> (||| id : diff(ThreadID, ts) @
         MapThread(id))
24  -- Interleave action threads with crash/persist events
25  Spec_with_crash=(AllMapThreads ||| crash -> SKIP) [| {crash} |>...
26  SpecThreads = (((Spec_with_crash [| threadSyncSet |] AllThreadHandler({}))
         ...) ||| Persist
27  -- Ensure actions update the states on do/crash/persist events.
28  Spec = (SpecThreads [| specSyncSet |] MapSpec) \ internalSpec
```

Listing 1.1. CSP Abstract Model. See the spec.csp file in [14] for the full model.

The MapOps process, shown in full, keeps track of the state variables (pmem and vmem) and updates them according to the effects of the do, crash and persist actions in the IOA. Specifically, we have three channels to model hash map do events: doRead, doUpdate, and doUpdateFull. Note the c and pmemc parameters are for managing model checker bounds only, and assume a concrete implementation of this specification has its size bound by the number of nodes. MapSpec initialises this process with the initial values of the memory states.

---

[3] CSPM stands for "machine-readable" CSP—a lazy functional language used by FDR for defining CSP models, hence used in our listings.

The `MapThread` process manages part of the transition relation of our IOA, specifically the external invocation and response actions for hash map operations on a given *Tid* (`me`), implicitly keeping track of thread state. The process waits (mimicking an *idle* or *notStarted* thread state) until an invocation event occurs (e.g., `invRead`)) which must then be followed by corresponding `do` (`doRead`) and response (`resRead`) events respectively before restarting the process to wait for the next invocation event. Once an invocation event occurs on a thread, the `AllThreadHandler` records that thread as used (i.e. in any state but *notStarted*). `AllMapThreads` (which restarts after each crash) concurrently starts a `MapThread` process for each *Tid* in a *notStarted* state, thus ensuring the thread state precondition for invocation actions in the IOA.

The `MapThread` processes are interleaved in parallel with both **persist** and **crash** events, which per the IOA can occur at any time. To conclude our CSP encoding, the transition processes are performed in parallel with the state managing processes (`MapOps` and `AllThreadHandler`), synchronising on **update, read, updateFull, persist** and **crash** events, to ensure the effects on the states are updated appropriately after each action. Importantly, the final **Spec** process hides the internal **do** and **persist** events, so its traces only contain a sequence of *external* events, in line with our definition of a trace for an IOA.

It would be straightforward to adapt this model to instantiate a different sequential object—namely by replacing the **inv**, **res** and **do** channels and updating the operation effects in `MapOps`. Thus this provides a blue-print for future automated verification of buffered durable linearizable data structures in FDR.

4   Modelling Dalí

Dalí [24] is a persistent hash map that was proposed to be buffered durable linearizable via an "informal" proof. As a case study for our trace refinement proof methodology, we intend to formally show that Dalí is indeed buffered durable linearizable, which first requires a formal model of Dalí and the underlying NVM memory features. We present an overview of the data structure in Sect. 4.1, a notion of locality for Dalí in Sect. 4.2 and the CSP encoding in Sect. 4.3.

4.1   Dalí Overview

The Dalí [24] hash map is implemented such that each hash value corresponds to a *bucket* implemented by a linked list of key-value nodes. An update operation simply adds a new node to the head of the list, while a read operation searches for the key in the list starting from the head, returning the value of the first node found (if the key exists). Interestingly, these operations only execute over volatile memory. Persistency is maintained by a separate worker thread periodically executing *global fences*. Each global fence starts a new *epoch*—noting this differs from an era which is a section of history without crashes. If a crash occurs in epoch E, Dalí only guarantees that updates in the current era corresponding to epoch $E - 2$ or earlier are persisted. Updates corresponding to epochs E and

$E-1$ are lost, even if the operations have returned. Such behaviour is allowed by buffered durable linearizability (though disallowed by durable linearizability).

```
 1  class node: <key k, val v, node* next>
 2  class status: <int a, int f, int c, int ss>
 3  class bucket: <mutex lock, status stat, node* ptrs[3]>
 4  class dali: <bucket buckets[N_BUCKTS], int list flist, int epoch>
 5
 6  bool bucket::curr_fail(status s):    // helper function
 7    return s.ss ∈ flist
 8
 9  bool bucket::prev_fail(status s):    // helper function
10    return s.ss-1 ∈ flist || s.f == ⊥
11
12  node* bucket::valid_head(status s): // helper function
13    if !curr_fail(s) then return ptrs[s.a]
14    elsif !prev_fail(s) then return ptrs[s.f]
15    else return ptrs[s.c]
16
17  status bucket::lookup(status s): // helper function
18    if s.ss = epoch then return s
19    if s.ss = epoch-1 then
20      if curr_fail(s) then return <s.a, ⊥, s.c, epoch>
21      if prev_fail(s) then // Change occurs for this case
22          if s.f == ⊥ then return <3 - s.a - s.c, s.a, s.c, epoch>
23          return <s.f, s.a, s.c, epoch>
24      return <s.c, s.a, s.f, epoch>
25    // here: s.ss < epoch-1
26    if !curr_fail(s) then return <s.a, ⊥, s.c, epoch>
27    if !prev_fail(s) then return <s.a, ⊥, s.f, epoch>
28    return <s.a, ⊥, s.c, epoch>
29
30  // bucket is assumed to be locked
31  val bucket::read(key k):
32    return search(k, valid_head(stat))
33
34  // bucket is assumed to be locked
35  void bucket::update(key k, val v):
36    node* n = new node(k, v, valid_head(stat))
37    status new_stat = lookup(stat)
38    ptrs[new_stat.a] = n
39    stat = new_stat
```

Listing 1.2. Dalí data types and **read**/**update** methods (refactored from [24]) with corrected **lookup** function. The change from the original version is described in §5.2.

Listing 1.2 gives an overview of the key data types and bucket operations (noting the global worker thread operations are not shown, but explained in the paragraphs on global fences, epochs, crash and recovery below). The top-level structure, dali, maintains an array of buckets, a failure list (**flist**) and a monotonically increasing epoch number (**epoch**). Each bucket contains a lock (**lock**), a status tuple (**stat**) and three node pointers (**ptrs**). Finally, each node comprises a key and value pair, together with a pointer to the next node. The **read** and **update** methods are executed by *application* threads. While simple in principle, the operations rely on a sophisticated underlying logic to manage global process interactions that is challenging to reason about, detailed below.

Active, In-flight and Committed Nodes. During epoch E, a node may be in one of three states: *active*, *in-flight* and *committed*, which are the nodes written in epochs E, $E-1$ and $E-2$, respectively. Epochs E and $E-1$ may be failed epochs and if they are, Dalí ensures that applications never access the nodes corresponding to these epochs. To achieve this, Dalí uses three pointers into the linked list, each of which may take a role: active (a), in-flight (f) or committed (c), as determined by the status indicator, stat. The status indicator also records a snapshot, ss, of the epoch where the most recent update took place.

Global Fences and Epochs. Note that none of the operations in Listing 1.2 perform any explicit persist operations. Instead, persists are performed asynchronously as part of the *global fence* that is executed by the worker thread. Specifically, the worker increments and persists the global epoch counter under the protection of a sequence lock, releasing the lock as soon as the persist has completed. Then, it waits for all other threads to complete their in-flight operations (on all buckets) before persisting the nodes corresponding to all updates in the current epoch. The worker thread can only execute one global fence at a time. The global fence (for epoch E) is non-atomic, and may overlap with the execution of new update operations in the next epoch (i.e., epoch $E + 1$).

Crash and Recovery. After a crash, a recovery operation is executed (to completion) before resuming normal operation. If a crash occurs during an epoch E, both epochs E and $E - 1$ are considered failed epochs, and these get recorded in flist (which is a persistent list of failed epoch numbers). Specifically, the recovery operation simply reads the persistent value of epoch and stores both epoch and epoch − 1 in the failure list, flist. Significantly, the recovery procedure does not delete or modify failed records - recovery is performed incrementally by application threads as they access data using the status indicator, with the lookup function playing a crucial role in updating this.

4.2   Locality of Dalí

Although Dalí is a generic hash map with operations across multiple buckets, this section notes that it is sufficient to only consider the behaviour of a single bucket in parallel with the worker thread using a locality property (see Theorem 2).

As already observed by Izraelevitz et al. [19], buffered durable linearizability is in general *not* local: an operation that does not persist before it returns, will not be able to ensure that it persists before any operation that follows it. However, Dalí's design is based on global fences (that are executed by a worker thread) that synchronise operations across all buckets, allowing us to obtain a locality property across buckets (i.e., hash values). Suppose h is a history of Dalí. For each hash value z, let $h_{|z}$ be the history h restricted to z, i.e., for each invocation and response event in $h_{|z}$, we have that $\mathsf{hash}(k) = z$ where k is the key corresponding to the event. We can now state the theorem formally below:

Theorem 2. *Let h be a history of Dalí. Then, h is buffered durable linearizable iff for each hash value z, $h_{|z}$ is buffered durably linearizable.*

Proof (Sketch). Suppose $h = h_1$ crash h_2 crash $\ldots$ crash h_n. Consider the era h_i of h. We assume that the epoch numbers at the beginning and end of h_i are

E_{i-1} and E_i, respectively. We take $p(h_i)$ to be the subsequence of all operations in h_i in epoch e, where $E_{i-1} \leq e \leq E_i - 2$. (Note the distinction between E_{i-1} and $E_i - 1$; the former is not necessarily equal to the latter.) Note that if fewer than two global fences have been executed in h_i, then $p(h_i)$ is empty. Each operation in $p(h_i)$ must have linearized and persisted. This is because a global fence waits for all operations on each bucket to complete their operation (but not necessarily return) before incrementing the value of the epoch number (to $E_i - 1$) and persisting the corresponding nodes of the linked list. Moreover, because the epoch number at the end of h_i is E_i, we know that a second global fence has been started, which means all persists corresponding to epoch $E_i - 2$ have completed.

Now, if h is buffered durably linearizable, trivially $h_{|z}$ for each hash value z is buffered durably linearizable. Namely, if h is buffered durably linearizable then by definition $h^m = p(h_1)\, p(h_2)\, \ldots h_m$ is linearizable for each $m \leq n$, and hence h^m restricted to each hash value z, i.e., $h^m_{|z}$ is also linearizable. Now consider $h_{|z} = h_{z1}$ crash h_{z2} crash $\ldots$ crash h_{zn} for each hash value z, where $h_{zi} = (h_i)_{|z}$. For each $m \leq n$ and $i < m$, we take the consistent cut to be $p(h_i)_{|z}$. By above, since $h^m_{|z}$ is linearizable (for each m), we have that $h_{|z}$ is buffered durably linearizable.

Conversely, suppose $h_{|z} = h_{z1}$ crash h_{z2} crash $\ldots$ crash h_{zn} is buffered durably linearizable for each hash value z. Thus, for $m \leq n$, we have that $h^m_{|z} = h'_{z1} h'_{z2} \ldots h_{zm}$ is linearizable and by the design of Dalí, we take $h'_{zi} = p(h_{zi})$ as a consistent cut, since the operations in epochs E_i and $E_i - 1$ are discarded after the crash in era h_i. Since this holds for all hash values z, by the compositionality of linearizability, $h^m = p(h_1)\, p(h_2)\, \ldots p(h_{m-1})h_m$ is linearizable. Moreover, each $p(h_i)$ is a consistent cut of h_i, and hence h is buffered durably linearizable. $\qquad\square$

4.3   CSP Model

The encoding of a concrete implementation into CSP involves significantly more internal events and processes than its abstract counterpart. We note that while parts of the model in this section are specific to Dalí, many aspects could be adapted to model other implementations of buffered durable linearizable data structures - such as handling nodes or persisted and volatile memory.

Overview. Our Dalí model has three main sections: (1) the application thread, which, given Theorem 2, models a single bucket's operations and data (e.g. status indicators); (2) the worker thread, including modelling of global fences and data (e.g. failure list); and (3) global processes to combine these, including modelling crash and recovery. There are three types of CSP processes used across these:

(i) *Method-based processes*, which are responsible for representing Dalí operations, structured similarly to the original pseudo-code (e.g., Listing 1.2, [24]);

(ii) *Handlers*, which are responsible for tracking object states and data;

(iii) *Combiners*, which bring the other two types together—ensuring that method-based processes and handlers are synchronised on certain events.

Listing 1.3 provides an overview of the main global processes, which are primarily represented by combiners (iii), along with select examples of methods (i) and handlers (ii) for both the application and worker thread sections. Numerous channels are used to model events (e.g., an event on the `getGlobalEpoch` channel fetches the current epoch `e` for an operation on thread `t`), supported by custom datatypes (e.g., `NodeIDType`). We note that while application thread method processes structurally resemble the original pseudocode provided and are Dalí specific, the handlers and combiners are more unique to the CSP model and could be adapted to other structures.

Application Threads. Modelling an application thread, i.e., a single bucket, is similar to modelling a linked-list queue implementation in CSP. There are four core handler processes: `BucketLockHandler`, `NodeHandler`, `PointerHandler`, and `BucketVarHandler`, which manage the state of the bucket lock, individual nodes, pointers, and the bucket status variables respectively. Several `NodeHandler` processes may run in parallel (for each active node), initialised by an `initNode` event. Notably, the latter three handlers both manage aspects of persistent memory (aka NVM): the `persisted` parameter in the `NodeHandler` is true only once the node's data has been persisted, and the `PointerHandler` and `BucketVarHandler` can (per the original paper [24]) be updated via atomic operations, hence in our model are always considered "persisted" memory.

Our method-based processes correspond to **read** and **update** from Listing 1.2. To model a read, we define a process for finding the valid head (see **Read** in [14]) and a search process (see **ReadSearch** in [14]). The former is the critical aspect of Dalí's read algorithm, and hence our model, as it is responsible for determining the node to search from based on the failure list and working bucket epoch.

```
1  --- APPLICATION THREADS
2  --Datatype and channel declaration examples
3  datatype NodeIDType = Null | N0 | N1 | N2
4  channel getGlobalEpoch : ThreadID . {2..maxEpoch}
5
6  --(ii) Bucket handler process example: track state of node 'me'
7  NodeHandler(me, key, value, next, persisted) = ...
8  --(i) Bucket method process example: Update initialises a new node if free,
       then Update' performs the method's functionality.
9  Update(me, key, val) =
10   lock -> getGlobalEpoch.me?e ->
11     (   (initNode?node!key!val -> Update'(me, node, e))
12     [] (noFreeNode -> resUpdateFull.me -> unlock -> Thread(me)))
13  Update'(me, node, gepoch) =
14   getBucketEpoch?SS ->
15   if (SS == 0) then
16     getActiveNode?headNode ->
17     Lookup(me, SS, false, false, node, headNode, gepoch)
18   else
19     ssFail.SS?currFail->
20     ssFail.(SS - 1)?prevFail ->
21     if not currFail then
22       getActiveNode?headNode ->
23       Lookup(me, SS, currFail, prevFail, node, headNode, gepoch)
24     else
25       getFlightNode?headNodef ->
```

```
26        if (not prevFail and headNodef != Bot) then
27           Lookup(me, SS, currFail, prevFail, node, headNodef, gepoch)
28        else
29           getCommittedNode?headNodec ->
30           Lookup(me, SS, currFail, prevFail, node, headNodec, gepoch)
31 ...
32 --- WORKER THREAD
33 --(ii) Worker handler example: track global epoch state in volatile (e) and
            persisted (pe) memory, as well as the lock (lt).
34 GlobalEpochHandler(e, pe, lt) =
35   (if lt then getGlobalEpoch?t!pe -> GlobalEpochHandler(e, pe, lt)
36   else getGlobalEpoch?t!e  -> GlobalEpochHandler(e, pe, lt) )
37   [] getGlobalEpochW!e -> GlobalEpochHandler(e, pe, lt)
38   [] incGlobalEpoch -> (if (e == maxEpoch) then SKIP
39                          else GlobalEpochHandler(e + 1, pe, lt))
40   [] persistGlobalEpoch -> GlobalEpochHandler(e, e, lt)
41   [] crash -> GlobalEpochHandler(pe, pe, false)
42   [] setEpochLock?l -> GlobalEpochHandler(e, pe, l)
43 --(i) Worker method example
44 WorkerThread() = getGlobalEpochW?e -> ...
45 ...
46 --- GLOBAL PROCESSES (iii)
47 -- Processes with interleave method threads
48 ApplicationThreads = pickFreeTID?t -> Thread(t) ||| ...
49 AllThreads = ApplicationThreads ||| WorkerThread()
50 -- Interleave handlers with synchronisation on crash events
51 GlobalProcesses = ((AllNodes [| {| crash |} |] ...
52
53 -- Select combination process examples, including crash interrupts
54 DaliMethods = (DaliArray [| alphaLock |] BucketLockHandler)
55 DaliRecovery = (Recovery ; DaliMethods)
56 DaliCrash = ((((DaliMethods) ||| crash -> SKIP)) [| {crash} |> DaliCrashR)
57 DaliCrashR = ((((DaliRecovery) ||| crash -> SKIP)) [| ...
58 Dali = (DaliCrash [| alphaG |] GlobalProcesses) \ internalEvents
```

Listing 1.3. CSP Process Overview. See the concrete.csp file in [14] for the full model

The update function is modelled over four processes (see Listing 1.3). It begins with **Update**, which, in addition to creating a new node (within model-checking bounds), also acquires the bucket lock and registers an operation with the global transaction array when fetching the global epoch—mentioned only in passing when describing the worker thread in the original Dalí paper. **Update'** then determines the valid head (similarly to **Read**), which in turn calls the **Lookup** and **setStat** processes, whose CSP encodings closely follow the pseudocode for the **lookup** function and **stat** variable assignment from Listing 1.2.

The **Read** and **Update** processes are triggered by the **invRead** and **invUpdate** invocation events respectively, and conclude with the respective response events. The invocation events occur in the **Thread** process—a model of an individual application thread offering the choice of either event. Our model considers up to two application threads running in parallel by interleaving events, with no direct synchronisation (e.g., **Thread(T0) ||| Thread(T1)**).

The Worker Thread. The worker thread requires four further handlers to model the global data: the **GlobalEpochHandler**, which keeps track of the value of the current global epoch; the **GlobalArrayHandler**, which keeps track of an array that indicates the epoch of each thread's current transaction (or 0 if not in a transaction); the **FailureListHandler** which keeps track of the list of failed epochs (in both persisted and volatile memory); and the **FreeTIDsHandler** which keeps track of available (i.e., unused) threads.

As previously mentioned for the `NodeHandler`, two of these notably consider both persisted and volatile memory, essential to accurately modelling data structures used in an NVM context. The `GlobalEpochHandler` (see Listing 1.3) provides a particularly interesting modelling example for Dalí. On the memory front, the `incGlobalEpoch` event—triggered after a global fence—increments (if possible) the *volatile* value of the global epoch. A `crash` event will then reset the volatile memory value back to the persisted value, or vice versa for a `persist` event.

The remaining `get` and `set` events require consideration of the epoch *sequence lock*. Our modelling revealed that this lock in its original form was somewhat heavy-handed. The purpose of the lock, as clarified with the original authors [24], is to prevent a *read-before-persist* problem, and while it does not prevent bucket operations accessing the epoch, if held, the *previous* epoch value should be used. To accurately model the lock in this current form, the epoch handler utilises a boolean parameter, `lt`, to keep track of the "lock" status of the epoch[4]. Thus the channel `setEpochLock` is used on either side of the `inc` and `persist` events in the worker thread, and the application thread `getGlobalEpoch` event returns the persisted or volatile lock value depending on the lock status. The remaining `getGlobalEpochW` channel is used only by the worker thread to obtain the current epoch value (thus cannot overlap with a worker thread `inc` event).

The worker thread executes the global fence using two key processes (following an epoch increment and persist): (i) `WaitOnTransactions` and (ii) `WriteBack`. The first (i) uses the `GlobalArrayHandler` to "wait" till no threads are performing an operation in the previous epoch (hence the aforementioned synchronisation), and (ii) then performs the fence by persisting all nodes between the current active node and committed node (which is already persisted).

Global Processes. The global processes carefully combine the worker and application thread processes. Method-based processes combine simply via parallel interleaving (e.g., the `AllThreads` combiner process in Listing 1.3), noting each application thread is assigned a unique *Tid* (picked from a pool of available threads). Comparatively, handlers are combined with methods such that they run in parallel *with* synchronisation on an event set. Any handlers which do not consider persisted memory are in the scope of the crash (`DaliMethods`), where as those that do will continue to run if a crash occurs, using event synchronisation on the `crash` event to model its effects (`Dali`).

We model a crash in the `DaliCrash` and `DaliCrashR` combiner processes (see Listing 1.3), which randomly interleave a crash event with the main process and use a CSP exception to move to the recovery process (see `Recovery` in [14]) after a crash. The recovery method, which follows the exact steps outlined in (Sect. 4.1), can be affected by a crash, but happens before the process restarts other method-based processes in `DaliCrashR`. Note that when application threads "restart" after a crash, they must pick a previously unused *Tid*. The final process `Dali` hides all internal events (i.e., all implementation details), leaving only the invocation, response, and crash events in the implementation's traces.

---

[4] Further discussion based on modelling observations also identified possible further simplifications to this locking process such as a bit-tagging or counter based solution.

Table 1. FDR Experiment Results

Parameters					Results		
#*Tids*	#Nodes	#Epochs	#Keys	#Threads	C. Time (s)	R. Time (s)	#States(M)
2	2	9	2	1	18.64	53.68	49.5
3	2	8	2	1	17.38	245.83	238.3
2	3	8	2	1	16.7	491.37	462.7
3	3	7	2	1	38.41	1935.51	1877.3
3	2	8	2	2	14.44	1770.58	946.4
3	3	6	1	2	1.75	1596.92	1032.2

5   Model Checking in FDR

We can now show Dalí is a buffered durable linearizable hash map [19] via an automated trace refinement proof in FDR4[5]. This ensures the traces of our Dalí implementation model (Sect. 4) are contained by our abstract specification (Sect. 3.2), and thus by Theorem 1, the Dalí model is buffered durable linearizable (within model checking bounds). We summarise the results of our experiments in Sect. 5.1, and highlight issues with the Dalí approach exposed by this process in Sect. 5.2.

5.1   Model Checking Results

The refinement check is performed with partial order reduction enabled, as well as the semantic-preserving compression functions `normal` and `dbisim` on certain processes. Our experiments considered several variations on the size of key datatypes from (Sect. 4): the number of TIDs (for application threads), the number of nodes, the maximum value of the global epoch, number of keys, and number of parallel application threads (noting the worker thread is additional to this).

Our experiments used FDR4 (v4.2.7) and took place on a 12th-Gen Intel Core i9-12900K CPU with 48 GB RAM running Ubuntu 22.04.5 LTS. Table 1 presents a selection of our results, showing compilation time (C. Time) and refinement checking time (R. Time) in seconds, and the number of states (millions) visited. Our timeout was 2000s, correlating to when checks were approaching the maximum available RAM. The number of keys was only varied to enable testing on three nodes in conjunction with parallel threads within computation limits.

Checking a single application thread is sufficient for testing the read and update algorithms given the bucket lock, however two parallel application threads (in addition to the worker thread) are useful to model check the linearizability of interactions with the global worker thread. As an application thread can never move from a crashed state back to *idle* or *notStarted*, it picks

---

[5] The assertions.csp file in [14] contains the trace refinement assertions.

a new *Tid* each time it starts, hence the number of *Tid*s limits the number of crashes. A minimum epoch of 5 ensures that at least one crash and recovery can occur (also requiring a minimum of 2 or 3 *Tid*s in the single and parallel cases respectfully). Considering up to three node IDs over 7 epochs on a single thread with up to three available *Tid*s (i.e., up to 2 crashes) allows the model to encounter all the cases described in the crucial lookup part of an update.

5.2 Dalí Issues and Insights

Our experiments identified three key issues occurring in the original Dalí specification [24][6]. Most critically, we observed an error in row 3 of the lookup table (corrected in line 21 of Listing 1.2). Recall the status indicator components `s.a`, `s.f`, and `s.c` are integers (between 0, 1, and 2) indicating the role of the pointer at the respective index in the `ptrs` array. Critically, only `s.f` can ever be invalid ($\perp$), and all role indicators maintain different values. Following the original code, if the old `s.f` is $\perp$ when $SS = E - 1$, the new `s.a` is assigned to `s.f`, i.e. would become $\perp$, which breaks this invariant. Instead, the new `s.a` should be the index to the currently unused pointer in the pointer array, which is immediately assigned a new value on the line following the lookup.

Next, our experiments highlighted the need for careful synchronisation between the transaction array, worker thread, and operation thread when fetching the global epoch during an operation to avoid a subtle error if a persist is occurring in parallel. In our model the threads sync on the event `getGlobalEpoch?t!e` to ensure that when thread t fetches the epoch value e, the global transaction array is updated (referenced in only a single sentence in [24]). If the transaction array is updated separately, the model checker identified a trace where thread t fetches the epoch value to start an operation on epoch E, the worker thread updates the epoch and begins a persist (which finds no ongoing transactions in epoch E), then the transaction array logs a transaction in epoch E after the worker thread has completed its checks - thus resulting in no "consistent cut".

Finally, while not mentioned in the original paper [24], it is critical that the global epoch is incremented during recovery as otherwise the later periodic recovery of nodes would break as the "current" epoch would be in the failure list. This combined with our earlier modelling observations on the epoch lock in Sect. 4.3 highlights the critical role global epoch management plays in ensuring buffered durable linearizability.

Our results thus show via trace refinement that Dalí (with the fixes above) is buffered durable linearizable under the model checking parameters in the table. The range of parameters explored provides confidence that this would be maintained more generally, supporting the original informal proofs [24]. We note that the full Dalí source code is closed-source, so while every effort has been made to follow the approach outlined in [24], this model checking approach is

---

[6] The Dalí code is closed-source, hence our model relies on the code snippets and explanations in the paper, along with correspondence with the authors.

also based on the assumptions outlined for our model, such as those highlighted in this section. An additional contribution of our CSP model is therefore an accessible process-based description for how to implement the Dalí approach for persistent data structures.

6   Conclusion and Related Work

In this paper, we have developed an IO-automaton for the persistent correctness condition of buffered durable linearizability. This can serve as an abstract specification for model checking, which, when encoded in the CSP process algebra alongside an encoding of a concrete implementation, enables automated proofs via trace refinement in the FDR4 model checker. We have demonstrated this methodology though our case study, Dalí, revealing several subtle (yet fixable) issues that occurred the original specification. We plan to furthermore employ our abstract specification to show that libraries like Montage [32] guarantee buffered durable linearizability of its (linearizable) clients. In addition to expanding on this paper's model-checking methodology, future work could extend to verification tools with stronger guarantees such as interactive proof assistants while reusing the IOA specification approach. Furthermore, the CSP models could continue to be useful alongside alternative verification tools to FDR4, noting, for example, a growing CSP toolkit in the Isabelle/HOL proof assistant [1].

Related Work. Several works propose notions of "persistent" linearizability, i.e., linearizability adapted to a setting with non-volatile memory. A survey and comparison of several such notions can be found in [2]. The development of abstract specifications like we do here has only been done for a few such notions, e.g., Khyzha and Lahav [20] propose an abstract specification for a strict version of buffered durable linearizability, but provide no proof thereof.

Verification via refinement has for instance also been studied by Derrick et al. [10] who show correctness of the durable linearizable queue of [15]. In [3–5], a similar technique has also been applied to *durable opacity*, an extension of the correctness criterion of opacity for software transactional memory to NVM. D'Osualdo et al. [13] develop a so-called path theorem which can help in developing refinement proofs (via simulation) for durable linearizability. There are works proving correctness of libraries like Flit [31] and Mirror [16] providing *transformations* to durable linearizability for linearizable data structures: Stefanesco et al. [29] base their approach on an axiomatic semantics for non-volatile memory while Bodenmüller et al. [6] work with an operational semantics.

Model checking concurrent correctness conditions like linearizability or opacity via CSP and FDR has already been studied in [12,21,22]. We note in particular that Lowe's work [22] on a lock-free linearizable queue provided a useful starting point for our models. However, none of these look at buffered durable linearizability or Dalí.

References

1. Ballenghien, B., Taha, S., Wolff, B., Ye, L.: Hol-csp version 2.0. Archive of Formal Proofs (2019). https://isa-afp.org/entries/HOL-CSP.html, Formal proof development

2. Ben-David, N., Friedman, M., Wei, Y.: Brief announcement: Survey of persistent memory correctness conditions. In: DISC. LIPIcs, vol. 246, pp. 41:1–41:4. Schloss Dagstuhl - Leibniz-Zentrum für Informatik (2022)

3. Bila, E., Doherty, S., Dongol, B., Derrick, J., Schellhorn, G., Wehrheim, H.: Defining and verifying durable opacity: correctness for persistent software transactional memory. In: Gotsman, A., Sokolova, A. (eds.) FORTE 2020. LNCS, vol. 12136, pp. 39–58. Springer, Cham (2020). https://doi.org/10.1007/978-3-030-50086-3_3

4. Bila, E., Derrick, J., Doherty, S., Dongol, B., Schellhorn, G., Wehrheim, H.: Modularising verification of durable opacity. Log. Methods Comput. Sci. **18**(3) (2022)

5. Bila, E.V.: Specifying and verifying persistent transactional memory. Ph.D. thesis, University of Surrey (2023)

6. Bodenmüller, S., Derrick, J., Dongol, B., Schellhorn, G., Wehrheim, H.: A fully verified persistency library. In: Dimitrova, R., Lahav, O., Wolff, S. (eds.) VMCAI. LNCS, vol. 14500, pp. 26–47. Springer (2024). https://doi.org/10.1007/978-3-031-50521-8_2

7. Brookes, S.D., Hoare, C.A.R., Roscoe, A.W.: A theory of communicating sequential processes. J. ACM **31**(3), 560–599 (1984). https://doi.org/10.1145/828.833

8. Cai, W., Wen, H., Maksimovski, V., Du, M., Sanna, R., Abdallah, S., Scott, M.L.: Fast nonblocking persistence for concurrent data structures. In: Gilbert, S. (ed.) DISC. LIPIcs, vol. 209, pp. 14:1–14:20. Schloss Dagstuhl - Leibniz-Zentrum für Informatik (2021). https://doi.org/10.4230/LIPIcs.DISC.2021.14

9. Choe, J.: Review and things to know: flash memory summit 2022. TechInsights (2022). https://www.techinsights.com/blog/review-and-things-know-flash-memory-summit-2022

10. Derrick, J., Doherty, S., Dongol, B., Schellhorn, G., Wehrheim, H.: Verifying correctness of persistent concurrent data structures. In: ter Beek, M.H., McIver, A., Oliveira, J.N. (eds.) FM 2019. LNCS, vol. 11800, pp. 179–195. Springer, Cham (2019). https://doi.org/10.1007/978-3-030-30942-8_12

11. Dongol, B., Derrick, J.: Verifying linearisability: a comparative survey. ACM Comput. Surv. **48**(2), 19:1–19:43 (2015). https://doi.org/10.1145/2796550

12. Dongol, B., Le-Papin, J.: Checking opacity and durable opacity with FDR. In: Calinescu, R., Pasareanu, C.S. (eds.) SEFM. LNCS, vol. 13085, pp. 222–242. Springer (2021). https://doi.org/10.1007/978-3-030-92124-8_13

13. D'Osualdo, E., Raad, A., Vafeiadis, V.: The path to durable linearizability. Proc. ACM Program. Lang. **7**(POPL), 748–774 (2023)

14. Edmonds, C., Dongol, B., Derrick, J., Wehrheim, H., Schellhorn, G.: CSP artifact for model checking buffered durable linearizability (2025). https://doi.org/10.5281/zenodo.14902055

15. Friedman, M., Herlihy, M., Marathe, V.J., Petrank, E.: A persistent lock-free queue for non-volatile memory. In: Krall, A., Gross, T.R. (eds.) PPoPP, pp. 28–40. ACM (2018). http://doi.acm.org/10.1145/3178487.3178490

16. Friedman, M., Petrank, E., Ramalhete, P.: Mirror: making lock-free data structures persistent. In: PLDI, pp. 1218–1232. ACM (2021)

17. Gibson-Robinson, T., Armstrong, P., Boulgakov, A., Roscoe, A.W.: FDR3 – A Modern Refinement Checker for CSP. In: Ábrahám, E., Havelund, K. (eds.)

Tools and Algorithms for the Construction and Analysis of Systems, pp. 187–201. Springer, Berlin (2014)

18. Herlihy, M., Wing, J.M.: Linearizability: a correctness condition for concurrent objects. ACM Trans. Program. Lang. Syst. **12**(3), 463–492 (1990)

19. Izraelevitz, J., Mendes, H., Scott, M.L.: Linearizability of Persistent Memory Objects Under a Full-System-Crash Failure Model. In: Gavoille, C., Ilcinkas, D. (eds.) DISC 2016. LNCS, vol. 9888, pp. 313–327. Springer, Heidelberg (2016). https://doi.org/10.1007/978-3-662-53426-7_23

20. Khyzha, A., Lahav, O.: Abstraction for crash-resilient objects. In: DISC 2016. LNCS, vol. 9888, pp. 262–289. Springer, Cham (2022). https://doi.org/10.1007/978-3-030-99336-8_10

21. Liu, Y., Chen, W., Liu, Y.A., Sun, J.: Model checking linearizability via refinement. In: Cavalcanti, A., Dams, D.R. (eds.) FM 2009. LNCS, vol. 5850, pp. 321–337. Springer, Heidelberg (2009). https://doi.org/10.1007/978-3-642-05089-3_21

22. Lowe, G.: Analysing lock-free linearizable datatypes using CSP. In: Gibson-Robinson, T., Hopcroft, P., Lazić, R. (eds.) Concurrency, Security, and Puzzles. LNCS, vol. 10160, pp. 162–184. Springer, Cham (2017). https://doi.org/10.1007/978-3-319-51046-0_9

23. WDAG 1996. LNCS, vol. 1151. Springer, Heidelberg (1996). https://doi.org/10.1007/3-540-61769-8_9

24. Nawab, F., Izraelevitz, J., Kelly, T., III, C.B.M., Chakrabarti, D.R., Scott, M.L.: Dalí: A periodically persistent hash map. In: Richa, A.W. (ed.) DISC. LIPIcs, vol. 91, pp. 37:1–37:16. Schloss Dagstuhl - Leibniz-Zentrum für Informatik (2017). https://doi.org/10.4230/LIPIcs.DISC.2017.37

25. Raad, A., Lahav, O., Wickerson, J., Balcer, P., Dongol, B.: Artifact report: intel PMDK transactions: specification, validation and concurrency. In: Weirich, S. (ed.) ESOP. LNCS, vol. 14577, pp. 180–184. Springer (2024). https://doi.org/10.1007/978-3-031-57267-8_7

26. Raad, A., Lahav, O., Wickerson, J., Balcer, P., Dongol, B.: Intel PMDK transactions: specification, validation and concurrency. In: Weirich, S. (ed.) ESOP. LNCS, vol. 14577, pp. 150–179. Springer (2024). https://doi.org/10.1007/978-3-031-57267-8_6

27. Roscoe, A.: Understanding Concurrent Systems, 1st edn. Springer-Verlag, Berlin, Heidelberg (2010). https://doi.org/10.1007/978-1-84882-258-0

28. Samsung Electronics: Samsung electronics unveils far-reaching, next-generation memory solutions at flash memory summit 2022 (2022)

29. Stefanesco, L., Raad, A., Vafeiadis, V.: Specifying and verifying persistent libraries. In: ESOP (2). LNCS, vol. 14577, pp. 185–211. Springer (2024). https://doi.org/10.1007/978-3-031-57267-8_8

30. Vafeiadi Bila, E., Dongol, B.: A verified durable transactional mutex lock for persistent x86-TSO. Form Methods Syst. Des. (2024). https://doi.org/10.1007/s10703-024-00462-1

31. Wei, Y., Ben-David, N., Friedman, M., Blelloch, G.E., Petrank, E.: Flit: a library for simple and efficient persistent algorithms. In: PPoPP, pp. 309–321. ACM (2022)

32. Wen, H., Cai, W., Du, M., Jenkins, L., Valpey, B., Scott, M.L.: A fast, general system for buffered persistent data structures. In: ICPP, pp. 73:1–73:11. ACM (2021)

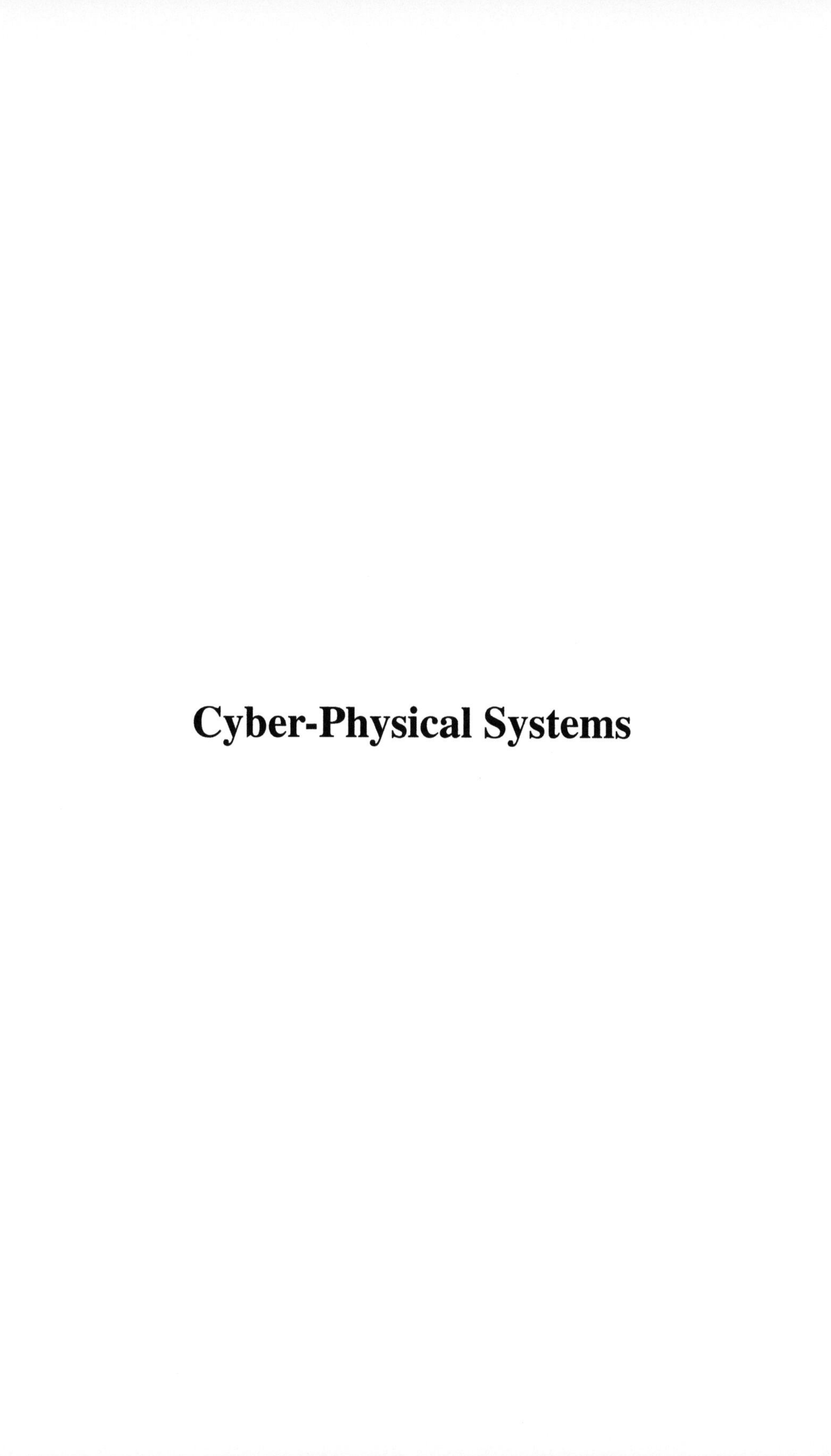

Cyber-Physical Systems

Safe Temperature Regulation: Formally Verified and Real-World Validated

Carlos Isasa[1]([✉])[iD], Noah Abou El Wafa[2]([✉])[iD], Claudio Gomes[1][iD],
Peter Gorm Larsen[1][iD], and André Platzer[2][iD]

[1] Aarhus University, Aarhus, Denmark
{cisasa,claudio.gomes,pgl}@ece.au.dk
[2] Karlsruhe Institute of Technology, Karlsruhe, Germany
{noah.abouelwafa,platzer}@kit.edu

Abstract. This paper presents a case study in the design and formal verification of a safe controller for the generic two-element lumped-capacitance model of temperature regulation, using formal cyber-physical system (CPS) theorem proving. The coupled dynamics and the absence of a fallback state reflect the complexities of real-world control systems and make it a representative challenge for theorem proving. A controller is developed by a design-by-invariant methodology. Verification using the axiomatic theorem prover KeYmaera X revealed critical assumptions for safety and pushes the frontier of CPS theorem proving. The parametric, general and provably safe controller can be applied to a wide range of temperature regulation tasks and is validated by deploying an instance of the verified controller on a physical system, demonstrating its robustness under model inaccuracies and confirming its real-world usability.

1 Introduction

From nuclear power plants to organ preservation, unsafe temperature changes lead to life-threatening outcomes. Despite the diverse domains, these systems share a common challenge: the need for safe and ideally verified controllers to maintain a safe temperature. Recent advances in formal theorem proving for cyber-physical systems (CPS) [20] offer a promising approach to finding a *generic* solution to this challenge by enabling formal verification through (computer-checkable) safety proofs for parametric controller specifications, that can be used practically in a wide array of applications and provide strong safety guarantees.

This paper presents a *generic temperature regulation controller*, that is *formally verified* through an integration of CPS theorem proving into the controller design process. Moreover, the controller design is validated experimentally on a *real-world instance* of the temperature regulation system, demonstrating how theorem proving as an approach to CPS verification can be *integrated end-to-end*: from the theoretical model and controller design via the formal safety proof to a real implementation on a physical system. The temperature changes of a generic heat-exchange system are modeled by linear ordinary differential

F. Damiani and M. Farrell (Eds.): iFM 2025, LNCS 16194, pp. 143–161, 2026.
https://doi.org/10.1007/978-3-032-10794-7_8

equations, which provide a practical trade-off between accuracy and complexity. While sufficiently accurate for many practical and industrial applications [4,7,9,15], designing a provably safe controller for this model is challenging. The proven controller is at the cutting edge of deductive verification, overcoming challenges that have not been addressed in this context previously, and provides valuable general insights for verifying more complex systems.

Differential dynamic logic (dL) [18] is used to model the controller and verify correctness in the axiomatic CPS theorem prover KeYmaera X [10]. The deductive approach enables formal verification for *unbounded time* and *generic parameters*, making it possible to find a versatile controller with very strong safety guarantees. Safety is fully addressed at design time, so that online safety checks or reachability analysis are no longer strictly needed. Nonetheless these can still increase the safety margin.

A new major difficulty of the considered system is the lack of a safe fallback action. The controller must always either choose to heat or not to heat. In the first case, it runs the risk that the temperature drops below a safe threshold and in the latter, the temperature may exceed the safe maximum. Thus, every action potentially leads to a state, from which a safety violation is inevitable. To tackle this, *directional invariants* are introduced as a new technique, which can be an ingredient in the verification of any system without a safe fallback action.

The successful validation of the verified controller on a real-world instance of the studied model confirms its correctness. By completing the circle (Fig. 1) from the physical system, through modeling, control design, formal safety proof, and implementation, back to the real-world system, this paper provides a first-of-its-kind, end-to-end case study paving the way for the verification of even more complex CPSs. Furthermore, the experiments enable an empirical analysis of how safety depends on system parameters, revealing a surprising robustness of the verified controller to both calibration and state estimation errors.

Summary of Contributions. The red arrows in Fig. 1 illustrate the contributions of this paper. A *generic provably safe controller* for temperature regulation is presented (①) and *formally verified* by a deductive proof in differential dynamic logic (②). Finally, an instance of the safe controller (③) is *validated on a real instance* of the model (④), which demonstrates both the practical feasibility of the deductive approach and the robustness of the generic approach to calibration and state estimation errors.

Related Work. The analyzed model has been used extensively in other scientific areas. Different techniques for the modeling of heat flow with lumped elements have been compared [1]. A similar model, including the estimation of its parameters and validation from data, was derived in detail [9], with the main difference that different types of heat transfer are considered (radiation). Model-based predictive control (MPC) approaches for heating in buildings are reviewed by Drgoňa et al. [6]. MPC is complementary to this work, since the control law (from Sect. 3.1) can be inserted as an additional constraint in deriving an MPC, to ensure safety (see [6, Section 2.3]).

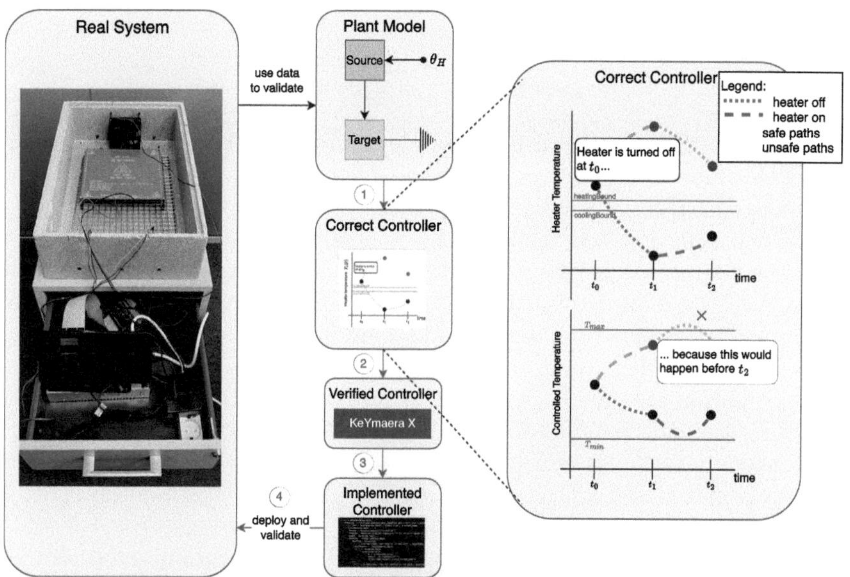

Fig. 1. Summary of the work. Contributions are marked by the red arrows. (Color figure online)

The lumped parameter model of temperature has been verified in specific instances via reachability analysis [15,24]. However, due to the need of instantiated parameters in order to carry a reachability analysis, no generic temperature regulation controller has been verified previously. Moreover, the safety guarantees presented here hold for an unbounded time horizon.

Other case studies for deductive CPS verification have been modeled and verified successfully in KeYmaera X [11,13,14,19] and using Hybrid CSP [25] and hybrid Hoare logic [16]. While end-to-end verification of CPSs has been considered [3], this work is the most complex model without fallback options using theorem proving, which is also evaluated on a real system.

2   Background

2.1   Deductive CPS Verification in dL

The formalization and verification in this paper is carried out in differential dynamic logic (dL), a language for describing models of hybrid systems with a proof calculus for the formal verification of safety properties. A brief introduction into the main ideas of dL is given here. For details see [10,18].

The logic dL can describe and reason about *discrete dynamics*, in the form of programs, combined with *continuous dynamics*, in the form of differential equations. The shape of a typical dL formula asserting the safety of a hybrid system model is

$$\text{assumptions} \rightarrow [(\text{ctrl}; \text{plant})^*]\, \text{safe} \tag{1}$$

This formula consists of assertions and hybrid programs. The system $(\text{ctrl}; \text{plant})^*$ is a *hybrid program* and serves as a nondeterministic over-approximation of a hybrid system. Hybrid programs are models, which do not deterministically describe one behavior, but rather describe a set of possible executions. In this way the model abstracts from minor details and focuses on the important aspects. And where deterministic models must consider modeling errors, a nondeterministic overapproximation should include the actual behaviour of the real system.

The condition safe and the assumptions are formulas in first-order logic (over $\mathbb{R}$) defining the safe region which the system should not leave (safe) and the initial assumptions under which this should be guaranteed. In this case study the formula safe will be $T_{\min} \leq T_c \wedge T_c \leq T_{\max}$ asserting that the controlled temperature T_c is in the range $[T_{\min}, T_{\max}]$.

Formula (1) combines these assertions and a hybrid program to formally state that under the assumptions every execution of the system $(\text{ctrl}; \text{plant})^*$ remains safe. (This is indicated by the square brackets $[\,]$ of the box-modality.)

Hybrid Program Syntax. The hybrid programs in (1) and at the heart of dL are described here briefly. Their syntax is given by the following grammar

$$\alpha ::= x := e \mid {?}\varphi \mid x' = f(x)\ \&\ \varphi \mid \alpha \cup \beta \mid \alpha; \beta \mid \alpha^*$$

where x is a variable, e a term in the variables and φ is a first-order formula. Assignments are represented as a hybrid program in dL by $x := e$, which discretely updates the value of the variable x to the value of the term e. The test program ${?}\varphi$ restricts the nondeterminism by removing all possible execution traces which do not satisfy the formula φ. Most important are the *continuous programs* $x' = f(x)\ \&\ \varphi$ of dL. These consist of an ordinary differential equation (ODE), which describes the continuous physical behavior of a CPS and are annotated with an *evolution domain constraint* formula φ to restrict the evolution of the dynamics to the set described by φ. The remaining hybrid programs are analogous to regular expressions. The choice program $\alpha \cup \beta$ introduces a nondeterministic choice between α and β and $\alpha; \beta$ is a composition indicating that β is run after α. The nondeterministic repetition program α^* means that α may be run repeatedly an arbitrary finite number of times.

The hybrid program model $(\text{ctrl}; \text{plant})^*$ describes a typical control cycle consisting of a discrete controller ctrl followed by the evolution of a continuous process described by plant in a loop of arbitrary length indicated by *. The discrete controller ctrl models all possible control decisions. It relies on information provided by the system as input, performs computations and makes choices for the future execution. The communication between the controller and the plant is handled through shared variables. The plant describes the physical evolution of the continuous system. Typically, this takes the form of a continuous program.

KeYmaera X. Differential dynamic logic is equipped with a proof calculus that enables *formal* (mechanized) safety proofs of formulas such as (1). The proof calculus for dL is implemented in the KeYmaera X theorem prover [10] for hybrid systems. It facilitates the *interactive* theorem proving of theorems formalized in dL and is equipped with powerful *automation* techniques for proving properties of continuous dynamics [20] and finding differential invariants [22]. Proofs developed with KeYmaera X provide a witness of correctness, that can be easily checked by the small soundness-critical core of KeYmaera X.

2.2   Lumped-Capacitance Model

The lumped-capacitance model (LCM) describes the transmission of heat between lumped elements, ignoring the inner heat dynamics of each element. Physically, the model describes the heat transfer akin to Newton's law of cooling [21]. By lumping elements together, the dynamics become significantly easier to handle through simulations and are simpler to study than the partial differential equations that can be used to model continuous heat distribution.

Here a controller for the two-element lumped-capacitance model (2ELCM) consisting of a heat source and a target whose temperature needs to stay between two bounds is verified. The heat source can either be powered on and thereby heat itself or be powered off. The target, under the assumption that the outside temperature is lower, continuously loses heat to the environment and heat is always transmitted from the heat source to the target.

In this model, a temperature controller cannot rely on a safe fallback action: turning off the heating is not a safe choice when the temperature is too low. Conversely, turning on the heating is not a safe choice when the temperature is too high (see Sect. 3.1).

The following lumped parameter heat transfer model is derived from the principles of thermodynamics [5]:

$$\begin{cases} T_h' = \dfrac{1}{C_h}(V \cdot I - G_h(T_h - T_c)) \\[2ex] T_{c'} = \dfrac{1}{C_c}(G_h(T_h - T_c) - G_c(T_c - T_s)) \end{cases} \tag{2}$$

where T_h is the heat source (e.g. a heater) temperature, T_c is the controlled temperature of the target, T_s is the (constant) temperature of a heat sink which models the environment, V, I are the voltage and current respectively and C_h, C_c, G_h, G_c are constant model parameters. Modeling the environment as a heat sink is justified when the environment is such that its temperature remains unaffected by temperature changes in the system. For example, the outside temperature of a building does not change (significantly) when the inside is heated up. The parameters C_h and C_c represent the heat capacitance (i.e. how fast energy is absorbed into temperature) of the heat source and the target, respectively, while the parameters G_h and G_c represent the heat transfer coefficients between the heat source and the target and between the target and the sink. Note that the rate of change of the controlled temperature T_c is proportional to the difference of the incoming heat, which itself is proportional to the temperature difference $T_h - T_c$, and the outgoing heat, which is itself proportional to the temperature difference $T_c - T_s$. The heat source temperature behaves similarly, where the incoming heat comes from the electric power $V \cdot I$ delivered. The parameters V, I, C_h, C_c, G_h, G_c are assumed to be positive and $T_s \leq T_c \leq T_h$ is assumed initially, so the heat is always transferred in the same direction. This model has been created and validated on a real-world prototype [7] and will be used to validate the safe controller in Sect. 4.

3   Verified Safe Controller

Section 3.2 will formally define the full hybrid systems model of the temperature regulation system consisting of a discrete controller defined in Sect. 3.1 running in a control loop (similar to Eq. (1)), in which plant follows the continuous dynamics Eq. (2) and the controller is executed at least every τ seconds. The verification of the model is discussed in Sect. 3.3.

3.1   Verifiably Safe Controller

Controller Requirements. A safe controller must ensure that the temperature T_c remains within the safe temperature range $T_{\min} \leq T_c \leq T_{\max}$. It receives the current heat source temperature T_h and the current temperature of the heated object T_c and decides whether the heat source should be powered on or off for the next cycle (up to τ seconds). We define the hybrid program on $\equiv I := I_{on}$, which sets the current I to I_{on}. This models turning on the heat source. Similarly, the hybrid program off $\equiv I := 0$ sets the electric current I to 0 to model turning off the heat source.

In order to obtain *provable* safety guarantees, the controller must make the choice whether to run on or off in a way that is safe and facilitates formal deductive reasoning. Abstractly, the controller (corresponding to the hybrid program ctrl in Eq. (1)) is of the form

$$\text{ctrl} \equiv \{\{?(\text{onSafe}(T_h)); \text{on}\} \cup \{?(\text{offSafe}(T_h)); \text{off}\}\} \tag{3}$$

This hybrid program ctrl describes a *nondeterministic* controller, which can be read as follows: the controller *may* turn the heat source on whenever the constraint onSafe(T_h) is satisfied and it *may* turn the heat source off if offSafe(T_h) is true. Theoretically the conditions can be arbitrarily complex and a significant part of the contribution is to obtain conditions onSafe and offSafe, which depend only (polynomially) on the heat source (not the regulated target) temperature. This ensures the controller is practical (can be checked quickly at runtime), verifiably safe, and always has at least one choice available (can not get stuck).

System Invariant. A provably safe controller can be found through *design-by-invariant* [18], where the invariant properties that should remain true for as long as the system is running are derived first and then guide the design of the controller. Proving safety formally requires an *inductive* invariant of the system, which is strong enough to ensure its own invariance. For example, it must prevent the temperature from reaching the upper limit of the safe range $T_c = T_{max}$ with too much energy in the heat source, which would make it impossible to cool down the system before safety is violated (Fig. 2).

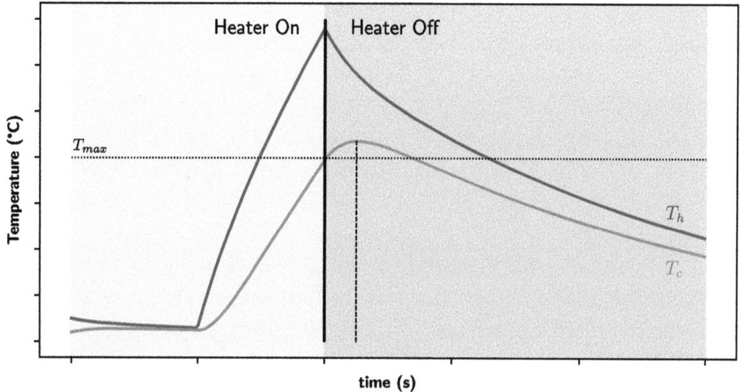

Fig. 2. T_c maximum reached after the heater is turned off (T_h maximum).

Clearly then, any invariant needs to ensure not only that T_c is in the safe region, but that it *will never* leave. Considering the upper and the lower limit of the safe region separately, this can be decomposed into two directional criteria that make up the following *directional invariant*:

(I) $T_{min} \leq T_c \leq T_{max}$
(II) if $T_c' \geq 0$ then the temperature will *never* exceed T_{max}
(III) if $T_c' \leq 0$ then the temperature will *never* drop below T_{min}

Combining (II)–(III) as a conjunction ensures that T_c never breaches the safety bounds, while crucially allowing reasoning about the bounds independently.

Directional Invariant Refinement. To describe an invariant formally, so that it is amenable to deductive verification, it is first necessary to capture '*never exceeding the bounds*' (as used in (II) and (III)) symbolically in the form of bounds on T_c. This is done by conservatively over/underestimating the maximum and minimum values of T_c that can be reached in the next control cycle, given the current state of the system. The controller temperature T_c is locally minimal or maximal only at times t_e where $T_{c'}(t_e) = 0$. By solving the equilibrium condition

$T_{c'} = 0$ (recall Eq. (2)) for T_c, the extremal values of T_c are seen to be of the form

$$\mathcal{E}(T_h(t_e)) \quad \text{with} \quad \mathcal{E}(T) := \frac{G_h T + G_c T_s}{G_c + G_h} \tag{4}$$

for some time t_e when the extremal value is attained. Because the exact expression for $T_h(t_e)$ involves exponentials, it cannot be used for a dL verifiable controller. However in the following a polynomial approximation is presented, that turns out to be practical and efficient as it is only used for short time (Sect. 4). Note that in case the heater is turned off (I $= 0$), T_h is decreasing ($T_h' = -G_h(T_h - T_c) \leq 0$ by Eq. (2)). Since $\mathcal{E}(T)$ is monotone, assuming that the controller can intervene at any time to turn off the heater, the maximal value of T_c is bounded above by $\mathcal{E}(T_h)$. As the invariant is evaluated at every point in time, the implication $T_{c'} \geq 0 \to \mathcal{E}(T_h) \leq T_{\max}$ ensures (II). However, the controller can only act at specific times, and its decisions will be restricted (onSafe and offSafe defined appropriately) to take into account reaction delay to make $\mathcal{E}(T_h) \leq T_{\max}$ invariant.

Similarly, (III) can be approximated by the implication $T_{c'} \leq 0 \to \mathcal{E}(T_h) \geq T_{\min}$. However, this implication will ensure (III) only in case the temperature T_h always rises, whenever the heater is turned on. This assumption is discussed below, since it depends in a surprising way on the controller constraint onSafe. In summary, the conjunction of the above conditions forms the invariant inv, presented in Invariant 1.

Invarient 1. Inductive Directional System Invariant.

$$\text{inv} \; \begin{cases} 1 & T_{\min} \leq T_c \leq T_{\max} \\ 2 & T_{c'} \geq 0 \to \mathcal{E}(T_h) \leq T_{\max} \\ 3 & T_{c'} \leq 0 \to \mathcal{E}(T_h) \geq T_{\min} \end{cases}$$

Safe Heating Condition. To verify that a condition onSafe maintains Invariant 1 inductively, the directionality of the invariant means that attention can be restricted to the upper bound $T_{\max}$. Specifically, Line 3 from Invariant 1 ensures that the lower bound is not violated and since T_h is rising, Line 3 remains true. Because every control cycle is of duration $\leq \tau$, a control decision at t_0 maintains the invariant, if the invariant holds at times $t \in [t_0, t_0 + \tau]$. Because $T_h' \leq \frac{VI}{C_h}$ (see Eq. (2)), the heat source temperature in this scenario can be bounded above:

$$\sup_{t \in [t_0, t_0 + \tau]} T_h(t) \leq \frac{VI_{on}}{C_h} \tau + T_h(t_0) = T_h^{\max}(T_h(t_0)) \tag{5}$$

where $T_h^{\max}(T) := \frac{\mathrm{VI}_{on}}{\mathrm{C_h}}\tau + T$. Consequently, by Eq. (4) it is safe to turn on the heater if $\mathcal{E}(T_h^{\max}(T_h(t_0))) \leq T_{\max}$. By solving this expression for $T_h(t_0)$, a *decision bound* B_{heat} (heating bound) is obtained such that $T_h(t_0) \leq B_{\mathsf{heat}}$ guarantees that the controlled temperature will not overshoot $T_{\max}$. Defining

$$\mathsf{onSafe}(T_h(t_0)) \equiv T_h(t_0) \leq B_{\mathsf{heat}} \tag{6}$$

where

$$B_{\mathsf{heat}} := \frac{T_{\max}(\mathrm{G_h} + \mathrm{G_c}) - \mathrm{G_c}\mathrm{T_s}}{\mathrm{G_h}} - \frac{\mathrm{VI}_{on}\tau}{\mathrm{C_h}}$$

ensures that for the controller (3) line 3 of Invariant 1 is an inductive invariant. Note that the heating bound conveniently depends only on the system parameters $\mathrm{G_h}$, $\mathrm{G_c}$, $\mathrm{C_h}$, V, I_{on}, $T_{\max}$, $\mathrm{T_s}$, τ and *not* on the system state T_c, T_h.

Safe Cooling Condition. The derivation of the condition $\mathsf{offSafe}$ is more subtle as it critically relies on the assumption that the temperature T_c rises immediately once the heater is turned on. Using the lower bound

$$\inf_{t\in[t_0,t_0+\tau]} T_h(t) \geq T_h(t_0) + \frac{\mathrm{G_h}T_h(t_0)}{\mathrm{C_h}} \cdot \tau = T_h^{\min}(T_h(t_0)) \tag{7}$$

where $T_h^{\min}(T) := T + \frac{\mathrm{G_h}T}{\mathrm{C_h}} \cdot \tau$, it is safe to turn off the heater if $\mathcal{E}(T_h^{\min}(T_h(t_0))) = T_{\min}$. Solving for $T_h(t_0)$ assuming $\mathrm{C_h} > \mathrm{G_h}\tau$ (see below), yields the (cooling) bound B_{cool}

$$B_{\mathsf{cool}} := \frac{T_{\min}(\mathrm{G_h} + \mathrm{G_c}) - \mathrm{G_c}\mathrm{T_s}}{\mathrm{G_h}} \frac{\mathrm{C_h}}{\mathrm{C_h} - \mathrm{G_h}\tau}$$

such that $\mathcal{E}(T_h^{\min}(T_h(t_0))) \geq T_{\min}$ is true exactly if the decision guard

$$\mathsf{offSafe}(s) \equiv T_h(t_0) \geq B_{\mathsf{cool}} \tag{8}$$

holds. This ensures that the temperature does not drop below the lower limit of the safe range. Like the heating bound, the cooling bound B_{cool} also depends only on the system parameters $\mathrm{G_h}$, $\mathrm{G_c}$, $\mathrm{C_h}$, $T_{\min}$, $\mathrm{T_s}$, τ.

The two decision guards, onSafe and $\mathsf{offSafe}$, completely define the non-deterministic controller ctrl. Invariance of inv and suitability of the controller are discussed in Sect. 3.3. The controller is simple to instantiate, as it only adds polynomial constraints (the decision bounds B_{heat} and B_{cool}) on turning the heat source on and off, which are easy to implement and can be verified via theorem proving.

Heater Power Assumption. For Line 2 of Invariant 1 it was assumed that the heater immediately starts heating up after being turned on. In order to formally verify the controller, this assumption needs to be made symbolically. Interestingly, this assumption can depend on the definition of the controller, since the heater temperature T_h does not need to rise immediately whenever the heater is turned on, but T_h must rise when the heater has been turned on *by the controller* and the invariant inv holds. In other words it suffices to show that in case the invariant inv holds ($T_c \geq T_{\min}$), the heating condition is satisfied ($\mathsf{onSafe}(T_h(t_0))$ is true) and the heater is turned on ($I = I_{on}$), the heater temperature rises immediately ($T_h'(t_0) \geq 0$). This implication is guaranteed by the following assumption on the heater power:

$$\mathrm{VI}_{on} \geq T_{\max}(\mathrm{G_h} + \mathrm{G_c}) - \mathrm{G_c}T_s - \mathrm{G_h}T_{\min} \tag{9}$$

Proof. It is shown that Eq. (9) implies that the heater has sufficient power to immediately heat the box once it is turned on. Observe first that

$$\mathrm{VI}_{on}\left(1 + \tfrac{\mathrm{G_h}}{\mathrm{C_h}}\tau\right) > \mathrm{VI}_{on} \geq T_{\max}(\mathrm{G_h} + \mathrm{G_c}) - \mathrm{G_c}T_s - \mathrm{G_h}T_{\min}$$

Rearranging gives

$$\begin{aligned}
\mathrm{VI}_{on} &> T_{\max}(\mathrm{G_h} + \mathrm{G_c}) - \mathrm{G_c}T_s - \mathrm{G_h}T_{\min} - \mathrm{VI}_{on}\tfrac{\mathrm{G_h}}{\mathrm{C_h}}\tau \\
&= \mathrm{G_h}\left(\tfrac{T_{\max}(\mathrm{G_h}+\mathrm{G_c})-\mathrm{G_c}T_s}{\mathrm{G_h}} - T_{\min} - \tfrac{\mathrm{VI}}{\mathrm{C_h}}\tau\right) \\
&= \mathrm{G_h}(B_{\mathsf{heat}} - T_{\min})
\end{aligned}$$

So since $\mathsf{onSafe}(T_h(t_0))$ is true, $\mathrm{VI}_{on} > \mathrm{G_h}(T_h(t_0) - T_{\min})$. By definition of the dynamics (Eq. (2)):

$$T_h'(t_0) = \mathrm{VI}_{on} - \mathrm{G_h}(T_h(t_0) - T_{\min}) > 0$$

Thus the heater temperature rises immediately when the heater is turned on. $\square$

The fact that the assumptions shown in Eq. (9) are parametric in the controller variables V, I_{on}, allows for flexibility in engineering the system. Depending on the system parameters the power of the heat source can be chosen to satisfy Eq. (9).

The derivation of the minimum heater power illustrates the power of the fully symbolic approach to verification. The increased complexity of the manual proof work is redeemed by its easy formal *interpretability*.

Liveness. For the verified model to be meaningful, the controller should always have a choice available. If $B_{\mathsf{heat}} \geq B_{\mathsf{cool}}$ is true, the controller can always safely turn the heater on or off. Since both constants depend only on the parameters, liveness of the controller does *not* depend on the state of the system and so can be established at design time. And conversely, the parametric expressions of B_{heat} and B_{cool} help with making appropriate choices of for the heater power to ensure liveness. This is the reason the safety conditions were expressed in the form of heating and cooling bounds For the real-system parameters used in the validation (see Table 1), it is the case that $B_{\mathsf{heat}} \geq B_{\mathsf{cool}}$.

Summary. The conditions onSafe(T_h) and offSafe(T_h) were defined in terms of the decision bounds, B_{heat} and B_{cool} (Fig. 1) and ensure that T_c will remain in the safe region. It is always possible to either cool down or heat up the system before T_c leaves the safe region. Which choice is available depends only on the temperature of the heat source, T_h. Perhaps surprisingly, restricting the controller decision guards, onSafe and offSafe to the heat source temperature makes the safety proof significantly easier, while still yielding a functional and safe controller, as will be demonstrated in Sect. 4.

3.2 Formal dL Model

The formal dL hybrid systems model of the 2ELCM is a control loop as in Eq. (1). The postcondition safe is the safety condition, which says that the temperature of the target remains within the safe range $T_{\mathsf{min}} \le T_c \le T_{\mathsf{max}}$, where T_c denotes the temperature of the heated object. The controller ctrl has been defined in Eq. (3) and the heat dynamics describes the physical evolution of the system according to Eq. (2). The precondition assumptions is the conjunction of the conditions listed in Listing 1, as obtained in the design process of the controller in Sect. 3.1 and the assumption that the system is in a safe starting state. (Line 3 captures the parametric liveness assumption as used in the derivation of B_{cool} and the heater power assumption from Eq. (9).) The precondition assumptions is a conjunction of the conditions in Listing 1.

Listing 1. Pre- and postconditions for safe controller.

assumptions	1	$G_h, G_c, C_c, C_h, I_{on}, V > 0 \,\land\, B_{\mathsf{cool}} \le T_h \le B_{\mathsf{heat}}$
	2	$T_{\mathsf{min}} \le T_c \le T_{\mathsf{max}} \,\land\, 0 \le T_s \le T_c \le T_h 0$
	3	$C_h > G_h \tau \,\land\, V I_{on} > T_{\mathsf{max}}(G_h + G_c) - G_c T_s - G_h \cdot T_{\mathsf{min}}$
safe	4	$T_{\mathsf{min}} \le T_c \le T_{\mathsf{max}}$

The formal model of the continuous heat dynamics side of the hybrid system model is shown in Listing 2. In order to include the time-triggered nature of the controller, an explicit timer is introduced ($t'{=}1$), which is reset ($t{:=}0$ in Line 5 of Listing 2) at the beginning of every control cycle. The timer is used inside the evolution domain constraint ($t \le \tau$) to ensure that the controller is executed at least τ seconds after the last controller execution. As the ODE has no explicit dependence on time, the timer does not affect the behaviour of the dynamics. The continuous plant dynamics are separated into two phases in order to make case-distinction reasoning possible in the verification process. It splits the phase tempRise in which the temperature is rising $T_{c'} \ge 0$ and the phase tempFall where it is falling $T_{c'} \le 0$. Switching between these phases (*ghost switching* [23]) is realized through the use of a nondeterministic choice facilitating the phase-transition and a loop allowing any execution to make an arbitrary (finite) number of phase transitions.

Listing 2. Continuous dynamics model with ghost switching.

$$
\begin{array}{r|l}
\text{ODE} & 1 \quad T_h' = 1/\mathrm{C_h}(\mathrm{VI} - \mathrm{G_h}(T_h - T_c)), \\
 & 2 \quad T_{c'} = 1/\mathrm{C_c}(\mathrm{G_h}(T_h - T_c) - \mathrm{G_c}(T_c - \mathrm{T_s})), \\
\text{tempFall} & 3 \quad \{\text{ODE}, t' = 1 \,\&\, t \leq \tau \wedge T_{c'} \leq 0\} \\
\text{tempRise} & 4 \quad \{\text{ODE}, t' = 1 \,\&\, t \leq \tau \wedge T_{c'} \geq 0\} \\
\text{plant} & 5 \quad \{t := 0; \{\text{tempFall} \cup \text{tempRise}\}^*\}
\end{array}
$$

3.3 Formal Verification of Safety

Any minor oversight in the design of the controller could lead to an unsafe controller leading to potentially dangerous outcomes. This possibility is excluded by a formal proof of safety carried out in KeYmaera X. The formal proofs are available in the repeatability package [12] and the proof tactic serves as an easily checkable witness of correctness. As such the proof also certifies the correctness of the controller to a third party, which would only need to trust the small proof-checking core of KeYmaera X [2] and the accuracy of the model itself.

This section describes some of the key challenges and insights required for the formal proof of safety and in particular their *general* lessons for modeling and verifying cyber-physical systems formally.

Verification Process. The correct controller was obtained through several design and proof iterations. Many critical assumptions were made implicitly in the design of the controller and were only revealed through the process of constructing a formal proof. (See for example the assumption on the minimum power of the heater on Sect. 3.1.)

Case Distinctions and Local Invariants. At the heart of the formal proof of safety lies the verification that Invariant 1 indeed is an *inductive invariant* of the system. Note that the invariant mentions $T_{h,\text{init}}$ as the initial temperature of the heat source at the beginning of the control cycle (which can be introduced as a constant using a discrete ghost argument [18]). Ghost switching enables a formal proof by case distinction into four distinct cases along two dimensions: The heat source may be powered on or off and the temperature may be rising or falling. The *directional invariants* are a new ingredient that fully leverage the case distinction to reduce a complex property to its core and discharge many proof obligations using the advanced automation of KeYmaera X. The idea to make the invariant conditional on the direction of the evolution (cf. Lines 4 and 5 in Invariant 2) constitutes a novel approach in deductive CPS verification and is promising for many other cases. In particular, it is a powerful technique for treating the challenges posed by the lack of a safe fallback controller action.

The effect of the case distinction and the directional invariant is that the temperature T_c and the heat source temperature T_h can be considered (temporarily) monotone, which enables formalization of symbolic estimates of the temperatures, as used in the design of onSafe and offSafe in Sect. 3.1. To exploit the monotonicity syntactically, a key ingredient in the proof are the two local invariants, which remain true of the physical system only for the duration of one control cycle, one for each of the two modes of the controller. These local invariants are essentially the invariants for the continuous dynamics (differential invariants), with the difference that, thanks to the ghost switching they only need to be verified until the temperature reaches a critical point. The local invariant for the heating cases (Invariant 2) captures additionally that the heater temperature will be hotter than it is initially throughout the control cycle and is based on the over-approximation argument of the temperature. The directional nature of the invariant determines whether the next extremal temperature is maximal or minimal. The local invariant for cooling is similar.

Invarient 2. Local Invariant for Heating Cycle.

---

heatingInv		
	1	$T_{\min} \leq T_c \leq T_{\max} \wedge 0 \leq t \leq \tau$
	2	$0 \leq T_s \leq T_c \leq T_h \wedge T_{h,\mathrm{init}} \leq T_h$
	3	$T_h^{\min}(T_{h,\mathrm{init}}) \leq T_h \leq T_h^{\max}(T_{h,\mathrm{init}})$
	4	$T_{c'} \leq 0 \rightarrow (T_c \geq \mathcal{E}(T_{h,\mathrm{init}}) \wedge \mathcal{E}(T_{h,\mathrm{init}}) \geq T_{\min})$
	5	$T_{c'} \geq 0 \rightarrow (T_c \leq \mathcal{E}(T_h^{\max}(T_{h,\mathrm{init}})) \wedge \mathcal{E}(T_h^{\max}(T_{h,\mathrm{init}})) \leq T_{\max})$

Proof Technology. The marked improvements in the theorem-proving technology for hybrid systems are critical for the successful formal verification. Of particular importance are recent advances in the automatic *complete* verification of differential invariants [20]. This obviates the need for complex reasoning about the continuous evolution. As long as a valid differential invariant can be found, it can be verified automatically. KeYmaera X implements invariance verification in the tactic `odeInvC`, which automatically proves any valid differential invariant for a system. However, for computational reasons, it is still necessary to simplify the invariance problem to avoid time outs. This requires controlling exactly which assumptions are required for invariance. In the artifact package [12] a part of the proof is explained in depth to illustrate the subtleties of reducing a complex problem to one that can be solved *efficiently* and *automatically*.

Another valuable tool in the verification process was the counterexample finding tool of KeYmaera X. In the process of designing and verifying the safe controller refinement, counterexamples made clear which assumptions were missing and highlighted possible scenarios that were overlooked.

4   Control Deployment and Validation

The controller was validated on the incubator described by Feng et al. [7] consisting of an insulated box containing a heater (the heat source in the 2ELCM) and a fan to distribute the heat (so that it can be modeled as a single lump). The heater can be turned on or off and the inside air temperature (T_c) is viewed as the average of two sensor readings.

An important feature of this case study is that the heatbed temperature T_h is not measured directly. Instead, it is estimated through a Kalman filter [8] that uses the same model used for the proof of the controller. We evaluate in practice the impact of the uncertainty in this estimation and the controller performance.

To test the limits of the bounds, the physical controller is a refinement of the (nondeterministic) dL specification, which heats for as long as possible and then cools for as long as possible, by activating the heater exactly if:

1. either the heater was previously on and it is safe to leave it on; or
2. the heater was previously off and it is unsafe to leave it off.

This example illustrates the flexibility of the generic, verified controller, which allows many alternative implementations, which optimize for other measures and can be designed manually. A correct-by-construction controller monitor that checks at runtime that any choice made by the controller is allowed by the specification can be obtained through Modelplex [17].

Table 1. Parameter sets used in the experiments. (The parameters are approximate and exact values can be found in the repeatability package [12].)

	Parameters				Power		Bounds		
	C_c	G_c	C_h	G_h	V	I_{on}	B_{heat}	B_{cool}	Source
Γ_1	24.59	0.16	47.26	0.22	12.17	1.55	49.47	49.17	Calibration Process
Γ_2	17.63	0.16	40.01	0.13	12.17	1.55	57.56	56.75	Calibration Process
Γ_3	34.63	0.16	40.01	0.13	12.17	1.55	58.02	57.22	Γ_2 with C_c Disturbed
Γ_4	24.59	0.25	47.26	0.22	12.17	1.55	55.92	55.24	Γ_1 with G_c Disturbed

Experimental Setup. Four distinct experiments with parameter sets $\Gamma_1, \Gamma_2, \Gamma_3$ and Γ_4, shown in Table 1, were conducted to validate the controller on a real system with tight safety margins (parameter sets Γ_1 and Γ_2), and to investigate the impact of modeling errors and parameter variations (parameter sets Γ_3 and Γ_4). The parameters are used in the controller decision process and in the Kalman filter for state estimation. For the experiments the temperature bounds $T_{\min} = 3.5\,^{\circ}\mathrm{C}$ and $T_{\max} = 37.75\,^{\circ}\mathrm{C}$ were used for a range of $1.25\,^{\circ}\mathrm{C}$. The first two parameter sets, Γ_1 and Γ_2 were obtained through a calibration process [7], which fits the parameters to an experimental run of the physical system. This process involves an underconstrained optimization problem, so that two different sets of parameters (Γ_1 and Γ_2), representing different, well-fitting models, are obtained. To study the effect of perturbations the most and least sensitive parameters were determined by a sensitivity analysis over B_{heat} and B_{cool} (computing partial derivatives of Eqs. (6 and (8)). Parameter set Γ_3, was obtained by adding 17 to the value of the least sensitive parameter C_c in Γ_2 (almost doubling it) and Γ_4 is Γ_1 with the value of the most sensitive parameter G_c multiplied by 1.5 in Γ_1.

The measured (average) air temperatures of the real-world experiments are overlaid in Fig. 3 from the moment both sensor readings first exceed $T_{\min}$.

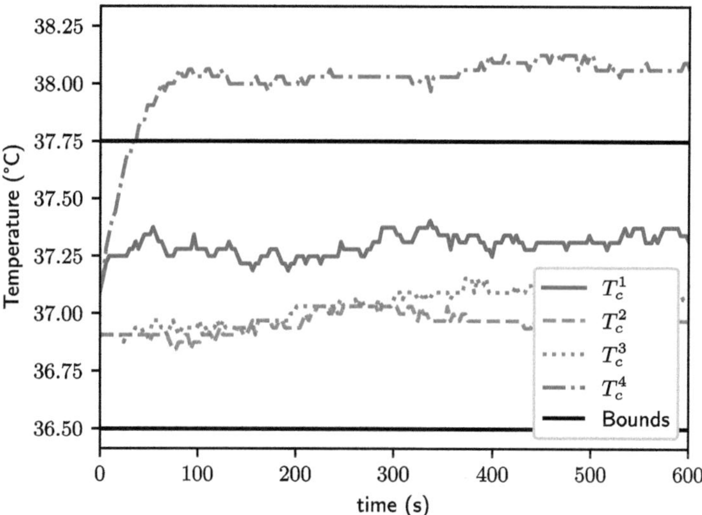

Fig. 3. Average incubator temperature T_c^i for each experiment with parameters Γ_i.

Discussion. As verified deductively, Fig. 3 shows that the controlled temperature (T_c^1 and T_c^2) remains within the bounds in both experiments (Γ_1, Γ_2). Interestingly the verification result applies to very different values for the decision bounds B_{heat} and B_{cool} (see Table 1). These experiments provide evidence that our controller remains safe, despite typical modeling, calibration, and estimation uncertainties.

Interestingly, the temperature T_c^3 also stays within the safety bounds. This is surprising, as a perturbation to one of the parameters (capacitance C_c) might intuitively make the system unsafe. However, the capacitance C_c does not affect the heating and cooling bounds at all, so that, according to the model and the experiment, safety is not affected by changes to the capacitance C_c, such as placing objects inside the air volume. This is particularly relevant for applications where it is unknown what objects will be placed inside the temperature controlled environment.

Finally, the temperature T_c^4 fails to stay within the safety bounds. The perturbation of the coefficient G_c (by 50%) makes the system unsafe, by virtue of the larger significance of the affected parameter. While the decision bound B_{heat} (see Table 1) is similar to the one in Γ_2 the reliance of the Kalman filter on the same parameters means that the estimate of the temperature T_h does not fit the model anymore.

5   Conclusion

This paper introduced a formally verified controller for temperature regulation in the two-element lumped-capacitance model. The requirements of formal verification guided the design of the controller and revealed all critical assumptions on the heating system for the system to be provably safe. The controller was designed using several correct-by-construction over-/under-approximations of the safety bounds in order to obtain verifiably correct decision bounds. These approximations are correct for the dynamical system that models the real-world dynamics and thus correct for the real world dynamics assuming that the approximation is good enough. This process ensures safety for unbounded time and presents a representative verification case study of a controller that does not rely on a safe fallback action. Safety is formalized in the hybrid systems theorem prover KeYmaera X, which delivers easily checkable correctness guarantees. The resulting controller is generic and allows for the straightforward implementation of a safe temperature-regulation unit in many application domains, as demonstrated by the real-world validation of the controller. The validation provides an end-to-end case study for CPS verification of a hybrid system with dynamics of general interest.

Furthermore, the validation on a real system shows the strength and applicability of this approach. The complexities of the formal approach are vindicated in the implementation and validation phase, where the verified bounds reveal which parameters are the most relevant to the inner workings of the system. This is validated by applying a large disturbance to the least relevant parameter (G_c) and showing that it does not influence the safety of the system. All in all, this process minimizes calibration problems and thus allows for more robust implementations. Initially, the potential of modeling discrepancies and the fact that the controller requires a Kalman filter, are concerning, since the correctness hinges on the 2ELCM being a good fit for the system. However, it is shown that controller safety is quite robust with respect to modeling inaccuracies.

Future Work. This work opens up several exciting areas of research. As a real-world case study, the 2ELCM model provides a valuable aid to the development of advanced hybrid systems verification techniques. The surprising robustness of the presented controller with respect to parameter errors suggest an investigation of the impact that calibration errors and state estimation (the Kalman filter) can have on the safety of a formally verified CPSs beyond 2ELCM.

The conditions on the safe controller use an overapproximation of the maximal heater temperature. Alternative controller bounds that are derived similarly could be explored, using alternative assumptions and better bounds. This could achieve practical improvements with more efficient control envelopes at the expense of increased proof complexity.

The presented controller solves many challenges at the heart of the heat-transmission problem. Although still challenging, increasing the complexity of the model to more elements is now possible on the basis of the verified two-element controller. This makes it an interesting object for further research into the composability of deductive hybrid systems verification.

The approach used in the deductive verification has many generalizable lessons and critical insights that are useful in other cases, in which safety can not be maintained by simply retaining a safe fallback option at all times. This is potentially useful for other verification tasks and could benefit from being studied more generally.

Acknowledgments. This research was supported by the RoboSAPIENS Project financed by the European Commission's Horizon Europe programme under Grant 101133807 and the Alexander von Humboldt Professorship program.

References

1. Afroz, Z., Shafiullah, G., Urmee, T., Higgins, G.: Modeling techniques used in building HVAC control systems: a review. Renew. Sustain. Energy Rev. **83**, 64–84 (2018). https://doi.org/10.1016/j.rser.2017.10.044
2. Bohrer, R., Rahli, V., Vukotic, I., Völp, M., Platzer, A.: Formally verified differential dynamic logic. In: Bertot, Y., Vafeiadis, V. (eds.) Certified Programs and Proofs - 6th ACM SIGPLAN Conference, CPP 2017, Paris, France, 16–17 January 2017, pp. 208–221. ACM (2017). https://doi.org/10.1145/3018610.3018616
3. Bohrer, R., Tan, Y.K., Mitsch, S., Myreen, M.O., Platzer, A.: VeriPhy: verified controller executables from verified cyber-physical system models. In: Grossman, D. (ed.) PLDI, pp. 617–630. ACM, Philadelphia (2018). https://doi.org/10.1145/3192366.3192406
4. Buhagiar, A.J., Freitas, L., III, W.E.S., Larsen, P.G.: Digital twins for organ preservation devices. In: Margaria, T., Steffen, B. (eds.) ISoLA 2022, Part IV. LNCS, vol. 13704, pp. 22–36. Springer, Cham (2022). https://doi.org/10.1007/978-3-031-19762-8_3

5. Cengel, Y.A., Boles, M.A., Kanoğlu, M.: Thermodynamics: An Engineering Approach, vol. 5. McGraw-Hill, New York (2011)

6. Drgoňa, J., et al.: All you need to know about model predictive control for buildings. Annu. Rev. Control. **50**, 190–232 (2020). https://doi.org/10.1016/j.arcontrol.2020.09.001

7. Feng, H., Gomes, C., Thule, C., Lausdahl, K., Sandberg, M., Larsen, P.G.: The incubator case study for digital twin engineering (2021). https://arxiv.org/abs/2102.10390

8. Feng, H., Gomes, C., Larsen, P.G.: Model-based monitoring and state estimation for digital twins: the Kalman filter (2023). https://arxiv.org/abs/2305.00252

9. Frahm, M., Langner, F., Zwickel, P., Matthes, J., Mikut, R., Hagenmeyer, V.: How to derive and implement a minimalistic RC model from thermodynamics for the control of thermal parameters for assuring thermal comfort in buildings. In: 2022 Open Source Modelling and Simulation of Energy Systems (OSMSES), pp. 1–6. IEEE, Aachen, Germany (2022). https://doi.org/10.1109/osmses54027.2022.9769134

10. Fulton, N., Mitsch, S., Quesel, J.-D., Völp, M., Platzer, A.: KeYmaera X: an axiomatic tactical theorem prover for hybrid systems. In: Felty, A.P., Middeldorp, A. (eds.) CADE 2015. LNCS (LNAI), vol. 9195, pp. 527–538. Springer, Cham (2015). https://doi.org/10.1007/978-3-319-21401-6_36

11. Garcia, L., Mitsch, S., Platzer, A.: HyPLC: hybrid programmable logic controller program translation for verification. In: Bushnell, L., Pajic, M. (eds.) ICCPS, pp. 47–56 (2019). https://doi.org/10.1145/3302509.3311036

12. Isasa, C., Abou El Wafa, N., Platzer, A., Larsen, P.G., Gomes, C.: Artifact for Safe Temperature Regulation: Formally Verified and Real-World Validated. https://doi.org/10.6084/m9.figshare.28869218

13. Jeannin, J., et al.: Formal verification of ACAS X, an industrial airborne collision avoidance system. In: Girault, A., Guan, N. (eds.) EMSOFT, pp. 127–136. IEEE Press, Amsterdam, Netherlands (2015). https://doi.org/10.1109/EMSOFT.2015.7318268

14. Kabra, A., Mitsch, S., Platzer, A.: Verified train controllers for the federal railroad administration train kinematics model: balancing competing brake and track forces. IEEE Trans. Comput. Aided Des. Integr. Circuits Syst. **41**(11), 4409–4420 (2022). https://doi.org/10.1109/TCAD.2022.3197690

15. Kapuria, A., Cole, D.G.: Formal verification of a nuclear plant thermal dispatch operation using system decomposition. In: 2024 IEEE 6th International Conference on Trust, Privacy and Security in Intelligent Systems, and Applications (TPS-ISA), pp. 543–548 (2024). https://doi.org/10.1109/TPS-ISA62245.2024.00074

16. Liu, J., Lv, J., Quan, Z., Zhan, N., Zhao, H., Zhou, C., Zou, L.: A calculus for hybrid CSP. In: Ueda, K. (ed.) APLAS 2010. LNCS, vol. 6461, pp. 1–15. Springer, Heidelberg (2010). https://doi.org/10.1007/978-3-642-17164-2_1

17. Mitsch, S., Platzer, A.: ModelPlex: verified runtime validation of verified cyber-physical system models. Formal Methods Syst. Des. 33–74 (2016). https://doi.org/10.1007/s10703-016-0241-z

18. Platzer, A.: Logical Foundations of Cyber-Physical Systems. Springer, Cham (2018). https://doi.org/10.1007/978-3-319-63588-0

19. Platzer, A., Quesel, J.-D.: European train control system: a case study in formal verification. In: Breitman, K., Cavalcanti, A. (eds.) ICFEM 2009. LNCS, vol. 5885, pp. 246–265. Springer, Heidelberg (2009). https://doi.org/10.1007/978-3-642-10373-5_13

20. Platzer, A., Tan, Y.K.: Differential equation invariance axiomatization. J. ACM **67**(1), 6:1–6:66 (2020). https://doi.org/10.1145/3380825
21. Serway, R.A., Faughn, J.S.: College Physics, 5th edn. Saunders College Publishing, Philadelphia (1999)
22. Sogokon, A., Mitsch, S., Tan, Y.K., Cordwell, K., Platzer, A.: Pegasus: a framework for sound continuous invariant generation. In: ter Beek, M.H., McIver, A., Oliveira, J.N. (eds.) FM 2019. LNCS, vol. 11800, pp. 138–157. Springer, Cham (2019). https://doi.org/10.1007/978-3-030-30942-8_10
23. Tan, Y.K., Mitsch, S., Platzer, A.: Verifying switched system stability with logic. In: Proceedings of the 25th ACM International Conference on Hybrid Systems: Computation and Control. HSCC 2022. Association for Computing Machinery, New York (2022). https://doi.org/10.1145/3501710.3519541
24. Wright, T., Gomes, C., Woodcock, J.: Formally verified self-adaptation of an incubator digital twin. In: Margaria, T., Steffen, B. (eds.) ISoLA 2022, Part IV. LNCS, vol. 13704, pp. 89–109. Springer, Cham (2022). https://doi.org/10.1007/978-3-031-19762-8_7
25. Zou, L., et al.: Verifying Chinese train control system under a combined scenario by theorem proving. In: Cohen, E., Rybalchenko, A. (eds.) VSTTE 2013. LNCS, vol. 8164, pp. 262–280. Springer, Heidelberg (2014). https://doi.org/10.1007/978-3-642-54108-7_14

Online Model Checking for Anomaly Detection in Industrial Control Systems

Douglas Fraser, Alice Miller(✉), Marco Cook, and Dimitrios Pezaros

University of Glasgow, Glasgow G12 8QQ, UK
`alice.miller@glasgow.ac.uk`

Abstract. Cyber attacks on Industrial Control Systems (ICSs) are becoming increasingly sophisticated, undermining the ability of these systems to manage critical processes and compromising the availability of key public infrastructure. Detecting system anomalies is an important element in the identification of cyber attacks, allowing the rapid deployment of crucial incident-response activities. In this paper, we introduce a novel anomaly detection approach that integrates SPIN model checking into ICS environments to detect anomalies in live system data. Our approach uses the application code extracted from Programmable Logic Controllers (PLCs) to generate the dynamic system model, requiring only a small amount of test data to validate their design. We evaluate our approach by generating models using a representative physical hydroelectric dam testbed containing real PLCs. These models are used to analyse synthetic data containing potential irregularities that could occur within the dam as a result of false data injection attacks. Our approach was shown to identify anomalies and verify normal system behaviour. Our evaluation shows that the models achieved high performance while maintaining explainability and delivering metrics of 99.99% precision, 99.05% recall, a 99.52% F1-score, and 99.05% accuracy.

Keywords: Industrial control systems · model checking · Promela · SPIN · anomaly detection · cyber security

1 Introduction

Industrial Control Systems (ICSs) underpin the operation of critical national infrastructure, including energy generation and distribution, chemical processing, water and wastewater management, telecommunications and defence. These systems perform a fundamental role in sustaining daily life, economic stability, and national security. However, as the operational technology (OT) used in ICSs becomes increasingly interconnected and digitised, these systems face a growing number of cyber threats that can disrupt operations, compromise safety, and cause significant financial damage [26]. Faced with increasingly sophisticated attacks targeting these critical systems, their safeguarding requires the development of innovative measures that can detect and mitigate potential intrusions without compromising their performance and reliability [7].

F. Damiani and M. Farrell (Eds.): iFM 2025, LNCS 16194, pp. 162–181, 2026.
https://doi.org/10.1007/978-3-032-10794-7_9

Statistical anomaly detection is the process of identifying device behaviours inconsistent with the system's regular operation [8]. These behaviours can occur either from a software bug or hardware fault, or through the malicious intervention of an attacker. When an anomaly is detected, an investigation must be conducted to determine the source of the anomalous behaviour and engage necessary mitigation strategies.

In this paper, we introduce a novel approach using model checking to validate industrial system behaviour through live process data. We use Promela [18] to represent a physical hydroelectric dam testbed. Our system comprises multiple co-executing devices, including real Programmable Logic Controllers (PLCs) and a Human Machine Interface (HMI) through which an operator provides commands to the system. Promela was chosen because it is designed to model concurrent processes and analyse their interactions. Using a Promela model allows us to specify all system components directly based on the logic of the executable code written to the PLCs. Using SPIN, the behaviours of all the components can be combined to define the complete set of reachable system states. This allows the model to extrapolate to unseen behaviours, reducing the requirement for extensive system baselining before deployment as system data is only required to test the created models. In addition, this approach is not limited to detecting known anomalies. We only need to specify the types of behaviour the system is programmed to perform and any deviations from that will be detected by the system.

Our main contributions are:

- An illustration of how PLC code can be formalised into Promela models for system validation.
- A method of integrating the SPIN model checker into a physical ICS environment, enabling it to perform validation on live system data.
- An evaluation of the effectiveness of our approach on live industrial system data from a physical hydroelectric dam testbed.

2   Related Work

The effectiveness of an Intrusion Detection System (IDS) can be assessed by comparing its classifications against a known ground truth. The primary evaluation metrics include false positives (incorrectly flagging benign activity as an intrusion) and false negatives (failing to detect an actual intrusion). Alongside true positives (correctly detected intrusions) and true negatives (correctly classified benign activity), these values are used to compute key performance indicators such as accuracy and F-score [9,34].

There are three main categories of intrusion detection methods, namely signature-based detection, statistical anomaly detection, and specification-based detection [16,24,27]. Signature-based detection methods search for known attack patterns in system behaviours [24]. Statistical anomaly-detection methods identify statistically significant deviations from normal system data as intrusions [3].

Specification-based detection uses a description of normal behaviour and identifies deviations from that as anomalies [20,24,29]. While each approach has its benefits and drawbacks, specification-based approaches are considered among the most reliable of the three categories [36]. They provide fewer false negatives than anomaly detection techniques while still being able to detect novel attacks, unlike signature-based methods [29]. Model checking, by its nature, is a specification-based approach that generates a model of a system containing a comprehensive representation of all system behaviours. Theoretically, any deviation from these behaviours can be identified as an anomaly. This approach, however, requires some level of abstraction in order for the model checker to be able to analyse the model within an acceptable period of time.

Several approaches use software validation through model checking to detect intrusions. In [15], the methodology developed in [1,13] was used to represent PLC code using UPPAAL. It was proposed that this representation of the operational PLC code could be compared to a trusted ground truth PLC program to detect modifications to the code and flag them as intrusions. This approach serves as a useful method of validating that the software in operation has not been tampered with. While program hashing could provide a similar function to this, most PLCs lack the computational power to generate program hashes [38]. Software validation methods will not be able to detect an attack that originates from the network outside the PLC [11], driving the need for a more active means of monitoring the operation of these devices.

Tracking the internal state or operating conditions of control systems is a common method of detecting anomalies and facilitating attack identification. In [12], an approach is proposed for fingerprinting PLC memory snapshots that are then analysed with machine learning. This was able to support the classification of attacks targeting PLCs through correlations between memory usage and PLC application code. Another approach uses state machine-based system design specification to detect intrusions in safety-critical medical environments via peer-to-peer monitoring [28]. It uses behaviour rules, threat models and defined attack states to distinguish attacks from bugs, reducing false positives.

Specification-based detection methods at a network-level have also been developed. The approach used in [6], originally developed for mobile networks in [33], describes a network-based detection method that analyses network packets to detect values outside the constraints of normal operation.

Our approach differs from existing methods in that it uses formal specifications of individual component behaviours to derive the reachable behaviours of the overall system, from which anomalies can be detected. We utilise memoisation and multithreading to enhance the performance of our approach, enabling it to be directly integrated with standard SCADA components during system operation.

3   Background

The Promela specification language [14] is used to describe the behaviour of concurrent processes. The SPIN model checker [17] allows the analysis of models constructed from these specifications. In this section, we use a minimal example to demonstrate the basic features of Promela that we use in our models and how SPIN is used to check properties expressed in Linear Time Temporal Logic (LTL).

There are many other model checking approaches that can be applied to modelling ICSs; however, all come with strengths and weaknesses that must be considered. UPPAAL [5,23] is a tool for modelling real-time systems as a network of timed automata, enabling it to represent the passage of time within the system. It is well-suited to the domains of real-time systems and has demonstrated applications in ICS environments [15,31,37]. However, it is less suited to the domain of concurrent systems, and for our purposes, we are primarily interested in the sequences of data exchanges instead of the time taken to perform them. The desire to examine the outcomes of the concurrent operation of ICS components motivated our decision to use Promela and SPIN. NuSMV [10] is a symbolic model checker based upon Binary Decision Diagrams (BDDs) [4]. Systems are specified as Kripke structures to represent finite state machines. Each process can be specified as a module consisting of variables using basic datatypes that can be modified during transitions. NuSMV [10] also provides a viable method of specifying a network of finite state machines that can be applied to represent ICS [21], where it has been used to verify the safety of PLC programs [22,32]. We used Promela/SPIN rather than NuSMV due to its more expansive data type system, combined with the ability to incorporate synchronous and asynchronous channels for interprocess communication.

In Promela, each process in the modelled system is represented via a `proctype` statement. Data types include integers, booleans and an enumerated type (`mtype`). Flow is controlled in various ways including: labels and `goto` statements, `if...fi` statements (in which a single executable statement is selected non-deterministically and executed) and `do...od` statements (which are similar, but statements are continuously selected until the loop is exited via, for example, a `goto` or `break` statement). Other features, such as communication via channels, are omitted here as we do not use them in our models. Note that although the use of the `goto` statement is often considered inelegant in other programming languages, in Promela it provides a natural way to express transitions in the underlying transition system and is therefore commonly used in specifications.

Consider the simple Promela example shown in Fig. 1. There are two processes, A and B which are defined to be `active`, i.e., initiated instantly. Process A executes its `if...fi` statement, choosing a statement for which the guard evaluates to `true`, repeating the process (as directed by the goto statement), until exiting, when and if the third statement is chosen, and proceeding to the `end` label. Process B simply executes its single statement and exits.

SPIN allows us to analyse the interleaving behaviour of the two processes using LTL. Suppose we were to naively assume that whenever a is equal to 3 and b is equal to 2 then `flag` is true. This property is expressed using the LTL property included in Fig. 1. LTL properties have an implicit *for all paths* operator, and the operator $\Box$ denotes *for all states*. So, the LTL property asserts that "for all paths, in every state, q is true" (where q is defined appropriately). SPIN checks all paths arising from the interleaved behaviour of A and B and returns an error path, i.e., a path for which q becomes false, as a counter-example, if there is one. An example here is one in which a is set to 3 and b set to 2 before `flag` is set to true.

It is possible to limit interleaving behaviour via the use of `atomic` and `d_step` statements which both prevent sequences of statements from being interrupted by another process unless the sequence is blocked. A `d_step` has the additional advantage that intermediate states are not visible to the LTL property. Were we to enclose the two statements in the final choice of the `if...fi` statement in our example within a `d_step`, our LTL property would now be true, as the flag would be set to `true` when a is set to 3.

```
1   byte a = 1; byte b = 1;
2   bool flag = false;
3   active proctype A(){
4       label1:
5       if
6       ::a==1 -> a=2
7       ::a==2 -> a=1
8       ::a=3; flag= true; goto end
9       fi;
10      goto label1;
11      end: skip
12  }
13  active proctype B(){b = 2;}
14
15  #define q ((a==3 && b==2) -> flag==true)
16  ltl property1 {[] q}
17  }
```

Fig. 1. A simple Promela example containing two processes and one global variable.

Because LTL properties apply to all paths, they cannot be used to express existential properties (i.e., of the form *for some path* ϕ, for a proposition ϕ). However, we can identify such a path by finding a counterexample to the negation of the property, i.e. $\Box!\phi$ (for all paths ϕ is never true).

Another process that we use in this paper arises from the fact that we generate models, in close to real time, from templates populated with observed data. For large SPIN models, compiling the Promela specification into the associated *state-space* can take several seconds, or even minutes. As it is likely that the same models will arise repeatedly, we use a process known as memoisation. This is a software optimisation technique that is used to speed up computer programs by storing the results of time-consuming or frequent function calls. We use it to store the results of calls to the SPIN model checker with an encoding of the variables in the system snapshot. This creates a look-up table of system states that have already been checked by the model checker since the system was initialised. Before analysing a new snapshot, our system first checks this table of memoised results; if a match is found, it instead returns the precomputed result without compiling and analysing a new model with SPIN. A similar approach (also using SPIN) was used in [25] when planning overtaking manoeuvres for autonomous vehicles.

4   Approach

In this section, we describe our overall method, including the design and integration of models into the ICS environment.

4.1   Development and Use of Models

Our method uses two Promela models derived from PLC ladder logic to identify anomalies in received system data using the SPIN model checker. SPIN was chosen as it is well-suited to analysing environments with multiple collaborating systems. The use of LTL properties allows us to efficiently hone in on paths of interest. The behaviour that we are interested in is temporal: specifically that two states are not only reachable, but one follows from the other within a defined number of operations (so use of, say a SAT solver, would not be sufficient).

While we do not discuss the specifics of ladder logic programming due to space constraints, in Sect. 4.2 we outline how we construct a Promela representation from the PLC code. We use a historian to collect system data from control systems. This data is then inserted into template versions of our Promela models to check system behaviour with the SPIN model checker, as shown in Fig. 2. Each time a new system snapshot is gathered, the placeholder values are updated to produce new instances of the models. If the state is not recognised in either model, an anomaly is flagged.

Our approach primarily analyses the state of the discrete variables within the ICS; analogue variables, such as measurements or timers, are either abstracted or discretised into intervals. Given two consecutive snapshots of state data our objective is to validate if each of the states contains valid system configurations and if the system can move from one state to the other within the elapsed time between snapshots. We validate the system state data observed in state snapshots using an inductive approach that splits this larger problem into two smaller problems with smaller search spaces. We use one model to check the validity of the state configurations and another to check the transitions between states; we respectively refer to these models as the *trunk* and *branch* models to reflect the tree structure of the possible system execution paths. The purpose of the trunk model is to validate whether an observed state is reachable via any valid execution trace from system initialisation. The branch model complements this by evaluating whether there is a valid sequence of actions that can occur within the time between snapshots that can transition the system between two observed states. Figure 3 shows how, given two states $S1$ and $S2$ that have been

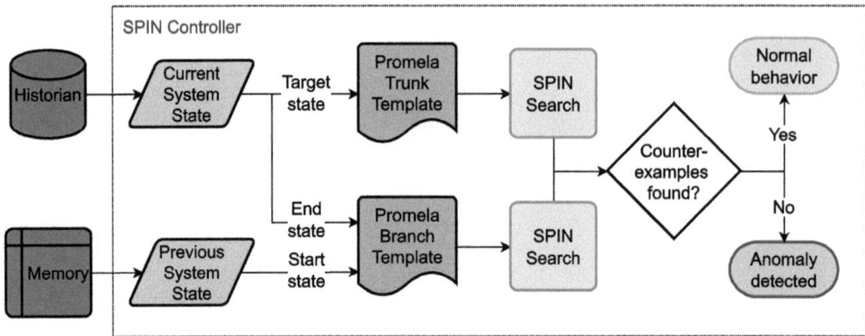

Fig. 2. The proposed approach inserts system state data into templates of the trunk and branch models. The instantiated models are then analysed by SPIN to identify anomalies.

observed to occur in sequence, the two models combine to search the tree of possible system executions. If a single large model were to be analysed, this would require searching the whole search tree for each occurrence of $S1$ and then continuing to search to see if $S2$ could occur within a specified window. To detect this behaviour would require a property of the form:

$$\Box\,(S_1 \rightarrow (\neg X S_2 \wedge \neg X(X S_2)))$$

Since SPIN has no built-in representation of time we use transitions (denoted using the **next-time** operator, X) to approximate how many changes the system can undergo between snapshots. This property translates to: *it is always the case that if S1 occurs, S2 does not occur within the next two transitions.* A counter-example would therefore consist of a trail where $S1$ occurs, followed by $S2$ within two actions. We note that, although the **next-time** operator is permitted, its use in SPIN is discouraged because interleaving process behaviour can make it difficult to ascertain what the *next* state actually represents. It also invalidates the use of the (extremely efficient) *partial order reduction* [19] optimisation method. We therefore want to avoid this operator.

Dividing this task into two sub-problems significantly reduces the search space. In each case, the property becomes a simple reachability property: $\neg\Diamond S_i$, i.e. *state S_i is never eventually reached.* The SPIN search of the trunk model can therefore terminate once it identifies the first matching $S1$ state without needing to search each for a subsequent occurrence of $S2$ since this is handled by the branch model that uses the assumption that $S1$ is reachable to reduce the search space. If SPIN fails to find such a state/transition (i.e., fails to find a counterexample path containing it, see Sect. 3) in either model, the system is deemed to be behaving anomalously.

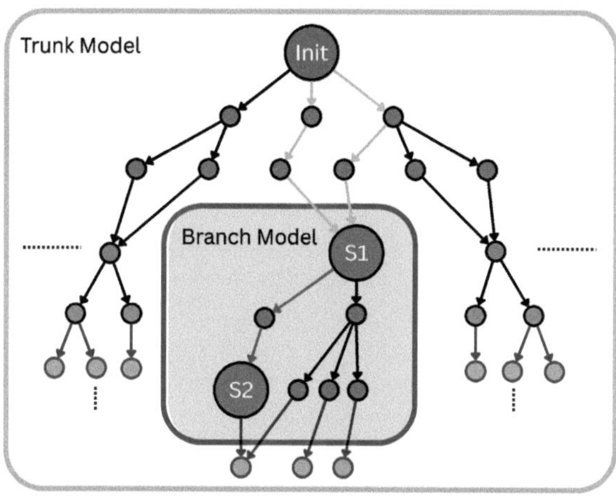

Fig. 3. Demonstration of how the trunk and branch models combine to validate system behaviour. $S1$ is the previous snapshot that was gathered from the system. $S2$ is the most recently collected system snapshot. The trunk model validates that S1 is a valid state, then the transition between $S1$ and $S2$ is validated using the branch model.

4.2   Modelling PLC Code in Promela

Our process for create template Promela models from PLC ladder logic is shown in Fig. 4. Translating PLC instructions to Promela comes with the challenge of capturing the simultaneous execution of the PLC instructions within the bounds of a sequential Promela program. This simultaneous assignment can be achieved through the appropriate use of `d_step` operations (see Sect. 3). Our design approach, therefore, is to perform the logical computations of the rung and then write the outcome as a single `d_step` operation.

Both models begin by identifying which of the rungs are active through an `if...fi` statement. This determines the subsequent direction of control.

When constructing our representations of the PLC, a key objective is to reduce the number of operations required to execute a piece of control logic.

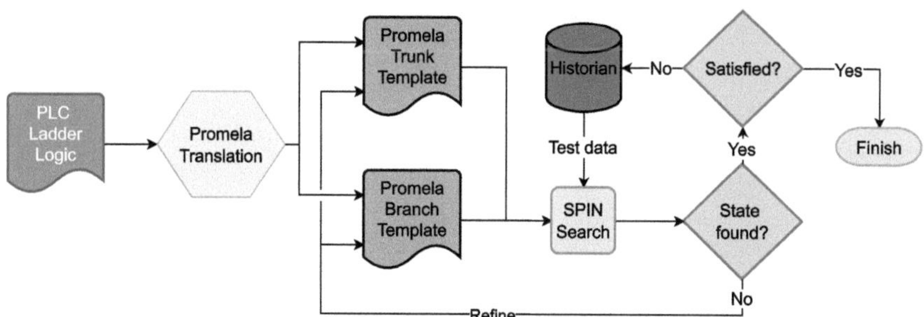

Fig. 4. The process used to translate ladder logic code to Promela models. Test data is used to check the performance of the models, ensuring that the system's behaviours are well understood and accurately represented before deployment.

While a PLC can execute the rungs of its ladder logic code multiple times a second, our SPIN representation cannot afford to perform the same number of actions. It is, therefore, essential to focus on the key behavioural changes that the code performs. In our trunk model, we include a discretised representation of continuous variables, such as timers, to reduce the size of the state space. While this comes at the cost of fidelity, it allows for the creation of a trunk model that captures control logic associated with continuous variables. In contrast, the branch model uses fully non-deterministic transitions between states to represent timers, as the historian does not gather timer data.

The objective of the branch model is to identify valid system states that are inconsistent with recently observed system behaviour. Whereas in the trunk model all possible sequences of execution exist, the branch model allows only a small number of state changes to occur after the initial state has been identified. By restricting the transitions that can occur in the model, we can identify dramatic changes in system behaviour that cannot occur between system snapshots.

4.3 Model Checking Integration

Establishing the true operating state of a system from data originating from multiple controllers requires aligning the state data from each source based on timestamps. Our approach collates received data to create snapshots of the overall system state. We use integration code written in Python 3 to connect to the Influx database. Our model checking integration follows a main operation loop that pulls new PLC data from the database. These data readings are then synchronised into state snapshots, which are translated from their binary values into a numerical representation and sent to worker threads for analysis with SPIN. We use a thread-safe queue to store these values until the worker threads are available to process them. Once a value is received by a worker, the thread checks if the value has been previously processed and, if so, returns the previously computed result. Otherwise, the thread extracts the state variable values and embeds them in the template Promela models. This is done by finding and replacing placeholder values used in initial variable assignments and the reachability properties within the model files. The models are then compiled and executed in a separate working directory for each thread using the subprocess Python module[1] to run SPIN and parse the output for the presence of counterexamples. If SPIN identifies a counterexample for both models, then the state data is considered normal. If SPIN cannot find a counterexample for one or both of the models, then a warning is raised to the user, alerting them that the system is behaving abnormally. The process of gathering data and analysing it with SPIN is performed automatically and continuously while the hydroelectric dam is in operation.

During each execution loop, our system pulls all data collected during the last second. The task is then to combine these collected datasets into a complete view of the system that can be inserted into the Promela models. We achieve

---

[1] https://docs.python.org/3/library/subprocess.html

this through a two-step process of merging and then sorting. We first combine measurements from different devices by those that have the closest timestamps to create a single combined dataset of candidate snapshots. We then evaluate these candidate snapshots using an appropriate score function to identify the best snapshots to use for our analysis.

5   Case Study: Hydroelectric Dam

We demonstrate our approach on a hydroelectric testbed constructed as part of the Glasgow Renewable Electrical Energy Security (GREENS) testbed at the University of Glasgow. The testbed is representative of a pumped-storage hydroelectric dam [30], a type of dam that operates as a large-scale electric battery using water to store electricity when demand is lower. The hydroelectric dam testbed is a scaled-down representative test environment containing the OT devices and networks used in industrial pumped-storage hydroelectric dams.

Figure 5 shows the testbed architecture with the two PLCs that control the testbed's operation. The generator PLC controls the normal water movement from the upper tank through two generator turbines to the lower tank. Within each penstock, the generator PLC controls the upper tank release valve and receives data from the flow rate sensor. In each turbine enclosure, the generator PLC controls the pump that pushes the water through the turbine (a requirement due to the small scale of the testbed) while receiving the turbine's voltage output and monitoring the temperature within the turbine enclosure. If the temperature in an enclosure increases too much, the PLC activates the appropriate cooling fan to reduce it. The control PLC manages the movement of water from the lower tank back up to the upper tank. The control PLC maintains the water levels between the two tanks and modifies its behaviour to increase the rate at which water is returned depending upon how many generators are active. When water is to be returned, the value on the lower tank is released, and the two sump pumps are activated to push the water up to the upper tank. Additionally, if the water level in the upper tank becomes too high, the control PLC can release an additional outflow valve in the upper tank, allowing water to be returned to the lower tank through the flood pipe.

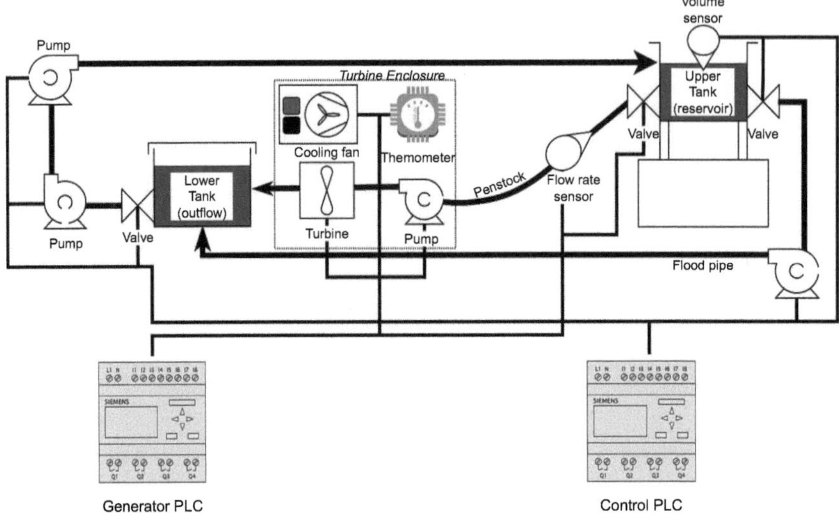

Fig. 5. System design of University of Glasgow GREENS hydroelectric dam.

We retrieve physical measurement data from the dam through a historian that gathers and collates data from the PLCs to monitor performance. Data is pulled approximately every 100 ms from the PLCs using GET requests in the S7 Communication protocol [2]. The retrieved data is then transformed into a JSON object that is then sent to and stored in InfluxDB.

A simplified excerpt of the Promela code for the trunk model of the dam is shown in Fig. 6. First, the state of the PLC controlling the generator is identified. Then control is directed to the appropriate label where variables are updated. A transition system for one of the PLCs in the finished branch model, with some branches and states removed for clarity, is shown in Fig. 7. In any trace through the diagram the generator can only change state once between system snapshots (i.e., during transitions originating from $S33$, $S48$ and $S90$). Since the system is operator-driven, we defined the number of transitions that can occur between snapshots on how quickly the operator can send commands using the HMI. Through testing, we concluded that an operator can interact with the system up to two times in the 800 ms between snapshots. These changes are initiated through a separate concurrent process that models our operator modifying the operational mode of either PLC or the values of **Gen_A_Active** and **Gen_B_Active**. Full Promela models of the hydroelectric dam (along with files used in the evaluation) are available from our online repository[2].

---

[2] https://doi.org/10.5281/zenodo.16811853.

```
 1  if
 2       /* Identify the combination of rungs to be executed */
 3       :: Gen_B_Active == true -> goto Generator_B_Control
 4       ...
 5  fi;
 6  ...
 7  /* Execute outcome */
 8  Generator_B_Control: skip
 9  d_step {
10      Gen_B_Valve = true;
11      Gen_B_Pump = true;
12      Gen_B_GreenLED = true;
13      Gen_B_RedLED = false;
14  }
```

Fig. 6. A simplified excerpt from the trunk PLC model in Promela, illustrating how a generator turbine is represented.

6   Evaluation

We tested how reliably our approach can identify anomalous system states from baseline states by repeatedly running the SPIN models in an isolated test environment to simulate the collection of different sets of system data.

A state consists of 23 binary variables yielding 2^{23} possible state variations and 2^{46} possible transitions between those states. Testing all of these is infeasible, so we use a more selective approach to create a set of test states that are closest to the baseline states observed during testing. Assuming that subtle variations of normal behaviours are where errors are most likely to be found, we test our approach on states that are slightly modified from baseline states. If the models can identify small behaviour changes, larger changes will also be identified.

We evaluate a set of states for the trunk model and a set of transitions for the branch model. Trunk model evaluation utilised variations of baseline states, where up to 4 of the 23 state bits were modified from their original values. This results in a set of $122,216$ previously unobserved test states. The exponential increase in size means that it is not viable to evaluate sets with a larger number of deviations. A subset of these states was then used to generate transitions between states to evaluate the branch model. The breakdown of the pairings in this test transition dataset is shown in Table 1. This includes states with 1 and 2-bit modifications, and all false negatives from the trunk model evaluation. It also contains 1054 fabricated transitions between baseline states. Transitions beginning and ending in 1 and 2-bit modified states that had already been detected by our trunk model were not included.

We evaluate each model's performance by how often it is correct. We classify the results of our evaluation into one of the four categories described in Sect. 2: true positive, false positive, true negative and false negative.

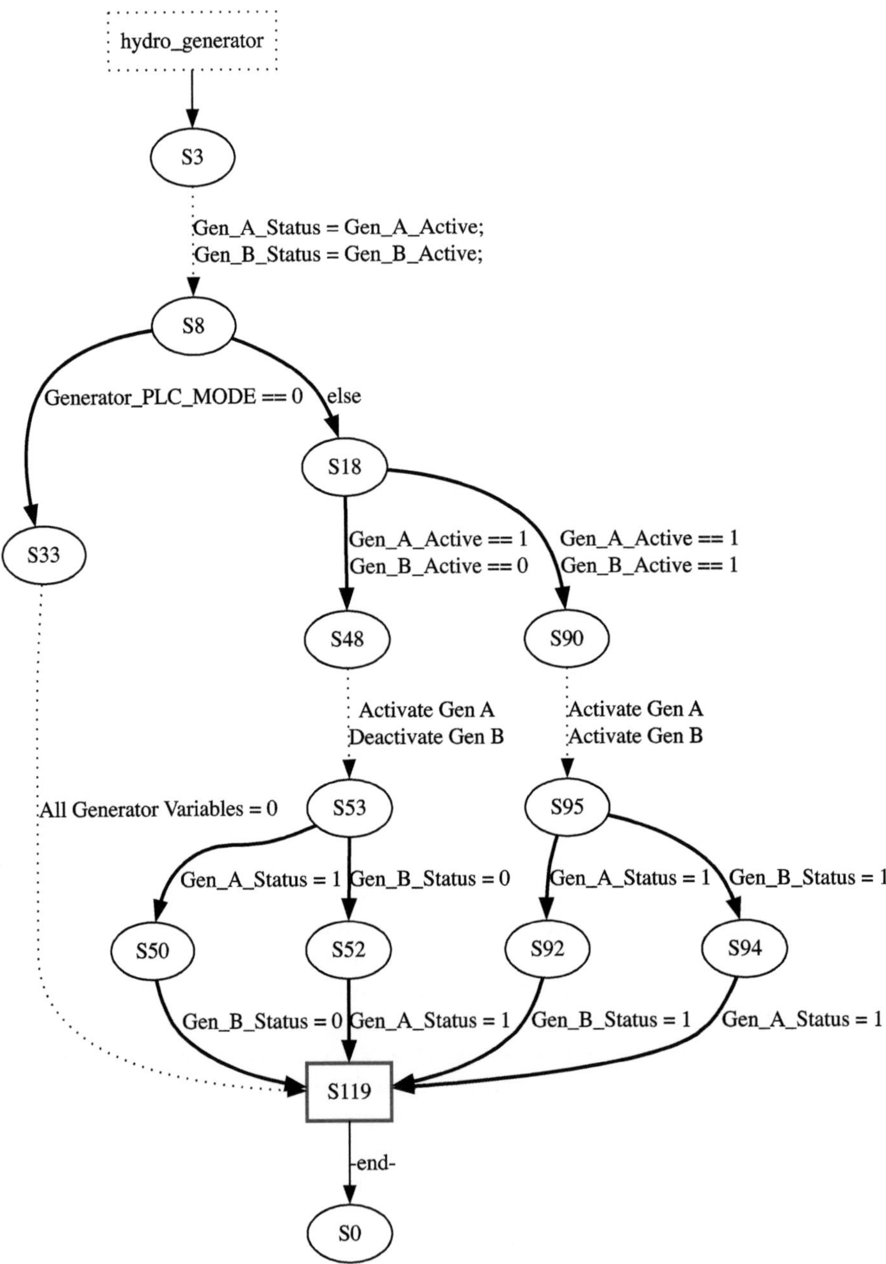

Fig. 7. A state transition diagram of the generator PLC modelled within the branch model. The model specifies behaviour changes, not the entire state space. Some additional states and branches have been omitted for readability.

Table 1. Table showing the composition of the test transitions set, summing to 558,038. Trunk false negatives consist of the states that were not flagged during the evaluation of the trunk model.

Start Set	End Set	Number of Transitions
Baseline	Baseline	1054
Baseline	Trunk false negatives	1768
Trunk false negatives	Baseline	1768
Trunk false negatives	Trunk false negatives	2704
Baseline	1-bit modified	9214
1-bit modified	Baseline	9214
Baseline	2-bits modified	99654
2-bits modified	Baseline	99654
Trunk false negatives	1-bit modified	14092
1-bit Modified	Trunk false negatives	14092
Trunk false negatives	2-bits modified	152412
2-bits modified	Trunk false negatives	152412

Table 2. Summary of the classification results for the individual trunk and branch models evaluations, along with totals for when the models are used together.

Model	True Positives	False Positives	True Negatives	False Negatives
Trunk	121,530	0	34	52
Branch	405,416	1	101	152,622
Combined	552,712	1	101	5,326

The false negative states from the trunk model evaluation were included in our evaluation of the branch model. Our branch model performed well at identifying invalid end-states when the initial state is valid, with 99.55% accuracy. When used alone, the branch model struggles to detect transitions from an invalid initial state to a valid end state with an accuracy of 51.55%. However, the branch model is designed to be used alongside the trunk model, so it is not designed to verify the validity of the initial state before beginning its search.

One transition from our set of baseline states was not recognised by the branch model. It arises as a result of unexpected pathological behaviour by an operator turning the generators rapidly on, off and on again. This contravenes our assumption that the operator can only perform two actions in the time taken to gather new data. It may be better to modify the model to allow three operator actions to occur, so that it can recognise this type of activity as normal. However, our assumption that an operator should only perform two actions per transition seems reasonable. It may be better for the system to flag this type of behaviour to ensure that operators are aware of its occurrence.

The objective of the branch model is to identify invalid transitions between valid states. Such a transition would indicate a rapid change in behaviour that is inconsistent with the regular operation of the system, even if it starts and ends with the system in a normal operating state. Of the 1054 fabricated baseline states, 250 were identified as anomalous, with 804 false negatives. Similar to the explanation for false negatives in the trunk model, this could be because these transitions are possible in the dam and have not been observed in testing. There are relatively few inputs that the operator can provide to modify the system state, and the length of the system's operational loop is short in terms of the number of distinct states involved. Therefore, it is likely that a significant number of these transitions can indeed occur with only two actions on the operator's part. This type of branch model may, therefore, perform better in an environment with a longer loop of system behaviours where the process proceeds through a sequence of stages.

7   Discussion

The results of our evaluation show that the two models complement each other. The trunk model detects many of the anomalous states involved in the transitions that the branch model does not detect. This means that despite the transition being recognised by the branch model, the trunk model will ensure that the behaviour is flagged as anomalous. In this way, the trunk model mitigates the relative weakness of the branch model for this type of transition. Conversely, the branch model can improve the performance of using the trunk model alone by identifying 1,968 transitions between states that the trunk model incorrectly recognises as normal operational states.

A summary table of the results of the two models and their combined performance is provided in Table 2. We use these values to calculate the precision, recall, accuracy and F1-score of each model and the two models combined to contextualise performance. These are metrics commonly used in the evaluation of classification systems, particularly in the field of machine learning. The computed metrics are presented in Table 3.

Table 3. Individual precision, recall, F-score and accuracy scores for trunk and branch models when used individually and when used together.

Category	Precision	Recall	F1-Score	Accuracy
Trunk	100%	99.96%	99.98%	99.96%
Branch	99.9998%	72.65%	84.15%	72.66%
Combined	99.9998%	99.05%	99.52%	99.05%

Precision measures the ratio of true positives to all positives, signifying how reliably a positive result identifies a true anomaly. Our approach scores close to 100%. Recall measures how many tested anomalies were correctly flagged as anomalies. The trunk model also performs extremely well in this regard, scoring almost 100%. The branch model scores less well, 72.65%, even though it correctly identified a large number of anomalies, it also allowed a large number of anomaly transitions to pass without being identified.

F1-score and accuracy are both metrics used to evaluate the overall performance of the classifier, considering each of the four outputs. Accuracy measures correct classifications (true positives and true negatives) and is reliable in balanced datasets but skewed in imbalanced ones, like ours, where 99% of states are anomalous. A model predicting anomalies 100% of the time would still score 99% accuracy, making alternative metrics more suitable. The trunk and combined models achieve high accuracy (99.96% and 99.05%), while the branch model scores lower (72.66%) due to false negatives. F1-score is a metric derived from precision and recall. It balances false positives and false negatives, assigning equal weight to both to provide a more reliable performance indicator for imbalanced datasets where distinguishing true negatives from anomalies is critical. The very high scores for the trunk model and the combination of both models (99.98% and 99.52%) reflect a strong indicator of the ability of our approach in these configurations to correctly classify the behaviours of the dam.

7.1   Operational Usage

The analysis performed by SPIN could not initially keep up with the rate at which data were retrieved from the system without modifications. Two enhancements to our design were used to mitigate this to an acceptable level. Firstly, a multithreaded approach was implemented where the retrieved states were pushed to a thread-safe queue to be processed by worker threads. Each worker thread can access a model template in its own working directory, embedding the state values before compiling the model and executing SPIN. This enabled an average search time of 7.9 s for the trunk model and 2.4 s for the branch model. The difference in these times is due to the increased complexity and scope of the trunk model. For each snapshot received, we search the trunk model first, then check the branch model for the transition from the previous snapshot to the new snapshot. During our testing, it took a worker thread an average of 10.3 s to complete both of these actions.

The key enabler of our approach is the use of memoisation optimisation techniques (see Sect. 3). This significantly reduces the computational load of our approach during operation. We use two Pandas DataFrames as memoisation tables that store the returned results from the worker threads. Initially, these tables are empty, and the rate at which new states are observed outpaces the speed at which SPIN can process them. As system data is received, numerical values encoding the binary values of state variables are stored in a multi-consumer queue for processing. This means new data must wait until any previous system data has been checked, leading to a delay in response but not the absence of a response. As the worker threads process the observed states and append their computed results to the memoisation tables, the system stabilises, and model checking searches are then only executed for previously unobserved data.

The performance of our model can be further improved by continuing the iterative refinement process shown in Fig. 4. The misclassified states can be used to identify flaws in the representation of the system. However, these changes should be made once it has been confirmed whether the identified states are anomalous or intended behaviours. It may be that they have not been observed in testing but are theoretically possible in practice, prompting a discussion about whether or not this behaviour is intended. Therefore, refinements to the model should be made jointly with the designers of the underlying system being modelled, who can determine the true nature of identified anomalies.

8   Conclusion

We have developed a specification-based approach for validating the behaviour of PLCs within an OT environment based on their code. We show how logical representations of PLC behaviours are derived from ladder logic code. We have demonstrated how SPIN can be integrated into an OT environment by embedding gathered state data within the Promela model. The embedded models are then checked to determine if the embedded state data represents normal system operation. We implemented this approach to perform anomaly detection in a physical hydroelectric dam testbed.

We evaluated our approach using modified baseline states to create sets of subtle anomalous states. Using standard classification metrics, both models proved effective at recognising normal behaviour. We calculated F1-score and accuracy for the two models to evaluate overall performance. Our trunk model achieved an accuracy score of 99.96%, while our branch model achieved an accuracy score of 72.66% due to the high number of false positives. Overall, our approach scored 99.05% accuracy. While our evaluation cannot practically evaluate the entire set of observable behaviours, the results of our evaluation on a representative subset suggest that this technique can deliver highly reliable identification of system anomalies.

While automatic transcription methods for converting PLC ladder logic to Promela do not currently exist, tools such as PLCverif [13,35] have demonstrated that specifications for NuSMV, nuXmv, Theta, and CBMC can be extracted from other PLC programming languages. Our results demonstrate that SPIN is also a viable tool for analysing ICS environments. However, PLC programming and model checking are two specialist fields, and transcription between the two paradigms requires detailed knowledge of both environments. Developing similar methods to extract Promela specifications from PLC programs is, therefore, critical to support further research into SPIN's utility in this domain.

We have shown that combining model checking with memoisation can be effective for anomaly detection in a small-scale representative ICS environment. Further applications should explore methods of scaling these approaches to the large environments commonly found in industrial settings and testing their effectiveness at detecting large-scale attacks across systems.

Acknowledgements. Douglas Fraser was funded by EPSRC Industrial Case account EP/V519686/1 and was sponsored by the Defence Science and Technology Laboratory (Dstl). This work was funded through the Glasgow Cyber Defence Lab supported by the Royal Academy of Engineering (grant number: RCSRF2223-1645), Dstl (order number: DSTL 0000014002) and EDF (order number: 4840659490). Alice Miller was funded by a Research Fellowship awarded by the Leverhulme Trust.

For the purpose of open access, the authors have applied a Creative Commons Attribution (CC BY) licence to any Author Accepted Manuscript version arising from this submission.

References

1. Adiego, B.F., Darvas, D., Tournier, J.C., Viñuela, E.B., Suárez, V.M.G.: Bringing automated model checking to PLC program development – a CERN case study –. IFAC Proc. Volumes **47**(2), 394–399 (2014)
2. AG, S.: S7 communication with PUT/GET. Tech. rep., Siemens AG (2020)
3. Ahmed, M., Naser Mahmood, A., Hu, J.: A survey of network anomaly detection techniques. J. Netw. Comput. Appl. **60**, 19–31 (2016)
4. Akers: binary decision diagrams. IEEE Trans. Comput. **100**(6), 509–516 (1978)
5. Behrmann, G., et al.: UPPAAL 4.0. In: QEST, vol. 6, pp. 125–126. Citeseer (2006)
6. Berthier, R., Sanders, W.H.: Specification-based intrusion detection for advanced metering infrastructures, pp. 184–193 (2011). https://doi.org/10.1109/PRDC.2011.30, https://www.scopus.com/inward/record.uri?eid=2-s2.0-84857771025&doi=10.1109%2fPRDC.2011.30&partnerID=40&md5=9973d92c8fafc0c467bbba326250508a
7. Bhamare, D., Zolanvari, M., Erbad, A., Jain, R., Khan, K., Meskin, N.: Cybersecurity for industrial control systems: a survey. Comput. Secur. **89**, 101677 (2020)
8. Chandola, V., Banerjee, A., Kumar, V.: Anomaly detection: a survey. ACM Comput. Surv. **41**(3) (2009). https://doi.org/10.1145/1541880.1541882
9. Chauhan, H., Kumar, V., Pundir, S., Pilli, E.S.: A comparative study of classification techniques for intrusion detection. In: 2013 International Symposium on Computational and Business Intelligence, pp. 40–43. IEEE (2013)
10. Cimatti, A., et al.: NuSMV 2: An OpenSource tool for symbolic model checking. In: Brinksma, E., Larsen, K.G. (eds.) CAV 2002. LNCS, vol. 2404, pp. 359–364. Springer, Heidelberg (2002). https://doi.org/10.1007/3-540-45657-0_29
11. Cook, M., Marnerides, A., Johnson, C., Pezaros, D.: A survey on industrial control system digital forensics: challenges, advances and future directions. IEEE Commun. Surv. Tutorials **25**(3), 1705–1747 (2023)
12. Cook, M.M., Marnerides, A.K., Pezaros, D.: Plcprint: Fingerprinting memory attacks in programmable logic controllers. IEEE Trans. Inf. Forensics Secur. **18**, 3376–3387 (2023)
13. Darvas, D., Blanco Vinuela, E., Fernández Adiego, B.: PLCverif: a tool to verify PLC programs based on model checking techniques, p. WEPGF092 (2015).https://doi.org/10.18429/JACoW-ICALEPCS2015-WEPGF092, https://cds.cern.ch/record/2213507
14. Gerth, R.: Concise promela reference (1997). https://spinroot.com/spin/Man/Quick.html. Accessed 8 Jan 2024

15. Hailesellasie, M., Hasan, S.R.: Intrusion detection in plc-based industrial control systems using formal verification approach in conjunction with graphs. J. Hardware Syst. Secur. **2**, 1–14 (2018)
16. Han, S., Xie, M., Chen, H.H., Ling, Y.: Intrusion detection in cyber-physical systems: techniques and challenges. IEEE Syst. J. **8**(4), 1052–1062 (2014). https://doi.org/10.1109/JSYST.2013.2257594
17. Holzmann, G.: The SPIN Model Checker: Primer and Reference Manual. Addison-Wesley Professional, 1st edn. (2011)
18. Holzmann, G.J.: The SPIN Model Checker: Primer and Reference Manual, vol. 1003. Addison-Wesley Reading (2004)
19. Holzmann, G.J., Peled, D.: An improvement in formal verification. In: Formal Description Techniques VII. IAICT, pp. 197–211. Springer, Boston, MA (1995). https://doi.org/10.1007/978-0-387-34878-0_13
20. Hotellier, E., Sicard, F., Francq, J., Mocanu, S.: Standard specification-based intrusion detection for hierarchical industrial control systems. Inf. Sci. **659**, 120102 (2024)
21. Khairullah, S.S.: Formal verification of a dependable state machine-based hardware architecture for safety-critical cyber-physical systems: analysis, design, and implementation. J. Electron. Test. **40**(4), 509–523 (2024)
22. Kottler, S., Khayamy, M., Hasan, S.R., Elkeelany, O.: Formal verification of ladder logic programs using NUSMV. In: SoutheastCon 2017, pp. 1–5 (2017). https://doi.org/10.1109/SECON.2017.7925390
23. Larsen, K.G., Pettersson, P., Yi, W.: UPPAAL in a nutshell. Int. J. Softw. Tools Technol. Transfer **1**, 134–152 (1997)
24. Liao, H.J., Richard Lin, C.H., Lin, Y.C., Tung, K.Y.: Intrusion detection system: a comprehensive review. J. Netw. Comput. Appl. **36**(1), 16–24 (2013)
25. Miller, A., Porr, B., Valkov, I., Fraser, D., Pagojus, D.: Model checking with memoisation for fast overtaking planning. Sci. Comput. Program. **244**, 103300 (2025)
26. Miller, T., Staves, A., Maesschalck, S., Sturdee, M., Green, B.: Looking back to look forward: Lessons learnt from cyber-attacks on industrial control systems. Int. J. Crit. Infrastruct. Prot. **35**, 100464 (2021)
27. Mitchell, R., Chen, I.R.: A survey of intrusion detection techniques for cyber-physical systems. ACM Comput. Surv. **46**(4) (2014). https://doi.org/10.1145/2542049
28. Mitchell, R., Chen, I.R.: Behavior rule specification-based intrusion detection for safety critical medical cyber physical systems. IEEE Trans. Dependable Secure Comput. **12**(1), 16–30 (2015). https://doi.org/10.1109/TDSC.2014.2312327
29. Nweke, L.O.: A survey of specification-based intrusion detection techniques for cyber-physical systems (2021)
30. Rehman, S., Al-Hadhrami, L.M., Alam, M.M.: Pumped hydro energy storage system: a technological review. Renew. Sustain. Energy Rev. **44**, 586–598 (2015)
31. Sakata, K., Fujita, S., Sawada, K., Iwasawa, H., Endoh, H., Matsumoto, N.: Model verification of fallback control system under cyberattacks via UPPAAL. Adv. Robot. **37**(3), 156–168 (2D023)
32. Shrestha, R., Mehrpouyan, H., Xu, D.: Model checking of security properties in industrial control systems (ICS). In: Proceedings of the Eighth ACM Conference on Data and Application Security and Privacy, pp. 164–166. CODASPY 2018, Association for Computing Machinery, New York, NY, USA (2018). https://doi.org/10.1145/3176258.3176949

33. Song, T., Ko, C., Tseng, C.H., Balasubramanyam, P., Chaudhary, A., Levitt, K.N.: Formal reasoning about a specification-based intrusion detection for dynamic auto-configuration protocols in ad hoc networks. In: Dimitrakos, T., Martinelli, F., Ryan, P.Y.A., Schneider, S. (eds.) Formal Aspects in Security and Trust: Thrid International Workshop, FAST 2005, Newcastle upon Tyne, UK, 18-19 July 2005, Revised Selected Papers, pp. 16–33. Springer (2006). https://doi.org/10.1007/11679219_3

34. Thakkar, A., Lohiya, R.: A survey on intrusion detection system: feature selection, model, performance measures, application perspective, challenges, and future research directions. Artif. Intell. Rev. **55**(1), 453–563 (2022)

35. Tournier, J.C., Fernández Adiego, B., Lopez-Miguel, I.D.: PLCverif: status of a formal verification tool for programmable logic controller. In: Proceedings of the 18th International Conference on Accelerator and Large Experimental Physics Control Systems ICALEPCS2021, China (2022).https://doi.org/10.18429/JACOW-ICALEPCS2021-MOPV042, https://jacow.org/icalepcs2021/doi/JACoW-ICALEPCS2021-MOPV042.html

36. Uppuluri, P., Sekar, R.: Experiences with specification-based intrusion detection. In: Lee, W., Mé, L., Wespi, A. (eds.) International Workshop on Recent Advances in Intrusion Detection, pp. 172–189. Springer (2001). https://doi.org/10.1007/3-540-45474-8_11

37. Wang, T., Su, Q., Chen, T.: Formal analysis of security properties of cyber-physical system based on timed automata. In: 2017 IEEE Second International Conference on Data Science in Cyberspace (DSC), pp. 534–540. IEEE (2017)

38. Wardak, H., Zhioua, S., Almulhem, A.: PLC access control: a security analysis. In: 2016 World Congress on Industrial Control Systems Security (WCICSS), pp. 1–6 (2016). https://doi.org/10.1109/WCICSS.2016.7882935

Using Bayesian Inference and Flowpipe Construction to Bound Predictions of Biogas Production at Wastewater Treatment Plants

Fletcher Chapin[1], Ankur Varma[2], Samuel Akinwande[1], Meagan Mauter[1], and Sriram Sankaranarayanan[2(✉)]

[1] Stanford University, Stanford, USA
[2] University of Colorado Boulder, Boulder, USA
srirams@colorado.edu

Abstract. In this paper, we use a novel combination of probabilistic programming and flowpipe construction to predict bounds on future biogas production for a wastewater treatment plant given operational data from the past. The operation of the anaerobic digester of a wastewater treatment plant is modeled through an Ordinary Differential Equation (ODE) model with unknown parameters and unobservable internal states. We are given data from the plant's operation that includes the daily measurement of the incoming waste volumes and concentrations along with the volume of biogas produced. We formalize our problem as first estimating the unknown parameters and initial conditions using Bayesian inference, such that the past behavior of the system is "compatible" with the observed data. Next, we propagate those input parameter estimates forward using flowpipe construction. To enable rapid and accurate flowpipe construction, we exploit the monotonicity property of the dynamical model of the plant. The procedure yields an over-approximation of the upper and lower bounds on biogas production, given the inputs. As a result, it can be used to formally bound future predictions that might inform facility operations. We implemented this procedure using a first-order kinetics model of hydrolysis to model the anaerobic digester of a real-world case study facility. We demonstrate how this method constructs realistic bounds for biogas prediction from the historical data that contain the actual ground-truth data 100% of the time. Our approach outperforms the standard approach that computes a posterior predictive distribution from samples both in terms of time and accuracy.

Keywords: Cyber-Physical Systems · Reachability Analysis · Flowpipe Construction · Monotone Systems · Wastewater treatment · Bayesian Inference

1 Introduction

This work uses a combination of probabilistic programming and reachability analysis to predict probabilistic bounds on the future biogas production of wastewater treatment plants (WWTP). WWTPs involve a *digester* that employs a process of anaerobic digestion to convert various input waste streams into biogas that can be used as a source of

F. Damiani and M. Farrell (Eds.): iFM 2025, LNCS 16194, pp. 182–201, 2026.
https://doi.org/10.1007/978-3-032-10794-7_10

renewable energy. The operation of WWTPs is rife with many sources of uncertainties. The process of digestion can be captured (approximately) by ordinary differential equation (ODE) models with uncertain rate parameters, and unobservable state variables. There is also uncertainty in the data, including the amount and concentration of wastes in the various input streams. Finally, data at WWTPs is measured at varying frequencies and accuracies. Some data is measured using real-time sensors, while other data is measured every few days by a laboratory technician. The differing frequency and accuracy in these measurements adds additional uncertainty to an already underspecified problem. Given all of these uncertainties, being able to obtain formal bounds on predictions of future conditions, such as anaerobic digester biogas production, would be useful to WWTP operators. For instance, the operator may wish to predict the biogas production over the near term for various future input scenarios.

In this paper, we use ideas from formal verification of cyber-physical systems (CPS) and probabilistic programming to analyze the operation of WWTPs. We wish to construct upper and lower bounds for the future biogas production of an anaerobic digester at a WWTP such that for an input probability level γ, the future biogas production should lie within the computed bounds with probability at least γ. Our method is a two-step approach. First, we use Bayesian modeling and inference to estimate a range of uncertain input parameters whose posterior probability exceeds γ [38]. Bayesian modeling and inference consists of specifying a generative model of the process of biogas production from the input waste streams. *Probabilistic programming* languages such as PyRO [10], Stan [13], Anglican [48] and Turing.jl [25] are commonly used to specify such models. We refer the reader to a survey by De Meent et al. [39] or the monograph edited by Barthe et al. [8] for a detailed introduction to probabilistic programming concepts. Our work uses the Julia programming language based Turing.jl to specify the model and perform inference [25]. The process of inference yields samples from the posterior distribution over the unknown parameters and initial conditions, conditioned on the observed data from plant operation. Second, we extract the *credible intervals* (the Bayesian analog of confidence intervals) over the input parameters and initial states such that the (sample-estimated) posterior probability of these intervals is at least γ [32]. Finally, given a planned future set of inputs, we perform reachability analysis over the differential equation model. Given a set of initial states and unknown parameters, reachability analysis constructs a flowpipe that is an over-approximation of all states reached over some finite time horizon of interest [4, 19]. By exploiting the monotonicity properties of the WWTP model, we show how to perform reachability analysis. Our approach here is a simplified version of a framework for reachability analysis proposed by Meyer et al. [40]. This approach reduces reachability analysis to a simulation of the upper and lower bound trajectories of the system, showing that all behaviors are contained "in between" these trajectories. As a result, we obtain an enormous speedup over existing approaches.

We evaluate our two-step approach against a standard approach based on simulation of the samples from the posterior over a dataset that spans three months of operational data consisting of waste inputs and gas production outputs for a WWTP in the San Francisco Bay Area. We evaluate our approach by splitting the data into 8-day segments wherein parameters and initial conditions are obtained by running Bayesian inference over data from 3 days and then using data from the subsequent 5 days as a prediction period. We assess the flowpipes constructed for various credible intervals against the ground truth data. In addition to measuring prediction accuracy, we also compare the flowpipe bounds and computational times against those obtained through the posterior simulation approach. We show that our approach is more accurate in terms of containing ground truth data within the predicted bounds but also quite fast when compared to posterior simulations. However, we also note that our approach to deriving credible intervals can be quite conservative, leaving room for future improvements. The bounds predictions obtained using our approach could be used by plant operators to formulate a cost-minimizing energy management plan, especially at facilities with highly variable electricity tariffs [15], gas storage resources like a biogas storage tank [11, 16], or energy storage resources like a Li-ion battery [11, 16, 41].

1.1 Related Work

Significance and Challenges: Recent research has highlighted the carbon emission reductions [16, 43] and electricity bill savings [11, 41, 50] potential of flexible operation of wastewater treatment plants (WWTPs). However, operational challenges make it difficult to realize those benefits in the real world [47]. Since WWTPs are critical infrastructure, facility operators are understandably risk-averse to modifying operations. Formal guarantees around predictions could help build operator confidence around novel control approaches such as model predictive control.

Reachability Analysis: This work builds upon the existing literature on computing reachable sets for cyber-physical systems described by ordinary differential equations [4, 19]. Reachability analysis techniques estimate bounds on the solutions to a differential equation model over a finite time horizon, given the set of initial conditions and unknown parameters. The problem of reachability analysis is known to be undecidable even for linear systems. However, recent approaches have provided computationally efficient and precise bounds to prove properties for systems with billions of state variables [6]. Unfortunately, these approaches are not directly applicable to our case due to the presence of uncertain parameters. Approaches that can handle non-linear systems can be used for our application. For non-linear systems, we have numerous approaches including Taylor-model based verified integration [9, 17, 18], or polynomial zonotopes [2], to mention a few. However, these approaches can be computationally expensive. Our work here uses a specialized approach that exploits monotonicity properties of the underlying model [40]. As a result, we obtain a precise bound that is also computationally inexpensive. Prior work has addressed the problem of reachability analysis for models with uncertainty by employing sampling-based approaches to reachability analysis as in [26, 36].

Sampling and Inference in Verification: The use of sampling and hypothesis testing to prove properties of stochastic systems has been explored extensively in the past through the statistical model checking approach [22, 33]. This has been applied in many domains, including biological systems [51]. Our approach is sample-based since we employ a Bayesian inference procedure that uses Monte Carlo methods to draw samples from the posterior [39]. Although inference approaches such as Hakaru can characterize the posterior distribution precisely [42], they are restricted to a relatively small class of programs, and cannot handle those involving differential equation models. As a result, our work employs Monte Carlo approaches with asymptotic guarantees that assume a sufficiently large number of samples. We emphasize that such an approach is very common in the probabilistic programming literature, wherein the properties of the posterior are inferred from a "large enough" number of samples. Our approach is in direct contrast to the standard statistical approach of constructing "posterior predictive samples" by simulating the posterior samples. However, we observe in our empirical evaluation that such an approach is relatively expensive since it involves simulation of a large number of samples and at the same time loses accuracy since it is unable to generalize effectively from the samples.

Prior work has explored the combination of reachability analysis and statistical inference for predictive monitoring of a variety of systems including road vehicles [3], stochastic processes [12], and human models [7]. Of these, our work is most closely related to the work of Chou et al. [20] in which the authors apply Bayesian approximation methods to estimate forward projection sets for a vehicle model.

2   Problem Statement and Approach

Ordinary differential equations (ODEs) are used to model a variety of natural and engineered systems in domains ranging from physics to ecology. Let $\mathbf{x} \in \mathbb{R}^n$ represent a vector of state variables $\mathbf{x} = (x_1, \ldots, x_n)$ and $f : \mathbb{R}^n \times \mathbb{R}^m \to \mathbb{R}^n$ be a Lipschitz continuous function wherein $f(\mathbf{x}, \theta)$ is dependent on parameters $\theta \in \Theta \subseteq \mathbb{R}^m$. An ODE is of the form $\frac{d\mathbf{x}}{dt} = f(\mathbf{x}, \theta)$, wherein the function f (also known as the vector field) maps each state $\mathbf{x}$ and parameter $\theta \in \Theta$ to a derivative $f(\mathbf{x}, \theta)$. The solution to the ODE given fixed parameter values $\theta \in \Theta$ and initial conditions $\mathbf{x}(0)$ is a trajectory $\varphi : [0, T) \to \mathbb{R}^n$ for some time horizon $T > 0$ such that (a) $\varphi(0) = \mathbf{x}(0)$ and (b) for all $t \in [0, T)$, $\frac{d\varphi}{dt} = f(\varphi(t), \theta)$. In other words, the derivative of the solution satisfies the differential equation for a fixed θ. Since f is assumed to be Lipschitz continuous, we know that the solution exists and is unique. In this paper, we will work with ODEs with inputs. Let $\mathbf{u} \in \mathbb{R}^k$ represent a vector of k inputs.

An ODE with inputs drawn from a domain $U \subseteq \mathbb{R}^k$ has the form $\frac{d\mathbf{x}}{dt} = f(\mathbf{x}, \mathbf{u}, \theta)$. In many ODE models of physical systems (including that studied here), the internal state $\mathbf{x}$ is not directly measurable. We will assume that $\mathbf{y} = g(\mathbf{x})$ is a measurable output. Given a fixed parameter $\theta \in \Theta$ and an input signal $\xi : [0, T] \to U$, the corresponding trajectory φ for initial condition $\mathbf{x}(0)$ satisfies $\varphi(0) = \mathbf{x}(0)$ and $\frac{d\varphi}{dt} = f(\varphi(t), \xi(t), \theta)$.

For notational convenience, given a set of values $\mathbf{u}_1, \ldots, \mathbf{u}_t \in \mathbb{R}^k$, we write $\mathbf{u}(1, \ldots, t)$ to denote the function $[0, t) \to \mathbb{R}^n$ wherein $\mathbf{u}(\tau) = \mathbf{u}_i$ if $i - 1 \leq \tau < i$.

Definition 1 (Problem Statement). *The problem of predicting future range of possible biogas production given past data and the model structure is as follows:*

Inputs: *Model structure $\langle f, \Theta, U, g \rangle$, past data $\langle \mathbf{u}(1, \ldots, t), \mathbf{y}(1, \ldots, t) \rangle$, future planned input signal $\mathbf{u}(t + 1, \ldots, t + k)$, and confidence level $\gamma \in (0, 1)$.*

Outputs: *Credible interval for parameters* : $[\theta_{lo}, \theta_{hi}]$ *and future output bounds* $[\mathbf{y}_{lo}(\tau), \mathbf{y}_{hi}(\tau)]$, *wherein* $\mathbf{y}_{lo}, \mathbf{y}_{hi} : [t, t+k) \to \mathbb{R}^{|\mathbf{y}|}$, *such that* $\forall \tau \in [t+1, t+k), \mathbf{y}_{lo}(\tau) \le \mathbf{y}_{hi}(\tau)$ *are bounds on the future outputs of the model.*

The specific wastewater treatment model is detailed in Sect. 3. It has $n = 7$ state variables, $k = 10$ inputs, $m = 7$ unknown parameters and a scalar ($|\mathbf{y}| = 1$) observable output which represents the gas production. Each parameter is known to belong to a large interval of possible values and the states of the plant $\mathbf{x}$ cannot be observed. As a result, the problem has two aspects to it: (a) given past data, find out possible values of parameters θ and possible initial states $\mathbf{x}(0)$; and (b) given future inputs, and the set of possible values of $\theta, \mathbf{x}(0)$, predict bounds on the outputs $\mathbf{y}$.

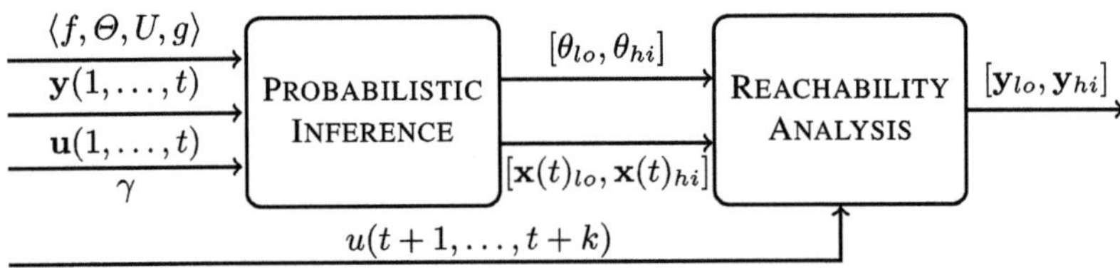

Fig. 1. Overall approach at a glance using a combination of probabilistic inference to estimate the parameter and initial condition posterior ranges while using reachability analysis to estimate bounds on future outputs.

Figure 1 summarizes the overall approach to the problem, which consists of two parts: (a) we run Bayesian inference through a probabilistic programming framework to compute posterior credible intervals over the unknown parameters and final states of the model; and (b) we perform a reachability analysis over the unknown parameters and initial conditions given the future inputs to compute the overall bounds.

Bayesian Inference: Bayesian inference inputs (a) the generative model given by the probability distribution $\mathbb{P}(\mathbf{y}(1, \ldots, t) \mid \theta, \mathbf{x}(0), \mathbf{u}(1, \ldots, t))$ which represents the probability of observing the output data, given the inputs to the plant, the unknown parameters θ and initial state $\mathbf{x}(0)$ for the model; and (b) the *prior distribution* $\pi(\theta, \mathbf{x}(0))$ with support over the set $\Theta \times \mathbb{R}^n$. We seek to compute a representation of the posterior distribution $\mathbb{P}(\theta, \mathbf{x}(0) \mid \mathbf{y}(1, \ldots, t), \mathbf{u}(1, \ldots, t))$ using Bayes' rule:

$$\mathbb{P}(\theta, \mathbf{x}(0) \mid \mathbf{y}(1, \ldots, t), \mathbf{u}(1, \ldots, t)) \propto \mathbb{P}(\mathbf{y}(1, \ldots, t) \mid \theta, \mathbf{x}(0), \mathbf{u}(1, \ldots, t)) \pi(\mathbf{x}(0), \theta).$$

There are many computational approaches to Bayesian inference, including techniques such as Markov chain Monte Carlo (MCMC), sequential Monte Carlo (SMC), Belief Propagation (BP), and Variational Inference (VI) [8,39]. Tools such as `Turing.jl` [25], `PyRo` [10] and `Stan` [13] support Bayesian inference by specifying the model, and the prior distribution as programs in a domain-specific language called a *probabilistic programming language.*

Our framework uses probabilistic programming to compute samples from the posterior distributions for $\mathbb{P}(\theta, \mathbf{x}(0) \mid \mathbf{y}(1, \ldots, t), \mathbf{u}(1, \ldots, t))$. Given the posterior and a confidence level $\gamma \in (0, 1)$, we extract *credible intervals* over $[\theta_{lo}, \theta_{hi}] \times [\mathbf{x}(t)_{lo}, \mathbf{x}(t)_{hi}]$ for $\theta, \mathbf{x}(t)$, such that the probability of drawing a sample from the credible interval is at least γ.

Reachability Analysis: We wish to predict bounds on the output $[\mathbf{y}_{lo}, \mathbf{y}_{hi}]$ such that for any choice of parameters $\theta \in [\theta_{lo}, \theta_{hi}]$, an initial state $\mathbf{x}(0) \in [\mathbf{x}(0)_{lo}, \mathbf{x}(0)_{hi}]$, an input signal $\mathbf{u}(1, \ldots, t + k)$, the resulting trajectories $\varphi : [0, t + k) \to \mathbb{R}^n$ is such that $\forall t \in [0, t + k), g(\varphi(t)) \in [\mathbf{y}_{lo}(t), \mathbf{y}_{hi}(t)]$. In other words, the reachability analysis returns a bound that accounts for all possible outputs that can be observed for the input parameter and initial condition ranges.

Overall Result: The Bayesian inference yields the following guarantee:

Theorem 1. *Assume that the observed data was generated by an instance of the model with parameter $\theta \in \Theta$ and $\mathbf{x}(0) \in \mathbb{R}^n$ that are sampled according to the prior distribution $(\theta^*, \mathbf{x}^*(0)) \sim \pi(\theta, \mathbf{x})$. Suppose, that we run a Bayesian inference procedure that generates N posterior samples. As $N \to \infty$, the probability that the $\theta^*, \mathbf{x}^*(0)$ lie within the credible intervals $[\theta_{lo}, \theta_{hi}]$ and $[\mathbf{x}(0)_{lo}, \mathbf{x}(0)_{hi}]$ is at least γ.*

The reachability analysis approach yields the following guarantee:

Theorem 2. *For any $\theta \in [\theta_{lo}, \theta_{hi}]$ and initial condition $\mathbf{x}(0) \in [\mathbf{x}(0)_{lo}, \mathbf{x}(0)_{hi}]$, the output obtained from the resulting trajectory $\varphi : [0, t + k) \to \mathbb{R}^n$ is contained in the computed reachable output bounds $[\mathbf{y}_{lo}, \mathbf{y}_{hi}]$:*

$$\forall \, t \in [0, t + k), \; \mathbf{y}_{lo}(t) \leq g(\varphi(t)) \leq \mathbf{y}_{hi}(t) \,.$$

Theorem 1 combined with the soundness guarantee of the reachability analysis from Theorem 2 yields the result that the bounds computed by our approach capture all possible future outputs of the system with probability at least γ.

3 Wastewater Treatment Model

The goal of our wastewater treatment model is to compute the biogas production in m^3/day based on the influent (incoming waste stream) concentrations and flow rates. We use a simplified first-order kinetics reaction to model the biogas production of an anaerobic digester. The anaerobic digester is modeled as a continuously stirred tank reactor (CSTR). Anaerobic digestion consists of three main steps. First, sludges and other wastes are hydrolyzed into simpler fats, acids, and proteins. Second, those simpler organic compounds are fermented into acetate and H_2. Third, acetate and H_2 are converted into CH_4 and CO_2 by acetotrophic or hydrogenotrophic methanogens [44]. Recent research has shown that hydrolysis can be rate limiting when there are high concentrations of volatile solids (VS) [44]. For example, Mahmood et al. found that hydrolysis was the rate-limiting step in the presence of high phosphine concentrations [37].

Since the rate-limiting step of anaerobic digestion depends on the wastewater's composition, our model incorporates two steps of the anaerobic digestion process: hydrolysis of complex wastes into simpler organic compounds and methane fermentation of those simple organics into CH_4. In other words, we combine fermentation and methanogenesis into a single step by assuming that methanogenesis is rate limiting. We model both steps using first-order kinetics models.

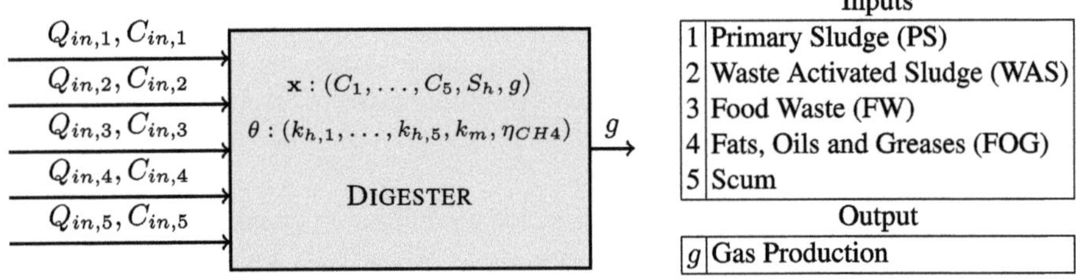

Fig. 2. Diagram of anaerobic digester at a wastewater treatment plant. The variables associated with each flow are labeled.

Figure 2 shows the overall model of the digester in terms of a block diagram. The model has 7 state variables $C_1, \ldots, C_5$ representing the concentration of the various wastes coming from the input streams numbered $1, \ldots, 5$ whose meanings are explained in Fig. 2, S_h representing the overall chemical oxygen on demand (COD), and the gas production g. The detailed explanation of the state variables, parameters and the differential equations is provided through the rest of this section.

3.1 Hydrolysis

We model reactions using first-order kinetics, meaning that the reaction rate is linearly dependent on the concentration of the reactant [49]. For our problem, there are j heterogeneous waste streams into the reactor. As a CSTR, we can assume that the effluent waste stream is fully mixed throughout the reactor. Let $Q_{in,j}$ be the influent flow rate of the jth waste stream in m^3/day, Q_{out} be the effluent flow rate of the well mixed sludge in m^3/day, V be the total volume of wastewater in the reactor in m^3, $C_{in,j}$ be the influent volatile solids (VS) concentration of the jth waste stream in mg / L, C_j be the VS concentration of the jth constituent within the reactor in mg / L, and $k_{h,j}$ be the hydrolysis rate of the jth waste stream in 1/day. Then, we can use mass balance to define dC_j/dt, the rate of change of the jth waste concentration, in mg/L/day as

$$\frac{dC_j}{dt} = \frac{Q_{in,j}}{V} C_{in,j} - (\frac{Q_{out}}{V} + k_{h,j}) C_j , \tag{1}$$

wherein, the term $\frac{Q_{in,j}}{V} C_{in,j}$ represents the influent flow of waste stream j, $\frac{Q_{out}}{V} C_j$ represents the effluent flow, and $k_{h,j} C_j$ represents the mass converted in the hydrolysis reaction. We assume that $Q_{out} = \sum_{j=1}^{5} Q_{in,j}$ and thus, the volume of the tank V remains constant throughout the operation of the digester.

3.2   Methanogenesis

In reality, methane fermentation (or methanogenesis) takes multiple steps. Hydrolyzed organic compounds are first fermented to acetate and H_2, then acetate and H_2 are fermented further to CO_2 and CH_4. To simplify our system of equations, we model the entire methane fermentation process from hydrolyzed organic compounds to CH_4 as a single first-order reaction.

We define the chemical oxygen demand (COD) of the homogeneous concentration of hydrolyzed substrate as S_h (in mg / L) and assume that S_h will be consumed during methanogenesis at rate of k_m (in 1/day), a first-order rate constant to approximate overall methane fermentation. Far more precise models of methanogenesis exist, but literature has shown that those models can be simplified considerably when the rate-limiting steps of anaerobic digestion are known [44]. In our case, we assume that hydrolysis or methanogenesis are the two potentially rate-limiting steps, so we believe that combining all fermentation into a single methanogenesis reaction is reasonable.

The rate of change in concentration, dS_h/dt, can be modeled as

$$\frac{dS_h}{dt} = \left(\sum_j k_{h,j}C_j\right) - \left(\frac{Q_{out}}{V} + k_m\right)S_h , \tag{2}$$

wherein, the first term, $\sum_j k_{h,j}C_j$, representing the specific hydrolysis rate of the digester as described by Guo et al. [28]

We rely on stoichiometry to estimate biogas production. There are $0.35\,\text{m}^3$ of CH_4 produced for every kg of COD at standard temperature and pressure [44]. Therefore, we can estimate the daily biogas production, dg/dt, in m^3/day using the equation

$$\frac{dg}{dt} = 0.00035 k_m V S_h / \eta_{CH_4} \tag{3}$$

where η_{CH_4} is the percent of methane in biogas by volume. The factor 0.00035 comes from converting $0.35\,\text{m}^3$ CH_4/kg COD to $0.00035\,\text{L}$ CH_4/mg COD to account for the units of V (m^3) and S_h (mg/L).

3.3   Sources of Uncertainty

The anaerobic digester receives five distinct waste streams: thickened primary sludge (TPS); thickened waste activated sludge (TWAS); food waste (FW); and fats, oils, and greases (FOG); and scum. As discussed above, each of these streams has a different influent flow rate ($Q_{in,j}$), concentration ($C_{in,j}$), and hydrolysis rate ($k_{h,j}$). Inline flow meters are installed at the facility, so $Q_{in,j}$ is well understood (Fig. 1).

The concentrations, $C_{in,j}$, are measured periodically by laboratory technicians, so the data has two potential issues. First, the concentrations vary with time, so this single sample is not representative of the temporal fluctuations in concentration. Second, the single grab sample may not be representative spatially, so that, for a given time it is only an estimate of the waste concentration.

The largest source of uncertainty is the hydrolysis ($k_{h,j}$) and methanogenesis (k_m) reaction rates. To preserve model simplicity, these reactions are modeled using first-order kinetics. In reality, a complex series of microbial kinetics involving growth and decay of biomass is at play. As a result, these reaction rates vary in time and do not have a true physical meaning (in the way a cell death rate would). Nonetheless, this approach excels at capturing various dimensions of uncertainty from the microbial kinetics in a single reaction term. One final source of uncertainty is the methane fraction of biogas by volume (η_{CH_4}), which varies between 45% and 75% depending on the ratio of acetotrophic to hydrogenotrophic methanogens [31].

Table 1. Parameters in the biogas production model and their range of values from the literature. We assumed an initial concentration of zero for parameters such as food waste concentration that are highly dependent on plant operation and not available from the literature as a result.

Parameter	Meaning	Range (Literature)	Units	Source
k_m	1st-order methanogenesis rate	0.05–0.3	1/day	[28,34]
$k_{h,1}$	1st-order TPS hydrolysis rate	0.286–3.0	1/day	[21,23]
$k_{h,2}$	1st-order TWAS hydrolysis rate	0.025–0.22	1/day	[27,28]
$k_{h,3}$	1st-order FW hydrolysis rate	0.2–0.8	1/day	[35]
$k_{h,4}$	1st-order FOG hydrolysis rate	0.333–50	1/day	[5,30]
$k_{h,5}$	1st-order scum hydrolysis rate	0.1–3.0	1/day	[21,23]
η_{CH_4}	Methane fraction of biogas by volume	0.45–0.75		[31]
$C_{1,0}$	Initial concentration of TPS	1,000–50,000	mg/L	[44,46]
$C_{2,0}$	Initial concentration of TWAS	1,000–50,000	mg/L	[44,46]
$C_{3,0}$	Initial concentration of FW	Not available		
$C_{4,0}$	Initial concentration of FOG	Not available		
$C_{5,0}$	Initial concentration of scum	Not available		
$S_{h,0}$	Initial hydrolyzed substrate in digester	100–10,000	mg/L	[1,29,45]

4　Bayesian Inference

As mentioned earlier in Sect. 2, we use Bayesian inference to compute intervals over parameters and the initial states, based on some past observations from the system. We assume that the process of biogas production is explained by the model in Sect. 3, but for unknown parameters and initial conditions. The ranges for these are shown in Table 1. In this section, we describe the overall structure of the probabilistic programming model for performing inference on the biogas production data. We will then briefly summarize the process of extracting posterior samples through a Bayesian inference procedure and the extraction of credible intervals from the samples.

The model used for specifying the prior probabilities $\pi(\theta, \mathbf{x}(0))$ and the generative model $\mathbb{P}(\mathbf{y}(1,\ldots,t) \mid \theta, \mathbf{x}(0), \mathbf{u}(1,\ldots,t))$ is shown in Fig. 3. It is a model expressed in the Julia-based Domain Specific Language (DSL) for the state-of-the-art probabilistic programming library `Turing.jl`. The model takes as inputs (Lines 1–6 in the listing of Fig. 3) the input data $\mathbf{u}(1,\ldots,t)$, the output data $\mathbf{y}(1,\ldots,t)$, the ranges for the

```
1   @model function gas_production_model(
2       inp_data::Matrix{Float64},      # data: inputs to model
3       output_data::Vector{Float64},   # data: gas production
4       param_ranges::Matrix{Float64},  # parameter ranges
5       init_ranges::Matrix{Float64},   # initial condition
6       ξ)                              # std. measurement error
7       # Prior distribution
8       k1 ~ uniform(param_ranges[1,1], param_ranges[1,2])
9       k2 ~ uniform(param_ranges[2,1], param_ranges[2,2])
10      # ... prior for parameters ...
11      # initial conditions
12      C10 ~ uniform(init_ranges[1,1], init_ranges[1,2])
13      # ... prior for initial conditions ...
14      params = [k1, k2, k3, k4, k5, k, eta, V]
15      x0 = [C10, C20, C30, C40, C50, S0, G0]
16      # Run a ODE simulator given
17      #      input data, parameter sample, initial cond. sample
18      daily_production = sim_ode(inp_data, params, x0)
19      for i in 1:n_days
20        # Condition the gas production on the output data
21        output_data[i] ~ daily_production[i] + Normal(0.0, ξ)
22      end
23      return params, init_ranges
```

Fig. 3. Probabilistic programming model in `Turing.jl` for specifying the generative model for the gas production data.

parameters and initial conditions, as specified in Table 1 and a parameter ξ that specifies the standard deviation for the measurement of the gas production output. Lines 7 - 13 specify the generation of the prior distribution. The function `sim_ode` in line 18 is not shown, but uses an off-the-shelf numerical ODE solver to solve the ODE given parameters, initial conditions and inputs. It then returns the total gas production aggregated for each day in the data. Line 21 conditions that model predicted gas production against the measurements from the data assuming that the measurement device has a known standard error of ξ.

Once the model has been specified, we can use a built-in inference engine in `Turing.jl` to return posterior samples. These samples are of the form

$$S = \{(\theta^{(1)}, \mathbf{x}^{(1)}(0)), \ldots, (\theta^{(N)}, \mathbf{x}^{(N)})\},$$

for a large sample size $N > 0$ (set to $25{,}000$ for our experiments). The available procedures in `Turing.jl` include Markov chain Monte Carlo (MCMC) methods, Sequential Monte Carlo (SMC) methods and other approaches such as Variational Inference (VI).

Next, given a confidence bound γ, we extract intervals $[\theta_{lo}, \theta_{hi}]$ and $[\mathbf{x}(0)_{lo}, \mathbf{x}(0)_{hi}]$ so that the probability that a given sample $(\theta, \mathbf{x}(t))$ from the posterior distribution belongs to the intervals is $\geq \gamma$,

$$\mathbb{P}(\theta \in [\theta_{lo}, \theta_{hi}] \mid \mathsf{data}) \geq \gamma, \mathbb{P}(\mathbf{x}(0) \in [\mathbf{x}(0)_{lo}, \mathbf{x}(0)_{hi}] \mid \mathsf{data}) \geq \gamma.$$

There are many ways of extracting such intervals. Consider the following scheme that works independently with each dimension of θ and $\mathbf{x}(0)$. Consider a dimension z_i of the vector θ or $\mathbf{x}(0)$. We estimate the $z_{i,lo} = \frac{1-\gamma}{2(n+m)}$ quantile and $z_{i,hi} = 1 - \frac{1-\gamma}{2(m+n)}$ quantile of all the values of the scalar z_i from the posterior samples S. Assume that the Bayesian inference procedure satisfies convergence in distribution to the true posterior and that the posterior CDF is continuous everywhere.

Lemma 1. *As the number of samples $N \to \infty$, the posterior probability $\mathbb{P}(z_i \notin [z_{i,lo}, z_{i,hi}]) \to \frac{1-\gamma}{(n+m)}$.*

Proof. This follows from the fact that the empirical distribution $Z_N^{(i)}$, formed by the samples $z_i^{(1)}, \ldots, z_i^{(N)}$ obtained by projecting the samples in set S along z_i, converges to the true posterior $Z^{(i)}$. As a result, the values of $z_{i,lo}$ and $z_{i,hi}$ converge to the $\frac{1-\gamma}{2(n+m)}$ and $1 - \frac{1-\gamma}{2(m+n)}$ quantiles since the CDF is assumed to be continuous as well. Therefore,

$$\mathbb{P}(z_i \notin [z_{i,lo}, z_{i,hi}]) = \mathbb{P}(z_i \leq z_{i,lo}) + \mathbb{P}(z_i \geq z_{i,hi}) = \frac{1-\gamma}{n+m}.$$

The bounds $[\theta_{lo}, \theta_{hi}] \times [\mathbf{x}_{lo}(0), \mathbf{x}_{hi}(0)]$ are obtained as a product over intervals $[z_{i,lo}, z_{i,hi}]$ wherein z_i ranges over the dimensions θ_j for $j = 1, \ldots, m$ and $x_{0,i}$ for $i = 1, \ldots, n$.

Lemma 2. *Assuming the conditions for the convergence in distribution of the Bayesian inference procedure and the continuity of the posterior CDF, as the number of samples $N \to \infty$, the posterior probability $\mathbb{P}((\theta, \mathbf{x}(0)) \notin [\theta_{lo}, \theta_{hi}] \times [\mathbf{x}_{lo}(0), \mathbf{x}_{hi}(0)]) \leq (1-\gamma)$.*

Proof. Proof is obtained by applying the union bound along each dimension to the inequality derived in Lemma 1.

Our approach for deriving the posterior is conservative since it ignores the correlations between the various components of $\theta, \mathbf{x}(0)$ in the posterior. Note that once we have bounds for $[\mathbf{x}_{lo}(0), \mathbf{x}_{hi}(0)]$ at time $t = 0$, we can obtain corresponding bounds at time t $[\mathbf{x}_{lo}(t), \mathbf{x}_{hi}(t)]$ using the reachability analysis algorithm that we will describe in the subsequent section. Finally, we will make the simplifying assumption that $[\theta_{lo}, \theta_{hi}] \subseteq \Theta$. Failing this, we will need to consider the set $[\theta_{lo}, \theta_{hi}] \cap \Theta$, which will be a hyper-rectangle if Θ is a hyper-rectangle.

5   Fast Reachability Analysis Using Monotonicity

Thus far, we have used Bayesian inference to obtain posterior bounds in the form of intervals over θ and $\mathbf{x}(0)$. We will now describe a reachability analysis procedure that infers bounds $[\mathbf{x}_{lo}(t), \mathbf{x}_{hi}(t)]$ for the states at time t and therefore results in output bounds $[\mathbf{y}_{lo}(t), \mathbf{y}_{hi}(t)]$. There are many reachability analysis tools that can be used off-the-shelf for such analysis including Flow* [18] and CORA [2]. Note that although the model presented in Sect. 3 is linear in the state-variables, the uncertainties in the parameters θ means that standard approaches to linear systems that have been shown to work for billions of state variables cannot be directly applied [6]. In this section, we present an efficient approach by exploiting some key physical properties of the wastewater model and ideas from the study of positive differential equations. Our approach is based on ideas presented by Meyer et al. [40]. The key contributions include showing that the WWTP model in Sect. 3 satisfies the necessary monotonicity conditions; and in doing so, adapting the ideas of Meyer et al. to systems with uncertain parameters.

The ODE model in Sect. 3 has the form $\frac{d\mathbf{x}}{dt} = A(\theta)\mathbf{x} + h(\mathbf{u})$, wherein $A(\theta)$ is a matrix whose entries are affine functions (linear plus constant) over the parameters θ and $h(\mathbf{u})$ is an input dependent term that is always non-negative.

Definition 2 (Metzler Matrix). *A matrix $M \in \mathbb{R}^{n \times n}$ is said to be* Metzler *(essentially positive) iff $M_{i,j} \geq 0$ for $i \neq j$.*

An ODE is positive iff whenever $\mathbf{x}(0) \geq 0$ then $\mathbf{x}(t) \geq 0$ for all time $t \geq 0$. The notion of positivity is significant because the wastewater treatment plant involves physical quantities such as concentration of effluents that are non-negative at all times (negative concentrations are not physically meaningful).

Theorem 3. *Consider the ODE $\frac{d\mathbf{x}}{dt} = M\mathbf{x} + \mathbf{b}$ for vector $\mathbf{b} \geq 0$ entrywise. The system is positive if and only if M is a Metzler matrix.*

Proof can be found in a standard textbook [24].

Lemma 3. *The model $\frac{d\mathbf{x}}{dt} = A(\theta)\mathbf{x} + h(\mathbf{u})$ defined in Sect. 3 satisfies the condition that $A(\theta)$ is Metzler for all $\theta \in [\theta_{lo}, \theta_{hi}]$ and $h(\mathbf{u}) \geq 0$ for all $\mathbf{u} \in U$.*

Proof is by verifying each entry $A_{i,j}(\theta) \geq 0$ for $i \neq j$ and $\theta \in [\theta_{lo}, \theta_{hi}]$. From Eq. 1, the off-diagonal terms include $\frac{Q_{in,j}}{V} \geq 0$ and from Eq. (2), the off-diagonal terms are $k_{h,j} \geq 0$ (see Table 1).

Lemma 4. *For any $\theta \in [\theta_{lo}, \theta_{hi}]$ such that $\theta_{hi} \geq \theta_{lo} \geq 0$, the matrix $A(\theta)$ for the model in Sect. 3 is Metzler. Also, there exists Metzler matrices L, U such that*

$$\forall \theta \in [\theta_{lo}, \theta_{hi}], \ L \leq A(\theta) \leq U,$$

wherein the inequality $\leq$ between matrices is interpreted entrywise.

Proof. The matrices L, U are obtained by computing for each entry in $A(\theta)$, $L_{i,j} = \min_{\theta \in [\theta_{lo}, \theta_{hi}]} A_{i,j}(\theta)$ and $U_{i,j} = \max_{\theta \in [\theta_{lo}, \theta_{hi}]} A_{i,j}(\theta)$. Since $[\theta_{lo}, \theta_{hi}]$ form a compact interval, it is easy to see that the minima and maxima exist. Furthermore, L is Metzler following Lemma 3 for each $i \neq j$, the minimum value of $A_{i,j}(\theta) \geq 0$. Since $L \leq U$ entrywise, U is Metzler as well.

Consider the time trajectories $\varphi_{lo}(t)$ of the initial value problem (IVP) $\frac{d\mathbf{x}_{lo}}{dt} = L\mathbf{x}_{lo} + h(\mathbf{u})$ for initial condition $\mathbf{x}_{lo}(0)$ and $\varphi_{hi}(t)$ for the IVP $\frac{d\mathbf{x}_{hi}}{dt} = U\mathbf{x}_{hi} + h(\mathbf{u})$ with initial condition $\mathbf{x}_{hi}(0)$.

Theorem 4. *For all $\theta \in [\theta_{lo}, \theta_{hi}]$, $\mathbf{x}(0) \in [\mathbf{x}_{lo}, \mathbf{x}_{hi}]$ and time $t \geq 0$, the solution $\psi(t)$ of the system $\frac{d\mathbf{x}}{dt} = A(\theta)\mathbf{x} + h(\mathbf{u})$ satisfies the bounds $\varphi_{lo}(t) \leq \psi(t) \leq \varphi_{hi}(t)$.*

Note that φ_{lo} is the solution of the system $\frac{d\mathbf{x}_{lo}}{dt} = L\mathbf{x}_{lo} + h(\mathbf{u}(t))$ with initial condition $\mathbf{x}_{lo}(0)$ while φ_{hi} is the solution of the system $\frac{d\mathbf{x}_{hi}}{dt} = U\mathbf{x}_{hi} + h(\mathbf{u}(t))$ with initial condition $\mathbf{x}_{hi}(0)$. For any fixed θ, let $M = A(\theta)$ be a Metzler matrix (by assumption).

Lemma 5. *If $L \leq M$ then for all $\mathbf{x} \geq 0$, $L\mathbf{x} \leq M\mathbf{x}$.*

Proof. Note that the matrix $M - L$ has all non-negative entries since $L \leq M$. Therefore, $(M - L)\mathbf{x} \geq 0$ whenever $\mathbf{x} \geq 0$. Thus, $L\mathbf{x} \leq M\mathbf{x}$.

We recall a well-known result known as the monotone comparison principle, that is also sometimes known as the Chaplygin's theorem. We specialize this for the case of linear systems in our presentation below.

Theorem 5 (Monotone Comparison Principle). *Consider a dynamical system $\frac{d\mathbf{x}}{dt} = M\mathbf{x} + h(\mathbf{u}(t))$, wherein M is Metzler and $h(\mathbf{u}) \geq 0$ for all $\mathbf{u}$. Consider a system $\frac{d\mathbf{z}}{dt} = L\mathbf{z} + h(\mathbf{u}(t))$, wherein $L \leq M$. If $\mathbf{z}(0) \leq \mathbf{x}(0)$ at time $t = 0$, then $\mathbf{z}(t) \leq \mathbf{x}(t)$ for all time.*

Note that L, M are both Metzler matrices. Furthermore, $\mathbf{x}_{lo}(0) \leq \mathbf{x}(0)$. As a result, applying the monotone comparison principle, yields the result that $\mathbf{x}_{lo}(t) \leq \mathbf{x}(t)$. Similarly, M, U are Metzler matrices and $\mathbf{x}(0) \leq \mathbf{x}_{hi}(0)$. Applying the theorem yields the result that $\mathbf{x}(t) \leq \mathbf{x}_{hi}(t)$. This concludes the proof of Theorem 4.

Theorem 4 is remarkable since it reduces the reachability analysis problem to that of computing the solutions of two linear systems for fixed matrices and initial conditions. We perform the reachability analysis as follows:

1. Compute the matrices L, U that form upper and lower bounds of $A(\theta)$.
2. Compute a rigorous lower-bound $\varphi_{lo}(t)$ for the system $\frac{d\mathbf{x}_{lo}}{dt} = L\mathbf{x}_{lo} + h(\mathbf{u})$ with initial condition $\mathbf{x}_{lo}(0)$.
3. Compute a rigorous upper-bound $\varphi_{hi}(t)$ for the system $\frac{d\mathbf{x}_{hi}}{dt} = U\mathbf{x}_{hi} + h(\mathbf{u})$ with initial condition $\mathbf{x}_{hi}(0)$.
4. The reachable set at time $t \geq 0$ is contained in $[\varphi_{lo}(t), \varphi_{hi}(t)]$.

6   Implementation and Data Sources

We have implemented both the Bayesian inference and flowpipe construction in Julia. The historical data used to evaluate our algorithm comes from a municipal WWTP in the San Francisco Bay Area (Cf. Sect. 6.1). The ability for our algorithm to perform on real-world data is vital given our industrial application.

6.1   Data Sources

We use historical data from our case study WWTP to evaluate our method. This data includes a variety of measurements from different sources and on different timescales. For example, flow rates of the various waste streams are recorded in close to real time by inline sensors, while the strength of each waste stream (i.e., concentration) is measured in a laboratory every few days. We perform our analysis on daily timesteps due to the different granularity of data. I.e., we sum or average the sub-daily flow rate data to daily values and linearly interpolate the concentration data between missing days so that all the data is on the same timescale. We do not clean the data besides interpolating missing values, so the typical noise and potential inaccuracies of real-world operational data are present in our dataset. Our combined method of Bayesian inference followed by flowpipe construction is especially suited to real-world data with large uncertainty such as this case study. Further description of specific data used are found in the Appendix (available upon request).

We use data from three sample months for our analysis: September 2018, January 2020, and March 2020. These months include different operating conditions, such as influent waste stream concentrations and reaction rate parameters, to demonstrate the generalizability of our method at each step.

6.2 Bayesian Inference

The first step of our two-step approach is Bayesian inference to determine the credible intervals of unknown parameters. We perform this Bayesian inference using an MCMC method (we use 25,000 iterations of the Metropolis Hastings algorithm) from the `Turing.jl` package [25]. In general, selecting the number of iterations for Bayesian inference is hard. We chose to perform 25,000 iterations after initial tuning experiments that compared the variability of the confidence intervals obtained after each run versus the time taken to run. For $25,000$ iterations, the results had no variation across multiple runs. We initialize the algorithm with the nominal parameters and initial values of concentrations that are available in the Appendix (available upon request).

We chunk the historical data into 8-day segments, wherein the first 3 days of data are used for Bayesian inference to determine the kinetic parameters and initial conditions of the wastewater model. We then construct an 8-day flowpipe from the beginning of the Bayesian inference, rejecting the first 3 days that overlap with the training period to produce a 5-day prediction. The prediction uses the ground truth inputs for the next 5 days but in an application, it may consist of a future scenario that the plant operators may consider for their analysis. We also use these samples to construct posterior predictive simulations for the next 5 days using an ODE solver and compare the flowpipe against the posterior predictive simulations. In Sect. 7, we evaluate our approach for 75%, 90%, and 99% credible intervals.

6.3 Flowpipe Construction

As mentioned in Sect. 5, we can leverage the monotonicity of the wastewater model presented in Sect. 3 to quickly over-approximate the bounds of biogas production. We begin the flowpipe construction by taking the parameter estimates from the Bayesian inference for the desired credible interval. Once we define the initial conditions using the output from the Bayesian inference, we simply propagate those bounds from the same start date as the Bayesian inference. We perform reachability analysis for a 8-day period, then ignoring the 3 days that overlap with the Bayesian inference, we evaluate the flowpipe on the final 5 days of the simulation period. Specific implementation details in Julia are described in the Appendix (available upon request).

7   Evaluation

We evaluate our two-step approach of Bayesian inference and flowpipe construction versus the standard approach of performing posterior predictive simulations. We compare the accuracy and computational time of our predictions for credible intervals (CI) of 75%, 90%, and 99%. The code used for evaluation can be found in the software artifact available on Zenodo [14].

Posterior Predictive Simulations: We compare our approach against a standard approach based on constructing the so-called "posterior predictive distribution" [38] through simulations. The posterior predictive simulations approach uses the samples computed through Bayesian inference to predict future states of the model through simulation. In our implementation, we simulate the samples computed by the Bayesian inference procedure using the ODE model to obtain sample values for gas production for the 5 days in the future. We then simply compute credible intervals for each of the future days as an alternative to flowpipe construction. Note that the simulation is performed for each sample obtained by the Bayesian inference algorithm.

In Fig. 4, we illustrate representative prediction outcomes across different time periods. Table 2 summarizes statistics across the entire data set spanning three months split into multiple 8 day segments. Both the two-step approach (Fig. 4, left) and the approach using posterior predictive simulations (Fig. 4, right) provide reasonable prediction bounds that capture the historical trajectory. Although the posterior predictive simulations produce tighter bounds, they fail to accurately predict the ground truth. Whereas, the approach proposed here using flowpipe construction is able to capture the ground truth data with very high accuracy.

We hypothesize that the use of credible intervals captures a simple but accurate set of point estimates from the posterior samples. The rest of the approach is entirely free of any randomness and therefore has generalized from the available samples to facts about the underlying probability distributions. On the other hand, the posterior simulations are tied to the samples and attempt to make complex inference (by propagating the samples through a differential equation model) that fails to generalize well. The high uncertainty in measurements and changing conditions of the wastewater treatment processes exacerbate the challenges faced by the posterior simulation approach.

Table 2 presents key performance statistics comparing the two methods. The two-step approach consistently outperforms Bayesian inference alone in terms of prediction *accuracy*, defined as the proportion of ground-truth gas production values captured within the predicted bounds. For example, the combined method captures 94% of samples at the 90% CI, while the posterior simulations method captures only 21% of the samples.

Table 2. Performance statistic comparing our two-step approach of Bayesian inference followed by flowpipe construction to posterior predictive simulations approach for various credible intervals (CIs). Legend: **Accuracy** refers to the percentage of samples where the historical (ground-truth) biogas production fell within the predicted bounds; **Uncertainty** refers to the average width of the bounds in m^3; **Bayesian Inference Time** refers to the amount of time it took to perform the 3-day initialization, and **Prediction Time** refers to the 8-day prediction. All computation times were gathered on a 2023 MacBook Pro using the Apple M2 Pro chip with 12 cores.

	Flowpipe Construction			Posterior Predictive Simulations		
	75% CI	90% CI	99% CI	75% CI	90% CI	99% CI
Accuracy	0.85	0.94	1.00	0.13	0.21	0.33
Uncertainty (m^3)	9220	13850	21290	330	490	770
Bayesian Inference Time (s)	64	64	64	64	64	64
Prediction time (s)	1.6	1.7	1.6	77	77	77

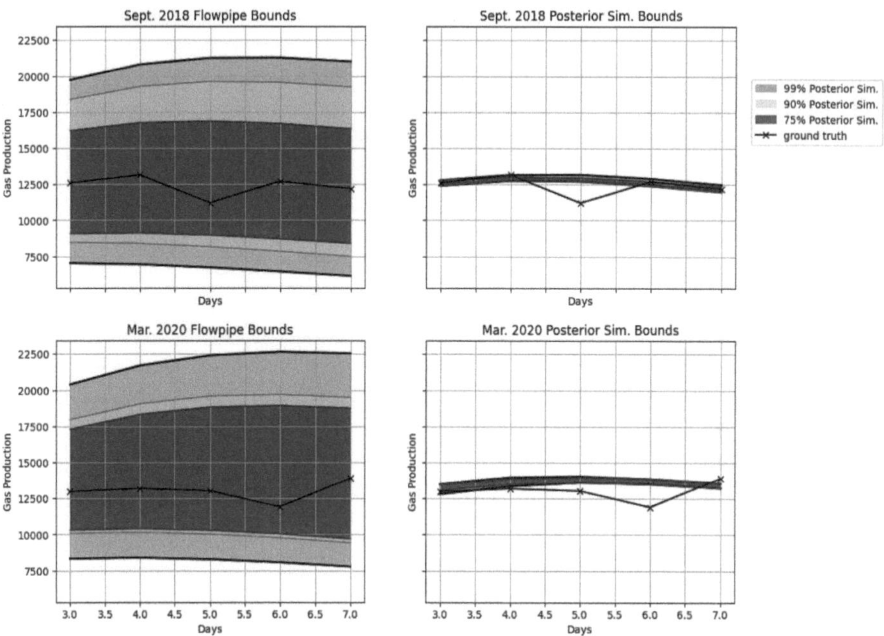

Fig. 4. Sample predictions for a single 8 day segment from September 2018 (top) and March 2020 (bottom) using various methods for various credible intervals (CIs). (Left) Upper and lower bounds from our two-step approach of Bayesian inference and flowpipe construction. (Right) Credible intervals from posterior prediction.

This improved accuracy comes with increased *uncertainty*, i.e., wider bounds. At the 99% CI, the combined method produces an average interval width of 21,290 m^3. However, the fact that the posterior predictive samples have a small credible interval is irrelevant since their accuracy is quite low.

Importantly, the *inference time* remains constant across both methods and all CIs (64 s), since both use the same Bayesian inference stage.

The most notable difference lies in *prediction time*: whereas posterior simulations takes over 75 s, the combined method completes in under 2 s, regardless of CI level. This 40× speedup enables the method to be used in time-sensitive applications without sacrificing reliability.

To conclude, our approach based on credible intervals and flowpipe computations yields not just a speedup but also captures the ground truth data well when compared to the standard approach of posterior predictive simulations.

8   Conclusion and Future Work

In this paper, we present a novel combination of two heavily researched mathematical topics: probabilistic programming and reachability analysis. Specifically, we use MCMC on 3-days of past data to create credible intervals for the unknown parameters and initial conditions of a first-order kinetics model of biogas production at a WWTP. We then exploit the monotonicity of this model to quickly compute upper and lower bounds for the next 5-days of biogas production at the WWTP. These formal bounds could be used to verify biogas production predictions at WWTPs, which in turn facilitates energy management plans.

We found it challenging to evaluate our results against previous publications given the dearth of prior research in this area. Instead, we perform posterior predictive simulations for the same 5-day period that we construct a flowpipe using reachability analysis. Across credible intervals from 75% to 99%, we found that posterior predictive simulations had an accuracy of 13–33% compared to 85–100% accuracy for our two-step Bayesian inference plus flowpipe construction. High accuracy is vital to building the trust of operators when deploying prediction algorithms in the context of automated control, especially for critical infrastructure like WWTPs. The much faster computation time of flowpipe construction versus posterior predictive simulations (approximately 40x in the prediction phase) makes it better suited for automated planning and closed-loop controls.

Our method seeks to construct formal bounds given the sensitive nature of WWTPs as critical infrastructure. We are successful, as we achieve a 100% accuracy for a 99% credible interval, but this comes with a large degree of uncertainty ($21{,}290\,\mathrm{m}^3$ for a 99% credible interval). Unfortunately, this large uncertainty makes the algorithm impractical to deploy in a real-world setting. The 75% credible interval is still quite accurate with the biogas production falling within the bounds 85% of the time, and it has less than half the uncertainty of the 99% credible interval.

More credible intervals could be tested, and the operators could give input on the balance of accuracy and uncertainty that their prefer at their WWTP. Future work will also study the effect of using inference algorithms other than MCMC such as sequential Monte Carlo and other methods. With further refinement, our combination of probabilistic programming and reachability analysis has the potential to verify predictions of biogas production at WWTPs. These predictions of biogas production are vital to successfully deploying cost- or emissions-minimizing operational strategies that have been recently studied at WWTPs [11, 16]. One challenge to deploying these optimal energy management plans is the role of WWTPs as critical infrastructure and subsequent risk aversion of operators, so formal methods offer a compelling approach to reassuring WWTP operators of the safety of these operational recommendations. This technique could also be applied to critical infrastructure outside of the water sector that can be modeled with ODEs, such as transportation and energy.

Acknowledgments. This work was funded, in part, by the Center for Integrated Facility Engineering at Stanford University as a part of CIFE Seed Proposal 2023–02, "Formal proofs of safe operating limits at wastewater resource recovery facilities"; the Stanford Woods Institute for the Environment as a part of Realizing Environmental Innovation Program (REIP) under award "Affordable, Sustainable, and Just Design of Next Generation Wastewater Resource Recovery Facilities"; and the US National Science Foundation (NSF) under awards # CCF-2422136 and CPS-1836900.

References

1. Ahnert, M., Schalk, T., Brückner, H., Effenberger, J., Kuehn, V., Krebs, P.: Organic matter parameters in WWTP-a critical review and recommendations for application in activated sludge modelling. Water Sci. Technol. **84**(9), 2093–2112 (2021)
2. Althoff, M.: An introduction to CORA 2015. In: Proceedings of Applied Verification for Continuous and Hybrid Systems (ARCH), pp. 120–151. EasyChair (2015). https://doi.org/10.29007/zbkv, https://easychair.org/publications/paper/xMm
3. Althoff, M., Dolan, J.M.: Online verification of automated road vehicles using reachability analysis. IEEE Trans. Rob. **30**(4), 903–918 (2014)
4. Althoff, M., Frehse, G., Girard, A.: Set propagation techniques for reachability analysis. Ann. Rev. Control Robot. Auton. Syst. **4**(1), 369–395 (2021). https://doi.org/10.1146/annurev-control-071420-081941
5. Baena, A., Orjuela, A., Rakshit, S.K., Clark, J.H.: Enzymatic hydrolysis of waste fats, oils and greases (FOGs): status, prospective, and process intensification alternatives. Chem. Eng. Process. Process Intensification **175**, 108930 (2022)
6. Bak, S., Tran, H.D., Johnson, T.T.: Numerical verification of affine systems with up to a billion dimensions. In: Proceedings of the 22nd ACM International Conference on Hybrid Systems: Computation and Control, pp. 23 – 32. HSCC '19, Association for Computing Machinery, New York, NY, USA (2019)
7. Bansal, S., Bajcsy, A., Ratner, E., Dragan, A.D., Tomlin, C.J.: A Hamilton-Jacobi reachability-based framework for predicting and analyzing human motion for safe planning. In: 2020 IEEE International Conference on Robotics and Automation (ICRA), pp. 7149–7155. IEEE (2020)
8. Barthe, G., Katoen, J.P., Silva, A.: Foundations of Probabilistic Programming. Cambridge University Press (2020)
9. Berz, M., Makino, K.: Verified integration of ODEs and flows using differential algebraic methods on high-order Taylor models. Reliable Comput. **4**(4), 361–369 (1998)
10. Bingham, E., et al.: Pyro: deep universal probabilistic programming. J. Mach. Learn. Res. **20**(1), 973–978 (2019)
11. Bolorinos, J., Mauter, M.S., Rajagopal, R.: Integrated energy flexibility management at wastewater treatment facilities. Environ. Sci. Technol. **57**(46), 18362–18371 (2023)
12. Cairoli, F., Paoletti, N., Bortolussi, L.: Conformal quantitative predictive monitoring of STL requirements for stochastic processes. In: Proceedings of the 26th ACM International Conference on Hybrid Systems: Computation and Control, pp. 1–11 (2023)

13. Carpenter, B., et al.: Stan: a probabilistic programming language. J. Stat. Softw. **76**(1) (2017)

14. Chapin, F., Varma, A., Akinwande, S., Mauter, M., Sankaranarayanan, S.: Software artifact for using Bayesian inference and Flowpipe construction to bound predictions of biogas production at wastewater treatment plants (2025). https://doi.org/10.5281/zenodo.16930822

15. Chapin, F.T., Bolorinos, J., Mauter, M.S.: Electricity and natural gas tariffs at united states wastewater treatment plants. Sci. Data **11**(1), 113 (2024)

16. Chapin, F.T., Wettermark, D., Bolorinos, J., Mauter, M.S.: Load-shifting strategies for cost-effective emission reductions at wastewater facilities. Environmental Science & Technology (2025)

17. Chen, X., Abraham, E., Sankaranarayanan, S.: Taylor model Flowpipe construction for non-linear hybrid systems. In: 2012 IEEE 33rd Real-Time Systems Symposium, pp. 183–192. IEEE (2012)

18. Chen, X., Ábrahám, E., Sankaranarayanan, S.: Flow*: an analyzer for non-linear hybrid systems. In: Computer Aided Verification: 25th International Conference, CAV 2013, Saint Petersburg, Russia, July 13-19, 2013. Proceedings 25, pp. 258–263. Springer (2013)

19. Chen, X., Sankaranarayanan, S.: Reachability analysis for cyber-physical systems: are we there yet? (invited paper). In: Proceedings of NASA Formal Methods Symposium. Lecture Notes in Computer Science, vol. 13260, pp. 109–130. Springer (2022)

20. Chou, Y., Yoon, H., Sankaranarayanan, S.: Predictive runtime monitoring of vehicle models using Bayesian estimation and reachability analysis. In: 2020 IEEE/RSJ International Conference on Intelligent Robots and Systems (IROS), pp. 2111–2118. IEEE (2020)

21. Christensen, M.L., et al.: Pilot-scale hydrolysis of primary sludge for production of easily degradable carbon to treat biological wastewater or produce biogas. Sci. Total Environ. **846**, 157532 (2022)

22. Clarke, E.M., Zuliani, P.: Statistical model checking for cyber-physical systems. In: International Symposium on Automated Technology for Verification and Analysis, pp. 1–12. Springer (2011)

23. Eastman, J.A., Ferguson, J.F.: Solubilization of particulate organic carbon during the acid phase of anaerobic digestion. Journal (Water Pollution Control Federation), pp. 352–366 (1981)

24. Farina, L., Rinaldi, S.: Positive Linear Systems: Theory and Applications. John Wiley & Sons, Inc. (2000). https://onlinelibrary.wiley.com/doi/book/10.1002/9781118033029

25. Ge, H., Xu, K., Ghahramani, Z.: Turing: a language for flexible probabilistic inference. In: International Conference on Artificial Intelligence and Statistics, AISTATS 2018, 9-11 April 2018, Playa Blanca, Lanzarote, Canary Islands, Spain, pp. 1682–1690 (2018). http://proceedings.mlr.press/v84/ge18b.html

26. Ghosh, B., Duggirala, P.S.: Reachability of linear uncertain systems: Sampling based approaches. arXiv preprint arXiv:2109.07638 (2021)

27. Gossett, J.M., Belser, R.L.: Anaerobic digestion of waste activated sludge. J. Environ. Eng. Div. **108**(6), 1101–1120 (1982)

28. Guo, H., et al.: Reconsidering hydrolysis kinetics for anaerobic digestion of waste activated sludge applying cascade reactors with ultra-short residence times. Water Res. **202**, 117398 (2021)

29. Henze, M., van Loosdrecht, M.C., Ekama, G.A., Brdjanovic, D.: Biological wastewater treatment. IWA publishing (2008)

30. Iasmin, M., Dean, L.O., Ducoste, J.J.: Quantifying fat, oil, and grease deposit formation kinetics. Water Res. **88**, 786–795 (2016)

31. International Energy Agency: Outlook for biogas and biomethane: prospects for organic growth. OECD Publishing, Paris (2020)

32. Jaynes, E.T.: Confidence intervals vs Bayesian intervals. In: Harper, W.L., Hooker, C.A. (eds.) Foundations of Probability Theory, Statistical Inference, and Statistical Theories of Science, pp. 175–. D. Reidel, Dordrecht (1976)

33. Jha, S.K., Clarke, E.M., Langmead, C.J., Legay, A., Platzer, A., Zuliani, P.: A Bayesian approach to model checking biological systems. In: Computational Methods in Systems Biology: 7th International Conference, CMSB 2009, Bologna, Italy, August 31-September 1, 2009. Proceedings 7, pp. 218–234. Springer (2009)

34. Koch, K., Drewes, J.E.: Alternative approach to estimate the hydrolysis rate constant of particulate material from batch data. Appl. Energy **120**, 11–15 (2014)

35. Koch, K., Helmreich, B., Drewes, J.E.: Co-digestion of food waste in municipal wastewater treatment plants: effect of different mixtures on methane yield and hydrolysis rate constant. Appl. Energy **137**, 250–255 (2015)

36. Lal, R., Prabhakar, P.: Bounded error Flowpipe computation of parameterized linear systems. In: 2015 International Conference on Embedded Software (EMSOFT), pp. 237–246. IEEE (2015)

37. Mahmood, Q., Ping, Z., Li, G.X., Mei, L.L.: The rate-limiting step in anaerobic digestion in the presence of phosphine. Toxicol. Ind. Health **22**(4), 165–172 (2006)

38. McElreath, R.: Statistical Rethinking: A Bayesian Course with Examples in R and STAN, 2nd edn. Chapman & Hall/CRC Texts in Statistical Science, Boca Raton, FL (2020)

39. van de Meent, J.W., Paige, B., Yang, H., Wood, F.: An introduction to probabilistic programming (2021). https://arxiv.org/abs/1809.10756

40. Meyer, P.J., Coogan, S., Arcak, M.: Sampled-data reachability analysis using sensitivity and mixed-monotonicity. IEEE Control Syst. Lett. **2**(4), 761–766 (2018). https://doi.org/10.1109/LCSYS.2018.2848280

41. Musabandesu, E., Loge, F.: Load shifting at wastewater treatment plants: a case study for participating as an energy demand resource. J. Clean. Prod. **282**, 124454 (2021)

42. Narayanan, P., Carette, J., Romano, W., Shan, C., Zinkov, R.: Probabilistic inference by program transformation in Hakaru (system description). In: Kiselyov, O., King, A. (eds.) Functional and Logic Programming. FLOPS 2016. Lecture Notes in Computer Science, vol. 9613, pp. 1–29. Springer, Cham (2016)

43. Reifsnyder, S., Cecconi, F., Rosso, D.: Dynamic load shifting for the abatement of GHG emissions, power demand, energy use, and costs in metropolitan hybrid wastewater treatment systems. Water Res. **200**, 117224 (2021)

44. Rittmann, B.E., McCarty, P.L.: Environmental Biotechnology: Principles and Applications. McGraw-Hill Education, New York, second edn (2020)

45. Roeleveld, P., Van Loosdrecht, M.: Experience with guidelines for wastewater characterisation in the netherlands. Water Sci. Technol. **45**(6), 77–87 (2002)

46. Sillanpää, M., Khadir, A., Gurung, K.: Resource Recovery in Drinking Water Treatment. Elsevier (2023)

47. Sowby, R.B.: Increasing water and wastewater utility participation in demand response programs. Energy Nexus **1**, 100001 (2021)

48. Tolpin, D., van de Meent, J.W., Wood, F.: Probabilistic programming in Anglican. In: Proceedings of the 2015th European Conference on Machine Learning and Knowledge Discovery in Databases, pp. 308–311. ECMLPKDD'15, Springer (2015)

49. Vavilin, V., Fernandez, B., Palatsi, J., Flotats, X.: Hydrolysis kinetics in anaerobic degradation of particulate organic material: an overview. Waste Manage. **28**(6), 939–951 (2008)

50. Zohrabian, A., Plata, S.L., Kim, D.M., Childress, A.E., Sanders, K.T.: Leveraging the water-energy nexus to derive benefits for the electric grid through demand-side management in the water supply and wastewater sectors. Wiley Interdiscip. Rev. Water **8**(3), e1510 (2021)

51. Zuliani, P.: Statistical model checking for biological applications. Int. J. Softw. Tools Technol. Transf. **17**(4), 527–536 (2015)

Reachability

CHC-Based Reachability Analysis
via Cycle Summarization

Konstantin Britikov[1]([✉]), Grigory Fedyukovich[1,2], and Natasha Sharygina[1]

[1] University of Lugano, Lugano, Switzerland
konstantin.britikov@usi.ch
[2] Florida State University, Tallahassee, FL, USA

Abstract. Modern reachability analysis techniques are highly effective when applied to software safety verification. However, they still struggle with certain classes of problems, particularly the verification of programs with complex control flow and deep nested loops. In this paper, we introduce Cycle Summarization-based Reachability Analysis (CSRA), a new Constrained Horn Clause (CHC) based approach for reachability analysis of nested-loop software. Our technique relies on the generation and refinement of cycle summaries within the CHC system. CSRA analyzes cycles in a modular manner, constructing summaries and cycle unrollings. Cycle summaries in our approach are used both to prove safety and detect potential safety violations. This enables more efficient exploration of nested loops. The prototype of CSRA is implemented within the Golem CHC solver. An empirical comparison with other reachability analysis techniques demonstrates that our approach is highly competitive in both proving safety and constructing counterexamples.

1 Introduction

Reachability analysis is a foundational technique providing a rigorous and systematic means of analyzing software with respect to specified safety properties. While it is undecidable in general, recent advances in Satisfiability Modulo Theories (SMT) and Constrained Horn Clause (CHC) solvers have enabled the development of efficient symbolic analysis techniques. However, when the program of interest has a complicated loop structure, the search space for possible property violations explodes quickly. Thus, the reachability analysis remains challenging even for advanced modern techniques.

State-of-the-art techniques such as Counter-Example Guided Abstraction Refinement (CEGAR) [3,15,29], IC3/Spacer [11,34], Accelerated Bounded Model Checking (ABMC) [25], and Transition Power Abstraction (TPA) [8,12] often struggle with nested loops and complex control flows. Although capable of some acceleration, approaches based on IC3/Spacer and CEGAR usually perform reachability analysis one step at a time, which is particularly taxing in the presence of deep loops. A recent TPA technique instead makes larger steps and handles deep loops more efficiently. However, it applies only to the analysis of

F. Damiani and M. Farrell (Eds.): iFM 2025, LNCS 16194, pp. 205–225, 2026.
https://doi.org/10.1007/978-3-032-10794-7_11

a single loop. To analyze nested loops, TPA relies on a preprocessing to merge them into a single loop, losing important structural information. ABMC under-approximates loop behavior and is more suited for bug finding than for proving safety. Specifically, ABMC attempts to generate blocking clauses to prove safety, but it can be challenging for programs with nested loops and complex execution flow.

We introduce a new approach of Cycle Summarization-based Reachability Analysis (CSRA) to target programs with nested loops and complex structures. Our algorithm operates within the framework of CHC solving, in which the program is modeled by logical implications over uninterpreted predicates. CHCs serve as an intermediate software representation, which enables reasoning about programs independently of their programming language. This paradigm is employed in a wide range of model checkers, such as SEAHORN [28], JAY-HORN [32], RUSTHORN [37], and KORN [19].

Our approach decomposes reachability analysis into the exploration of different cycle-free paths through the CHC system. The algorithm traverses each path independently, analyzing cycles and constructing cycle unrollings when needed. The core procedure of our approach is the computation and refinement of cycle summaries. CSRA uses TPA engine *modularly*, to analyze cycles, produce cycle summaries and unrollings. The constructed cycle summaries serve as abstractions that describe any possible cycle unrolling and as components for the construction of other cycle summaries. The use of cycle summaries enables efficient reasoning about potentially infinite sets of paths in the system and facilitates safety verification. Additionally, once learned, these summaries can be reused in the analysis of other paths through the CHC system.

A prototype of our technique has been implemented in the GOLEM [6] CHC solver and evaluated on benchmarks from CHC-Comp-2024 [17], aeval-bench-marks [21], and a set of instances synthesized from real C++ code from repositories of Z3 [5], SEAHORN [28], OPENSMT [30] and GOLEM. Our results show that the approach is competitive with other state-of-the-art reachability analysis techniques. Specifically, CSRA solved a significant number of instances uniquely. On average, CSRA is $2.5\times$ faster than ELDARICA and $1.9\times$ faster than SPACER.

The main contributions of this paper are: (1) a novel CHC-based reachability analysis approach for nested-loop programs, (2) a new TPA-based compositional approach for the generation and refinement of cycle summaries that uses inner cycle summaries to produce outer cycle summaries, (3) a technique for decomposing CHC reachability analysis into the exploration of cycle-free paths through the CHC system, (4) formalization and proof of soundness for our method, and (5) an extensive empirical evaluation of CSRA in comparison with other state-of-the-art approaches for reachability analysis.

Motivating Example

Figure 1 gives a C program with a nested loop structure. The outer loop increments x1 by the value of x2 and assigns 0 to x2, while the inner loop increments x2 by 2 until $x2 \geq 32$. When execution of the loops is finished, x1 equals 512, so the program is safe.

```
1 int x1 = 0, x2 = 0;
2 while (x1 < 512) {
3   while(x2 < 32) { x2 = x2 + 2; }
4   x1 = x1 + x2; x2 = 0;
5 }
6 assert(x1 == 512);
```

Fig. 1. A C program with nested loops.

$$
\begin{array}{lll}
x_1 = 0 \wedge x_2 = 0 & \implies p_1(x_1, x_2) & (c_1) \\
p_1(x_1, x_2) \wedge x_1 < 512 \wedge x_1' = x_1 \wedge x_2' = x_2 & \implies p_2(x_1', x_2') & (c_2) \\
p_2(x_1, x_2) \wedge x_2 < 32 \wedge x_1' = x_1 \wedge x_2' = x_2 + 2 & \implies p_2(x_1', x_2') & (c_3) \\
p_2(x_1, x_2) \wedge x_2 \geq 32 \wedge x_1' = x_1 + x_2 \wedge x_2' = 0 & \implies p_1(x_1', x_2') & (c_4) \\
p_1(x_1, x_2) \wedge x_1 \geq 512 \wedge x_1 \neq 512 & \implies \bot & (c_5)
\end{array}
$$

Fig. 2. CHC representation of the program in Fig. 1.

When applied to this program, state-of-the-art reachability analysis techniques behave as follows. In the worst-case scenario, CEGAR and Spacer/IC3 would need to traverse all 16 outer and 256 inner loop iterations one by one to synthesize *inductive invariants* for both inner and outer loops. In contrast, TPA would proceed using *transition invariant* generation, but in order to apply it, one would need to merge both loops into a single one, losing structural information of the program and thus degrading efficiency. For this specific example, ABMC would underapproximate inner and outer loop behavior, successfully deriving blocking clauses that prove the safety of the program. However, as shown by our evaluation, it often struggles, especially if the control flow is more complex or the program contains multiple nested loops.

In contrast, CSRA leverages the program's structural information to efficiently prove safety and handle deep loops. First, CSRA constructs a cycle summary that overapproximates the behavior of the inner loop. Then, using this summary as an abstraction of any possible inner loop traversal, CSRA employs TPA to analyze the outer loop and prove the safety of the system. The use of the inner cycle summary eliminates the need to produce exact traces through the loop, making our approach significantly more efficient compared to classical TPA.

2   Preliminaries

This section introduces the definitions and formalisms needed to describe our algorithm and prove its correctness. We represent programs symbolically by mapping control flow to first-order logic formulas, restricted to Linear Integer Arithmetic (LIA).

A set of Constrained Horn Clauses (CHCs) models programs and safety properties as first-order logic formulas. We focus on linear CHCs:

Definition 1 (Linear CHC). *A linear CHC is a universally quantified first-order logic formula over a set of uninterpreted predicates $\mathcal{P}$ that takes one of the following three forms:*

$$
\begin{aligned}
\forall x.\phi_1(x) &\implies p_1(x) &\quad \text{fact} \\
\forall x, x'.p_1(x) \wedge \phi_2(x, x') &\implies p_2(x') & \\
\forall x.p_1(x) \wedge \phi_3(x) &\implies \bot &\quad \text{query}
\end{aligned}
$$

where $p_1, p_2 \in \mathcal{P}$, x, x' are sets of variables, and ϕ_1, ϕ_2, and ϕ_3 are first-order logic formulas that do not have occurrences of any predicates from $\mathcal{P}$.

Throughout, we omit universal quantifiers in CHCs for readability. A *fact* is a CHC without an uninterpreted predicate in the premise, while a *query* has $\bot$ in the conclusion. For a CHC c, $src(c)$ denotes the predicate in the premise (or $\top$ if c is a fact), $trg(c)$ denotes the predicate in the conclusion (or $\bot$ if c is a query), and $constr(c)$ denotes the interpreted part ϕ of the clause. We write c_t^s to denote a CHC with $src(c_t^s) = s$ and $trg(c_t^s) = t$.

An example of a CHC system is given in Fig. 2. Each loop in the corresponding program has a dedicated predicate, e.g., the loop with head at Line 2 in Fig. 1 corresponds to p_1, and the loop with head at Line 3 to p_2. The *query* CHC c_5 encodes the negation of the assertion (i.e., violation of the safety property).

CHC paths are analogous to queries in Bounded Model Checking [14]. They represent finite sequences of CHCs, each of which encodes a program fragment.

Definition 2 (CHC path, path predicates, path condition). *Given a CHC system S over a set of uninterpreted predicates $\mathcal{P}$ with predicates $s, t \in \mathcal{P}$, a CHC path $h_t^s = [c_1, \ldots, c_n]$ is a vector of CHCs $c_1, \ldots, c_n \in S$ such that (1) for all i, $1 \leq i < n$: $trg(c_i) = src(c_{i+1})$, (2) $src(c_1) = s$, and (3) $trg(c_n) = t$. Additionally, for h_t^s, we define the path predicates $preds(h_t^s) = \{p \in \mathcal{P} : \exists c \in h_t^s$ s.t. $p = src(c) \vee p = trg(c)\}$ and its path condition π as follows:*

$$
\pi(h_t^s)(x^{(0)}, \ldots, x^{(n)}) = \bigwedge_{i=1}^{n} constr(c_i)(x^{(i-1)}, x^{(i)}).
$$

The length of a path $|h_t^s| = n$ is the number of CHCs $c_1, \ldots, c_n$ in the path. Path h_p^p is called a *cycle path* over predicate p. Cycle paths are constructed using *unrolling*, which is similar to loop unrolling in BMC. A cycle path $h_p^p = [c_1, \ldots, c_n]$ is called an *iteration* path if $\forall i.1 < i \leq n, src(c_i) \neq p$. Path h_t^s is called *simple* if for any two CHCs $c_i, c_j \in h_t^s$, $src(c_i) \neq src(c_j) \wedge trg(c_i) \neq trg(c_j) \wedge i \neq j$ (i.e., there are no inner cycles in the path). We denote simple paths by η and iteration paths by γ. For example, the CHC system in Fig. 2 has a single *simple* path from p_1 to itself: $\eta_{p_1}^{p_1} = [c_2, c_4]$, and its path condition $\pi(\eta_{p_1}^{p_1}) = (x_1 < 512 \wedge x_1' = x_1 \wedge x_2' = x_2 \wedge x_2' \geq 32 \wedge x_1'' = x_1' + x_2' \wedge x_2'' = 0)$. A path h_t^s is called *feasible* if its path condition $\pi(h_t^s)$ is satisfiable. If the initial CHC of a feasible path is a *fact* and the final CHC is a *query*, then the CHC system S is called unsatisfiable. If such a path through the CHC system does not exist, then it is called satisfiable[1].

Definition 3 (Expansion of path). *Given a CHC system S over a set of uninterpreted predicates $\mathcal{P}$ with $s, t \in \mathcal{P}$, and a path[2] $h_t^s = [c_1, \ldots, c_{i-1}] \oplus [c_i, \ldots, c_n]$ where $1 \leq i \leq n$, an expansion of h_t^s over i is a new path $\exp(h_t^s, i)$ such that:*
$$\exp(h_t^s, i) = [c_1, \ldots, c_{i-1}] \oplus h_{src(c_i)}^{src(c_i)} \oplus [c_i, \ldots, c_n].$$

A cycle summary is a formula that overapproximates the path conditions of any possible cycle path, ignoring paths through specific predicates. A cycle summary for a transition system would be its transition invariant [42].

Definition 4 (Cycle summary). *Given a CHC system S over a set of uninterpreted predicates $\mathcal{P}$, $p \in \mathcal{P}$, and a set of predicates $\mathcal{P}_b \subset \mathcal{P}$ (called* blocked*), a cycle summary for p and $\mathcal{P}_b$ is a formula $\sigma(x, x')$ such that for any cycle path h_p^p with $preds(h_p^p) \cap \mathcal{P}_b = \emptyset$ it holds that $\pi(h_p^p)(x, \ldots, x') \implies \sigma(x, x')$. If no cycles h_p^p such that $preds(h_p^p) \cap \mathcal{P}_b = \emptyset$ exist, then conventionally $\sigma(x, x') = \bot$.*

Blocked predicates are used to restrict the set of cycle paths through the predicate. In the CHC system in Fig. 2, the cycle summary for predicate p_2 with blocked predicates $\mathcal{P}_b = \{p_1\}$ is $\sigma_{p_2} = (x_2' \leq 33 \wedge x_1' = x_1)$. There are two possible iteration paths over p_2: $[c_3]$ and $[c_4, c_2]$. However, the path $[c_4, c_2]$ is not overapproximated by σ_{p_2} because $src(c_2) = p_1$ and $p_1 \in \mathcal{P}_b$. For any cycle path $h_{p_2}^{p_2} = [c_3, \ldots, c_3]$, it holds that $\pi(h_{p_2}^{p_2})(x, \ldots, x') \implies \sigma_{p_2}(x, x')$.

Cycle summaries can be generated using a recent technique called Transition Power Abstraction (TPA) [7,8].

Definition 5 (TPA). *TPA is a function that takes a triple of logic formulas over a set of variables x and x': $\langle \phi_{pre}(x), \phi_{tr}(x, x'), \phi_{post}(x) \rangle$, and decides the satisfiability of the following CHC system:*

$$
\begin{aligned}
\phi_{pre}(x) &\implies p(x) & (c_p^\top)\\
p(x) \wedge \phi_{tr}(x, x') &\implies p(x') & (c_p^p)\\
p(x) \wedge \phi_{post}(x) &\implies \bot & (c_\bot^p)
\end{aligned}
$$

If TPA terminates, it returns a tuple $\langle h, \sigma \rangle$. If the CHC system is unsatisfiable, then h is a path $[c_p^p \ldots, c_p^p]$ such that $\phi_{pre}(x) \wedge \pi(h)(x, \ldots, x') \wedge \phi_{post}(x')$ is satisfiable, and $\sigma(x, x') = \bot$. If the CHC system is satisfiable, then $h = \emptyset$, and $\sigma(x, x')$ is a formula such that for any $h_p^p = [c_p^p \ldots, c_p^p]$, it holds that $\pi(h_p^p)(x, \ldots, x') \implies \sigma(x, x')$ and $\phi_{pre}(x) \wedge \sigma(x, x') \wedge \phi_{post}(x')$ is unsatisfiable.

Intuitively, the CHC system in the definition is a transition system, and the formula σ produced by TPA is its transition invariant. It is also a cycle summary over the predicate p in the CHC system.

---

[1] The satisfiability differs from one used in CHC solving, as it does not require to compute interpretations for uninterpreted predicates.

[2] We write $\oplus$ to denote the concatenation of vectors.

3   Cycle Summarization-Based Reachability Analysis

We present the Cycle Summarization-based Reachability Analysis (CSRA) to systematically explore expansions of all simple paths through the CHC system. Upon termination, it either finds a feasible path from a fact to a query or proves that no such path exists. CSRA incrementally builds feasible paths starting from the facts, constructing and utilizing cycle summaries that speed up analysis of the CHC system. Cycle summaries enable efficient reasoning about potentially infinite sets of paths, as they overapproximate any possible cycle traversal. Due to this property, they are used to prove the absence of feasible "bad" paths through the CHC system. Summaries also enable the detection of possible feasible "bad" paths, which are then validated by building a corresponding concrete feasible path. Additionally, cycle summaries are used in the compositional construction of other cycle summaries (for example, if a cycle contains inner cycles).

Our approach consists of three main procedures: CSRA, EXPANDPATH, and ANALYZECYCLES. CSRA receives a CHC system and uses depth-first search (DFS) to enumerate all simple (cycle-free) paths from $\top$ to $\bot$. For each simple path $\eta_\bot^\top$, it invokes EXPANDPATH that attempts to construct a feasible expansion of this path by analyzing inner cycles. If such an expansion exists for some simple path, the CHC system is unsatisfiable and CSRA returns UNSAT; otherwise, it returns SAT.

The core functionality of EXPANDPATH is the construction of a feasible expansion of the given path. This function serves two purposes: first, it attempts to construct a feasible expansion of a simple path $\eta_\bot^\top$ (when called from CSRA), and second, it attempts to construct a feasible cycle path with a specific number of iterations (when called from ANALYZECYCLES). The path is built incrementally, by appending CHCs one at a time. If a CHC cannot be added, the algorithm backtracks and attempts to unroll cycles in the preceding path to enable appending the CHC. For cycle unrolling and analysis, EXPANDPATH calls ANALYZECYCLES. If no feasible path expansion exists, this procedure returns cycle summaries, refined during cycle analysis.

The ANALYZECYCLES function attempts to construct a feasible cycle path over a specified predicate. To find it, ANALYZECYCLES constructs a formula from iteration overapproximations that overapproximates the encoding of any possible iteration path over the predicate. It uses this formula in an attempt to find a feasible cycle path, composed of iteration overapproximations. If such a path exists, the algorithm calls EXPANDPATH to produce the corresponding concrete cycle path. If no feasible cycle path exists, it employs TPA to produce a cycle summary capturing the reason for this.

3.1   Cycle Analysis

Algorithm 1 gives pseudocode of function ANALYZECYCLES. It takes the following inputs: a CHC system S, a set of blocked predicates $\mathcal{P}_b$ (possibly, empty), a map of summaries Σ, formulas *pre* and *post*, and a predicate p. Specifically, $\Sigma : \langle p, \mathcal{P} \rangle \to \sigma$ maps a predicate and a set of blocked predicates to an existing

---

Algorithm 1: ANALYZECYCLES$(S, \mathcal{P}_b, \Sigma, pre, post, p)$

Input : CHC system S, set of blocked predicates $\mathcal{P}_b$, map of cycle summaries
      $\Sigma : \langle p, \mathcal{P} \rangle \to \sigma$, pre and $post$ formulas, predicate p

Output: feasible cycle path h_p^p, updated summaries Σ

1   **while** $\top$ **do**
2   let $\mu \leftarrow$ SUMMARIZEITERATION$(S, \mathcal{P}_b, \Sigma, p)$
3     $\langle a_p^p, \sigma_p \rangle \leftarrow$ TPA$(pre, \mu, post)$
4   **if** $a_p^p \notin \emptyset$ **then**   // if overapproximated cycle path exists
5       $[\eta_1, \ldots, \eta_n] \leftarrow$ EXTRACTPATHS$(S, \mathcal{P}_b, pre \wedge \pi(a_p^p) \wedge post)$
6   **if** $SAT(pre \wedge \pi(\eta_1 \oplus \cdots \oplus \eta_n) \wedge post)$ **then return** $\langle \eta_1 \oplus \cdots \oplus \eta_n, \Sigma \rangle$
7       $\langle h_p^p, \Sigma \rangle \leftarrow$ EXPANDPATH$(S, \mathcal{P}_b \cup \{p\}, \Sigma, pre, post, \eta_1 \oplus \cdots \oplus \eta_n)$
8   **if** $h_p^p \notin \emptyset$ **then return** $\langle h_p^p, \Sigma \rangle$;   // return concrete path
9   **else**
10      $\Sigma(p, \mathcal{P}_b)(x, x') \leftarrow \Sigma(p, \mathcal{P}_b)(x, x') \wedge \sigma_p(x, x')$
11   **return** $\langle \emptyset, \Sigma \rangle$ // return refined cycle summaries

---

cycle summary ($\top$ if no summary exists). Formula *pre* encodes a satisfiable path condition of a prefix path $h_p^\top$. Formula *post* encodes a constraint that must be met under *pre* for some cycle path h_p^p over p. In other words, a path $h_p^\top \oplus h_p^p$ must be feasible, and it must meet *post* after h_p^p. The algorithm returns such a feasible cycle path h_p^p, i.e., such that $pre(\ldots, x) \wedge \pi(h_p^p)(x, \ldots, x') \wedge post(x')$ is satisfiable. In addition, the returned h_p^p does not contain CHCs over predicates $\mathcal{P}_b$. If no such path exists, then the returned h_p^p is conventionally empty. The algorithm also returns a refined map of summaries Σ.

If no feasible cycle path can be determined, the algorithm generates a cycle summary σ_p that overapproximates all possible cycle paths over p (still, not containing blocked predicates $\mathcal{P}_b$). Intuitively, this summary gives a reason for why *post* never holds for any cycle path over p under the given *pre*.

The algorithm builds an auxiliary formula μ that overapproximates any possible cycle iteration. It uses TPA to determine existence of a feasible path $a_p^p = [c_p^p, \ldots, c_p^p]$, such that $pre(\ldots, x) \wedge \pi(a_p^p)(x, \ldots, x') \wedge post(x')$ is satisfiable, where c_p^p is defined as $p(x) \wedge \mu(x, \ldots, x') \implies p(x')$. Approaches like BMC or Spacer can be used, however, TPA is particularly suitable as it can generate and refine cycle summaries. Additionally, TPA is efficient in deep reachability checks. If a path a_p^p exists, ANALYZECYCLES attempts to build a concrete cycle path h_p^p that corresponds to it. This h_p^p is composed of CHCs that are present in the CHC system. When h_p^p cannot be constructed, summaries of inner cycles are refined by TPA, and formula μ is updated to block the previously found a_p^p, and the algorithm is restarted. If no feasible a_p^p exists, TPA returns a cycle summary σ_p.

We proceed with illustrating the construction of formula μ on our running example and give the formal definition of μ afterwards.

Example 1. Recall the CHC system in Fig. 2. Suppose we wish to overapproximate all possible iteration paths over the predicate p_1. There are two classes,

γ_1 and γ_2, of iteration paths over p_1: (1) simple path $\gamma_1 = [c_2, c_4]$, with path condition $\pi(\gamma_1) = constr(c_2) \wedge constr(c_4)$, and (2) path with inner cycles $\gamma_2 = [c_2] \oplus h_{p_2}^{p_2} \oplus [c_4]$, where $h_{p_2}^{p_2} = [c_3, \dots, c_3]$. The corresponding path condition is $\pi(\gamma_2) = constr(c_2) \wedge \pi(h_{p_2}^{p_2}) \wedge constr(c_4)$. It is known that the cycle summary $\sigma_{p_2}(x, x') = x_2' \leq 33 \wedge x_1' = x_1$ overapproximates any path condition $\pi(h_{p_2}^{p_2})$ such that $p_1 \notin \mathcal{P}(h_{p_2}^{p_2})$. Therefore, the path condition of any iteration path over p_1 can be overapproximated by the following formula[3]: $\mu(x^{(0)}, x^f, x^{(2)}) =$

$$\overbrace{constr(c_2)(x^{(0)}, x^{(1)})}^{A} \wedge \Big(\underbrace{constr(c_4)(x^{(1)}, x^{(2)})}_{C} \vee \underbrace{(\sigma_{p_2}(x^{(1)}, x^f) \wedge constr(c_4)(x^f, x^{(2)}))}_{D} \Big)^{B}$$

Here, conjunct A captures the traversal of CHC c_2, shared between both iteration classes. Conjunct B encodes two cases: either only c_4 is traversed without entering the cycle (captured by C), or the cycle over p_2 is traversed, followed by the traversal of CHC c_4 (captured by D). The formula μ overapproximates the simple path $[c_2, c_4]$ or any iteration path. The concrete formula would look as follows (with variable sets $x^{(0)}, x^{(2)}$ substituted by x, x'): $\mu(x, x^f, x') =$

$$\overbrace{\Big(x_1 < 512 \wedge x_1^{(1)} = x_1 \wedge x_2^{(1)} = x_2 \Big)}^{A} \wedge \Big(\overbrace{\big(x_2^{(1)} \geq 32 \wedge x_1' = x_1^{(1)} + x_2^{(1)} \wedge x_2' = 0 \big)}^{C} \vee$$
$$\underbrace{\big((x_2^f \leq 33 \wedge x_1^f = x_1^{(1)}) \wedge (x_2^f \geq 32 \wedge x_1' = x_1^f + x_2^f \wedge x_2' = 0) \big) \Big)}_{D}$$

Definition 6 (SummarizeIteration). *Given a CHC system S, a set of blocked predicates $\mathcal{P}_b$, a map of cycle summaries Σ, a predicate p, and the set Θ of all simple paths over predicate p, $\Theta = \{\eta_p^p \mid preds(\eta_p^p) \cap \mathcal{P}_b = \emptyset\}$, SummarizeIteration produces a formula $\mu(x, \dots, x')$[4]:*

$$\bigvee_{\eta \in \Theta} \Big(\bigwedge_{i=1}^{|\eta|} \big((constr(c_i)(x^{(i-1)}, x^{(i)})) \vee (\Sigma(src(c_i), \mathcal{P}_b^i)(x^{(i-1)}, x^f) \wedge constr(c_i)(x^f, x^{(i)})) \big) \Big)$$

where $\mathcal{P}_b^i = \mathcal{P}_b \cup \{p\} \cup \big(preds(\eta_{src(c_i)}^p) \setminus \{src(c_i)\} \big)$ and[5] $\eta_{src(c_i)}^p \subset \eta$. For each disjunct, the set of variables $x^{(0)}$ is substituted by x and the last set $x^{(|\eta|)}$ by x'.

In the rest of this subsection, we give more details on Algorithm 1. It starts by calling SummarizeIteration to build the formula μ (Line 2), which overapproximates any iteration path γ_p^p with $preds(\gamma_p^p) \cap \mathcal{P}_b = \emptyset$: $\pi(\gamma_p^p)(x, \dots, x') \implies \mu(x, \dots, x')$. For every simple path η_p^p, SummarizeIteration constructs the corresponding disjunct in μ. The first conjunct in every disjunct in μ is always of the form $constr(c)(x^{(0)}, x^{(1)})$ since $\Sigma(p, \{p\}) = \bot$.

---

[3] Throughout, x^f is a fresh copy of variables x.

[4] x^f is an auxiliary copy of variables x which is unique for each conjunct. It is needed to ensure the equivalence of the variable versions of the first and last set of variables within each conjunct.

[5] For two vectors h_1, h_2, we use $h_1 \subset h_2$ to denote that $h_2 = [\dots] \oplus h_1 \oplus [\dots]$.

Afterwards, the algorithm attempts to construct a path a_p^p using TPA (Line 3). If a_p^p exists, then by the definition of TPA: $pre(\ldots, x) \wedge \pi(a_p^p)(x, \ldots, x') \wedge post(x')$ is satisfiable, where $a_p^p = [c_p^p, \ldots, c_p^p]$ and c_p^p is defined as $p(x) \wedge \mu(x, \ldots, x') \implies p(x')$. Intuitively, path a_p^p overapproximates any cycle path h_p^p of $|a_p^p|$ iterations.

Definition 7 (ExtractPaths). *Given a CHC system S, a set of blocked predicates $\mathcal{P}_b$, a satisfiable formula $\phi = (pre \wedge \pi(a_p^p) \wedge post) = (pre(\ldots, x^{(0)}) \wedge (\bigvee_{i=1}^m \mu_{\eta_i})(x^{(0)}, \ldots, x^{(1)}) \wedge \cdots \wedge (\bigvee_{i=1}^m \mu_{\eta_i})(x^{(n-1)}, \ldots, x^{(n)}) \wedge post(x^{(n)}))$ where $n = |a_p^p|$, and a set of simple paths $\Theta = \{\eta_p^p \mid preds(\eta_p^p) \cap \mathcal{P}_b = \emptyset\}$, let $M \models \phi$ be a model of ϕ. ExtractPaths returns the vector of simple paths $\Theta_p^p = \{[\eta_1, \ldots, \eta_n] \mid M \models pre \wedge \mu_{\eta_1} \cdots \wedge \mu_{\eta_n} \wedge post,\ s.t.\ for\ all\ i \in [1, n], \eta_i \in \Theta\ and\ \mu_{\eta_i}\ is\ disjunct\ in\ \mu\}$.*

ANALYZECYCLES calls EXTRACTPATHS at Line 5 to extract a vector of simple iteration paths over predicate p which potentially can be expanded into a feasible path. If the formula $pre \wedge \pi(\eta_k \oplus \cdots \oplus \eta_j) \wedge post$ is satisfiable, then a feasible cycle path is found. Otherwise, the EXPANDPATH call at Line 7 attempts to expand the extracted simple paths into the concrete cycle path $h_p^p = \gamma_1 \oplus \cdots \oplus \gamma_{|a_p^p|}$ such that $preds(h_p^p) \cap \mathcal{P}_b = \emptyset$ and $pre(\ldots, x) \wedge \pi(h_p^p)(x, \ldots, x') \wedge post(x')$ is satisfiable. Predicate p is added to the set of blocked predicates in the call to EXPANDPATH to restrict h_p^p to exactly $|a_p^p|$ iterations over p. If a concrete feasible path h_p^p does not exist, EXPANDPATH refines the summaries of inner cycles and the algorithm restarts, rebuilding μ.

If feasible path a_p^p cannot be determined, then no concrete path h_p^p exists either. The summary for $\langle p, \mathcal{P}_b \rangle : \Sigma(p, \mathcal{P}_b)(x, x') \leftarrow \Sigma(p, \mathcal{P}_b)(x, x') \wedge \sigma_p(x, x')$ is **strengthened**, and the algorithm returns a pair $\langle \emptyset, \Sigma \rangle$ at Line 11. This indicates that no feasible cycle path satisfying *pre* and *post* formulas exists.

Example 2. Consider ANALYZECYCLES called over the CHC system in Fig. 2 with $\mathcal{P}_b = \{\top\}$, summaries map Σ: $\{\Sigma(p_1, \{\top\}) = \top, \Sigma(p_2, \{\top, p_1\}) = \top\}$, *pre* formula $pre = (x_1 = 0 \wedge x_2 = 0)$, formula $post = x_1 \geq 512$, and predicate $p = p_1$.

ANALYZECYCLES starts by calling SUMMARIZEITERATION to build μ at Line 2. The formula μ is equivalent to the formula in Example 1 with the exception that σ_{p_2} (formula C) is currently set to $\top$. At Line 3, TPA tries to produce an overapproximating path $a_{p_1}^{p_1} = [c_{p_1}^{p_1}, \ldots, c_{p_1}^{p_1}]$, such that $(x_1 = 0 \wedge x_2 = 0) \wedge \pi(a_{p_1}^{p_1})([x_1, x_2], \ldots, [x_1', x_2']) \wedge (x_1' \geq 512)$. The path $a_{p_1}^{p_1} = [c_{p_1}^{p_1}]$ satisfies this formula. Afterwards, at Line 5, EXTRACTPATHS would return $\Theta_{p_1}^{p_1} = [[c_2, c_4]]$ since μ is composed from a single simple path. The algorithm calls EXPANDPATH at Line 7 to produce a single iteration path $\gamma_{p_1}^{p_1}$ such that $pre \wedge \gamma_{p_1}^{p_1} \wedge post$ would be SAT. This iteration path does not exist. EXPANDPATH updates $\Sigma(p_2, \{\top, p_1\})(x, x') = (x_2' \leq 33 \wedge x_1' = x_1)$ and returns an empty path $\emptyset$. ANALYZECYCLES will roll back and call SUMMARIZEITERATION to produce a different μ (same as in Example 1). The call to TPA at Line 3 constructs new overapproximating path $a_{p_1}^{p_1}$ of at least 16 iterations that reaches *post*. The call at Line 5 returns new $\Theta_{p_1}^{p_1} = [[c_2, c_4], \ldots, [c_2, c_4]]$—16 simple paths $\eta_{p_1}^{p_1}$. Finally,

EXPANDPATH produces a concrete feasible path of 16 iterations composed from expansions of $\eta_{p_1}^{p_1}$, which would be returned at Line 8.

3.2   Path Expansion

This subsection describes the EXPANDPATH procedure which is outlined in Algorithm 2. It aims to construct a feasible expansion of a path $h_t^s = [c_1, c_2, \ldots, c_n]$. The path h_t^s is either a simple path $\eta_\perp^\top$ (when called from CSRA), or a path composed of multiple simple cycle paths $h_p^p = \eta_p^p \oplus \cdots \oplus \eta_p^p$ (when called from ANALYZECYCLES). EXPANDPATH incrementally builds a feasible expansion by constructing feasible subpaths $h_{trg(c_1)}^s, h_{trg(c_2)}^s, \ldots, h_t^s$ one by one. If appending a CHC c_i to the feasible path $h_{trg(c_{i-1})}^s$ yields an unfeasible path $h_{trg(c_i)}^s$, then the algorithm attempts to unroll cycles over predicates in the preceding path $h_{trg(c_{i-1})}^s$ to construct $h_{trg(c_{i-1})}'^s$, such that $h_{trg(c_{i-1})}'^s \oplus [c_i]$ is feasible.

The algorithm takes as input a CHC system S, a set of blocked predicates $\mathcal{P}_b$, a map of summaries $\Sigma : \langle p, \mathcal{P} \rangle \to \sigma$, formulas pre and $post$, and the path h_t^s to expand. It returns a pair $\langle h, \Sigma \rangle$. The path h is either an expansion of h_t^s, satisfying $pre(\ldots, x) \wedge \pi(h)(x, \ldots, x') \wedge post(x', \ldots)$ and $preds(h) \cap \mathcal{P}_b = \emptyset$, or $\emptyset$ if no such expansion exists. Σ is the refined map of summaries. EXPANDPATH maintains the following auxiliary variables for each CHC $c_j \in h_t^s$:

- formulas $pre(c_j)$ and $post(c_j)$ to capture constraints that must be satisfied before and after the cycle unrolling over $src(c_j)$, respectively, to ensure the existence of a feasible expansion of h_t^s;
- path h_j to reach $src(c_j)$ from s which is built by multiple consecutive expansions of $h_{src(c_j)}^s \subset h_t^s$;
- cycle path h_j^j over $src(c_j)$ such that $\pi(h_j \oplus h_j^j)(x, \ldots, x') \wedge post(c_j)(x')$ is satisfiable.

Initially, $h_j = \emptyset$, $h_j^j = \emptyset$, $pre(c_j) = \top$, and $post(c_j) = \top$ for all j, $1 < j \leq n$. One extra variable $pre(c_{n+1})$, is initialized to the input $post$ formula.

EXPANDPATH starts by building a path from the first CHC $c_1 \in h_t^s$ at Line 4. It proceeds in two stages for each CHC: *path traversal* and *cycle unrolling*, as denoted throughout the section. To avoid revisiting paths considered previously, it maintains an auxiliary subpath[6] denoted $\eta_p^s = [c_j, \ldots] \subseteq h_t^s$ (Line 6). Using η_p^s, the algorithm constructs a set of blocked predicates $\mathcal{P}_b' = (preds(\eta_p^s) \setminus \{p\}) \cup \mathcal{P}_b$.

Path Traversal: If the path $h_i \oplus h_i^i \oplus [c_i]$ is feasible (i.e., the formula at Line 8 is satisfiable) the algorithm extends the path with c_i (Line 9). If $i = n$ (Line 10), then this feasible path is returned. Otherwise, i is incremented to process the next CHC in the path h_t^s (Line 11).

If the formula at Line 8 is unsatisfiable, then the feasible path cannot be extended by appending c_i. The algorithm updates $post$ formula using a Craig

---

[6] When EXPANDPATH is called from CSRA, η_p^s is a prefix simple path $\eta_p^\top \subset \eta_\perp^\top$.

Algorithm 2: EXPANDPATH$(S, \mathcal{P}_b, \Sigma, pre, post, h_t^s)$

Input : CHC system S, blocked predicates $\mathcal{P}_b$, map of summaries
$\Sigma : \langle p, \mathcal{P} \rangle \to \sigma$, formulas $pre, post$, path to expand $h_t^s = [c_1, \ldots, c_n]$
Output: Feasible expansion h, refined summaries Σ

1   let $h_j = \emptyset$, $h_j^j = \emptyset$, $pre(c_j) = \top$, and $post(c_j) = \top$ for all j, $1 < j \leq n$
2   let $pre(c_{n+1}) = post$
3   let $i = 1$ `// index of a considered CHC`
4   **while** $\top$ **do**
5   let $p \leftarrow src(c_i)$
6   let $\eta_p^s \leftarrow [c_j, \ldots, c_i] \subseteq h_t^s$ s.t. $src(c_j) = s$ and $\forall k.j < k \leq i, src(c_k) \neq s$
7   let $\mathcal{P}_b' \leftarrow (preds(\eta_p^s) \setminus \{p\}) \cup \mathcal{P}_b$ `// path traversal`
8   **if** $SAT(pre \wedge \pi(h_i \oplus h_i^i) \wedge constr(c_i) \wedge pre(c_{i+1}))$ **then**
9          $h_{i+1} \leftarrow h_i \oplus h_i^i \oplus [c_i]$
10   **if** $i = n$ **then return** $\langle h_{i+1}, \Sigma \rangle$;
11         $i \leftarrow i + 1$
12   **else**
13         $post(c_i) \leftarrow post(c_i) \wedge \neg Itp(pre \wedge \pi(h_i \oplus h_i^i), constr(c_i) \wedge pre(c_{i+1}))$
14   **if** $\Sigma(p, \mathcal{P}_b') \neq \bot$ **then**   `// cycle unrolling`
15          $\langle h_i^i, \Sigma \rangle \leftarrow$ ANALYZECYCLES$(S, \mathcal{P}_b', \Sigma, pre \wedge \pi(h_i), post(h_i), p)$
16   **if** $h_i^i \in \emptyset$ **then**
17   **if** $i = 1$ **then return** $\langle \emptyset, \Sigma \rangle$;
18   **if** $\Sigma(s, \mathcal{P}_b') = \bot$ **then** $pre(c_i) \leftarrow post(c_i)$
19   **else** $pre(c_i) \leftarrow pre(c_i) \wedge \neg Itp(pre \wedge \pi(h_i), \Sigma(s, \mathcal{P}_b') \wedge post(c_i))$
20          $i \leftarrow i - 1$

---

interpolant[7] that explains why path $h_i \oplus h_i^i$ cannot be extended with c_i. Since *post* generalizes all paths that can be potentially extended with c_i in the next iterations, additional constraints make the generalization more precise.

Cycle Unrolling: If a cycle over p exists (i.e., $\Sigma(p, \mathcal{P}_b') \neq \bot$), ANALYZE-CYCLES attempts to construct a cycle path to satisfy $post(c_i)$ (Line 15). This procedure attempts to produce a cycle path h_i^i such that $pre(\ldots, x) \wedge \pi(h_i \oplus h_i^i)(x, \ldots, x') \wedge post(c_i)(x')$ is satisfiable. If such a path does not exist, it refines the cycle summary $\Sigma(p, \mathcal{P}_b)(x, x')$ in a way that $pre(\ldots, x) \wedge \pi(h_i)(x, \ldots, x') \wedge \Sigma(p, \mathcal{P}_b)(x', x'') \wedge post(c_i)(x'')$ becomes unsatisfiable. If a path h_i^i is found, the algorithm attempts to append c_i again.

When no path h_i^i exists (Line 16), the algorithm updates *pre* formula for the CHC c_i and rolls back to produce a path that would satisfy updated $pre(c_i)$. When $i = 1$, the formula $pre(\ldots, x) \wedge constr(c_1)(x, x') \wedge pre(c_2)(x')$ is unsatisfiable. Therefore, no feasible expansion of h_t^s exists, and $\langle \emptyset, \Sigma \rangle$ is returned. If $i \neq 1$, the algorithm updates formula $pre(c_i)$ depending on existence of a

---

[7] Given two logical formulas (A, B) such that $A \wedge B$ is unsatisfiable, a Craig interpolant [16] I is a logical formula such that $I \wedge B$ is unsatisfiable and $A \implies I$ is valid. I contains only common variables of A and B.

cycle path over $src(c_i)$. If no cycle path exists over $src(c_i)$, then $pre(c_i)$ is set to $post(c_i)$. This is because the $pre(c_i)$ formula captures the constraints that must hold before cycle unrolling over $src(c_i)$ (and no such unrolling exists). Otherwise, $pre(c_i)$ is updated using Craig interpolation (Line 19). Formula $pre(c_i)$ describes all paths that potentially can be extended into a feasible path, by appending a cycle path h_i^i and expansion of $[c_i, \ldots, c_n] \subseteq h_t^s$. The algorithm backtracks to try to construct a path h_i that would satisfy the refined formula $pre(c_i)$.

Example 3. Consider EXPANDPATH called for the CHC System in Fig. 2, with $\mathcal{P}_b = \{\top\}$, summaries $\Sigma = \{(p_1, \{\top\}) \mapsto \top, (p_2, \{\top, p_1\}) \mapsto \top\}$, formula $pre = \top$, formula $post = \top$ and path to expand $\eta_\perp^\top = [c_1, c_2]$ where $c_1 = c_1$ and $c_2 = c_5$ in the CHC system. The algorithm initializes $pre(c_1), pre(c_2), post(c_1)$, and $post(c_2)$ to $\top$; h_1, h_2, h_1^1, and h_2^2 to $\emptyset$; and $pre(c_3) \leftarrow \top$.

For $i = 1$ at Line 5 the algorithm sets $p = src(c_1) = \top$ and $\mathcal{P}_b' = \{\top\}$. Then since $\big(pre \wedge \pi(h_1 \oplus h_1^1) \wedge constr(c_1) \wedge pre(c_2)\big) = \big(\top \wedge \top \wedge x_1 = 0 \wedge x_2 = 0 \wedge \top\big)$ is satisfiable, the feasible path h_2 is updated to $[c_1]$ (Line 9) and i is incremented.

For $i = 2$, $p = src(c_5) = p_1$ and $\mathcal{P}_b' = \{\top\}$. The algorithm tries to traverse CHC c_5 at Line 8. However, since $\big(pre \wedge \pi(h_2 \oplus h_2^2) \wedge constr(c_5) \wedge pre(c_3)\big) = \big(\top \wedge (x_1 = 0 \wedge x_2 = 0) \wedge (x_1 \geq 512 \wedge x_1 \neq 512) \wedge \top\big)$ is unsatisfiable, formula $post(c_2)$ is updated to $x_1 \geq 512$ (Line 13).

The algorithm enters the check at Line 14 since there exists a cycle, $\eta_{p_1}^{p_1} = [c_2, c_4]$. The ANALYZECYCLES call (described in Example 2) returns a path $h_2^2(x, \ldots, x')$ of 16 iterations on p_1 which would satisfy $post(c_2)$ and updates summaries $\Sigma(p_2, \{\top, p_1\})(x, x') = (x_2' \leq 33 \wedge x_1' = x_1)$. However, the formula at Line 8 $\big(pre \wedge \pi(h_2 \oplus h_2^2) \wedge constr(c_5) \wedge pre(c_3)\big) = \big(\top \wedge (x_1 = 0 \wedge x_2 = 0) \wedge \pi(h_2^2)([x_1, x_2], \ldots, [x_1', x_2']) \wedge (x_1' \geq 512 \wedge x_1' \neq 512) \wedge \top\big)$ is still unsatisfiable since the only satisfying assignment for $(x_1 = 0 \wedge x_2 = 0) \wedge \pi(h_2^2)(x, \ldots, x')$ can be represented by a formula $(x_1' = 512 \wedge x_2' = 0)$, but $constr(c_2)(x, x') = (x_1 \geq 512 \wedge x_1 \neq 512)$. $post$ formula is updated $post(c_2)(x) = (x_1 \geq 512 \wedge x_1 \neq 512)$. Thus, ANALYZECYCLES is called at Line 15. No cycle path to satisfy $post(c_2)$ exists, therefore $h_2^2(x, \ldots, x') = \emptyset$ and ANALYZECYCLES updates the summary: $\Sigma(p_1, \{\top\})(x, x') = x_1' \leq 512 \wedge x_2' = 0$. Formula $pre(c_2) = x_1 \neq 0$ is updated at Line 19, backtracking to CHC c_1. The formula at Line 8 for c_1 is now unsatisfiable. Formula $post(c_1) = \top \wedge x_1 \neq 0$ and, since $i = 1$ at Line 17, the algorithm returns $\langle \emptyset, \Sigma \rangle$. No feasible expansion of path $[c_1, c_5]$ exists.

3.3   Core Procedure

We finally get all subroutines together for our reachability analysis. The central idea of our approach is to systematically explore the *expansions* of all possible simple paths $\eta_\perp^\top$ within the CHC system. Algorithm 3 gives pseudocode of the CSRA algorithm. It takes as input a CHC system S.

The algorithm begins by enumerating all simple paths $\eta_\perp^\top$ through the CHC system (Line 1). During execution, it maintains a map of summaries $\Sigma : \langle p, \mathcal{P}_b \rangle \rightarrow \sigma$ which overapproximate all cycle paths over $p : h_p^p$ such that

---

Algorithm 3: CSRA (S)

    Input   : CHC system S
    Output: SAT/UNSAT

1 let $\Theta_\bot^\top \leftarrow [\eta_1, ..., \eta_n]$ where $\eta_1, ..., \eta_n$ are all *simple* paths $\eta_\bot^\top$ in S
2 let $\Sigma : \langle p, \mathcal{P}_b \rangle \rightarrow (\top$ if $\exists h_p^p$ s.t. $preds(h_p^p) \cap \mathcal{P}_b = \emptyset,\ \bot$ otherwise$)$
3 **for** $\eta_\bot^\top \in \Theta_\bot^\top$ **do**
4 | $\langle h_\bot^\top, \Sigma \rangle \leftarrow$ EXPANDPATH$(S, \emptyset, \Sigma, \top, \top, \eta_\bot^\top)$
5 | **if** $h_\bot^\top \neq \emptyset$ **then return** UNSAT;
6 **return** SAT

$preds(h_p^p) \cap \mathcal{P}_b = \emptyset$. Initially, cycle summaries are set to $\top$ if there exists a cycle path h_p^p with $preds(h_p^p) \cap \mathcal{P}_b = \emptyset$, and to $\bot$ otherwise.

The loop at Line 3 iterates over all simple paths $\eta_\bot^\top \in \Theta_\bot^\top$. For each path, CSRA calls EXPANDPATH attempting to construct a feasible path $h_\bot^\top$ by expanding specific simple path. During execution, EXPANDPATH additionally refines the map of cycle summaries Σ. If a feasible path $h_\bot^\top \neq \emptyset$ is found, the algorithm returns UNSAT at Line 5. Otherwise, it continues to explore the next simple path, reusing the updated summaries. If no feasible expansion is found for any simple path, CSRA concludes that no feasible path through the CHC system exists and returns SAT. For example, in Fig. 2, there is only a single simple path $[c_1, c_5]$ for which EXPANDPATH would be invoked. This call is detailed in Example 3.

3.4 Soundness

We first establish correctness for the case when Algorithm 3 terminates and returns UNSAT. Important to note that CSRA not necessarily terminates, as TPA can diverge and nonterminate.

Theorem 1 (UNSAT soundness). *If CSRA, applied to a CHC system S over a set of predicates $\mathcal{P}$, returns UNSAT, then there exists a feasible path $h_\bot^\top$ through the CHC system.*

Proof. If CSRA returns UNSAT, then EXPANDPATH has successfully constructed a feasible path through the CHC system S. In Algorithm 2, the path is built incrementally. Each time a CHC c_i is added to the path at Line 9, the algorithm checks that $pre(\ldots, x) \wedge \pi(h_i \oplus h_i^i)(x, \ldots, x') \wedge constr(c_i)(x', x'') \wedge pre(c_{i+1})(x'')$ is satisfiable (Line 8). If a path $h_\bot^\top$ is returned at Line 10, then by construction the path condition $\pi(h_\bot^\top)$ is satisfiable, so $h_\bot^\top$ is a feasible path.

Next, we show that if Algorithm 3 terminates and returns SAT, then **no feasible path** $h_\bot^\top$ exists.

Theorem 2 (SAT soundness). *If Algorithm 3 returns SAT, then there does not exist a feasible path $h_\bot^\top$ through the CHC system S.*

Proof Sketch. This theorem follows from the following facts. *First,* any possible feasible path within the CHC system is an expansion of a simple path $\eta_\perp^\top$, and can be constructed using ExpandPath. *Second,* when ExpandPath returns $\langle \emptyset, \Sigma \rangle$, there does not exist a feasible expansion of a simple path $\eta_\perp^\top$. Therefore, if ExpandPath cannot produce a feasible expansion for any simple path $\eta_\perp^\top$, then a feasible path through the CHC system does not exist, meaning the system is SAT.

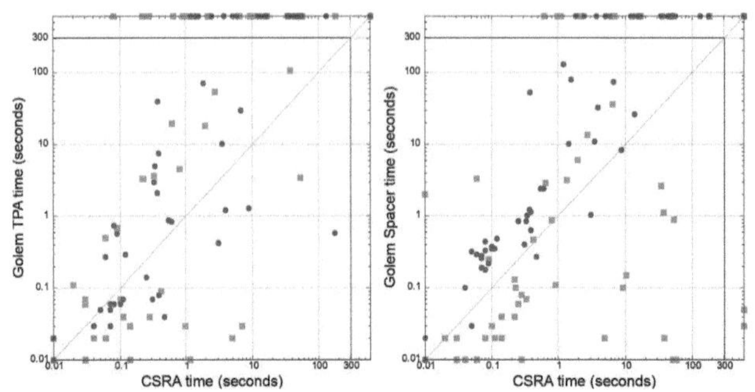

Fig. 3. Comparison of CSRA with other engines in Golem.

4 Evaluation

We implemented Algorithm 3 in the Golem CHC solver [6]; we refer to this implementation as CSRA. We compare CSRA to several state-of-the-art tools: Spacer [34] (implemented in Z3, v4.13.1), Eldarica [29] (v2.2.0), LoAT - ABMC [26] (v0.7.0), and to existing Golem engines, namely Golem-TPA and Golem-Spacer. Evaluation focuses on complex linear CHC instances encoding programs with nested loops. Experiments were conducted on Ubuntu 20.04 machine with an AMD EPYC 7452 32-core processor and 8×32 GiB RAM (the artifact is in open access[8]). Our evaluation addresses the following research questions:

- **RQ1:** How does the new algorithm compare to other engines in Golem?
- **RQ2:** How does CSRA perform against state-of-the-art tools?

The benchmark suite[9] is composed of nested-loop instances selected from the LIA category of CHC-COMP 2024 [17] and aeval-benchmarks [21]. Additionally, we extracted nested-loop functions from the source code of several tools: Z3 [41], OpenSMT [30], SeaHorn [28], and Golem and encoded them as LIA CHC instances using Korn [19] and SeaHorn. Benchmark selection is based on the

---

[8] https://doi.org/10.5281/zenodo.17055558.

[9] https://github.com/BritikovKI/pretzel-benchmarks/tree/main.

presence of nested loops in the original program, for the instances without nested loops CSRA performs similar to GOLEM-TPA (for example on LIA-lin benchmarks from CHC-Comp which mainly contain single loops, CSRA is on average 20% faster compared to GOLEM-TPA and solves 20 more instances). The final set contains 130 CHC instances (68 SAT, 62 UNSAT).

Figure 3 gives scatter plots comparing CSRA to GOLEM-TPA and GOLEM-SPACER. Each point (x, y) in the plots represents the solving times of a particular CHC instance, with x being the execution time of CSRA and y the execution time of the competitor. Green squares are SAT, and red circles are UNSAT instances. Points above the diagonal indicate cases where CSRA outperformed the competitor. Points beyond 300 s are timeouts for at least one of the engines.

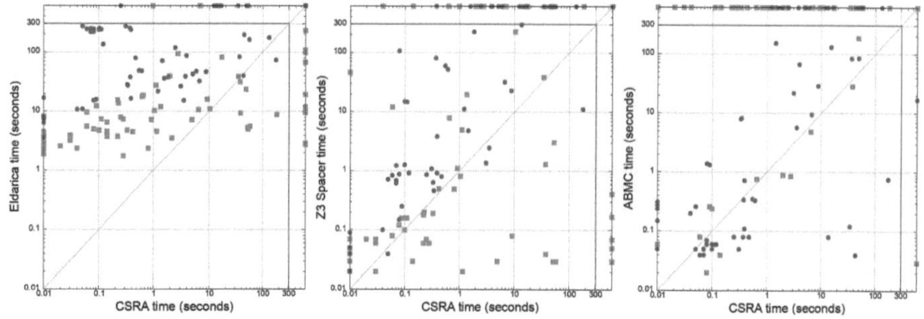

Fig. 4. Comparison of CSRA with state-of-the-art.

Our results indicate that CSRA consistently outperforms both GOLEM-SPACER and GOLEM-TPA for SAT and UNSAT instances. We attribute this to the modular nature of our algorithm, which decomposes the reachability analysis task into multiple, smaller subproblems—thereby reducing the overall complexity of reasoning. CSRA leverages structural information and explicitly analyzes cycles separately, which benefits both SAT and UNSAT performance. In contrast, GOLEM-TPA merges the entire CHC system into a CHC cycle composed from a single clause, losing structural information. GOLEM-SPACER, while effective in many scenarios, struggles with deep nested loops. In particular, as the number of loop iterations increases, GOLEM-SPACER frequently times out. Overall, CSRA solved 118/130 instances, compared to 78 for GOLEM-TPA and 93 for GOLEM-SPACER. To answer **RQ1**, we conclude that the compositional strategy of CSRA leads to better performance. We attribute this to the *modular* summarization-based approach, which uses TPA for fast deep reachability checks and summarization, while maintaining structural information about the system.

Figure 4 gives comparison charts for CSRA to other state-of-the-art CHC solvers. CSRA solves the most benchmarks (118), followed by ELDARICA (111), SPACER (91), and LoAT - ABMC (55). The listed approaches are somewhat orthogonal, as ELDARICA solves 6 SAT and 1 UNSAT instance uniquely, and

SPACER solves 3 unique SAT problems. CSRA significantly outperforms all competitors for the UNSAT systems. In analysis of SAT instances CSRA is competitive with other techniques, it is only slightly outperformed by ELDARICA, which solves 6 more SAT problems. To address **RQ2**, our evaluation shows that CSRA not only solves the highest number of benchmarks but also does so more efficiently. On average, for instances solved by both solvers, CSRA is $2.5\times$ faster than ELDARICA and $1.9\times$ faster than SPACER. In summary, the proposed algorithm achieves strong performance on both SAT and UNSAT CHC instances, outperforming existing GOLEM engines and other state-of-the-art solvers.

5   Related Work

Invariant Generation. Inductive invariant generation is a widely used technique for reasoning about loops by producing an overapproximation of program states, such that any loop iteration remains within the same overapproximation. Multiple approaches include CEGAR and predicate abstraction [29,38], IC3/PDR [34], program transformation-based methods [31], syntax-guided synthesis [20], and machine learning/neural networks [33,43]. One of the most popular approaches, used in a wide variety of algorithms, is interpolation-based invariant generation [7,29,34,36,38–40]. A recent advancement in this direction is Multiloop TPA [12], which specifically targets multi-loop programs. However, unlike CSRA, this method does not support software with nested loops or gotos and cannot be applied to general linear CHC systems.

Single-Loop Transformation. A common strategy for analyzing complex systems is to transform them into a single-loop representation [1,13,18]. This enables the application of techniques such as IMC or TPA, optimized for single-loop analysis [4], allowing them to reason over the original complex structure.

Loop Acceleration. Techniques [2,10,22–24,26] aim to produce quantifier-free first-order formulas that are equivalent to or underapproximate a loop's behaviour. These methods are motivated by improving the scalability of safety verification, attempting to replace a loop with a concrete formula. State-of-the-art acceleration approaches predominantly rely on underapproximation and can struggle with proving safety.

Loop Summarization. A group of approaches overapproximating loop execution by constructing a symbolic relation between loop inputs and outputs, allowing the loop to be abstracted away in subsequent analysis. Common methods include symbolic abstraction [9,35,44] and symbolic execution [27,45,46]. However, such approaches are typically property-agnostic and unaware of the surrounding system, which can reduce their effectiveness. Some of the approaches above also do not support summarization of nested loops. In contrast, our method performs property-guided summary generation and handles nested loops.

6 Conclusion

This paper introduces Cycle Summarization-based Reachability Analysis (CSRA), a new CHC-based reachability analysis approach designed for software with diverging control flow and nested loops. The key insight is to analyze cycles modularly and construct/reuse cycle summaries on the fly. CSRA decomposes the reachability analysis of a system into the exploration of separate simple paths through the CHC system. Applying TPA modularly allows our approach to efficiently unroll cycle paths and produce property-specific cycle summaries. Modular application of TPA together with maintaining the structural information about the CHC system, enables our technique to efficiently verify complex programs. We proved the algorithm's correctness and conducted an extensive experimental evaluation that demonstrates the efficiency of CSRA compared to state-of-the-art competitors and reachability analysis engines in Golem on challenging nested-loop systems.

References

1. Aho, A.V., Sethi, R., Ullman, J.D.: Compilers: Principles, Techniques, and Tools. Addison-Wesley series in computer science/World student series edition, Addison-Wesley (1986). https://www.worldcat.org/oclc/12285707
2. Bardin, S., Finkel, A., Leroux, J., Petrucci, L.: FAST: acceleration from theory to practice. Int. J. Softw. Tools Technol. Transf. **10**(5), 401–424 (2008). https://doi.org/10.1007/s10009-008-0064-3
3. Beyer, D., Keremoglu, M.E., Wendler, P.: Predicate abstraction with adjustable-block encoding. In: Bloem, R., Sharygina, N. (eds.) Proceedings of 10th International Conference on Formal Methods in Computer-Aided Design, FMCAD 2010, Lugano, Switzerland, October 20-23, pp. 189–197. IEEE (2010), https://ieeexplore.ieee.org/document/5770949/
4. Beyer, D., Lee, N., Wendler, P.: Interpolation and sat-based model checking revisited: Adoption to software verification. CoRR abs/2208.05046 (2022). https://doi.org/10.48550/arXiv.2208.05046
5. Bjørner, N.S., Gurfinkel, A., McMillan, K.L., Rybalchenko, A.: Horn clause solvers for program verification. In: Beklemishev, L.D., Blass, A., Dershowitz, N., Finkbeiner, B., Schulte, W. (eds.) Fields of Logic and Computation II - Essays Dedicated to Yuri Gurevich on the Occasion of His 75th Birthday. Lecture Notes in Computer Science, vol. 9300, pp. 24–51. Springer (2015). https://doi.org/10.1007/978-3-319-23534-9_2
6. Blicha, M., Britikov, K., Sharygina, N.: The golem horn solver. In: Enea, C., Lal, A. (eds.) Computer Aided Verification - 35th International Conference, CAV 2023, Paris, France, July 17-22, 2023, Proceedings, Part II. Lecture Notes in Computer Science, vol. 13965, pp. 209–223. Springer (2023). https://doi.org/10.1007/978-3-031-37703-7_10
7. Blicha, M., Fedyukovich, G., Hyvärinen, A.E.J., Sharygina, N.: Split transition power abstraction for unbounded safety. In: Griggio, A., Rungta, N. (eds.) 22nd Formal Methods in Computer-Aided Design, FMCAD 2022, Trento, Italy, pp. 349–358. IEEE (2022). https://doi.org/10.34727/2022/isbn.978-3-85448-053-2_42

8. Blicha, M., Fedyukovich, G., Hyvärinen, A.E.J., Sharygina, N.: Transition power abstractions for deep counterexample detection. In: Fisman, D., Rosu, G. (eds.) Tools and Algorithms for the Construction and Analysis of Systems - 28th International Conference, TACAS 2022. Lecture Notes in Computer Science, vol. 13243, pp. 524–542. Springer (2022). https://doi.org/10.1007/978-3-030-99524-9_29

9. Blicha, M., Kofron, J., Tatarko, W.: Summarization of branching loops. In: Hong, J., Bures, M., Park, J.W., Cerný, T. (eds.) SAC '22: The 37th ACM/SIGAPP Symposium on Applied Computing, Virtual Event, April 25 - 29, 2022, pp. 1808–1816. ACM (2022). https://doi.org/10.1145/3477314.3507042

10. Bozga, M., Iosif, R., Konecný, F.: Fast acceleration of ultimately periodic relations. In: Touili, T., Cook, B., Jackson, P.B. (eds.) Computer Aided Verification, 22nd International Conference, CAV 2010, Edinburgh, UK, July 15-19. Lecture Notes in Computer Science, vol. 6174, pp. 227–242. Springer (2010). https://doi.org/10.1007/978-3-642-14295-6_23

11. Bradley, A.R., Manna, Z.: Property-directed incremental invariant generation. Formal Aspects Comput. **20**(4-5), 379–405 (2008). https://doi.org/10.1007/S00165-008-0080-9

12. Britikov, K., Blicha, M., Sharygina, N., Fedyukovich, G.: Reachability analysis for multiloop programs using transition power abstraction. In: Platzer, A., Rozier, K.Y., Pradella, M., Rossi, M. (eds.) Formal Methods - 26th International Symposium, FM 2024, Milan, Italy, September 9-13, 2024, Proceedings, Part I. Lecture Notes in Computer Science, vol. 14933, pp. 558–576. Springer (2024). https://doi.org/10.1007/978-3-031-71162-6_29

13. Bueno, D.: Horn2VMT: Translating horn reachability into transition systems. Tech. rep., Sandia National Lab. (SNL-NM), Albuquerque, NM (United States) (2020)

14. Clarke, E.M., Biere, A., Raimi, R., Zhu, Y.: Bounded model checking using satisfiability solving. Formal Methods Syst. Des. **19**(1), 7–34 (2001). https://doi.org/10.1023/A:1011276507260

15. Clarke, E.M., Grumberg, O., Jha, S., Lu, Y., Veith, H.: Counterexample-guided abstraction refinement. In: Emerson, E.A., Sistla, A.P. (eds.) Computer Aided Verification, 12th International Conference, CAV 2000, Chicago, IL, USA, July 15-19, 2000, Proceedings. Lecture Notes in Computer Science, vol. 1855, pp. 154–169. Springer (2000). https://doi.org/10.1007/10722167_15

16. Craig, W.: Three uses of the Herbrand-Gentzen theorem in relating model theory and proof theory. J. Symbolic Logic **22**(3), 269–285 (1957)

17. De Angelis, E., K., H.G.V.: CHC-COMP 2023: competition report. In: Kutsia, T., Ventura, D., Monniaux, D., Morales, J.F. (eds.) Proceedings 18th International Workshop on Logical and Semantic Frameworks, with Applications and 10th Workshop on Horn Clauses for Verification and Synthesis, LSFA/HCVS 2023, and 10th Workshop on Horn Clauses for Verification and SynthesisRome, Italy & Paris, France, 1-2 July, 2023 & 23rd April 2023. EPTCS, vol. 402, pp. 83–104 (2023). https://doi.org/10.4204/EPTCS.402.10

18. Donaldson, A.F., Kroening, D., Rümmer, P.: Automatic analysis of DMA races using model checking and k-induction. Formal Methods Syst. Des. **39**(1), 83–113 (2011). https://doi.org/10.1007/s10703-011-0124-2

19. Ernst, G.: Korn - software verification with horn clauses (competition contribution). In: Sankaranarayanan, S., Sharygina, N. (eds.) Tools and Algorithms for the Construction and Analysis of Systems - 29th International Conference, TACAS 2023, Held as Part of the European Joint Conferences on Theory and Practice of Software, ETAPS 2022, Paris, France, April 22-27, 2023, Proceedings, Part II. Lec-

ture Notes in Computer Science, vol. 13994, pp. 559–564. Springer (2023). https://doi.org/10.1007/978-3-031-30820-8_36

20. Fedyukovich, G., Kaufman, S.J., Bodík, R.: Learning inductive invariants by sampling from frequency distributions. Formal Methods Syst. Des. **56**(1), 154–177 (2020). https://doi.org/10.1007/s10703-020-00349-x

21. Fedyukovich, G., Prabhu, S., Madhukar, K., Gupta, A.: Quantified invariants via syntax-guided synthesis. In: Dillig, I., Tasiran, S. (eds.) Computer Aided Verification - 31st International Conference, CAV 2019, New York City, NY, USA, July 15-18, 2019, Proceedings, Part I. Lecture Notes in Computer Science, vol. 11561, pp. 259–277. Springer (2019). https://doi.org/10.1007/978-3-030-25540-4_14

22. Frohn, F.: A calculus for modular loop acceleration. In: Biere, A., Parker, D. (eds.) Tools and Algorithms for the Construction and Analysis of Systems - 26th International Conference, TACAS 2020. Lecture Notes in Computer Science, vol. 12078, pp. 58–76. Springer (2020). https://doi.org/10.1007/978-3-030-45190-5_4

23. Frohn, F., Giesl, J.: Proving non-termination via loop acceleration. CoRR abs/1905.11187 (2019). http://arxiv.org/abs/1905.11187

24. Frohn, F., Giesl, J.: Proving non-termination and lower runtime bounds with LoAT (system description). In: Blanchette, J., Kovács, L., Pattinson, D. (eds.) Automated Reasoning - 11th International Joint Conference, IJCAR 2022, Haifa, Israel, August 8-10, 2022, Proceedings. Lecture Notes in Computer Science, vol. 13385, pp. 712–722. Springer (2022). https://doi.org/10.1007/978-3-031-10769-6_41

25. Frohn, F., Giesl, J.: Accelerated bounded model checking. CoRR abs/2401.09973 (2024). https://doi.org/10.48550/ARXIV.2401.09973

26. Frohn, F., Giesl, J.: Integrating loop acceleration into bounded model checking. In: Platzer, A., Rozier, K.Y., Pradella, M., Rossi, M. (eds.) Formal Methods - 26th International Symposium, FM 2024, Milan, Italy, September 9-13, 2024, Proceedings, Part I. Lecture Notes in Computer Science, vol. 14933, pp. 73–91. Springer (2024). https://doi.org/10.1007/978-3-031-71162-6_4

27. Godefroid, P., Luchaup, D.: Automatic partial loop summarization in dynamic test generation. In: Dwyer, M.B., Tip, F. (eds.) Proceedings of the 20th International Symposium on Software Testing and Analysis, ISSTA 2011, Toronto, ON, Canada, pp. 23–33. ACM (2011). https://doi.org/10.1145/2001420.2001424

28. Gurfinkel, A., Kahsai, T., Komuravelli, A., Navas, J.A.: The seahorn verification framework. In: Kroening, D., Pasareanu, C.S. (eds.) Computer Aided Verification - 27th International Conference, CAV 2015, San Francisco, CA, USA, July 18-24, 2015, Proceedings, Part I. Lecture Notes in Computer Science, vol. 9206, pp. 343–361. Springer (2015). https://doi.org/10.1007/978-3-319-21690-4_20

29. Hojjat, H., Rümmer, P.: The ELDARICA horn solver. In: Bjørner, N.S., Gurfinkel, A. (eds.) Formal Methods in Computer Aided Design, FMCAD 2018, Austin, TX, USA, pp. 1–7. IEEE (2018). https://doi.org/10.23919/FMCAD.2018.8603013

30. Hyvärinen, A.E.J., Marescotti, M., Alt, L., Sharygina, N.: OpenSMT2: an SMT solver for multi-core and cloud computing. In: Creignou, N., Berre, D.L. (eds.) Theory and Applications of Satisfiability Testing - SAT 2016 - 19th International Conference, Bordeaux, France, July 5-8, 2016, Proceedings. Lecture Notes in Computer Science, vol. 9710, pp. 547–553. Springer (2016). https://doi.org/10.1007/978-3-319-40970-2_35

31. Kafle, B., Gallagher, J.P., Morales, J.F.: Rahft: a tool for verifying horn clauses using abstract interpretation and finite tree automata. In: Chaudhuri, S., Farzan, A. (eds.) Computer Aided Verification - 28th International Conference, CAV 2016, Toronto, ON, Canada. Lecture Notes in Computer Science, vol. 9779, pp. 261–268. Springer (2016). https://doi.org/10.1007/978-3-319-41528-4_14

32. Kahsai, T., Rümmer, P., Sanchez, H., Schäf, M.: Jayhorn: a framework for verifying java programs. In: Chaudhuri, S., Farzan, A. (eds.) Computer Aided Verification - 28th International Conference, CAV 2016, Toronto, ON, Canada, July 17-23, 2016, Proceedings, Part I. Lecture Notes in Computer Science, vol. 9779, pp. 352–358. Springer (2016). https://doi.org/10.1007/978-3-319-41528-4_19

33. Kamath, A., et al.: Finding inductive loop invariants using large language models. CoRR abs/2311.07948 (2023). https://doi.org/10.48550/arXiv.2311.07948

34. Komuravelli, A., Gurfinkel, A., Chaki, S.: SMT-based model checking for recursive programs. Formal Methods Syst. Des. **48**(3), 175–205 (2016). https://doi.org/10.1007/S10703-016-0249-4

35. Kroening, D., Sharygina, N., Tonetta, S., Tsitovich, A., Wintersteiger, C.M.: Loop summarization using abstract transformers. In: Cha, S.D., Choi, J., Kim, M., Lee, I., Viswanathan, M. (eds.) Automated Technology for Verification and Analysis, 6th International Symposium, ATVA 2008, Seoul, Korea. Lecture Notes in Computer Science, vol. 5311, pp. 111–125. Springer (2008). https://doi.org/10.1007/978-3-540-88387-6_10

36. Lin, S., Sun, J., Xiao, H., Liu, Y., Sanán, D., Hansen, H.: FiB: squeezing loop invariants by interpolation between forward/backward predicate transformers. In: Rosu, G., Penta, M.D., Nguyen, T.N. (eds.) Proceedings of the 32nd IEEE/ACM International Conference on Automated Software Engineering, ASE 2017, Urbana, IL, USA, pp. 793–803. IEEE Computer Society (2017). https://doi.org/10.1109/ASE.2017.8115690

37. Matsushita, Y., Tsukada, T., Kobayashi, N.: RustHorn: CHC-based verification for rust programs. In: Müller, P. (ed.) Programming Languages and Systems - 29th European Symposium on Programming, ESOP 2020, Held as Part of the European Joint Conferences on Theory and Practice of Software, ETAPS 2020, Dublin, Ireland, April 25-30, 2020, Proceedings. Lecture Notes in Computer Science, vol. 12075, pp. 484–514. Springer (2020). https://doi.org/10.1007/978-3-030-44914-8_18

38. McMillan, K., Rybalchenko, A.: Computing relational fixed points using interpolation. Technical report, January 2013. MSR-TR-2013-6 (2013)

39. McMillan, K.L.: Interpolation and sat-based model checking. In: Jr., W.A.H., Somenzi, F. (eds.) Computer Aided Verification, 15th International Conference, CAV 2003, Boulder, CO, USA, July 8-12, 2003, Proceedings. Lecture Notes in Computer Science, vol. 2725, pp. 1–13. Springer (2003). https://doi.org/10.1007/978-3-540-45069-6_1

40. McMillan, K.L.: Lazy abstraction with interpolants. In: Ball, T., Jones, R.B. (eds.) Computer Aided Verification, 18th International Conference, CAV 2006, Seattle, WA, USA, August 17-20, 2006, Proceedings. Lecture Notes in Computer Science, vol. 4144, pp. 123–136. Springer (2006). https://doi.org/10.1007/11817963_14

41. de Moura, L.M., Bjørner, N.S.: Z3: an efficient SMT solver. In: Ramakrishnan, C.R., Rehof, J. (eds.) Tools and Algorithms for the Construction and Analysis of Systems, 14th International Conference, TACAS 2008. Lecture Notes in Computer Science, vol. 4963, pp. 337–340. Springer (2008). https://doi.org/10.1007/978-3-540-78800-3_24

42. Podelski, A., Rybalchenko, A.: Transition invariants. In: 19th IEEE Symposium on Logic in Computer Science (LICS 2004), 14-17 July 2004, Turku, Finland, Proceedings, pp. 32–41. IEEE Computer Society (2004). https://doi.org/10.1109/LICS.2004.1319598

43. Ryan, G., Wong, J., Yao, J., Gu, R., Jana, S.: CLN2INV: learning loop invariants with continuous logic networks. In: 8th International Conference on Learning Representations, ICLR 2020, Addis Ababa, Ethiopia. OpenReview.net (2020). https://openreview.net/forum?id=HJlfuTEtvB
44. Silverman, J., Kincaid, Z.: Loop summarization with rational vector addition systems. In: Dillig, I., Tasiran, S. (eds.) Computer Aided Verification - 31st International Conference, CAV 2019. Lecture Notes in Computer Science, vol. 11562, pp. 97–115. Springer (2019). https://doi.org/10.1007/978-3-030-25543-5_7
45. Strejcek, J., Trtík, M.: Abstracting path conditions. In: Heimdahl, M.P.E., Su, Z. (eds.) International Symposium on Software Testing and Analysis, ISSTA 2012, Minneapolis, MN, USA, pp. 155–165. ACM (2012). https://doi.org/10.1145/2338965.2336772
46. Xie, X., Chen, B., Zou, L., Liu, Y., Le, W., Li, X.: Automatic loop summarization via path dependency analysis. IEEE Trans. Software Eng. **45**(6), 537–557 (2019). https://doi.org/10.1109/TSE.2017.2788018

Reachability Analysis
of Function-as-a-Service Scheduling
Policies

Giuseppe De Palma[1,2], Saverio Giallorenzo[1,2], Jacopo Mauro[3], Matteo Trentin[1,2,3], and Gianluigi Zavattaro[1,2(✉)]

[1] Università di Bologna, Bologna, Italy
{giuseppe.depalma2,saverio.giallorenzo2,matteo.trentin2, gianluigi.zavattaro}@unibo.it
[2] OLAS Research Team, INRIA, Sophia Antipolis, France
[3] University of Southern Denmark, Odense, Denmark
mauro@imada.sdu.dk

Abstract. Functions-as-a-Service (FaaS) is a Serverless Cloud paradigm where a platform manages the execution (e.g., scheduling, runtime environments) of stateless functions. Recently, domain-specific languages like APP and aAPP have been developed to express per-function scheduling policies, e.g., enforcing the allocation of functions on nodes that enjoy low data-access latencies thanks to proximity and connection pooling.

Reachability analysis of FaaS scheduling policies is fundamental to check quality-of-service properties, like preventing the scheduling of functions on workers which cannot sustain expected performance levels, or verifying security properties, e.g., that safety-critical functions cannot run on nodes with untrusted ones. We investigate the complexity of reachability analysis for APP and aAPP– the latter extends APP with constraints for placing functions according to the absence/presence of other (anti-)affine functions on workers. We show that reachability analysis has linear time complexity in APP, while the addition of affinities (in aAPP) makes reachability PSPACE. Given the computational complexity correspondence between reachability analysis in aAPP and automatic planning problems (both are in PSPACE), we investigate the exploitability of planners, i.e., tools specialised for solving planning problems for the realisation of static analysers of reachability-like problems for aAPP.

1 Introduction

Functions-as-a-Service (FaaS) is a programming paradigm supported by the Serverless Cloud execution model [30]. In FaaS, developers implement a distributed architecture by composing stateless functions and delegate concerns like execution runtimes and resource allocation to the serverless platform, thus focusing on writing code that implements business logic rather than worrying about infrastructure management. The main cloud providers offer FaaS [5,25,38] and open-source alternatives exist too [6,22,27,42].

F. Damiani and M. Farrell (Eds.): iFM 2025, LNCS 16194, pp. 226–247, 2026.
https://doi.org/10.1007/978-3-032-10794-7_12

A common denominator of these platforms is that they manage the allocation of functions over the available computing resources, also called *workers*, following opinionated policies that favour some performance principle. Indeed, effects like *code locality* [27] – due to latencies in loading function code and runtimes – or *session locality* [27] – due to the need to authenticate and open new sessions to interact with other services – can substantially increase the run time of functions. The breadth of the design space of serverless scheduling policies is witnessed by the growing literature focused on techniques that mix one or more of these locality principles to increase the performance of function execution, assuming some locality-bound traits of functions [1,9,10,12,29,31–33,35,40,41,45,47,48,50–55]. Besides performance, functions can have functional requirements that the scheduler shall consider. For example, users might want to ward off allocating their functions alongside "untrusted" ones – common threat vectors in serverless are limited function isolation and the ability of functions to (surreptitiously) gather weaponisable information on the runtime, the infrastructure, and the other tenants [4,8,15,57].

Although one can mix different principles to expand the profile coverage of a given platform-wide scheduler policy, the latter hardly suits all kinds of scenarios. This shortcoming motivated the introduction of a domain-specific, platform-agnostic, declarative language for expressing *Allocation Priority Policies* (which inspired the name of the language APP), for specifying custom function allocation policies [17,21]. Thanks to APP, the same platform can support different scheduling policies, each tailored to meet the specific needs of a set of related functions. APP has been validated by implementing a serverless platform as an extension of the open-source Apache OpenWhisk project – the APP-based variant outperforms vanilla OpenWhisk in several locality-bound scenarios [17,21].

Recently, De Palma et al. [20] presented an extension of APP for expressing *affinity-aware* policies for serverless function scheduling (the addition of affinity-awareness to APP inspired the name aAPP for this language extension). Specifically, aAPP extends APP with the possibility to impose that one function can be placed on a worker only if another function is present (affinity) or absent (anti-affinity) on that worker. These constraints are useful to avoid the co-location of functions (e.g., trusted functions cannot be placed on a worker which is executing untrusted ones) or to guarantee their co-location (e.g., a function accessing a database can be placed on a worker only if it hosts a function able to open a connection with that database).

Contributions. APP and its extension aAPP have been validated experimentally [17,20,21] via FaaS benchmarks and case studies. However, there is no formal study nor comparison between the two. We cover this gap by presenting the aAPP-calculus, in Sect. 2, which is an abstract formal model of function scheduling in FaaS systems where functions are scheduled following aAPP scripts. Since aAPP is an extension of APP, we identify a fragment of the aAPP-calculus corresponding to APP, that we name APP-calculus. We use our formal model to investigate whether aAPP is *more expressive* than APP by showing that static verification of properties of policies, relevant in the context of function scheduling, is *more complex* in aAPP than in APP. Namely, we formally define, in Sect. 5, the properties of *reachability*, i.e., checking if a function f can be deployed on a targeted worker, and of *co-occurrence*, i.e., checking if two functions f and g can be co-located, so they can run simultaneously on a targeted worker.

In Sect. 4, we start by investigating reachability and co-occurrence in the APP-calculus, and we prove that both problems have linear-time complexity. Then, in Sect. 5, we show that the problems become PSPACE-complete when we move to the aAPP-calculus – for presentation, here we discuss proof strategy insights while detailed proofs can be found in the companion paper [19]. These results formally witnesses the increase in expressiveness from APP to aAPP, given that the latter can specify scheduling policies much harder to formally verify. In Sect. 6, we further solidify the above results by showing that the jump in complexity comes from affinity constraints. Indeed, we show that in aAPP *without affinity* reachability and co-occurrence preserve a linear complexity while in aAPP *without anti-affinity* the problems become NP-hard.

The proof of PSPACE-completeness of the reachability problems in the aAPP-calculus formalises a complexity correspondence with automated planning problems [24]. In the light of the rich literature on automated planning and the availability of *planners* (tools for solving such problems), in Sect. 7, we introduce a static analyser for aAPP scripts which leverages planners. In particular, our analyser translates both the semantics of aAPP (scripts) and the reachability problems of interest into PDDL [23], the de-facto standard input language for planners. In this way, the analyser can use any planner capable of solving the problems we express in *PDDL with numeric fluents* – the latter are necessary for modelling function occurrences on workers and their resource usage.

We position our contributions in Sect. 8 and discuss future steps in Sect. 9.

2   Preliminaries: The **APP** Language and the **aAPP** Extension

We present APP [17,21] and its affinity-aware extension aAPP [20].

Since aAPP is a syntactic extension of APP, we directly report in Fig. 1 the syntax of aAPP, which APP shares, except for the `affinity` clause in the syntax of *blocks*. From here on, we indicate syntactic units in *italics*, optional fragments in *grey*, terminals in `monospace`, and lists with $\overline{bars}$. The syntax draws inspiration from YAML [58], a renowned data-serialisation language for configuration files—e.g., many modern tools use the format, like Kubernetes, Ansible, and Docker.[1] The idea is that an APP/aAPP script defines a scheduling policy where functions have associated a tag that identifies their scheduling information. Essentially, a *tag* corresponds to a list of *blocks* that indicate either some collection of workers, each identified by a worker *id*, or the universal *.

---

[1] While aAPP scripts are YAML-compliant, for presentation, we slightly stylise the syntax to increase readability. For instance, we omit quotes around strings, e.g., * instead of "*".

The scheduling of a function works by retrieving its tag and then its scheduling information, which includes one or more blocks of possible workers. Worker selection happens by iteratively checking the blocks from top to bottom, picking the first block with a non-empty list of valid workers and selecting one worker of that list according to the strategy defined by the block (described later).

In case all the blocks associated with a tag fail, the `followup` clause specifies what to do next: either `fail`, to terminate the attempt to schedule the function, or `default`, to try scheduling the function as if associated with the special `default` tag. More precisely, we consider `default` as a special tag name with which we can associate generic scheduling policies which are independent of the function peculiarities; if the specific function scheduling policies fail, the `followup` clause set to `default` indicates that the generic `default` policy can be used.

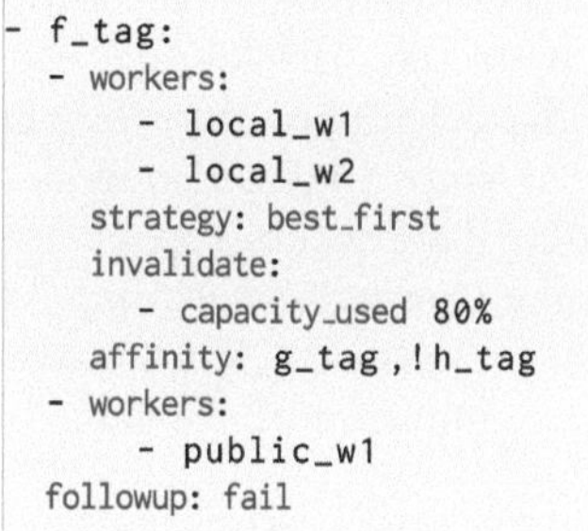

Fig. 1. aAPP syntax (APP omits the affinity clause).

Fig. 2. Example aAPP script.

Each block can define a `strategy` for worker selection (`any` selects one of the available workers non-deterministically from the list; `best_first` selects the first available worker in the list), a list of constraints that `invalidate`s a worker for the allocation (`capacity_used` invalidates a worker if its resource occupation reaches the set threshold; `max_concurrent_invocations` invalidates a worker if it hosts more than the specified number of functions). The aAPP extension includes the `affinity` clause, which carries a list containing affine tag identifiers id and anti-affine tags, represented by negated tag identifiers $!id$. This clause introduces an invalidation condition determined by the absence (affinity) or presence (anti-affinity) of functions on workers.

As an example, Fig. 2 shows an aAPP script carrying the scheduling information for functions tagged `f_tag`, which includes two blocks. The first restricts the allocation of the function on the workers labelled `local_w1` and `local_w2` and the second on `public_w1`. The first block specifies as invalid (i.e., unable to host the function under scheduling) the workers that reach a memory consumption above 80%. Since the strategy is `best_first`, we allocate the function on the first valid worker; if none are valid, we proceed with the next block. The function has affinity with g_tag and anti-affinity with h_tag. Hence, a worker is valid if it hosts at least a function with tag g_tag and no functions with tag h_tag. If both the first and second blocks did not find a valid worker, the scheduling of the function `fails`.

As a final remark, note that the (anti-)affinity relation in aAPP is "directional"—similarly to the one introduced by Microsoft in its IaaS offering [37]. In particular, it does not impose any properties like symmetry on affinity or anti-affinity. The reason for avoiding these additional constraints is to allow aAPP to capture as many useful scenarios as possible, which imposing properties like symmetry would prevent.[2]

3   The aAPP-Calculus and its Fragment APP-Calculus

We introduce the aAPP-calculus to formally model function scheduling in FaaS systems governed by aAPP scripts. We represent the states of the FaaS systems with pairs $\langle N, \Delta \rangle$ where N is a *network of workers* and Δ is a *scheduling policy*. The calculus defines labelled transitions $\langle N, \Delta \rangle \xrightarrow{\alpha} \langle N', \Delta \rangle$ that indicate that the state $\langle N, \Delta \rangle$ can change into $\langle N', \Delta \rangle$ as effect of the occurrence of the event α. The events ranged by α are either $f \downarrow w$, denoting the scheduling of function f on worker w, and $f \uparrow w$, representing the removal of function f from worker w because f terminated its execution.

The definition of the calculus is parametric w.r.t. the workers and the functions.

Definition 1 (Workers and Functions). *We assume given the set $\mathcal{W}$ (ranged over by w) of the* worker *identifiers and the set $\mathcal{F}$ (ranged over by f) of the* function *identifiers. For each $w \in \mathcal{W}$ we use* **cap**(w) *to denote the capacity of the worker w (i.e., a strictly positive number quantifying the total resources of the worker w) and for each $f \in \mathcal{F}$ we use* **res**(f) *to denote the resources needed by the function f (i.e., a strictly positive number quantifying the resources that the function f must acquire from the worker where it is scheduled).*

We also use two additional sets: the *selection strategies*, $\mathcal{S} \triangleq \{$`any`, `best_first`$\}$ (ranged over by s), and the set of the *invalidation conditions*, $\mathcal{I} \triangleq \{$`capacity_used` $n\%$, `max_concurrent_invocations` n, `affine` F, `anti_affine` $F \mid n \in \mathbb{N}$, F $\subseteq \mathcal{F}\}$ (ranged over by i). Note that the selection strategies, `any` and `best_first`, as well as the invalidation conditions, `capacity_used` $n\%$, `max_concurrent_invocations` n, precisely correspond to the syntactic elements of aAPP/APP (cf. Fig. 1). Contrarily to aAPP's syntax, we do not treat `affinity` as a separate entity and include it with the other invalidation conditions by

---

adding **affine** F, meaning that at least one function in F should be present, and **anti_affine** F, requiring the absence of all the functions in F.

We start by defining the network of workers N, which intuitively associates to each worker the list of functions currently scheduled on it.

Definition 2 (Network of workers). *A network of workers $N \in \mathcal{N} \triangleq \mathcal{W} \to List(\mathcal{F})$ is a function that associates to a worker the list $\overline{f}$ of functions currently scheduled on that worker.*

In the following, $N \cup (w \mapsto \overline{f})$ denotes a network of workers obtained by extending the network N with the mapping from the worker w to the list of functions $\overline{f}$.[3]

Moving on to the definition of the scheduling policy Δ, it intuitively associates to each function its list of scheduling blocks, each carrying the list of workers, strategies, and invalidation conditions that determine the scheduling of the function.

Definition 3 (Scheduling blocks and policy). *A scheduling block $b \in \mathcal{B} \triangleq (List(\mathcal{W}), \mathcal{S}, List(\mathcal{I}))$ is a triple $(\overline{w}, s, \overline{i})$ where $\overline{w}$ is a list of workers, s is a selection strategy, and $\overline{i}$ is a list of invalidation conditions. A scheduling policy $\Delta \in \mathcal{D} \triangleq \mathcal{F} \to List(\mathcal{B})$ is a mapping that associates to each function $f \in \mathcal{F}$ the list $\overline{b}$ of blocks that define the scheduling of f on workers.*

As for networks, in the following, we denote with $\Delta \cup (f \mapsto \overline{b})$ a policy obtained by extending the policy Δ with the mapping from function f to the the list of blocks $\overline{b}$.[4]

$$[\![\overline{-\ tag} :: -\textbf{default:}\overline{-\ block}]\!] = [\![\overline{-\ tag} :: -\textbf{default:}\overline{-\ block}\ \ \texttt{followup: fail}]\!]$$

$$[\![\overline{-\ tag} :: -\textbf{default:}\overline{-\ block}\ \ \texttt{followup: } f\_opt]\!] = \bigcup_{t\ \in\ \overline{tag}} \left\{ [t]_{\overline{[block]}} \right\}$$

$$[\![id : \overline{-\ block}]\!]_{\overline{b}} = [\![id : \overline{-\ block}\ \ \texttt{followup : default}]\!]_{\overline{b}} = \bigcup_{f\ \in\ id} \left\{ (f \mapsto \overline{[block]} :: \overline{b}) \right\}$$

$$[\![id : \overline{-\ block}\ \ \texttt{followup : fail}]\!]_{\overline{b}} = \bigcup_{f\ \in\ id} \left\{ (f \mapsto \overline{[block]}) \right\}$$

$$[\text{workers: } w\_opt \ \ \bullet] = \begin{cases} ([w\_opt], s, i) & \text{if } (s,i) = [\bullet] \\ ([w\_opt], \text{any}, \varepsilon) & \text{otherwise} \end{cases} \qquad [\text{strategy : } s\_opt \ \ \bullet] = \begin{cases} (s\_opt, i) & \text{if } (-,\overline{i}) = [\bullet] \\ (s\_opt, \varepsilon) & \text{otherwise} \end{cases}$$

$$[\![\text{invalidate : } \overline{-\ i\_opt} \ \ \bullet]\!] = \begin{cases} (\text{any}, \overline{i\_opt} :: \overline{i}) & \text{if } (-,\overline{i}) = [\bullet] \\ (\text{any}, \overline{i\_opt}) & \text{otherwise} \end{cases} \qquad [\![\text{affinity: } \overline{a\_opt}]\!] = (\text{any}, [\![\overline{a\_opt}]\!])$$

$$[\![a\_opt :: \overline{a\_opt}]\!] = \begin{cases} \text{affine } id :: [\![\overline{a\_opt}]\!] & \text{if } a\_opt = id \\ \text{anti\_affine } id :: [\![\overline{a\_opt}]\!] & \text{if } a\_opt = !id \end{cases} \qquad \begin{array}{c} [\varepsilon] = \varepsilon \qquad\qquad [\![\overline{-\ id}]\!] = \overline{id} \\ [*] = w_1 :: w_2 :: \cdots :: w_n \quad \text{with } \mathcal{W} = \{w_1, w_2, \cdots, w_n\} \end{array}$$

Fig. 3. aAPP syntax encoding.

From aAPP to Δ The straightforward encoding $[\![\ ]\!]$ – defined inductively in Fig. 3 – determines the relationship between an aAPP script and its formal representation within a policy Δ in the aAPP-calculus. The encoding formalises the translation

---

[3] The notation assumes that w does not belong to the domain of N.

[4] The notation assumes that f does not belong to the domain of Δ.

from aAPP to Δ, assuming a sorting of aAPP scripts where the default tag is the last element – to keep the definition in Fig. 3 compact, we use • as a pattern-matching variable. We slightly abuse the notation so that a tag f_tag denotes also the set of functions tagged with f_tag. Moreover, we extend the notation of lists, denoting with ε the empty list and with $e :: l$ a list obtained by adding the element e in front of the list l.

For instance, $f \in$ f_tag means that f has tag f_tag. For each $f \in$ f_tag we simply add in Δ a mapping from f to the list of blocks associated with f_tag in the aAPP script. We implement the semantics of the followup clause – where the policy follows the logic of the default blocks if none of the tag's blocks led to a successful scheduling – by appending the list of blocks of the default tag to the tag's blocks. This concatenation happens only when the followup value of the tag is set to default.

Formally, for each block in the aAPP script, we consider a corresponding aAPP-calculus block $(\overline{w}, s, \overline{i})$, where $\overline{w}$ is the list of the specified workers (all the workers, in case of $\ast$), s is the selection strategy, and $\overline{i}$ contains all the invalidation conditions in the aAPP script. These conditions include the sequence of affinity-based invalidations of the form affine g_tag and anti_affine h_tag resp. for each g_tag and !h_tag occurring in the affinity clause – affine g_tag indicates affinity with functions tagged g_tag and anti_affine h_tag indicates anti-affinity with functions tagged h_tag.

Operational Semantics. We are ready to define the operational semantics of aAPP-calculus. Formally, we define a labelled transition system on the set of states $States \triangleq \{\langle N, \Delta \rangle \mid N \in \mathcal{N}, \Delta \in \mathcal{D}, \}$ (which contains the set of possible configurations of the modelled FaaS system represented as pairs $\langle N, \Delta \rangle$ where N is a network of workers and Δ is a scheduling policy) and the set of labels $Labels \triangleq \{f{\downarrow}w, f{\uparrow}w \mid f \in \mathcal{F}, w \in \mathcal{W}\}$ (where $f{\downarrow}w$ represents the scheduling of an instance of function f on worker w while $f{\uparrow}w$ represents the removal of f from w, occurring when the execution of f on w terminates).

$$[start] \; \frac{\overline{b} \triangleright (w,s,\overline{i}) :: \overline{b'} \quad \textbf{valid}(f,w,\overline{i},\overline{f})}{\langle N \cup (w \mapsto \overline{f}),\, \Delta \cup (f \mapsto \overline{b}) \rangle \xrightarrow{f\downarrow w} \langle N \cup (w \mapsto f::\overline{f}),\, \Delta \cup (f \mapsto \overline{b}) \rangle}$$

$$[rm] \; \frac{f \in \overline{f}}{\langle N \cup (w \mapsto \overline{f}),\, \Delta \rangle \xrightarrow{f\uparrow w} \langle N \cup (w \mapsto \overline{f}\backslash f),\, \Delta \rangle}$$

$$[next] \; \frac{\langle N,\, \Delta \cup (f \mapsto \overline{b'}) \rangle \xrightarrow{f\downarrow w} \langle N',\, \Delta' \rangle \quad \overline{b} \triangleright (w',s,\overline{i}) :: \overline{b'} \quad \neg\textbf{valid}(f,w',\overline{i},N(w'))}{\langle N,\, \Delta \cup (f \mapsto \overline{b}) \rangle \xrightarrow{f\downarrow w} \langle N',\, \Delta \cup (f \mapsto \overline{b}) \rangle}$$

———— $\triangleright$ relation ————

$$\frac{\big(s=\texttt{any} \wedge w \in \overline{w}\big) \vee \big(s=\texttt{best\_first} \wedge \overline{w}=w::\overline{w'}\big)}{(\overline{w},s,\overline{i})::\overline{b} \triangleright (w,s,\overline{i}) :: (\overline{w}\backslash w,s,\overline{i})::\overline{b}} \qquad \frac{\overline{b} \triangleright (w,s,\overline{i}) :: \overline{b'}}{(\varepsilon,s',\overline{i'})::\overline{b} \triangleright (w,s,\overline{i}) :: \overline{b'}}$$

———— valid predicate ————

$$\textbf{valid}(f,w,i_1::\cdots::i_n,\overline{f}) \;=\; \textbf{occ}(f::\overline{f}) \leq \textbf{cap}(w) \;\wedge\; \bigwedge_{j \in \{1,..,n\}} \textbf{check}(f,w,i_j,\overline{f})$$

$$\textbf{check}(f,w,i,\overline{f}) = \begin{cases} \text{true} & \text{if } i=\texttt{capacity\_used } n\% \wedge 100*\textbf{occ}(f::\overline{f})/\textbf{cap}(w) \leq n \\ \text{true} & \text{if } i=\texttt{max\_concurrent\_invocations } n \wedge |f::\overline{f}| \leq n \\ \text{true} & \text{if } i=\texttt{anti\_affine } F \wedge \forall g \in F.g \notin \overline{f} \\ \text{true} & \text{if } i=\texttt{affine } F \wedge \exists g \in F.g \in \overline{f} \\ \text{false} & \text{otherwise} \end{cases}$$

$$\textbf{occ}(\overline{f}) = \sum_{f \in \overline{f}} \textbf{res}(f)$$

Fig. 4. aAPP semantics.

Definition 4 (aAPP-calculus and APP-calculus). *The aAPP-calculus models function scheduling in FaaS systems by means of a labelled transition system (States × Labels × States) defined as the minimal transition system satisfying the rules in Fig. 4. We call APP-calculus the fragment of the aAPP-calculus where the invalidation conditions* `affine` *F and* `anti_affine` *F are not used.*

Before discussing the formal definition of the semantics of the calculus, we extend the notation for lists so that: $e \in l$ means that e belongs to l ($e \notin l$ is its negation), $l \setminus e$ is a list obtained by removing the first occurrence of e from l, and $|l|$ is the length of l.

In the definition, we use the auxiliary $\triangleright$ relation and **valid** predicate, specified in Fig. 4. The relation $\triangleright$ is defined on lists of scheduling blocks with the aim of extracting, from a given list, one worker to be considered for scheduling. Namely, $\overline{b} \triangleright (w,s,\overline{i})::\overline{b'}$ means that w is one of the workers that can be selected from the first (non-empty) scheduling block of $\overline{b}$, and s and $\overline{i}$ are the selection strategy and the invalidation conditions of the block from which w has been extracted. The list $\overline{b'}$ contains the remaining workers and scheduling blocks. The predicate

234   G. De Palma et al.

valid$(f, w, i_1 :: \cdots :: i_n, \overline{f})$ checks whether a function f can be scheduled on w assuming invalidation conditions $i_1 :: \cdots :: i_n$, and that the worker w currently hosts the functions $\overline{f}$, i.e., $N(w) = \overline{f}$. In the definition of the predicate, **occ** returns the occupancy of a list of functions (using **res** to obtain the occupancy of a single function), **cap** calculates the capacity of a worker, and **check** verifies whether a condition i the scheduling of a function f on a worker w, given a list of functions $\overline{f}$ already present on w.

We are now ready to discuss the operational semantics rules. Rule $[start]$ states that if the worker w (extracted from the list of scheduling blocks of f via the $\triangleright$ relation) is valid for the scheduling of the function f (validity is checked with the **valid** predicate) then the current state can evolve by adding an instance of f to the list of functions currently scheduled on w. Rule $[rm]$ simply removes an instance of function f from the list of functions currently scheduled on a worker w. This rule models the removal of a function from a worker when its execution has been completed. Lastly, rule $[next]$ models the case when an attempt to schedule a function f fails (due to the invalidation conditions) and it allows the remaining workers/scheduling blocks to schedule f.

We present a couple of examples of derivations which involve the rules $[start]$ and $[next]$ (rule $[rm]$ has a rather straightforward application). We consider the function f with consumed resources **res**$(f) = 5$ and scheduling policy $\Delta = (f \mapsto b)$, where $b = (w :: w',\ \texttt{best\_first},\ \texttt{capacity\_used}\ 50\%)$, and initial network $N = (w \mapsto \varepsilon) \cup (w' \mapsto \varepsilon)$, with workers w and w' with capacity **cap**$(w) =$ **cap**$(w') = 10$.

First, we can schedule f on w using the rule $[start]$ (for brevity, we use f to denote the list $f :: \varepsilon$ in networks).

$$[start]\ \frac{b \triangleright (w,\texttt{best\_first},\texttt{capacity\_used}\ 50\%) :: (w',\texttt{best\_first},\texttt{capacity\_used}\ 50\%) \quad \textbf{valid}(f,w,\texttt{capacity\_used}\ 50\%,\varepsilon)}{\langle (w \mapsto \varepsilon) \cup (w' \mapsto \varepsilon),\ (f \mapsto b) \rangle \xrightarrow{f \downarrow w} \langle (w \mapsto f) \cup (w' \mapsto \varepsilon),\ (f \mapsto b) \rangle}$$

Let N' be the reached network $(w \mapsto f) \cup (w' \mapsto \varepsilon)$. If we try to schedule f in $\langle N',\ (f \mapsto b) \rangle$, we will allocate it on w' since w cannot host f without exceeding the $\texttt{capacity\_used}\ 50\%$ condition. This is formalised by the transition below, where $s = \texttt{best\_first}$ and $i = \texttt{capacity\_used}\ 50\%$, for brevity.

$$[next]\ \frac{b \triangleright (w,s,i) :: (w',s,i) \quad \neg\textbf{valid}(f,w,i,f) \quad [start]\ \dfrac{b \triangleright (w',s,i) :: \varepsilon \quad \textbf{valid}(f,w',i,\varepsilon)}{\langle N',\ (f \mapsto (w',s,i)) \rangle \xrightarrow{f \downarrow w'} \langle (w \mapsto f) \cup (w' \mapsto f),\ (f \mapsto (w',s,i)) \rangle}}{\langle N',\ (f \mapsto b) \rangle \xrightarrow{f \downarrow w'} \langle (w \mapsto f) \cup (w' \mapsto f),\ (f \mapsto b) \rangle}$$

In the remainder, we use the following notation: given the sequence of labels $\overline{\alpha} = \alpha_1 \ldots \alpha_n$, we use $\langle N, \Delta \rangle \xrightarrow{\overline{\alpha}} \langle N_n, \Delta \rangle$ to denote that $\langle N, \Delta \rangle \xrightarrow{\alpha_1} \langle N_1, \Delta \rangle \ldots \xrightarrow{\alpha_n} \langle N_n, \Delta \rangle$.

We close the section with the definition of the problems we consider in our development: *reachability* concerns checking whether a function f can be scheduled on a worker w starting from an initial network of workers, while *co-occurrence* checks whether two functions f and g can be both present in the list of functions scheduled on a worker w. By *initial* network of workers, we mean a network N where all workers have no functions already scheduled, i.e., $N(w) = \varepsilon$ for every available worker w.

Definition 5 (Reachability). *Given a scheduling policy Δ, an initial network N, a function f, and a worker w, the* reachability *problem* $\mathsf{Reach}(\Delta, N, f, w)$ *consists of checking if there exists a sequence of labels $\overline{\alpha}$ such that $\langle N, \Delta \rangle \xrightarrow{\overline{\alpha}} \langle N', \Delta \rangle$ with $N'(w) = \overline{f}$ such that $f \in \overline{f}$.*

Definition 6 (Co-occurrence). *Given a scheduling policy Δ, an initial network N, two functions f and g, and a worker w, the* co-occurrence *problem* $\mathsf{CoOccur}(\Delta, N, f, g, w)$ *consists of checking if there exists a sequence of labels $\overline{\alpha}$ such that $\langle N, \Delta \rangle \xrightarrow{\overline{\alpha}} \langle N', \Delta \rangle$ with $N'(w) = \overline{f}$ such that $f \in \overline{f}$ and $g \in \overline{f} \setminus f$.*

4 Reachability and Co-occurrence in the **APP**-Calculus

We prove that both reachability and co-occurrence have linear time complexity in the APP-calculus.[5] The result follows from two properties formalised in Lemmas 1 and 2.

Lemma 1 formalises a sort of anti-monotonic property of scheduling: if we can schedule a function f on a worker, we can do it even if the worker hosted fewer functions.

Lemma 1. *Let $\overline{i}$ be a list of invalidation conditions that does not contain invalidations of the kind* $\mathtt{affine}\ F$, *N a network of workers, Δ a scheduling policy, w a worker belonging to the domain of N, and f, g functions belonging to the domain of Δ. We have that* $\mathbf{valid}(f, w, \overline{i}, \overline{f})$ *implies* $\mathbf{valid}(f, w, \overline{i}, \overline{f} \setminus f')$, *for every function f'.*

Notice that Lemma 1 does not hold if we consider also the invalidation conditions $\mathtt{affine}\ F$. In fact, if $f \in F$, the **check** predicate in Fig. 4 checks whether $f \in \overline{f}$, and if there is only one occurrence of f in $\overline{f}$ we have that $f \notin (\overline{f} \setminus f)$. We can then conclude that the property stated by the above lemma does not hold in the full aAPP-calculus due to the presence of the invalidation conditions $\mathtt{affine}\ F$, while it holds in the APP-calculus (and in a fragment of the aAPP-calculus which does not use $\mathtt{affine}\ F$, named negatively-polarised fragment of aAPP in Sect. 6).

Lemma 2 intuitively states that, when considering the reachability on a worker w, we can consider a simpler script with only the blocks that involve w and remove the other workers from said blocks; as defined by the auxiliary function $\mathtt{simple}$. Formally, $\mathtt{simple}(\Delta, w) = \Delta'$ where Δ' has the same

---

[5] We recall that details about the proofs of our results are in the companion paper [19]. In this paper, we give an idea of the proof structure and discuss the proof techniques.

domain as Δ and if $\Delta(f) = \overline{b}$ then $\Delta'(f) = \mathtt{fltr}(\overline{b}, w)$ where $\mathtt{fltr}(\varepsilon, w) = \varepsilon$ and $\mathtt{fltr}((\overline{w}, s, \overline{i}) :: \overline{b}, w) = \begin{cases} (w, s, \overline{i}) :: \mathtt{fltr}(\overline{b}, w) & \text{if } w \in \overline{w} \\ \mathtt{fltr}(\overline{b}, w) & \text{otherwise} \end{cases}$ Intuitively, Lemma 2 holds because the other workers (not w) that have higher priority than w can be invalidated by assigning functions to them until they reach full capacity.

Lemma 2. *Given a scheduling policy Δ, an initial network of workers N, a function f, and a worker w, we have that* $\mathsf{Reach}(\Delta, N, f, w)$ *iff* $\mathsf{Reach}(\mathtt{simple}(\Delta, w), N, f, w)$.

We now move to the proof that the reachability problem has linear time complexity in the APP-calculus. Intuitively, the proof proceed as follows. In the light of Lemma 2 we can restrict to the simplest $\mathtt{simple}(\Delta, w)$ scheduling policy which considers only the target worker w. If $\mathtt{simple}(\Delta, w)$ contains at least one scheduling block capable of scheduling the function f on w when w is empty, then we know that $\mathsf{Reach}(\mathtt{simple}(\Delta, w), N, f, w)$. On the opposite direction, if $\mathsf{Reach}(\mathtt{simple}(\Delta, w), N, f, w)$ we know that there is a sequence of scheduling events ending with the scheduling of f on w. By the anti-monotonic property formalized in Lemma 1, we have that the scheduling of f on w can be anticipated at the beginning (when w is empty). Verifying whether there is a scheduling block for function f on an empty worker w in $\mathtt{simple}(\Delta, w)$ corresponds to a linear-time check of the lists of invalidation policies associated with blocks of f and check if the invalidation conditions are not met.

Theorem 1. $\mathsf{Reach}(\Delta, N, f, w)$ *has linear time complexity in the APP-calculus.*

Similarly, we prove that also co-occurrence has linear time complexity by reducing the problem to solving the reachability problem twice.

Theorem 2. $\mathsf{CoOccur}(\Delta, N, f, g, w)$ *has linear time complexity in the APP-calculus.*

5   Reachability and Co-occurrence in the aAPP-Calculus

We now prove that both reachability and co-occurrence become PSPACE-complete in the full aAPP-calculus, i.e., when consider (anti-)affinity constraints. While this result formalises the expressiveness gap – i.e., aAPP can specify more sophisticated scheduling policies than APP– it severely complicates reachability verification, which motivates the introduction of our planner-based tool in Sect. 7.

To prove that reachability is PSPACE-complete in the aAPP-calculus we first need to show that the problem is in PSPACE. This first result follows from the following observations: (i) a network $N \in \mathcal{N}$ can be represented in memory by a matrix (with a row for each worker, a column for each function, and the number of instances of a function on a worker stored in the corresponding cell) which occupies a polynomial amount of space; (ii) reachability can be detected with a nondeterministic algorithm using that amount of space; (iii) NPSPACE coincides with PSPACE [46]. Then we need to prove that the problem is PSPACE-hard. This can be proved by reduction from the single post-condition variant of PLANSAT which was proved to be PSPACE-hard by Bylander [11]. In a few words, this problem consists of checking whether a target state can be reached starting from an initial state represented by a finite set of ground atomic conditions that are considered initially true, by applying operators that change the current state by checking some positive and negative pre-conditions (the positive ones should hold, the negative ones should not hold) and then modifying the state by making a ground atomic condition either true or false. This problem can be modeled in aAPP by means of an appropriate encoding which represents each ground atomic condition with two possible functions, one representing the condition true and one representing the condition false. The operators are modeled by means of a scheduling policy capable of: (i) scheduling a specific function f_o representing one operator o only if the functions representing the corresponding pre-conditions are already scheduled, and (ii) scheduling the function representing the post-condition of o only if the function f_o is already scheduled. We use affinity to check the presence of the functions representing the pre-conditions, while anti-affinity is used to guarantee that if the post-condition requires to change the value of a ground atomic condition, the function representing the new value true (resp. false) is not scheduled contemporaneously with the opposite previous value false (resp. true).

Theorem 3. Reach(Δ, N, f, w) *is PSPACE-complete in the aAPP-calculus.*

We have that the co-occurrence problem can be reduced to the reachability problem. This allows us to conclude the following.

Corollary 1. CoOccur(Δ, N, f, g, w) *is   PSPACE-complete   in   the   aAPP-calculus.*

6   Reachability and Co-occurence with Polarised Affinities

We move to investigate *polarised* aAPP sublanguages, where one can express either affinity or anti-affinity but not mix them. Practically, we want to understand if we can use algorithmically tractable analyses with fragments of aAPP, e.g., when a script uses only the syntax of a polarised fragment. We call *positively-polarised* aAPP the variant with only affinity and *negatively-polarised* aAPP the one with only anti-affinity.

The calculus corresponding to positively-polarised aAPP is the fragment of the aAPP-calculus that does not contain invalidation conditions of the kind `anti_affine` F (generated by the forbidden anti-affinity requirements); while the calculus corresponding to negatively-polarised aAPP is the fragment of the aAPP-calculus that does not contain invalidation conditions of the kind `affine` F (generated by the forbidden affinity requirements). We study the complexity of the reachability and co-occurrence problems for the two fragments. We show that in the positively-polarised fragment the problems are NP-hard (hence not tractable unless P=NP), while in the negatively-polarised fragment both problems have linear time complexity.

First, we prove that in the positively-polarised fragment of the aAPP-calculus the reachability and co-occurrence problems are NP-hard. The proof is by reduction from 3SAT, a well known NP-hard problem [14] consisting of checking the satisfiability of a boolean formula in conjunctive normal form, where each clause has at most three literals (where a literal is a boolean variable or its negation). The reduction is based on a scheduling policy which allows for the initial scheduling of functions which represent a possible assignment of boolean values to the variables in the formula. Then, affinity is used to allow the scheduling of functions representing whether a given clause is satisfied by the assignment. These functions are forced to be scheduled in sequence, from the first clause to the last one. In this way, the functions corresponding to the last clause can be scheduled if-and-only-if all the clauses can be satisfied, i.e., the formula is satisfiable.

Theorem 4. Reach(Δ, N, f, w) *and* CoOccur(Δ, N, f, g, w) *are NP-hard in the positively-polarised fragment of the* **aAPP-calculus**.

```
1 (:goal
2    (= (number_of_f_in_W f w) 1)
3 )
```

```
1 (:goal
2    (and (= (number_of_f_in_W f1 w) 1)
3         (= (number_of_f_in_W f2 w) 1)
4 ))
```

Fig. 5. Encoding of Reach and CoOccur in PDDL, on the left and right side respectively.

Note that the proof of linear time complexity of Reach(Δ, N, f, w) and CoOccur(Δ, N, f, g, w) cannot be applied to the positively-polarised fragment of the aAPP-calculus because Lemma 1 considers scheduling policies that do not contain invalidations of the kind `affine` F. On the other hand, the proof can be applied to the negatively-polarised fragment of the aAPP-calculus, thus we can conclude the following.

Theorem 5. Reach(Δ, N, f, w) *and* CoOccur(Δ, N, f, g, w) *have linear time complexity in the negatively-polarised fragment of the* **aAPP-calculus**.

7   Automated Verification of **aAPP** Scripts

Given the results of the Reach and CoOccur problems for APP and aAPP, we have a firmer grasp of how to automate their analysis, provided an initial configuration. Since we proved that the complexity of this analysis for aAPP is PSPACE-hard, we present a proof-of-concept solution developed on existing solvers for that class of problems.

Specifically, we encode the Reach and CoOccur problems as automated planning tasks. We choose to use PDDL [23], i.e., the de-facto standard for encoding planning problems. Mainly, PDDL specifications include two parts: a domain description, regarding all available actions and their preconditions and effects, and a problem description, modelling the initial state of the specific problem instance and the desired goals.

The choice of PDDL has many advantages, the main ones include: *i*) it lets us use different dedicated and efficient planning solvers, *ii*) it naturally provides a witness (i.e., a sequence of actions) leading to the violation of some desired property (e.g., if two functions shall be anti-affine and we find an instance where they co-occur, we can see a trace that produces the offending result), and *iii*) it lets users express more elaborate goal configurations than reachability and co-occurrence (e.g., we can ask if there exists a worker that can host a given set of functions and still preserve a certain capacity).

7.1   Encoding of the PDDL Domain

To define the domain, we encoded the semantic rules reported in Fig. 4. The two main encoded actions are the *(start, _, _)* and *(done, _, _)* transitions. Each action alters the state appropriately, e.g., removing a function from a worker increases its available capacity accordingly. The encoding of the rules uses a combination of boolean predicates (e.g., for the affinity of a block) and numerical functions (e.g., for capacity constraints). We did not encode the *(fail, _, _)* transition since it does not affect the state – it is equivalent to a null operation in the context of a plan.

7.2   Encoding of the PDDL Problems

Since aAPP's semantics works on aAPP scripts and configurations (cf. Fig. 4), we define the problem by encoding an input aAPP script with a companion configuration definition, which describes the existing workers and functions with the respective capacities/occupancies – the latter, defined using PDDL *numeric fluents* to model non-binary, discrete resources. Given a configuration, in its initial state workers have no allocated functions and maximal capacity. We define the Reach and CoOccur problems using of the proposition *number_of_f_in_W*, which indicates the number of copies of a function on a given worker in the final state. The code on the left of Fig. 5 exemplifies the Reach problem, where we check if we can satisfy the goal of allocating at least one copy of function f on worker w; on the right of Fig. 5, we realise CoOccur as the conjunction of two *number_of_f_in_W*, checking if worker w can host both functions f1 and f2.

7.3   Tool Components and Support for Advanced Queries, an Example

To provide a smoother experience to users, we provide users with a simple, YAML-like notation for configurations (exemplified in Fig. 6) and translators that generate the PDDL encoding of part of the problem, given a configuration

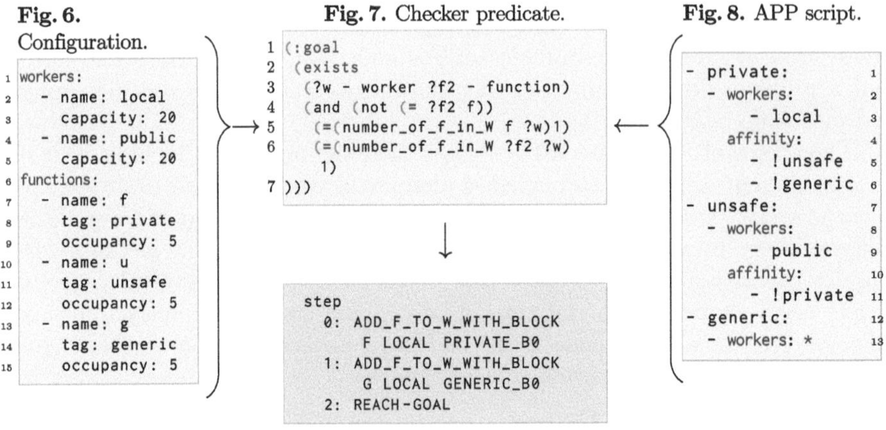

Fig. 9. Fixed APP script.

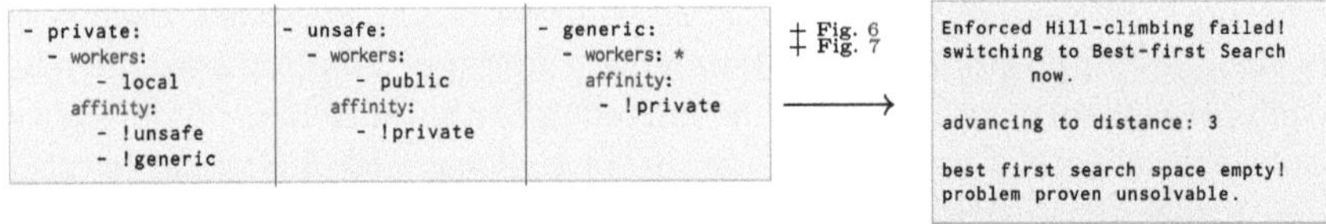

Fig. 10. Example of incorrect aAPP script for the *singleton* example (top) and fix (bottom). (Color figure online)

file and an aAPP script. The last piece of the problem, required from the user, is the definition of the goal, which uses the PDDL notation. The encoding and its companion tools are available at [16].

We illustrate the experience of using our analysis tool by defining a configuration, an aAPP script, and a property. Let us consider the configuration in Fig. 6, with two workers, local and public, and three functions f, u and g, resp. tagged private, unsafe, and generic. We want to define an aAPP script such that *it never happens that we allocate* f*s with other non-*f *functions*. We encode this property in Fig. 7, where we use existential quantifiers to range over both workers and functions and check whether we can find a worker that can host both f and a function different from f. If the planner is unable to find a solution, the property holds for the provided aAPP script.

In Fig. 8, we show a possible candidate script. Running the planner with (the encodings of) the excerpts in Fig. 6 and Fig. 8 and the goal from Fig. 7, we obtain the output in the red box at the centre of Fig. 10. The output is a trace of actions that satisfies the goal; namely, the allocation of f with another function on the same worker. Specifically, we found that f can co-occur with a function g, tagged generic, on the local worker. Hence, we need to fix our candidate aAPP script to prevent the allocation of generic functions with fs. Looking closely at Fig. 8, we indeed notice that we forgot to indicate that also the generic (tagged) functions are anti-affine with the private ones. Remember that affinity in aAPP is not symmetric, so, to ensure that private functions are anti-affine with the other functions, we need to mark also all the latter anti-affine with the private ones.

Figure 9 shows a fixed version of the aAPP script from Fig. 8 where we add mutual anti-affinity – the new affinity clause under the generic block. The new constraint makes the goal from Fig. 7 unsatisfiable, as shown in the green box next to Fig. 9.

Performance-wise, we tested our encoding using the MetricFF [28] planner on examples similar to Fig. 10, obtaining results (either providing a solution or proving its non-existence) within a few milliseconds – we obtain a solution in 2.4 ms for the script in Fig. 8 and the exhaustion for the one in Fig. 9 in 4 ms, averaged over 10^4 runs.

Here, we focus on the feasibility of our approach based on using off-the-shelf planning solvers, hence we leave as future work the study of which planners work best and how well they scale under different cases. Like SAT solvers, which can solve large SAT problems despite their NP-hardness, we conjecture that planners can efficiently solve the majority of reachability and co-occurrence problems. Intuitively, except for those combinations of configuration, script, and predicates that require the saturation of workers to reach the goal, the plan to prove the violation of the property is rather short and therefore solvers can find it quickly.[6]

8   Related Work and Discussion

Common scheduling problems are renownedly NP-complete [56]. However, we are not aware of results on the complexity of scheduling problems where affinity is the key point for turning the complexity of the problem from linear-time to PSPACE-hard (as formalised by Theorems 4 and 3). We consider these result an interesting point to highlight in relation to other computational models. We initially thought that the source of the increase of complexity was mainly due to anti-affinity (i.e., check the absence of a set of functions F before scheduling another function g on a worker). In fact, in many computational models, "negative" tests increase the complexity of verifying properties. For example, it is well-known that in register-based computational models (RAMs) the ability to test whether a register is empty is necessary for RAMs to be Turing complete, while in Petri nets reachability and coverability problems are decidable, but they become undecidable in Petri nets extended with inhibitor arcs (i.e., the ability to test whether a place is empty).

Regarding Petri nets, it is interesting to observe that our results exhibit notable differences compared to the known complexity/undecidability results in that context. Our reachability problems are expressed as the possibility to reach a configuration with at least some given functions on some given worker. This

---

[6] The complexity of the planning problem becomes pseudo-polynomial with bounded plan length – $O(n^k)$ with n size of the planning encoding and k maximal length of the plan.

formulation has a strong correspondence with the coverability problem in Petri nets, consisting of checking the reachability of a marking with at least a given amount of tokens in some given places. Coverability is EXPSPACE-hard in Petri nets [36] while our reachability problems are PSPACE-complete as in 1-safe Petri nets [13], the fragment of Petri nets where places can contain at most one token. Our calculus is significantly different from 1-safe Petri nets because we need to count how many instances of a function are present in a worker. Moreover, our semantics also incorporates priorities because the scheduling blocks must be considered in order, i.e., a block is considered only if the previous ones fail. Differently from our context, the addition of priorities to Petri nets makes them Turing complete [26], hence coverability becomes undecidable.

Another interesting highlight concerns the linear time complexity of co-occurrence in the APP-calculus (Theorem 2) and in negatively-polarised aAPP (Theorem 4). On the positive side, we have that we can efficiently check possible violations of security properties of scripts, like the co-location of "trusted" and "untrusted" functions. However, this efficiency comes at a cost, i.e., the impossibility to express any reasonable form of affinity. As a corollary of Lemma 1, we have that if $\langle N, \Delta \rangle \xrightarrow{f \downarrow w} \langle N_1, \Delta \rangle$ in a network N where the worker w already hosts instances of g, we have that also $\langle N', \Delta \rangle \xrightarrow{f \downarrow w} \langle N_1', \Delta \rangle$ where $\langle N', \Delta \rangle$ is the same as $\langle N, \Delta \rangle$, but with all occurrences of g removed from w. Such property implies that scheduling policies expressed in APP, or in the negatively-polarised fragment of aAPP, cannot admit the scheduling of a function f in case we want f to be affine with g, i.e., we want the guarantee that f can be scheduled only on workers which already host instances of another function g.

Looking at the industry, we see platforms using both affinity and anti-affinity. Azure Service Fabric [39] provides a notion of *service affinity* that ensures the placement of replicas of a service on the same nodes as those of another, affine service. Another example is Kubernetes, which has a notion of *node affinity* and *inter-pod (anti-)affinity* to express advanced scheduling logic for the optimal distribution of pods [34]. Affinity and anti-affinity have been also studied in the context of microservices. Proposals in this direction are by Baarzi and Kesidis [7], who present a framework for the deployment of microservices that infers and assigns affinity and anti-affinity traits to microservices to orient the distribution of resources and microservices replicas on the available machines; Sampaio et al. [44], who introduce an adaptation mechanism for microservice deployment based on microservice affinities (e.g., the more messages microservices exchange the more affine they are) and resource usage; Sheoran et al. [49], who propose an approach that computes procedural affinity of communication among microservices to make placement decisions. Overall, the mentioned work proves the usefulness of affinity-aware deployments at lower layers than FaaS (e.g., VMs, containers, microservices) but we are not aware of any formal study on the semantics and expressiveness of these constructs.

In the literature on serverless, proposals might adopt affinity and anti-affinity relations to encode and complement desirable properties of function scheduling, otherwise implemented via ad-hoc, platform-wide policies. For instance, some works present serverless architectures that enable the efficient composition of functions co-located on the same host [3,43,50]. Here, aAPP can help to parametrise the co-location of functions, expressed in terms of affinity and anti-affinity constraints. Another example regards security, e.g., Pubali et al. [15] present a serverless platform where developers can constrain the information flow among functions to avoid attacks due to container reuse and data exfiltration. In this case, aAPP can complement flow policies with affinity and anti-affinity constraints that restrict the co-tenancy of functions and their flows of communication. Another interesting proposal, Palette [2], uses optional opaque parameters in function invocations to inform the load balancer of Azure Functions on the affinity with previous invocations and the data they produced. While Palette does not support (anti-)affinity constraints, it allows users to express which invocations benefit from running on the same node. We deem an interesting future work extending aAPP to support a notion of (anti-)affinity that considers the history of scheduled functions.

Closing our revision of related work, we mention our previous publication [18], that presents an alternative definition of a semantics for the APP language. The differences between that work and the aAPP-calculus we present are twofold. First, we consider also affinity-aware scheduling policies, i.e., we model APP's semantics and extend it with affinities, giving us the aAPP language. Second, we define a more elegant and simplified semantics. Indeed, the previous semantics definition [18] considers three distinct layers (for [*Workers*], [*Blocks*], and [*Configurations*]), while the semantics we propose has just one layer. Moreover, our semantics omits the transition $(fail, f)$ – used in the alternative semantics [18] to model the failure of an attempt to schedule a function f – because it is irrelevant for the study of the reachability and co-occurrence problems.

9   Conclusion and Future Work

We shed some light on formal characterisations of reachability analysis of FaaS scheduling policies and show immediate application of these mathematical results. We first introduce the aAPP-calculus to rigorously reason on the semantics of function scheduling that includes affinity constraints and then proceed to study the expressiveness of aAPP. We start with APP, which is a subset of aAPP that does not express either affinity or anti-affinity constraints. Performing our analysis of APP, we show that it is unfit for expressing interesting (anti-)affinity constraints between functions. Turning to aAPP, we formally prove the increment of expressiveness of adding affinity by showing that affinity-aware reachability problems, having linear time complexity in APP, turn out to be PSPACE-complete in aAPP. The proof of PSPACE-hardness is by reduction from PLANSAT, a well-known planning problem. We complement the above results by studying fragments of aAPP that can only express either affinity or anti-affinity constraints, proving that the complexity increase derives from affinity.

We summarise the complexity bounds of the co-occurrence (and reachability) problem of APP, aAPP, and the latter's affinity-only and anti-affinity-only fragments.

	APP	neg. polarised aAPP	pos. polarised aAPP	aAPP
Lowerbound	Linear	Linear	NP	PSPACE
Upperbound	Linear	Linear	PSPACE	PSPACE

Given the above results, we define a relationship from aAPP to PDDL – a standard language for planning problems – and realise a tool for automatic verification of scheduling properties for aAPP that exploits off-the-shelf PDDL solvers.

Directions for future work include capturing configurations whose workers can change, i.e., when workers (dis)appear while the platform is running. In such dynamic scenarios, the configuration space is infinite, which could have repercussions on the complexity/decidability of the reachability and co-occurrence problems. We also plan to define a timed semantics for aAPP, e.g., to specify the expected execution time of functions on workers. One such model could support quantitative analysis, e.g., to estimate the completion time of a FaaS application or the distribution of workers' load over time, i.e., it would allow us to quantitatively reason on policies, e.g., whether they could lead to bad performance or underutilisation of workers.

Acknowledgement. Research partly supported by project PNRR CN HPC - SPOKE 9 - Innovation Grant LEONARDO - TASI - RTMER funded by the NextGenerationEU European initiative through the MUR, Italy (CUP: J33C22001170001).

References

1. Abad, C.L., Boza, E.F., Eyk, E.V.: Package-aware scheduling of FaaS functions. In: Proceedings of ACM/SPEC ICPE, pp. 101–106. ACM (2018). https://doi.org/10.1145/3185768.3186294
2. Abdi, M., et al.: Palette load balancing: locality hints for serverless functions. In: Proceedings of the Eighteenth European Conference on Computer Systems, pp. 365–380 (2023)
3. Akkus, I.E., et al.: SAND: towards high-performance serverless computing. In: 2018 Usenix Annual Technical Conference (USENIX ATC 2018), pp. 923–935 (2018)
4. Alpernas, K., et al.: Secure serverless computing using dynamic information flow control. Proc. ACM Program. Lang. **2**(OOPSLA), 1–26 (2018)
5. Amazon Web Services: AWS Lambda Getting Started (2024). https://aws.amazon.com/lambda/getting-started/. Accessed Aug 2025
6. Apache Software Foundation: Apache OpenWhisk (2025). https://openwhisk.apache.org/. Accessed Aug 2025
7. Baarzi, A.F., Kesidis, G.: Showar: right-sizing and efficient scheduling of microservices. In: Proceedings of the ACM Symposium on Cloud Computing, pp. 427–441 (2021)

8. Baldini, I., et al.: Serverless computing: current trends and open problems. In: Chaudhary, S., Somani, G., Buyya, R. (eds.) Research Advances in Cloud Computing, pp. 1–20. Springer, Singapore (2017). https://doi.org/10.1007/978-981-10-5026-8_1

9. Banaei, A., Sharifi, M.: ETAS: predictive scheduling of functions on worker nodes of Apache OpenWhisk platform. J. Supercomput. (2021). https://doi.org/10.1007/s11227-021-04057-z

10. Baresi, L., Quattrocchi, G.: PAPS: a serverless platform for edge computing infrastructures. Front. Sustain. Cities **3**, 690660 (2021)

11. Bylander, T.: The computational complexity of propositional STRIPS planning. Artif. Intell. **69**(1-2), 165–204 (1994). https://doi.org/10.1016/0004-3702(94)90081-7

12. Casale, G., et al.: Radon: rational decomposition and orchestration for serverless computing. SICS Softw.-Intensive Cyber-Phys. Syst. **35**(1), 77–87 (2020)

13. Cheng, A., Esparza, J., Palsberg, J.: Complexity results for 1-safe nets. In: Shyamasundar, R.K. (ed.) FSTTCS 1993. LNCS, vol. 761, pp. 326–337. Springer, Heidelberg (1993). https://doi.org/10.1007/3-540-57529-4_66

14. Cook, S.A.: The complexity of theorem-proving procedures. In: Harrison, M.A., Banerji, R.B., Ullman, J.D. (eds.) Proceedings of the 3rd Annual ACM Symposium on Theory of Computing, 3–5 May 1971, Shaker Heights, Ohio, USA, pp. 151–158. ACM (1971). https://doi.org/10.1145/800157.805047

15. Datta, P., Kumar, P., Morris, T., Grace, M., Rahmati, A., Bates, A.: Valve: securing function workflows on serverless computing platforms. In: Proceedings of the Web Conference 2020, pp. 939–950 (2020)

16. De Palma, G., Giallorenzo, S., Mauro, J., Trentin, M., Zavattaro, G.: Reachability Analysis of Function-as-a-Service Scheduling Policies (Artifact). https://zenodo.org/records/17047090. Accessed Aug 2025

17. De Palma, G., Giallorenzo, S., Mauro, J., Trentin, M., Zavattaro, G.: A declarative approach to topology-aware serverless function-execution scheduling. In: IEEE International Conference on Web Services, ICWS 2022, Barcelona, Spain, 10–16 July 2022, pp. 337–342. IEEE (2022). https://doi.org/10.1109/ICWS55610.2022.00056

18. De Palma, G., Giallorenzo, S., Mauro, J., Trentin, M., Zavattaro, G.: Function-as-a-service allocation policies made formal. In: Margaria, T., Steffen, B. (eds.) Leveraging Applications of Formal Methods, Verification and Validation. REoCAS Colloquium in Honor of Rocco De Nicola - 12th International Symposium, ISoLA 2024, Crete, Greece, 27–31 October 2024, Proceedings, Part I. Lecture Notes in Computer Science, vol. 15219, pp. 306–321. Springer, Cham (2024). https://doi.org/10.1007/978-3-031-73709-1_19

19. De Palma, G., Giallorenzo, S., Mauro, J., Trentin, M., Zavattaro, G.: On the Complexity of Reachability Properties in Serverless Function Scheduling. CoRR abs/2407.14159 (2024). https://doi.org/10.48550/ARXIV.2407.14159

20. De Palma, G., Giallorenzo, S., Mauro, J., Trentin, M., Zavattaro, G.: Affinity-aware serverless function scheduling. In: 22nd IEEE International Conference on Software Architecture, ICSA 2025, Odense, Denmark, 31 March–4 April 2025, pp. 49–59. IEEE (2025). https://doi.org/10.1109/ICSA65012.2025.00015

21. De Palma, G., Giallorenzo, S., Mauro, J., Zavattaro, G.: Allocation priority policies for serverless function-execution scheduling optimisation. In: Kafeza, E., Benatallah, B., Martinelli, F., Hacid, H., Bouguettaya, A., Motahari, H. (eds.) ICSOC 2020. LNCS, vol. 12571, pp. 416–430. Springer, Cham (2020). https://doi.org/10.1007/978-3-030-65310-1_29

22. Fission Project: Fission (2024). https://fission.io/. Accessed Aug 2025
23. Fox, M., Long, D.: PDDL2. 1: an extension to PDDL for expressing temporal planning domains. J. Artif. Intell. Res. **20**, 61–124 (2003)
24. Ghallab, M., Nau, D.S., Traverso, P.: Automated planning - theory and practice. Elsevier (2004)
25. Google: Google Cloud Functions (2024). https://cloud.google.com/functions/. Accessed Aug 2025
26. Hack, M.: Petri net language. Technical report, USA (1976)
27. Hendrickson, S., Sturdevant, S., Harter, T., Venkataramani, V., Arpaci-Dusseau, A.C., Arpaci-Dusseau, R.H.: Serverless computation with openlambda. In: 8th USENIX Workshop on Hot Topics in Cloud Computing (HotCloud 2016) (2016)
28. Hoffmann, J.: Extending FF to numerical state variables. In: Proceedings of the 15th European Conference on Artificial Intelligence (ECAI 2002), pp. 571–575. wil, Lyon, France (2002)
29. Jia, Z., Witchel, E.: Boki: stateful serverless computing with shared logs. In: Proceedings of ACM SIGOPS SOSP, pp. 691–707. ACM, New York (2021). https://doi.org/10.1145/3477132.3483541
30. Jonas, E., et al.: Cloud programming simplified: a Berkeley view on serverless computing. Technical report UCB/EECS-2019-3, EECS Department, University of California, Berkeley (2019)
31. Kehrer, S., Scheffold, J., Blochinger, W.: Serverless skeletons for elastic parallel processing. In: 2019 IEEE 5th International Conference on Big Data Intelligence and Computing (DATACOM), pp. 185–192. IEEE (2019)
32. Kelly, D., Glavin, F., Barrett, E.: Serverless computing: behind the scenes of major platforms. In: 2020 IEEE 13th International Conference on Cloud Computing (CLOUD), pp. 304–312. IEEE (2020)
33. Kotni, S., Nayak, A., Ganapathy, V., Basu, A.: Faastlane: accelerating function-as-a-service workflows. In: Proceedings of USENIX ATC, pp. 805–820. USENIX Association (2021)
34. Kubernetes: Assign Pods to Nodes using Node Affinity (2025). https://kubernetes.io/docs/tasks/configure-pod-container/assign-pods-nodes-using-node-affinity/. Accessed Aug 2025
35. Kuntsevich, A., Nasirifard, P., Jacobsen, H.A.: A distributed analysis and benchmarking framework for apache OpenWhisk serverless platform. In: Proceedings of Middleware (Posters), pp. 3–4 (2018)
36. Lipton, R.: The reachability problem requires exponential space. Research report (Yale University. Department of Computer Science), Department of Computer Science, Yale University (1976). https://books.google.it/books?id=7iSbGwAACAAJ
37. Microsoft: Configuring and using service affinity in Service Fabric (2025). https://learn.microsoft.com/en-us/azure/service-fabric/service-fabric-cluster-resource-manager-advanced-placement-rules-affinity. Accessed Aug 2025
38. Microsoft: Microsoft Azure Functions (2025). https://azure.microsoft.com/. Accessed Aug 2025
39. Microsoft: Microsoft Azure Service Fabric Overview (2025). https://learn.microsoft.com/en-us/azure/service-fabric/service-fabric-overview. Accessed Aug 2025
40. Mohan, A., Sane, H., Doshi, K., Edupuganti, S., Nayak, N., Sukhomlinov, V.: Agile cold starts for scalable serverless. In: Proceedings of HotCloud 19. USENIX Association, Renton, WA (2019)

41. Oakes, E., et al.: SOCK: rapid task provisioning with serverless-optimized containers. In: 2018 USENIX Annual Technical Conference (USENIX ATC 2018), pp. 57–70 (2018)

42. OpenFaaS Ltd.: OpenFaaS (2024). https://www.openfaas.com/. Accessed Aug 2025

43. Sabbioni, A., Rosa, L., Bujari, A., Foschini, L., Corradi, A.: A shared memory approach for function chaining in serverless platforms. In: 2021 IEEE Symposium on Computers and Communications (ISCC), pp. 1–6. IEEE (2021)

44. Sampaio, A.R., Rubin, J., Beschastnikh, I., Rosa, N.S.: Improving microservice-based applications with runtime placement adaptation. J. Internet Serv. Appl. **10**(1), 1–30 (2019)

45. Sampé, J., Sánchez-Artigas, M., García-López, P., París, G.: Data-driven serverless functions for object storage. In: Middleware, Middleware 2017, pp. 121–133. ACM (2017). https://doi.org/10.1145/3135974.3135980

46. Savitch, W.J.: Relationships between nondeterministic and deterministic tape complexities. J. Comput. Syst. Sci. **4**(2), 177–192 (1970). https://doi.org/10.1016/S0022-0000(70)80006-X

47. Shahrad, M., Balkind, J., Wentzlaff, D.: Architectural implications of function-as-a-service computing. In: Proceedings of MICRO, pp. 1063–1075 (2019)

48. Shahrad, M., et al.: Serverless in the wild: characterizing and optimizing the serverless workload at a large cloud provider. In: Proceedings of USENIX ATC, pp. 205–218 (2020)

49. Sheoran, A., Fahmy, S., Sharma, P., Modi, N.: Invenio: communication affinity computation for low-latency microservices. In: Proceedings of the Symposium on Architectures for Networking and Communications Systems, pp. 88–101 (2021)

50. Shillaker, S., Pietzuch, P.: Faasm: lightweight isolation for efficient stateful serverless computing. In: Proceedings of USENIX ATC, pp. 419–433. USENIX Association (2020)

51. Silva, P., Fireman, D., Pereira, T.E.: Prebaking functions to warm the serverless cold start. In: Proceedings of Middleware, Middleware 2020, pp. 1–13. ACM, New York (2020). https://doi.org/10.1145/3423211.3425682

52. Smith, C.P., Jindal, A., Chadha, M., Gerndt, M., Benedict, S.: Fado: Faas functions and data orchestrator for multiple serverless edge-cloud clusters. In: 2022 IEEE 6th International Conference on Fog and Edge Computing (ICFEC), pp. 17–25. IEEE (2022)

53. Solaiman, K., Adnan, M.A.: WLEC: a not so cold architecture to mitigate cold start problem in serverless computing. In: 2020 IEEE International Conference on Cloud Engineering (IC2E), pp. 144–153 (2020). https://doi.org/10.1109/IC2E48712.2020.00022

54. Sreekanti, V., et al.: Cloudburst: stateful functions-as-a-Service. Proc. VLDB Endow. **13**(12), 2438–2452 (2020). https://doi.org/10.14778/3407790.3407836

55. Suresh, A., Gandhi, A.: FnSched: an efficient scheduler for serverless functions. In: WOSC@Middleware, pp. 19–24. ACM (2019). https://doi.org/10.1145/3366623.3368136

56. Ullman, J.D.: NP-complete scheduling problems. J. Comput. Syst. Sci. **10**(3), 384–393 (1975). https://doi.org/10.1016/S0022-0000(75)80008-0

57. Wang, L., Li, M., Zhang, Y., Ristenpart, T., Swift, M.: Peeking behind the curtains of serverless platforms. In: 2018 USENIX Annual Technical Conference (USENIX ATC 2018), pp. 133–146 (2018)

58. YAML: YAML Specification (2025). https://yaml.org/spec/. Accessed Aug 2025

From Zonotopes to Proof Certificates: A Formal Pipeline for Safe Control Envelopes

Jonathan Hellwig[1]([✉]) [iD], Lukas Schäfer[2] [iD], Long Qian[3] [iD], André Platzer[1] [iD], and Matthias Althoff[2] [iD]

[1] Karlsruhe Institute of Technology, Karlsruhe, Germany
{jonathan.hellwig,platzer}@kit.edu
[2] Technical University of Munich, Garching, Germany
{lukas.schaefer,althoff}@tum.de
[3] Carnegie Mellon University, Pittsburgh, USA
longq@andrew.cmu.edu

Abstract. Synthesizing controllers that enforce both safety and actuator constraints is a central challenge in the design of cyber-physical systems. While zonotope-based reachability methods deliver impressive scalability, only parts of these methods have been formalized. Consequently, no practical tool provides a fully verified end-to-end pipeline, leaving an assurance gap for safety-critical systems. Deductive verification with the hybrid system prover KeYmaera X could, in principle, resolve this assurance gap, but the high-dimensional set representations required for reachability analysis overwhelm its reasoning based on quantifier elimination. To close this gap, we develop a verification pipeline that combines scalability with formal rigor by computing control-invariant sets using high-performance reachability algorithms and verifying them using novel logical proof rules. Computationally intensive zonotope containment tasks are offloaded to efficient numerical backends, which return compact witnesses that KeYmaera X can validate rapidly. We show the practical utility of our approach through representative case studies.

Keywords: deductive verification · reachability analysis · zonotopes · robust control invariant sets · differential dynamic logic

1 Introduction

Autonomous vehicles, aircraft, and other cyber-physical systems increasingly demand advanced control algorithms while never violating stringent safety specifications. Control-envelope synthesis has become a central problem at the intersection of formal verification and control theory [8,30]. Rather than synthesizing a single monolithic controller, in control-envelope synthesis, the goal is to compute a set of control inputs whose execution traces satisfy a formal safety

F. Damiani and M. Farrell (Eds.): iFM 2025, LNCS 16194, pp. 248–267, 2026.
https://doi.org/10.1007/978-3-032-10794-7_13

specification. As a result, control envelopes enable decoupling safety from performance: the precomputed control envelope guarantees that *every* admissible input meets the specification, while at runtime an optimization routine can freely sample concrete control signals with respect to a secondary performance objective. A promising recent line of work [47] frames control envelope synthesis as the computation of the maximal *robust control invariant* sets (RCI) [10,41,45]— the set of states from which at each sampling instant, there exists a control action that keeps the system in it—thereby guaranteeing safety by construction. Building on this insight, the authors rely on efficient over-approximations of reachable sets as the main computational workhorse. The efficiency of their computations is achieved by symbolic set representations, e.g., zonotopes [4], support functions [2,54], or ellipsoids, that are either closed or can be tightly over-approximated under Minkowski addition and affine transformations, realizing an efficient computation of the reachable set [3]. However, despite their scalability, this reachability-based approach raises two concerns in safety-critical fields:

1. Floating-point uncertainty: Current reachability tools perform every operation with finite precision, so the end result does not have any end-to-end guarantee that rounding errors have not led to a violation of the safety specification.
2. Formally unverified implementations: The highly-tuned numerical kernels are optimized for speed, not transparency. Proving the correctness of their implementations is prohibitively expensive.

Mission-critical control systems—like aircraft, autonomous robots, or self-driving cars—would benefit greatly from numerical pipelines that provide end-to-end correctness guarantees. One way to obtain such rigorous guarantees is to use a theorem prover like KeYmaera X [22] that implements differential dynamics logic (dL) [38,39], a specialized logic designed for specification and deductive verification of cyber-physical systems. Unlike numerical reachability tools [5,18, 21], which aim to provide fast but conservative over-approximations of reachable sets, a theorem prover like KeYmaera X works with a symbolic proof calculus whose goal is to construct fully machine-checkable proofs that a control system satisfies its specification.

The key difficulty in combining techniques lies in the fundamental difference of formalisms of dL and classical reachability analysis. In reachability analysis, one works with highly specialized set representations that admit efficient "push-button" computations, but at the price of modelling restrictions. In dL, specifications are expressed as fully general semi-analytic formulas, resulting in a much richer specification language. However, verification in this expressive framework typically demands substantial interactive proof effort for complicated systems. As a result, tasks that are easy on one side, such as scalable numerical over-approximations, can be arduous on the other, such as manual proof construction, and vice versa. Indeed, the theorem-proving and the reachability analysis research fields have been developed largely in parallel, with little cross-pollination.

Thus, our goal with this paper is to build a bridge between the two research fields. Specifically, we formalize the control-envelope synthesis approach using RCIs in dL. By doing so, we enable end-to-end correctness guarantees for an envelope computed by an independent numerical reachability tool. This integration of numerical reachability and deductive verification achieves something neither approach could accomplish alone: efficient numerical computation paired with fully rigorous, machine-checked correctness. During formalization, we encountered the following challenges:

1. *Linking safety specifications to RCIs.* Although RCIs are commonly used as terminal constraints in model predictive control [12,49], no formal dL proof has yet shown that an RCI necessarily satisfies a given safety specification.
2. *Treatment of continuous dynamics.* The algorithms utilized by reachability tools are inherently delicate due to their numerical nature, therefore difficult to implement directly in dL. Whilst the completeness of dL [40] essentially guarantees that all true numerical properties can be deductively proven in principle, more efficient methods are desired for practical problems.
3. *Scalable verification of set containment.* Rigorous proofs of set containment— a central step in reachability analysis methods—involve large arithmetic formulas that are often intractable to verify without specialized methods. KeY-maera X uses a general decision procedure for real-arithmetic formulas, which does not scale to large verification problems.

Our Contribution is to build a formal link between reachability analysis and deductive verification by introducing a dL-based verification pipeline for control-envelopes addressing all three challenges. Specifically, we provide a syntactic derivation showing that if a control envelope is a robust control invariant set, then it automatically satisfies the dL specification. In addition, we leverage Taylor Models in dL, which is general enough to validate the invariant sets synthesized by numerical methods while also having rigorous error bounds that are deductively proven in dL. Finally, to overcome the scalability bottleneck in set containment proofs, we focus on zonotopic control envelopes and extend a known witness theorem for zonotope containment. This enables fast floating-point search for a candidate witness followed by a lightweight certification in KeYmaera X without relying on the slow, general-purpose decision procedure.

2   Preliminaries

This section first recalls the control envelope synthesis problem and then distills the basic principles of differential dynamic logic that support our verification approach. Let $\mathcal{X}_0 \subseteq \mathbb{R}^n$ denote the set of initial states, $\mathcal{X} \subseteq \mathbb{R}^n$ the set of admissible states and $\mathcal{U} \subseteq \mathbb{R}^m$ the set of admissible control inputs. For a *sampling period* $\Delta t > 0$ the *sampled-data system* is given by the ordinary differential equation (ODE)

$$x'(t) = f(x(t), u_{\lfloor t/\Delta t \rfloor}), \quad x_0 \in \mathcal{X}_0, \tag{1}$$

where the control input is zero-order-hold: for each integer $k \geq 0$ we sample at $t_k = k\Delta t$ a feedback law $\mu : \mathbb{R}^n \to \mathbb{R}^m$ generates $u_k := \mu(x(t_k))$, which is held constant on $[t_k, t_{k+1}]$. In the classical control, problem we seek to find one concrete feedback law $\mu : \mathbb{R}^n \to \mathbb{R}^m$ such that every control input is admissible,

$$\mu(x(k\Delta t)) \in \mathcal{U}, \tag{2}$$

and every trajectory of the closed-loop system remains in the admissible set of states,

$$x(t) \in \mathcal{X} \tag{3}$$

for all $t \geq 0$. The control envelope problem lifts this problem from finding a single control law to a family of laws. Concretely, we seek to construct a relation $\mathcal{E} \subseteq \mathbb{R}^n \times \mathbb{R}^m$ between states and control inputs such that *every* feedback law whose sampled control inputs stay within the envelope, automatically satisfy the admissibility and safety specifications.

In reachability analysis, one over-approximates ODE trajectories by a set-valued abstraction, a perspective that yields efficient computational properties. This viewpoint naturally leads to the following notion of reachable sets.

Definition 1 (Reachable set). *Let $\Delta t > 0$ be the sampling period and let $\mathcal{E} \subseteq \mathbb{R}^n \times \mathbb{R}^m$ be a control envelope: $\mathcal{E}_x := \{u \in \mathbb{R}^m \mid (x, u) \in \mathcal{E}\}$ denotes the set of control outputs at $x \in \mathbb{R}^n$. Given an initial set $\mathcal{X}_0$, the reachable set at time $t \in [0, \Delta t]$ is the set of states*

$$\mathcal{R}(t, \mathcal{X}_0, \mathcal{E}) := \left\{ x \in \mathbb{R}^n \mid \exists x_0 \in \mathcal{X}_0 \exists u \in \mathcal{E}_{x_0} : x = x_0 + \int_0^t f(x(s), u)ds \right\}.$$

The reachable set over the time interval $[0, t]$ is the union of reachable sets, i.e.,

$$\mathcal{R}([0, t], \mathcal{X}_0, \mathcal{E}) = \bigcup_{s \in [0, t]} \mathcal{R}(s, \mathcal{X}_0, \mathcal{E}).$$

The difficulty with reachable-set computations is that we can only evaluate them over finite time horizons. How can we verify that a proposed control envelope $\mathcal{E}$ satisfies the safety property (3) for all $t \geq 0$? The key is to use an inductive argument: leverage finite-horizon reachable-set computations to establish an invariant that guarantees safety over an infinite time horizon. This leads us to the definition of robust control invariants.

Definition 2 (Robust control invariant set [47]). *A set $\mathcal{S} \subset \mathbb{R}^n$ is called a robust control invariant set if there exists a control envelope $\mathcal{E} \subset \mathbb{R}^n \times \mathbb{R}^m$ such that*

1. One-step invariance: $\mathcal{R}(\Delta t, \mathcal{S}, \mathcal{E}) \subseteq \mathcal{S}$,
2. One-step safety: $\mathcal{R}([0, \Delta t], \mathcal{S}, \mathcal{E}) \subseteq \mathcal{X}$,
3. Control-admissibility: $\forall x_0 \in \mathcal{S} : \mathcal{E}_{x_0} \subseteq \mathcal{U}$.

The central claim is that the existence of a robust control invariant $\mathcal{S}$ and its associated control envelope $\mathcal{E}$, implies the safety property (3) for all $t \geq 0$. We prove this claim formally in Sect. 3.

2.1   Differential Dynamic Logic

To formally verify a control envelope, we must first introduce differential dynamic logic: its hybrid-program modeling language, its formula specification language, and the proof calculus that enables deductive verification. For a more detailed introduction the reader is referred to the literature [38,39].

Hybrid Programs. The language of hybrid programs is generated by the following grammar, where x is a variable, e is a dL term, Q is a formula of first-order real arithmetic:

$$\alpha, \beta ::= x := e \mid x := * \mid x' = f(x) \,\&\, Q \mid ?P \mid \alpha; \beta \mid \alpha \cup \beta \mid \alpha^*.$$

Continuous dynamics are modeled by $x' = f(x) \,\&\, Q$ evolving in the domain Q. Discrete dynamics are modeled by *assignments* $x := e$, which instantaneously assign the term e to x and *tests* $?Q$, which check whether the formula Q is true in the current state. The *nondeterministic assignment* $x := *$ assigns an arbitrary value to x. Throughout this paper we always use such assignments in conjunction with a test $?Z(x)$, to model non-deterministic assignment restricted to a formula $Z(x)$. To combine the discrete and continuous fragments, there are three program combinators: *sequential composition* $\alpha; \beta$, which first runs α then β; *nondeterministic choice* $\alpha \cup \beta$, which runs either α or β; and finally *nondeterministic repetitions* α^*, which repeats α an arbitrary number of times.

Formulas. The formulas of dL are defined by the following grammar where e, g are terms, P, Q are formulas, x is a variable, and α is a hybrid program:

$$P, Q ::= e \leq g \mid \neg P \mid P \wedge Q \mid P \rightarrow Q \mid \forall x P \mid [\alpha]P.$$

A dL formula combines first-order arithmetic with model operators that refers to program behavior. Atomic formulas are inequalities $e \leq g$ between real-valued terms. These atomic formulas are composed with Boolean connectives such as $\neg$, $\wedge$ and $\rightarrow$, together with the first-order quantifier $\forall$. Connectives such as $\vee$ and the quantifier $\exists$ are definable from these primitives. The only distinctive construct is the *box modality* $[\alpha]P$, which asserts that after every execution of the hybrid program α the post-condition P holds.

2.2   Deductive Verification

Formula verification in dL is carried out within a sequent-calculus framework built on sound axioms and inference rules. We write $\Gamma \vdash \Delta$ if the formula Δ is provable from the assumption Γ in the dL proof calculus. The calculus includes propositional rules such as

$$\rightarrow \! \mathrm{R} \frac{\Gamma, P \vdash Q, \Delta}{\Gamma \vdash P \rightarrow Q, \Delta} \qquad\qquad \wedge \mathrm{R} \frac{\Gamma \vdash P, \Delta \quad \Gamma \vdash Q, \Delta}{\Gamma \vdash P \wedge Q, \Delta}$$

The $\rightarrow$ R rule decomposes the implication $P \rightarrow Q$ by adding P in the list of assumptions, while the $\wedge$R rule splits the conjunctive formula $P \wedge Q$ into two separate proof goals. Similarly, there are rules that decompose every other logical construct. These inference rules are applied bottom-up, but provability is read top-down: if the premises at the top of each rule are provable, then the conclusion is provable as well.

Box modalities of hybrid program are treated with an axiomatic proof calculus that strips away the program structure step by step, leaving simpler proof goals. A few representative axioms illustrate this:

$$[\alpha; \beta]P \leftrightarrow [\alpha][\beta]P \qquad\qquad [;]$$

$$[\alpha \cup \beta]P \leftrightarrow [\alpha]P \wedge [\beta]P \qquad\qquad [\cup]$$

The $[;]$ axiom unfolds the sequential composition into successive modalities, while the $[\cup]$ axiom reduces the nondeterministic choice $\alpha \cup \beta$ to a conjunction over two branches.

By combining the inference rules with the axioms, we can derive new theorems, and every step of the resulting derivation can be mechanically verified by a proof checker. Transformation steps on logical connectives and box modalities are applied until the renaming goal is purely arithmetic. Then, we can invoke a trusted decision procedure, such as quantifier elimination [19]. In the example, we first apply the propositional rule $\rightarrow$ R, then the $[;]$ axiom. After a few further transformation steps we reach purely arithmetic formulas $Q_1(x), \ldots, Q_n(x)$, at which point we hand the proof obligations to the trusted decision procedure, finishing the proof.

$$
\textbf{Deduction} \qquad
\dfrac{
\vdash Q_1(x) \quad \cdots \quad \vdash Q_n(x)
}{
\rightarrow\!\text{R} \dfrac{ [;] \dfrac{ \vdots \;\; \dfrac{\Gamma \vdash [\alpha][\beta]\varphi}{\Gamma \vdash [\alpha; \beta]\varphi} }{ \vdash \Gamma \rightarrow [\alpha; \beta]\varphi } }{}
}
$$

3   Control Envelope Verification Framework

In this section, we first formalize the control *envelope* synthesis problem from Sect. 2 in dL. To do so, we first model sampled-data systems (1) as a hybrid program. We can then state the safety property (3) formally in dL. Once these components are formalized, we present several key theorems which, taken together, yield a deductive proof of the safety property. This allows us to take a control envelope produced numerically and rigorously verify its adherence to the specification.

3.1   Control Envelope Synthesis Problem in dL

We adopt the following conventions: for a function symbol h, let $\partial_t h$ denote syntactic partial derivative with respect to t, and we use ∇_x to denote the syntactic partial gradient with respect to x. We use $\|\cdot\|_\infty$ to denote the infinity norm of $\mathbb{R}^n$. In Sect. 2, we used a calligraphic font to denote semantic sets, e.g. $\mathcal{E}$ for the control envelope, $\mathcal{S}$ for the robust control invariant set, $\mathcal{X}_0$ for the set of initial states, $\mathcal{X}$ for the safety set and $\mathcal{U}$ for the control constraint set. Hereafter, we write the corresponding uppercase predicates, e.g. $E(x, u)$, $S(x, u)$, $X_0(x)$, $X(x)$ and $U(u)$, to denote their syntactic formula counterparts in dL.

We now formulate sampled-data systems. Let x be the state vector, u the control input, and $E(x, u)$ a control envelope formula, and $\Delta t > 0$ the sampling period. We define the *initialization, controller* and *plant* components as follows:

$$\text{init} \equiv u := *; ?\exists x E(x, u),$$
$$\text{ctrl} \equiv (?t = \Delta t; u := *; ?E(x, u); t := 0 \,) \cup (?t \neq \Delta t),$$
$$\text{plant} \equiv \{x' = f(x, u), t' = 1 \,\&\, t \leq \Delta t\}.$$

The controller nondeterministically chooses between two branches. If the current time t has not yet reached the sampling period Δt, it does nothing. Once the sampling instant is reached, a new control action is chosen nondeterministically from within the control envelope E based on the current state x. Note that this controller is an abstraction of any concrete implementation. By isolating only the aspects relevant to safety verification, we simplify reasoning in dL. Any actual controller would, of course, adhere to additional performance criteria. The plant is modeled by the differential equation $x' = f(x, u), t' = 1$ subject to the constraint $t \leq \Delta t$ to ensure a duration of evolution of at most Δt. In dL, differential equations are non-deterministic: the continuous evolution may stop at any state that still satisfies the constraint $t \leq \Delta t$. The dL *sampled-data system* for one sampling period is

$$\text{sys} \equiv \text{ctrl}; \text{plant}.$$

The corresponding dL closed-loop system is the nondeterministic repetition of this program sys*. Thus, the dL *control envelope synthesis* problem is to determine an envelope predicate $E(x, u)$ such that the *control-admissibility formula*

$$\exists x E(x, u) \rightarrow U(u), \tag{4}$$

and the *closed-loop safety formula*

$$X_0(x) \wedge t = 0 \rightarrow [\text{init}; \text{sys}^*]X(x) \tag{5}$$

are valid, i.e., true in all states. These two formulas are the formalized counterparts to (2) and (3).

3.2   Deductive Verification of Control Envelopes

Having posed the control envelope synthesis problem in dL, we can take an envelope computed by an unverified numerical tool, formalize its specification in dL, and certify its correctness through an independent verification process.

When carrying out deductive verification, several key considerations arise: The control-admissibility formula (4) is purely a first-order statement over the reals, so it can be proved without invoking any of dL's hybrid system axioms. In contrast, the system-safety formula (5) is more challenging: it combines discrete and continuous dynamics, a nondeterministic repetition, and may contain a high-dimensional control envelope. To tackle this challenge for generic sampled-data system, we present a systematic verification strategy. Specifically, we present a sequence of theorems that, when composed, yield a rigorous proof of the desired safety property. The following five theorems outline the high-level structure of our argument:

1. Theorem 3.1: Relates closed-loop safety (5) to the invariance and safety properties of robust control invariant sets.
2. Theorem 3.2: Connects finite-horizon box modalities for continuous systems to Taylor models.
3. Theorem 3.3: A special case of Theorem 3.2 that establishes the RCI invariance condition for zonotopic control envelopes.
4. Theorem 3.4: A special case of Theorem 3.2 used to establish the RCI safety condition for zonotopic control envelopes.
5. Theorem 3.5: Connects the zonotope-containment problem to an efficiently implementable witness-checking problem.

Detailed derivations and proofs of soundness for these theorems are provided in [28].

The first theorem shows that, in dL, the invariance and safety property of robust control invariants imply the closed-loop safety property (5):

Theorem 3.1. *The following is a derived proof rule of* dL*:*

$$\frac{E(x,u), t = 0 \;\vdash\; [\text{plant}]X(x) \qquad E(x,u), t = 0 \;\vdash\; [\text{plant}](t = \Delta t \rightarrow \exists u E(x,u))}{X_0(x), t = 0 \;\vdash\; [\text{init}; \text{sys}^*]X(x)}$$

Informally, the bottom premise states that whenever an initial control-state pair satisfies $E(x,u)$, then, after one continuous evolution lasting Δt, we can choose a new control action to remain in $E(x,u)$. The top premise encodes the safety property: if the start in $E(x,u)$, then we always remain in the safety constraint $X(x)$ after running the plant. The safety property is enforced continuously; not just at the sampling points. Taken together, these two properties entail the safety of the closed-loop system for an arbitrary number of execution steps. The premises are much easier to discharge, because they only involve ordinary differential equations. The two main challenges in proving the premises in Theorem 3.1 are

1. constructing rigorous reachable set over-approximations,
2. efficiently discharging the resulting proof obligations, which involve large arithmetic formulas.

We address the first challenge by introducing generalized Taylor models and showing how they can be derived in dL. Before introducing Taylor models, we briefly review the necessary background Picard iteration and interval arithmetic.

Picard Iteration. Picard iteration is a classical technique that successively constructs polynomial approximations to the solutions of ordinary differential equations. They can be carried out to arbitrarily high order, resulting approximations of whatever precision is required. Let h be a function symbol and let λ be a variable vector such that $\|\lambda\|_\infty \leq 1$. Further, let $x' = f(x)$ be an ODE system with parameter-dependet initial value $x_0 = h(\lambda)$. The sequence of *Picard iterates* $(p_k)_{k\geq 0}$ is recursively defined by

$$p_0(t,\lambda) := h(\lambda), \quad p_{k+1}(t,\lambda) := h(\lambda) + \int_0^t f(p_k(s,\lambda))ds, \quad k \geq 0.$$

Interval Arithmetic. A foundational concept we are making use of to discharge arithmetic proof obligations is *interval arithmetic* [37]. We write $\mathbb{IQ}^n$ to denote the set of rational intervals in the n-dimensional vector space $\mathbb{Q}^n$. We write $\mathbf{I} = [\underline{\mathbf{I}}, \overline{\mathbf{I}}] \in \mathbb{IQ}^n$, where $\underline{\mathbf{I}} \in \mathbb{Q}^n$ and $\overline{\mathbf{I}} \in \mathbb{Q}^n$ are the lower and upper bound respectively. In order to simplify, notation we write

$$\mathrm{mid}(\mathbf{I}) := \frac{\overline{\mathbf{I}} + \underline{\mathbf{I}}}{2},$$

$$\mathrm{rad}(\mathbf{I}) := \overline{\mathbf{I}} - \underline{\mathbf{I}},$$

for an intervals *mid-point* and *radius*. For a variable x and concrete dL term e, we write $[e]_x^{\mathbf{I}}$ to denote its interval evaluation with respect to the interval $\mathbf{I}$.

Taylor Models. Equipped with interval arithmetic and Picard polynomial approximations, we are now ready to define Taylor models in dL [11].

Definition 3 (Taylor models). *Let* $p(t,\lambda)$ *be a concrete* dL *term and* $\mathbf{I}(t)$ *a* dL *interval. Then a* dL *Taylor model is a tuple* $(p,\mathbf{I})$ *whose associated formula is*

$$\mathrm{TM}_{p,\mathbf{I}}(x,\lambda,t) \;\equiv\; \underline{\mathbf{I}}(t) \leq x - p(t,\lambda) \leq \overline{\mathbf{I}}(t).$$

For its derivative formula, we write

$$\mathrm{TM}_{p,\mathbf{I}}(x,\lambda,t) \;\equiv\; \partial_t\underline{\mathbf{I}}(t) < f(x) - \partial_t p(t,\lambda) < \partial_t\overline{\mathbf{I}}(t).$$

Theorem 3.2. *Let* $(p,\mathbf{I})$ *be a Taylor model. Let* h *be a function symbol and* $X_0(x) \equiv \exists\lambda\,(x = h(\lambda) \wedge \|\lambda\|_\infty \leq 1)$. *The following is a sound derived proof rule of* dL*:*

$$\exists\lambda\exists t(\mathrm{TM}_{p,\mathbf{I}}(x,\lambda,t) \wedge 0 \leq t \leq \Delta t \wedge \|\lambda\|_\infty \leq 1) \vdash P(x)$$

$$X_0(x) \vdash \exists\lambda\,(\mathrm{TM}_{p,\mathbf{I}}(x,\lambda,0) \wedge \|\lambda\|_\infty \leq 1)$$

$$\frac{\mathrm{TM}_{p,\mathbf{I}}(x,\lambda,t),\; 0 \leq t \leq \Delta t,\; \|\lambda\|_\infty \leq 1 \vdash \mathrm{TM}_{p,\mathbf{I}}(x,\lambda,t)}{X_0(x),\; t = 0 \vdash [x' = f(x), t' = 1\ \&\ t \leq \Delta t]P(x)}$$

Zonotope Reachable Set. We now focus our attention on the zonotope case and set out to prove premise 1 of Theorem 3.1. Our strategy is to successively rewrite the proof goal until it is an instance of zonotope containment. Once in that form, a lightweight numerical solver can supply a witness that one zonotope is contained in the other.

Definition 4 (Zonotope). *Let G be an $n \times p$ generator* dL *matrix, c an n center* dL *vector, and let λ be a p* dL *vector. The* zonotope formula *associated with $\langle c,\, G \rangle$ is given by*

$$\langle c,\, G \rangle(x) \;\equiv\; \exists \lambda \bigl(x = c + G\lambda \wedge \|\lambda\|_\infty \le 1 \bigr).$$

In order to simplify arithmetic reasoning, our goal is to linearize the Picard iterates. This helps us to over-approximate the reachable set at the time instance Δt by a zonotope. We have the following theorem:

Lemma 3.1 (Linear interval abstraction). *Let $p(x)$ be a concrete* dL *polynomial in x. Then, for the interval $\mathbf{I} \in \mathbb{IQ}^n$ and the interval remainder*

$$\mathbf{R} = \bigl[p(x) - p(0) - \nabla_x p(0)^\top x \bigr]_x^{\mathbf{I}}$$

the following formula is a sound axiom of dL*:*

$$\underline{\mathbf{I}} \le x \le \bar{\mathbf{I}} \to \exists \xi \bigl(p(x) = p(0) + \nabla_x p(0)^\top x + \mathrm{mid}(\mathbf{R}) + \frac{1}{2}\,\mathrm{rad}(\mathbf{R})\xi \wedge \|\xi\|_\infty \le 1 \bigr).$$

Theorem 3.3 (Zonotope reachable set for discrete time instance). *Let $(p, \mathbf{I})$ be a Taylor model of the ODE system $x' = f(x) \;\&\; t \le \Delta t$. Let*

$$\mathbf{R} = \bigl[p(t, \lambda) - p(t, 0) - \nabla_\lambda p(t, 0)^\top \lambda \bigr]_{(t, \lambda)}^{[0, \Delta t] \times [-1, 1]^n}$$

be the remainder of its linear interval abstraction. Finally, we define the dL *center vector and generator matrix*

$$b := p(\Delta t, 0) + \mathrm{mid}(\mathbf{I}(\Delta t)) + \mathrm{mid}(\mathbf{R}),$$

$$H := [\nabla_\lambda p(\Delta t, 0),\ \frac{1}{2}\,\mathrm{rad}(\mathbf{I}(\Delta t)),\ \frac{1}{2}\,\mathrm{rad}(\mathbf{R})].$$

Then, the following is a sound derived proof rule of dL:

$$\langle b,\, H \rangle(x, u) \vdash \langle c_x,\, G_x \rangle(x, u)$$

$$\langle c,\, G \rangle(x, u) \vdash \exists \lambda \bigl(\mathrm{TM}_{p, \mathbf{I}}(x, u, \lambda, t)[0] \wedge \|\lambda\|_\infty \le 1 \bigr)$$

$$\frac{\mathrm{TM}_{p, \mathbf{I}}(x, u, \lambda, t),\ 0 \le t \le \Delta t,\ \|\lambda\|_\infty \le 1 \vdash \mathrm{TM}_{p, \mathbf{I}}(x, u, \lambda, t)}{\langle c,\, G \rangle(x, u), t = 0 \vdash [\mathrm{plant}]\,(t = \Delta\ t \to \exists u\, \langle c,\, G \rangle(x, u))}$$

We now turn our attention to second premise in Theorem 3.1. Unlike the first premise, which involves a single sampling instant, this condition must hold for every $t \in [0, \Delta t]$. In other words, we must enclose the entire time-tube of states captured by $\mathcal{R}([0, \Delta t], \mathcal{X}_0, \mathcal{E})$. We tackle this problem by constructing a single zonotope that encloses the reachable set at every time instant $t \in [0, \Delta t]$.

Theorem 3.4 (Zonotope reachable set for time intervals). *Let $(p, \mathbf{I})$ be a Taylor model for the ODE system $x' = f(x)$ & $t \leq \Delta t$. We define the remainder polynomial*

$$r(t, \lambda, \xi) := p(t, \lambda) + \mathrm{mid}(\mathbf{I}(t)) + \frac{1}{2}\,\mathrm{rad}(\mathbf{I}(t))^\top \xi - p(0,0) - \mathrm{mid}(\mathbf{I}(0))$$
$$- \partial_t p(0,0)\, t - \partial_t \mathrm{mid}(\mathbf{I}(t))\big|_{t=0}\, t - \nabla_\lambda p(0,0)^\top \lambda - \tfrac{1}{2}\,\mathrm{rad}(\mathbf{I}(0))^\top \xi.$$

To bound its range over the domain $\mathbf{J} := [0, \Delta t] \times [-1, 1]^n \times [-1, 1]^n$, we introduce the error interval

$$\mathbf{R} := \left[\, r(t, \lambda, \xi) \,\right]_{(t, \lambda, \xi)}^{\mathbf{J}}.$$

Finally, we define the dL *center vector and generator matrix*

$$b := p(0,0) + \mathrm{mid}(\mathbf{I}(0)) + \mathrm{mid}(\mathbf{R}),$$

$$H := [\partial_t p(0,0) + \partial_t \mathrm{mid}(\mathbf{I}(t))|_{t=0},\ \nabla_\lambda p(0,0),\ \tfrac{1}{2}\,\mathrm{rad}(\mathbf{I}(0)),\ \tfrac{1}{2}\,\mathrm{rad}(\mathbf{R})].$$

Then, the following is a sound derived proof rule of dL*:*

$$\frac{\begin{array}{l}\langle b,\ H\rangle(x) \vdash X(x) \\[4pt] \langle c,\ G\rangle(x, u) \vdash \exists \lambda \left(\mathrm{TM}_{p,\mathbf{I}}(x, u, \lambda, t)[0] \wedge \|\lambda\|_\infty \leq 1\right) \\[4pt] \mathrm{TM}_{p,\mathbf{I}}(x, u, \lambda, t),\ 0 \leq t \leq \Delta t,\ \|\lambda\|_\infty \leq 1 \vdash \mathrm{TM}_{p,\mathbf{I}}(x, u, \lambda, t)\end{array}}{\langle c,\ G\rangle(x, u),\ t = 0 \vdash [\mathrm{plant}]X(x)}$$

Witness Checks for Arithmetic Goals. Recall that our earlier theorems translate the reachability problem into a single question of zonotope containment. In practice, the zonotopes that bound control envelopes usually involve on the order of ten to twenty generators. Consequently, the resulting formulas can become quite large. A straightforward quantifier-elimination procedure is not a good fit for this problem, because its computational costs are prohibitive. A common approach in reachability analysis is to invoke a witness theorem [46, Cor. 4]: for zonotopes $\langle c,\ G\rangle(x)$, $\langle b,\ H\rangle(x)$ the containment

$$\forall x \big(\langle c,\ G\rangle(x) \rightarrow \langle b,\ H\rangle(x) \big)$$

holds whenever one can find a matrix Γ and vector β that satisfy

$$H\Gamma = G, \quad b - c = H\beta, \quad \|(\Gamma, \beta)\|_\infty \leq 1. \tag{6}$$

These linear formulas define a witness (Γ, β), which can be computed with an efficient linear program. To obtain a rigorous proof, we must produce an exact witness. That means solving the linear program with exact rational arithmetic—an operation that is orders of magnitude slower than solving with floating-point numbers. Instead of insisting on exact equality, we weaken the witness condition slightly, allowing for small perturbations. These relaxed conditions can be solved efficiently in floating-point arithmetic with a numerical linear programming solver and then rationalized with the residual margin ensuring the conditions still hold.

Theorem 3.5 (Zonotope containment). *The following is a derived proof rule of* dL*:*

$$
\frac{\begin{array}{l} \vdash HH^+ = I \\ \vdash b - c = H\beta \\ \vdash \|H\Gamma - G\|_\infty \leq \varepsilon \\ \vdash \|(\Gamma, \beta)\|_\infty \leq 1 - \varepsilon \|H^+\|_\infty \end{array}}{\langle c,\ G\rangle(x) \vdash \langle b,\ H\rangle(x)}
$$

Equipped with Theorem 3.1 to Theorem 3.5, we have all the necessary ingredients to carry out an end-to-end verification of a concrete system.

4   Evaluation

In this section, we compute the control envelopes of two examples and demonstrate how to verify them using the theorem from Sect. 3. The key challenge here is to handle the different representations that are used in reachability tools and the theorem prover KeYmaera X.

To compute RCI sets for sampled-data systems, we use the approach by Schäfer et al. [47]. The authors represent both the RCI and over-approximations of the reachable sets as zontopes. Using the witness conditions (6), the one-step invariance, the one-step safety and control-admissibility in Definition 2 are formulated as constraints in an optimization problem returning an RCI set with maximum volume. In order to verify the envelope in dL's formalism, we need a post-processing step: we rationalize center vector and generator matrix of the output zonotopes[1]. Then, we compute a provably correct dL Taylor model using the approach implemented in KeYmaera X[2]. Finally, we verify the zonotope containment.

4.1   Double Integrator

The dynamics of the double integrator are governed by the following differential equations [25, Sec. V.A]:

$$
x_1' = x_2 + w_1,
$$

$$
x_2' = \frac{1}{m}u + w_2,
$$

where the system states are the position x_1 and the velocity x_2 of the point-mass, the system input is the force $u = F$, and the weight of the point-mass is $m = 1\text{kg}$. The state constraints are $|x_1| \leq 1\text{m}$ and $|x_2| \leq 1\text{m/s}$, the input

---

[1] A suitable operator is implemented in the MATLAB function **rat**, see https://de.mathworks.com/help/matlab/ref/rat.html.

[2] https://github.com/LS-Lab/KeYmaeraX-release/blob/master/keymaerax-core/src/main/scala/org/keymaerax/btactics/TaylorModel.scala.

constraint is $|u| \leq 1\mathrm{N}$, and the set of disturbances is $w_1 \in [-0.1, 0.1]\mathrm{m/s}$ and $w_2 \in [-0.1, 0.1]\mathrm{m/s^2}$. The sampling time is $\Delta t = 0.1\,\mathrm{s}$. In dL, we use a slightly enlarged initial condition given by the formula

$$X_0(x, u) \equiv \exists \lambda \left(x_1 = \frac{11}{10}\lambda_1 \wedge x_2 = \frac{11}{10}\lambda_2 \wedge u = \frac{11}{10}\lambda_3 \wedge \|\lambda\|_\infty \leq 1 \right).$$

By Picard iteration we obtain the following polynomial approximation

$$p_{x_1}(t, \lambda) = \lambda_1 + t\lambda_2 + \frac{t^2}{2}\lambda_3,$$

$$p_{x_2}(t, \lambda) = \lambda_2 + t\lambda_3,$$

$$p_u(t, \lambda) = \lambda_3.$$

With interval arithmetic we then obtain the following provable error bounds:

$$\underline{\mathbf{I}}_{x_1}(t) = -101020 \cdot 10^{-11}t \quad \overline{\mathbf{I}}_{x_1}(t) = 101020 \cdot 10^{-11}t,$$

$$\underline{\mathbf{I}}_{x_2}(t) = -10^{-6}t \quad \overline{\mathbf{I}}_{x_2}(t) = 10^{-6}t,$$

$$\underline{\mathbf{I}}_u(t) = -10^{-6}t \quad \overline{\mathbf{I}}_u(t) = 10^{-6}t.$$

Together, the polynomial p and the error interval $\mathbf{I}(t)$ yield the Taylor model $(p, \mathbf{I})$ on $[0, \Delta t]$. We numerically compute an RCI set and, using the Taylor model, check the premises of Theorem 3.3 and Theorem 3.4 (See Fig. 1a). Note that, although we visually verify containment here, a formal proof can be derived directly by applying Theorem 3.5.

4.2 Controlled Jet Engine

Next, we consider the Moore-Greitzer model of a jet engine [33, 40] whose dynamics are governed by

$$\begin{aligned} x_1' &= -x_2 - \frac{3}{2}x_1^2 - \frac{1}{2}x_1^3 + w, \\ x_2' &= u, \end{aligned} \tag{7}$$

where the system states are the mass flow x_1 and the pressure rise x_2. The state constraints are $|x_1| \leq 0.2$ and $|x_2| \leq 0.2$, the input constraint is $|u| \leq 0.3$, and the set of disturbances is $w \in [-0.025, 0.0.025]$. Measurements are taken with a sampling time of $\Delta t = 0.1$ time units. Computing the associated dL Taylor model with conservative initial conditions

$$X_0(x, u) \equiv \exists \lambda \left(x_1 = \frac{3}{10}\lambda_1 \wedge x_2 = \frac{3}{10}\lambda_2 \wedge u = \frac{3}{10}\lambda_3 \wedge \|\lambda\|_\infty \leq 1 \right)$$

yields the following provable polynomial approximation

$$p_{x_1}(t, \lambda) = \lambda_1 - t\lambda_2 + \frac{3t}{2}\lambda_1^2 - \frac{t^2}{2}\lambda_3 - \frac{3t^2}{2}\lambda_1\lambda_2 - \frac{t}{2}\lambda_1^3,$$

$$p_{x_2}(t, \lambda) = \lambda_2 + t\lambda_3,$$

$$p_u(t, \lambda) = \lambda_3,$$

with error bounds

$$\underline{\mathbf{I}}_{x_1}(t) = -28605705206 \cdot 10^{-11}t \quad \overline{\mathbf{I}}_{x_1}(t) = 27585076206 \cdot 10^{-11}t,$$
$$\underline{\mathbf{I}}_{x_2}(t) = -10^{-6}t \quad \overline{\mathbf{I}}_{x_2}(t) = 10^{-6}t,$$
$$\underline{\mathbf{I}}_{u}(t) = -10^{-6}t \quad \overline{\mathbf{I}}_{u}(t) = 10^{-6}t.$$

Again, using the Taylor model $(p, \mathbf{I})$, we can compute the zonotopes form Theorem 3.3 and Theorem 3.4 (See Fig. 1b).

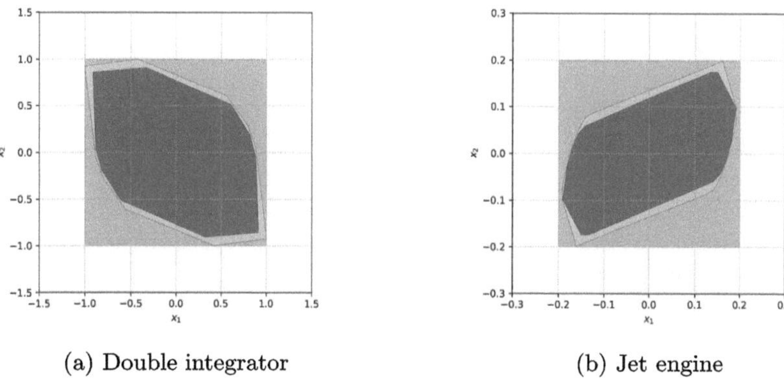

(a) Double integrator　　　　　　(b) Jet engine

Fig. 1. Comparison of the numerically computed robust control-invariant set (blue), its Taylor-model reachability over-approximation after one sampling period (red), and the safety region (gray). (Color figure online)

5 Related Work

Reachability Analysis. Reachability analysis itself can be categorized into several techniques: simulation-based techniques [24], Hamilton-Jacobi techniques [16], and set propagation techniques [3]. The disadvantage of simulation-based techniques and Hamilton-Jacobi techniques is that they scale exponentially in the number of continuous state variables, while many set propagation techniques scale polynomially [3]. Because the main purpose of including reachability analysis into theorem proving is to deduce properties of complex dynamics with potentially many continuous state variables, we will focus on set propagation techniques. This technique is also currently predominantly used in the International Competition on Verifying Continuous and Hybrid Systems [6,23]. Further advantages of set-based reachability analysis are that it can be fully automated [54,55] and easily interpreted due to its resemblance with the numerical simulation of systems.

Computing Invariant Sets Using Reachability Analysis. Computing invariant sets has a rich history in control theory due to their many applications: they serve as terminal regions in model predictive control [44] or are employed as part of supervisory safety-filters in, e.g., learning-based control [36,53]. Since we aim at reducing conservatism, we focus on the computation of the largest invariant set, also known as the maximal invariant set. The maximal invariant set can be obtained using the standard set recursion introduced in [10,45]. However, this procedure usually fails to terminate in finite time and the computational complexity of the required set operations restricts the applicability to low-dimensional systems.

The latter also holds for algorithms for approximating the maximal invariant set by gridding the sate space [14,15]. Thus, most approaches in the literature formulate an optimization problem to compute a possibly large invariant set.

The most popular set representations of the invariant set are ellipsoids [17,35] and polytopes [9,20,27,41]. Due to their low representation complexity, algorithms using ellipsoids as the set representation scale better to higher-dimensional systems at the cost of more conservative results. On the other hand, polytopic invariant sets enable more flexibility and, thus, larger invariant sets while sacrificing computational efficiency.

Level sets are an even more flexible representation of invariant sets that can be computed using Hamilton-Jacobi reachability analysis [57,58] and control-barrier functions [7,43,56]. To circumvent the exponential complexity of solving the associated partial differential equation numerically (Hamilton-Jacobi reachability analysis) or synthesizing the barrier certificate from simulations [7], the computation of an invariant set can be relaxed into a (sequence of) semidefinite program(s) using sum-of-squares programming. However, an invariance-enforcing controller must be designed prior to computing the invariant set [57,58] or the approach suffers from poor scalability due to the large number of variables of the semi-definite program [1,32].

The approaches reviewed above typically either consider discrete-time systems, e.g., [20,35] and, thus, do not check constraint satisfaction in between sampling times, or enforce invariance for the continuous-time dynamical system, e.g., [7,9], which is unnecessarily conservative. As an alternative, invariant sets for sampled-data systems have been characterized in [42]: sampled-data systems are continuous-time systems that are controlled by a digital controller; similarly, measurements are only taken at discrete points in time [36]. Crucially, the system can leave the invariant set in between sampling times, which reduces conservatism. This notion of invariance has been employed in [26] to introduce so-called safe sets of linear systems. Since this approach represents the invariant set as a zonotope, invariant sets of high-dimensional systems can be computed efficiently. This concept has been extended to ellipsoidal sets in [34] and nonlinear systems in [47,48].

Deductive Verification of Control Problems. Differential dynamic logic (dL) has been successfully applied in several control domains, including air traffic control, train control, and ground robots to formally prove safety properties [13,29,31]. It has also been employed for the deductive verification of control system stability [51,52]. The control-system meta-model has been extended to incorporate the environment, with a focus on identifying conditions that prevent proofs of safety from being invalidated by modeling errors [50]. In contrast, our work focuses on a simplified controller-plant model and formalizes in dL the verification of synthesized controllers by reducing closed-loop analysis to continuous-time safety and discrete-time invariance.

The problem of control-envelope synthesis has been studied in the context of dL before [8,30]. Both of these works approach the problem from a logical perspective and do not leverage existing techniques and tools developed in the field of reachability analysis field. By comparison, our work integrates these two viewpoints by combining established numerical methods.

6   Conclusion

In this paper, we established a link between two traditionally separate research fields: reachability analysis and theorem proving. We showed how zonotope-based reachable-set computations can be encoded in the dL formalism and how a control envelope can be formally verified. Although the differing levels of representation between these tools posed nontrivial technical challenges, our case studies demonstrate that these obstacles can be overcome. By combining the computational efficiency of reachability analysis with the deductive rigor of theorem proving, we achieve a verification workflow that is both scalable and formally sound. This work represents only the first step toward a more unified formal-methods ecosystem. In future work, we plan to explore how reachability methods can be even more tightly integrated, reducing the boundaries between research fields.

Acknowledgements. This work was supported by the German Research Foundation - SFB 1608 - under grant number 501798263 and by an Alexander von Humboldt Professorship. Additionally, we would like to thank Fabian Immler for his valuable Taylor model implementation in KeYmaera X.

References

1. Ahmadi, A.A., Hall, G., Papachristodoulou, A., Saunderson, J., Zheng, Y.: Improving efficiency and scalability of sum of squares optimization: Recent advances and limitations. In: IEEE Conference on Decision and Control, pp. 453–462 (2017). https://doi.org/10.1109/CDC.2017.8263706
2. Althoff, M., Frehse, G.: Combining zonotopes and support functions for efficient reachability analysis of linear systems. In: Proceedings of the 55th IEEE Conference on Decision and Control, pp. 7439–7446 (2016). https://doi.org/10.1109/CDC.2016.7799418
3. Althoff, M., Frehse, G., Girard, A.: Set propagation techniques for reachability analysis. Annu. Rev. Control Robot. Auton. Syst. 4(1), 369–395 (2021). https://doi.org/10.1146/annurev-control-071420-081941

4. Althoff, M., Krogh, B.H.: Zonotope bundles for the efficient computation of reachable sets. In: Proceedings of the 50th IEEE Conference on Decision and Control, pp. 6814–6821 (2011). https://doi.org/10.1109/CDC.2011.6160872

5. Althoff, M.: An introduction to CORA 2015. In: ARCH14-15. 1st and 2nd International Workshop on Applied veRification for Continuous and Hybrid Systems, pp. 120–151 (2015). https://doi.org/10.29007/zbkv

6. Althoff, M., Forets, M., Schilling, C., Wetzlinger, M.: ARCH-COMP24 category report: continuous and hybrid systems with linear continuous dynamics. In: Frehse, G., Althoff, M. (eds.) Proceedings of the 11th International Workshop on Applied Verification for Continuous and Hybrid Systems. EPiC Series in Computing, vol. 103, pp. 15–38. EasyChair (2024). https://doi.org/10.29007/7xf3

7. Ames, A.D., Coogan, S., Egerstedt, M., Notomista, G., Sreenath, K., Tabuada, P.: Control barrier functions: theory and applications. In: European Control Conference, pp. 3420–3431 (2019). https://doi.org/10.23919/ECC.2019.8796030

8. Aréchiga, N., Krogh, B.: Using verified control envelopes for safe controller design. In: 2014 American Control Conference, pp. 2918–2923 (2014). https://doi.org/10.1109/ACC.2014.6859307

9. Ben Sassi, M.A., Girard, A.: Controller synthesis for robust invariance of polynomial dynamical systems using linear programming. Syst. Control Lett. **61**(4), 506–512 (2012). https://doi.org/10.1016/j.sysconle.2012.01.004

10. Bertsekas, D.: Infinite time reachability of state-space regions by using feedback control. IEEE Trans. Autom. Control **17**(5), 604–613 (1972). https://doi.org/10.1109/TAC.1972.1100085

11. Berz, M., Makino, K.: Verified integration of ODEs and flows using differential algebraic methods on high-order taylor models. Reliable Comput. **4**(4), 361–369 (1998). https://doi.org/10.1023/A:1024467732637

12. Blanchini, F.: Set invariance in control. Automatica **35**(11), 1747–1767 (1999)

13. Bohrer, R., Tan, Y.K., Mitsch, S., Sogokon, A., Platzer, A.: A formal safety net for waypoint-following in ground robots. IEEE Robot. Autom. Lett. **4**(3), 2910–2917 (2019). https://doi.org/10.1109/LRA.2019.2923099

14. Bravo, J., Limon, D., Alamo, T., Camacho, E.: On the computation of invariant sets for constrained nonlinear systems: an interval arithmetic approach. Automatica **41**(9), 1583–1589 (2005). https://doi.org/10.1016/j.automatica.2005.04.015

15. Brown, S., Khajenejad, M., Yong, S.Z., Martínez, S.: Computing controlled invariant sets of nonlinear control-affine systems. In: IEEE Conference on Decision and Control, pp. 7830–7836 (2023). https://doi.org/10.1109/CDC49753.2023.10383613

16. Chen, M., Tomlin, C.J.: Hamilton–Jacobi reachability: some recent theoretical advances and applications in unmanned airspace management. Annu. Rev. Control Robot. Auton. Syst. **1**, 333–358 (2018). https://doi.org/10.1146/annurev-control-060117-104941

17. Chen, W.H., O'Reilly, J., Ballance, D.: On the terminal region of model predictive control for non-linear systems with input/state constraints. Int. J. Adapt. Control Signal Process. **17**, 195–207 (2003). https://doi.org/10.1002/acs.731

18. Chen, X., Ábrahám, E., Sankaranarayanan, S.: Flow*: an analyzer for non-linear hybrid systems. In: Sharygina, N., Veith, H. (eds.) CAV 2013. LNCS, vol. 8044, pp. 258–263. Springer, Heidelberg (2013). https://doi.org/10.1007/978-3-642-39799-8_18

19. Collins, G.E.: Quantifier elimination for real closed fields by cylindrical algebraic decompostion. In: Brakhage, H. (ed.) GI-Fachtagung 1975. LNCS, vol. 33, pp. 134–183. Springer, Heidelberg (1975). https://doi.org/10.1007/3-540-07407-4_17

20. Fiacchini, M., Alamo, T., Camacho, E.: On the computation of convex robust control invariant sets for nonlinear systems. Automatica **46**(8), 1334–1338 (2010). https://doi.org/10.1016/j.automatica.2010.05.007

21. Frehse, G., et al.: SpaceEx: scalable verification of hybrid systems. In: Gopalakrishnan, G., Qadeer, S. (eds.) CAV 2011. LNCS, vol. 6806, pp. 379–395. Springer, Heidelberg (2011). https://doi.org/10.1007/978-3-642-22110-1_30

22. Fulton, N., Mitsch, S., Quesel, J.-D., Völp, M., Platzer, A.: KeYmaera X: an axiomatic tactical theorem prover for hybrid systems. In: Felty, A.P., Middeldorp, A. (eds.) CADE 2015. LNCS (LNAI), vol. 9195, pp. 527–538. Springer, Cham (2015). https://doi.org/10.1007/978-3-319-21401-6_36

23. Geretti, L., et al.: ARCH-COMP24 category report: continuous and hybrid systems with nonlinear dynamics. In: Frehse, G., Althoff, M. (eds.) Proceedings of the 11th International Workshop on Applied Verification for Continuous and Hybrid Systems. EPiC Series in Computing, vol. 103, pp. 39–63. EasyChair (2024). https://doi.org/10.29007/21ch

24. Girard, A., Pappas, G.J.: Verification using simulation. In: Hespanha, J.P., Tiwari, A. (eds.) HSCC 2006. LNCS, vol. 3927, pp. 272–286. Springer, Heidelberg (2006). https://doi.org/10.1007/11730637_22

25. Gruber, F., Althoff, M.: Computing safe sets of linear sampled-data systems. IEEE Control Syst. Lett. **5**(2), 385–390 (2021). https://doi.org/10.1109/LCSYS.2020.3002476

26. Gruber, F., Althoff, M.: Scalable robust output feedback MPC of linear sampled-data systems. In: IEEE Conference on Decision and Control, pp. 2563–2570 (2021). https://doi.org/10.1109/CDC45484.2021.9683384

27. Gupta, A., Falcone, P.: Full-complexity characterization of control-invariant domains for systems with uncertain parameter dependence. IEEE Control Syst. Lett. **3**(1), 19–24 (2019). https://doi.org/10.1109/LCSYS.2018.2849714

28. Hellwig, J., Schäfer, L., Qian, L., Platzer, A., Althoff, M.: From Zonotopes to Proof Certificates: A Formal Pipeline for Safe Control Envelopes (2025). https://doi.org/10.48550/arXiv.2509.20301

29. Jeannin, J.B., et al.: Formal verification of ACAS X, an industrial airborne collision avoidance system. In: 2015 International Conference on Embedded Software (EMSOFT), pp. 127–136 (2015). https://doi.org/10.1109/EMSOFT.2015.7318268

30. Kabra, A., Laurent, J., Mitsch, S., Platzer, A.: CESAR: control envelope synthesis via angelic refinements. In: Finkbeiner, B., Kovács, L. (eds.) Tools and Algorithms for the Construction and Analysis of Systems, pp. 144–164. Springer, Cham (2024). https://doi.org/10.1007/978-3-031-57246-3_9

31. Kabra, A., Mitsch, S., Platzer, A.: Verified train controllers for the federal railroad administration train kinematics model: balancing competing brake and track forces. IEEE Trans. Comput. Aided Des. Integr. Circuits Syst. **41**(11), 4409–4420 (2022). https://doi.org/10.1109/TCAD.2022.3197690

32. Korda, M., Henrion, D., Jones, C.N.: Convex computation of the maximum controlled invariant set for polynomial control systems. SIAM J. Control. Optim. **52**(5), 2944–2969 (2014). https://doi.org/10.1137/130914565

33. Krstic, M., Kanellakopoulos, I., Kokotovic, P.V.: Nonlinear and Adaptive Control Design, 1 edn. Wiley-Interscience (1995)

34. Kulmburg, A., Schafer, L., Althoff, M.: Approximability of the containment problem for zonotopes and ellipsotopes. IEEE Trans. Autom. Control 1–16 (2025). https://doi.org/10.1109/TAC.2025.3583624

35. Lazar, M., Tetteroo, M.: Computation of terminal costs and sets for discrete–time nonlinear MPC. IFAC-PapersOnLine **51**(20), 141–146 (2018). https://doi.org/10.1016/j.ifacol.2018.11.006
36. Mitchell, I.M., Yeh, J., Laine, F.J., Tomlin, C.J.: Ensuring safety for sampled data systems: an efficient algorithm for filtering potentially unsafe input signals. In: IEEE Conference on Decision and Control, pp. 7431–7438 (2016). https://doi.org/10.1109/CDC.2016.7799417
37. Moore, R.E., Kearfott, R.B., Cloud, M.J.: Introduction to Interval Analysis. Other Titles in Applied Mathematics, Society for Industrial and Applied Mathematics (2009). https://doi.org/10.1137/1.9780898717716
38. Platzer, A.: A complete uniform substitution calculus for differential dynamic logic. J. Autom. Reason. **59**(2), 219–265 (2017). https://doi.org/10.1007/s10817-016-9385-1
39. Platzer, A.: Logical Foundations of Cyber-Physical Systems. Springer, Cham (2018). https://doi.org/10.1007/978-3-319-63588-0
40. Platzer, A., Qian, L.: Axiomatization of compact initial value problems: open properties. J. ACM. https://doi.org/10.1145/3763228
41. Rakovic, S.V., Baric, M.: Parameterized robust control invariant sets for linear systems: theoretical advances and computational remarks. IEEE Trans. Autom. Control **55**(7), 1599–1614 (2010). https://doi.org/10.1109/TAC.2010.2042341
42. Raković, S., Fontes, F., Kolmanovsky, I.: Reachability and invariance for linear sampled–data systems. IFAC-PapersOnLine **50**(1), 3057–3062 (2017). https://doi.org/10.1016/j.ifacol.2017.08.675
43. Rauscher, M., Kimmel, M., Hirche, S.: Constrained robot control using control barrier functions. In: IEEE/RSJ International Conference on Intelligent Robots and Systems, pp. 279–285 (2016). https://doi.org/10.1109/IROS.2016.7759067
44. Rawlings, J.B., Mayne, D.Q., Diehl, M.M.: Model Predictive Control: Theory, Computation, and Design. Nob Hill Publishing, LLC (2022)
45. Rungger, M., Tabuada, P.: Computing robust controlled invariant sets of linear systems. IEEE Trans. Autom. Control **62**(7), 3665–3670 (2017). https://doi.org/10.1109/TAC.2017.2672859
46. Sadraddini, S., Tedrake, R.: Linear encodings for polytope containment problems. In: 2019 IEEE 58th Conference on Decision and Control (CDC), pp. 4367–4372 (2019). https://doi.org/10.1109/CDC40024.2019.9029363
47. Schäfer, L., Gruber, F., Althoff, M.: Scalable computation of robust control invariant sets of nonlinear systems. IEEE Trans. Autom. Control **69**(2), 755–770 (2024). https://doi.org/10.1109/TAC.2023.3275305
48. Schäfer, L., Althoff, M.: Computing robust control invariant sets of nonlinear systems using polynomial controller synthesis. In: Proceedings of the American Control Conference (2024). https://doi.org/10.23919/ACC60939.2024.10644939
49. Schürmann, B., Kochdumper, N., Althoff, M.: Reachset model predictive control for disturbed nonlinear systems. In: 2018 IEEE Conference on Decision and Control (CDC), pp. 3463–3470 (2018). https://doi.org/10.1109/CDC.2018.8619781
50. Selvaraj, Y., Krook, J., Ahrendt, W., Fabian, M.: On proving that an unsafe controller is not proven safe. J. Log. Algebraic Methods Program. **137**, 100939 (2024). https://doi.org/10.1016/j.jlamp.2023.100939
51. Tan, Y.K., Mitsch, S., Platzer, A.: Verifying switched system stability with logic. In: Proceedings of the 25th ACM International Conference on Hybrid Systems: Computation and Control, HSCC 2022, pp. 1–11. Association for Computing Machinery, New York (2022). https://doi.org/10.1145/3501710.3519541

52. Tan, Y.K., Platzer, A.: Deductive stability proofs for ordinary differential equations. In: TACAS 2021. LNCS, vol. 12652, pp. 181–199. Springer, Cham (2021). https://doi.org/10.1007/978-3-030-72013-1_10

53. Wabersich, K.P., Zeilinger, M.N.: Linear model predictive safety certification for learning-based control. In: 2018 IEEE Conference on Decision and Control (CDC), pp. 7130–7135 (2018). https://doi.org/10.1109/CDC.2018.8619829

54. Wetzlinger, M., Kochdumper, N., Bak, S., Althoff, M.: Fully-automated verification of linear systems using reachability analysis with support functions. In: Proceedings of the 26th ACM International Conference on Hybrid Systems: Computation and Control (2023). https://doi.org/10.1145/3575870.3587121

55. Wetzlinger, M., Kulmburg, A., Althoff, M.: Adaptive parameter tuning for reachability analysis of nonlinear systems. In: Proceedings of the 24th International Conference on Hybrid Systems: Computation and Control. HSCC 2021. Association for Computing Machinery (2021). https://doi.org/10.1145/3447928.3456643

56. Xu, X., Tabuada, P., Grizzle, J.W., Ames, A.D.: Robustness of control barrier functions for safety critical control. IFAC-PapersOnLine 48(27), 54–61 (2015). https://doi.org/10.1016/j.ifacol.2015.11.152

57. Xue, B., Wang, Q., Zhan, N., Wang, S., She, Z.: Synthesizing robust domains of attraction for state-constrained perturbed polynomial systems. SIAM J. Control. Optim. 59(2), 1083–1108 (2021). https://doi.org/10.1137/19M125220X

58. Xue, B., Wang, Q., Zhan, N., Fränzle, M.: Robust invariant sets generation for state-constrained perturbed polynomial systems. In: International Conference on Hybrid Systems: Computation and Control, pp. 128–137 (2019). https://doi.org/10.1145/3302504.3311810

Autonomous Systems

Formal Modeling of Trust in Autonomous Delivery Vehicles

Manar Altamimi[1(✉)], Asieh Salehi Fathabadi[2], and Vahid Yazdanpanah[2]

[1] School of Computer and Information Sciences, Princess Nourah bint Abdulrahman University, Riyadh, Saudi Arabia
`mmaltamimi@pnu.edu.sa`
[2] School of Electronics and Computer Science, University of Southampton, Southampton, UK
`{a.salehi-fathabadi,v.yazdanpanah}@soton.ac.uk`

Abstract. Trust modeling is critical for the safe deployment of autonomous systems, yet existing approaches that rely primarily on historical performance data fail to capture dynamic operational contexts and real-time agent capabilities. This paper introduces a formal framework for modeling actual trust in Autonomous Delivery Vehicles (ADVs)—a context-aware trust model that evaluates an agent's current ability, knowledge state, and commitment to task completion rather than relying solely on past behavior. We present a systematic refinement-based approach using Event-B formal methods to model trust in ADV task delegation scenarios. Our methodology progresses through five refinement levels, transitioning from an untrusted baseline model to a comprehensive trust framework that integrates three key dimensions: (1) strategic trust (capability verification), (2) epistemic trust (knowledge-based assessment), and (3) commitment trust (availability and willingness evaluation). Each refinement level addresses specific failure modes identified in traditional delegation systems where tasks may be assigned to incapable, unknown, or unavailable vehicles. The formal model is verified using the Rodin theorem prover with 93 proof obligations, achieving 90% automatic verification. Our approach demonstrates how actual trust can be systematically integrated into autonomous systems through correctness-by-construction refinement, ensuring that task assignments occur only when trust conditions are formally verified. The framework provides a foundation for trustworthy task delegation in multi-agent autonomous systems and offers insights for developing reliable AI-driven delivery networks.

Keywords: Autonomous Systems · Formal Methods · trust · Event-B · trustworthy AI

1 Introduction

Trust in autonomous systems is a multifaceted and context-dependent concept that remains difficult to formalize, interpret, and verify [1,2]. Within Multi-

F. Damiani and M. Farrell (Eds.): iFM 2025, LNCS 16194, pp. 271–289, 2026.
https://doi.org/10.1007/978-3-032-10794-7_14

Agent Systems (MAS), trust plays a crucial role in enabling effective coordination and task delegation [3]. Early research in MAS, such as Ramchurn et al. [4], emphasized the complexity of trust modeling, typically relying on agents' historical behavior to infer trustworthiness. [5,6] continue to focus on retrospective reasoning, maintaining the assumption that trust can be adequately captured through analysis of past interactions. However, traditional approaches that rely solely on past interactions are often inadequate in real-time and dynamic environments, where agents must make decisions based on their current beliefs, situational awareness, and evolving goals. This approach often conflate trust, which is the delegator's belief in another agent's future performance, with trustworthiness, which refers to the agent's inherent properties such as capability, availability, and commitment.

Addressing this limitation, Akintunde et al. [7] introduced the concept of *actual trust*. It spans both trust and trustworthiness: the agent's knowledge represents the epistemic trust held by the trustor, while capability and commitment reflect the trustworthiness of the trustee. Salehi et al. [8] proposed formal Event-B [9] model that formalise an agent's knowledge, capability, and commitment at the time of delegation. These dimensions represent a dynamic model, focusing on causality [10] rather than static. This paper extends the formal model of actual trust by grounding it in a practical, real-world case study: Autonomous Delivery Vehicles (ADVs). ADVs are a compelling domain due to their reliance on real-time decision-making, decentralized control, and varying operational conditions. The use of formal methods to verify trust-related behavior in such systems is crucial for ensuring safety, reliability, and accountability.

While prior work introduced the foundational theory of actual trust in Multi-Agent Systems [15] and briefly demonstrated three abstract levels of refinement using Event-B as a modeling toolset for formalizing actual trust in autonomous systems [9], this paper makes three novel contributions: (1) it presents a complete refinement-based of actual trust applied to a real-world case study, Autonomous Delivery Vehicles (ADVs); (2) it develops five Event-B refinement levels that systematically introduces the trust dimensions (strategic, epistemic, and commitment); and (3) it provides a step-wise verification through theorem proving in Rodin, demonstrating the applicability of trust in ADVs.

To illustrate the limitations of traditional trust models, consider a scenario in which a delivery agent must delegate a package delivery to one of several autonomous vehicles. A traditional trust model might select a vehicle based on past successful deliveries. However, this could result in assigning the task to a vehicle that is currently unavailable, malfunctioning, or unaware of its own limitations. This mismatch can lead to delivery failure despite the vehicle's favorable history. In contrast, a trust model that considers current capability, current knowledge, and explicit task commitment is essential to make reliable delegation decisions.

Such limitations motivate the following research question, which builds on the theoretical foundation established in [8]:

- How can refinement-based formal methods ensure that trust assumptions remain consistent across evolving system states and interactions?

To address this research question, we extend the model of actual trust introduced in [8] by applying it to a real-world case study involving Autonomous Delivery Vehicles (ADVs), enabling a contextualized and operational evaluation of trust dimensions. This is achieved by formally developing a refinement-based model of actual trust tailored to ADVs, demonstrating how trust reasoning—grounded in dimensions such as capability, knowledge, and commitment—can be preserved in dynamic and decentralized contexts. Through a systematic refinement strategy in Event-B, the model captures the progression from abstract task delegation to trust-informed decision-making. Furthermore, the use of theorem proving within the Rodin platform ensures the consistency of trust invariants across refinements, supporting both automatic proof discharge and manual validation for complex proof obligations. The resulting model provides a rigorous and formally verified foundation for building trust in autonomous systems that operate under uncertainty.

The paper is structured as follows: Sect. 2 presents background knowledge on the applied modelling approach and outlines the refinement-based strategy used to incorporate actual trust into the ADV system and background of the Event-B formal method. Section 3 describes the abstract model, establishing the foundational representation of tasks and agent interactions in an untrusted cases. Section 4 elaborates on the series of refinements that incrementally introduce and verify trust dimensions—capability, epistemic knowledge, and commitment—along with ADV state transitions. Section 5 summarizes the verification process, including the theorem proving and proof obligation analysis conducted using the Rodin platform. Section 6 discusses related work and reflects on how our model advances the current state of research in trust modeling. Finally, Sect. 7 concludes the paper and outlines future directions.

2 Background and Overview of Approach

This section provides the necessary background on modeling trust in autonomous systems and introduces the formal methods employed in this work. In particular, we adopt a case study of Autonomous Delivery Vehicles (ADVs) to investigate the formalization of actual trust, building upon the refinement-based modeling framework [9]. The model is specified using Event-B and is formally verified using the Rodin tools in conjunction with the iUML-B tool set [11].

2.1 Modeling Approach: Modeling Actual Trust in Autonomous Systems

We adopt a correct-by-construction refinement strategy [12,13] approach using Event-B to formally model the notions of trust in Autonomous Delivery Vehicles (ADVs). This approach allows us to incrementally incorporate trust-related properties across multiple levels of abstraction. Detailed of this abstraction is provided in Sect. 3

We begin with an abstract model representing the *untrusted* state of the system –capturing task assignment, agent capabilities, and ADV availability –as illustrated in Fig. 1, where no trust assumptions have yet been enforced (solid black line). This baseline model allows tasks to be assigned to any ADV, regardless of its current capabilities, availability, or commitment to perform the task.

We then progressively integrate dimensions of *actual trust*—strategic, epistemic, and commitment trust—across multiple refinement levels. Each refinement incrementally strengthens the model, as highlighted in the blue dashed lines in Fig. 1.

Figure 1 thus consolidates the refinement hierarchy, showing the model's progression from abstract task delegation to a fully trust-integrated ADV system:

1. **Model Task** Define tasks that need to be accomplished.
2. **Model Agent Capabilities** Define the agent's capabilities.
3. **Strategic Trust** Verifies ADV capabilities before assignment.
4. **Epistemic Trust** Models the agent's knowledge of ADV capabilities.
5. **Commitment Trust** Ensures the ADV is committed to accomplishing the task.
6. **ADV Availability** Ensures the ADV is available to perform the task.

This approach is motivated by potential failures in traditional delegation systems and incrementally addresses those failures using *actual trust* constraints. The figure serves both as a roadmap and as an architectural summary of our approach. Detailed formalization of each refinement level is provided in Sect. 4.

2.2 Event-B Formal Method

Event-B [9,14] is a formal method for system development, particularly suitable for safety-critical and reliable systems. It supports rigorous specification and refinement through mathematical reasoning. An Event-B model is composed of two core components:

- Contexts: which define the static aspects of the system, such as carrier sets, constants, and axioms that constrain them.
- Machines: which capture dynamic behavior through variables, invariants, and events. Events describe state transitions using guards (preconditions) and actions (state updates).

Modeling and verification in Event-B is supported by the Rodin platform [9,14], an open-source toolset built on the Eclipse framework. Rodin provides:

- Automated and interactive proof support, ensuring model consistency, invariant preservation, and refinement correctness through proof obligations.
- Model validation tools, including model checking and animation, to verify that the system behaves as expected with respect to the specified properties.

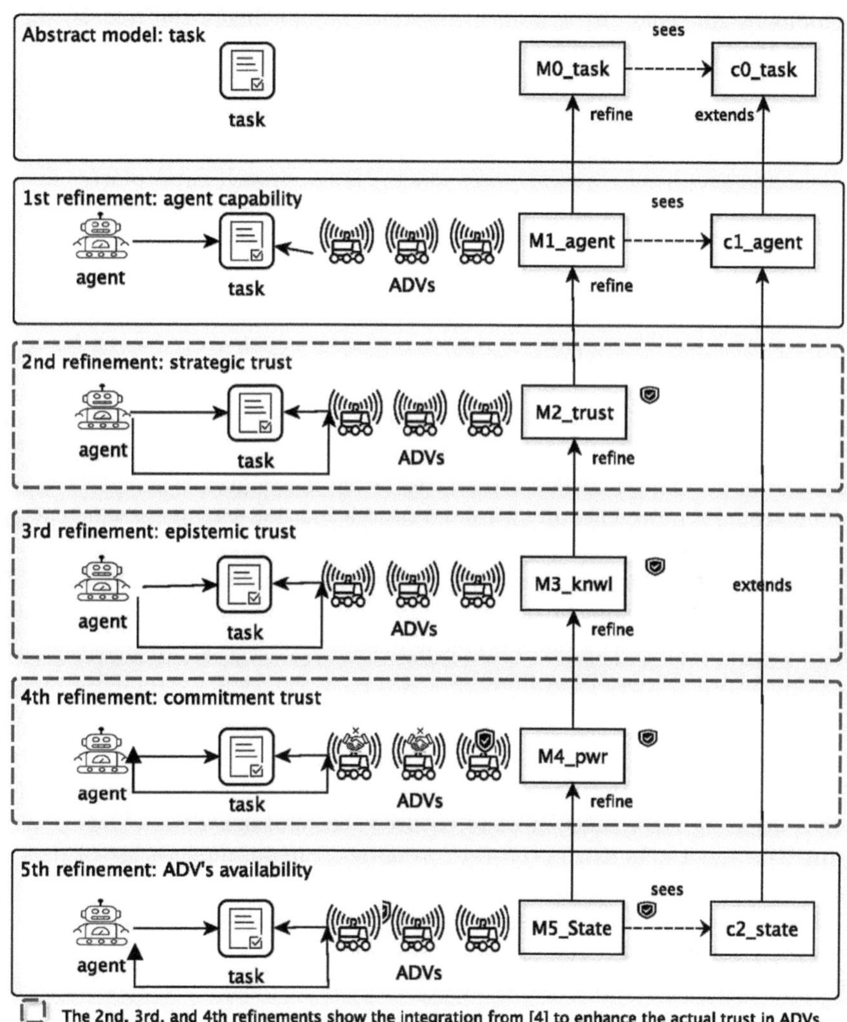

Fig. 1. Refinement Strategy to model actual trust in ADVs.

To manage the complexity of modeling actual trust in autonomous systems, especially between multiple refinement layers, we adopt iUML-B [15–17], a diagrammatic modeling notation integrated with Event-B, designed to enhance the visual expressiveness of formal models. It provides two key diagram types:

- State machines, to capture system behavior through states and transitions;
- Class diagrams, to structure data and define relationships between components.

iUML-B automatically generates corresponding Event-B elements from these diagrams, maintaining semantic consistency while improving readability and development efficiency. Its graphical interface complements the textual nature of Event-B, making the refinement process more accessible and intuitive.

Event-B, supported by the Rodin platform and extended with the diagrammatic notation iUML-B, provides a rigorous and scalable framework for correct-by-construction modeling. The integration of formal reasoning, automated verification, and graphical expressiveness makes this approach particularly effective for representing and verifying trust reasoning in autonomous systems.

3   Modelling Abstract ADVs

In a basic autonomous delivery system, tasks are dispatched to available vehicles based solely on accessibility, with no evaluation of suitability or operational readiness. The agent responsible for delegation assumes that any ADV can perform any task, regardless of its current state in terms of capability limitations, awareness of its ability, or commitment to achieving a given task.

This scenario represents an untrusted task delegation setting, in which assignments occur without validating whether the ADV is capable of completing the task, known to be reliable, or presently available and committed. The absence of such trust assessments makes the system vulnerable to task failures, inconsistent performance, and reduced operational dependability. The primary components involved in this setting are as follows:

Tasks Each task is defined by a set of specifications, such as delivery destination, time constraints, and required capabilities (e.g., payload capacity, route range). These specifications implicitly establish a minimum threshold that the executing ADV must meet to ensure successful delivery.

Agent The agent acts as the central coordinator, maintaining a list of pending tasks and assigning them to ADVs based on accessibility alone. It lacks visibility into the internal states of the ADVs and does not evaluate whether a selected vehicle meets the task's requirements.

Autonomous Delivery Vehicle (ADV) Each ADV is assumed to be capable of executing any given task and is expected to proceed with the delivery immediately upon assignment. The vehicle is also expected to return to its origin after task completion and be ready for subsequent assignments, without the system validating its operational status or readiness.

Operating under these assumptions, the system frequently encounters task execution failures. An ADV may be assigned a delivery it cannot complete due to unmet capability requirements (e.g., insufficient payload capacity or battery range), lack of real-time availability (e.g., already engaged in another task), or internal conditions not visible to the agent (e.g., navigation errors or degraded performance). Because the agent neither verifies the ADV's suitability nor confirms its willingness or readiness to perform the task, assignments may lead to delays, incomplete deliveries, or the need for manual intervention. These outcomes not only reduce the system's efficiency but also undermine its reliability and scalability in real-case scenario.

To formally capture this failure behavior, we develop an initial untrusted Event-B model of the ADV system, in which task assignments proceed without enforcing trust notions, Fig. 1. This abstract model is composed of three levels that reflect the potential for task failure due to the absence of strategic, epistemic, and commitment guarantees, detailed in Sect. 4. These abstract levels are:

The abstract refinement: task defines the foundational structure of the ADV system at a high level. The *context* introduces the static elements:

- SETS: TASKS These represent the set of deliverable tasks where autonomous delivery vehicles (ADVs) that carry them.

The *machine* defines the dynamic behavior of the system using:

- VARIABLES: taskComp $\in$ tasks $\to$ BOOL, taskStart $\in$ tasks $\to$ BOOL, where taskComp indicates whether a task has been completed, and taskStart indicates whether a task has been started.
- INVARIANT: $\forall t \cdot t \in$ tasks $\wedge t \in$ dom(taskComp) $\wedge t \in$ dom(taskStart) $\wedge$ taskComp(t)= TRUE $\Rightarrow$ taskStart(t) = TRUE ensures that a task cannot be completed unless it has already been started.
- EVENTS: define_task introduces a new task to the system with its associated specifications, start_task transitions a task into execution, and complete_task marks the task as completed and frees the ADV.

The 1st refinement: agent's capability introduces the ADV and agent sets and refines the behavior of task delegation.

The *context* introduces additional sets:

- SETS: AGENTS, ADVS
  These represent the agents responsible for task delegation and the autonomous delivery vehicles (ADVs) that perform deliveries.

The *machine* introduces:

- VARIABLES: assignedTask $\in$ advs $\nrightarrow$ tasks, capabilities $\in$ advs $\leftrightarrow$ CAPABILITY, requiresMin $\in$ tasks $\leftrightarrow$ CAPABILITY, where CAPABILITY is a set of capabilities.
- EVENTS: In addition to the refined events from the previous refinement, new events are introduced such as add_adv_Capability, which refines the task assignment logic to include capability checks, and assign_advs_task to delegate tasks to capable ADVs.

The 2nd refinement: agent's states extends the system to account for the operational state of each autonomous delivery vehicle (ADV). It introduces a dynamic view of ADVs by distinguishing between different phases in their task lifecycle, such as being *available*, *ready*, *delivering*, or *returning*. This refinement allows the model to reason about the ADV's availability and readiness before task delegation.

In a subsequent section, we progressively introduce these trust dimensions to support safer and more reliable task delegation.

4   Modelling Actual Trust in ADVs

To overcome the limitations of the untrusted model described earlier in Sect. 3, we integrate the formal notion of trust proposed in [8], which defines trust as a relation grounded in an agent's assessment of an ADV's capability, knowledge, and commitment to perform a given task. Guided by this definition, our refinement strategy, illustrated in Fig. 1, introduces three key dimensions of actual trust: **strategic trust** (trust in the ADV's capabilities), **epistemic trust** (trust based on the agent's knowledge of those capabilities), and **commitment trust** (trust in the ADV's readiness and willingness to execute the task).

Each refinement level addresses one of the failure scenarios identified in the abstract model in Sect. 3 and incrementally constrains the conditions under which task delegation can occur. This refinement development process ensures that the model evolves correctly by construction, with each level preserving the soundness and consistency of the previous one. The formal development is structured through these successive refinements, each capturing a distinct dimension of actual trust.

The integration of these trust dimensions into the formal model is achieved through a combination of carefully defined invariants and event refinement. Each dimension; strategic, epistemic, and commitment trust; is involved as a set of invariants that are proved to be preserved across all refinement levels. Additional invariants are introduced to capture other essential properties of the ADV system, ensuring consistency and firm throughout the development.

Among the events in the model in the abstract refinements, assign_task plays a central role. It holds the assignment of a task to an ADV and acts as the essential point for enforcing trust conditions. However, assign_task does not work in isolation: it depends on the successful occurrence of prior events such as define_task, which establishes the task and its requirements, and trust, which reflects the trustor's decision to rely on a given ADV.

As trust dimensions are introduced through successive refinements, the assign_task, and trust events are incrementally strengthened to reflect the evolving trust notions. They ensure that trust-related invariants are preserved and that task delegation only occurs under verified conditions. The last refinement of this event is presented in the following and will be explained throughout the remainder of this section[1].

---

[1] The full model can be accessed here: https://shorturl.at/NiIkb.

```
EVENT assign_task
ANY i j t
WHERE
@grd01: j ∈ advs                    // j is the trustee ADV (M1)
@grd02: t ∈ tasks                   // t is a defined task (M1)
@grd03: capabilities[{j}] ∩ requires[{t}] ≠ ∅   // ADV j is capable of t (M1)
@grd04: taskComp(t) = FALSE               // t has not been completed (M1)
@grd05: adv(j) = TRUST            // ADV j is trusted (M2)
@grd06: j ∈ dom(adv)             // ADV j has a defined state (M2)
@grd07: j ↦ t ∈ ran(trustor_trustee_task)     // j is trusted by some agent for task t (M2)
@grd08: adv_states(j) = available        // ADV j is currently available (M4/M5)
THEN
@act01: assignedTask(j) := t         // Assign t to ADV j (M1)
@act02: adv_states(j) := ready        // Update ADV state to 'ready' (M4/M5)
END
```

4.1   2nd Refinement: Strategic Trust

The second refinement follows the first refinement on agent capability. It introduces the notion of strategic trust, which ensures that an ADV is only assigned a task if it possesses the necessary capabilities to perform it. We assume that all ADVs are initially in an untrusted state, and only transition to the trusted state once they satisfy the conditions for all three trust dimensions, illustred in Fig. 2. This addresses the first failure scenario identified in the abstract model, where tasks may be assigned to any available ADV regardless of its suitability. In such cases, the assignment may fail because the selected ADV is unfit to complete the given task.

```
@inv01: ∀ i , j · i ∈ agents ∧ j ∈ advs ∧ i ∈ dom(trustor_trustee_task) ⇒ i ≠ j
@inv02: ∀ i , t · t ∈ tasks ∧ i ∈ agents ⇒ requiresMin[{t}] ⊆ capabilities[advs]
@inv03: dom(assignedTask) ⊆ dom(trustees_task)
```

```
EVENT trust
ANY i j t
WHERE
@grd01: j ∈ advs                  // j is the trustee ADV (M2)
@grd02: i ∈ agents                // i is the trustor agent (M2)
@grd03: t ∈ tasks                 // t is a task requested by i (M2)
@grd04: t ∈ trustees_task[{j}]         // ADV j is assigned task t (M2)
@grd05: i ≠ j              // An agent cannot trust itself (M2)
@grd06: i ∉ dom(trustor_trustee_task)     // i hasn't trusted any ADV yet (M2)
@grd07: adv(j) = NOT_TRUST            // ADV j is not yet trusted (M2)
@grd08: j ∈ knowledge[{i}]          // Agent i knows ADV j (M3)
@grd09: adv_untrusted(j) = committed     // ADV j has declared commitment (M4)
@grd10: (i ↦ (j ↦ t)) ∈ dom(commitments)     // Commitment exists (M4)
@grd11: commitments(i ↦ (j ↦ t)) = TRUE     // Commitment is confirmed (M4)
THEN
@act01: adv(j) := TRUST             // Set ADV j to trusted (M2)
@act02: trustor_trustee_task :=
    trustor_trustee_task ∪ {i ↦ (j ↦ t)}   // Register trust relationship (M2)
@act03: adv_untrusted(j) := adv_untrusted_NULL   // Reset untrusted state (M4)
@act04: adv_states(j) := available        // ADV becomes available to act (M4)
END
```

To formally capture strategic trust M2, we introduce invariant @inv01, @inv02, and @inv03 that constrains task assignment to only those ADVs capable of fulfilling the task requirements. Each task is associated with a capability requirement, and each ADV is modeled with its own set of capabilities. Invariant inv01 ensures that a trustor agent does not assign a task to itself as a trustee ADV, maintaining the separation of delegation roles. Invariant inv02 ensures that every task required by an agent is matched against the set of capabilities possessed by available ADVs, ensuring capability feasibility across all tasks. Lastly, Invariant inv03 restricts the domain of assigned tasks to those ADVs that are already recognized as trustees, thereby ensuring that task assignments are only made to trusted and validated ADVs. These invariants collectively preserve trust correctness even as ADVs transition between operational states. The assign_task event is refined at this level by incorporating additional guards @grd05,@grd06, @grd07 which enforces the strategic trust notions.

Specifically, this guard @grd05 checks that the ADV j is in a trusted state, which introduced the trust variable adv. This means j has already been evaluated its capability and has been formally marked as TRUSTED. This is necessary to proceed with actions that should only involve trusted ADVs. @grd06 ensures that ADV j has a valid entry in the adv variable, i.e., it has a known trust status (TRUST, NOT_TRUST). Without this, referencing adv(j) would be undefined, possibly causing a well-definedness proof of obligation in Event-B. @grd07 confirms that the pair $(j \mapsto t)$ meaning ADV j is responsible for task t exists within the range of the trustor−to−trustee−task mapping. It shows that some agent has explicitly trusted ADV j for task t, and this trust is recorded in the relation trustor_trustee_task. This ensures that j is not just generally trusted, but trusted specifically for this task. In this refinement, the trust event enables the agent to establish reliance on an ADV, based on its verified ability to complete the task successfully guard from @grd01 to @grd06.

At this stage, trust is interpreted in terms of capability: an ADV is considered trustworthy if it has the means to complete the task, regardless of whether the agent is aware of this capability or whether the ADV has committed to performing the task.

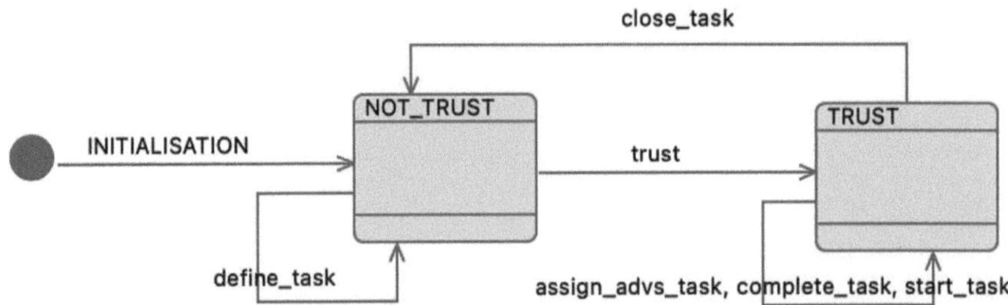

Fig. 2. State machine diagram illustrating the second refinement, which classifies ADVs as trusted or not based on their capabilities.

4.2   3rd Refinement: Epistemic Trust

The third refinement introduces the concept of epistemic trust, which ensures that the agent assigns a task to an ADV only if it has sufficient knowledge of the ability of the ADV to perform that task. This refinement addresses the second failure scenario from the abstract model, where an agent may assign a task to an ADV whose capabilities are suitable in principle, but are unknown or unverifiable to the agent at the time of delegation. In the absence of verified knowledge, the assignment decision becomes speculative and may lead to failures if the agent's assumptions are incorrect.

```
@inv04: knowledge ∈ agents ↔ advs
@inv05: ∀i, t · i ∈ agents ∧ t ∈ tasks ∧ t ∉ dom(definedTask) ∧ t ∈ ran(trustees_task) ⇒
  (∃j · j ∈ dom(trustees_task) ∧ trustees_task(j) = t ∧ requiresMin[{t}] ⊆ capabilities[{j}] ∧ j ∈
    knowledge[{i}])
```

To formally capture epistemic trust, we refine the model by introducing new invariants that represent the agent's knowledge of the ADVs' capabilities and by extending relevant events to reflect this trust dimension.

Invariant inv04 defines knowledge as a binary relation between agents and ADVs, capturing which ADVs are known to which agents. Invariant inv05 ensures that an agent delegates a task only if it knows an ADV whose capabilities satisfy the task's minimum requirements. Specifically, for any task not yet defined but already present in the trustees list, there must exist a trustee ADV whose capability set meets the task's requirements and is known to the delegating agent. Together, these invariants guarantee that task delegation is not only strategically feasible but also epistemically justified based on the agent's knowledge.

This refinement also affects the behavior of the trust event by introducing grd08, which restricts task assignment to only those ADVs that the agent knows are capable. In this way, trust is grounded in verified knowledge rather than assumption. Even if an ADV meets the strategic requirements, it cannot be selected unless the agent possesses the epistemic justification to trust it. By enforcing epistemic trust, the model ensures that task assignments are knowledge-aware, thereby eliminating delegation based on uncertainty.

4.3   4th Refinement: Commitment Trust

The fourth refinement introduces commitment trust, which ensures that an ADV is assigned a task only if it is intentionally committed to carrying it out. This addresses the third failure scenario identified in the abstract model, where an ADV may be capable and known to the agent but is either burdened with existing tasks, experiencing operational failure, or lacking sufficient time to complete the assigned task.

```
@inv06: commitments ∈ trustor_trustee_task → BOOL
@inv07: ∀i, t · i ∈ agents ∧ t ∈ tasks ∧ taskStart(t) = TRUE ⇒ (∃j · j ∈ advs ∧
  (j ↦ t) ∈ assignedTask ∧
  adv(j) = TRUST)
```

To formally capture commitment trust, the model is extended with a new state component that tracks the commitment status of each ADV. This includes whether an ADV is explicitly committed to executing a given task, describe in Fig. 3. Invariant inv06 defines commitments as a total function from the set trustor_trustee_task to BOOL. This means that for every trust relationship between an agent (the trustor) and an ADV (the trustee) with respect to a task, there is an associated Boolean value indicating whether the ADV is committed TRUE or not FALSE to performing that task. Invariant inv07 ensures that any task marked as started (i.e., taskStart(t) = TRUE) must meet two conditions:

1. It is assigned to some ADV j, such that $(j \mapsto t) \in$ assignedTask, and
2. ADV j must currently be in the TRUSTED state, i.e., adv(j) = TRUST.

This invariant guarantees that no task can be initiated unless it has been formally assigned to a trusted ADV. It enforces the core principle of commitment trust: task execution may only begin if the vehicle is explicitly trusted and has committed to carrying out the task. This reduces the risk of premature or unreliable task starts.

At this level, the trust event reflects a comprehensive trust relation: the agent may only trust an ADV if it is (1) capable of performing the task (strategic trust), (2) known to be capable (epistemic trust), and (3) available and committed to carry it out (commitment trust). This layered model of trust ensures that task assignments are not only feasible and informed but also actionable and reliable at the moment of delegation.

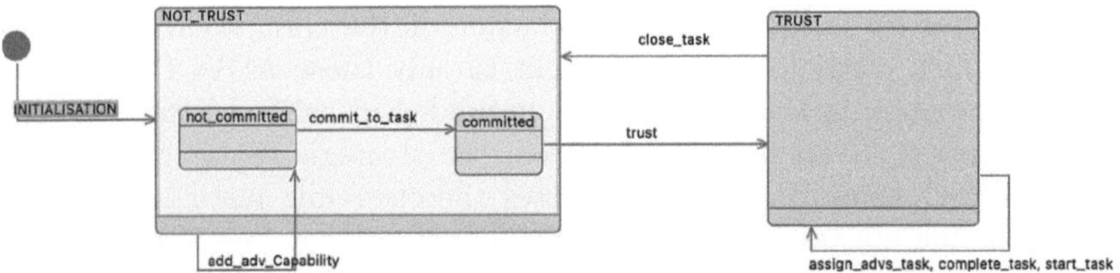

Fig. 3. State machine diagram illustrating the fourth refinement, which enforces Commitment Trust in ADV task delegation.

4.4 5th Refinement: ADV's States

The fifth refinement ensures the state consistency of trust notions as the ADV's state is updated during operation. While previous refinements introduced capability, knowledge, and commitment trust dimensions, this refinement verifies that those invariants continue to hold across dynamic ADV states such as available, ready, delivering, and returning.

@inv08: $\forall i, j, t \cdot i \in$ agents $\wedge\, j \in$ advs $\wedge\, t \in$ tasks $\wedge$
$j \in$ dom (trustees_task) $\wedge$ trustees_task$(j) = t \wedge$ adv$(j) =$ TRUST
$\Rightarrow j \in$ knowledge$[\{i\}] \wedge i \mapsto (j \mapsto t) \in$ dom(commitments) $\wedge$
commitments$(i \mapsto (j \mapsto t)) =$ TRUE $\wedge (i \mapsto (j \mapsto t)) \in$ trustor_trustee_task

In this refinement, the model is extended to incorporate ADV state transitions that reflect the operational scenario depicted in Fig. 4. These transitions introduce potential changes in availability and engagement, which may affect the trust assumptions made at the time of task assignment. Therefore, it becomes essential to prove that previously established invariants remain preserved as the ADV's state changes over time.

To formally guarantee this, we refine relevant events such as start_task, complete_task, trust, and close_task, to ensure they do not violate trust-related invariants. This involves checking that:

Task assignments remain valid as ADVs move between states;
No tasks are lost or reassigned during transitions;
The ADV's trust status remains aligned with its actual state.

By maintaining trust invariant preservation throughout the ADV's lifecycle, this refinement reinforces the model's robustness in practical deployment scenarios, where trust must be preserved.

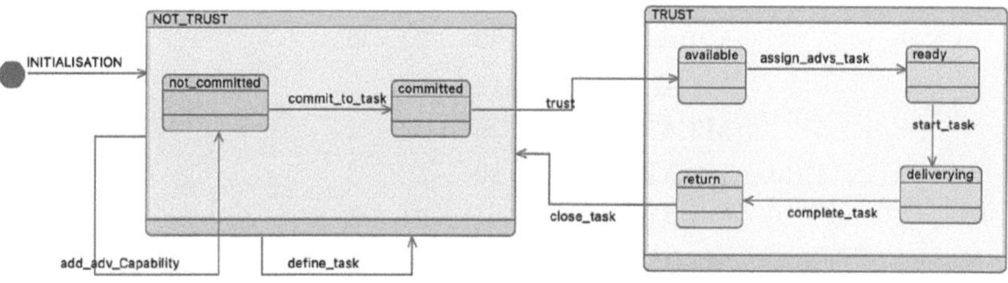

Fig. 4. State machine diagram illustrating the fifth refinement, where trust-related invariants are preserved across dynamic ADV states such as delivering and returning.

5 Verification and Proof of Trust Properties

The trusted ADV Event-B model is verified using theorem proving techniques embedded in the Event-B toolset, called Rodin [18]. These proofs ensure the correctness of the model and consistency between different refinements, especially in terms of enforcing and preserving trust properties.

The Rodin tool automatically generates a set of proofs obligation(POs) to verify:

- invariant preservation (e/v/INV) ensures that every invariant v holds after execution of event e.

- The guard strengthening (e/g/GRD) ensures that the guard of refined (concrete) event is stronger than those of the abstract event, preserving behavioral consistency.

As an example of POs, the assign_task/inv08/INV ensures that tasks are only assigned to ADVs that are explicitly marketed as trusted. Here, the invariant inv08 requires that a trusted ADV must be in a valid operational state (e.g., available), and this is enforced in the assign_task event through guard grd10. Thus, trust is not just assumed but it is formally required and verified.

- **Quantified Invariants**: Such as ensuring that for all tasks, a corresponding ADV in a trusted state exists trust/inv08/INV. These often cannot be resolved automatically due to variable scoping or dependency on other events.
- **Guard-Strengthening**: For example, in the fifth refinements, where the ADV's state dynamically changes, guard strengthening POs were manually proven to ensure that trust-preserving behavior holds across states like delivering, returning, etc.

Table 1. Proving effort summary

Refinement name	Total	Auto	Manual
trust_ADV	131	117	13
M0_tasks	20	20	0
M1_agents	17	17	0
M2_ADV_trust	29	27	2
M3_ADV_knwl	10	7	3
M4_ADV_com	31	24	6
M5_ADV_states	24	22	2

As summarized in Table 1, a total of 131 POs were generated throughout the refinement process. Approximately 90% were discharged automatically by Rodin. The remaining 13 POs were proven manually, underscoring the rigor required to ensure that the model accurately captures trust-aware behavior under refinement.

Manual proofs were often concentrated in later refinements, particularly in the modeling of commitment and strategic. Proving guard strengthening obligations in these contexts required careful reasoning about state-dependent behavior, especially when modeling transitions such as delivering, returning, or reavailability of ADVs. Additionally, quantified invariants introduced subtle proof challenges due to the need to generalize correctness properties across all agents and tasks.

Modeling actual trust within ADVs revealed how each trust dimension reflects different system concerns. Epistemic trust, for example, captures the agent's internal state of belief about the ADV's capabilities and availability. In contrast, strategic trust (based on advertised capabilities) and commitment trust (based on intention to deliver) reflect objective system properties associated with trustworthiness. The verification process enforced these distinctions by requiring that delegation only occurs when both trust (agent-side reasoning) and trustworthiness (ADV-side guarantees) are satisfied. The model thus ensures that trust is not assumed naively, but is formally substantiated through both knowledge and operational constraints.

6   Related Work and Discussion

Trust modeling in autonomous systems draws from formal methods, multi-agent systems, and human-computer interaction research. Traditional approaches have relied on statistical and reputation-based models [1,19], with recent work shifting toward dynamic trust frameworks using simulation models [20] and machine learning [21]. However, these approaches primarily focus on empirical observation rather than formal verification guarantees. Formal methods for autonomous systems have gained significant attention [22], with formal verification recognized as essential for regulatory acceptance [23]. Dennis et al. [24] demonstrate formal verification of ethical decision-making, extending formal methods beyond traditional safety properties. Trust research in multi-agent systems provides foundational concepts through cognitive, game-theoretic, and socio-cognitive paradigms [25]. Recent advances include Trust Computation Tree Logic (TCTL) for formal trust reasoning [26] and combined trust-commitment verification frameworks [27]. However, these approaches address trust between software agents rather than trust in autonomous capabilities of physical systems. Event-B has been successfully applied to safety-critical domains [28], context-aware systems [29], and enhanced through graphical tools [30] and hybrid system extensions [31]. Despite this progress, several gaps remain: most trust models rely on probabilistic [32] rather than formal guarantees, traditional approaches model trust as static rather than dynamic [33], existing models focus on historical performance rather than current capabilities, and integration of trust reasoning with system verification remains limited [34].

6.1   Contribution and Novelty

Our work addresses these gaps by introducing a formal framework for "actual trust" that evaluates current system state and capabilities rather than historical performance. Unlike statistical models, our Event-B formalization provides mathematical guarantees through theorem proving. The key contributions include: (1) a novel three-dimensional trust model integrating strategic, epistemic, and commitment trust; (2) a systematic refinement-based approach ensuring correctness-by-construction; and (3) formal verification of trust properties with 93 proof obligations achieving 90% automatic verification.

6.2 Evaluation and Limitations

The verification results demonstrate the feasibility of our approach, with the Rodin theorem prover successfully handling the majority of proof obligations automatically. The 11 manual proofs primarily involved complex invariant preservation across state transitions, indicating areas where automated reasoning reaches its limits. Compared to similar Event-B developments, our proof effort is reasonable for the complexity of trust reasoning integrated with autonomous system behavior. However, several limitations exist. First, our evaluation relies solely on formal verification without empirical validation in real deployment scenarios. The model assumes perfect communication and does not address potential security threats or malicious agents. The trust dimensions are currently treated as boolean properties rather than continuous measures, which may limit applicability in scenarios requiring nuanced trust assessment.

The scalability of our approach presents both opportunities and challenges. The refinement-based methodology scales well to additional trust dimensions or more complex ADV behaviors through systematic model extension. However, the computational complexity of proof verification may increase significantly with larger fleets or more sophisticated trust reasoning. This increase in computational complexity arises due the presence of quantified invariants and the dependency of event guards on evolving trust notations—all of which contribute to larger state spaces and more intricate proof obligations [35]. Future work should investigate distributed verification approaches and automated proof strategy generation. For practical deployment, our framework provides a foundation for trustworthy task delegation but requires integration with runtime monitoring and adaptation mechanisms. The static nature of our current model could be extended with dynamic trust update mechanisms that respond to changing operational conditions while preserving verified trust properties.

7 Conclusion and Future Direction

The case study provided valuable insights into the practical modeling of trust in ADVs by assessing their perceptions according to actual trust notions. The trust notions must be explicitly decoupled—an agent might be capable but unaware of its own limitations, or willing but not committed. Modeling these distinctions required progressively layering trust notions across separate refinements. It uses Event-B to represent ADVs's capabilities, awareness of their ability to achieve the task, and knowledge of their current state at different refinement levels. Additionally, the evaluation reveals that incorporating more information into the refinement, such as the ADVs capabilities and their status, enhances the possibilities of achieving the task and developing trust.

While modelling used to evaluate actual trust, it can also be embedded in task allocation systems for task assignment to trustworthy delivery vehicles, integrated into smart user assistants for task evaluation, and embedded in organisational settings for task delegation when a vehicle struggles to deliver due to unexpected issues.

Modelling of actual trust formally in ADVs can be expanded in multiple directions. One direction is to investigate cases in which achieving a task requires collaboration among multiple ADVs, hence the need for verification of actual trust on the coalitional level. Further research can also investigate modelling actual trust in ADV organisations with a hierarchical structure and the possibility of task delegation among ADVs. In such settings, we envisage that trust may propagate through the chain of task delegation.

Several research directions emerge from this work. Extending the framework to multi-ADV collaboration scenarios would require modeling coalitional trust and distributed decision-making. Integration with machine learning components for dynamic capability assessment while maintaining formal guarantees presents an interesting challenge. Additionally, developing domain-specific trust models for other autonomous systems (aerial vehicles, maritime systems) could demonstrate the broader applicability of our approach. The relationship between formal trust verification and regulatory compliance deserves investigation, particularly how our mathematical guarantees can support certification processes for autonomous delivery systems. Finally, empirical studies comparing our approach with existing trust models in real-world scenarios would provide valuable validation of the practical benefits of formal trust modeling.

Acknowledgments. This work is supported by the UK Engineering and Physical Sciences Research Council (EPSRC) through the UKRI Trustworthy Autonomous Systems Hub (EP/V00784X/1) and a Turing AI Fellowship (EP/V022067/1) on Citizen-Centric AI Systems.

References

1. Kohn, S.C., De Visser, E.J., Wiese, E., Lee, Y.-C., Shaw, T.H.: Measurement of trust in automation: a narrative review and reference guide. Front. Psychol. **12**, 604977 (2021)
2. Afroogh, S., Akbari, A., Malone, E., Kargar, M., Alambeigi, H.: Trust in AI: progress, challenges, and future directions. Humanit. Soc. Sci. Commun. **11**(1) (2024)
3. Barbosa, R., Santos, R., Novais, P.: Trust-based negotiation in multiagent systems: a systematic review. In: International Conference on Practical Applications of Agents and Multi-Agent Systems, pp. 133–144 (2023). Springer
4. Ramchurn, S.D., Huynh, T.D., Jennings, N.R.: Trust in multi-agent systems. Knowl. Eng. Rev. **19**(1), 1–25 (2004)
5. Bentahar, J., Drawel, N., Sadiki, A.: Quantitative group trust: a two-stage verification approach. In: Proceedings of the 21st International Conference on Autonomous Agents and Multiagent Systems, pp. 100–108 (2022)
6. Drawel, N., Laarej, A., Bentahar, J., El Menshawy, M.: Transformation-based model checking temporal trust in multi-agent systems. J. Syst. Softw. **192**, 111383 (2022). https://doi.org/10.1016/j.jss.2022.111383
7. Akintunde, M., Yazdanpanah, V., Salehi Fathabadi, A., Cirstea, C., Dastani, M., Moreau, L.: Actual trust in multiagent systems. In: Proceedings of the 23rd International Conference on Autonomous Agents and Multiagent Systems (AAMAS

2024). IFAAMAS '24, pp. 2114–2116. International Foundation for Autonomous Agents and Multiagent Systems, Auckland, New Zealand (2024). https://doi.org/10.5555/3635637.3663078 . Extended Abstract

8. Salehi Fathabadi, A., Yazdanpanah, V.: Trust modelling and verification using Event-B. (2023)

9. Abrial, J.-R.: Modeling in Event-B: System and Software Engineering. Cambridge University Press, Cambridge (2010)

10. Halpern, J.Y.: Actual Causality. MIT Press, Cambridge, MA (2016)

11. Snook, C., Butler, M., Hoang, T.S., Fathabadi, A.S., Dghaym, D.: Developing the UML-B modelling tools. In: International Conference on Software Engineering and Formal Methods, pp. 181–188 (2022). Springer

12. Dghaym, D., Poppleton, M., Snook, C.: Diagram-led formal modelling using iUML-B for hybrid ERTMS level 3. In: Abstract State Machines, Alloy, B, TLA, VDM, and Z: 6th International Conference, ABZ 2018, Southampton, UK, June 5–8, 2018, Proceedings 6, pp. 338–352 (2018). Springer

13. Dghaym, D., Hoang, T.S., Turnock, S.R., Butler, M., Downes, J., Pritchard, B.: An STPA-based formal composition framework for trustworthy autonomous maritime systems. Saf. Sci. **136**, 105139 (2021)

14. Hoang, T.S.: An introduction to the Event-B modelling method. Industrial Deployment of System Engineering Methods, pp. 211–236 (2013)

15. Said, M.Y., Butler, M., Snook, C.: A method of refinement in UML-B. Softw. Syst. Model. **14**(4), 1557–1580 (2015)

16. Snook, C.: iUML-B state machines new features and usage examples. In: Proceedings of the 5th Rodin User and Developer Workshop, University of Southampton (2014). https://eprints.soton.ac.uk/365301/

17. Snook, C., Butler, M.: UML-B: formal modeling and design aided by UML. ACM Trans. Softw. Eng. Methodol. (TOSEM) **15**(1), 92–122 (2006)

18. Abrial, J.-R., Butler, M., Hallerstede, S., Hoang, T.S., Mehta, F., Voisin, L.: Rodin: an open toolset for modelling and reasoning in Event-B. Softw. Tools Technol. Transfer **12**(6), 447–466 (2010). https://doi.org/10.1007/s10009-010-0145-y

19. Hoff, K.A., Bashir, M.: Trust in automation: integrating empirical evidence on factors that influence trust. Hum. Factors **57**(3), 407–434 (2015)

20. Poornikoo, M., Gyldensten, W., Vesin, B., Overgård, K.I.: Trust in automation (TiA): simulation model, and empirical findings in supervisory control of maritime autonomous surface ships (MASS). Int. J. Hum. Comput. Interact. 1–18 (2024)

21. Zhang, X., Wang, Y., Li, J.: Human-autonomous teaming framework based on trust modelling. IEEE Trans. Hum. Mach. Syst. **52**(6), 1273–1284 (2022)

22. Luckcuck, M., Farrell, M., Dennis, L.A., Dixon, C., Fisher, M.: Formal specification and verification of autonomous robotic systems: a survey. ACM Comput. Surv. **52**(5), 1–41 (2019)

23. Farrell, M., Luckcuck, M., Fisher, M.: Robotics and integrated formal methods: necessity meets opportunity. In: Proceedings of the International Conference on Integrated Formal Methods (iFM). Lecture Notes in Computer Science, vol. 11023, pp. 161–171. Springer, Cham (2018). https://doi.org/10.1007/978-3-319-98938-9_10

24. Dennis, L., Fisher, M., Slavkovik, M., Webster, M.: Formal verification of ethical choices in autonomous systems. Robot. Auton. Syst. **77**, 1–14 (2016)

25. Pinyol, I., Sabater, J.: Computational trust and reputation models for open multiagent systems: a review. Artif. Intell. Rev. **40**(1), 1–25 (2013)

26. Drawel, N., Laarej, A., Bentahar, J., El Menshawy, M.: Specification and automatic verification of trust-based multi-agent systems. Futur. Gener. Comput. Syst. **107**, 1047–1060 (2020)
27. Bentahar, J., Drawel, N., Sadiki, A.: Model checking combined trust and commitments in multi-agent systems. In: Proceedings of the 22nd International Conference on Autonomous Agents and Multiagent Systems, pp. 100–108 (2023). ACM
28. Singh, N.K., Aït-Ameur, Y., Pantel, M., Dieumegard, A., Jenn, E.: Formal domain-driven system development in Event-B: application to interactive critical systems. J. King Saud Univ. Comput. Inf. Sci. **35**(9), 101722 (2023)
29. Le, H.A., Truong, N.T.: Formal modeling and verification of context-aware systems using Event-B. In: Proceedings of the 9th International Conference on Evaluation of Novel Software Approaches to Software Engineering, pp. 133–141 (2014). SCITEPRESS
30. Karmakar, R., Datta, S.: A graphical tool for formal verification using Event-B modeling. Multimedia Tools Appl. 1–24 (2023)
31. Banach, R.: Autonomous system safety properties with multi-machine hybrid Event-B. In: Proceedings of the Sixth International Workshop on Formal Methods for Autonomous Systems, pp. 45–62 (2024). EPTCS
32. Vogiatzis, G., MacGillivray, I., Chli, M.: A probabilistic model for trust and reputation. In: Proceedings of the 9th International Conference on Autonomous Agents and Multiagent Systems, Volume 1, pp. 225–232 (2010)
33. Lygizou, Z., Kalles, D.: A biologically inspired trust model for open multi-agent systems that is resilient to rapid performance fluctuations. Appl. Sci. **15**(11), 6125 (2025). https://doi.org/10.3390/app15116125
34. Jonker, C.M., Treur, J.: Formal analysis of models for the dynamics of trust based on experiences. In: Proceedings of the 9th European Workshop on Modelling Autonomous Agents in a Multi-Agent World (MAAMAW '99). Lecture Notes in Computer Science, vol. 1647, pp. 221–232. Springer, Berlin, Heidelberg (1999). https://doi.org/10.1007/3-540-48437-X_18
35. Déharbe, D.: Integration of SMT-solvers in B and Event-B development environments. Sci. Comput. Program. **78**(3), 310–326 (2013)

The **CAISAR** Platform: Extending the Reach of Machine Learning Specification and Verification

Michele Alberti[1]([✉])[iD], François Bobot[1][iD], Julien Girard-Satabin[1][iD], Alban Grastien[1][iD], Aymeric Varasse[2][iD], and Zakaria Chihani[1][iD]

[1] Université Paris-Saclay, CEA, List, Palaiseau 91120, France
{michele.alberti,francois.bobot,julien.girard2,alban.grastien,
zakaria.chihani}@cea.fr
[2] Software Heritage, Rocquencourt, France
aymeric.varasse@softwareheritage.org

Abstract. The formal specification and verification of machine learning models have advanced remarkably in less than a decade, leading to a profusion of verification tools that provide mathematical guarantees about model properties. However, this growing diversity risks ecosystem fragmentation, making it difficult to compare tools beyond narrowly defined benchmarks. Moreover, much of the progress to date has focused on a limited class of properties, particularly *local robustness*. While existing tools are increasingly effective at verifying such properties, more complex ones, such as those involving multiple neural networks, remain beyond their capabilities: these properties cannot currently be expressed in their specification languages, nor can they be directly verified. This applies even to the winning verification tools of the International Verification of Neural Networks Competition (**VNN-Comp**).

In this tool paper, we present **CAISAR**, an open-source platform for specifying and verifying properties of machine learning models, with particular focus on neural networks and support vector machines. **CAISAR** provides a high-level language for specifying complex properties and integrates several state-of-the-art verifiers for their automatic verification. Through concrete use cases, we show how **CAISAR** leverages automated graph-editing techniques to translate high-level specifications into queries for the supported verifiers, bridging the (embedding) gap between user specifications and the corresponding ones that are actually verified.

Keywords: Formal Specification and Verification · Machine Learning

1 Introduction

In recent years, the formal methods (FM) community has made significant progress, going from the very first neural network (NN) verifiers [28,33], suffering from scalability issues, to a wide range of tools capable of handling increasingly large NNs [4,24,29,31,35,40][1] and diverse machine learning (ML) models, like Support Vector Machines (SVM) [20,34] and boosted trees [3].

---

[1] For a comprehensive overview of the field, we refer readers to the survey in [38].

F. Damiani and M. Farrell (Eds.): iFM 2025, LNCS 16194, pp. 290–309, 2026.
https://doi.org/10.1007/978-3-032-10794-7_15

From this Cambrian explosion of tools, we draw the following observations:

A Focus on a Narrow Set of Properties. Research on the formal verification of ML models has largely concentrated on a restricted class of properties, most notably *local robustness*. Given an input x, a model f, and a perturbation bound $\epsilon \in \mathbb{R}$, local robustness is defined as the requirement that

$$\forall x'. \ \|x - x'\| \leq \epsilon \implies f(x) = f(x').$$

Several variants of this definition have been proposed [13], including *K-Lipschitz robustness* [5] and *strong classification robustness* [26]. The emphasis on local robustness is motivated by the nature of modern ML models, which frequently operate on high-dimensional inputs such as images or text. In such settings, formulating functional specifications is often impractical—if not impossible— whereas local robustness remains applicable and well-defined. While this has not prevented researchers from proposing higher-level specifications—including fairness constraints [37], semantic transformations robustness [6] or providing formally-grounded explanations [8,42]—we argue that the field remains primarily centered on robustness properties. As previously noted [19], there is an urgent need for more expressive specification languages that would enable the formal verification of a broader range of semantic properties of ML models.

Limitations on the Expressiveness of Input Languages. The current de-facto standard for specifying properties is the VNN-LIB language, adopted by the Verification of Neural Network Competition (VNN-Comp) [10–12]. As the VNN-LIB was originally designed to handle the community focus towards the specification and verification of *local robustness* properties of NNs, it exhibits certain limitations. First, the size of specification increases with the size of the NN, making it cumbersome for a human to write, and even more so to read and maintain. Second, VNN-LIB restricts specifications to conjunctions of linear arithmetic constraints over inputs and outputs, which are the only authorized free variables.

More formally, let $x \in \mathbb{R}^d$ be a vector and x_c its c-th element, $f : \mathbb{R}^d \mapsto \mathbb{R}^p$ be a function representing an NN that takes a d-dimensional vector as input and returns a p-dimensional vector, $\boldsymbol{K} \subseteq \{1, \ldots, p\}$ be a (possibly empty) set of integers, and $a, b \in \mathbb{R}^d$ and $c, d \in \mathbb{R}^p$ be vectors. A VNN-LIB specification is then equivalent to the following formula:

$$\forall x \in \mathbb{R}^d. \ \forall y \in \mathbb{R}^p. \ y = f(x) \implies$$

$$\bigwedge_{i=0..d} a_i \leq x_i \leq b_i \implies (\bigwedge_{j=0..p} c_j \leq y_j \leq d_j \wedge \bigwedge_{k \in \boldsymbol{K}} y_p \leq y_k),$$

which specifies that if the input is within a polyhedron defined by a and b, then the output should be within the polyhedron defined by c and d, and its p-th element should be lower than all others in $\boldsymbol{K}$.

Such a formulation prevents expressing properties on multiple NNs [2], hyperproperties [9,43], or any specification yielding uninterpreted functions. Promising high-level specification languages exist, notably the one in Vehicle [21], that need to be both expressive enough *and* compile down to a vast range of verifiers to take advantage of the profusion of existing tools.

Difficulty to Compare and Select a Verifier. A profusion of solutions implies the burden of choice. For now, this burden is mostly taken by the end-user of verification tools. Comparing the capabilities of tools is a first prerequisite to lift that burden. This need for comparison is partially addressed with the VNN-Comp, where tools are evaluated against benchmarks proposed by the community. However, as displayed in [30], this is but one of the numerous facets for evaluating the quality of verifiers. Indeed, depending on the property to check or the implementation specifics of a ML model, some verifiers may not be suitable, or underperform compared to others [30], making it difficult to assess the strengths and weaknesses of specific verifiers. It is thus necessary to provide a systematic and principled way to compare verifiers against the same basis.

A Gap Between the Specified and Proven Programs. Formal verification is a multifaceted activity that usually involve multiple steps: writing a specification, developing a program, encoding the specification into a suitable tool and ensuring the program is correct regarding the encoded specification.

A common struggle is to ensure that each step of the process is trustworthy and coherent one with another, that is to say, that the proof run on a particular program is meaningful with regard to a specification that was provided. One possible solution is to couple writing the specification *and* generating the code, like in the industrial software SCADE[2]. However, machine learning has its own peculiarities. For instance, it is common to apply transformations on the inputs of a neural network during the evaluation pipeline to normalize inputs regarding a certain training set distribution. Such transformations are not specified inside the NN, but done at runtime. Furthermore, most tools express specifications with real arithmetic, whereas NNs compute floating points numbers. VNN-LIB assumes that the companion program to verify is a NN, but without specifying anything towards it, or the transformations on inputs. This creates an *embedding gap* [19,22]: the specification the program is checked against follows an unspecified transformation. Ideally, a complete specification should be unambiguous on the transformations applied to an input.

In this paper, we present a way to lift these limitations within the open-source verification platform CAISAR [1]. We present and implement a higher-level specification language that allows users to express complex properties, including properties with multiple ML models. CAISAR proposes an automated and principled way to translate specifications written in a higher-level language to 9 verification tools—including the winners of the VNN-Comp. CAISAR is thus able to express properties and send them to existing off-the-shelf verification tools *without modifying them.* Its maturity allowed it to be used in industrial settings on non-public use-cases, although this paper focuses on illustrating the platform through simple examples (see Sect. 3).

---

[2] https://www.ansys.com/en-gb/products/embedded-software/ansys-scade-suite.

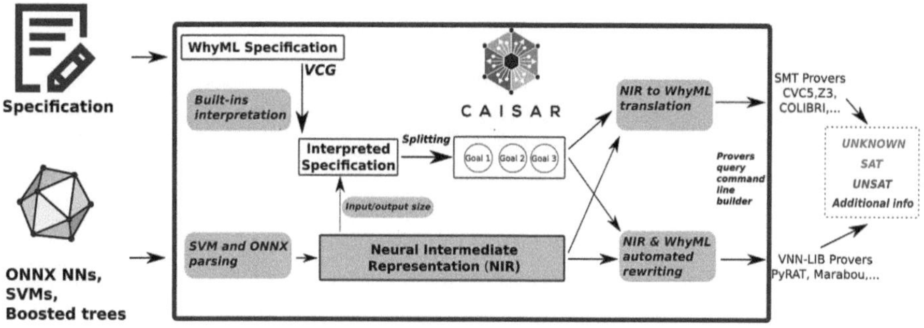

Fig. 1. The overall functional architecture of CAISAR. Significant extensions to the original Why3 platform are outlined in shaded rectangles.

Artifact Availability Statement. An artifact—including instructions, datasets, and experiment scripts—reproducing the results in this paper is publicly available at https://doi.org/10.5281/zenodo.16902886.

2   General Architecture and Core Components

The general architecture of CAISAR is depicted in Fig. 1. CAISAR builds upon the design of Why3 [25] and makes extensive use of the Why3 API. Why3 is a mature platform for deductive program verification, applied across a wide range of domains, from robotic navigation algorithms [36] to the formalization and verification of quantum programs [14]. It provides a rich input language for specifying, implementing, and formally verifying the correctness of algorithms. Verification proceeds by generating verification conditions, which are dispatched to a variety of automated and interactive provers via composable transformations. A dedicated verification condition generator (VCG) translates a program together with its specifications into logical goals. Finally, Why3 offers a unified text-based configuration mechanism for each supported solver.

CAISAR adapts those components to the specific needs of verification of ML models. To include ML into the specification and ease vector computation, we extend the Why3 input language with several *built-ins* as described in Sect. 2.1. To handle those extensions, we modify the internal Why3 interpretation engine as described in Sect. 2.3. To represent ML components in Why3, we build a Neural Intermediate Representation (NIR) described in Sect. 2.2; Sect. 3.2 describes how to translate SVMs to valid NIR representations. High-level specifications are currently not directly amenable for provers. In such cases, we translate part of the Why3 specification directly as a new NIR as explained in Sect. 2.3, using automated graph editing that incorporates part of Why3 terms within the NIR. Finally, a list of supported provers is presented in Sect. 2.3.

2.1 The Specification Language

CAISAR supports specifications written in WhyML[3], the specification and programming language of Why3. It exhibits three key qualities: it is *strongly typed* to prevent type errors, *expressive* to specify properties beyond local robustness, and *high-level* to bridge the embedding gap inherent of VNN-LIB (see Sect. 1). Specifically, WhyML enables writing properties of (multiple) ML models, treating them as *pure* (*i.e.* side-effect free), *abstract* functions that operate on vectors.

To support this abstraction, CAISAR extends the Why3 standard library with dedicated *theories*, such as the theory `Model` of ML models, and `Vector` of finite-length arrays. These theories define types, predicates and functions necessary to specify properties about ML models, vectors and their operations.

We present the grammar of the language in Fig. 2. A CAISAR specification is then a WhyML sequence of type, predicate and function definitions.

$$
\begin{array}{rcl}
\langle decl\rangle &::=& \textbf{type } \langle tId\rangle = \langle type\rangle \\
&\mid& \textbf{predicate } \langle id\rangle \\
& & \quad \langle binder\rangle^* = \langle expr\rangle \\
&\mid& \textbf{function } \langle id\rangle \\
& & \quad \langle binder\rangle^* \langle spec\rangle^* = \langle expr\rangle \\[4pt]
\langle type\rangle &::=& \langle tId\rangle \\
&\mid& \langle type\rangle \to \langle type\rangle \\
&\mid& (\langle type\rangle,\dots,\langle type\rangle) \\
&\mid& \texttt{vector } \langle type\rangle \\
&\mid& \texttt{int}\mid\texttt{bool}\mid\texttt{float}\mid\texttt{string} \\
&\mid& \texttt{model} \\[4pt]
\langle binder\rangle &::=& \langle id\rangle \mid (\langle id\rangle : \langle type\rangle) \\[4pt]
\langle spec\rangle &::=& \textbf{requires } \{\langle expr\rangle\} \\
&\mid& \textbf{ensures } \{\langle expr\rangle\} \\[4pt]
\langle bop\rangle &::=& \le \mid \ge \mid < \mid > \\
&\mid& + \mid - \mid \times \mid / \\
&\mid& \wedge \mid \vee \mid \to
\end{array}
$$

$$
\begin{array}{rcl}
\langle expr\rangle &::=& \langle id\rangle \\
&\mid& \langle built\text{-}in\rangle \\
&\mid& \langle expr\rangle\langle expr\rangle \\
&\mid& (\langle expr\rangle,\dots,\langle expr\rangle) \\
&\mid& \textbf{let } \langle id\rangle = \langle expr\rangle \textbf{ in} \\
&\mid& \textbf{if } \langle expr\rangle \textbf{ then } \langle expr\rangle \\
& & \textbf{else } \langle expr\rangle \\
&\mid& \langle expr\rangle\langle bop\rangle\langle expr\rangle \\
&\mid& \textbf{forall}\langle binder\rangle.\langle expr\rangle \\
&\mid& \textbf{exists}\langle binder\rangle.\langle expr\rangle \\
&\mid& \textbf{not}\langle expr\rangle \\
&\mid& \texttt{i} \in \textbf{Integer} \\
&\mid& \{\textbf{true},\textbf{false}\} \in \textbf{Boolean} \\
&\mid& \texttt{f} \in \textbf{Float} \mid \texttt{s} \in \textbf{String} \\[4pt]
\langle built\text{-}in\rangle &::=& \texttt{read\_model } \langle expr\rangle \\
&\mid& \texttt{length } \langle expr\rangle \\
&\mid& \texttt{has\_length } \langle expr\rangle\ \langle expr\rangle \\
&\mid& \langle expr\rangle[\langle expr\rangle] \\
&\mid& \langle expr\rangle\texttt{@@}\langle expr\rangle
\end{array}
$$

Fig. 2. Grammar of CAISAR's high-level specification language. The nonterminal $\langle built\text{-}in\rangle$ denotes WhyML functions having a special interpretation in CAISAR.

Examples of specifications are shown in Fig. 3 and Fig. 4. Fig. 3 shows a specification where the output of a first NN is perturbed and then passed as an input to a second NN, requiring the classification of the second NN to be a certain class. This example illustrates how to naturally express properties involving multiples NN, intermediate computations on inputs and outputs, and NN composition. On the other hand, property in Fig. 4 specifies that two NNs produce output vectors that differ by at most δ over their entire, valid input domain.

---

[3] https://www.why3.org/doc/syntaxref.html.

```
1    goal sequencing:
2      let nn1 = Model.read_model "path/to/nn1.onnx" in
3      let nn2 = Model.read_model "path/to/nn2.onnx" in
4      let dataset = Dataset.read_dataset "path/to/csv" in
5      let eps = (0.01:t) in
6      CSV.forall_ dataset (fun l e ->
7        forall perturbed_e.
8          has_length perturbed_e (length e) ->
9          FeatureVector.valid feature_bounds perturbed_e ->
10         let perturbation = perturbed_e - e in
11         ClassRobustVector.bounded_by_epsilon perturbation eps ->
12         let out_1 = nn_1@@perturbed_e in
13         let out_2 = nn_2@@out_1 in
14         forall j. Label.valid label_bounds j -> j != 1 ->
15         out_2[1] .>= out_2[j]
16       )
```

Fig. 3. CAISAR specification about the output prediction of a composition of NNs. The specification begins by declaring a verification goal named `sequencing`. Lines 2-4 introduce two NNs and the dataset by loading their **ONNX** model and CSV files, followed by line 5 which sets the perturbation ϵ of the first input to 0.01. Line 6 ensures the specification will be checked against all samples in the dataset. Lines 7-11 define a perturbed vector that has the same length of the original vector and have the same bounded values. Lines 12-13 describe the computation: the input of the first NN is perturbed, then the computation is performed, and the composition by the second NN takes place. Finally, line 14-15 assert that the prediction for the given output label is always the preferred one.

```
1    goal equality_up_to_delta:
2      let nn1 = Model.read_model "path/to/nn1.onnx" in
3      let nn2 = Model.read_model "path/to/nn2.onnx" in
4      let delta = (0.125:t) in
5      forall input. Vector.has_length input 5 ->
6        (forall i. 0 <= i < Vector.length input -> 0.0 .<= input[i] .<= 1.0) ->
7          let output1 = nn1 @@ input in
8          let output2 = nn2 @@ input in
9          .- delta .<= output1[0] .- output2[0] .<= delta
```

Fig. 4. CAISAR specification about the output equality up-to δ between two NNs. The specification begins by declaring a verification goal named `equality_up_to_delta`. Lines 2-3 introduce two NNs by loading their **ONNX** model files, followed by line 4 which sets the tolerance threshold δ to 0.125. Lines 5-6 constraint the input vector to be of length 5 with elements in $[0.0, 1.0]$. Lines 7-8 then apply both NNs to this input using the `@@` operator for model application. Finally, line 9 asserts that the absolute difference between the first output components of both networks is bounded by δ.

The *built-ins* currently have no explicit definition inside WhyML; rather their semantics is determined via interpretation, a process described in more detail in Sect. 2.3. For instance, the `Model` theory provides the built-ins `read_model` s, which introduces a model in a specification by reading the filename s, and m `@@` v, which returns a (output) vector obtained by applying model m to (input) vector v. Similarly, the `Vector` theory provides several built-ins such as, among others, `length` v to return the length of vector v, `has_length` v i to check whether vector v has length i, $v[i]$ to retrieve the element at position i of vector v, and `forall_` v f to verify that predicate f holds for every element of vector v.

2.2   The Neural Intermediate Representation

Preliminaries on ONNX. The Open Neural Network Exchange (ONNX) is an intermediate representation described via the *Protocol Buffer*[4] interface language. It is vastly supported within state-of-the-art machine learning frameworks like PyTorch or TensorFlow. ONNX describes a directed acyclic graph (DAG) whose nodes are operators describing computations on multidimensional arrays, called *tensors*, and edges describe the flow of data. An example of ONNX graph is available in Fig. 5.

At the time of writing, ONNX defines 193 operators[5]. Below, we provide an informal semantics for a subset of these operators used later in the paper:

- **Add**(x, y) (respectively, **Sub**, **Mul**, **Div**) performs element-wise addition (respectively, subtraction, multiplication, and division) of tensors x and y, which are assumed to have the same shape;
- **Concat**(x, y) appends tensor y to tensor x along a specified axis;
- **Gather**(x, y) selects values from tensor x at indices specified by tensor y, that is, **Gather**$(x, y) = x_{y_i}$;
- **Gemm**(x, y) performs matrix multiplication of tensors x and y, optionally followed by the addition of a bias term c;
- **Sign**(x) returns an integer tensor y such that $y_i = 1$ whenever $x_i > 0$, $y_i = -1$ whenever $x_i < 0$, and $y_i = 0$ otherwise;
- **ReLU**(x) applies to tensor x the rectified linear function $\max(0, x)$ element-wise;
- **Input** designates the entry point of the graph[6].

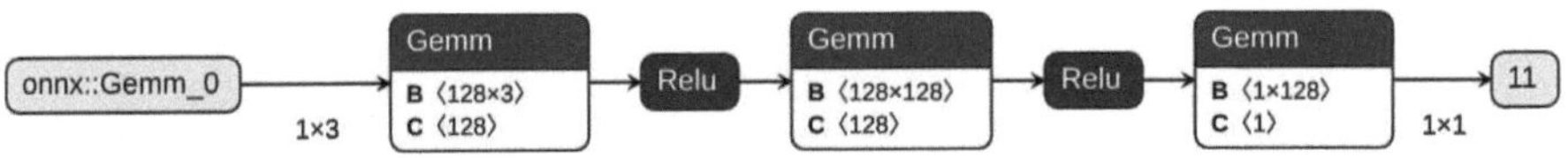

Fig. 5. Example of an ONNX graph, obtained using the netron tool. **Gemm** stands for GEneralized Matrix Multiplication, while **Relu** is the Rectified Linear Unit function.

Representing Machine Learning Components. CAISAR defines a Neural Intermediate Representation (NIR) to model machine learning components. Similar to ONNX, a NIR is a DAG, where each node encodes an operation, its input and output shapes, and the computation type. The NIR language supports a subset of the ONNX Intermediate Representation v8 and ONNX Opset v13 standards[7]. The full list of supported operators is available in the CAISAR source code.

---

[4] https://protobuf.dev/.

[5] https://github.com/onnx/onnx/blob/main/docs/Operators.md.

[6] In plain ONNX, the entry point is specified via graph metadata. We define an operator **Input** explicitly here for clarity.

[7] https://onnx.ai/onnx/operators/index.html.

CAISAR can parse various machine learning models into NIR, including neural networks in the ONNX and NNet formats, and support vector machines exported in a format compliant with the scikit-learn [39] framework. Gradient boosting machines are currently handled via a separate pipeline.

The NIR is implemented as a pure recursive OCaml variant type. Its signature is compatible with the ocamlgraph [17] library, enabling efficient graph traversal and transformation.

CAISAR also supports back-translation from NIR into multiple target formats. It can generate valid ONNX models, and leverages prior work [27] to compile control-flow representations of neural networks into the SMT-LIB (and its subset, VNN-LIB) format, enabling interoperability with a range of off-the-shelf solvers.

Automated Transformations of SVM to NIR. CAISAR is able to reason about Support Vector Machines (SVM) by translating them into equivalent NIR.

SVMs are classical ML models used for classification. Given an input vector x and assuming m classes, the model outputs a vector $y \in \mathbb{R}^m$ where each component y_{cl} is the *score* associated with the class $cl \in \{1, \dots, m\}$.

We first consider the binary case ($m = 2$). In this setting, training identifies a subset of the samples, called *support vectors*, that lie on or near the margin of separation between the two classes. Together with their learned coefficients, these vectors define a hyperplane that partitions the input space into two regions, one for class cl_1 and the other for class cl_2.[8]

Multiple support vectors can contribute to the separation of the two classes. Each class cl_j has a (possibly different) number k_j of support vectors, denoted $S_{cl_j,1}, \dots, S_{cl_j,k_j}$. Classification is based on the (signed) distance between the input x and each hyperplane defined by the support vectors, denoted $x \otimes S_{cl_j,\ell}$, indicating how *confidently* the corresponding support vector classifies the input.

An optional non-linear function f can be applied to these distances, which are then scaled by a scalar $c_{cl_j,\ell}$, called the *dual coefficient*. The resulting values are summed over all support vectors of the class, and a bias term i, called the *intercept*, is added. This leads to the following formula:

$$i + \sum_{\ell \in \{1, \dots, k_1\}} (c_{cl_1,\ell} * f(x \otimes S_{cl_1,\ell})) - \sum_{\ell \in \{1, \dots, k_2\}} (c_{cl_2,\ell} * f(x \otimes S_{cl_2,\ell})).$$

The input x is classified as belonging to class cl_1 if the sum is positive, and to class cl_2 if it is negative (the probability that it equals zero is negligible).

For SVMs with more than two classes, we adopt the one-versus-one (OVO) scheme. A binary classifier is trained for each pair of classes, using dual coefficients and intercepts specific to that pair. (The support vectors associated with each class remain the same, although some dual coefficients may be zero, effectively ignoring certain support vectors in a given comparison.) For each input,

---

[8] This geometric interpretation is valid for the linear case; for models using Radial Basis Function (RBF) kernels, the separation is non-linear, which we omit here for simplicity.

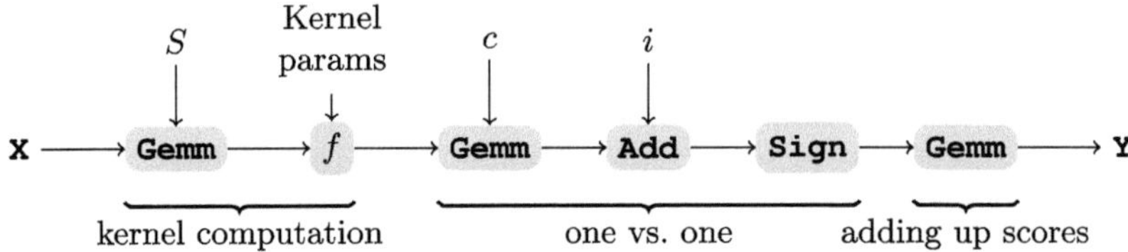

Fig. 6. NIR representation of an SVM.

the SVM counts how many times each class is selected in these pairwise comparisons. For instance, with 10 classes, the output is a vector of 10 integers, each between 0 and 9. It should be clear that ties—where two or more classes share the highest score—can occur, but are rare in the case of binary classification.

The translation of an SVM into a NIR is illustrated in Fig. 6. The first stage computes the *kernel*, which involves taking the product of the support vectors with the input, optionally followed by the non-linear function f. The second stage performs the one-versus-one comparisons: kernel values are multiplied by the dual coefficients, the intercept is added, and a positivity check determines the predicted class for each pair of classes. Finally, the last layer aggregates these pairwise scores to produce a final score for each class.

CAISAR currently supports Linear and Polynomial kernels, as well as Radial Basis Function (RBF) kernels.

2.3   The Verification Module

CAISAR leverages the Why3 architecture to generate verification conditions for its supported provers. A high-level WhyML specification first undergoes an interpretation phase, during which constants and computable expressions are evaluated and lifted to the top level. This is followed by a series of formula-wide transformations, handled by Why3's modular infrastructure. Prover-specific transformations may then be applied before translating the result into the input format of the target prover. Finally, Why3 coordinates the execution of provers and collects their results, presenting them back to the user.

The remainder of this section describes how this general workflow is adapted to ML programs.

Interpretation of Built-Ins. To convert a high-level WhyML specification into lower-level VNN-LIB conditions accepted by existing verifiers, CAISAR interprets the *built-ins* defined in Sect. 2.1 as follows:

- *Reading models and datasets.* The built-in function `read_model` is treated as a pure function that loads an ONNX model from a given file path. Note that we do not add I/O capabilities to Why3 as `read_model` only performs read-only access to the file system. Semantically, it is modeled as a mathematical function mapping valid ONNX file paths to their corresponding parsed models.

Similarly, `read_dataset` reads a labeled dataset from a CSV file and returns a vector of label-features pairs. Accessing this vector at a fixed index yields the corresponding data point.

- *Vector computation and access.* To manipulate vectors, `mapi` applies a user-defined function to each element of a vector whose size is statically known. The operator `@@` applies a ML model—obtained via `read_model`—to a vector of inputs and returns an output vector. Standard indexing `v[i]` retrieves the i-th element of the vector `v`.
- *Quantification.* Bounded quantifications over vectors are interpreted as quantifications over their individual elements, assuming the vector's size is fixed and known—either explicitly provided or inferred from hypotheses. The reduction engine in Why3 maintains symbolic representations of each vector element, enabling the interpretation of `mapi` and similar higher-order constructs.

Limitations. While interpretation enables the expression of rich specifications, some WhyML constructs remain outside its scope. Specifically, universal quantification over vectors is unsupported when the vector's shape cannot be determined statically. Since VNN-LIB is a fragment of the SMT-LIB theory of Quantifier-Free Linear Real Arithmetic (QF_LRA), quantifiers must be eliminated to generate valid verification conditions. In particular, formulas involving alternating quantifiers are not directly supported.

Embedding Specifications within Neural Networks

Illustrative Example. Let nn_1 and nn_2 be two NNs with one (resp. two) inputs and one output each. Consider the following WhyML expression:

$$nn_2@@(nn_1@@(x_1), x_1 + \epsilon) + nn_1@@(x_0)$$

In this expression, nn_1 is applied to both x_0 and x_1; the result of $nn_1@@(x_1)$ is used as the first input to nn_2, whose second input is $x_1 + \epsilon$. Let H be a valid QF_LRA formula defining bounds on x_1, x_2 and ϵ. Then, the formula

$$\forall x_0, x_1, \epsilon.\ H(x_0, x_1, \epsilon) \rightarrow \underbrace{nn_2@@(\overbrace{nn_1@@(x_1),\ \ \underbrace{x_1 + \epsilon}_{\text{operation on the input}}}^{\text{composition of nns}})}_{\text{multiple networks}} + nn_1@@(x_0) > 0 \tag{1}$$

illustrates several limitations of the VNN-LIB format discussed in Sect. 1:

1. It includes a nontrivial computation on the input, $x_1 + \epsilon$;
2. It composes multiple networks, nn_1 and nn_2;
3. It feeds the output of one network (nn_1) into another (nn_2).

These constructs are not directly supported by VNN-LIB, preventing the specification and verification of such formulas.

However, it is possible to lift these limitations by *embedding* part of the specification within a new neural network, say nn_3. The resulting formula becomes:

$$\forall x_0, x_1, \epsilon.\ H(x_0, x_1, \epsilon) \to nn_3@@(x_0, x_1, \epsilon) > 0 \tag{2}$$

Here, nn_3 encodes the entire computation: the arithmetic on inputs, the nested evaluation of networks, and the final comparison. A representation of the NIR corresponding to nn_3 is shown in Fig. 7. Embedding multiple networks within a single NIR allows specifications that involve their composition, while incorporating fragments of WhyML expressions into the NIR enables more expressive specifications that capture computations over both inputs and outputs.

The key insight is that *certain WhyML expressions can be encoded as ONNX operators*, effectively relocating parts of the specification into the neural network itself. This approach not only enables the expression of richer specifications that are otherwise inexpressible in VNN-LIB, but also leverages the fact that ONNX operators are more widely supported by state-of-the-art verifiers. Combined with the interpretation mechanism introduced in Sect. 2.3, this strategy significantly broadens the class of properties that can be formally specified and verified for machine learning programs.

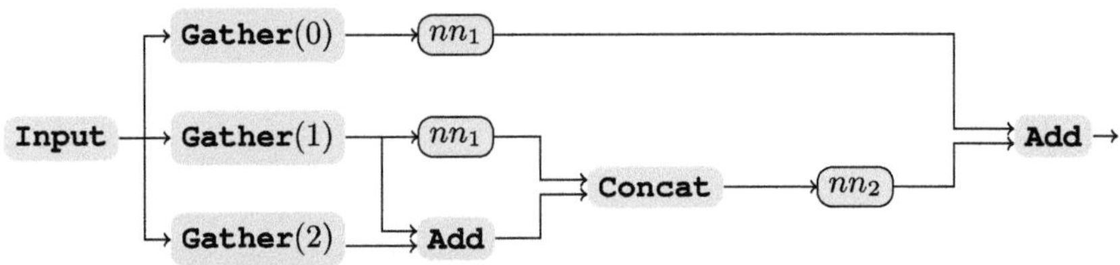

Fig. 7. **Gather** (0) (resp. **Gather** (1)) extracts x_0 (resp. x_1) and **Gather** (2) extracts ϵ from the **Input** node. The first **Add** node computes $x_1 + \epsilon$. Nodes nn_1 nn_2 represents inlined nn_1 and nn_2 control flows. Finally, **Concat** prepares the inputs of nn_2.

Integrating WhyML Terms into NIR. Given a WhyML formula $\phi(S, \mathcal{N}, P, Q)$, with $\mathcal{N}$ a non-empty set of NNs, S a set of universally quantified variables that represents both inputs and outputs of NNs, P a precondition and Q a postcondition, the goal is to write a new formula $\phi'(S', \mathcal{N}', P', Q')$, equivalent to ϕ, with $\mathcal{N}'$ consisting of a single NN.

To do so, we perform a structural analysis of ϕ, heavily relying on OCaml pattern-matching capabilities. First, WhyML terms t describing operations not supported by VNN-LIB are matched. Then, subterms t_is are selected top-down. If t_i can be translated into NIR nodes, then CAISAR generates a new NIR with the properly inserted nodes, removes the computation from the Why3 formula and replaces the proper symbols. A table representing the correspondance between WhyML terms and NIR operators is shown in Fig. 8.

$$[\![e_1 + e_2]\!]_M = \mathbf{Add}([\![e_1]\!]_M, [\![e_2]\!]_M)$$
$$[\![e_1 - e_2]\!]_M = \mathbf{Sub}([\![e_1]\!]_M, [\![e_2]\!]_M)$$
$$[\![e_1 * e_2]\!]_M = \mathbf{Mul}([\![e_1]\!]_M, [\![e_2]\!]_M)$$
$$[\![e_1/e_2]\!]_M = \mathbf{Div}([\![e_1]\!]_M, [\![e_2]\!]_M)$$
$$[\![-e_1]\!]_M = \mathbf{Mul}([\![-1.]\!]_M, [\![e_2]\!]_M)$$
$$[\![\langle id \rangle]\!]_M = \mathbf{Gather}(\mathbf{Input}, M(\langle id \rangle))$$
$$[\![nn@@(e_1, \ldots, e_n)[c]]\!]_M = \mathbf{Gather}(\mathtt{Apply}(nn, \mathbf{Concat}([\![e_1]\!]_M, \ldots, [\![e_n]\!]_M)), c)$$
$$\mathtt{Apply}(nn, g) = Parser(nn)[\mathbf{Input} \leftarrow g]$$

Fig. 8. Mapping between WhyML expressions and NIR nodes. All nodes are one-dimensional tensors. A transformation $[\![\cdot]\!]_M$ is parametrized by a mapping of input symbols $\langle id \rangle \in S$ towards NIR input indices. For NNs nn_1 and nn_2, $nn_1[\mathbf{Input} \leftarrow nn_2]$ builds a copy of nn_1 where the input g is replaced by nn_2.

Limitations. In principle, our approach applies to any WhyML expression that can be encoded as NIR nodes. For instance, ONNX includes an **If** operator for representing conditionals. However, such constructs are rarely supported by existing verifiers, often requiring formula splitting and thereby increasing the number of generated verification conditions. Consequently, we restrict ourselves to simple arithmetic operations expressible within the QF_LRA fragment.

Moreover, the translation of WhyML formulas relies on a flattened representation of the inputs, requiring the insertion of multiple one-dimensional NIR nodes. Since NN verifiers are typically optimized for high-dimensional tensor computations, this flattening introduces overhead, as empirically evaluated in Sect. 3.1.

More broadly, the question of how much of the specification should be embedded within the neural network itself remains open. There is an inherent trade-off between, on the one hand, the expressiveness and conciseness afforded to the user, and on the other hand, the tractability of the resulting verification conditions.

Provers. CAISAR supports the following ML-specific verification tools: α-β-CROWN [40], PyRAT [31], Marabou [29,41], nnenum [4], AIMOS [32], SAVer [34]. Thanks to the Why3 platform and the NIR, it supports translating specifications into the SMT-LIB format, compliant with CVC5 [7], Z3 [23] and Alt-Ergo [16] provers. It also supports gradient-boosted trees generated with the XGBoost library [15]. Each prover is automatically detected by CAISAR if installed. An experimental distribution of CAISAR using the Nix declarative package manager bundles CAISAR, Marabou and Python-based provers. By default, CAISAR brings an appropriate configuration for each prover. It is possible for the user to define alternative prover configurations in the `caisar-detection-data.conf` file. The user only needs to specify the desired command-line options in this file, a name for the custom configuration, and run CAISAR by specifying said name.

3 Use Cases and Evaluation

CAISAR provides a publicly available manual[9], including classical examples from the ACAS Xu benchmark and local robustness on MNIST. It was also used in industrial contexts [18], for instance in the DeepGreen[10] project and Confiance.ai[11] program. In the following, we also illustrate CAISAR capabilities to specify properties beyond local robustness properties.

3.1 Formal Verification of **ACAS Xu** with Unnormalized Inputs

We consider the classical ACAS Xu benchmarks, originally presented in [28] with a subtle, but important difference. The original paper presents the benchmark with unnormalized values. For instance, property ϕ_1 is written as follows:

$$\mathcal{P}(x) = x[\rho] \geq 55947.691 \;\wedge\; x[vown] \geq 1145 \;\wedge\; x[vint] \leq 60$$
$$\implies \mathcal{Q}(y) = y[coc] < 1500$$

However, the actual property specifications encoded in Marabou exhibit normalized values[12]. As neural networks require normalized inputs, this is expected; however it creates a gap between the specification expressed in terms of expert-domain knowledge and the actual values checked during verification. This *embedding gap* was identified as a major obstacle [19] to actionable formal specification.

Fortunately, specifying the normalization process inside the WhyML specification will produce an ONNX file *that normalizes its input according to the specification*. The network will then compute normalized results, which can then be returned to the original output space. As long as the normalization and denormalization processes are well-specified, the specification can be expressed on the original input and output. Fig. 9 provides a WhyML excerpt of such specification.

In Table 1, we report runtimes on the original (normalized) ACAS Xu properties as well as their unnormalized counterparts. For PyRAT, our graph-editing technique preserves the verification outcome for all properties. However, the additional overhead is significant enough to cause many timeouts within the allocated runtime budget. For nnenum, results remain consistent except for occasional crashes, which stem from a known bug in its ONNX parsing module. By contrast, maraboupy, the Python wrapper of Marabou, exhibits incorrect behavior: it reports counterexamples for properties ϕ_4, ϕ_5, and ϕ_9, where none should exist according to the original specification. Even more concerning, maraboupy finds a counterexample for the normalized version of ϕ_{10}, in direct contradiction with Marabou itself, which correctly verifies the property. During our experiments, maraboupy raised degradation warnings about floating-point arithmetic on ϕ_{10}, which may explain this discrepancy. In particular, CAISAR outputs specifications using IEEE 754 double-precision floating-point arithmetic, whereas

---

[9] https://caisar-platform.com/documentation.
[10] https://deepgreen.ai.
[11] https://confiance.ai.
[12] Values available on the Marabou GitHub repository.

```
1    let function normalize_t i mean range = (i .- mean) ./ range
2    let function denormalize_t i mean range = (i .* range) .+ mean
3    let function normalize_input i = Vector.mapi i normalize_by_index
4
5    let function denormalize_output_t o =
6      denormalize_t o
7        (7.5188840201005975316661533724982291460037231445312 5:t)
8        (373.9499200000000200816430151462554931640625:t)
9
10   let runP1 (i: input) : t
11     requires { has_length i 5 ∧ valid_input i }
12     requires { intruder_distant_and_slow i }
13     ensures { result .≤ (1500.0:t) }  =
14       let j = normalize_input i in
15       let o = (nn @@ j)[clear_of_conflict] in
16       (denormalize_output_t o)
```

Fig. 9. A WhyML specification for the unnormalized ACAS Xu ϕ_1 property.

the ACAS Xu networks—and the instances generated from them—operate exclusively in single precision. Further investigation revealed an inconsistency between the plain Marabou solver, which supports only a limited set of ONNX operators, and its maraboupy, which supports a broader set. This issue was reported to the Marabou developers[13].

Nevertheless, this example displays how CAISAR allows users to compare multiple provers on the same specification; further helping to build a case on the correctness of a program.

3.2 On the Correctness of SVM Parsing

In the context of one-versus-one (OVO) classification, consider an SVM f, a point $x \in \mathbb{R}^d$, a class $cl \in \mathbb{N}$, and a perturbation bound $\epsilon \in \mathbb{R}$. The *local robustness* property requires that for all $x' \in \mathbb{R}^d$ such that $\|x - x'\| \leq \epsilon$, the class maximizing the output of f remains cl.

For evaluation, we considered the model `linear-1k` from the MNIST domain provided by the developers of SAVer[14] with the associated dataset[15]. We provided the robustness property to CAISAR using the translation from SVM to NIR described in Sect. 2.2, and used PyRAT as verifier. We then compared the results with those produced by SAVer.

The results are presented in Table 2. The answers produced by CAISAR are consistent with those of SAVer, but obtained at a runtime approximately two orders of magnitude higher, independently of whether the robustness property holds. It should be noted, however, that SAVer was designed specifically for the verification of robustness properties and cannot be applied to other classes of properties. In addition, SAVer no longer appears to be under active development, casting doubts on its long-term usability. By contrast, CAISAR is designed as

---

[13] https://github.com/NeuralNetworkVerification/Marabou/issues/882.

[14] The model is available at https://github.com/abstract-machine-learning/data-collection/tree/master/domains/mnist/models/svm/linear-1k.dat.zip.

[15] The dataset is available at https://github.com/abstract-machine-learning/data-collection/blob/master/domains/mnist/datasets/test-set.csv.zip.

Table 1. ACAS Xu benchmarks on selected verifiers, averaged over three runs. The string next to the property indicates the Reluplex [28] neural network it was verified against. Columns T_n (resp. T_u) report the time (in seconds) required by verifiers to answer on the original (resp. the unnormalized) queries, while columns A_n (resp. A_u) report the actual answers on the original (resp. the unnormalized) queries. A ✓ indicates that a property is satisfied, a ✗ that a counterexample has been found, a ⏱ that a timeout is reached, and a ? that a runtime crash occurred. Failures of Marabou are expected on unnormalized properties, as the **Concat** operator, mandatory for our approach, is not supported.

Property	Marabou				maraboupy				PyRAT				nnenum			
	T_n	A_n	T_u	A_u	T_n	A_n	T_u	A_u	T_n	A_n	T_u	A_u	T_n	A_n	T_u	A_u
ϕ_1	3.00	(?)	3.00	(?)	5.00	(✓)	243.00	(⏱)	8.00	(✓)	11.00	(✓)	4.00	(✓)	4.00	(✓)
ϕ_2	37.00	(✓)	3.00	(?)	26.00	(✓)	243.00	(⏱)	19.00	(✓)	38.00	(✓)	4.00	(✓)	6.00	(?)
ϕ_3	243.00	(⏱)	5.00	(?)	243.00	(⏱)	243.00	(⏱)	246.00	(⏱)	246.00	(⏱)	4.00	(✓)	4.00	(✓)
ϕ_4	44.00	(✓)	5.00	(?)	36.00	(✓)	4.00	(✗)	25.00	(✓)	246.00	(⏱)	4.00	(✓)	4.00	(✓)
ϕ_5	102.00	(✓)	5.00	(?)	93.00	(✓)	5.00	(✗)	246.00	(⏱)	246.00	(⏱)	4.00	(✓)	5.00	(✓)
ϕ_6	558.00	(✓)	5.00	(?)	566.00	(✓)	1925.00	(⏱)	156.00	(✓)	426.00	(⏱)	7.00	(✓)	13.00	(?)
ϕ_7	485.00	(⏱)	5.00	(?)	484.00	(⏱)	484.00	(⏱)	246.00	(⏱)	246.00	(⏱)	119.00	(✗)	4.00	(?)
ϕ_8	485.00	(✗)	5.00	(?)	8.00	(✗)	248.00	(⏱)	246.00	(⏱)	246.00	(⏱)	4.00	(✗)	4.00	(✗)
ϕ_9	182.00	(✓)	5.00	(?)	222.00	(✓)	5.00	(✗)	61.00	(✓)	246.00	(⏱)	6.00	(✓)	9.00	(✓)
ϕ_{10}	83.00	(✓)	3.00	(?)	151.00	(✗)	245.00	(✗)	13.00	(✓)	246.00	(⏱)	4.00	(✓)	5.00	(✓)

a general specification and verification framework, and ongoing work aims to improve its performance on this class of problems.

3.3   Composition of Neural Networks

We evaluated CAISAR on two illustrative specifications concerning multiple NNs: a property about the output of the sequential composition of two NNs (Fig. 3) and the comparison of outputs between two NNs (Fig. 4). Both serve as representative examples of practical verification tasks, such as quantifying the effect of quantization or ensuring correctness of composed models.

Table 2. Runtime comparison between SAVer and CAISAR. *Valid* indicates that robustness holds for the instance. The two solvers agree on the result.

Instance	Result	SAVer (ms)	PyRAT via CAISAR (ms)
0	Valid	35	19,101
1	Invalid	49	20,740
2	Valid	53	18,552
3	Valid	41	22,001
4	Valid	45	20,464
5	Valid	47	19,300
6	Valid	43	20,546
7	Valid	48	19,802
8	Invalid	43	20,111
9	Valid	42	20,957

Table 3. Verification results of the sequential composition property of Fig. 3.

Prover	Result
maraboupy	Invalid
nnenum	Timeout
PyRAT	Timeout

For the first specification (see Fig. 3), which involves sequential composition of NNs, we evaluated CAISAR with maraboupy, nnenum and PyRAT as verifiers. Within a runtime budget of one hour, maraboupy could not prove the property (most likely by finding a counterexample), while both nnenum and PyRAT timed out (see Table 3). It is worth noting that Marabou cannot be used as a backend prover for this property, since it does not support all ONNX operators required to encode the sequential combination of the two networks.

For the second specification (see Fig. 4), the results are not revealing, as all provers ultimately reach timeouts without producing a conclusive answer.

Overall, these experiments demonstrate that CAISAR can express non-trivial properties beyond local robustness, dispatching their verification to multiple backend tools, though performance and conclusiveness remain highly dependent on the underlying prover.

4   Conclusion

Historically, the formal verification of human-written software evolved from tools able to verify simple properties to large-scale platforms (*e.g.* Why3) capable of handling higher-level properties, decomposing them into smaller properties, and dispatching them to back-end solvers and analyzers. The AI field, and in particular ML, already advanced to the first stage of such evolution. We present the extensible, open-source CAISAR platform, that aims to embody the next stage of that similar evolution, with emphasis on an expressive language where higher-level properties can be described, as well as the compilation of these properties into inputs that existing solvers can handle. We also expanded the range of what is possible to specify with the clear goal of encouraging the community to target such specifications in the next versions of their solvers. The authors are keen for any request for collaboration or special needs, such as handling particular model architectures or properties.

Of particular interest is the integration of confidence-based properties, as well as expanding the set of supported tools. We are also actively developing heuristics to inform the validation process, particularly through past accumulated knowledge of successful runs (*e.g.* on use-cases involving X type of properties on Y type of model with Z activation functions, provers A gave the best results with configuration C, therefore a suggested strategy is to start with A on use-cases with similar characteristics to X, Y and Z). An ongoing collaboration is focused on bridging the validation process with requirement-based engineering.

CAISAR is made available online, with clear documentation as well as tutorials that can be used in teaching classes to infuse the paramount importance of safety in the minds of future generations of ML developers. CAISAR's existence goes beyond this sole publication: it has the durable support of CEA-List and a dedicated developing team, giving the platform the stable future necessary for long-term support.

Acknowledgements. This work was partially supported by the SAIF project (ANR-23-PEIA-0006) and the DeepGreen project (ANR-23-DEGR-0001) funded by the "France 2030" government investment plan managed by the French National Research Agency (ANR).

The authors thank Serge Durand for his help with Marabou and PyRAT, and Augustin Lemesle and Julien Lehmann for fruitful discussions.

References

1. Alberti, M., Bobot, F., Chihani, Z., Girard-Satabin, J., Lemesle, A.: CAISAR: a platform for characterizing artificial intelligence safety and robustness. In: AISafety. CEUR-Workshop Proceedings, Vienne, Austria (2022). https://hal.archives-ouvertes.fr/hal-03687211

2. Athavale, A., Bartocci, E., Christakis, M., Maffei, M., Nickovic, D., Weissenbacher, G.: Verifying global two-safety properties in neural networks with confidence. In: Gurfinkel, A., Ganesh, V. (eds.) Computer Aided Verification, pp. 329–351. Springer Nature Switzerland, Cham (Jun 2024). https://doi.org/10.48550/arXiv.2405.14400, http://arxiv.org/abs/2405.14400, zSCC: 0000000 arXiv:2405.14400 [cs] type: article

3. Audemard, G., Lagniez, J.M., Marquis, P.: On the computation of contrastive explanations for boosted regression trees. IOS Press (2024). https://doi.org/10.3233/faia240600

4. Bak, S.: nnenum: verification of ReLU neural networks with optimized abstraction refinement. In: Dutle, A., Moscato, M.M., Titolo, L., Muñoz, C.A., Perez, I. (eds.) NASA Formal Methods, pp. 19–36. Lecture Notes in Computer Science, Springer International Publishing, Cham (2021). https://doi.org/10.1007/978-3-030-76384-8_2

5. Balan, R., Singh, M., Zou, D.: Lipschitz properties for deep convolutional networks (2017). https://doi.org/10.48550/ARXIV.1701.05217

6. Balunovic, M., Baader, M., Singh, G., Gehr, T., Vechev, M.: Certifying geometric robustness of neural networks. In: Advances in Neural Information Processing Systems. vol. 32. Curran Associates, Inc. (2019). https://papers.nips.cc/paper/2019/hash/f7fa6aca028e7ff4ef62d75ed025fe76-Abstract.html

7. Barbosa, H., et al.: cvc5: a versatile and industrial-strength SMT solver. In: Fisman, D., Rosu, G. (eds.) Tools and Algorithms for the Construction and Analysis of Systems - 28th International Conference, TACAS 2022, Held as Part of the European Joint Conferences on Theory and Practice of Software, ETAPS 2022, Munich, Germany, April 2-7, 2022, Proceedings, Part I. Lecture Notes in Computer Science, vol. 13243, pp. 415–442. Springer (2022). https://doi.org/10.1007/978-3-030-99524-9_24

8. Bassan, S., Katz, G.: Towards Formal XAI: Formally Approximate Minimal Explanations of Neural Networks, pp. 187–207. Springer Nature Switzerland (2023). https://doi.org/10.1007/978-3-031-30823-9_10

9. Boetius, D., Leue, S.: Verifying global neural network specifications using hyperproperties (2023)

10. Brix, C., Bak, S., Johnson, T.T., Wu, H.: The fifth international verification of neural networks competition (VNN-COMP 2024): Summary and results (2024). https://doi.org/10.48550/ARXIV.2412.19985, https://arxiv.org/abs/2412.19985

11. Brix, C., Bak, S., Liu, C., Johnson, T.T.: The fourth international verification of neural networks competition (VNN-COMP 2023): Summary and results (2023)

12. Brix, C., Müller, M.N., Bak, S., Johnson, T.T., Liu, C.: First three years of the international verification of neural networks competition (VNN-COMP) (2023)

13. Casadio, M., et al.: Neural network robustness as a verification property: a principled case study. In: International Conference on Computer Aided Verification, pp. 219–231. Springer (2022)

14. Chareton, C., Bardin, S., Bobot, F., Perrelle, V., Valiron, B.: An Automated Deductive Verification Framework for Circuit-building Quantum Programs, pp. 148–177. Springer International Publishing (2021). https://doi.org/10.1007/978-3-030-72019-3_6

15. Chen, T., Guestrin, C.: XGBoost: a scalable tree boosting system. In: Proceedings of the 22nd ACM SIGKDD International Conference on Knowledge Discovery and Data Mining, pp. 785–794. KDD '16, ACM, New York, NY, USA (2016). https://doi.org/10.1145/2939672.2939785

16. Conchon, S., Coquereau, A., Iguernlala, M., Mebsout, A.: Alt-Ergo 2.2. In: SMT Workshop: International Workshop on Satisfiability Modulo Theories. Oxford, United Kingdom (2018). https://hal.inria.fr/hal-01960203

17. Conchon, S., Filliâtre, J.C., Signoles, J.: Designing a generic graph library using ML functors. In: Morazán, M.T., Nilsson, H. (eds.) The Eighth Symposium on Trends in Functional Programming. vol. TR-SHU-CS-2007-04-1, pp. XII/1–13. Seton Hall University, New York, USA (2007). https://usr.lmf.cnrs.fr/~jcf/publis/ocamlgraph-tfp07.ps

18. "Confiance.ai": "methodological guideline for assessing the trustworthiness of models of artificial intelligence with caisar" (2024). https://catalog.confiance.ai/records/wqm9q-cnv75

19. Cordeiro, L.C., et al.: Neural network verification is a programming language challenge (2025). https://doi.org/10.48550/ARXIV.2501.05867

20. Cristianini, N., Ricci, E.: Support Vector Machines, pp. 928–932. Springer US, Boston, MA (2008). https://doi.org/10.1007/978-0-387-30162-4_415

21. Daggitt, M.L., Kokke, W., Atkey, R., Arnaboldi, L., Komendantskya, E.: Vehicle: Interfacing neural network verifiers with interactive theorem provers (2022). https://doi.org/10.48550/ARXIV.2202.05207

22. Daggitt, M.L., Kokke, W., Atkey, R., Slusarz, N., Arnaboldi, L., Komendantskaya, E.: Vehicle: Bridging the embedding gap in the verification of neuro-symbolic programs (2024). https://doi.org/10.48550/ARXIV.2401.06379

23. de Moura, L., Bjørner, N.: Z3: an efficient SMT solver. In: Ramakrishnan, C.R., Rehof, J. (eds.) Tools and Algorithms for the Construction and Analysis of Systems, pp. 337–340. Lecture Notes in Computer Science, Springer, Berlin, Heidelberg (2008). https://doi.org/10.1007/978-3-540-78800-3_24

24. Durand, S., Lemesle, A., Chihani, Z., Urban, C., Terrier, F.: ReCIPH: relational coefficients for input partitioning heuristic. WFVML 2022 (2022). https://inria.hal.science/hal-03926281, poster

25. Filliâtre, J.C., Paskevich, A.: Why3 - where programs meet provers. In: Felleisen, M., Gardner, P. (eds.) Programming Languages and Systems, pp. 125–128. Lecture Notes in Computer Science, Springer, Berlin, Heidelberg (2013). https://doi.org/10.1007/978-3-642-37036-6_8
26. Fischer, M., Balunovic, M., Drachsler-Cohen, D., Gehr, T., Zhang, C., Vechev, M.: DL2: training and querying neural networks with logic. In: Chaudhuri, K., Salakhutdinov, R. (eds.) Proceedings of the 36th International Conference on Machine Learning. Proceedings of Machine Learning Research, vol. 97, pp. 1931–1941. PMLR (2019). https://proceedings.mlr.press/v97/fischer19a.html
27. Girard-Satabin, J., Charpiat, G., Chihani, Z., Schoenauer, M.: CAMUS: a framework to build formal specifications for deep perception systems using simulators. In: ECAI 2020 - 24th European Conference on Artificial Intelligence. Santiago de Compostela, Spain (2020). https://hal.inria.fr/hal-02440520
28. Katz, G., Barrett, C., Dill, D.L., Julian, K., Kochenderfer, M.J.: Reluplex: An Efficient SMT Solver for Verifying Deep Neural Networks, pp. 97–117. Springer International Publishing (2017). https://doi.org/10.1007/978-3-319-63387-9_5
29. Katz, G., et al.: The marabou framework for verification and analysis of deep neural networks. In: Dillig, I., Tasiran, S. (eds.) Computer Aided Verification, vol. 11561, pp. 443–452. Springer International Publishing, Cham (2019). https://doi.org/10.1007/978-3-030-25540-4_26
30. König, M., Bosman, A.W., Hoos, H.H., van Rijn, J.N.: Critically assessing the state of the art in neural network verification. J. Mach. Learn. Res. **25**(12), 1–53 (2024). http://jmlr.org/papers/v25/23-0119.html
31. Lemesle, A., Lehmann, J., Gall, T.L.: Neural network verification with PyRAT (2024). https://doi.org/10.48550/ARXIV.2410.23903
32. Lemesle, A., Varasse, A., Chihani, Z., Tachet, D.: AIMOS: Metamorphic Testing of AI - An Industrial Application. WAISE 2023 (2023)
33. Pulina, L., Tacchella, A.: NeVer: a tool for artificial neural networks verification. Ann. Math. Artif. Intell. **62**(3–4), 403–425 (2011). https://doi.org/10.1007/s10472-011-9243-0
34. Ranzato, F., Zanella, M.: Robustness verification of support vector machines. In: Chang, B.Y.E. (ed.) Static Analysis, pp. 271–295. Springer International Publishing, Cham (2019)
35. Singh, G., Ganvir, R., Püschel, M., Vechev, M.: Beyond the single neuron convex barrier for neural network certification. In: Wallach, H., Larochelle, H., Beygelzimer, A., Alché-Buc, F.d., Fox, E., Garnett, R. (eds.) Advances in Neural Information Processing Systems 32, pp. 15098–15109. Curran Associates, Inc. (2019). http://papers.nips.cc/paper/9646-beyond-the-single-neuron-convex-barrier-for-neural-network-certification.pdf
36. Trojanek, P., Eder, K.: Verification and testing of mobile robot navigation algorithms: a case study in spark. In: 2014 IEEE/RSJ International Conference on Intelligent Robots and Systems, pp. 1489–1494. IEEE (2014). https://doi.org/10.1109/iros.2014.6942753
37. Urban, C., Christakis, M., Wüstholz, V., Zhang, F.: Perfectly Parallel Fairness Certification of Neural Networks. arXiv:1912.02499 [cs] (2019)
38. Urban, C., Miné, A.: A Review of Formal Methods applied to Machine Learning. arXiv:2104.02466 [cs] (2021)
39. van der Walt, S., et al.: scikit-image: image processing in Python. PeerJ **2**, e453 (2014). https://doi.org/10.7717/peerj.453

40. Wang, S., et al.: Beta-CROWN: Efficient Bound Propagation with Per-neuron Split Constraints for Complete and Incomplete Neural Network Robustness Verification. http://arxiv.org/abs/2103.06624
41. Wu, H., et al.: Marabou 2.0: A versatile formal analyzer of neural networks (2024). https://doi.org/10.48550/ARXIV.2401.14461
42. Wu, M., Wu, H., Barrett, C.: VeriX: Towards verified explainability of deep neural networks (2023)
43. Xie, X., Kersting, K., Neider, D.: Neuro-symbolic verification of deep neural networks. In: Raedt, L.D. (ed.) Proceedings of the Thirty-First International Joint Conference on Artificial Intelligence, IJCAI-22, pp. 3622–3628. International Joint Conferences on Artificial Intelligence Organization (2022). https://doi.org/10.24963/ijcai.2022/503, main Track

Security and Blockchain

Security of the Lightning Network: Model Checking a Stepwise Refinement with TLA$^+$

Matthias Grundmann$^{(\boxtimes)}$ and Hannes Hartenstein

KASTEL Security Research Labs, Karlsruhe Institute of Technology, Karlsruhe, Germany
{matthias.grundmann,hannes.hartenstein}@kit.edu

Abstract. Payment channel networks such as the Lightning Network are an approach to improve the scalability of blockchain-based cryptocurrencies. The complexity of Lightning, the Lightning Network's protocol, makes it hard to assess whether the protocol is secure. To enable computer-aided security verification of Lightning, we formalize the protocol in TLA$^+$ and formally specify the security property that honest users are guaranteed to retrieve their correct balance. Model checking provides a fully automated verification of the security property, however, the state space of the protocol's specification is so large that model checking is unfeasible. We make model checking of Lightning possible using two refinement steps that we verify using proofs. In a first step, we abstract the model of time and in a second step we use compositional reasoning to separately model check a single payment channel and multi-hop payments. These refinements reduce the state space sufficiently to allow for model checking Lightning with small finite models. Our results indicate that the current specification of Lightning is secure.

Keywords: Model checking · Compositional verification · TLA$^+$ · Payment Channel · Temporal logic · Real-time systems · Bitcoin · Security

1 Introduction

Blockchain-based cryptocurrencies do not scale well with respect to their transaction throughput. One approach to improve said scalability are Payment Channel Networks – a second layer on top of a blockchain that processes payments without writing a transaction for each payment to the blockchain. A *payment channel* between two users is opened by publishing one transaction on the underlying blockchain. Once a payment channel is open, it allows for performing an unlimited number of payments between its two users. Finally, a payment channel is closed by publishing a second transaction. In a payment channel *network*, the participating users are connected by payment channels and can perform multi-hop payments using a path between a payment's sender and recipient over a set of payment channels. The Lightning Network [47] is a payment channel network built on top of Bitcoin [44]. It is being used and experiences a rising adoption [5].

F. Damiani and M. Farrell (Eds.): iFM 2025, LNCS 16194, pp. 313–335, 2026.
https://doi.org/10.1007/978-3-032-10794-7_16

Our goal is to verify that Lightning, the Lightning Network's protocol, is secure, i.e., an honest user finally retrieves on the blockchain the user's correct balance in the payment channel even if other users do not cooperate or are actively malicious. Lightning disincentivizes malicious behavior using a mechanism that allows honest parties to detect and punish malicious behavior. The punishment mechanism as well as Lightning's reliance on time and the number of involved parties make it difficult to assess whether Lightning actually fulfills the security property. Such an assessment might be facilitated by computer-aided methods. In particular, model checking can automatically verify that a protocol fulfills a property and provide a counterexample if the checked property does not hold. Lightning is defined by an official specification [62] that describes all aspects of the protocol and partially the intuition behind the protocol. The specification is not directly usable for a security analysis because the specification contains many implementation details and is not formalized. To enable the use of model checking for Lightning, we contribute a *specification of Lightning* in the formal language TLA^+ [33,34] that formalizes all protocol steps and messages that users send during opening, updating, and closing a payment channel as well as for multi-hop payments. We also contribute a *specification of the security property* of a payment channel network by defining a secure payment system in TLA^+. Our security model allows parties to become adversarial. Adversarial parties may omit sending messages or publishing transactions required by the protocol and may publish additional transactions not specified by the protocol.

However, the state space of the specification of Lightning with a model of time and multiple users is so large that model checking is unfeasible. We make model checking of Lightning possible using a stepwise refinement (see Fig. 1). We verify general abstractions with hand-written proofs and use model checking to verify the actual Lightning protocol. We prove that the model of time used in the protocol can be abstracted (①&③) using ideas from the research of timed automata [3]. This proof generalizes to other explicit real-time specifications in TLA^+. In a second step, we prove that it suffices to model check the protocol for single payment channels ②a and the protocol for multi-hop payments ④ separately. These refinements reduce the state space sufficiently to allow for model checking Lightning with the model checker TLC [64]. We use TLC to fully explore the state space of models with payments over up to four hops and with two concurrent payments. To check also larger models as well as the whole stepwise refinement, we use simulation which is a lightweight alternative to model checking where only some random behaviors are explored as opposed to checking the complete state space. While our approach does not give comprehensive formal correctness guarantees, it gives confidence that the specification of Lightning is secure. We leave verifying all refinements with a theorem prover for future work.

We describe Lightning in more detail and give an introduction to TLA^+ in Sect. 2. Related work follows in Sect. 3. Our approaches for the specification of Lightning and for the specification of the security property are presented in Sect. 4 and Sect. 5. In Sect. 6, we explain our approach for verifying that Lightning fulfills the security property and sketch the ideas behind each abstraction step. We present the results of model checking in Sect. 7 and discuss limitations of our approach and ideas for future work in Sect. 8.

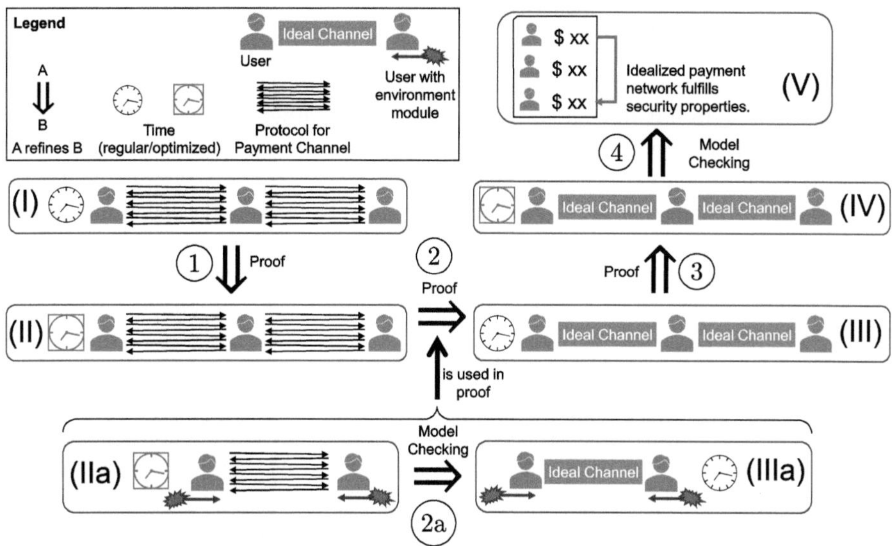

Fig. 1. Structure of the stepwise refinement to show that the Lightning protocol (I) (see Sect. 4) implements the security property (V) (see Sect. 5). In ① & ③, we prove that time can be modeled more efficiently. We model check individual payment channels in ②a and interaction of channels in ④. The environment module in spec. (IIa) models the interaction with other channels, ensuring that a channel in spec. (IIa) can be composed with other channels in spec. (II).

2 Fundamentals

In this section, we briefly introduce Lightning and TLA$^+$. For a more detailed introduction, we refer to the extended version of this paper [22].

2.1 Lightning Payment Channel Network

We aim to give an overview of the main ideas of Lightning that contribute to the protocol's complexity. A payment channel is opened by publishing a funding transaction on the blockchain that defines the initial distribution of funds between the two parties. For each payment being made, the two parties agree on a new distribution of funds. Lightning ensures that a user can close a payment channel independently of the other party by asserting that a user always has a valid closing transaction that could be published on the blockchain and distributes the funds according to the latest distribution of funds. After each payment, previously valid closing transactions become outdated but these transactions could still be published on the blockchain. To disincentivize a dishonest user Alice from publishing an outdated closing transaction, the other user, Bob, receives revocation secrets when the closing transaction is outdated. These revocation secrets enable Bob to punish Alice by retrieving not only his assets but also the assets of Alice, if Alice were to publish an outdated closing transaction.

If two users do not have a common payment channel but they are connected over a path of payment channels of other users, they can make multi-hop payments between each other. Intermediate users forward the payment over their channels and receive a small fee for their service. To prevent intermediaries from stealing or losing coins, it must be guaranteed that each intermediary receives an incoming payment on one channel if and only if the intermediary forwards the payment on another channel. Lightning uses Hash Timelocked Contracts (HTLCs) to achieve this atomicity. An HTLC is a contract that encodes the agreement that the recipient receives a specified amount if the recipient proves knowledge of a preimage to a specified hash before a specified time has passed. The recipient of a payment draws a random value x, calculates the hash value $y = H(x)$, and sends y to the sender of the payment. The sender of the payment creates an HTLC with the first intermediary using y as the hash condition for the HTLC. The intermediary creates an HTLC with the next hop and each intermediary repeats this process until the last intermediary creates an HTLC with the recipient of the payment. The recipient fulfills the HTLC by sending x to the last intermediary. Thereby, the payment's recipient receives the payment's amount from the last intermediary. Each intermediary forwards the secret value x back along the route until the sender receives x. Then, all HTLCs are fulfilled and all intermediaries have received and forwarded the payment's amount. The timelocks of the HTLCs are chosen in a descending order from the sender to the recipient, so that each intermediary has enough time to fulfill the incoming HTLC from the previous hop if the next hop fulfills the outgoing HTLC.

2.2   TLA$^+$

We specify Lightning and the security property in TLA$^+$. The Temporal Logic of Actions (TLA) [33] is a temporal logic. The language TLA$^+$ is based on TLA and used to formalize the behavior of a system. TLA$^+$ has been used repeatedly to reason about properties of systems and protocols (see [11,40]). We chose TLA$^+$ because, as a general purpose language, TLA$^+$ allows for specifying arbitrary protocols although abstractions are required for modeling cryptographic primitives (see Sect. 4) and because there are tools supporting different verification methods from model checking [63,64] to theorem proving [41].

In TLA$^+$, the state of a system is described by a set of variables v. Formally, a state is an assignment of values to variables. The state space of a system is the set of all reachable states. A behavior is a sequence of states. A system is described by defining the set of valid behaviors of the system. A step is a pair of successive states in a behavior. An *action* is a function that maps a step to a boolean value. If an action A maps a step to TRUE, then this step is an A step. An action A is enabled in a state s if there exists an A step starting at state s.

The definition of a system in TLA$^+$ is the set of all valid behaviors of the system. A system is described inductively by a set of initial states and an action that determines valid steps of the system. The set of initial states is defined by a formula *Init* that defines the values that each variable can have in an initial state. An action that commonly has the name *Next* determines which steps are allowed for the system to change its state. By starting in an initial state and performing steps allowed by the action *Next*, the behaviors of the system can be generated. A system with variables v is represented as a formula $Spec = Init \wedge \square[Next]_v$ where $\square$ is the *always* operator of temporal logic and $[Next]_v$ means *Next* or a stuttering step in which all variables v are unchanged. An additional conjunct may be a fairness condition, e.g., $WF_v(A)$ which asserts that an A step is taken if the action A is enabled continuously. The *Next* action is typically a disjunction of multiple subactions that define different ways for the system's state to be updated. An action A is described as a conjunction of multiple conjuncts that describe the state in which the action A is enabled and the new state that is reached by an A step. Primed variables (e.g., v') are used to describe the values of the variables in the new state and unprimed variables (e.g., v) describe the values of the variables in the current state.

The variables of a system can be internal or external. From the outside, what a system does is described by the external variables only. A specification S_1 implements (or, equally, refines) specification S_2, noted $S_1 \Rightarrow S_2$, if all external variables of specification S_1 are also external variables of specification S_2 and, when restricting the specifications to these external variables, every behavior of specification S_1 must also be a behavior of specification S_2.

3   Related Work

Aspects of Bitcoin and Lightning were formally analyzed in previous work. Andrychowicz et al. [4] modeled Bitcoin contracts as timed automata and verified them using the UPPAAL model checker [36]. Setzer [54] modeled Bitcoin transactions in Agda [13]. Boyd et al. [14] created a model of a blockchain in Tamarin and analyzed Hash Timelocked Contracts, a primitive that is used by Lightning. Hüttel and Staroveški [27,28] formalized four subprotocols of Lightning and analyzed these protocols using ProVerif for secrecy and authenticity properties. These works on Lightning are complementary to the problem definition in Sect. 1 as they show lower level properties of subprotocols but not the security of the combined protocol. Rain et al. [16,48] formalized two subprotocols of Lightning and conducted an automated analysis for game-theoretic security. Their work is also complementary to the problem definition above as their formalization of the protocol assumes that an honest party actually can punish a dishonest party. This assumption is a property that we aim to prove. Weintraub et al. [65] analyzed the messages exchanged in Lightning during a single-hop payment. They found an ambiguity in the official specification and show two scenarios in which parties might loose their funds if they do not follow the protocol correctly. In particular, parties may not prematurely consider a payment processed and may not agree out-of-band about a payment's outcome.

The security of Lightning was analyzed before by Kiayias and Thyfronitis Litos [31]. They specified an ideal functionality and used the UC framework [17] to prove that Lightning securely implements this ideal functionality. Compared to our formalization, the protocol definition of [31] considers more details about the cryptographic aspects. While working on our TLA$^+$ formalization of Lightning, we found two subtle flaws in the description of [31] of Lightning that render the formalized protocol insecure. The first flaw concerns an incomplete description of how a user reacts to maliciously published outdated transactions. The second flaw is more subtle and concerns how the data in an input is linked to the spending methods of an output that is spent by this input. A detailed description of the flaws can be found in the appendix and in the extended version of this paper [22]. While we found the first flaw by comparing our formalization to the definitions in [31], we found the second flaw only by model checking when we had a similar flaw in a draft of our formalization. We believe that the specific flaws can be corrected and Lightning actually fulfills the ideal functionality. However, it is difficult and tedious to manually find such flaws in a proof. Using model checking, such issues can be revealed automatically.

Concurrently to our work, Fabiański et al. [21] used the deductive program verification platform Why3 [10] to formalize and verify a simplified variant of Lightning. They also formalized the informal security property that honest users do not loose money. In contrast to our approach of defining the security property by defining the behavior of a secure system, they use a game-based definition which is more complex. While we assume an adversary with limited capabilities, they verified that the formalized protocol is secure even in the presence of arbitrary behavior. Their work shows that a formal verification of even a variant of Lightning considering only single payment channels without HTLCs is a challenging effort.

4   Formalization of Lightning

To verify the security properties of Lightning, we need to formalize Lightning first. In this section, we explain important aspects of our TLA$^+$ formalization of Lightning to show the assumptions and the abstraction layer of the formalization. The complete formalization is available as accompanying artifact [23].

The TLA$^+$ formalization specifies a system with an arbitrary number of users. The behavior of a user is specified as in the official specification [62] with some simplifications that we detail below. The key task of Lightning is to ensure that each user can spend the right transaction output at the right time. Therefore, our model of Lightning focuses on the protocol logic in which users exchange data to build transactions, publish transactions, and observe transactions on the blockchain. To keep the complexity at a manageable level, we do not model fees and we abstract cryptographic primitives like signatures and hash functions.

To ensure that our TLA$^+$ formalization of Lightning captures the behavior of Lightning as closely as possible, the TLA$^+$ formalization follows the structure of the official specification. We make use of the same identifiers for messages as in the official specification, and the states of HTLCs in the formalization can be mapped to those used in Core Lightning [60], an implementation of Lightning.

Lightning uses primitives such as signatures and hash functions that are not directly available in TLA$^+$. For the formalization, we make the perfect cryptography assumption that the adversary cannot break cryptographic primitives, and we use a symbolic representation of cryptographic keys and signatures as done in previous work (e.g., [4,14]). We abstract these primitives by focusing on their relevant properties that are used in Lightning. For example, Lightning is based on the assumption that a hash function is deterministic and easy to evaluate given the preimage but cannot be reverted given a hash value and that two different inputs to a hash function result in two different outputs. In the TLA$^+$ formalization, the preimages that are used for multi-hop payments are not randomly generated but are deterministically assigned based on the associated payment. We model the hash value of a preimage to be equal to the preimage itself and distinguish hashes and preimages by the names of the variables in which a preimage or hash value is stored. In Bitcoin, transaction identifiers are defined as a hash over the transaction. In the formalization, we model transaction identifiers by drawing a new unique value for each transaction when the transaction is created and including that identifier in the transaction.

The TLA$^+$ formalization contains a model of the blockchain and all transaction types used in Lightning defining the conditions how each transaction output can be spent. We model publishing a transaction on the blockchain by a single step that happens instantly, i.e., we assume that users have blockchain connectivity and we make the simplifying assumption that each transaction to be published is included in the next block being created. For the communication between users, we model that messages are delivered reliably and in order but can be arbitrarily delayed.

In Lightning, the height of the blockchain is used as logical time that is relevant for the timeout of HTLCs. We refer to the height of the blockchain as time, which is formalized as a variable that is advanced by integer steps. Thus, our specification of Lightning is a real-time specification. While there are languages especially for modeling real-time systems (e.g., KRONOS [15], UPPAAL [36]), we use TLA$^+$, a general purpose language. Real-time systems can be modeled in TLA$^+$ using explicit real-time specifications [35] that we define as follows. An *explicit real-time specification* has a set of variables for clocks. Because time is defined in Lightning by the height of the blockchain, we restrict all clocks to have discrete values. Progress of time is modeled by a *Tick* action that advances each clock by the same non-negative integer value and leaves all other variables unchanged. In the specification of Lightning, we model time using a clock representing the height of the blockchain and, for each published transaction, a specific clock which models the time since the transaction's publication and is used to determine whether a timelocked transaction is valid. Some actions in the protocol are urgent (see [12]) meaning that they need to happen before a certain point in time, e.g., a user has to fulfill a HTLC before the HTLC's timeout. We model this by letting each user specify deadlines and not letting time advance beyond a deadline until a step is taken that removes the deadline.

The TLA$^+$ formalization also models adversarial behavior. The adversary model allows the adversary to omit sending messages or publishing transactions. Also, the adversary is allowed to create and publish transactions other than those specified by the protocol. Transactions published by an adversary are only relevant if they spend an output of a transaction that is related to the payment channel. In the formalization, an action models that the adversary publishes transactions in two ways: First, by finding all outputs that are spendable for the adversary and publishing a new transaction that spends these outputs and sends the funds to the adversary. Second, by signing and publishing a transaction that the adversary has already received the other user's signature for (e.g., an outdated commitment transaction). We do not model that the adversary sends messages with arbitrary content because this would significantly increase the specification's complexity. In practice, the effect of the adversary sending messages with arbitrary content is limited because users validate every message they receive. Messages that have an invalid payload or that are received at an invalid point in the protocol execution are ignored. To verify the validation of messages, we explicitly model the validation of every received message and the message's payload, e.g., the validation of signatures and preimages.

We model that any user in the specification can become adversarial. However, we do not allow information exchange between adversarial users which would model a single adversarial entity controlling multiple users. This limitation simplifies the verification of the specification and we consider it future work to extend the specification with a broader adversary model.

5   Security Property

Our goal is to model check the security of Lightning. Our notion of security is captured by the following informal definition. We define a user as being honest if the user behaves as required by the specification of Lightning.

Definition 1 (informal security). *An honest user will finally get paid out on the blockchain at least the user's correct balance.*

This informal definition implicitly concerns four variables: 1. Whether a user is honest. 2. A user's balance in a channel which defines the correct balance that a user expects to have. This balance is affected by the deposited amount and the processed payments. 3. A user's view on whether a payment has been sent or received. 4. A user's balance on the blockchain. To formalize the informal definition, we use TLA$^+$ to define how these four variables are allowed to change by defining the behavior of a secure payment system. The security property is shown in Figs. 2 and 3. The security property has four variables matching the variables described above and is divided into three modules: The module

─────────────────── MODULE *IdealPaymentNetwork* ───────────────────

VARIABLES *BlockchainBalances, ChannelBalances, Payments, Honest*
CONSTANTS *UserIds, InitialPayments, Numbers*

$IdealUser(user) \triangleq$ INSTANCE *IdealUser* WITH
    $UserId \leftarrow user,$
    $ChannelBalance \leftarrow ChannelBalances[user],$
    $BlockchainBalance \leftarrow BlockchainBalances[user],$
    $Payments \leftarrow Payments[user],$
    $Honest \leftarrow Honest[user]$

$IdealPayments \triangleq$ INSTANCE *IdealPayments*

$Spec \triangleq$
    $\wedge\ \forall\, user \in UserIds : IdealUser(user)!\,Spec$
    $\wedge\ IdealPayments!\,Spec$

─────────────────────── MODULE *IdealPayments* ───────────────────────

EXTENDS *Integers*
VARIABLE *Payments*
CONSTANTS *UserIds, Numbers*

$Pay \triangleq$
    $\wedge\ \forall\, user \in UserIds :$
        $\vee$ UNCHANGED $Payments[user]$
        $\vee\ \exists\, P \in$ SUBSET $\{p \in Payments[user] : p.state = \text{"NEW"}\} :$
            $\wedge\ \exists\, nState \in [P \rightarrow \{\text{"ABORTED"}, \text{"PROCESSED"}\}] :$
                $\wedge\ \forall\, p \in P :$
                    $(nState[p] = \text{"PROCESSED"} \wedge p.sender = user)$
                        $\implies \exists\, rp \in Payments'[p.receiver] :$
                              $rp.id = p.id \wedge rp.state = \text{"PROCESSED"}$
                $\wedge\ Payments[user]' = (Payments[user] \setminus P)$
                            $\cup\ \{[p$ EXCEPT $!.state = nState[p]] : p \in P\}$

$Spec \triangleq Init \wedge \square[Pay]_{Payments}$

Fig. 2. Formal definition of the security property as a secure payment network. The module *IdealPaymentNetwork* specifies that each user behaves as specified by the module *IdealUser* (see Fig. 3) and that the users' views on which payments have been processed are consistent as specified in the module *IdealPayments* which ensures that a payment can be seen as processed by the payment's sender only if it is seen as processed by the payment's receiver.

IdealUser describes changes to the variables of a single user, the module Ideal-Payments ensures that the users' views on which payments have been processed are consistent, and the module IdealPaymentNetwork defines that for all users the specification of the module IdealUser must hold and that the specification of the module IdealPayments must hold. The action *Deposit* describes a deposit as a user's blockchain balance decreasing by an amount and the user's channel

───────────────────── MODULE *IdealUser* ─────────────────────

EXTENDS *Integers*, *SumAmounts*
VARIABLES *BlockchainBalance*, *ChannelBalance*, *Payments*, *Honest*
CONSTANTS *UserIds*, *UserId*, *InitialPayments*, *Numbers*
ASSUME *Numbers* $\subseteq$ *Int*

$Init \triangleq$
    $\land$ *BlockchainBalance* $\in$ *Numbers*
    $\land$ *ChannelBalance* $= 0$
    $\land$ *Payments* $= \{pmt \in InitialPayments :$
                    $pmt.sender = UserId \lor pmt.receiver = UserId\}$
    $\land$ *Payments* $\in$ SUBSET $[amount : Numbers,$
                          $sender : UserIds, receiver : UserIds, id : Numbers,$
                          $state : \{\text{“NEW”}, \text{“ABORTED”}, \text{“PROCESSED”}\}]$
    $\land$ *Honest* $\in \{\text{TRUE}, \text{FALSE}\}$

$Deposit \triangleq$
    $\land \exists\, amount \in 1 .. BlockchainBalance :$
        $\land$ *BlockchainBalance$'$* $= BlockchainBalance - amount$
        $\land$ *ChannelBalance$'$* $= ChannelBalance + amount$
        $\land$ *ChannelBalance$'$* $\in$ *Numbers*
    $\land$ UNCHANGED $\langle Payments, Honest \rangle$

$Pay \triangleq$
    $\land \exists\, P \in$ SUBSET $\{pmt \in Payments : pmt.state = \text{“NEW”}\} :$
        $\exists\, nState \in [P \to \{\text{“ABORTED”}, \text{“PROCESSED”}\}] :$
            $\land$ *Payments$'$* $= (Payments \setminus P) \cup \{[p \text{ EXCEPT } !.state = nState[p]] : p \in P\}$
           $\land$ LET $ProcPmts \triangleq \{p \in P : nState[p] = \text{“PROCESSED”}\}$
                   $recAmts \triangleq SumAmounts(\{p \in ProcPmts : p.receiver = UserId\})$
                   $sentAmts \triangleq SumAmounts(\{p \in ProcPmts : p.sender = UserId\})$
             IN $\land$ *ChannelBalance* $- sentAmts \geqslant 0$
                     $\land$ *ChannelBalance$'$* $= ChannelBalance + recAmts - sentAmts$
                     $\land$ *ChannelBalance$'$* $\geqslant 0$
    $\land$ UNCHANGED $\langle Honest, BlockchainBalance \rangle$

$Withdraw \triangleq$
    $\land$ *BlockchainBalance$'$* $\in$ *Numbers*
    $\land$ *BlockchainBalance$'$* $\geqslant BlockchainBalance$
    $\land \exists\, amount \in 0 .. ChannelBalance :$
        $\land$ *ChannelBalance$'$* $= ChannelBalance - amount$
        $\land$ *Honest* $\implies BlockchainBalance' \geqslant BlockchainBalance + amount$
    $\land$ UNCHANGED $\langle Payments, Honest \rangle$

$Next \triangleq Deposit \lor Pay \lor Withdraw$
$vars \triangleq \langle BlockchainBalance, ChannelBalance, Payments, Honest \rangle$
$Spec \triangleq$
    $\land$ *Init*
    $\land \Box[Next]_{vars}$
    $\land \text{WF}_{vars}(ChannelBalance > 0 \land Honest \land Withdraw)$

───

Fig. 3. Part of the security property defining how a user's variables may change.

balance increasing by the same amount. The action *Withdraw* describes a withdraw by defining that a user's channel balance is reduced by an amount and, for an honest user, the user's blockchain balance increases by at least the same amount. The action *Pay* of the module IdealUser describes the execution of a set of payments by defining that the sending users' channel balances are decreased by the amounts of payments sent and the receiving users' channel balances are increased by the respective amounts. Payments can be aborted keeping channel balances unchanged. Intuitively, one expects from a secure payment network that the sender of a payment sees the payment as sent (and the payment's balance deducted from the user's channel balance) only if the receiver of the payment sees the payment as received. This condition is enforced by the action *Pay* in the module IdealPayments. The fairness condition of the module IdealUser ensures that the system does not terminate before all honest users have been paid out.

In our formalization of Lightning, the BlockchainBalances variable is refined as the sum of unspent transaction outputs on the blockchain that a user can exclusively spend. In the view of each user, the state of a payment is changed from NEW to PROCESSED when the corresponding HTLC is fulfilled. Because our specification of the protocol allows for adversarial behavior, the result that the protocol specification implements the secure payment system means that no modeled adversarial behavior can break the security property, i.e., the countermeasures implemented in the protocol are sufficient.

6   Verification of Security Properties of Lightning

The state space of the TLA$^+$ specification of Lightning (see Sect. 4) is too large for model checking. We use stepwise refinement to reduce the specification's state space so that we can model check that it fulfills the security property (see Sect. 5). In this section, we give an overview of the refinement steps. One reason for the large state space is that there are many equivalent states that only differ by their value of time. In a first abstraction step ① (depicted in Fig. 1), we reduce the number of equivalent states by modeling progress of time more efficiently in specification (II) (see Sect. 6.1). To further reduce the state space, we abstract the payment channels from being updated by the concrete steps of the Lightning protocol to being updated by idealized steps that merge the effects of multiple protocol steps (see Sect. 6.2). We model check for a single channel that the protocol steps refine the idealized steps (②a). Based on this result, we prove that specification (II) modeling a network composed of payment channels implements specification (III) modeling a network of idealized payment channels. Because specification (III) uses the original model of time, we again optimize the modeling of time (see Sect. 6.3). Finally, we model check (see ④) that specification (IV) implements the security property defined in specification (V). In this section, we present the ideas behind the proofs. The full proofs can be found in the extended version [22].

6.1 Improved Model of Time

The protocol as specified in specification (I) is too complex for model checking because of the large number of possible states of the protocol. One reason for the huge state space is the modeling of time. There are many bisimilar states that only differ by the value of the clocks. Bisimilarity defines two states s_1 and s_2 to be equivalent if, informally stated, they have the same futures, i.e., for every behavior that starts in state s_1 there exists a matching behavior of steps of the same actions starting at state s_2. Consequently, it suffices to consider only one of the states s_1 and s_2 during model checking. In the area of timed automata [3], this notion of bisimilarity is usually referred to as untimed bisimilarity [2] or time-abstracting bisimilarity [59]. Prior work (e.g. [3,59]) has proposed to improve model checking of timed automata by grouping all states that are bisimilar in an equivalence class, referred to as a *zone*. A zone graph is constructed by connecting zone z_1 to zone z_2 if zone z_1 contains a state from which a step to a state of zone z_2 exists. During model checking, it suffices to explore the zone graph as a time-optimized specification instead of the possibly much larger state graph of the original specification. To illustrate the effect of the approach, imagine a specification with an initial time value of 1, a single HTLC with timelock 7, and an action with a condition that checks whether the HTLC has timed out. While the original specification would include each state with every possible time value, the time-optimized specification would include only states with time value 1 in which the HTLC has not timed out and time value 7 when the HTLC has reached its timelock. With this approach, the time-optimized specification is bisimilar to the original specification which means that for every behavior in the original specification there exists a behavior in the time-optimized specification *and vice versa*. For the stepwise refinement mapping, we only need the direction that the original specification implements the time-optimized specification. We reduce the state space to an even greater extent by letting the time-optimized specification be a more abstract over-approximation and allowing for behaviors that are not possible in the original specification. More specifically, the zones in the time-optimized specification encode the order in which the outputs of timelocked transactions become spendable. As Lightning does not depend on this order, we reduce the number of zones and allow timelocked transaction outputs to become spendable in any order.

We prove for a general explicit real-time specification that the original specification refines the time-optimized specification by defining a refinement mapping and proving its correctness. The proof can be found in the extended version [22] of this paper. The refinement mapping maps a state s to a state s_R that is the zone representative of the respective zone by setting each clock in state s_R to the lowest value that the clock can have in the respective zone. The idea of the proof is to show that each step of the original specification starting in state s is mapped to a step of the time-optimized specification starting in state s_R. Having proven the optimization in a generalized setting, we prove that the general proof applies to the abstraction from specification (I) to specification (II). Therefore, we explicitly define the zones for specification (I) and prove for every action A

and every pair of points in time t_1 and t_2 that if there exists a reachable state so that the action A is enabled at time t_1 but not at time t_2, then the points in time t_1 and t_2 are in different zones.

6.2   Abstraction of Protocol Steps in Payment Channels

Having applied the time optimization, the state space of specification (II) is still too large to be explored by model checking. To prune the state space, we divide the model checking problem into two separate refinement steps by specifying an intermediate specification. The intermediate specification specifies idealized channels that abstract from the concrete payment channel protocol. The idealized channels omit protocol details that play a role only for a specific channel and describe only those aspects that are relevant for channels to interact with each other during multi-hop payments, e.g. how the states of HTLCs are updated. Having the intermediate idealized channel specification (III), it has to be checked that the protocol specification (II) refines the idealized channel specification (III) and that the idealized channel specification (III) fulfills the security property. Model checking the two refinement steps is a smaller problem than directly checking that specification (II) refines the security property for the following reasons: For the second step, the model checker has to explore the states of a specification in which the complex individual channel management has been abstracted. This leads to a much smaller state space. The first step can be checked efficiently because we use ideas from compositional reasoning [1,19] to check that the channel protocol refines the idealized channels by model checking just a single payment channel. In the following, we explain the idea behind this step. In specification (II), payment channels are composed in a network. To separate this network into single channels, we have to consider how channels affect each other. Two channels of the same user can affect each other because they share variables, e.g., a variable for the set of preimages known to the user. If a user learns a preimage in one channel, this preimage becomes also available in all other channels of the user. We explicitly specify how a channel can be affected by the channels in its environment by specifying an environment module that contains an action for each step outside the channel that can affect the channel's variables. We specify a single channel with the environment module in specification (IIa). Because specification (IIa) contains the environment module and the same module for describing a channel's possible actions as in specification (II), every step of a channel in specification (II) is also possible in specification (IIa). We specify a refinement mapping ②a that maps the state of specification (IIa) to a state of specification $(IIIa)$ which specifies a single idealized channel. By model checking, we verify that the refinement mapping is correct (see Sect. 7). We define a refinement mapping ② from the protocol specification (II) to specification (III) with idealized channels that uses the refinement mapping ②a to map each channel in the protocol specification (II) to the corresponding idealized channel in specification (III). This refinement mapping is correct because every behavior of a channel in specification (II) is described by a behavior of specification (IIa) which is mapped to a behavior of an idealized channel by the refinement mapping ②a. In the extended version [22], we prove that the environment module describes all steps that can affect a payment channel and we prove that the refinement mapping ② is correct based on the assumption that the refinement mapping ②a is correct which we verify by model checking.

6.3   Refinement of Security Property

Specification (III) is defined as a real-time specification in which time can advance by arbitrary natural numbers. This facilitates the refinement mapping ② from specification (II) to specification (III) because it ensures that every step that advances time in specification (II) is also allowed in specification (III). For efficient model checking, we apply the same optimization for time as used above (see Sect. 6.1) by defining specification (IV) where equivalent states are grouped. By a proof analogously to the proof of Sect. 6.1, specification (III) implements specification (IV) and, by transitivity, specification (I) implements specification (IV). Finally, we can model check that specification (IV) using idealized channels implements the security property defined in specification (V).

7   Results of Model Checking

We verify the refinement mappings ②a and ④ by model checking and use simulation for additional verification for the manual proof steps ①, ② and ③.

Table 1. Model checking of refinement mapping ②a from specification (IIa) to specification $(IIIa)$

ID	Model	# States	Runtime
C1	Payment from user A to user B	$\sim 10^5$	$\sim 3\,\text{min}$
C2	Payment from user A over B to C	$\sim 10^5$	$\sim 8\,\text{min}$
C3	Payment from user C over A and B to D	$\sim 10^5$	$\sim 8\,\text{min}$
C4	Two payments: Payment from user A to B and payment from user B over A to C	$\sim 10^7$	$\sim 8\,\text{h}$
C5	Two concurrent payments from user A to B	$\sim 10^8$	$\sim 8\,\text{wks}$

To model check the refinement mapping ②a from specification (IIa) to specification $(IIIa)$, we use the model checker TLC that explores all reachable states, calculates the refinement mapping on these states and verifies that the mapped states and steps fulfill specification $(IIIa)$. Specification (IIa) models two users and a payment channel and is parameterized by the information about the context of this payment channel, i.e., the other users in the payment channel network, and the payments to be processed. As there are infinitely many possible ways to parameterize specification (IIa), we only check a small selection of configurations that we deem representative. We model check configurations for five different models that are listed in Table 1. To give an impression, the table also shows the magnitude of the number of distinct states that were explored and the time used by TLC (run on 96 CPU cores). Each model starts with two users (A and B) prepared to open a payment channel and TLC explores all possible behaviors for the two users to open the channel, communicate with users in the environment where applicable, process payments, and close the channel. Each checked behavior ends with the channel being closed and the two users having their funds paid out on the blockchain. The simplest model listed in Table 1 is a payment from user A who funded the channel to the other user. Models C2 and C3 are models in which the channel between users A and B is an intermediate hop on a payment that includes users in the environment. Model C4 models two payments: A payment from user A to user B and a payment that user B sends to user C over user A as an intermediate. There are many more states to explore in model C4 as in the previous models because the two payments can partially interleave: After user B has fulfilled the HTLC for the payment from user A to user B, user B can already start sending the payment to user C while the fulfilled HTLC is removed. Model C5 models two payments from user A to user B which is an even larger model as the two payments can interleave from the beginning. By taking about eight weeks to model check, this model is at the limits of what we can model check in reasonable time.

Table 2. Model checking of refinement mapping ④ from specification (IV) to security property (V)

ID	Model	# States	Runtime
M1	Payment from user A over B to user C	$\sim 10^5$	$\sim 1\,\text{min}$
M2	Two payments: Payment from user A over B to C and payment from user C over B to A	$\sim 10^7$	$\sim 45\,\text{min}$
M3	Two concurrent payments: Payment from user A over B to C and payment from user A to B	$\sim 10^7$	$\sim 1\,\text{h}$
M4	Three payments: Payment from user A over B to C, payment from user B to A, and payment from user B to C	$\sim 10^8$	$\sim 13\,\text{h}$
M5	Payment from user A over B and C to user D	$\sim 10^8$	$\sim 13\,\text{h}$

The models that we model check to verify the refinement mapping ④ from specification (IV) to specification (V) are listed in Table 2. In all models except the last one, we model three users (A, B, and C) and two payment channels: one channel between user A and user B and the other between user B and user C. In the last model, we model four users (A to D) and three payment channels so that a payment from user A to user D is possible. In all these models, we model check multi-hop payments to check that specification (IV) implements the secure payment network in specification (V).

Model checking of larger models than the models described above becomes impractical. We can partially check larger models by using TLC's simulation mode in which the model checker starts in an initial state and chooses each next state randomly. Recent work has shown that using simulation as a 'lightweight' verification where more rigorous methods are not practical can be successful at finding critical flaws [26]. While we specified the refinement mappings and wrote the proofs, we used simulation to check the abstractions ①, ②, and ④ and the whole stepwise refinement which helped to find flaws in our drafts within few minutes. Further, we used simulation to check the abstractions ②a and ④ also for larger models with more users and payments.

8   Discussion and Conclusion

Choice of Formalization Language and Tools. Protocol verifiers such as Tamarin [39] and ProVerif [8] have successfully been used for unbounded verification of a number of security protocols [6]. These verifiers support modeling cryptographic primitives, allow for stronger adversary models, and can reason about a protocol's properties without the limitations of finite model checking. These tools have successfully been used to verify subprotocols of Lightning [14,27,28]. However, it is challenging to model natural numbers with addition and subtraction of two variables (see [56, page 35] and [9, page 18]) which is required for modeling blockchain transactions with amounts as in our TLA$^+$ specification. While we had to abstract cryptographic primitives (see Sect. 4), the generality of TLA$^+$ allowed us to model all relevant aspects of Lightning. We modeled Lightning in TLA$^+$ because TLA$^+$ does not restrict the way properties are proven, whether manually, using an explicit-state [64] or a symbolic model checker [63], or a tool for automated reasoning [41]. We used the explicit-state model checker TLC. The automated model checking process and the generation of counterexamples facilitated our process of defining the intermediate specification (III) and the complex refinement mapping from specification (II) to specification (III). Because we used model checking, we could only verify the security for a number of four users. There might be attacks that only apply when there are more than four users; these attacks would not be discovered by our approach. A further consequence of the choice for model checking was that we had to restrict the adversary model to restrict the messages that an adversary can send. However, the TLA$^+$ specification could also be verified using unbounded verification with a theorem prover [41]. Currently, writing such a proof seems too effortful. However, it will be facilitated by future advancements in assistance and automation for theorem proving.

Limitations and Future Work. To formalize Lightning, we left out aspects that are not required for security, e.g., the fees that the sender of a payment pays to intermediate hops, key rotation and onion-routing for increased privacy, and route finding for multi-hop payments. Also, the model of the blockchain could be augmented by considering reorganizations and delays for transaction inclusion. Our adversary model restricts the capabilities of an adversary by disallowing the sending of messages with arbitrary content and the exchange of information between adversarial users. While we had to make these restrictions to keep the specification's state space at a manageable level, follow up work could find optimizations that allow for making the adversary stronger. While this work was in progress, the official Lightning specification was extended to allow both parties to deposit coins into a channel during opening (see [61, Channel Establishment v2]). Our method can be used to formalize and analyze the security of this advancement as well. While we put a focus on a security property, future work could also use the same approach to analyze other properties. For example, it could be shown that, assuming honest and cooperating users and timely delivery of messages, payments are guaranteed to succeed.

Known Attacks on Lightning. Prior work has identified several attacks on the assumptions of Lightning and properties that are not included in our security definition. Several works discuss griefing [37,42,46,50] and other denial-of-service attacks [58] in which no funds are stolen but the regular operation is disturbed. In the wormhole attack [38,57], an attacker reroutes a payment and receives the fees intended for other intermediate hops, however, the actual amount of the payment is unconcerned. Extending the TLA^+ formalization of Lightning with fees would allow for modeling the wormhole attack. Further, there are attacks on privacy [7,20,25,29,32,45,51,52] which is a property that is not included in the security definition used in this work. Other works [24,43,49,55] discuss the violation of the assumption that users can timely publish a transaction on the blockchain. In practice, security flaws are also based on implementations not following the specification, e.g., by missing verification checks [53].

Evaluation of Protocol Modifications. Besides proving that the formalization of Lightning fulfills the security property, the TLA^+ formalization of Lightning can also be used to test proposed modifications of Lightning. To quickly find flaws, it can suffice to model check only a subset of the specification (e.g., a single channel) and check just lower-level invariants. Such an approach can accelerate protocol development by providing a short feedback loop to developers. To evaluate this idea, we introduced flaws by adapting the formalization of Lightning and verified that the introduced flaws are detected by model checking. As an example, we tested whether the, so called, second-stage transactions for HTLCs can be removed by including the conditions of the outputs of HTLC second-stage transactions directly in a commitment transaction's outputs. Verification with the model checker showed within a few minutes that this makes the protocol insecure and, thus, Lightning cannot be simplified in this way.

Connecting the Specification to an Implementation. There exist multiple implementations of Lightning. While the TLA^+ specification of Lightning is not an executable implementation, it can be used to validate the correctness of existing implementations. Cirstea et al. [18] have recently shown a lightweight way to connect implementations in imperative languages to a TLA$^+$ specification. Their approach is to collect traces of program executions and check these traces against traces described by the corresponding TLA$^+$ specification. Transferring their approach, is an opportunity for follow up work.

Conclusion. We have formalized Lightning and a secure payment system that captures the security property of Lightning. Using stepwise refinement, we were able to check the security of Lightning for small models. The approach could enable specifications of other protocols to be model checked. In particular, the abstraction of time can be generalized as well as the approach of separating model checking of local behavior and behavior in a network. Thus, our approach can be a valuable tool to analyze new versions of Lightning or similar protocols.

Acknowledgement. This work was supported by funding from the topic Engineering Secure Systems of the Helmholtz Association (HGF) and by KASTEL Security Research Labs. The authors thank the anonymous reviewers for their helpful comments.

Appendix: On the Formalization of [31]

We found the following two flaws in the formalization of [31]. While these flaws render the formalized protocol insecure, they are easy to fix and it seems that the security proof could work for the corrected protocol. The following references to figures and page numbers refer to [30, version 20220217:205237].

The first flaw concerns the punishment of the publication of an outdated commitment transaction for which the protocol is specified in Fig. 37, lines 21–25 (page 64). A problem arises in the following situation: An HTLC from user Alice to user Bob was off-chain fulfilled and removed. Now, the HTLC's absolute timelock has passed. Alice is malicious and publishes the outdated commitment transaction that commits the HTLC and the associated HTLC timeout transaction. Bob runs the protocol specified in Fig. 37. In line 22, a revocation transaction is created whose inputs spend all outputs of the outdated commitment transaction. In the situation described, this revocation transaction is invalid. Instead of an input referencing the outdated commitment transaction's HTLC output, the revocation transaction must have an input that references the output of the HTLC timeout transaction. While the protocol as formalized in Fig. 37 is incorrect, the security proof on page 90 does not mention the case that a second-stage (timeout or success) HTLC transaction might have been published for an outdated commitment transaction and, thus, the protocol seems correct.

For a scenario that shows the impact of the second flaw, assume that in the payment channel between users Alice and Bob there is an unfulfilled HTLC for a payment from Alice to Bob. After the HTLC's absolute timelock has passed, Bob closes the payment channel by publishing the latest commitment transaction which contains an output o for the HTLC with the spending method $pt_{\mathrm{rev},n+1} \vee$ $(pt_{\mathrm{htlc},n+1}, \mathtt{CltvExpiry}\ \text{absolute}) \vee (pt_{\mathrm{htlc},n+1} \wedge ph_{\mathrm{htlc},n+1}, \text{on preimage of } h)$ (see Fig. 40, line 8) where pt (resp. ph) are public keys for which Alice (resp. Bob) has the private key and $\mathtt{CltvExpiry}$ is the HTLC's absolute timelock. Alice could spend the output o by creating a transaction with an input that uses the disjunct $(pt_{\mathrm{htlc},n+1}, \mathtt{CltvExpiry}\ \text{absolute})$. Bob holds the HTLC success transaction that was signed by Alice with the private key for $pt_{\mathrm{htlc},n+1}$ (Fig. 43, line 13). Because the HTLC success transaction, which is meant to spend the third disjunct, also fulfills the conditions of the disjunct $(pt_{\mathrm{htlc},n+1}, \mathtt{CltvExpiry}\ \text{absolute})$, Bob could receive the amount of the HTLC without knowing the preimage. One way to correct this problem would be to transform the disjunction in Fig. 40, line 8 into a list of spending methods and add the corresponding indices to the inputs in Fig. 43, line 13. Another way is taken by Lightning which uses the operator $\mathtt{CHECKLOCKTIMEVERIFY}$ that verifies that a spending transaction has a certain $\mathtt{locktime}$ set. As Bob's HTLC success transaction has the $\mathtt{locktime}$ set to 0, the success transaction cannot fulfill the spending method meant for the timeout.

References

1. Abadi, M., Lamport, L.: Conjoining specifications. ACM Trans. Program. Lang. Syst. **17**(3), 507–535 (1995). https://doi.org/10.1145/203095.201069
2. Alur, R., Courcoubetis, C., Henzinger, T.A.: The observational power of clocks. In: Jonsson, B., Parrow, J. (eds.) CONCUR 1994. LNCS, vol. 836, pp. 162–177. Springer, Heidelberg (1994). https://doi.org/10.1007/978-3-540-48654-1_16
3. Alur, R., Dill, D.: Automata for modeling real-time systems. In: Paterson, M.S. (ed.) ICALP 1990. LNCS, vol. 443, pp. 322–335. Springer, Heidelberg (1990). https://doi.org/10.1007/BFb0032042
4. Andrychowicz, M., Dziembowski, S., Malinowski, D., Mazurek, Ł.: Modeling bitcoin contracts by timed automata. In: Legay, A., Bozga, M. (eds.) Formal Modeling and Analysis of Timed Systems, pp. 7–22. Springer International Publishing, Cham (2014). https://doi.org/10.1007/978-3-319-10512-3_2
5. Barbaravičius, V.: Year-over-Year Data Shows Rising Lightning Network Adoption|CoinGate (2024). https://coingate.com/blog/post/lightning-network-year-over-year-data
6. Basin, D., Cremers, C., Dreier, J., Sasse, R.: Tamarin: verification of large-scale, real-world, cryptographic protocols. IEEE Secur. Priv. **20**(3), 24–32 (2022). https://doi.org/10.1109/MSEC.2022.3154689
7. Biryukov, A., Naumenko, G., Tikhomirov, S.: Analysis and probing of parallel channels in the lightning network. In: Eyal, I., Garay, J. (eds.) Financial Cryptography and Data Security, pp. 337–357. Springer International Publishing, Cham (2022). https://doi.org/10.1007/978-3-031-18283-9_16
8. Blanchet, B.: Modeling and verifying security protocols with the applied pi calculus and ProVerif. Foundations Trends Priv. Secur. **1**(1–2), 1–135 (2016). https://doi.org/10.1561/3300000004
9. Blanchet, B.: The security protocol verifier ProVerif and its horn clause resolution algorithm. Electron. Proc. Theoret. Comput. Sci. **373**, 14–22 (2022). https://doi.org/10.4204/EPTCS.373.2

10. Bobot, F., Filliâtre, J.C., Marché, C., Paskevich, A.: Why3: shepherd Your Herd of Provers. In: Boogie 2011: First International Workshop on Intermediate Verification Languages, p. 53 (2011). https://inria.hal.science/view/index/identifiant/hal-00790310

11. Bögli, R., Lerena, L., Tsigkanos, C., Kehrer, T.: A Systematic literature review on a decade of industrial TLA+ practice. In: Kosmatov, N., Kovács, L. (eds.) Integrated Formal Methods, pp. 24–34. Springer Nature Switzerland, Cham (2025). https://doi.org/10.1007/978-3-031-76554-4_2

12. Bornot, S., Sifakis, J., Tripakis, S.: Modeling urgency in timed systems. In: de Roever, W.P., Langmaack, H., Pnueli, A. (eds.) Compositionality: The Significant Difference, pp. 103–129. Springer, Berlin, Heidelberg (1998). https://doi.org/10.1007/3-540-49213-5_5

13. Bove, A., Dybjer, P., Norell, U.: A brief overview of Agda – a functional language with dependent types. In: Berghofer, S., Nipkow, T., Urban, C., Wenzel, M. (eds.) Theorem Proving in Higher Order Logics, pp. 73–78. Springer, Berlin, Heidelberg (2009). https://doi.org/10.1007/978-3-642-03359-9_6

14. Boyd, C., Gjøsteen, K., Wu, S.: A blockchain model in tamarin and formal analysis of hash time lock contract. In: DROPS-IDN/v2/document/10.4230/OASIcs.FMBC.2020.5. Schloss Dagstuhl – Leibniz-Zentrum für Informatik (2020). https://doi.org/10.4230/OASIcs.FMBC.2020.5

15. Bozga, M., Daws, C., Maler, O., Olivero, A., Tripakis, S., Yovine, S.: Kronos: a model-checking tool for real-time systems. In: Ravn, A.P., Rischel, H. (eds.) FTRTFT 1998. LNCS, vol. 1486, pp. 298–302. Springer, Heidelberg (1998). https://doi.org/10.1007/BFb0055357

16. Brugger, L.S., Kovács, L., Petkovic Komel, A., Rain, S., Rawson, M.: CheckMate: automated game-theoretic security reasoning. In: Proceedings of the 2023 ACM SIGSAC Conference on Computer and Communications Security, pp. 1407–1421. CCS '23, Association for Computing Machinery, New York, NY, USA (Nov 2023). https://doi.org/10.1145/3576915.3623183

17. Canetti, R.: Universally composable security: a new paradigm for cryptographic protocols. In: Proceedings 42nd IEEE Symposium on Foundations of Computer Science, pp. 136–145 (2001). https://doi.org/10.1109/SFCS.2001.959888

18. Cirstea, H., Kuppe, M.A., Loillier, B., Merz, S.: Validating traces of distributed programs against TLA+ specifications. In: Madeira, A., Knapp, A. (eds.) Software Engineering and Formal Methods, pp. 126–143. Springer Nature Switzerland, Cham (2025). https://doi.org/10.1007/978-3-031-77382-2_8

19. Clarke, E., Long, D., McMillan, K.: Compositional model checking. In: [1989] Proceedings. Fourth Annual Symposium on Logic in Computer Science, pp. 353–362 (1989). https://doi.org/10.1109/LICS.1989.39190

20. van Dam, G., Kadir, R.A., Nohuddin, P.N.E., Zaman, H.B.: Improvements of the balance discovery attack on lightning network payment channels. In: Hölbl, M., Rannenberg, K., Welzer, T. (eds.) ICT Systems Security and Privacy Protection, pp. 313–323. Springer International Publishing, Cham (2020). https://doi.org/10.1007/978-3-030-58201-2_21

21. Fabiański, G., Stefański, R., Thyfronitis Litos, O.S.: A Formally Verified Lightning Network (2025). https://fc25.ifca.ai/preproceedings/63.pdf

22. Grundmann, M., Hartenstein, H.: Model Checking the Security of the Lightning Network (2025). https://doi.org/10.48550/arXiv.2505.15568

23. Grundmann, M., Hartenstein, H.: TLA+ specification of lightning, security property, and refinement mappings. Zenodo (2025). https://doi.org/10.5281/zenodo.17206471
24. Harris, J., Zohar, A.: Flood & loot: a systemic attack on the lightning network. In: Proceedings of the 2nd ACM Conference on Advances in Financial Technologies, pp. 202–213. AFT '20, Association for Computing Machinery, New York, NY, USA (2020). https://doi.org/10.1145/3419614.3423248
25. Herrera-Joancomartí, J., Navarro-Arribas, G., Ranchal-Pedrosa, A., Pérez-Solà, C., Garcia-Alfaro, J.: On the difficulty of hiding the balance of lightning network channels. In: Proceedings of the 2019 ACM Asia Conference on Computer and Communications Security, pp. 602–612. Asia CCS '19, Association for Computing Machinery, Auckland, New Zealand (2019). https://doi.org/10.1145/3321705.3329812
26. Howard, H., Kuppe, M.A., Ashton, E., Chamayou, A., Crooks, N.: Smart casual verification of the confidential consortium framework. In: Proceedings of the 22nd USENIX Symposium on Networked Systems Design and Implementation, pp. 259–276. USENIX Association, Philadelphia, PA, USA (2025)
27. Hüttel, H., Staroveški, V.: Secrecy and Authenticity Properties of the Lightning Network Protocol, pp. 119–130 (2020). https://www.scitepress.org/Link.aspx?doi=10.5220/0008974801190130
28. Hüttel, H., Staroveški, V.: Key agreement in the lightning network protocol. In: Furnell, S., Mori, P., Weippl, E., Camp, O. (eds.) Information Systems Security and Privacy, pp. 139–155. Communications in Computer and Information Science, Springer International Publishing, Cham (2022). https://doi.org/10.1007/978-3-030-94900-6_7
29. Kappos, G., et al.: An empirical analysis of privacy in the lightning network. In: Borisov, N., Diaz, C. (eds.) Financial Cryptography and Data Security, pp. 167–186. Springer, Berlin, Heidelberg (2021). https://doi.org/10.1007/978-3-662-64322-8_8
30. Kiayias, A., Thyfronitis Litos, O.S.: A Composable Security Treatment of the Lightning Network (2019). https://eprint.iacr.org/2019/778
31. Kiayias, A., Thyfronitis Litos, O.S.: A composable security treatment of the lightning network. In: 2020 IEEE 33rd Computer Security Foundations Symposium (CSF), pp. 334–349 (2020). https://doi.org/10.1109/CSF49147.2020.00031
32. Kumble, S.P., Epema, D., Roos, S.: How lightning's routing diminishes its anonymity. In: Proceedings of the 16th International Conference on Availability, Reliability and Security, pp. 1–10. ARES '21, Association for Computing Machinery, New York, NY, USA (2021). https://doi.org/10.1145/3465481.3465761
33. Lamport, L.: The temporal logic of actions. ACM Trans. Program. Lang. Syst. **16**(3), 872–923 (1994). https://doi.org/10.1145/177492.177726
34. Lamport, L.: Specifying Systems: The TLA+ Language and Tools for Hardware and Software Engineers. Addison-Wesley Longman Publishing Co., Inc, USA (2002)
35. Lamport, L.: Real-time model checking is really simple. In: Borrione, D., Paul, W. (eds.) Correct Hardware Design and Verification Methods. pp. 162–175. Lecture Notes in Computer Science, Springer, Berlin, Heidelberg (2005). https://doi.org/10.1007/11560548_14
36. Larsen, K.G., Pettersson, P., Yi, W.: UPPAAL in a Nutshell. Int. J. Softw. Tools Technolo. Transfer **1**(1-2), 134–152 (1997). https://doi.org/10.1007/s100090050010

37. Lu, Z., Han, R., Yu, J.: General congestion attack on HTLC-based payment channel networks. In: DROPS-IDN/v2/document/10.4230/OASIcs.Tokenomics.2021.2. Schloss Dagstuhl – Leibniz-Zentrum für Informatik (2022). https://doi.org/10.4230/OASIcs.Tokenomics.2021.2
38. Malavolta, G., Moreno-Sanchez, P., Schneidewind, C., Kate, A., Maffei, M.: Anonymous multi-hop locks for blockchain scalability and interoperability. In: Proceedings 2019 Network and Distributed System Security Symposium. Internet Society, San Diego, CA (2019). https://doi.org/10.14722/ndss.2019.23330
39. Meier, S., Schmidt, B., Cremers, C., Basin, D.: The TAMARIN prover for the symbolic analysis of security protocols. In: Sharygina, N., Veith, H. (eds.) Computer Aided Verification, pp. 696–701. Springer, Berlin, Heidelberg (2013). https://doi.org/10.1007/978-3-642-39799-8_48
40. Merz, S.: Formal specification and verification. In: Concurrency: the Works of Leslie Lamport, pp. 103–129. Association for Computing Machinery, New York, NY, USA (2019). https://doi.org/10.1145/3335772.3335780
41. Microsoft Research – Inria Joint Centre: TLA+ Proof System (2025). https://proofs.tlapl.us/doc/web/content/Home.html
42. Mizrahi, A., Zohar, A.: Congestion attacks in payment channel networks. In: Borisov, N., Diaz, C. (eds.) Financial Cryptography and Data Security, pp. 170–188. Springer, Berlin, Heidelberg (2021). https://doi.org/10.1007/978-3-662-64331-0_9
43. Nadahalli, T., Khabbazian, M., Wattenhofer, R.: Timelocked bribing. In: Borisov, N., Diaz, C. (eds.) Financial Cryptography and Data Security, pp. 53–72. Springer, Berlin, Heidelberg (2021). https://doi.org/10.1007/978-3-662-64322-8_3
44. Nakamoto, S.: Bitcoin: A Peer-to-Peer Electronic Cash System. Tech. rep. (2008)
45. Ndolo, C., Tschorsch, F.: On the (Not So) surprising impact of multi-path payments on performance and privacy in the lightning network. In: Katsikas, S., et al. (eds.) Computer Security. ESORICS 2023 International Workshops, pp. 411–427. Springer Nature Switzerland, Cham (2024). https://doi.org/10.1007/978-3-031-54204-6_25
46. Pérez-Solà, C., Ranchal-Pedrosa, A., Herrera-Joancomartí, J., Navarro-Arribas, G., Garcia-Alfaro, J.: LockDown: balance availability attack against lightning network channels. In: Bonneau, J., Heninger, N. (eds.) Financial Cryptography and Data Security, pp. 245–263. Lecture Notes in Computer Science, Springer International Publishing, Cham (2020). https://doi.org/10.1007/978-3-030-51280-4_14
47. Poon, J., Dryja, T.: The Bitcoin Lightning Network: Scalable Off-Chain Instant Payments. Tech. rep. (2016)
48. Rain, S., Avarikioti, G., Kovács, L., Maffei, M.: Towards a game-theoretic security analysis of off-chain protocols. In: 2023 IEEE 36th Computer Security Foundations Symposium (CSF), pp. 107–122 (2023). https://doi.org/10.1109/CSF57540.2023.00003
49. Riard, A., Naumenko, G.: Time-Dilation Attacks on the Lightning Network. arXiv:2006.01418 [cs] (2020). http://arxiv.org/abs/2006.01418
50. Rohrer, E., Malliaris, J., Tschorsch, F.: Discharged payment channels: quantifying the lightning network's resilience to topology-based attacks. In: 2019 IEEE European Symposium on Security and Privacy Workshops (EuroS PW), pp. 347–356 (2019). https://doi.org/10.1109/EuroSPW.2019.00045
51. Rohrer, E., Tschorsch, F.: Counting down thunder: timing attacks on privacy in payment channel networks. In: Proceedings of the 2nd ACM Conference on

Advances in Financial Technologies, pp. 214–227. AFT '20, Association for Computing Machinery, New York, NY, USA (2020). https://doi.org/10.1145/3419614.3423262

52. Romiti, M., et al.: Cross-layer deanonymization methods in the lightning protocol. In: Borisov, N., Diaz, C. (eds.) Financial Cryptography and Data Security, pp. 187–204. Lecture Notes in Computer Science, Springer, Berlin, Heidelberg (2021). https://doi.org/10.1007/978-3-662-64322-8_9

53. Russell, R.: Full Disclosure: CVE-2019-12998 / CVE-2019-12999 / CVE-2019-13000 (2019). https://lists.linuxfoundation.org/pipermail/lightning-dev/2019-September/002174.html

54. Setzer, A.: Modelling Bitcoin in Agda (2018). https://doi.org/10.48550/arXiv.1804.06398

55. Sguanci, C., Sidiropoulos, A.: Mass exit attacks on the lightning network. In: 2023 IEEE International Conference on Blockchain and Cryptocurrency (ICBC), pp. 1–3 (2023). https://doi.org/10.1109/ICBC56567.2023.10174926

56. The Tamarin Team: Tamarin-Prover Manual (2024). https://tamarin-prover.com/manual/master/tex/tamarin-manual.pdf

57. Tikhomirov, S., Moreno-Sanchez, P., Maffei, M.: A quantitative analysis of security, anonymity and scalability for the lightning network. In: 2020 IEEE European Symposium on Security and Privacy Workshops (EuroS&PW), pp. 387–396 (2020). https://doi.org/10.1109/EuroSPW51379.2020.00059

58. Tochner, S., Zohar, A., Schmid, S.: Route hijacking and DoS in off-chain networks. In: Proceedings of the 2nd ACM Conference on Advances in Financial Technologies, pp. 228–240. AFT '20, Association for Computing Machinery, New York, NY, USA (2020). https://doi.org/10.1145/3419614.3423253

59. Tripakis, S., Yovine, S.: Analysis of timed systems using time-abstracting bisimulations. Formal Methods Syst. Design $18(1)$, 25–68 (2001). https://doi.org/10.1023/A:1008734703554

60. Various: Core Lightning, htlc_state.h (2018). https://github.com/ElementsProject/lightning/blob/master/common/htlc_state.h

61. Various: BOLT 2: Peer Protocol for Channel Management (2024). https://github.com/lightning/bolts/blob/master/02-peer-protocol.md

62. Various: BOLT: Basis of Lightning Technology (Lightning Network In-Progress Specifications) (2024). https://github.com/lightning/bolts

63. Various: Apalache | The Symbolic Model Checker for TLA+ (2025). https://apalache-mc.org/

64. Various: TLA+ Toolbox (2025). https://github.com/tlaplus/tlaplus

65. Weintraub, B., Kumble, S.P., Nita-Rotaru, C., Roos, S.: Payout races and congested channels: a formal analysis of security in the lightning network. In: Proceedings of the 2024 on ACM SIGSAC Conference on Computer and Communications Security, pp. 2562–2576. CCS '24, Association for Computing Machinery, New York, NY, USA (2024). https://doi.org/10.1145/3658644.3670315

Formal Verification of PKCS#1 Signature Parser Using Frama-C

Martin Hána[1] , Nikolai Kosmatov[2]([⊠]) , Virgile Prevosto[3] ,
and Julien Signoles[3]

[1] Thales Cybersecurity and Digital Identity, Prague, Czechia
`martin.hana@thalesgroup.com`
[2] Thales Research and Technology, cortAIx Labs, Palaiseau, France
`nikolai.kosmatov@thalesgroup.com`
[3] Université Paris-Saclay, CEA, List, Palaiseau, France
`{virgile.prevosto,julien.signoles}@cea.fr`

Abstract. Message parsing represents a complex security-critical problem. It has been demonstrated by numerous real-world exploits on parsers, e.g. on PKCS#1 (Public-Key Cryptography Standard) v1.5 signature, X.509 certificate chain, or infamously on a TLS extension during the Heartbleed attack. In this case study, we perform formal verification of a PKCS#1 v1.5 signature parser using Frama-C, where the verification of the parser is realized for the first time directly over the actual implementation in C. This brings highest guarantees of security and functional properties, while leaving developers the flexibility to adapt the code to the project's specific requirements. We present the proven properties, our verification approach and results. In particular, this work rules out applications of any variants of Bleichenbacher's signature forgery and ensures that we are able to detect potential parser incompatibilities. This work opens the door to future extensions to other protocols, for example, for parsing DER ASN.1 encoding of X.509 certificates and CRLs (Certificate Revocation Lists).

1 Introduction

As increasingly many aspects of public and private life are digitalized and moved into cyberspace, digital security becomes a major concern. The persistence of some families of bugs shows that code review and testing are not sufficient to reliably clean up the code even from publicly known vulnerabilities. One of the most risky attack vectors is related to the *message parsing problem*. Indeed, parsers are very often involved in processing of input data on external interfaces, where attackers have some level of control. Hence, parsers must apply a *rigorous defensive approach* and provide a high assurance that any malicious input is detected. It motivates the application of formal verification, capable to provide strong security guarantees.

An example of a long-lasting parsing problem—PKCS#1 v1.5 signature forging—was originally described by Bleichenbacher [28] in 2006, while exploitable

F. Damiani and M. Farrell (Eds.): iFM 2025, LNCS 16194, pp. 336–358, 2026.
https://doi.org/10.1007/978-3-032-10794-7_17

variants have been reported in popular open-source libraries in 2021, 15 years later [57]! During PKCS#1 v1.5 signature verification, due to a complex structure of the signed message, a dedicated parser must be applied to extract necessary data (such as the hash of the message and the hash function identifier) from the signature. An unsecured implementation of the parser opens the door to signature forgery. This case study paper addresses this problem.

Goals and Approach. Our main goal is to demonstrate that it is achievable to perform formal verification of a PKCS#1 v1.5 signature parser [47] directly on the parser's C code. We formally specify *functional and security properties* of the parser and prove them in the **Frama-C** verification platform [5,41]. These properties exclude any variant of Bleichenbacher attack or unauthorized memory access. Next to that, they ensure *parser compatibility* (with small limitations, discussed later in Sect. 5), i.e., the guarantee that correctly formatted messages are not refused by the parser. To illustrate that, we provide several buggy variants of the parser, for which—as expected—the proof with our specification fails.

Applying formal verification directly on the C implementation bridges the gap between a—typically, more abstract—formal model and the concrete code of the parser executed in practice, thus avoiding any non-trusted or laborious steps (such as code generation or refinement). In addition, it brings further practical advantages. For example, the code can be iteratively optimized or customized, as long as it is proved that each new modification retains all necessary properties and thus does not introduce vulnerabilities. On the other hand, it is often more difficult to verify real-life code than a more abstract high-level model. Further discussion about pros and cons of deductive verification on the source code level can be found in [23].

We select PKCS#1 v1.5 signature as a good representative of the TLV (Tag-Length-Value triple) tree structure, frequently used in parsers. In a TLV, the tag field defines the type of the data, and its length field defines the size of its value field. The PKCS#1 v1.5 signature has a non-trivial complexity yet is simple enough to tackle all methodological questions of parser verification. For the same reason, we develop a representative PKCS#1 v1.5 parser in C, for which we perform the proof, while keeping in mind the need of extension to other TLV-based protocols. This parser is capable of parsing the message structure specified in [47] almost completely (it is not compliant only to the fact that the NULL field can be *optional*). The annotated code of the verified parser and its buggy variants are available in a companion artifact [33].

The proposed specification approach of the message structure carefully combines *inductive predicates*—defined in a generic way—and a separate *ghost model* used in the inductive predicates and encoding a concrete TLV-based tree structure to be parsed. This separation appears to be practical and user-friendly. The proposed inductive predicates allow for a generic specification of different TLVs inside the same message and are expected to remain suitable for other message structures. It is an important benefit: such predicates are difficult to write correctly for a non-expert. The proposed ghost encoding of the TLV structure should be updated to parameterize the specification for other TLV structures. Closer to regular C data structures, it can be more easily written by engineers who are not experts in formal verification. It is another advantage of our approach.

Contributions. This verification case study presents the following contributions:

- a formal specification and proof—directly over the C code—of security and functional properties for a representative PKCS#1 v1.5 signature parser;
- an illustration by examples that the proposed specification rules out various variants of Bleichenbacher signature forgery [28] and ensures compatibility;
- a verification methodology based on the definition of inductive predicates, capable to conveniently express complex relations between particular TLVs in a generic way;
- an innovative usage of *ghost code* (see Sect. 2) to specify the target TLV structure and the application of cryptographic operations on concrete input data;
- a report of verification effort, results, faced difficulties and used workarounds.

Outline. Section 2 introduces Frama-C and the ACSL specification language. Section 3 presents some parser attacks and expected security and compatibility properties to guard against them. Section 4 details PKCS#1 v1.5 signature and known attacks. Section 5 describes our verification approach and proven properties. Section 6 provides a proof report. Finally, Sect. 7 presents related work and a conclusion.

2   Frama-C Verification Framework

Frama-C [5,41] is a state-of-the-art modular verification framework for C code developed and maintained by CEA List. Its modular structure allows application and collaboration of various analyzers—implemented as plugins—and eases the introduction of new ones. This combination of plugins offers a large variety of verification and analysis approaches. In our work we use the WP and RTE plugins, which perform, resp., *deductive verification* (based on *weakest precondition* calculus) and generation of annotations whose validity implies the absence of *runtime errors.*

Deductive verification with WP is conducted in a modular way: each C function is proved to respect its function contract (and additional annotations in the function body), specified in ACSL (ANSI/ISO C Specification Language [4]) using typed first-order logic formulas. A *function contract* includes preconditions (**requires** clauses) and postconditions (**ensures** clauses). In addition, variables and memory locations the function is allowed to modify are listed in **assigns** clauses. Loops require additional annotations (**loop invariant** and **loop assigns** clauses). The reader can find more information on ACSL in [8,12]. To show that the given C program respects the behavior specified by its annotations, the WP plug-in [9] generates *proof goals* (also called *proof* *obligations* or *verification conditions*). Such goals are mostly proven automatically, either by internal formula simplifier Qed [19] or external SMT solvers, but in some cases manual intervention is required to help the simplifier and the solvers by creating a *proof script*, a sequence of applications of predefined proof tactics. Examples of tactics include splitting a composed formula into simpler ones, unfolding a definition, instantiating a universally quantified formula with a concrete value (e.g. an index), rewriting bit-level operations, reasoning by case, etc.

Sometimes, it is also possible to circumvent the (time-consuming) development of such a proof script by adding assertions (using an **assert** clause), which must hold at a precise program point inside the function and can act as intermediate lemmas for the proof of complex goals. One example is to state an assertion that is useful to prove a predicate by explicitly providing a hypothesis. In some cases, **assert** clauses can also be generated by other plugins. In particular, the RTE plug-in [32] automatically emits **assert** clauses that are necessary to prove the absence of runtime errors (also known as *undefined behaviors*, as defined in the C standard [35], such as invalid memory accesses or some kinds of arithmetic overflows). Indeed, they must be avoided to ensure the soundness of the verification and exclude potential security vulnerabilities they can enable (notably via invalid memory accesses such as *buffer overflows*). WP generates proof goals for all assertions.

As illustrated in [10], there is a risk to introduce logical inconsistencies into specifications that are assumed, e.g. in entry-point function preconditions, environment hypotheses or postconditions of stub functions. WP can generate additional assertions to *try to detect* potential inconsistencies leading to logical contradictions. While very useful, this feature cannot guarantee the absence of inconsistencies, thus such specifications still must be carefully reviewed.

Verification can often benefit from *ghost code* [11,22,27], that is, additional C code added in annotations and used for verification only. It can create ghost C structures, possibly referring to structures of the original C code. Frama-C ensures non-interference of the ghost world into the non-ghost world: the semantics of the C code is not modified by ghost code (in particular, ghost instructions can read the content of C variables, but not modify it).

Our decision to use Frama-C is due to its capacity to successfully verify industrial C code and the fact that it is currently the only tool for C code verification recognized by ANSSI, the French Common Criteria certification body, as an acceptable formal verification technique for the highest levels of certification [23].

3   Parser Security and Related Requirements

Parsers are generally complex and dangerous software. Indeed, parsed messages can contain a lot of interdependencies between particular message elements. The attacker's control—full or even partial—over the parsed message can allow them to lead the processing system to unintended states and achieve practical exploits. This control can depend on the used cryptographic protections, the distance between the vulnerable parser and external interfaces, and other factors.

The most frequent parsing bugs are related to memory safety. All parsing steps must therefore carefully check that they access only valid memory of all involved buffers, in particular if this access is dependent on input data.

Numerous real-world exploits have been reported in last decades due to memory safety issues. For example, a simple overflow can lead to a segmentation error and a system crash, which can be exploited by attackers for denial-of-service attacks [16]. A buffer overflow during a reading operation, which relies on an incorrect buffer length from a malformed input message, can copy sensitive data from the victim's memory and return it to the attacker, like in the HeartBleed vulnerability [2]. A buffer overflow during a writing operation can allow attackers to rewrite system metadata and get control over the subsequent execution [1].

Even when a message is cryptographically protected, a wrong interplay between the parser and the cryptographic module can lead to a loss of protection, for example, with an acceptance of unauthenticated data. Mechanisms of such a wrong cooperation differ. For example, the parser can return different data than what was previously authenticated by the module [29]. For the case of PKCS#1 v1.5 signature, RSA cryptographic strength is dependent on added padding that enforces modular exponentiation, a key operation used in RSA. The security of the whole signature scheme is thus dependent on the security of its message parser. Many bugs also come from arithmetic overflows [46], which can lead the program to unintended states and trigger some of the previous issues.

Let us state general requirements that will be refined and formalized below for the PKCS#1 v1.5 case ("sec" and "comp" stand for security and compatibility).

$\mathcal{R}_{mem}$: Parser processing must be memory-safe. All memory accesses must be done to valid memory.

$\mathcal{R}_{arith}$: Parser processing must be free of arithmetic overflows, except well-justified cases.

$\mathcal{R}_{sec}$: If the parser accepts a message (and extracts its data), it must enforce all checks necessary to ensure it has correct format and content.

$\mathcal{R}_{comp}$: If the parser refuses an input message, it must be based on a check, clearly showing that the message's format or content is incorrect.

4 PKCS#1 Signature Parser and Its Security

PKCS#1 (Public-Key Cryptography Standard) [47] specifies the usage of RSA algorithm [54], in particular for creation and verification of signatures. PKCS#1 signatures are used to protect X.509 certificates [18]. To enforce security, *padding schemes* (defining how additional padding should be used) are prescribed to be applied with an RSA operation. Although PKCS#1 v1.5 is an older signature padding scheme[1], it is still widely used for backward-compatibility. For example, the newest version of TLS [53] still mandates its support for certificate signature verification. Next to that, it is also still a valid option within SSH [58] and IPSec protocols [40, 48]. For those reasons, it still remains a target for attackers today.

---

[1] for new applications, it is superseded by PKCS#1-PSS.

4.1 TLV-Based Message Structure

TLV-Based Structure. We denote the byte length of a data structure v by $\mathrm{len}(v)$. The structure of messages manipulated by parsers is often based on *Tag-Length-Value triples*, or *TLVs*. A TLV $\theta = (t, l, v)$ contains three consecutive fields: a tag t used to identify the type of the TLV, a length field l containing the byte length of its value field, and a value field v containing the value. In other words, we have $l = \mathrm{len}(v)$. The byte length of the whole TLV θ is the sum of the lengths of its fields, that is, $\mathrm{len}(\theta) = \mathrm{len}(t) + \mathrm{len}(l) + \mathrm{len}(v) = \mathrm{len}(t) + \mathrm{len}(l) + l$.

TLVs can be nested. Following [36], we say that a TLV is *constructed* if its value field contains a sequence of one or several TLVs. Otherwise, a TLV is called *primitive*. A TLV structure creates a tree, where constructed and primitive TLVs correspond, resp., to parent nodes and to leaves. Using this tree-based terminology we can speak of a TLV *level* (i.e., a depth in the tree) and define a parent-child relation between TLVs.

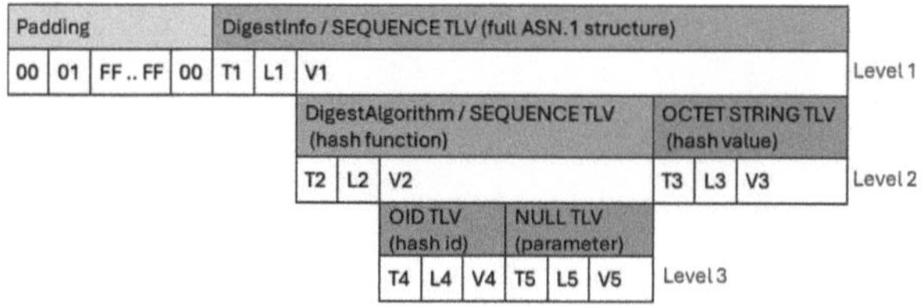

Fig. 1. PKCS#1 v1.5 signature: an ASN.1 structure with 5 nested TLVs preceded by a padding.

Example of TLVs. Consider the signature structure illustrated in Fig. 1, which is used by the target parser as detailed below. For the moment, we ignore the padding bytes on the left. At the upper level—Level 1—TLV $\theta_1 = (T_1, L_1, V_1)$ (of type DigestInfo/SEQUENCE in the standard) is constructed. It contains in its value field V_1 two other TLVs at Level 2: a TLV $\theta_2 = (T_2, L_2, V_2)$ (of type DigestAlgorithm/SEQUENCE in the standard) and a TLV $\theta_3 = (T_3, L_3, V_3)$ with a string of bytes (of type OCTET STRING in the standard). It means that V_1 consecutively stores the fields of θ_2 and θ_3. The latter is primitive. θ_2 is constructed again and contains two TLVs at Level 3, $\theta_4 = (T_4, L_4, V_4)$ (of type Object Identifier, or OID, in the standard) and $\theta_5 = (T_5, L_5, V_5)$ (of type NULL in the standard) containing a value V_5 of length $L_5 = 0$, i.e., an empty value with no bytes.

Correct Message Format and Content. Following [15], we informally define two properties. A message has a *correct format* if it has the expected TLV structure (with tags specified in [47]), and its constructed TLVs verify property $\mathcal{P}_{\mathrm{tree}}$:

$\mathcal{P}_{\text{tree}}$: For a constructed TLV $\theta = (t, l, v)$ whose value contains a sequence of n TLVs θ_i $(1 \leq i \leq n)$, the length of the value field of θ is the sum of lengths of its children θ_i, that is, $l = \sum_{i=1}^{n} \text{len}(\theta_i)$.

A message has a *correct content* if all its primitive TLVs have expected content, i.e. expected values of its length and value fields.

4.2   Algorithm Description

Overview. PKCS#1 v2.2 specification defines PKCS#1 v1.5 signature scheme as a *signature with appendix*. As depicted in Fig. 2, during the signature creation

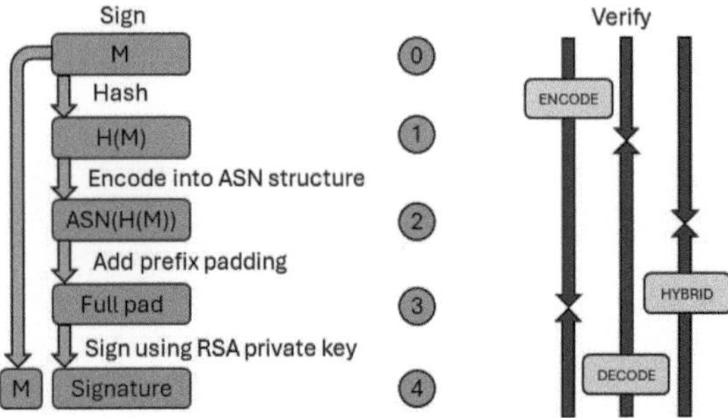

Fig. 2. PKCS#1 v1.5: creating a signature for message M (on the left) and three approaches for verification of the signature of message M (on the right).

procedure, the input message M is hashed, encoded, padded, and signed. The signature is the result of the RSA private key operation on a fully padded encoded message. This signature is then attached to the input message. Both are later required for signature verification, which can be done in several ways.

Signature Creation. First, the hash operation (going from Step 0 to 1) provides a hash $H(M)$. It is then encoded into a so-called ASN.1 structure (Step 1 to 2). This is the nested TLVs structure shown in Fig. 1, which contains two main pieces of information: the OID identifier of the used hash function (θ_4) and the resulting hash value $H(M)$ of the input message (θ_3). An additional tag (θ_5) can host a hash parameter. For the SHA family of hashes, it should be NULL.

Next, a padding is added as a prefix to the ASN.1 structure (Step 2 to 3). It consists of two fixed bytes 0x00 and 0x01, followed by a variable-length sequence of padding bytes 0xFF, and finished by a delimiter byte 0x00, which separates it from the ASN.1 structure. The implementation of the resulting padded message is shown in Fig. 1. The number of padding bytes is chosen to achieve the message size required by the following RSA operation, that is, the size of RSA modulus.[2]

---

[2] this size defines the strength of an RSA operation, e.g. 1024 bits or 2048 bits.

Correct signatures must satisfy two properties. First, the OID TLV must correspond to the ID of a hash function in the standard, and known to the parser. Second, the size of the hash value must correspond to this hash function.

Signature Verification. Because of the deterministic nature of PKCS#1 v1.5 signature padding, it is possible to apply different approaches to signature verification, as depicted in Fig. 2. First, the Encoding approach—the main procedure presented in [47]—does not actually involve any parsing. Given an input message M and a hash function, M is re-encoded (Steps 0 to 3) and then compared byte-by-byte with the result of the RSA operation (using a public key to reverse from signature to padded message, Step 4 to 3). Omitting the parsing steps avoids a difficult situation, where all variants of Bleichenbacher's attack were reported.

However, the specification [47] also allows an alternative, the Decoding approach. There, the padded message content is parsed to extract the message hash (Steps 4 to 1). If the extracted hash is equal to the re-computed one (Step 0 to 1), the signature is accepted. To be secure, the parser must check for correctness of the message format and content. Compared to the previous one, this approach avoids allocating space for the re-encoded message, which has the RSA modulus size.

As reported in [57], many libraries use a Hybrid approach. They parse only the padding (cf. Fig. 1) and then extract the entire ASN.1 structure (Steps 4 to 2). The latter is not parsed, but instead compared, as in the Encoding approach, against the re-encoded structure (Steps 0 to 2). This approach seems a reasonable trade-off. Parsing of ASN.1, which is structurally complex, is avoided, resulting in a higher security assurance. At the same time, the ASN.1 structure is relatively small compared to modulus size, thus reducing memory space overhead.

The different approaches of the signature verification also impact the proof. If the Decoding approach is used, $\mathcal{P}_{\mathrm{sec}}$ and $\mathcal{P}_{\mathrm{comp}}$ are deduced from applied parsing steps. For the Encoding approach, the same properties would have to be proven based on a successfully matched re-encoded padded message (Step 3).[3] In this work, we focus on the Decoding approach, which contains complex parsing steps and is therefore the more bug prone and the most relevant for formal verification.

DER Encoding and Unique Binary Representation. One possible way to encode TLVs at binary level is defined by *DER (Distinguished Encoding Rules)* [36]. We also use it in our parser. The latest standard [47] mandates the use of DER for the creation of new signatures. DER ensures a *unique binary representation* of the data in the TLVs. When DER is used in PKCS#1 v1.5 to encode ASN.1, each of the tag and length fields of its TLVs is stored in *exactly one byte*.

Backward-Compatibility. As it often happens in practice, evolution of software impacts compatibility. To ensure backward-compatibility, the standard [47] contains two requirements, which break the uniqueness of binary representation of

---

[3] This approach actually exploits the uniqueness of the padded message for particular hash function and input message M, which is discussed in the next sections.

the message: an *optional* presence of the NULL TLV[4] and support of another encoding, *BER (Basic Encoding Rules)* [36]. For simplicity, we do not support these requirements in this work (see also Sect. 4.4).

4.3   Signature Security

As already mentioned in Sect. 3, RSA security depends on the padding scheme. If the parser does not strictly check correct format and content of the padded message (State 3 of Fig. 2), it may lead to *universal signature forgery*, meaning that the attacker is able to create another actor's signature for *any* given message so that the resulting signature will be accepted by signature verification.

Since Bleichenbacher's original attack [28] reported in 2006, many variants have been found for the Decoding and Hybrid approaches. The attack is possible under the following two conditions. First, the signature must be verified using a public key of a specific small size—typically with public key exponent equal to 3. While rarely seen in practice currently [57], it can still be found in sensitive parts of the cryptographic ecosystem. For example, in 2021, Debian trust-anchor certificate bundle (ca-certificate) contained two certificates with such keys [57]. Four years later, they are still present on Ubuntu LTS 22.04.4.

Second, the verification procedure must ignore a sufficient number of bytes inside a padded message. Using the ignored bytes, an attacker can manage to compute a fake signature such that a public key operation on it—that is, taking a power of 3 *without modulo computation* in this case due to a small value— matches the data inside the checked bytes, such as the input message's hash. Note that it is impossible to avoid modulo computation if no byte inside a padded message is ignored and all are checked to some concrete values. Such a computation is then considered infeasible without knowledge of the private key.

Bleichenbacher's attack variants differ in locations that the buggy parser ignores. The original report [28] found parsers that ignored trailing bytes at the end of the padded message, i.e., after a correct ASN.1 structure. In [42,49], the length field in the NULL TLV was not checked and its value skipped. Another variant [34] ignored bytes in an extended form of the length field due to an arithmetic overflow. In yet another variant [15], padding bytes were not checked.

We can now formulate a security property, which refines $\mathcal{R}_{\text{sec}}$ for the PKCS#1 v1.5 parser and gives a sufficient condition to rule out such attacks.

$\mathcal{P}_{\text{uniq}}$: The parser accepts a padded message (depicted at State 3 in Fig. 2) only if it checks each of its bytes for a unique correct value determined by input message M and hash function according to the PKCS#1 v1.5 specification.

4.4   Target Parser Implementation

For the sake of simplicity, we verify a representative PKCS#1 v1.5 signature parser that we implemented in C. It follows the Decoding approach, which is

---

[4] This requirement is ignored by many open-source libraries [57] including OpenSSL v3.5, see https://openssl-library.org/source.

more bug-prone and thus more relevant for verification. Three main functions perform the parsing. Function `pars_PKCS1_lev1` is the parser's entry point. It removes the padding and realizes checks for the TLV at Level 1 (cf. Fig. 1). It expects two buffers (see line 649 of Fig. 7): the padded message (`pad_msg` of size `pad_msg_sz`), which is the output of an RSA operation on signature (State 3 in Fig 2), and the input message M (`in_msg` of size `in_msg_sz`). Its callee, function `pars_PKCS1_lev2`, handles the nested TLVs (Levels 2 and 3) and makes all semantic checks for the primitive TLVs' content. Repetitive steps for parsing a TLV are encapsulated in function `read_one_tlv`. The value returned by the parser either indicates that all checks pass, or provides an error code.

Our verification perimeter does not include the RSA operation, but includes a call to a hash computation (modeled by one of the three stub functions `stub_shaX`). This allows us to extend our properties to check that a proper hash function was indeed applied. As it is common for open-source libraries, the chosen hash function is indicated by an input parameter (`expect_hash_ind`,

```
 6  typedef unsigned char ul;
 7  typedef unsigned int uint;

70  /*@ ghost
71  const uint g_tlv_1[4] = {1, TAG_SEQ, CONSTR, 1};
72  const uint g_tlv_2[7] = {2, TAG_SEQ, CONSTR, 2, TAG_OCT,  PRIM, 0};
73  const uint g_tlv_3[7] = {2, TAG_OID, PRIM,   0, TAG_NULL, PRIM, 0};
74
75  \ghost const uint* const g_tlv_spec[3] =
76    { &g_tlv_1[0], &g_tlv_2[0], &g_tlv_3[0] };
77
78  ul* g_tlv_1_p[1]; ul* g_tlv_2_p[2]; ul* g_tlv_3_p[2];
79
80  ul* \ghost * const g_tlv_p[3] =
81    { &g_tlv_1_p[0], &g_tlv_2_p[0], &g_tlv_3_p[0] };  */
```

Fig. 3. Basic types and a ghost model of the TLV structure of ASN.1. Each `g_tlv_N` contains the specification of one TLV sequence.

see lines 649–650 of Fig. 7), expected to be a valid index in the list of supported hashes (see line 597). It allows the parser to check the hash function used inside the signature (as stored in the OID TLV) to any declaration external to PKCS#1 (e.g., the hash function declaration in the field of a X.509 certificate).

As it is essential for secure parsing programming, we chose a clear parsing pattern for our code, i.e., it parses all TLVs of the same sequence and checks $\mathcal{P}_{tree}$ property with respect to its parent before starting to parse its children. Similarly, before starting to read a new TLV—in functions `read_one_tlv` and `pars_PKCS1_lev1`—we check that the read indices are inside the entire parsed message (for Levels 2 and 3, it is done indirectly by checking the inclusion inside the value field of the parent TLV).

Our parser supports three hash functions (SHA256, SHA512, and, for backward compatibility, SHA1). Adding new functions is straightforward. The complete code is provided in the companion artifact. For lack of space, only essential

346   M. Hána et al.

(slightly simplified) parts are presented in Figs. 3–7, in which we preserve the line numbers of the complete file for convenience of the readers.

5   Formal ACSL Properties and Verification Approach

Correct Message Format (incl. $\mathcal{P}_{\text{tree}}$). To describe TLV-based structures, our methodology strongly relies on *inductive predicate* definitions in ACSL. Indeed, due to the structural nature of $\mathcal{P}_{\text{tree}}$, it is convenient to inductively define the correctness of a parsing step, as well as to maintain information about the already (correctly) parsed elements of the structure in the form of an inductive predicate. An interesting feature of the approach is that those predicates are *generic*, and are parameterized by a concrete TLV structure, defined as a *ghost model*.

Figure 3 presents the ghost model of the ASN.1 structure (cf. Fig. 1). The ghost models of the sequences of TLVs at Levels 1–3 are encoded, resp., in arrays `g_tlv_`N with $N \in \{1, 2, 3\}$ (see lines 71–73 in Fig. 3). The first byte indicates the number of TLVs in the sequence. The next bytes store the descriptions for each TLV of the sequence. Each description is composed of three bytes. The first and the second bytes indicate, resp., the expected tag and TLV type (constructed or primitive). For a primitive TLV, the third byte contains a dummy value (here,

```
86   inductive valid_tlv(u1* start, integer prev_pars, integer size_pars,
87     integer tlv_num_pars, integer tlv_id, boolean with_children)
88   {
89   case empty: \forall u1* start, integer tlv_id;
90     valid_tlv(start, 0, 0, 0, tlv_id, \true);
91
92   case new_tlv_child_not_incl:
93     \forall u1* start, integer prev_pars, integer size_pars,
94       integer tlv_num_pars, integer tlv_id;
95     \let tlv_cur = g_tlv_spec[tlv_id];
96     0 <= tlv_num_pars < tlv_cur[0] &&
97     valid_tlv(start, prev_pars, size_pars, tlv_num_pars, tlv_id, \true) &&
98     start[size_pars] == (u1)tlv_cur[1 + tlv_num_pars*3]
99     ==>
100    valid_tlv(start, size_pars, size_pars + 2 + start[size_pars + 1],
101      tlv_num_pars+1, tlv_id, \false);
       ...
113  case last_tlv_constr_incl_child:
114    \forall u1* start, integer prev_pars, integer size_pars,
115      integer tlv_num_pars, integer tlv_id, integer nest_prev_pars;
116    \let tlv_cur = g_tlv_spec[tlv_id];
117    \let tlv_link = tlv_cur[3 + (tlv_num_pars-1)*3];
118    1 <= tlv_num_pars &&
119    valid_tlv(start, prev_pars, size_pars, tlv_num_pars, tlv_id, \false) &&
120    (u1)tlv_cur[2 + (tlv_num_pars-1)*3] == CONSTR &&
121    valid_tlv(start + prev_pars + 2, nest_prev_pars, start[prev_pars + 1],
122      g_tlv_spec[tlv_link][0], tlv_link, \true)
123    ==>
124    valid_tlv(start, prev_pars, size_pars, tlv_num_pars, tlv_id, \true); }
```

Fig. 4. Inductive predicate for correct message format (`start`: parsing beginning, `prev_pars`: previous number of consumed (parsed) bytes, `size_pars`: number of consumed bytes, `tlv_num_pars`: number of parsed TLVs, `tlv_id`: TLV index inside `g_tlv_spec`, `with_children`: child TLV sequence checked).

0, cf. lines 72, 73). For a constructed TLV, the third byte is used to find the ghost model of the child sequence of TLVs. It is indicated indirectly,[5] as an index in the ghost array g_tlv_spec (cf. lines 75–76) that stores pointers to the ghost models of TLV sequences. For instance, index 2 on line 72 refers to the sequence of Level 3 since the element of index 2 in g_tlv_spec is &g_tlv_3[0]. The \ghost keyword indicates that the pointed arrays are also ghost. As shown in Fig. 1, each TLV level contains one sequence of TLVs in our case[6]. Lines 78–81 of Fig. 3 will be explained below.

The valid_tlv inductive predicate defined in Fig. 4 states that a given TLV sequence has a correct format (so far). It takes 6 arguments. First, parameter start points to a location where the parsing of the TLV sequence begins. The number of already consumed bytes and already parsed TLVs are given, resp., in size_pars and tlv_num_pars. The ghost model of the target TLV sequence is indicated as its index within g_tlv_spec by tlv_id. The last two parameters are more technical, related to the current stage of the parsing. Parameter with_children indicates whether child TLV sequences were already resolved (i.e., checked) for the last parsed TLV, as described below. Lastly, prev_pars is the number of bytes consumed before parsing the last parsed TLV.

For example, consider the TLV structure of Fig. 1 and assume θ_1 starts at p. When the parsing of TLV θ_1 is correctly finished at Level 1, before checking the child sequence, we have (i) valid_tlv(p,0,2+L1,1,0,\false), and (ii) valid_tlv(p,0,2+L1,1,0,\true) after checking the child sequence. The latter step requires a correct format of the sequence at Level 2, leading after parsing θ_2 (and its child sequence) to (iii) valid_tlv(p+2,0,2+L2,1,1,\true) and finally to (iv) valid_tlv(p+2,2+L2,4+L2+L3,2,1,\true) after parsing θ_3. Recall that the ghost models of Levels 1, 2 are, resp., at indices 0, 1 in g_tlv_spec. To respect $\mathcal{P}_{\text{tree}}$, L_1 must be equal to $4 + L_2 + L_3$.

Each induction step is defined by one case. Case empty initializes the induction for a starting pointer and a ghost model, with no parsed bytes and no parsed TLVs (lines 89–90 in Fig. 4). Next, case new_tlv_child_not_incl (lines 92–101) parses the next TLV in the sequence. The tag and the number of TLVs are checked against the ghost model (lines 95–96, 98), the size of the new TLV is added to the number of parsed bytes and the number of parsed TLVs is incremented (lines 100–101). After this step, with_children is false, indicating that for the last parsed TLV, the child sequence has still to be checked.

To deduce a full validity (i.e., with with_children set to true) for the last parsed TLV, we introduce two other cases, resp., for a constructed and a primitive TLV. Case last_tlv_constr_incl_child is applied if the last parsed TLV θ is constructed and its child sequence has not yet been checked (lines 119–120). We identify the ghost model of this child sequence (line 117), and check that the child TLVs are correct with respect to this model, including

---

⁵ An alternative way of encoding was suggested by a reviewer. The investigation of such alternative approaches is left for future work.

⁶ In general, there will be n sequences of TLVs at Level $k + 1$ if at Level k we have n TLVs having a child sequence.

their own children if any (lines 121–122). Property $\mathcal{P}_{\text{tree}}$ is then ensured for θ and its children. The case for a primitive TLV is trivial (switching `with_children` to `true`), and is omitted here.

In the previous example, step `last_tlv_constr_incl_child` is used to deduce (ii) from (i) and (iv). The reader can check by a step-by-step application that it works only if $L_1 = 4 + L_2 + L_3$, thus ensuring $\mathcal{P}_{\text{tree}}$.

Correct Message Content. According to [47] (and using the notation of Fig. 1), a valid message content must satisfy the following properties for primitive TLVs. (These properties are specific for the considered message structure.)

$\mathcal{P}_1$: The parsed OID (fields L_4 and V_4) corresponds to the indicated hash function (parameter `expect_hash_ind` in the entry point function).

$\mathcal{P}_2$: The length of NULL TLV (field L_5) is equal to 0.

$\mathcal{P}_3$: The length of the parsed hash value (L_3) corresponds to the parsed OID.

$\mathcal{P}_4$: The function used for hash re-computation corresponds to the parsed OID.

$\mathcal{P}_5$: Hash re-computation is applied on input message M (parameter `in_msg` in the entry point function).

```
193  predicate prim_tlv_oid_param(integer exp_hash_ind) =
194    \let oid_len = *(g_tlv_p[2][0]+1);                                  // Reads L4
195    \let oid_val_p = g_tlv_p[2][0]+2;                                   // Points to V4
196    \let param_len = *(g_tlv_p[2][1]+1);                               // Reads L5
197    (oid_len == OID_list[exp_hash_ind][0]) &&                          // En-
198    same_content(OID_list[exp_hash_ind]+1, oid_val_p, oid_len) &&  //   sures P1
199    param_len == 0;                                                    // Ensures P2
```

Fig. 5. $\mathcal{P}_1$ and $\mathcal{P}_2$: content properties related to OID and NULL TLVs.

$\mathcal{P}_6$: The parsed hash value (V_3) is equal to the re-computed hash value.

Since our inductive predicate `valid_tlv` focuses on the correct format in a generic way and does not trace particular TLVs, we cannot use it to identify, e.g., θ_4 for validating $\mathcal{P}_1$ when looking at the message as a whole. Similarly, as we can see for example for $\mathcal{P}_3$, there are dependencies between different TLVs, sometimes from different TLV levels. We detail here only $\mathcal{P}_1$, $\mathcal{P}_2$ and $\mathcal{P}_5$.

To express these properties, we introduce a ghost array `g_tlv_p` (see lines 78–81 of Fig. 3), whose structure and size are similar to `g_tlv_spec`. During parsing, we store—via ghost code—pointers to the beginning of each primitive TLV at the corresponding locations of this array. Once parsing is completed successfully, it allows us to refer to any primitive TLV. For instance, `g_tlv_p[2][0]` stores a pointer to the first TLV (second index 0) in the TLV sequence at Level 3 (first index 2), that is, to θ_4. Added ghost code is simple—it stores a pointer to each primitive TLV into the corresponding array element. It is however crucial to capture all primitive TLVs. To avoid any mistake, we introduce a second inductive predicate `prim_gh_set`. Structurally, it mimics `valid_tlv` presented above, with two important differences: it does not check again the expected tag, and it requires `g_tlv_p` to be correctly assigned with pointers to primitive TLVs. Maintaining `prim_gh_set` together with `valid_tlv` ensures that the message was checked for correct format and all pointers to primitive TLVs were correctly set, being readily available for content verifications.

Figure 5 shows a predicate to check $\mathcal{P}_1$ and $\mathcal{P}_2$. On lines 194–196, the OID and NULL TLVs (θ_4 and θ_5) are accessed. To get the OID length L_4 we first find θ_4, the first TLV at level 3, using pointer `g_tlv_p[2][0]`. This gives us the address of T_4. We increment it by 1 to get the address of L_4, that we dereference to get its value. Using our list `OID_list` of IDs of supported hash functions, line 197 checks that L_4 is the expected length of the ID, while line 198 verifies that V_4 contains the expected ID. On line 199 we then check L_5 to be 0.

```
227  /*@ ghost
228  ul g_backup_mes_to_hash[INT_MAX];
229  uint g_backup_len;
230
231  /@ requires \valid_read(msg + (0 .. msg_sz-1));
232     terminates \true; exits \false;
233     assigns g_backup_mes_to_hash[0 .. msg_sz-1];
234     ensures same_content(msg, &g_backup_mes_to_hash[0], msg_sz);
235     ensures g_backup_len == msg_sz; @/
236  void g_make_backup(ul* msg, int msg_sz); */
```

Fig. 6. Ghost array and function for creating a memory snapshot.

Ghost code is also used to store necessary information for the proof of $\mathcal{P}_4$ and $\mathcal{P}_5$. Let us detail $\mathcal{P}_5$ here. It requires to check that the hash function is applied indeed on the *original* message. To keep a copy of the message, we introduce a ghost array `g_backup_mes_to_hash` and a stub function `g_make_backup` (see Fig. 6). Its contract ensures that the function copies the content of the input into the ghost array. We call it at the very beginning of the entry point function (line 652 of Fig. 7). To verify $\mathcal{P}_5$ at a hash computation, typically realized by a crypto library call, it is sufficient to add a precondition checking that the content of its input array is identical to the one saved in `g_backup_mes_to_hash`. The strong separation[7] of the non-ghost world from the ghost one enforced by **Frama-C** [4] excludes unintended modifications of `g_backup_mes_to_hash` in the C code, thus making this approach consistent.

Entry Point Function Contract. Figure 7 shows the contract for the entry point function, `pars_PKCS1_lev1`. Several predicates are introduced to deal with the padding shown in Fig. 1. Predicate `prefix_prop` expresses the presence of the two fixed prefix bytes (lines 557–558). Then, `padding_prop` requires a variable length sequence containing (at least `MIN_FF_COUNT`) times 0xFF and finished by a delimiter byte (at offset `pad_bound`). Predicate `asn_prop` states that the Level 1 ASN.1 TLV is correctly formatted (using `valid_tlv`)

---

[7] Indeed, the C code cannot see ghost variables at all, while the ghost code can only read non-ghost variables but cannot modify them.

and occupies the entire space between the delimiter and the end of the padded message. As we already explained, it is valid only if all its TLV descendants were correctly parsed too. Predicate `ghost_set_prop` ensures that referenced ghost pointers were set correctly. Regarding message content properties, $\mathcal{P}_1$–$\mathcal{P}_4$ and $\mathcal{P}_6$ are regrouped in predicate `prim_tlv` (not detailed here, used on line 625), while $\mathcal{P}_5$ is ensured at another location.

$\mathcal{R}_{\text{sec}}$ *and* $\mathcal{P}_{\text{uniq}}$. As we can see on lines 614–625 of Fig. 7, if the parser accepts the message, the conjunction of all predicates above must hold. We recall there are 3 primitive TLVs within ASN.1 structure: θ_3, θ_4 and θ_5. One can easily see that properties $\mathcal{P}_1$–$\mathcal{P}_6$ specify all bytes of fields L_i, V_i for $3 \leq i \leq 5$[8] by making them uniquely determined by the input message and expected hash function. Indeed, for example on lines 197–198 of Fig. 5, we specify all bytes of L_4 and V_4 when we match parsed OID against parser list of supported OIDs. Inductive predicate `valid_tlv` then provides unique specification for all TLV tags. Next to that, due to $\mathcal{P}_{\text{tree}}$, lengths of constructed TLVs are uniquely determined by the contained primitive TLVs. Based on this analysis of our properties, we see that the proved parser indeed *accepts only one padded message* for each input message and expected hash function and so it fulfills $\mathcal{P}_{\text{uniq}}$.[9] As explained in Sect. 4.3, this guarantees its security against Bleichenbacher's attack family.

$\mathcal{R}_{\text{comp}}$. We formalize our properties for $\mathcal{R}_{\text{comp}}$ on lines 627–647 of Fig. 7. The specification is split based on the error type: for example, if an error is returned for insufficient space during the parsing of a new TLV, an unexpected tag or an inconsistent TLV structure (with regard to $\mathcal{P}_{\text{tree}}$), it implies a falsification of `valid_tlv` (lines 635–638). In case an error indicates a wrong content, we prove a correct setting of ghost pointers and a falsification of content properties (lines 640–647). An additional reason to split `prim_gh_set` and `valid_tlv` into two separate predicates—despite their similar structure—is the following. Predicate `prim_gh_set` can be falsified also by a buggy ghost code, (i.e. a mistake made during proof development). On the other hand, $\mathcal{R}_{\text{comp}}$ requires that the parser returns an error code only based on a wrong message format or content. Inside our specification, we therefore cannot allow the parser to refuse the message based on a failure of `prim_gh_set`.

$\mathcal{R}_{\text{mem}}$ *and* $\mathcal{R}_{\text{arith}}$. $\mathcal{R}_{\text{mem}}$ and $\mathcal{R}_{\text{arith}}$ are checked by annotations automatically generated by RTE (see Sect. 3). We specify a precondition of the entry point function, claiming memory validity of both input buffers (lines 595–596 of Fig. 7). Regarding $\mathcal{R}_{\text{arith}}$, as explained in [32], some arithmetic overflows (e.g. for char or unsigned integers) fall into the category of implementation-defined or even well-

---

[8] V_5 is absent as L_5 is equal to 0.

[9] An explicit specification and verification of $\mathcal{P}_{\text{uniq}}$ in Frama-C may be performed using the RPP plug-in [13], which allows users to express *relational properties* between two runs of the parser. It could be used to prove that if the parser accepts two padded messages for a given message M and a given hash function, then these two padded messages are necessarily identical. This extension is left for future work.

```
556  /*@ ghost uint pad_bound; */
557  /*@ predicate prefix_prop(u1* pad_msg) =
558    pad_msg[OFF_B1] == EXP_B1 && pad_msg[OFF_B2] == EXP_B2;
559  predicate padding_prop(u1* pad_msg, integer pad_msg_sz, integer pad_bound)=
560    2+ MIN_FF_COUNT <= pad_bound < pad_msg_sz &&
561    (\forall integer padd_off; 2 <= padd_off < pad_bound ==>
562      pad_msg[padd_off] == EXP_FF) && pad_msg[pad_bound] == EXP_DELIM;
563  predicate asn_prop(u1* pad_msg, integer pad_msg_sz, integer pad_bound,
564    integer tlv_num) =
565    2+ MIN_FF_COUNT <= pad_bound < pad_msg_sz &&
566    \exists integer prev_pars; valid_tlv(pad_msg + pad_bound + 1, prev_pars,
567      pad_msg_sz - pad_bound - 1, tlv_num, 0, \true);
568  predicate ghost_set_prop(u1* pad_msg, integer pad_msg_sz, integer pad_bound,
569    integer tlv_num)=
570    2+ MIN_FF_COUNT <= pad_bound < pad_msg_sz &&
571    \exists integer prev_pars; prim_gh_set(pad_msg + pad_bound + 1, prev_pars,
572      pad_msg_sz - pad_bound -1, tlv_num, 0, \true); */

       ...

595  requires \valid(pad_msg + (0 .. pad_msg_sz-1));
596  requires \valid(in_msg + (0 .. in_msg_sz - 1));
597  requires 0 <= expect_hash_ind < SUPP_OID_COUNT;

       ...

614  // ======== SECURITY PART ========
615  behavior sec_format:
616    ensures prefix: \result == PASS_OK ==> prefix_prop(pad_msg);
617    ensures pad: \result == PASS_OK ==>
618      padding_prop(pad_msg, pad_msg_sz, pad_bound);
619    ensures asn: \result == PASS_OK ==>
620      asn_prop(pad_msg, pad_msg_sz, pad_bound, g_tlv_1[0]);
621
622  behavior sec_prim_tlv:
623    ensures ghost_set: \result == PASS_OK ==>
624      ghost_set_prop(pad_msg, pad_msg_sz, pad_bound, g_tlv_1[0]);
625    ensures prim_tlv:  \result == PASS_OK ==> prim_tlv(expect_hash_ind);
626
627  // ======== COMPATIBILITY (ACCEPTANCE) PART ========
628  behavior acc_format:
629    ensures prefix:
630      \result == ERR_B1||\result == ERR_B2 ==> !prefix_prop(pad_msg);
631    ensures pad:
632      \result == ERR_FF_COUNT||\result == ERR_DELIM ==>
633      \forall uint pad_bound; !padding_prop(pad_msg, pad_msg_sz, pad_bound) ||
634      !asn_prop(pad_msg, pad_msg_sz, pad_bound, g_tlv_1[0]);
635    ensures asn:
636      \result == ERR_LEN||\result == ERR_TAG||\result == ERR_TLV_LEN_CONSIST ==>
637      \forall uint pad_bound; !padding_prop(pad_msg, pad_msg_sz, pad_bound) ||
638      !asn_prop(pad_msg, pad_msg_sz, pad_bound, g_tlv_1[0]);
639
640  behavior acc_prim_tlv:
641    ensures ghost_set:
642      \result == ERR_HASH_SZ||\result == ERR_HASH_OID||\result == ERR_HASH_VAL||
643      \result == ERR_NULL_SZ ==>
644      ghost_set_prop(pad_msg, pad_msg_sz, pad_bound, g_tlv_1[0]);
645    ensures prim_tlv:
646      \result == ERR_HASH_SZ||\result == ERR_HASH_OID||\result == ERR_HASH_VAL||
647      \result == ERR_NULL_SZ ==> prim_tlv_neg(expect_hash_ind);
648  */
649  int pars_PKCS1_lev1(u1* pad_msg, int pad_msg_sz, u1* in_msg, int in_msg_sz,
650    uint expect_hash_ind)
651  {
652    //@ ghost g_make_backup(in_msg, in_msg_sz);
```

Fig. 7. Entry point parser contract, where pad_msg and pad_msg_sz denote the padded message and its size, in_msg and in_msg_sz, the input message M and its size, and expect_hash_ind is the index of the used hash function.

defined behavior and thus are not checked by RTE by default. In our verification, we also activate the corresponding checks to avoid any overflows.

Current Limitations and Perspectives of Extension. While this case study already targets a representative parser, our approach may require extensions for the verification of other PKCS#1 v1.5 parser implementations or different TLV-based protocol. We currently consider the Decoding approach, with 1-byte fields both for a tag and a length field, and a mandatory presence of a NULL TLV. Extensions to support other choices are left as future work.

6   Proof Results

Summary of results. We use Frama-C v. 29.0 (Copper) with external SMT prover Alt-Ergo 2.5.4. on a VM running Ubuntu 24.04 under VirtualBox (running on a host PC under Windows 10 with Intel(R) Core(TM) i7 CPU @ 2.70 GHz) with 4 processors and 8 GB dedicated to the VM. The verified parser (155 lines of C code) includes seven C functions (including three stubs) annotated with 364 lines[10] of ACSL, giving a 2.35 spec-to-code ratio. To show the absence of runtime errors, we use the RTE plugin, which automatically generates 52 asserts.

Overall, the WP plugin generates and successfully proves 434 proof goals. Among them, reachability analysis proves 4 goals. The internal WP simplifier, Qed, discharges 251 goals. Alt-Ergo solves 176 goals. 3 goals require manually created WP proof scripts. The whole proof (with additional 60 consistency checks activated by `-wp-smoke-tests`) takes 2 min 8 s, with up to 14.2 s for one proof goal. We estimate the total effort to perform the verification case study (incl. creating a suitable methodology for a new kind of target code, identifying properties, annotating code and creating necessary proof scripts) as 6 person-months. Acquiring necessary expertise in cybersecurity and proof is not included in it.

Selected Difficulties. The created proof scripts instantiate the most complex induction steps of `valid_tlv` (see line 113 in Fig. 4) and `prim_gh_set`, which check the nested TLV structure. Next to that, we use several **assert** clauses, which further help us to instantiate other steps of these inductive predicates. It is for example necessary for each TLV sequence to initialize induction.

In our work, we experienced a specific difficulty with proofs involving inductive predicates. Indeed, in some cases, an assignment to an unrelated memory location would cause previously established instances of the inductive predicate to be "forgotten" by the prover. We worked around this issue by adding **assert** clauses for initial induction steps after the writing. This is not a universal solution and another methodology might be needed in other cases.

---

[10] We apply cloc utility. It considers ACSL annotations as other C comments. We thus removed classical C comments to count ACSL. Empty lines in C code are ignored.

7   Related Work and Conclusion

Related Work. Various approaches using formal methods were already applied on parsers. Symbolic execution and adaptive combinatorial testing were used to generate test suites and to discover a significant number of bugs in PKCS#1 v1.5 signature verification of public cryptographic libraries [15,57]. Formal verification was deployed [21,57] using Coq and Agda, providing test oracles and a reference implementation of PKCS#1 v1.5 signature and X.509 certificate validation logic. A formally proven PKCS#1 v1.5 signature verification procedure was further extracted to OCaml source code [57]. However, the proof was not performed for efficient real-life parsers. Our approach is on the contrary suitable for proving optimized parsers in C. Ramananandro et al. developed an automatic parser generator, formally proven in F*, and extracted C code using a non-verified tool [52]. Although it can serve to generate a big amount of parser code automatically [55], some validation logic is not expressible and the corresponding code must be added manually [21]. Li et al. used ACL2 formal language and developed a formally verified PDF parser and a semantic validator [45]. However, the correspondence between a formally verified ACL2 code and an efficient C code was not proved.

More generally, this work is related to other verification case studies [31]. Various verification tools were applied to verify real-life code, including KeY [7, 20], VerCors [3,50], Frama-C [22,24,26], SPARK [17,25], VCC [43], Dafny [14,44], VeriFast [37,51] and many others. Each new case study contributes to enhance verification tools by identifying their limitations and to push further the frontiers of what is achievable for formal verification.

Conclusion and Future Work. We have proposed a *methodology for formal verification* of a PKCS#1 v1.5 parser in Frama-C, and successfully *verified a representative parser* written in C. The proven properties include *security*, protecting against any variant of *Bleichenbacher's attack* and ensuring *memory safety*, and *compatibility*, i.e. non-rejection of a correct signature. To the best of our knowledge, it is the first time that formal verification is applied directly on the C implementation of such a parser. We proposed an original specification approach that relies on *inductive predicates*—defined in a generic way—and a separate *ghost model* encoding a concrete TLV-based structure to be parsed. We believe that this separation brings benefits for future extensions and industrial applications. The inductive predicates—more difficult to write—can be reused, whereas the ghost model should be adapted for another structure, that can be done more easily by non-experts.

Future work includes extensions to support additional features (see the end of Sect. 5), and formal verification of real-life open-source C parsers. A comparison of our parser with other similar parsers (in particular, regarding their performances) is another interesting work perspective. We believe that our methodology also provides a basis for future extensions to other TLV-based formats, like X.509 certificates [18]. A study of applications of Large Language Models (LLMs) to generate (candidate) specifications for parsers is another future work direction, which becomes popular today [6,30,38,39,56]. Finally, an easy integration of the proposed methodologies into industrial workflows should remain an important point of attention.

Data Availability Statement. The companion artifact [33] contains the annotated code of the parser, examples of its buggy versions, proof scripts, and a virtual machine (with all necessary tools installed), ready to reproduce the proof.

Acknowledgments. Parts of this work have been funded by the French National Research Agency (ANR) through PEPR Cyber Secureval (Grant ANR-22-PECY-0005), EMASS (Grant ANR-22-CE39-0014), CoMeMov (Grant ANR-22-CE25-0018), VeDySec (Grant ANR-24-ASM2-0001), and the European Union's Horizon Europe projects SecOPERA (Grant 101070599) and VASSAL (Grant 101160022). We would also like to thank the Frama-C team for their support and the reviewers for their insightful comments.

References

1. CVE-2002-0639 (2002). https://cve.mitre.org/cgi-bin/cvename.cgi?name=CVE-2002-0639
2. Heartbleed bug (2014). https://www.heartbleed.com
3. Armborst, L., et al.: The VerCors verifier: a progress report. In: Proceedings of the 36th International Conference on Computer Aided Verification (CAV 2024). LNCS, vol. 14682, pp. 3–18. Springer (2024). https://doi.org/10.1007/978-3-031-65630-9_1
4. Baudin, P., Filliâtre, J.C., Marché, C., Monate, B., Moy, Y., Prevosto, V.: ACSL: ANSI/ISO C Specification Language. http://frama-c.com/acsl.html
5. Baudin, P., et al.: The dogged pursuit of bug-free c programs: the Frama-c software analysis platform. Commun. ACM (2021). https://doi.org/10.1145/3470569
6. Beckert, B., Klamroth, J., Pfeifer, W., Röper, P., Teuber, S.: Towards combining the cognitive abilities of large language models with the rigor of deductive program verification. In: Proceedings of the 12th International Symposium on Leveraging Applications of Formal Methods, Verification and Validation (ISoLA 2024). LNCS, vol. 15222, pp. 242–257. Springer (2024). https://doi.org/10.1007/978-3-031-75387-9_15
7. Beckert, B., Sanders, P., Ulbrich, M., Wiesler, J., Witt, S.: Formally verifying an efficient sorter. In: Proceedings of the 30th International Conference on Tools and Algorithms for the Construction and Analysis of Systems (TACAS 2024). LNCS, vol. 14570, pp. 268–287. Springer (2024). https://doi.org/10.1007/978-3-031-57246-3_15
8. Blanchard, A.: Introduction to C program proof with Frama-C and its WP plugin (2020). https://allan-blanchard.fr/publis/frama-c-wp-tutorial-en.pdf
9. Blanchard, A., Bobot, F., Baudin, P., Correnson, L.: Formally verifying that a program does what it should: the Wp plug-in. In: Guide to Software Verification with Frama-C. Core Components, Usages, and Applications, pp. 187–261. Springer (2024). https://doi.org/10.1007/978-3-031-55608-1_4

10. Blanchard, A., Correnson, L., Djoudi, A., Kosmatov, N.: No smoke without fire: detecting specification inconsistencies with Frama-C/WP. In: Proceedings of the 18th International Conference on Tests and Proofs (TAP 2024), co-located with the 26th International Symposium on Formal Methods (FM 2024). LNCS, vol. 15153, pp. 65–83. Springer (2024). https://doi.org/10.1007/978-3-031-72044-4_4

11. Blanchard, A., Loulergue, F., Kosmatov, N.: Ghosts for lists: a critical module of Contiki verified in Frama-C. In: Proceedings of the 10th NASA Formal Methods Symposium (NFM 2018). LNCS, vol. 10811, pp. 37–53. Springer (2018). https://doi.org/10.1007/978-3-319-77935-5

12. Blanchard, A., Marché, C., Prevosto, V.: Formally expressing what a program should do: the ACSL language. In: Guide to Software Verification with Frama-C. Core Components, Usages, and Applications, pp. 3–80. Springer (2024). https://doi.org/10.1007/978-3-031-55608-1_1

13. Blatter, L., Kosmatov, N., Prevosto, V., Robles, V.: Chapter 10: specification and verification of high-level properties. In: Guide to Software Verification with Frama-C. Core Components, Usages, and Applications, pp. 457–486. Springer (2024). https://doi.org/10.1007/978-3-031-55608-1_10

14. Cassez, F., Fuller, J., Quiles, H.M.A.: Deductive verification of smart contracts with Dafny. In: Proceedings of the 27th International Conference on Formal Methods for Industrial Critical Systems (FMICS 2022). LNCS, vol. 13487, pp. 50–66. Springer (2022). https://doi.org/10.1007/978-3-031-15008-1_5

15. Chau, S.Y., Yahyazadeh, M., Chowdhury, O., Kate, A., Li, N.: Analyzing semantic correctness with symbolic execution: a case study on PKCS#1 v1.5 signature verification. In: Proceedings of the 26th Annual Network and Distributed System Security Symposium (NDSS 2019). The Internet Society (2019). https://doi.org/10.14722/ndss.2019.23430

16. Cisco Talos: WolfSSL library X509 Certificate Text Parsing Code Execution Vulnerability (2017). https://talosintelligence.com/vulnerability_reports/TALOS-2017-0293

17. Cluzel, G., Georgiou, K., Moy, Y., Zeller, C.: Layered formal verification of a TCP stack. In: Proceedings of the IEEE Secure Development Conference (SecDev 2021), pp. 86–93. IEEE (2021). https://doi.org/10.1109/SecDev51306.2021.00028

18. Cooper, D., Santesson, S., Farrell, S., Boeyen, S., Housley, R., Polk, W.: Internet X. 509 Public Key Infrastructure Certificate and Certificate Revocation List (CRL) Profile (2008). https://doi.org/10.17487/RFC5280, RFC 5280

19. Correnson, L.: QED. Computing what remains to be proved. In: Badger, J.M., Rozier, K.Y. (eds.) NFM 2014. LNCS, vol. 8430, pp. 215–229. Springer, Cham (2014). https://doi.org/10.1007/978-3-319-06200-6_17

20. de Boer, M., de Gouw, S., Klamroth, J., Jung, C., Ulbrich, M., Weigl, A.: Formal specification and verification of JDK's identity hash map implementation. Formal Aspects Comput. **35**(3), 18:1–18:26 (2023). https://doi.org/10.1145/3594729

21. Debnath, J., Jenkins, C., Sun, Y., Chau, S.Y., Chowdhury, O.: ARMOR: a formally verified implementation of X.509 certificate chain validation. In: Proceedings of the IEEE Symposium on Security and Privacy (SP 2024), pp. 1462–1480. IEEE (2024). https://doi.org/10.1109/SP54263.2024.00220

22. Djoudi, A., Hána, M., Kosmatov, N.: Formal verification of a JavaCard virtual machine with Frama-C. In: Proceedings of the 24th International Symposium on Formal Methods (FM 2021). LNCS, vol. 13047, pp. 427–444. Springer (2021). https://doi.org/10.1007/978-3-030-90870-6_23, long version available at https://nikolai-kosmatov.eu/publications/djoudi_hk_fm_2021.pdf

23. Djoudi, A., et al.: A bottom-up formal verification approach for common criteria certification: application to JavaCard virtual machine. In: Proceedings of the 11th European Congress on Embedded Real-Time Systems (ERTS 2022) (2022). https://hal.science/hal-03695829
24. Dordowsky, F.: An experimental study using ACSL and Frama-C to formulate and verify low-level requirements from a DO-178C compliant avionics project. Electron. Proc. Theoret. Comput. Sci. **187**, 28–41 (2015). https://doi.org/10.4204/EPTCS.187.3
25. Dross, C., Moy, Y.: Auto-active proof of red-black trees in SPARK. In: Barrett, C., Davies, M., Kahsai, T. (eds.) NFM 2017. LNCS, vol. 10227, pp. 68–83. Springer, Cham (2017). https://doi.org/10.1007/978-3-319-57288-8_5
26. Ebalard, A., Mouy, P., Benadjila, R.: Journey to a RTE-free X.509 parser. In: Symposium sur la sécurité des technologies de l'information et des communications (SSTIC 2019) (2019). https://www.sstic.org/media/SSTIC2019/SSTIC-actes/journey-to-a-rte-free-x509-parser/SSTIC2019-Article-journey-to-a-rte-free-x509-parser-ebalard_mouy_benadjila_3cUxSCv.pdf
27. Filliâtre, J.-C., Gondelman, L., Paskevich, A.: The spirit of ghost code. Formal Methods Syst. Design **48**(3), 152–174 (2016). https://doi.org/10.1007/s10703-016-0243-x
28. Finney, H.: Bleichenbacher's RSA signature forgery based on implementation error (2006). https://mailarchive.ietf.org/arch/msg/openpgp/5rnE9ZRN1AokBVj3VqblGlP63QE/
29. Forristal, J.: Android: One Root to Own Them All (2013). https://www.youtube.com/watch?v=mCF5kaCt4NI
30. Granberry, G., Ahrendt, W., Johansson, M.: Specify what? Enhancing neural specification synthesis by symbolic methods. In: Proceedings of the 19th International Conference on Integrated Formal Methods (iFM 2024). LNCS, vol. 15234, pp. 307–325. Springer (2024). https://doi.org/10.1007/978-3-031-76554-4_19
31. Hähnle, R., Huisman, M.: Deductive software verification: from pen-and-paper proofs to industrial tools. In: Computing and Software Science – State of the Art and Perspectives, LNCS, vol. 10000, pp. 345–373. Springer (2019). https://doi.org/10.1007/978-3-319-91908-9_18
32. Herrmann, P., Signoles, J.: RTE Runtime Error Annotation Generation (2024). https://frama-c.com/download/frama-c-rte-manual.pdf
33. Hána, M., Kosmatov, N., Prevosto, V., Signoles, J.: Formal Verification of PKCS#1 Signature Parser using Frama-C. Companion Artifact for the Paper Submitted to iFM 2025 (2025). https://doi.org/10.5281/zenodo.16919839
34. Intel Security: BERserk Vulnerability – Part 2: Certificate Forgery in Mozilla NSS (2014). https://bugzilla.mozilla.org/attachment.cgi?id=8499825
35. ISO/IEC JTC 1/SC 22: ISO/IEC 9899:1999 Programming languages — C. Standard 9899:1999, International Standard Organisation (1999). https://www.iso.org/standard/29237.html
36. ITU: X.690: Information Technology - ASN.1 Encoding Rules: Specification of Basic Encoding Rules (BER), Canonical Encoding Rules (CER), and Distinguished Encoding Rules (DER). Tech. rep. (2021). https://www.itu.int/rec/T-REC-X.690/
37. Jacobs, B., Smans, J., Philippaerts, P., Vogels, F., Penninckx, W., Piessens, F.: VeriFast: a powerful, sound, predictable, fast verifier for C and Java. In: Bobaru, M., Havelund, K., Holzmann, G.J., Joshi, R. (eds.) NFM 2011. LNCS, vol. 6617, pp. 41–55. Springer, Heidelberg (2011). https://doi.org/10.1007/978-3-642-20398-5_4

38. Janßen, C., Richter, C., Wehrheim, H.: Can ChatGPT support software verification? In: Proceedings of the 12th International Conference on Fundamental Approaches to Software Engineering (FASE 2024). LNCS, vol. 14573, pp. 266–279. Springer (2024). https://doi.org/10.1007/978-3-031-57259-3_13

39. Kamath, A., et al.: Leveraging LLMs for program verification. In: Proceedings of the 24th Conference on Formal Methods in Computer-Aided Design (FMCAD 2024), pp. 107–118. IEEE (2024). https://doi.org/10.34727/2024/ISBN.978-3-85448-065-5_16

40. Kaufman, C., Hoffman, P., Nir, Y., Eronen, P., Kivinen, T.: Internet Key Exchange Protocol Version 2 (IKEv2) (2014). https://doi.org/10.17487/RFC7296, RFC 7296

41. Kosmatov, N., Prevosto, V., Signoles, J. (eds.): Guide to Software Verification with Frama-C. Core Components, Usages, and Applications. Computer Science Foundations and Applied Logic Book Series, Springer (2024). https://doi.org/10.1007/978-3-031-55608-1

42. Kühn, U., Pyshkin, A., Tews, E., Weinmann, R.P.: Variants of Bleichenbacher's Low-exponent Attack on PKCS# 1 RSA Signatures. In: Sicherheit 2008: Sicherheit, Schutz und Zuverlässigkeit. Konferenzband der 4. Jahrestagung des Fachbereichs Sicherheit der Gesellschaft für Informatik e.V. (GI) (2008). https://download.hrz.tu-darmstadt.de/pub/FB20/Dekanat/Publikationen/CDC/sigflaw.pdf

43. Leinenbach, D., Santen, T.: Verifying the microsoft Hyper-V hypervisor with VCC. In: Proceedings of the Second World Congres on Formal Methods (FM 2009). LNCS, vol. 5850, pp. 806–809. Springer (2009). https://doi.org/10.1007/978-3-642-05089-3_51

44. Leino, K.R.M.: Program Proofs. The MIT Press (2023)

45. Li, L.W., Eakman, G., Garcia, E.J.M., Atman, S.: Accessible formal methods for verified parser development. In: Proceedings of the IEEE Security and Privacy Workshops (SP Workshops 2021), pp. 142–151. IEEE (2021). https://doi.org/10.1109/SPW53761.2021.00028

46. Mitre: CWE-190: Integer overflow or wraparound. https://cwe.mitre.org/data/definitions/190.html

47. Moriarty, K., Kaliski, B., Jonsson, J., Rusch, A.: PKCS #1: RSA Cryptography Specifications, Version 2.2 (2016). https://doi.org/10.17487/RFC8017, RFC 8017

48. Nir, Y., Kivinen, T., Wouters, P., Migault, D.: Algorithm Implementation Requirements and Usage Guidance for the Internet Key Exchange Protocol Version 2 (IKEv2) (2017). https://doi.org/10.17487/RFC8247, RFC 8247

49. Oiwa, Y., Kobara, K., Watanabe, H.: A new variant for an attack against RSA signature verification using parameter field. In: Lopez, J., Samarati, P., Ferrer, J.L. (eds.) EuroPKI 2007. LNCS, vol. 4582, pp. 143–153. Springer, Heidelberg (2007). https://doi.org/10.1007/978-3-540-73408-6_10

50. Oortwijn, W., Huisman, M.: Formal verification of an industrial safety-critical traffic tunnel control system. In: Ahrendt, W., Tapia Tarifa, S.L. (eds.) IFM 2019. LNCS, vol. 11918, pp. 418–436. Springer, Cham (2019). https://doi.org/10.1007/978-3-030-34968-4_23

51. Philippaerts, P., Mühlberg, J., Penninckx, W., Smans, J., Jacobs, B., Piessens, F.: Software verification with VeriFast: industrial case studies. Sci. Comput. Program. **82**, 77–97 (2014). https://doi.org/10.1016/J.SCICO.2013.01.006

52. Ramananandro, T., et al.: EverParse: verified secure zero-copy parsers for authenticated message formats. In: Proceedings of the 28th USENIX Conference on Security Symposium (SEC 2019) (2019). https://www.microsoft.com/en-us/research/wp-content/uploads/2019/05/20190601everparse.pdf

53. Rescorla, E.: The Transport Layer Security (TLS) Protocol Version 1.3 (2018). https://doi.org/10.17487/RFC8446, RFC 8446
54. Rivest, R.L., Shamir, A., Adleman, L.M.: A method for obtaining digital signatures and public-key cryptosystems. Commun. ACM **21**(2), 120–126 (1978). https://doi.org/10.1145/359340.359342
55. Swamy, N., et al.: Hardening attack surfaces with formally proven binary format parsers. In: Proceedings of the 43rd ACM SIGPLAN International Conference on Programming Language Design and Implementation (PLDI 2022) (2022). https://doi.org/10.1145/3519939.3523708
56. Wen, C., et al.: Enchanting program specification synthesis by large language models using static analysis and program verification. In: Proceedings of the 36th International Conference on Computer Aided Verification (CAV 2024). LNCS, vol. 14682, pp. 302–328. Springer (2024). https://doi.org/10.1007/978-3-031-65630-9_16
57. Yahyazadeh, M., et al.: Morpheus: bringing The (PKCS) One To Meet the Oracle. In: Proceedings of the 2021 ACM SIGSAC Conference on Computer and Communications Security (CCS 2021), pp. 2474–2496 (2021). https://doi.org/10.1145/3460120.3485382
58. Ylonen, T., C. Lonvick, E.: The Secure Shell (SSH) Transport Layer Protocol (2006). https://doi.org/10.17487/RFC4253, RFC 4253

Game Modeling of Blockchain Protocols

Sophie Rain[1](✉) ⓘ, Anja Petković Komel[1] ⓘ, Michael Rawson[2] ⓘ,
and Laura Kovács[3] ⓘ

[1] Argot Collective, Zug, Switzerland
sophie.rain@argot.org
[2] University of Southampton, Southampton, UK
[3] TU Wien, Vienna, Austria

Abstract. Reasoning about incentives in a blockchain protocol can be captured by game-theoretic modeling. We present modeling principles sufficient to create a faithful representation of a blockchain protocol as an extensive form game. Such games are then suitable for automatically establishing game-theoretic security. We showcase the semi-automated generation of the game models for two parts of Bitcoin's Lightning protocol: the closing of a channel and the routing of a payment along channels. Additionally, we provide a domain-specific language, which eases the implementation of the games. We believe our modeling principles and guidelines strengthen machine-supported modeling practices.

Keywords: Game Theory · Formal Models · Modeling Template · Protocol Modeling

1 Introduction

Users of decentralized economic systems, such as cryptocurrencies, demand security guarantees of the system as a whole. This includes *cryptographic* security [1,13,18], which ensures that the cryptographic premises of the protocol are secure, *implementation* security [4,6,12], which ensures the implementation of the protocol does not allow any unexpected behavior, and *game-theoretic* security [2,25], which ensures that cryptographically and implementationally possible but undesired behavior, such as collusion, is economically disincentivized. This paper focuses on the rigorous modeling of protocols as games, in order to automatically assess their game-theoretic security.

To say that a protocol is *game-theoretically secure* means that it has various desirable properties. Notably, we are interested in capturing that protocol users/participants cannot be economically harmed, and that a group of players cannot collaborate to gain an advantage. These properties are called *Byzantine-fault tolerance* and *incentive compatibility* [20] and revised in [2]: These properties are implemented through the game-theoretic concepts *weak immunity*, respectively *weaker immunity*, for Byzantine-fault tolerance, and *collusion resilience* and *practicality* for incentive compatibility. Manually checking

F. Damiani and M. Farrell (Eds.): IFM 2025, LNCS 16194, pp. 359–377, 2026.
https://doi.org/10.1007/978-3-032-10794-7_18

that a game has a particular game-theoretic property is, however, tedious and often not viable. Protocols may allow many possible options at each step, producing game trees with millions of paths, as showcased in [2]. To overcome the burden of manual and notoriously error-prone protocol analysis, automated approaches arose to check the game-theoretic properties for a given protocol [2], which work – in essence – by an exhaustive symbolic enumeration of all paths through the game tree. In this setting, game-theoretic security derived by an automated formal approach increases user trust in the protocol under analysis.

Tacit in game-theoretic security is the expertise and work required to model a protocol as a game rather than only as a list of specifications. *Extensive form games* (EFGs) turn out to offer suitable expressivity for modeling protocols using a tree-like data structure capturing actions between protocol users. Ensuring, though, that protocol requirements are best represented by EFGs is, however, challenging: it is reminiscent of the formalization of mathematics in that hidden details must be recovered, but with the added challenge of managing very large game trees. To the best of our knowledge, game-theoretic modeling of protocols has remained mostly manual to date, partially due to the fact that – until recently – automated methods did not scale to very large trees found in real-world protocols.

Our paper addresses this key missing bit in game-theoretic security: *provide (semi-)automated methods to represent protocols as games*, upon which game-theoretic analysis can be performed. We present a network of techniques (Sect. 3) to partially automate and accelerate the development of game models, while increasing trust in their construction. Using these techniques, we have successfully encoded very large games, such as those required to model a phase of Bitcoin's Lightning protocol [19], and the large proprietary protocol FAsset [7] on the *Flare* blockchain [8] for digital currency exchange. Our resulting models were then handed to the automated game-theoretic security tool CHECKMATE [21], as this framework allows automatically analyzing the Byzantine-fault tolerance and incentive compatibility of game models of very large protocols, and further supports models containing *conditional actions* (Sect. 7).

In summary, the main contributions of our paper come with (i) providing general principles guiding the automated synthesis of games from protocols (Sect. 3); (ii) introducing a domain specific language for game modeling (Sect. 4); and (iii) illustrating the generation of games from protocols on various examples (Sect. 5).

Related Work. The modeling principles described in Sect. 3 rely on the definition of an EFG as a suitable model for the game-theoretic security analysis as introduced in [20, 25], that can be automatically processed by CHECKMATE [2, 21]. While [20, 25] introduce manually made models, our semi-automated approach enables exhausting all parameter options systematically in a machine supported manner, and thus refines these models, making fewer assumptions on the way.

Extensive form games can be translated to Open games with agency [3, 10, 11]. The utilities in Open games are restricted to constant numeric utilities, and rational behavior of players is assumed. We, however, work with symbolic utilities and capture honest/rational behavior, and hence game-theoretic security. PRISM-games [14], offer a modeling language for concurrent stochastic multiplayer games (CSGs), thus capturing probabilistic behavior. They are also limited to constant numeric utilities, as opposed to the symbolic ones.

The manual game-theoretic models as static noncooperative games, such as a model for shard-based permissionless blockchains [16], the griefing attack in blockchain mining [5,17], the mining strategy for Bitcoin-NG blockchain protocol [24], the reward distribution in Algorand [9], use many of the modeling principles presented in Sect. 3. The authors of these models detail the assumptions and design decisions in forming a static game model. They are also able to use symbolic utilities in their (manual) game-theoretic security analysis. As opposed to the approach described in the present paper, these games were modeled manually and are not amenable to automatic processing.

2 Preliminaries

This section introduces relevant aspects for game-theoretic *modeling* of (blockchain) security, complementing the automated *verification* of game-theoretic security, and in particular the CHECKMATE framework [2].

2.1 Protocols

Blockchain protocols are a natural use for game-theoretic security, and in particular for the CHECKMATE framework [2], as they formalize economic incentives within strict formal rules. We, therefore, introduce an interesting Bitcoin protocol called Lightning [19] as a running example. It enables users to safely send numerous transactions while only having to publish two of them on the blockchain. This saves transaction fees and time. The protocol is based on so-called channels, each connecting two users. The part of the protocol we focus on is called *routing*: it enables Lightning users to *route* money from a user A to another user B (who do not share a channel) along a path of channels.

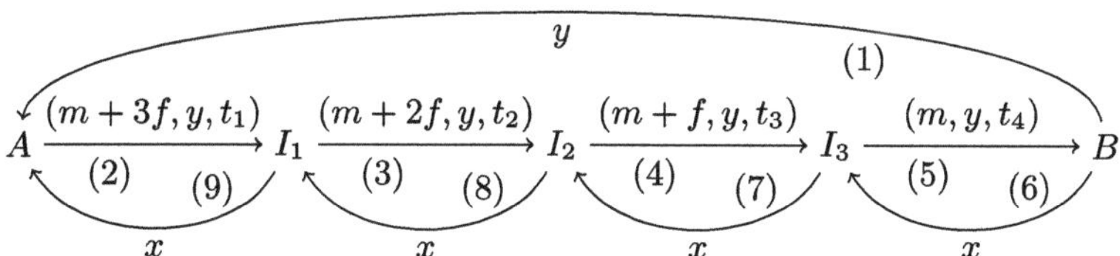

Fig. 1. Routing in Lightning, where hash$(x) = y$.

Example 1 (Routing in Lightning). Figure 1 illustrates the routing of transactions from a user A to a user B with the three intermediaries I_1, I_2, and I_3, where all *neighbors* (i.e. A and I_1, I_1 and I_2, etc.) have a *Lightning* channel. To route money from A to B using Lightning, B has to (1) define a secret x and send its hash value y to A. Next, (2) A locks some amount in the channel with I_1, which can only be unlocked with the secret x before a timeout t_1. The locked amount should be the amount m to be sent to B plus a fee f for each intermediary. The intermediaries proceed accordingly in steps (3–5), each reducing the amount by f. Then (6), as B knows the secret, they can unlock the money in their channel with I_3, thereby revealing the secret to I_3. Knowing the secret x, the intermediaries continue to unlock the money in their respective channels (7–9). For the sake of simplicity, in this paper we focus mostly on the *unlocking phase*, i.e., steps (6 – 9). Steps 1–5 are referred to as the *locking phase*.[1]

Closing a Lightning Channel. As mentioned above, the Lightning protocol is based on channels that each connect two users. Such a channel can be closed at any time by the users, releasing the money that was locked inside. Either user can unilaterally close the channel by posting the latest distribution state they agreed upon on the blockchain; we refer to this as *honest unilateral closing*. However, a user can also take an outdated distribution state and publish it on the blockchain to close the channel; we call this *dishonest unilateral closing*. After dishonest unilateral closing, the other channel user has the option to prove that the posted distribution state was outdated and evoke a punishment mechanism that keeps the other one from getting their assets. This is done through a so-called *revocation transaction.*

Further, the channel users can also collaboratively close their channel: this can be achieved through both signing and publishing the same transaction that distributes their assets. The distribution transaction proposed by one of them can be both honest (using the values of the latest agreed distribution state) or dishonest (using any other distribution values). The other user has to decide whether or not they agree to the distribution by signing or not signing the transaction. If none of the users ever close the channel in any way, their money will stay locked forever.

2.2   Game-Theoretic Concepts and CHECKMATE Input Structure

As detailed in [21], game-theoretic security verification relies on inputs given as *extensive form games* (EFGs) with *symbolic utilities*.

Definition 1 (Extensive Form Game –EFG).   *An extensive form game (EFG) is a finite tree G together with a finite set of players N, where*

- *each path in G that starts from the root is called* history*;*
- *each internal node has a* player *– the one whose turn it is – assigned;*

---

[1] The model of the full routing protocol and its generation code are available at [22].

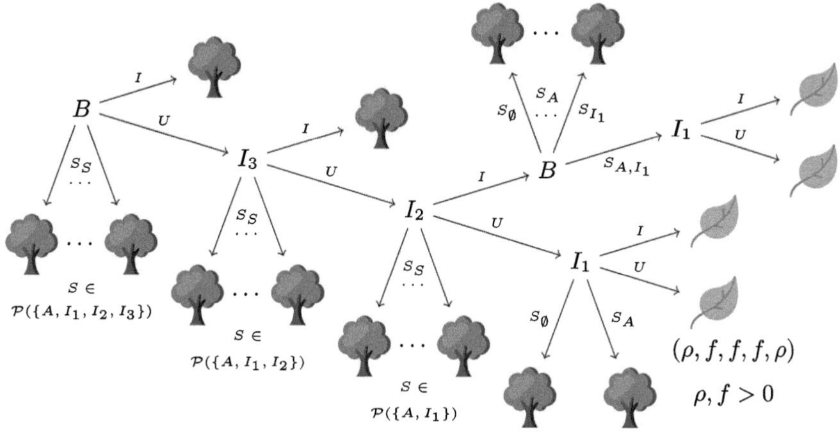

Fig. 2. Sketch of Lightning's Routing Unlocking phase. Tree icons by Freepik - Flaticon.

- *the set of edges at each internal node is called* actions *and are the options the assigned player can choose from;*
- *each leaf has a* utility *assigned and represents a possible end of the game. The utility specifies the pay-off for each player in N after this history (root to this leaf);*
- *there is at least one history to a leaf that represents the expected behavior of the underlying protocol, called* honest history.

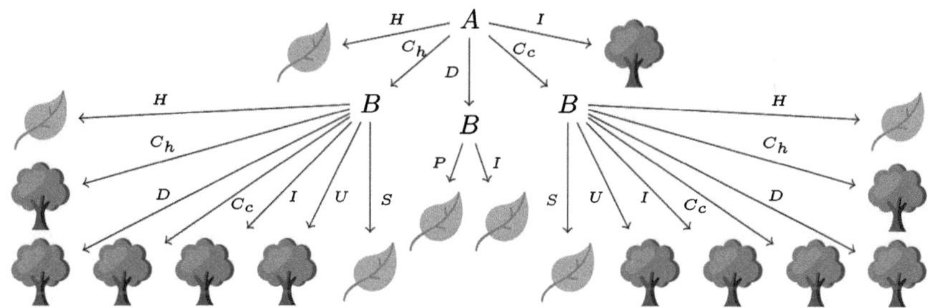

Fig. 3. Sketch of Lightning's Closing phase. Tree icons by Freepik - Flaticon.

Example 2 (Routing EFG). Figure 2 illustrates an EFG modelling *routing unlocking* in Fig. 1. At the root, it is player B's turn to choose between the actions U (unlocking), I (ignoring), or one of the S_S choices, representing B's option to share their secret x. We assume history (U, U, U, U) to be the honest history leading to utility ρ for A and B and f for the intermediaries I_1, I_2, I_3.

Example 3 (Closing EFG). Figure 3 shows an EFG model of closing a Lightning channel. We call the two users of a channel player A and player B. Without loss of generality, we assume player A has the first turn. Players can choose between action H (closing unilaterally and honestly), action C_h (closing the channel honestly and collaboratively, which requires player B to react), action D (dishonest unilateral closing, allowing B to post a revocation transaction – action P – or to ignore it – action I), action C_c (dishonest collaborative closing, again requiring B to react), or action I (not closing the channel).

If player A chose action C_h or C_c, player B gets to react. They have the same choices as player A before, but they additionally can pick action U (propose an update to the channel) or action S (signing player A's closing proposal).

We fix both ways of closing honestly: history (H) and history (C_h, S) to be honest histories.

The *symbolic utilities* are terms with two kinds of variables: *constants* and *infinitesimals*. Both types are interpreted over the reals, but the *infinitesimals* are assumed to be closer to 0 than any of the *constants* and are supposed to represent subjective motivation. This is achieved by interpreting utilities as constant-infinitesimal pairs, which are ordered lexicographically, thereby achieving infinitesimality. Further, to allow for more realistic models, the values of the constants and infinitesimals can be restricted through *initial constraints*.

Example 4 (Symbolic Utilities). The utility after the honest history in Fig. 2 contains one constant f and one infinitesimal ρ. For each variable, its type has to be specified. For example, A's utility ρ will be interpreted as the pair $(0, \rho)$ since it does not contain any *constant* variable. Further, it is assumed in Fig. 2 that both ρ and f are positive, hence the initial constraints $\rho > 0$, $f > 0$.

3   Modeling Principles for Game-Theoretic Security

Usually, several EFGs can serve as game-theoretic models for a blockchain protocol, so that they faithfully represent the protocol itself and adequately capture its security properties. While modeling protocols, we are therefore making some assumptions and design choices (see Sect. 3.3) that allow us to construct one such finite model of a possibly infinite protocol. These design choices and assumptions have to be thoroughly documented to ensure transparency of the model's limitations with regard to how accurately it corresponds to the protocol (and its potential implementation).

In this section, we present our guidelines towards faithful game-theoretic modeling of (blockchain) protocols. Our modeling principles yield a possible approach that was feasible to construct sufficient models for the CHECKMATE framework. To ensure faithful representations of protocols that are also aligned with the presuppositions on the CHECKMATE inputs, our models have the following three properties:

1. **Relative Utilities.** The utilities awarded to each player are relative to what they were assumed to have initially.

2. **Ghosting.** At every internal node of the game tree, it is possible to do nothing, i.e., to not respond in any way. It is crucial to account for such behavior, as it can easily happen in the decentralized and pseudonymous setting.
3. **Actual Choice.** At every internal node, there have to be at least two actions available. It is not possible to have just one, as this player does not have an actual choice.

Example 5 (Model Properties). In Example 2, *relative utility* means that player A in *Routing Unlocking* does not receive utility $-m$ in the honest case, even though A's balance is decreased by a value of m; instead, they receive an infinitesimal but positive utility ρ. This is due to our assumption that there is a fair trade of an asset in some form for Bitcoin, giving A some form of benefit. Otherwise, A would not route the money to the player B.

Next, *ghosting* means that at every internal node in the game tree, there has to be an "ignore" action that corresponds to inaction. For readability, it is useful to specify what task the current player is ignoring. In *Routing Unlocking*, players can "ignore to unlock" their HTLC (action I) or choose not to share their secrets with others, which we call "ignore the option to share a secret" (action $S_\emptyset$). In the *Closing game* players also have an "ignore" action, signifying doing nothing.

At every point in time in *Routing Unlocking* and in *Closing game*, there are always at least two available choices, doing something or ignoring to do something, ensuring *actual choice*.

3.1   Game Modeling Setup

We next summarize the setup we propose and use for modeling (blockchain) protocols as games. Our modeling principles listed below form instructions on how to model a decentralized protocol as an EFG, which we further translate into a modeling template as discussed next; for concrete design/implementation details on our template we refer to [22].

Define Players. Fix the number and names of players. Each agent who can make active choices in the protocol or impact it through their choices should be represented as a player.

Example 6 (Modeling Players). In Example 2 of Lightning's routing, we considered the player who wants to route money to another one, called A; the one who is supposed to receive the routed value, called B; and we chose to study the case where we have 3 intermediaries, named I_1, I_2 and I_3. In our modeling implementation, this is defined as

```
PLAYERS = players('A', 'I1', 'I2', 'I3', 'B')
```

In the Closing game of Example 3, we have two players, A and B, who share a channel.

We note that, within a protocol, there is potentially an unspecified number of players. It is then possible to create a model for each number instance of players. For example, the routing protocol of Example 2 has three intermediaries, but could have also just had one, two, or even more players (four, five, etc.). A good representation of players, therefore, depends on the protocol itself, and the number of players should be documented as an explicit assumption on the model.

Exhaust Parameter Options. One has to pay attention to the parameters in a protocol and vary them in all combinations exhaustively. Within CHECKMATE, all possible real values in players' utilities can be considered by construction, as CHECKMATE supports symbolic utilities. In addition to symbolic utilities, other parameters also need to be varied. For example, in our routing protocol from Example 2, relevant parameters include time (and time-outs), secret sharing, wrong addresses, wrong amounts, and all other possible ways of acting, including locking funds using a wrong secret hash.

Further, one also has to separate which model parameters can be tackled through symbolic utilities and which have to be studied as distinct actions that players can take. For instance, locking the wrong amount will introduce a new symbol for the utilities to the model (the amount to lock), but also a different action from locking the correct amount. In the closing protocol of Example 3, closing dishonestly also introduces a new symbol: the proposed cheating factor. Note that some parameters require additional constraints and assumptions, such as the symbol representing the wrong amount locked being different from the correct one, see Sect. 3.3.

Define a State. It is necessary to identify the values, storage slots, and facts about previous choices that suffice to compute utility in each EFG leaf. Constructing a state to keep track of these values/facts throughout the game tree generation is equally important. A state, then, usually includes at least all the varied parameters mentioned before. We define the initial values in the state and define a deep copy function. Note that during the design of EFG tree generation, the state might need to be refined with more information to ease the tree generation process.

Example 7 (Modeling States). For Routing unlocking in Example 2, our state contains the following information for each player: whether the contract they can possibly unlock is `locked`, `unlocked`, or `expired`, the amount locked in this contract `amountToUnlock`, whether they know the secret to unlock the contract `secret`, and with whom they have decided not to share the secret with (`ignoreshare`). Additionally, we keep track of whether player B has ever shared the secret (`BShared`), as any participation from player B requires them to send the goods to A. In our modeling template, we store the Routing unlocking state as a Python dictionary as follows:

```
initial_state = {"B_shared": False}
for player in PLAYERS:
```

```
initial_state[player] = {}
initial_state[player]["contract"] = "locked"
initial_state[player]["amount_to_unlock"] =
                m + (len(PLAYERS)-PLAYERS.index(player)-1)*f
initial_state[player]["secret"] = False
initial_state[player]["ignoreshare"] = {p: False for p in PLAYERS}
initial_state[PLAYERS[-1]]["secret"] = True
initial_state[PLAYERS[0]]["contract"] = "null"
initial_state[PLAYERS[0]]["amount_to_unlock"] = None
```

For the Closing game of Example 3, the model state contains for each player whether they closed unilateraly (if yes, then value by which they tried to enrich themselves, 0 if honest), published a revocation transaction, made a collaborative attempt (if yes, then value by which they tried to enrich themselves, 0 if honest), signed a collaborative closing, proposed an update (if yes, then value by which current balance of player changes), or agreed to an update. We also keep their current `balance`.

3.2   Generate the Game Tree of the Model

Define Final States. We fix the criteria under which an EFG is over, that is, when a final state is reached. In the routing phase of Example 2, this is when no contract is locked anymore, i.e., when all contracts are either expired or unlocked. Our model template uses a `isFinal` function to decide this, as follows

```
def is_final(state):
for p in PLAYERS:
    if state[p]["contract"] == "locked":
        return False
return True
```

Define the Utility Function. For every final state, that is, at each EFG leaf, the utility for each player has to be defined. The information in the state should suffice for this step. In the Routing unlocking protocol of Example 2, an intermediate player (I1 - I3) gets the utility of the amount in the contract they unlocked minus what they locked in their contract and the previous player unlocked. Players A and B are expected to make a fair trade of money and goods, which, in case it goes through (when B participates in the unlocking through either unlocking I_3's contract or sharing the secret), leads to a small positive utility ρ for both A and B. Our modeling template suggests a function `compute_utility(state)`.

Collect Actions. We collect all possible actions in the protocol and decide in which scenarios they are possible. Note that often variations of parameters can be grouped into a small set of actions depending on what impact choosing a specific value for a variable has. In our model template, the actions are collected in `ACTIONS` and the tree is produced by a `generate_tree` function.

Example 8 (Model Actions). In the Routing unlocking protocol of Example 2, besides the always-present action of ignoring (I), there is also unlocking (U) when the player knows the hashed secret, and sharing said secret with other players. For simplicity, we model secret sharing by each player choosing a subset of other players, who do not know the secret yet, and with whom they share it. An empty subset thus corresponds to ignoring sharing the secret.

For the Closing protocol of Example 3, the actions are listed in Example 3.

Fix Player Precedence. Next, an ordering of players has to be fixed, such that we can decide which player's turn it is at every point in the game. That means their precedence has to be established. In Example 2, we decided to give precedence according to the following three criteria:

- **Priority 1**: The next player is the one with the next time-out ($=$ right-most in Fig. 1) who knows the secret and whose current state of the contract is locked.
- **Priority 2**: The next player is the one with the earliest time out who can share the secret.
- **Priority 3**: If there is no such player, all locked contracts expire.

Our modeling template suggests defining the next player in a dedicated function NextPlayer, given below.

```python
def next_player(state):
    # prio1:
    for p in PLAYERS[::-1]:
        if state[p]["secret"] and state[p]["contract"] == "locked":
            return p, state


    # prio2:
    for p in PLAYERS[::-1]:
        if state[p]["secret"]:
            for share_with in PLAYERS:
                if (not state[p]["ignoreshare"][share_with] and
                    not state[share_with]["secret"]):
                    return p, state


    # prio3:
    state1 = copy_state(state)
    for p in PLAYERS:
        if state1[p]["contract"] == "locked":
            state1[p]["contract"] = "expired"
    return None, state1
```

3.3   Declare Assumptions and Design Choices

Some of the modeling steps from Sects. 3.1–3.2 require making assumptions. One has to pay special attention to such assumptions and document them thoroughly.

Some assumptions only need to be documented, such as choosing to require player B in the Routing game of Example 2 to send the goods in case they share the secret. Others, like assumptions on utility variables (e.g. $f > 0$), have to be explicitly listed as an INITIAL CONSTRAINT. Design choices usually also influence the shape and the size of the game tree: in the Routing unlocking of Example 2 the choice of how we set priorities for the player precedence enables us to model a protocol where in practice simultaneous actions are possible (sharing secrets could in principle happen at the same time), but the EFG does not allow for it.

4   Domain Specific Language for Game Modeling

Section 3 summarizes our guidelines to model protocols as EFGs. Our modeling template is designed such that the resulting (EFG) model is parsable by our CHECKMATE tool, which takes a '.json' file as input. To ease the process of model generation in a suitable format, we designed a simple domain-specific language (DSL), written in Python, that enables game tree generation. The usage of this DSL is discussed next and exemplified in the modeling template available [22].

To handle real-valued expressions in the utilities of the EFG players, appearing in the leaves of the game trees, and the constraints imposed on the symbols, our DSL introduces a class of expressions Expr, which includes a NameExpr to handle the symbols. The class overloads the usual arithmetic operators ($+$, $-$, $*$, $/$) and establishes their precedence. Further, the DSL defines a class of constraints, with subclasses for disequation constraints, conjunctions, and disjunctions, and defines their string representations. For convenience, the comparison operators ($<$, $>$, $=$) are also overloaded. Dedicated functions define constants and infinitesimals, and turn them into expressions. Similarly, players and actions turn them into a list of members of classes Player and Action, respectively. The class of trees is defined, with subclasses Leaf (containing a dictionary of utilities) and Branch (containing the player and a dictionary mapping actions to trees); and a dedicated json method, which produces a tree representation suitable to serve as CHECKMATE input. Finally, a function finish can be called to output the data into an appropriate '.json' file that can be piped directly to CHECKMATE.

5   Examples of Generated Game Models

Using the modeling principles specified in Sect. 3, the DSL of Sect. 4, and our modeling template available in [22], we generated game-theoretic models in the form of an EFG for the protocols listed in Table 1.

The Closing and Routing protocols listed in Table 1 are described in Examples 2–3 and explained in Sect. 2.1. A short description of the fAsset protocol can be found in Sect. 7. The other game-theoretic models of Table 1 are not modeling blockchain protocols, but rather simpler games, illustrating the variety to which our modeling principles apply. Here we give a short explanation of those models and refer to [22] for the full implementation.

Table 1. Examples of game-theoretic models. The full implementation of the models can be found at [22]. Columns 2–3 list respectively the number of EFG nodes and players of the games listed in Column 1. Column 4 specifies the intended honest history of the EFG, whereas Column 5 gives the lines of code (LOC) in our model templates.

Game	Nodes	Players	Honest histories	LOC
Closing	2131	2	$(H), (C_h, S)$	265
Routing	21688	3	(S_H, L, L, U, U)	487
	144342306	4	(S_H, L, L, L, U, U, U)	487
Routing Unlocking	18707	5	(U, U, U, U)	271
fAsset[a]	1805409	6	(CRTc+pp)	4300
Auction	81	4	(L, E, I, I)	131
EBOS	31	4	(Mine, Mine, Mine, Mine)	123
Tic-Tac-Toe	549946	2	$(CM, RU, LU, RD, RM, LM, CU, CD, LD)$	126
Tic-Tac-Toe (concise)	58748	2	$(CM, LU, RU, LD, LM, RM, CU, CD, RD)$	182
Pirate	161	4	$(y, y), (y, n, y)$	193

[a] The model of the fAsset protocol uses conditional actions defined in Sect. 7. The model implementation is currently not public, as the security analysis is still in process, but it will be made available once the analysis is terminated.

The Auction model represents a simple auction with 4 players involved - an auctioneer and three bidders. The auctioneer sets an initial price for the item to be sold. This can be less than what the item is worth in the auctioneer's opinion, exactly what they think it is worth, or more than what they think it is worth. As usual, the auctioneer also has the choice not to put it up for auction. Then the three bidders have the option to – one after the other – bid a price that is higher than the previous one, which can be lower than what they think the item is worth; exactly what the item is worth; or higher than what it is worth. In this model, each player can bid at most once. Their utility depends on whether they received the item or not. If the item was sold, the bidder who buys it receives what they think it is worth minus what they paid; the other bidders receive a very small (infinitesimal) negative utility for not getting an item they wanted; the auctioneer receives what they sold it for minus what they think it was worth. If the item was not bought, everyone receives a small (infinitesimal) negative utility, because it is assumed they wanted to sell/buy the item. Finally, if the auctioneer never put it up for auction, everyone receives utility 0.

The EBOS game is an extended version of the game-theoretic problem known as the battle of the sexes. In the Extended Battle Of the Sexes (EBOS), there are 4 players, which model two couples. Each player can choose between two activities: one they like but their partner does not, and one they do not like but their partner does. Their utility depends on whether they do the activity they prefer and with whom they do it.

The Tic-Tac-Toe game is enhanced with an end utility for each player: the player that wins receives a reward $w > 0$, reduced by the penalty s for every move required. The constraint $w > 9s$ is an initial constraint of the model. The player who loses the game is compensated by the utility $k \cdot s - w$, where k is the number of moves played. In the case of a draw, both players get utility 0. The concise version identifies equivalent actions and thus reduces the size of the model by breaking the symmetry. For example, the first player making a move can choose to pick a corner, but it does not matter whether it is the top left, top right, bottom left, or bottom right. These 4 actions are equivalent. Both versions of the model are faithful representations of a Tic-Tac-Toe game and hence also bear the same game-theoretic properties.

The Pirate game is an adapted version of the "puzzle for pirates" introduced in [23]. It follows a voting scenario: there are 4 players (A, B, C, and D) and each player proposes a distribution of a joint utility g. First, the players vote whether to accept A's proposed distribution, in alphabetical order. If the majority of players are in favor of the proposal (indicated by taking action y when it is their turn), the game ends with the proposed utilities. Otherwise, i.e., if the majority votes no (action n), player A is eliminated from the game, which results in the utility $-d$ for player A when the game ends, with $d > 0$. The process repeats with the joint utility proposed by player B, and then C. In case of a tie, the decision of the proposing player is the casting vote.

6   Evaluation of Modeling Principles

Comparison to Manual Games. The Closing and the Routing protocol, as explained in Sect. 2.1, have previously been modeled manually [20, 25]. We now compare the game models generated in Sect. 5 to their manually modeled counterparts. We note that in the related approach of [25], the Closing protocol is modeled as a Normal form game (NFG) with two players rather than an EFG. That means that in [25], both players only get to choose an action once and simultaneously, which drastically simplifies the protocol. The manual model of the Closing protocol in [20], which is modeled as an EFG with 221 nodes, provides a more thorough view when compared to [25]. However, compared to our generated model with 2131 nodes, the approach of [20] still misses several possible sequences of choices, such as player B proposing their own collaborative closing (actions C_c and C_h after player A chose C_c or C_h in Fig. 3). While these additional choices arose naturally when following the modeling template, since player B as well has the option to close the channel at any point in time, they were overlooked in [20]. Nonetheless, the manual model of [20] and the one generated using our modeling principles yield the same security result when analyzed by CHECKMATE.

Similar observations and improvements are also true for the Routing protocol (see Sect. 2.1). This protocol is modeled as an EFG with 3 players in [25], where each player only ever has 2 options: to lock the money or to not lock the money in the *locking phase* of the protocol (steps 1–5 in Fig. 1); and to unlock the money or to not unlock the money in the *unlocking phase* (steps 6–9 in Fig. 1), thereby ignoring all possible deviations such as sharing secrets or locking the wrong amount of money. The work of [20] aimed to consider these deviations in an EFG model of the Routing protocol with 5 players; however, due to the sheer size of the resulting game tree, the method of [20] only presents a partial manual model of the Routing protocol.

Assumptions. The fact that we need to make assumptions is not specific to the introduced modeling principles, but a natural consequence of abstraction. We work with two kinds of assumptions:

1. Assumptions on the *occurring variables*, listed as INITIAL CONSTRAINTS. These assumptions are typically driven either by (i) the protocol itself: excluding impossible values for variables, such as routing a negative amount in the routing protocol, Sect. 2.1; or by (ii) the modeling as an EFG: restrictions on values may be necessary to ensure all the given choices are possible for all allowed values of the variables.
2. Assumptions that are just *documented in words, but are not part of the generated EFG*. These assumptions usually stem from two considerations: (i) to decrease the size of the game tree, without violating the faithfulness of the generated model; or (are necessary) (ii) to accommodate the community's choice to use EFGs for game-theoretic security analyses, as discussed in Sect. 7.

Example 9 (Game Modeling Assumption). As an example of an assumption of the kind of (2i) discussed above, we study *secret sharing* in our model of the routing protocol (Fig. 2). We allow each player P to share the secret (actions S_S in Fig. 2) once with a subset of players S. Player P can never, in the future, share the secret with further players. Sharing the secret at most once and with a set of players, rather than with one player at a time, significantly reduces the size of the game tree, while arguably not impacting its faithfulness: a player should, in principle, not share the secret. However, if another one does so while refusing to unlock (e.g., to perform a Wormhole attack [15], where an intermediary's participation fee f is stolen), our approach allows the others to rectify the situation by sharing the secret with the deceived intermediary.

Required Domain Knowledge. Even when following our modeling principles, constructing game models still requires extensive domain knowledge. For example, the choice of parameters and the encoding of constraints need to be designed in a faithful way, and expertise is required for this. However, the manual effort is now semi-automated, reducing the errors during modeling and scaling. It further allows the user to focus on the technicalities of the protocol to be modeled rather than on defining their own modeling strategy.

7   Limitations of EFGs as Game-Theoretic Models

When considering EFGs as game-theoretic models of blockchain protocols, there are certain limitations, which also imply limitations on the modeling principles from Sect. 3. First of all, we consider deterministic models, rather than probabilistic ones - for security analysis, we ask whether the honest players could lose money, which depends on all possibilities of the other players' behavior and is fundamentally deterministic, thereby circumventing probabilistic effects. We assume that at every given point, full information about which previous actions were taken is known to the current player. Further, no simultaneous actions or choices of different players are permitted in the model. While in the protocol, it is often the case that any player could take action, an EFG model has to pose some assumptions on the order in which players act. Thus, the modeling principles require the user to define the player precedence (also in the modeling template), which affects the assumptions and the tree generation. Similarly, EFGs model finite games, and the modeling principles reflect that by checking whether a final state has been reached or the tree generation continues.

In an EFG with symbolic utilities, the actions available to the players cannot depend on the actual values of symbolic expressions and parameters. Further, there could be outside – possibly stochastic – effects from the environment that influence players' choices, but have no agenda on their own. Examples of such an effect would be time or price changes of the currencies, assuming players in the protocol are not moving the market. Modeling such effects as another player would compromise the definition of game-theoretic security as defined in [20]. In the modeling principles, this limitation is reflected in exhausting parameter options, where more actions are necessary to distinguish available choices. To enable more leeway in modeling, we propose the following extension to EFGs.

7.1   Extending EFGs to Conditional Actions

In this section, we introduce a generalization to EFGs to allow for actions that can only be taken if some (uncontrollable by the players, possibly probabilistic) condition is met. We call such actions *conditional actions*.

Definition 2 (EFGs with Conditional Actions). *An extensive form game with conditional actions is an EFG with the following adaptations:*

- *every non-terminal history h is assigned a set of constraints $CA(h)$ called conditions;*
- *every action a from an internal node belonging to history h is assigned one condition $c(a)$ from $CA(h)$;*
- *let $h = (a_1, a_2, \ldots, a_k)$ be a non-terminal history. Then the following holds:*
  1. the conditions in $CA(h)$ are mutually exclusive:

$$\left(\bigvee_{c \in CA(h)} c \wedge (\forall c, c' \in CA(h).c \neq c') \right) \implies \neg(c \wedge c');$$

2. *the conditions are collectively exhaustive (i.e. span the whole subspace):*

$$(c(a_1) \wedge c(a_2) \wedge \ldots \wedge c(a_k)) \iff \left(\bigvee_{c \in CA(h)} c \wedge c(a_1) \wedge c(a_2) \wedge \ldots \wedge c(a_k) \right);$$

3. *conditions along h are non-contradictory:* $(c(a_1) \wedge c(a_2) \wedge \ldots \wedge c(a_k)) \neq \bot$.
   - *honest behavior is captured by an* honest subtree*: At the root node, one action is chosen for every condition. Then, recursively, at every node that belongs to a chosen action, for every condition, one action is chosen.*

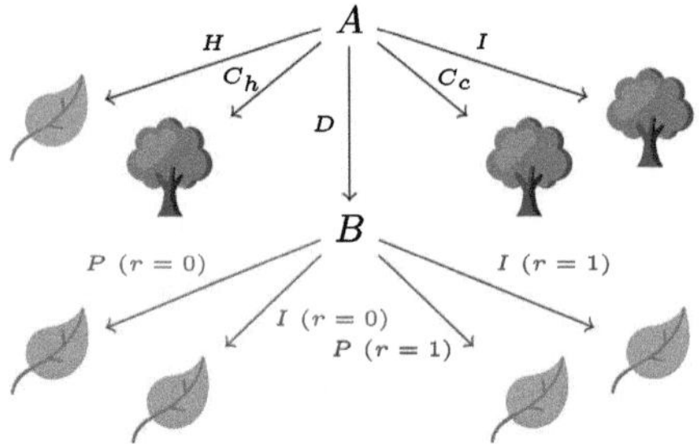

Fig. 4. Sketch of Lightning's Closing phase with conditional actions. Tree icons by Freepik - Flaticon.

Example 10 (Closing Game as an EFG with Conditional Actions). Let us revisit the Closing game from Example 3, but this time suppose that proving dishonest behavior is additionally rewarded by the system. If a player behaves dishonestly (chooses action D), and the other player proves it on chain (action P), the system will not require the transaction fee f for this proof for every other such player. The players have no control over whether the system will pardon the fee or not. We model this behavior by introducing a new symbolic value r, requiring in the initial constraints that $r = 0 \vee r = 1$ and in the utility multiplying the transaction fee by this factor, so $r \cdot f$. After a dishonest action D, we encounter conditional actions, as depicted in Fig. 4. There are two conditions ($r = 0$ depicted with teal actions and $r = 1$ depicted with blue actions), each having two actions possible (proving dishonest behavior P, or ignoring to prove I). These conditions are mutually exclusive and exhaustive. They are also non-contradictory when paired with the additional initial constraint. Note that in the nodes that do not require a conditional split of actions, we can assign the trivial condition $\top$.

The requirements on the conditions (mutually exclusive, exhaustive, non-contradictory) are, in practice, not difficult to meet and are relevant for subsequent security analysis: the definitions of the security properties need to be adapted for these extended models.

Our main motivation for defining EFGs with conditional actions is modeling the fAsset protocol on the Flare network. This decentralized finance platform enables communication of different blockchains through wrapped tokens: the assets (like Bitcoin, XRP, Eth, Dodgecoin, etc.) can be represented as fAssets on the Flare ecosystem and can be redeemed to reclaim the original assets. Such representation is sensitive to the price changes on the market, so the fAssets are collateralized during minting to ensure the redemption can always be performed for the original assets or for collateral. If the collateral drops below a certain threshold due to market fluctuations or misbehavior of the agents, a so-called liquidation phase is entered, where users are encouraged to redeem the fAssets in exchange for the collateral. The conditional actions in an EFG model play a natural role here, representing the changes in the market that can either trigger the liquidation of fAssets or not.

8   Conclusion

The modeling principles introduced in this paper rely on the definition of an EFG as a suitable model for the game-theoretic security analysis and can be automatically processed by game-theoretic security checks in CHECKMATE [2,21]. While previous work [20,25] introduced manually made models, to the best of our knowledge, our work provides the first semi-automated approach in generating games modeling protocols. Our approach enables exhausting all parameter options systematically in a machine-supported manner, thereby refining existing models, while also making fewer assumptions along the modeling process.

The modeling support presented in this paper makes automated game-theoretic security analyses much more accessible, as it eases the modeling process and automates the mechanical part of error-prone game tree generation. While the semi-automatic approach described here is already quite beneficial, (automatically) synthesizing game models from the protocol's specification, respectively source code in the case of smart contracts, is a challenge we aim to address in the future, in addition to the extension to conditional actions.

Acknowledgments. The work on extensive form games with conditional actions in Sect. 7 involved joint work with Ivana Bocevska during her master thesis project at TU Wien. The model of the fAsset protocol was developed in collaboration with Filip Koprivec. The research presented in this paper was funded in whole or in part by the ERC Consolidator Grant ARTIST 101002685, the Austrian Science Fund (FWF) SPyCoDe Grant 10.55776/F85, the WWTF Grant ForSmart 10.47379/ICT22007, the TU Wien Doctoral College SecInt, the Amazon Research Award 2023 QuAT, and a Netidee Fellowship 2022.

Disclosure of Interests. The authors have no competing interests to declare that are relevant to the content of this article.

References

1. Blanchet, B.: Automatic verification of security protocols in the symbolic model: the verifier ProVerif. In: Aldini, A., Lopez, J., Martinelli, F. (eds.) FOSAD 2012-2013. LNCS, vol. 8604, pp. 54–87. Springer, Cham (2014). https://doi.org/10.1007/978-3-319-10082-1_3
2. Brugger, L.S., Kovács, L., Petkovic Komel, A., Rain, S., Rawson, M.: CheckMate: automated game-theoretic security reasoning. In: Proceedings of the 2023 ACM SIGSAC Conference on Computer and Communications Security, CCS '23, pp. 1407–1421. Association for Computing Machinery, New York (2023).https://doi.org/10.1145/3576915.3623183
3. Capucci, M., Ghani, N., Ledent, J., Nordvall Forsberg, F.: Translating extensive form games to open games with agency. Electron. Proc. Theor. Comput. Sci. **372**, 221–234 (2022). https://doi.org/10.4204/eptcs.372.16
4. Nandi, C., Mooly Sagiv, D.J.: Certora Technology White Paper: Unveiling the Power and Limitations of Certora's Smart Contract Verification Technology. https://www.certora.com/blog/white-paper
5. Cheung, Y.K., Leonardos, S., Piliouras, G., Sridhar, S.: From griefing to stability in blockchain mining economies (2021). https://arxiv.org/abs/2106.12332
6. Dxo, Soos, M., Paraskevopoulou, Z., Lundfall, M., Brockman, M.: Hevm, a fast symbolic execution framework for evm bytecode. In: Gurfinkel, A., Ganesh, V. (eds.) Computer Aided Verification, pp. 453–465. Springer, Cham (2024). https://doi.org/10.1007/978-3-031-65627-9_22
7. FAssets. https://dev.flare.network/fassets/overview/
8. Flare: The Blockchain for Data. https://flare.network/
9. Fooladgar, M., Manshaei, M.H., Jadliwala, M., Rahman, M.A.: On incentive compatible role-based reward distribution in algorand. In: 2020 50th Annual IEEE/IFIP International Conference on Dependable Systems and Networks (DSN), pp. 452–463 (2020). https://doi.org/10.1109/DSN48063.2020.00059
10. Ghani, N., Hedges, J., Winschel, V., Zahn, P.: Compositional game theory. In: Proceedings of the 33rd Annual ACM/IEEE Symposium on Logic in Computer Science, LICS '18, pp. 472–481. Association for Computing Machinery, New York (2018). https://doi.org/10.1145/3209108.3209165
11. Ghani, N., Kupke, C., Lambert, A., Nordvall Forsberg, F.: Compositional game theory with mixed strategies: probabilistic open games using a distributive law. Electron. Proc. Theor. Comput. Sci. 323, 95–105 (2020). https://doi.org/10.4204/eptcs.323.7
12. Holler, S., Biewer, S., Schneidewind, C.: Horstify: sound security analysis of smart contracts. In: 36th IEEE Computer Security Foundations Symposium, CSF 2023, Dubrovnik, Croatia, 10–14 July 2023, pp. 245–260. IEEE (2023). https://doi.org/10.1109/CSF57540.2023.00023
13. Kobeissi, N., Nicolas, G., Tiwari, M.: Verifpal: cryptographic protocol analysis for the real world. In: Proceedings of the 2020 ACM SIGSAC Conference on Cloud Computing Security Workshop, CCSW'20, p. 159. Association for Computing Machinery, New York (2020). https://doi.org/10.1145/3411495.3421365
14. Kwiatkowska, M., Norman, G., Parker, D., Santos, G.: PRISM-games 3.0: stochastic game verification with concurrency, equilibria and time. In: Lahiri, S.K., Wang, C. (eds.) CAV 2020. LNCS, vol. 12225, pp. 475–487. Springer, Cham (2020). https://doi.org/10.1007/978-3-030-53291-8_25
15. Malavolta, G., Moreno-Sanchez, P., Schneidewind, C., Kate, A., Maffei, M.: Anonymous multi-hop locks for blockchain scalability and interoperability. In: Network and Distributed System Security Symposium. The Internet Society, San Diego (2019)

16. Manshaei, M.H., Jadliwala, M., Maiti, A., Fooladgar, M.: A game-theoretic analysis of shard-based permissionless blockchains. IEEE Access **6**, 78100–78112 (2018). https://doi.org/10.1109/ACCESS.2018.2884764
17. Mazumdar, S., Banerjee, P., Sinha, A., Ruj, S., Roy, B.K.: Strategic analysis of griefing attack in lightning network. IEEE Trans. Netw. Serv. Manag. **20**(2), 1790–1803 (2023). https://doi.org/10.1109/tnsm.2022.3230768
18. Meier, S., Schmidt, B., Cremers, C., Basin, D.: The TAMARIN prover for the symbolic analysis of security protocols. In: Sharygina, N., Veith, H. (eds.) CAV 2013. LNCS, vol. 8044, pp. 696–701. Springer, Heidelberg (2013). https://doi.org/10.1007/978-3-642-39799-8_48
19. Poon, J., Dryja, T.: The Bitcoin Lightning Network: Scalable Off-Chain Instant Payments. white paper (2016). https://lightning.network/lightning-network-paper.pdf
20. Rain, S., Avarikioti, G., Kovács, L., Maffei, M.: Towards a game-theoretic security analysis of off-chain protocols. In: 2023 IEEE 36th Computer Security Foundations Symposium (CSF), pp. 107–122. IEEE Computer Society, Los Alamitos (2023).https://doi.org/10.1109/CSF57540.2023.00003
21. Rain, S., Brugger, L.S., Komel, A.P., Kovács, L., Rawson, M.: Scaling checkmate for game-theoretic security. In: Bjørner, N., Heule, M., Voronkov, A. (eds.) Proceedings of 25th Conference on Logic for Programming, Artificial Intelligence and Reasoning. EPiC Series in Computing, vol. 100, pp. 222–231. EasyChair, Stockport (2024). https://doi.org/10.29007/llnq
22. Rain, S., Komel, A.P., Rawson, M., Kovács, L.: Game Modeling of Blockchain Protocols – Artifact (2025). https://zenodo.org/records/16925288
23. Stewart, I.: A puzzle for pirates. Sci. Am. **280**(5), 98–99 (1999)
24. Wang, T., Bai, X., Wang, H., Liew, S.C., Zhang, S.: Game-theoretical analysis of mining strategy for bitcoin-ng blockchain protocol. IEEE Syst. J. **15**(2), 2708–2719 (2021). https://doi.org/10.1109/JSYST.2020.3004468
25. Zappalà, P., Belotti, M., Potop-Butucaru, M.G., Secci, S.: Game theoretical framework for analyzing Blockchains Robustness. IACR Cryptol. ePrint Arch. **2020** (2020). https://api.semanticscholar.org/CorpusID:219616790

Concurrency Under Control: Systematic Analysis of SDN Races Hazards

Georgiana Caltais[1], Andrei Covaci[1], and Hossein Hojjat[2]([✉])

[1] University of Twente, Enschede, The Netherlands
g.g.c.caltais@utwente.nl, a.covaci@student.utwente.nl
[2] Tehran Institute for Advanced Studies, Khatam University, Tehran, Iran
h.hojjat@teias.institute

Abstract. Race conditions in Software-Defined Networks (SDNs) pose a significant threat to the correctness and reliability of network behavior, particularly in dynamic and distributed control plane environments. This paper presents a formal approach to identifying and analyzing races in SDNs using vector clocks and DyNetKAT, a domain-specific language for specifying and reasoning about dynamic packet-processing policies. By modeling network execution traces with vector clocks, we detect concurrent events through incomparable clock states, which signal potential races. We then assess the harmfulness of these races by comparing the DyNetKAT expressions associated with the corresponding transitions, determining if the race affects the network's behaviour. Our methodology enables systematic detection of harmful races that lead to packet drops, policy violations, or inconsistent forwarding behaviors. Through case studies and experimental validation on real network topologies, we demonstrate the effectiveness of our approach in uncovering subtle concurrency bugs that are often missed by traditional testing. This work provides a foundation for more robust SDN verification tools and contributes to the safe evolution of programmable network infrastructures.

Keywords: Race Condition · Software-defined Networking · Kleene Algebra · Process Algebra

1 Introduction

Race conditions occur when the outcome of concurrent operations depends on their unpredictable execution order [20]. Without proper synchronization, shared resource access may lead to failures such as data corruption, security breaches, or system crashes. These issues are especially problematic in distributed systems like Software-Defined Networking (SDN), where non-determinism and decentralized control make them hard to reproduce and debug. SDN decouples control and data planes, enabling centralized and programmable network control, but also introducing risks: concurrent control operations (e.g., flow rule updates) can cause packet loss, misrouting, or outages. An early ONOS release suffered intermittent traffic loss due to uncoordinated flow table updates [22].

© The Author(s), under exclusive license to Springer Nature Switzerland AG 2026
F. Damiani and M. Farrell (Eds.): iFM 2025, LNCS 16194, pp. 378–397, 2026.
https://doi.org/10.1007/978-3-032-10794-7_19

We aim to not only detect race conditions, but to identify those that violate system requirements. Even single-controller setups can be vulnerable. For instance, unsynchronized rule propagation in distributed firewalls can violate security policies. Detecting such violations is critical for secure SDN deployments.

Many verification tools exist for SDN reliability [16], but few address race conditions specifically between control and data planes. While dynamic analysis [10,25], model checking [24], and hybrid approaches [17] have been used, symbolic techniques are rare. Among them, TRACER [7] extends the semantics of DyNetKAT [6] (a domain-specific language for modeling SDN behavior) with Lamport-style vector clocks [15]. Each switch (or data-plane element) and controller is assigned one clock, to capture causal relationships between actions. TRACER also modifies the DyNetKAT semantics to operate without injecting concrete network packets, but instead reasoning over all packets that could hypothetically be processed according to the installed flow tables. However, Tracer does not focus on harmful races and lacks performance evaluation.

This work builds on [7] by introducing a symbolic execution framework that identifies harmful control-data plane races using the *big switch abstraction* [13]. It simplifies the network to a single logical switch, reducing state space. We further reduce overhead by using symbolic flow tables and associating one vector clock per big switch, improving scalability.

We make the following **contributions**: **(1)** enhance the DyNetKAT modeling accuracy by encoding the data plane as a single big switch, and **(2)** model controller-switch interactions through a communication mechanism inspired by the OpenFlow protocol (Sect. 4). **(3)** define a new symbolic semantics for DyNetKAT that operates over symbolic flow tables, rather than over individual packets, improving scalability (Sect. 6). **(4)** formalize three distinct classes of harmful SDN races, and **(5)** prove that our symbolic semantics enables detecting all such harmful races (Sect. 7). **(6)** implement our framework as a new prototype tool, RACELOOM [9], for automated symbolic race detection, and present the first DyNetKAT benchmark based on real-world topologies from the Topology Zoo dataset [14] and use it to evaluate the tool's performance (Sect. 8).

2   Related Work

Both static and dynamic analysis techniques have been used to detect races in SDNs [16]. Dynamic analysis inspects execution traces to infer concurrency errors, typically offering low false-positive rates but limited coverage. In contrast, static analysis explores all possible executions, enabling the detection of rare races at the cost of increased overhead and potential false alarms [11]

Dynamic approaches include SDNRacer [10], which detects races between the control and data planes by deriving a custom happens-before relation from the OpenFlow specification. ConGuard [25] similarly uses happens-before reasoning to detect races within the control plane, focusing on shared memory operations and validating harmful interleavings through source code instrumentation. SDN-predict [17] complements these tools by using SMT solvers [4] to analyze all valid reorderings of observed traces, detecting races missed by trace-limited approaches like SDNRacer. While the addition of SMT solvers improves the SDN race detection, SDN-predict still relies on the real execution traces of the network devices in order to perform the analysis.

Static methods for detecting SDN races often rely on model checking. Tools such as Kuai [18] and CMurphi [23], although not directly focused on concurrency in SDNs, apply general-purpose model checkers to verify safety properties in SDN programs, using domain specific abstractions to reduce state space. An approach focused more on SDN races is introduced in [24], which formulates three types of races as Linear Temporal Logic (LTL) properties verified with the SPIN model checker [12]. Although model checking is effective for detecting race hazards, it requires highly specific property formalizations and typically produces only a single, non-minimal counterexample. From a practical standpoint, this makes it harder to understand how a race hazard arises when the execution trace is unnecessarily long.

VeriCon [3] uses invariant checking and SMT solving to verify SDN programs over all topologies and event sequences, though it depends on user-defined invariants to expose harmful SDN races.

3   (Dy)NetKAT

In this section we provide a brief overview of (Dy)NetKAT [1] [6]. DyNetKAT is a formal language and algebraic model developed to reason about dynamic SDNs. It extends NetKAT [1], a domain-specific language based on Kleene Algebra with Tests (KAT), by introducing new constructs for control-plane actions, dynamic and stateful behaviors. We begin by introducing the key concepts that underpin the rest of the paper.

Network Packets. Let $F = \{f_1, \ldots, f_n\}$ be a finite set of field names. A *network packet* is a partial function $\sigma : F \rightarrow \mathbb{N}$, mapping fields to values. We write σ, σ' for packets. A condition $\sigma(f_i) = v_i$ checks if field f_i has value v_i; $\sigma[f_i := n_i]$ denotes the update assigning n_i to f_i. The *empty list* is $\langle \rangle$, and $\sigma :: l$ prepends σ to list l. Lists of packets are also referred to as *histories* in [1].

DyNetKAT Syntax. The syntax of DyNetKAT builds on NetKAT, a formal language for specifying network behavior using predicate logic and regular expressions. NetKAT expressions (cf. (1)) define how packets are transformed as they traverse the network. The language supports field tests ($f = n$), updates ($f \leftarrow n$), sequential ($\cdot$) composition, union ($+$) and iteration ($*$) for multi-hop forwarding. Constants **0** and **1** denote packet-dropping and identity policies, respectively. These constructs enable specification of routing, filtering, and access control. While standard NetKAT includes the **dup** operator for history-sensitive policies, DyNetKAT restricts to the dup-free fragment NetKAT$^{-\mathbf{dup}}$. The semantic map $[\![-]\!]$ of NetKAT denotes a function that takes a NetKAT policy p, a history H and produces a (possibly empty) set of histories $\{H_1, \ldots, H_n\}$.

$$Pr ::= \mathbf{0} \mid \mathbf{1} \mid f = n \mid Pr + Pr \mid Pr \cdot Pr \mid \neg Pr$$
$$N ::= Pr \mid f \leftarrow n \mid N + N \mid N \cdot N \mid N^* \mid \mathbf{dup} \tag{1}$$

For example, consider the following program: $(inport = 1 \cdot dst = 10.0.0.1 \cdot outport \leftarrow 2) + (inport = 2 \cdot dst = 10.0.0.2 \cdot outport \leftarrow 3)$. This NetKAT program performs the following. If a packet arrives on port 1 and its destination is 10.0.0.1, it forwards it to $outport$ 2. If a packet arrives on port 2 and its destination is 10.0.0.2, it forwards it to $outport$ 3. Let N be the dup-free fragment of NetKAT (NetKAT$^{-\mathbf{dup}}$).

Let $F = \{f_1, \ldots, f_n\}$ be a set of fields with values in V_i for $i \in \{1, \ldots, n\}$. A *complete test* (resp., *complete assignment*) is an expression $f_1 = v_1 \cdot \ldots \cdot f_n = v_n$ (resp., $f_1 \leftarrow v_1 \cdot \ldots \cdot f_n \leftarrow v_n$), where $v_i \in V_i$ [1]. NetKAT has a sound and complete axiomatization E_{NK} [1]. As shown in [6], any NetKAT$^{-\mathbf{dup}}$ policy d can be normalized via E_{NK} to $n.f.(d) \triangleq \sum_{i \in I} \alpha_i \cdot \pi_i$, where each α_i and π_i are complete tests and assignments, respectively. Given a packet σ such that $\sigma(f_i) = v_i$, we write α_σ (resp., π_σ) for the complete test (resp., assignment) $f_1 = v_1 \cdot \ldots \cdot f_n = v_n$ (resp., $f_1 \leftarrow v_1 \cdot \ldots \cdot f_n \leftarrow v_n$) induced by σ.

The syntax of DyNetKAT is built on top of N with the following constructs:

$$D ::= \bot \mid N\,;D \mid x?N\,;D \mid x!N\,;D \mid DD \mid D \oplus D \mid X \quad \text{with } X \triangleq D \tag{2}$$

The symbol $\bot$ denotes a dummy policy representing absence of behavior. Sequential composition $N\,;D$ means the NetKAT$^{-\mathbf{dup}}$ policy N must succeed on the current packet before applying D to the next. Communication is modeled via $x!N\,;D$ and $x?N\,;D$, denoting sending and receiving N over channel x, followed by D. Concurrent execution, written $D \,\|\, D$, allows synchronization between parallel components while ensuring per-packet consistency [21] -each packet follows a single NetKAT$^{-\mathbf{dup}}$ policy. $D \oplus D$ denotes non-determinism. X stands for variables defined via equations $X \triangleq D$. We omit trailing "; $\bot$" when implicit.

DyNetKAT Semantics. Figure 1 specifies the semantics of DynetKAT operators through a set of inference rules, following the conventional approach in process algebra [2]. Every rule captures how a DyNetKAT program p evolves into p' while consuming input packets H_i and emitting output packets H_o $((p, H_i, H_o) \xrightarrow{\gamma} (p', H_i', H_o'))$. In particular, the rule $(cpol^{\checkmark}\,,)$ makes the connection between the NetKAT denotational semantics and the DyNetKAT operational semantics: whenever σ' is the result of processing σ according to p, a corresponding step labeled $\xrightarrow{(\sigma,\sigma')}$ is observed as DyNetKAT behaviour. The operational semantics in Fig. 1 entails Labelled Transition System (LTS) behavioural models of DyNetKAT expressions, with bisimilarity as the standard notion of equivalence. Furthermore, DyNetKAT has a sound and complete axiomatisation E_{DNK} w.r.t. bisimilarity.

Example 1. Consider a switch with two modes of operation. In the first mode, upon receiving a packet destined for 10.0.0.1, the switch sets the output port field

$$(\mathbf{cpol}^{\curvearrowright};)\dfrac{\sigma' \in \llbracket p \rrbracket(\sigma::\langle\rangle)}{(p;q,\sigma::H,H') \xrightarrow{(\sigma,\sigma')} (q,H,\sigma'::H')} \qquad (\mathbf{cpolx})\dfrac{(p,H_0,H_1) \xrightarrow{\gamma} (p',H_0',H_1')}{(X,H_0,H_1) \xrightarrow{\gamma} (p',H_0',H_1')} X \triangleq p$$

$$(\mathbf{cpol}\_\oplus)\dfrac{(p,H_0,H_0') \xrightarrow{\gamma} (p',H_1,H_1')}{(p \oplus q,H_0,H_0') \xrightarrow{\gamma} (p',H_1,H_1')} \qquad (\mathbf{cpol}\_{||})\dfrac{(p,H_0,H_0') \xrightarrow{\gamma} (p',H_1,H_1')}{(p||q,H_0,H_0') \xrightarrow{\gamma} (p'||q,H_1,H_1')}$$

$$(\mathbf{cpol}_\bullet)\dfrac{}{(x \bullet p;q,H,H') \xrightarrow{x \bullet p} (q,H,H')} \qquad \bullet \in \{?,!\}$$

$$(\mathbf{cpol}_{\clubsuit\spadesuit})\dfrac{(q,H,H') \xrightarrow{x\clubsuit p} (q',H,H') \quad (s,H,H') \xrightarrow{x\spadesuit p} (s',H,H')}{(q||s,H,H') \xrightarrow{\mathbf{rcfg(x,p)}} (q'||s',H,H')} \qquad \begin{array}{l} \clubsuit = ? \quad \spadesuit = ! \\ \text{or} \\ \clubsuit = ! \quad \spadesuit = ? \end{array}$$

$$\gamma ::= (\sigma,\sigma') \mid x!q \mid x?q \mid \mathbf{rcfg(x,q)}$$

Fig. 1. DyNetKAT: Operational Semantics (relevant excerpt)

to 1. In the second mode, the switch drops all packets destined for 10.0.0.1. A controller runs in parallel with the switch and non-deterministically changes the mode between these two options. The complete system is the parallel composition of the switch (SW) and the controller (CT), expressed as:

$$SW \triangleq (dst = 10.0.0.1) \cdot (pt \leftarrow 1)\,;SW \oplus (x?1)\,;SW'$$
$$SW' \triangleq (dst = 10.0.0.1) \cdot \mathbf{0}\,;SW \oplus (x?0)\,;SW$$
$$CT \triangleq x!0\,;CT \oplus x!1\,;CT$$

Example 2. Consider a switch SW_N that operates based on the $\mathrm{NetKAT}^{-\mathbf{dup}}$ expression N. Let $FT \subseteq \mathrm{NetKAT}^{-\mathbf{dup}}$ represent the set of all possible configurations for SW_N. A controller non-deterministically selects a behavior N' from FT and instructs the switch SW_N via channel Ch to update itself, transforming into $SW_{N'}$. This behavior can be represented by the DyNetKAT expressions in (3); The SDN is defined as $SW_N \,||\, CT$.

$$SW_N \triangleq N \oplus \Sigma_{N' \in FT}^{\oplus} Ch?N'\,;SW_{N'} \qquad CT \triangleq \Sigma_{N' \in FT}^{\oplus} Ch!N'\,;CT \qquad (3)$$

4   One Big Switch Abstraction

The "One Big Switch" abstraction [13] simplifies SDN programming by modeling the entire network as a single logical switch. Instead of configuring individual devices, operators define high-level forwarding policies between end hosts. This

$$SW_N \triangleq N \,;\, SW_N \oplus$$
$$\Sigma_{i \in I}^{\oplus} \, FM_i \,?\, N_i \,;\, SW_{N_i} \oplus$$
$$\Sigma_{j \in J}^{\oplus} \, PI_j \,!\, M_{1j} \,;\, SWR_{N,j}$$
$$C \triangleq \Sigma_{i \in I}^{\oplus} \, FM_i \,!\, N_i \,;\, C \oplus$$
$$\Sigma_{j \in J}^{\oplus} \, PI_j \,?\, M_{1j} \,;\, CR_j$$

$$SWR_{N,j} \triangleq N \,;\, SWR_{N,j} \oplus$$
$$\Sigma_{i \in I}^{\oplus} \, FM_i \,?\, N_i \,;\, SWR_{N_i,j} \oplus$$
$$PO_j \,?\, M_{2j} \,;\, SW_{M_{2j}}$$
$$CR_j \triangleq \Sigma_{i \in I}^{\oplus} \, FM_i \,!\, N_i \,;\, CR_j \oplus$$
$$PO_j \,!\, M_{2j} \,;\, C$$

$$SDN \triangleq SW_N \parallel C$$

Fig. 2. $I, J \subseteq \mathbb{N}, \forall k \in I \cup J : M_{1k}, M_{2k},\ N, N_k \in \text{NetKAT}^{-\mathbf{dup}}, PI_k, PO_k,\ FM_k -$ DyNetKAT channels

approach improves scalability, simplifies management, and reduces configuration errors. We model SDNs under the one-big-switch abstraction in DyNetKAT to obtain a formal representation that simplifies reasoning about controller-dataplane races.

The "big switch" abstraction treats the network as a single switch with multiple ports, abstracting away the distributed behavior of individual switches. Let the network have n switches with topology t. Each switch $i \in \{1, \ldots, n\}$ has a configuration X_i, a NetKAT term over its packet fields and local ports. The entire data plane is encoded as $SW_N \triangleq (N \cdot t)^*$ with $N \triangleq (X_1 + \ldots + X_n)$.

DyNetKAT also models communication between SW_N and a controller C in line with OpenFlow. The required messages are: (i) **flow-mod** messages $FM_i!N_i$ (for $i \in I \subseteq \mathbb{N}$), where the controller instructs switch SW_N via channel FM_i to install forwarding behavior N_i (of the same form as N); (ii) **packet-in** messages $PI!M_1$, sent by SW_N to C when no matching flow entry exists; (iii) **packet-out** messages $PO!M_2$, sent by C to SW_N to forward packets received via packet-in. Packet-out must be preceded by a corresponding packet-in. With these ingredients at hand, OpenFlow inspired switches and controllers can be encoded in DyNetKAT as in Fig. 2. In words, SW_N can: (i) forward packets according to the NetKAT policy N and behave recursively as SW_N afterwards, (ii) update its behaviour according to flow-mod messages, or (iii) communicate with the controller via packet-in or packet-out messages.

5   Vector Clocks

We propose the use of Lamport vector clocks [15] as a mechanism for detecting races in DyNetKAT. A vector clock is typically defined as an array of logical clocks, one per concurrent process, and is commonly used to track racing behaviour in distributed systems. For a system with k concurrent processes, each process P_i (where $i \in \{1, \ldots, k\}$) is associated with a k-dimensional vector clock $\vec{c_i}$, initialized as: $\langle 0, \ldots, 0 \rangle$. We briefly outline the core vector clock update rules in the context of DyNetKAT. Case (i): When a local event occurs at process P_i, the i-th component of its vector clock is incremented by 1. In DyNetKAT, such events correspond to packet transformations within a switch

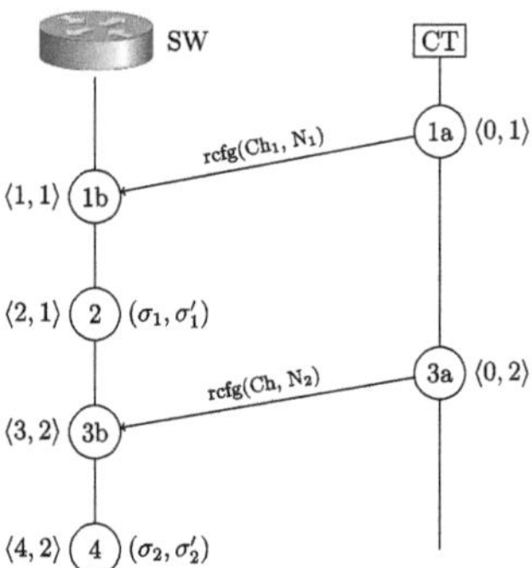

Fig. 3. Switch-Controller race; $\sigma_1' \in [\![N_1]\!](\sigma_1)$ and $\sigma_2' \in [\![N_2]\!](\sigma_2)$.

-formally represented by a label (σ, σ') in Fig. 1. Case (ii): For inter-process communication, represented by labels $\mathrm{rcfg}(Ch, N)$ in Fig. 3, the sender increments its own clock component, attaches its vector clock to the message, and sends it. Upon receipt, the receiving process updates each entry in its vector clock by taking the element-wise maximum (i.e., for each component, the larger value between its own clock and the received clock) with the received clock, and then increments its own component.

For an example, Fig. 3 gives the vector clocks (and associated messages and events) corresponding to a concurrent scenario within the SDN in example 2. In the rest of the paper, we use $\vec{c}_i[j]$ to refer to the value at index j of the vector clock $\vec{c}_i$. Assigning a value v_j to this position is written as $\vec{c}_i[j] = v_j$. To increment the value at index j by v_j, we write $\vec{c}_i[j]\mathrel{+}= v_j$, while $\vec{c}_i[j]\mathrel{+}{+}$ denotes a unit increment. Given two vector clocks $\vec{c}_i$ and $\vec{c}_j$ of dimension k, we denote by $\vec{c} = \max(\vec{c}_i, \vec{c}_j)$ the component-wise maximum vector, i.e., $\vec{c}[l] = \max(\vec{c}_i[l], \vec{c}_j[l])$ for each $l \in \{1, \ldots, k\}$.

Vector clocks can be compared to determine concurrency between events. For two vector clocks $\vec{c}$ and $\vec{c'}$ of equal length k, we define:

$$\vec{c} = \vec{c'} \text{ iff } \vec{c}[i] = \vec{c'}[i] \quad \text{for all } i \in \{1, \ldots, k\}$$
$$\vec{c} \leq \vec{c'} \text{ iff } \vec{c}[i] \leq \vec{c'}[i] \quad \text{for all } i \in \{1, \ldots, k\}$$
$$\vec{c} \| \vec{c'} \text{ iff } \vec{c} \not\leq \vec{c'} \text{ and } \vec{c'} \not\leq \vec{c}$$

The partial order $\leq$ represents the *happens-before* relation between events or messages tracked by vector clocks. The relation $\|$ identifies events that are concurrent, signaling potential undesired behaviour in the system.

Finally, we define:

$$c \underset{(i,j)}{\|} c' \text{ iff } ((\vec{c}_{[i]} < \vec{c'}_{[i]}) \wedge (\vec{c}_{[j]} > \vec{c'}_{[j]})) \vee ((\vec{c}_{[i]} > \vec{c'}_{[i]}) \wedge (\vec{c}_{[j]} < \vec{c'}_{[j]}))$$

for some $i, j \in \{1 \ldots k\}$, for any vector clocks c and c' of size k. Intuitively, this states that c and c' are incomparable with respect to some positions i and j.

In Fig. 3 the incomparable vector clocks $\langle 0, 2 \rangle$ and $\langle 2, 1 \rangle$ witness a race between the switch processing a packet according to N_1, and the controller installing the update N_2.

6 Symbolic DyNetKAT

The framework presented in this section introduces a set of DyNetKAT symbolic execution rules, enriched with vector clocks, which can be used to detect SDN races. As discussed later in the paper, races in SDN arise from concurrency between the control and data planes, as well as between multiple controllers that may interact or update one another. We represent SDNs using DyNetKAT policies of the following form:

$$S_1 \,||\, \ldots \,||\, S_n \,||\, C_1 \,||\, \ldots \,||\, C_m \tag{4}$$

where each S_i and C_j is a DyNetKAT expression (or process) corresponding to a big switch and a controller, respectively, as defined in Fig. 2, for all $i \in \{1, \ldots, n\}$ and $j \in \{1, \ldots, m\}$. Note that big switches and controllers as above are free of the parallel composition operator ($||$).

The symbolic execution rules ordering the events within an SDN as in (4) will be defined over tuples, or *symbolic configurations* of shape:

$$S_{1\vec{c_1}} \,||\, \ldots \,||\, C_{m\vec{c_m}} \tag{5}$$

In (5), each concurrent process S_i (for $i \in \{1, \ldots, n\}$) and C_j (for $j \in \{1, \ldots, m\}$) is associated with a vector clock $\vec{c_k}$ of size $n + m$.

The symbolic operational semantics of DyNetKAT in Fig. 4 is defined over symbolic configurations, based on *symbolic normal forms*: expressions capturing all first-step actions in an SDN. These include: (i) packet forwarding via a NetKAT expression N, (ii) message exchange between control and data planes, and (iii) synchronous reconfiguration. Our approach symbolically identifies action traces witnessing racing behaviour, without injecting actual network packets, unlike [6].

Definition 1 (Symbolic normal forms). *A DyNetKAT expression p is in symbolic normal form (s.n.f.) if it is of shape:*

$$\Sigma_{i \in I}^{\oplus} N_i; d_i \oplus \Sigma_{j \in J}^{\oplus} c_j; d_j \, (\oplus \bot) \tag{6}$$

where N_i ranges over NetKAT$^{-\mathbf{dup}}$ *policies, d_i, d_j range over* DyNetKAT *policies and $c_j :: = x?q \mid x!q \mid \mathbf{rcfg}(\mathbf{x}, \mathbf{q})$ with q denoting terms in* NetKAT$^{-\mathbf{dup}}$ *and x ranging over communication channels.*

Without loss of generality, we consider *guarded* DyNetKAT policies [6] encoding S_i and C_j as in (4). A DyNetKAT policy p is guarded if and only if all occurrences of all variables X in p are guarded. An occurrence of a variable X in a policy p is guarded if and only if: (i) p has a subterm of shape p'; t such that either p' is variable-free, or all the occurrences of variables Y in p' are guarded, and X occurs in t, or (ii) p is of shape $y?X$; t, $y!X$; t, or $\mathbf{rcfg}(\mathbf{X}, \mathbf{t})$.

Lemma 1 (E_{DNK}symbolic normalization / Lemma 7 in [6]). *Any guarded DyNetKAT expression p can be reduced, according to the axiomatization E_{DNK} of DyNetKAT, to an equivalent expression p' in symbolic normal form:* $E_{DNK} \vdash p = p'$.

Symbolic Semantics. Figure 4 shows a relevant excerpt of the DyNetKAT symbolic semantic rules. This semantics follows closely the original DyNetKAT semantics in [6] (or Fig. 1). Here we write $P_{i\vec{c_i}} \,||\, \Pi_{1 \leq j \leq k} P_{j\vec{c_j}}$ $(j \neq i)$ to denote $P_{1\vec{c_1}} \,||\, \ldots \,||\, P_{k\vec{c_k}}$. Rules $(\mathbf{Symb}_{\checkmark})$ and $(\mathbf{Symb}_{||})$ implement the semantics of vector clocks as described in Sect. 5. Note that we only consider synchronous communication in rule $(\mathbf{Symb}_{||})$. We are not interested in a symbolic semantics of asynchronous communication as asynchrony does not entail forwarding updates of switches. For technical reasons, we needed $(\mathbf{Symb}_{||})$ to also capture the indices of the sender l and the receiver k on the communication transition label.

$$(\mathbf{Symb}_{\checkmark}) \; \frac{N_i \in \mathrm{NetKAT}^{-\mathbf{dup}}}{(N_i\,;\,q_i)_{\vec{c_i}} \,||\, \Pi_{\substack{1 \leq j \leq n \\ j \neq i}} d_{j\vec{c_j}} \xrightarrow{N_i} (q_i)_{\vec{c_i}[i]++} \,||\, \Pi_{\substack{1 \leq j \leq n \\ j \neq i}} d_{j\vec{c_j}}}$$

$$(\mathbf{Symb}_{\mathbf{X}}) \; \frac{(p_i)_{\vec{c_i}} \,||\, \Pi_{\substack{1 \leq j \leq n \\ j \neq i}} d_{j\vec{c_j}} \xrightarrow{N_i} (p_i')_{\vec{c_i'}} \,||\, \Pi_{\substack{1 \leq j \leq n \\ j \neq i}} d_{j\vec{c_j}}}{(X_i)_{\vec{c_i}} \,||\, \Pi_{\substack{1 \leq j \leq n \\ j \neq i}} d_{j\vec{c_j}} \xrightarrow{N_i} (p_i')_{\vec{c_i'}} \,||\, \Pi_{\substack{1 \leq j \leq n \\ j \neq i}} d_{j\vec{c_j}}} \, X_i \triangleq p_i$$

$$(\mathbf{Symb}_{\oplus}) \; \frac{(p_i)_{\vec{c_i}} \,||\, \Pi_{\substack{1 \leq j \leq n \\ j \neq i}} d_{j\vec{c_j}} \xrightarrow{N_i} (p_i')_{\vec{c_i'}} \,||\, \Pi_{\substack{1 \leq j \leq n \\ j \neq i}} d_{j\vec{c_j}}}{(p_i \oplus q_i)_{\vec{c_i}} \,||\, \Pi_{\substack{1 \leq j \leq n \\ j \neq i}} d_{j\vec{c_j}} \xrightarrow{N_i} (p_i')_{\vec{c_i'}} \,||\, \Pi_{\substack{1 \leq j \leq n \\ j \neq i}} d_{j\vec{c_j}}}$$

$$(\mathbf{Symb}_{||}) \; \frac{s.n.f(q_i) \triangleq x\,!\,N\,;\,d_i \oplus r_i \qquad s.n.f(q_k) \triangleq x\,?\,N\,;\,d_k \oplus r_k}{(q_1)_{\vec{c_1}} \,||\, \cdots \,||\, (q_i)_{\vec{c_i}} \,||\, \cdots \,||\, (q_k)_{\vec{c_k}} \,||\, \cdots \,||\, (q_n)_{\vec{c_n}} \xrightarrow{\mathbf{rcfg(x, N, i, k)}} (q_1)_{\vec{c_1}} \,||\, \cdots \,||\, (d_i)_{\vec{c_i}[i]++} \,||\, \cdots \,||\, (d_k)_{max(\vec{c_i}[i]++,\vec{c_k})[k]++} \,||\, \cdots \,||\, (q_n)_{\vec{c_n}}}$$

Fig. 4. (Modified) symbolic semantics of DyNetKAT (relevant excerpt). For simplicity, the symmetric rules associated with $\mathbf{Symb}_{\oplus}$ and $\mathbf{Symb}_{||}$ were ommitted. $(N, N_i \in \mathrm{NetKAT}^{-\mathrm{dup}}$, x is a communication channel)

Given an initial SDN configuration as in (5), we can derive a symbolic LTS, according to the rules in Fig. 4, in the standard fashion.

Definition 2 (Symbolic LTS). *Let $d = \prod_{i=1}^{n} d_i$ be a DyNetKAT expression where d_i is free of $||$ for all $i \in \{1, \ldots, n\}$. We call $T = (S, s_0, \Sigma, \rightarrow)$ the symbolic LTS associated with d where:*

- *S is a set of states of shape $\prod_{i=1}^{n} d'_{i\vec{c}'_i}$ with:*
  - *d'_i as a DyNetKAT expression free of $\parallel$ for $i \in \{1, \ldots, n\}$*
  - *$\vec{c}'_i$ as a vector clock of size n for $i \in \{1, \ldots, n\}$*
- *$s_0 = \prod_{i=1}^{n} d_{i\vec{c}_i}$ with $\vec{c}_i = \langle 0, \ldots, 0 \rangle$ for $i \in \{1, \ldots, n\}$*
- *$\Sigma \subseteq \text{NetKAT}^{-\mathbf{dup}} \cup \{\mathbf{rcfg}(\mathbf{X}, \mathbf{N}, \mathbf{l}, \mathbf{t}) \mid X$ a variable denoting a communication channel, $N \in \text{NetKAT}^{-\mathbf{dup}}$, and $l, t \in \{1, \ldots, n\}$ indicies of the sender, respectively, the receiver of the communication\}*
- *$\rightarrow\, \subseteq S \times \Sigma \times S$ is the transition relation where $s \xrightarrow{l \in \Sigma} s'$ denotes a transition according to the symbolic rules of DyNetKAT when starting in s, for $s, s' \in S$*

For a state $s \triangleq \prod_{i=1}^{n} d_{i\vec{c}_i} \in S$, we call $d_{i\vec{c}_i}$ an *element* of s, denoted by $s \downarrow i$. By abuse of notation, we let $d_{i[j]}$ represent the value at position j in the vector clock of element $d_{i\vec{c}_i}$ (this simplifies notation in definitions 5, 6, and 7). We sometimes refer to the vector clock of element $d_{i\vec{c}_i}$ as the vector clock i of state s.

We call a *trace of T* a sequence $tr \triangleq s_0 \xrightarrow{l_0} s_1 \xrightarrow{l_1} \ldots$ in T, and we write $tr \in T$. We write $s \in tr$ whenever $s \xrightarrow{l} s'$ or $s' \xrightarrow{l} s$ is a transition in tr. We call a *finite trace of T* a finite sequence $tr \triangleq s_0 \xrightarrow{l_0} s_1 \xrightarrow{l_1} \ldots \xrightarrow{l_k} s_{k+1}$ in T, and we write $tr \in T$. For two traces $tr_1 \triangleq v_0 \xrightarrow{l_0} v_1 \xrightarrow{l_1} \ldots \xrightarrow{l_k} v_{k+1}$, $tr_2 \in T$, we call tr_1 a *subtrace of tr_2* and write $tr_1 \subseteq tr_2$ whenever $tr_2 \triangleq s_0 \xrightarrow{\cdots} \ldots \xrightarrow{\cdots} v_0 \xrightarrow{l_0} v_1 \xrightarrow{l_1} \ldots \xrightarrow{l_k} v_{k+1} \xrightarrow{\cdots} \ldots$.

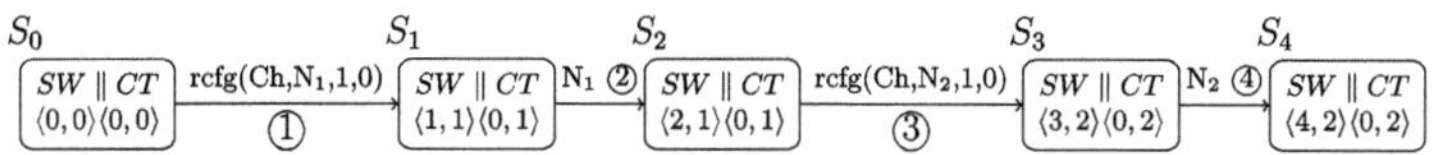

Fig. 5. Switch-Controller symbolic trace.

For example, the symbolic trace corresponding to the race in Fig. 3 is in Fig. 5.

Remark 1. The semantics in this paper differ from that of the tool in [7]. First, we define rules over big switches rather than modeling individual switches concurrently, better reflecting SDN practice and reducing the symbolic state space. Second, we analyze races at the level of full forwarding behaviors N_i (via symbolic normal forms), rather than individual packet steps, which suffices to detect races and further reduces the state space.

Let d range over DyNetKAT expressions $\prod_{i=1}^{n} d_i$ as in (4), where d_i is free of $\parallel$ for all $i \in \{1, \ldots, n\}$ and arbitrary n. Let H range over packet histories. We call an LTS *synchronous* whenever it is derived starting from d and H based on the DyNetKAT semantic rules in Fig. 1 excluding the asynchronous steps in $(cpol_\bullet)$.

Definition 1 (Simulation up-to forwarding). Let $T = (S,\, s_0,\, \Sigma,\, \rightarrow)$ be a synchronous DyNetKAT LTS derived according to Fig. 1. Consider a symbolic LTS $T' = (S',\, s_0',\, \Sigma',\, \rightarrow')$ derived according to Fig. 4. A relation $R \subseteq S \times S'$ is a *simulation up-to forwarding* whenever for all $(s, s') \in R$:

- if $s \xrightarrow{(\sigma, \sigma')} p$ then exists $s' \xrightarrow{N}{}' p'$ s.t. $\alpha_\sigma \cdot \pi_{\sigma'} \in n.f.(N)$ and $(p, p') \in R$.
  In words, if σ is processed into σ' in T, then there exists a forwarding policy N enabling the same processing in T'.
- if $s \xrightarrow{\mathbf{rcfg(x,\, N)}} p$ then exists $s' \xrightarrow{\mathbf{rcfg(x,\, N,\, l,\, t)}}{}' p'$ and $(p, p') \in R$.
  In words, if a reconfiguration $\mathbf{rcfg(x, N)}$ is enabled in T, then it also holds for T'.

We say that T and T' are *similar up-to forwarding*, written $T \precsim_f T'$, whenever they entail a relation R as above.

Lemma 2 (Symbolic similarity). *Let $T = (S,\, s_0,\, \Sigma,\, \rightarrow)$ be a synchronous DyNetKAT LTS from d and H. Consider the corresponding symbolic LTS $T' = (S',\, s_0',\, \Sigma',\, \rightarrow')$. It holds that $T \precsim_f T'$. Furthermore, each trace $tr \in T$ corresponds to a symbolic trace $tr' \in T'$ enriched with vector clocks and where transitions are labeled $\xrightarrow{N}{}'$, instead of $\xrightarrow{(\sigma, \sigma')}$, for $\alpha_\sigma \cdot \pi_{\sigma'} \in n.f.(N)$, and $\xrightarrow{\mathbf{rcfg(X,\, N,\, l,\, t)}}{}'$ instead of $\xrightarrow{\mathbf{rcfg(X,\, N)}}$. In this context, we abuse notation and write $tr \precsim_f tr'$.*

Proof sketch. The proof follows directly from the semantic rules in Fig. 1, the symbolic rules in Fig. 4, Lemma 1 and the existence of NetKAT$^{-\mathbf{dup}}$ normal forms as defined in [6]. ∎

Remark 2. Lemma 2 ensures that all potential racing behaviors (i.e., concurrency interleavings) are preserved within the symbolic LTS, thereby establishing the correctness of our approach as in Corollary 1.

7   DyNetKAT Races

Intuitively, a race occurs in a trace tr of a symbolic LTS if there exists a pair of states in tr whose vector clocks are incomparable (see Definition 3). Such a race is considered *harmful* with respect to a *forwarding* property ϕ if it alters the packet processing behavior of the network in a way that leads to the violation of ϕ. In our setting, a *forwarding* property ϕ specifies whether packets can traverse the network from a designated *ingress* point to a designated *egress* point. To verify if a race is harmful, we have to check whether the packet processing of the network satisfies ϕ before and after the race manifested.

We distinguish three types of races. (1) Controller→Switch (**CT→SW**): a race between a switch SW processing packets under policy N and a controller CT reconfiguring SW to N'. (2) Controller→Switch←Controller (**CT→SW←CT**): a race between two controllers CT_1 and CT_2 concurrently reconfiguring the same switch SW. (3) Controller→Controller→Switch (**CT→CT→SW**): a race where CT_2 reconfigures CT_1, which in turn reconfigures switch SW. Note that we do not consider races between switches, as our big switch encodings do not allow for communication between switches.

Definition 3 (Race). *Let* $T = (S, s_0, \Sigma, \rightarrow)$ *be the symbolic LTS of* $d \triangleq \prod_{i=1}^{n} d_i$ *as in (4), where* d_i *is free of* $\parallel$ *for all* $i \in \{1, \ldots, n\}$ *and* $tr \in T$. *We say that* tr *exhibits a* race *whenever:*

$$\exists \left(s = \prod_{i=1}^{n} d^s_{ic^{\vec{s}}_i}, v = \prod_{i=1}^{n} d^v_{ic^{\vec{v}}_i} \right) \in tr. \ \exists \vec{c^s_p} \in \{\vec{c^s_1}, \ldots, \vec{c^s_n}\}. \ \exists \vec{c^v_q} \in \{\vec{c^v_1}, \ldots, \vec{c^v_n}\}. \ \vec{c^s_p} \underset{(p,q)}{\parallel} \vec{c^v_q}$$

Definition 4 (Forwarding property). *A* forwarding property *is a function* $\phi^{\alpha_{out}}_{\alpha_{in}} : \text{NetKAT}^{-\textbf{dup}} \rightarrow \mathbb{B}$ *such that* $\phi^{\alpha_{out}}_{\alpha_{in}}(N) = \texttt{false}$ *whenever* E_{NK} *entails* $\alpha_{in} \cdot N \cdot \alpha_{out} \equiv \mathbf{0}$, *and* $\texttt{true}$ *otherwise. Here,* α_{in} *and* α_{out} *are NetKAT complete tests encoding ingress/egress conditions, and* N *is a NetKAT expression for data plane forwarding behaviour.*

A forwarding property $\phi^{\alpha_{out}}_{\alpha_{in}}(N)$ is $\texttt{false}$ ($\equiv \mathbf{0}$) if the policy fails and drops all packets; it is true ($\not\equiv \mathbf{0}$) if packets are forwarded according to the complete tests α_{in} and α_{out}.

We now specify assumptions and notation used in Definitions 5, 6 and 7. Let $T = (S, s_0, \Sigma, \rightarrow)$ be the symbolic LTS of $d \triangleq \prod_{i=1}^{n} d_i$ as in (4), $\phi^{\alpha_{out}}_{\alpha_{in}}$ be a forwarding property, and $tr \in T$. Suppose that $\exists \ v, v', u, u' \in tr$ such that $v = \prod_{i=1}^{n} d^v_{ic^{\vec{v}}_i}$, $v' = \prod_{i=1}^{n} d^{v'}_{ic^{\vec{v'}}_i}$, $u = \prod_{i=1}^{n} d^u_{ic^{\vec{u}}_i}$, $u' = \prod_{i=1}^{n} d^{u'}_{ic^{\vec{u'}}_i}$, and $\exists \ p, q \in \{1, \ldots, n\}$ such that $\vec{c^{v'}_p} \underset{(p,q)}{\parallel} \vec{c^{u'}_q}$. This formula identifies two elements with incomparable vector clocks, i.e. elements that run concurrently.

Definition 5 (Harmful CT→SW race). *We say that* tr *exhibits a* harmful CT→SW race *with respect to* $\phi^{\alpha_{out}}_{\alpha_{in}}$ *whenever:*

$$(v \xrightarrow{N_1} v' \xrightarrow{\cdots} \ldots \xrightarrow{\cdots} u \xrightarrow{\text{rcfg}(X,N_2,q,p)} u') \subseteq tr \tag{7a}$$

$$\wedge \ (v \downarrow p)_{[p]} \neq (v' \downarrow p)_{[p]} \wedge (v' \downarrow p)_{[p]} = (u \downarrow p)_{[p]} \tag{7b}$$

$$\wedge \ (u \downarrow q)_{[q]} \neq (u' \downarrow q)_{[q]} \tag{7c}$$

$$\wedge \ (\phi^{\alpha_{out}}_{\alpha_{in}}(N_1) \neq \phi^{\alpha_{out}}_{\alpha_{in}}(N_2)) \tag{7d}$$

For this definition, the elements that run concurrently are a switch SW_p and a controller CT_q. The formulas in (7a)–(7c) capture the corresponding transitions that caused these incomparable clocks, specifically, the transitions that modified position p of $\vec{c^{v'}_p}$ and position q of $\vec{c^{u'}_q}$, respectively. Finally, (7d) checks whether the forwarding behavior changes: only one of N_1 or N_2 enables forwarding from *in* to *out*.

Remark 3. Definition 5 covers only one ordering of the two transitions, i.e. $\ldots v \xrightarrow{N_1} v' \xrightarrow{\cdots} \ldots \xrightarrow{\cdots} u \xrightarrow{\text{rcfg}(X,N_2,q,p)} u' \ldots$. The ordering $\ldots u \xrightarrow{\text{rcfg}(X,N_2,q,p)} u' \xrightarrow{\cdots} \ldots \xrightarrow{\cdots} v \xrightarrow{N_1} v' \ldots$, such that the assumptions made in the beginning of the section and formulas (7b) and (7c) hold, is not possible for the switch and controller expressions that we consider. If the reconfiguration transition happens first, it means that SW_p has already updated its policy to N_2, so it cannot produce packet processing transitions that are labeled N_1 anymore.

Definition 6 (Harmful CT→SW←race). *We say that tr exhibits a* harmful *$CT{\rightarrow}SW{\leftarrow}CT$ race with respect to $\phi_{\alpha_{in}}^{\alpha_{out}}$ whenever:*

$$(v \xrightarrow{rcfg(X_1,N_1,p,t)} v' \xrightarrow{\cdots} \ldots \xrightarrow{\cdots} u \xrightarrow{rcfg(X_2,N_2,q,t)} u') \subseteq tr \tag{8a}$$

$$\wedge \; (v \downarrow p)_{[p]} \neq (v' \downarrow p)_{[p]} \wedge (v' \downarrow p)_{[p]} = (u' \downarrow p)_{[p]} \tag{8b}$$

$$\wedge \; (u \downarrow q)_{[q]} \neq (u' \downarrow q)_{[q]} \tag{8c}$$

$$\wedge \;\; \forall u_1, u_2 \in (v' \xrightarrow{\cdots} \ldots \xrightarrow{\cdots} u), \; \forall i \in \{1 \ldots n\}.$$

$$(i \neq t) \Rightarrow (u_1 \downarrow t)_{[i]} = (u_2 \downarrow t)_{[i]} \tag{8d}$$

$$\wedge \; \phi_{\alpha_{in}}^{\alpha_{out}}(N_1) \neq \phi_{\alpha_{in}}^{\alpha_{out}}(N_2) \tag{8e}$$

For this definition, the elements that run concurrently are two controllers CT_p and CT_q updating a switch SW_t. Formulas (8b) and (8c) ensure that the reconfiguration transitions from (8a) correspond to these elements and trigger the incomparable vector clocks. In (8d), we ensure that SW_t is only processing packets in between the updates and no other reconfigurations target it. Finally, (8e) checks whether the forwarding behavior changes: only one of the controllers' updates, i.e., N_1 or N_2, enables forwarding from *in* to *out*.

Definition 7 (Harmful CT→CT→SW race). *We say that tr exhibits a* harmful $CT{\rightarrow}CT{\rightarrow}SW$ *race with respect to $\phi_{\alpha_{in}}^{\alpha_{out}}$ whenever:*

$$(v \xrightarrow{rcfg(X_1,N_1,p,t)} v' \xrightarrow{\cdots} \ldots \xrightarrow{\cdots} u \xrightarrow{rcfg(X_2,N_2,q,p)} u') \subseteq tr \tag{9a}$$

$$\wedge \; (v \downarrow p)_{[p]} \neq (v' \downarrow p)_{[p]} \wedge (v' \downarrow p)_{[p]} = (u \downarrow p)_{[p]} \tag{9b}$$

$$\wedge \; (u \downarrow q)_{[q]} \neq (u' \downarrow q)_{[q]} \tag{9c}$$

$$\wedge \;\; \forall u_1, u_2 \in (v' \xrightarrow{\cdots} \ldots \xrightarrow{\cdots} u), \; \forall i \in \{1 \ldots n\}.$$

$$(i \neq t) \Rightarrow (u_1 \downarrow t)_{[i]} = (u_2 \downarrow t)_{[i]} \tag{9d}$$

$$\wedge \; \phi_{\alpha_{in}}^{\alpha_{out}}(N_1) \neq \phi_{\alpha_{in}}^{\alpha_{out}}(N_2) \tag{9e}$$

For this definition, the elements that run concurrently are a controller CT_q reconfiguring another controller CT_p while it updates the forwarding policy of a switch SW_t. Formulas (9a)–(9c) ensure that the reconfiguration transitions from (9a) correspond to these elements and cause the incomparable vector clocks. In (9d), we ensure that SW_t is not the target of any updates in between the racing transitions and may only process packets. Finally, (9e) checks whether the forwarding behavior changes: only one of the controllers' updates, i.e., N_1 or N_2, enables forwarding from *in* to *out*.

Remark 4. Analogously to Definition 5, Definition 7 covers only one ordering of the two transitions, i.e. $v \xrightarrow{rcfg(X_1,N_1,p,t)} v' \xrightarrow{\cdots} \ldots \xrightarrow{\cdots} u \xrightarrow{rcfg(X_2,N_2,q,p)} u'$. The other ordering $v \xrightarrow{rcfg(X_2,N_2,q,p)} v' \xrightarrow{\cdots} \ldots \xrightarrow{\cdots} u \xrightarrow{rcfg(X_1,N_1,p,t)} u'$, such that the assumptions made in the beginning of the section and formulas (9b) and (9c) hold, is not possible for the switch and controller expressions that we consider. If CT_q reconfigures CT_p first, then CT_p would use the new policy N_2 when reconfiguring switches, including SW_t.

Corollary 1 (Completeness). *Let $T = (S, s_0, \Sigma, \rightarrow)$ be a synchronous DyNetKAT LTS from d and H. Consider the corresponding symbolic LTS $T' = (S', s'_0, \Sigma', \rightarrow')$. All concurrent behaviours (interleavings) in T are characterised by races in T' as in Definition 3.*

Proof sketch.   The result follows directly from Lemma 2, as every $tr \in T$ corresponds to a $tr' \in T'$ such that $tr \lesssim tr'$.   ∎

8   Experimental Evaluation

Building on the theoretical foundations presented in this paper, we implemented RACELOOM [9], a tool for detecting and illustrating harmful races in SDNs via symbolic traces. The tool implementation integrates Python, Maude [8], and KATch [19]. Given a DyNetKAT model, a forwarding property, and a depth bound, RaceLoom uses Maude to generate all symbolic traces up to the specified depth, and applies KATch to check any racing transitions found along these traces against the forwarding property. Depending on the type of race, the concurrent transitions are identified using the conditions specified in definitions 5, 6, and 7. During the implementation of the tool, we observed that the same harmful race can appear at different depths across execution traces. This is why, unlike model checking approaches, RaceLoom outputs all minimal execution traces, terminating the analysis as soon as a harmful race is detected.

Our experimental evaluation answers the following research question **RQ:** *What is the performance of RaceLoom on DyNetKAT models based on real world network topologies of various sizes?* We begin by showcasing how RaceLoom captures CT→SW←CT races on the independent controllers example from [6]. Then, we continue with the performance evaluation of the tool.

Independent Controllers Example. One of the illustrative example presented in [5] (Example 2) consists of a network updated non-deterministically by two controllers, leading to a misconfiguration that cause the network traffic to be forwarded to the wrong host. The illustration is in Fig. 6.

The network connects four hosts through six switches, evenly divided between two controllers. $C1$ manages switches $S1$, $S3$, and $S5$, while $C2$ manages $S2$, $S4$, and $S6$. Initially, packets are forwarded from $H1$ to $H2$. The controllers then reconfigure the switches to forward traffic from $H3$ to $H4$. The network is considered "safe" provided no packets are forwarded from $H3$ to $H2$ or from $H1$ to $H4$.

We check whether RaceLoom detects harmful races between the two controllers, which, depending on the update order, violate the forwarding constraint by allowing packets from H3 (port 1) to reach H2 (port 16). To achieve this, we use the following forwarding property: $\phi_{\alpha_{in}}^{\alpha_{out}}(N) \triangleq (port = 1) \cdot N \cdot (port = 16)$. In words, applying the forwarding policy N of the network on a packet received on port 1 must not forward that packet to port 16.

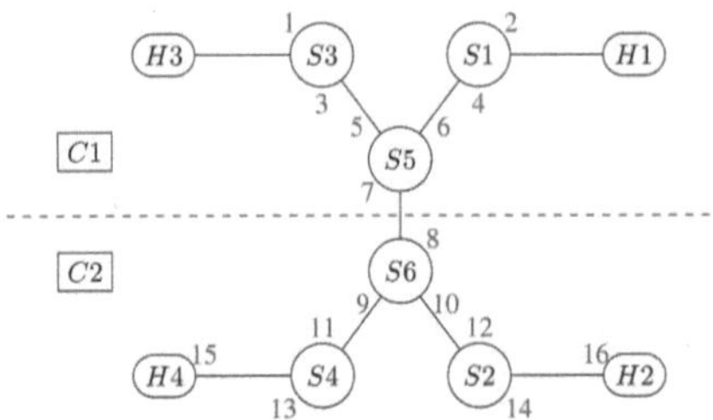

Fig. 6. Network with 6 switches controlled by 2 independent controllers forwarding traffic between 4 hosts [6].

With a trace depth of 7, we run RaceLoom on the DyNetKAT model and the forwarding property from above using a laptop running Linux Mint 21.3 with an Intel Core i7-10750H and 16GB of RAM. The analysis finishes in approx. 128 s. Unlike in the performance evaluation, the tool efficiently handles many complex examples without requiring a powerful computing cluster.

The tool reports 16 traces with harmful CT→SW races and 8 with harmful CT→SW←CT races. One such CT→SW←CT trace is shown in Fig. 7. After C_1 reconfigures S_5 to forward packets to port 7, RaceLoom detects two concurrent transitions: C_1 updating S_3 and C_2 updating S_2. A harmful CT→SW←CT race (6) arises because the update to S_3 occurs first, allowing packets to reach $H2$ ($\phi_{\alpha_{in}}^{\alpha_{out}}(N)$ is true), before S_2 is reconfigured, which would otherwise block packet delivery to $H2$ ($\phi_{\alpha_{in}}^{\alpha_{out}}(N)$ is false).

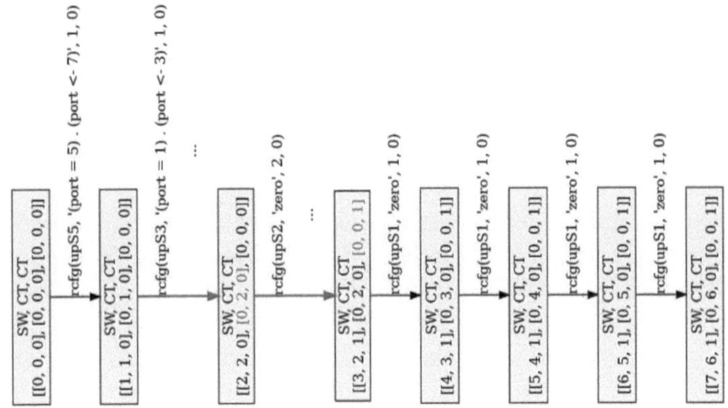

Fig. 7. Trace generated by RaceLoom exhibiting a harmful CT→SW←CT race on the Independent Controllers example ([6]). The top row of each state lists the type of elements in the encoded network. (relevant excerpt)

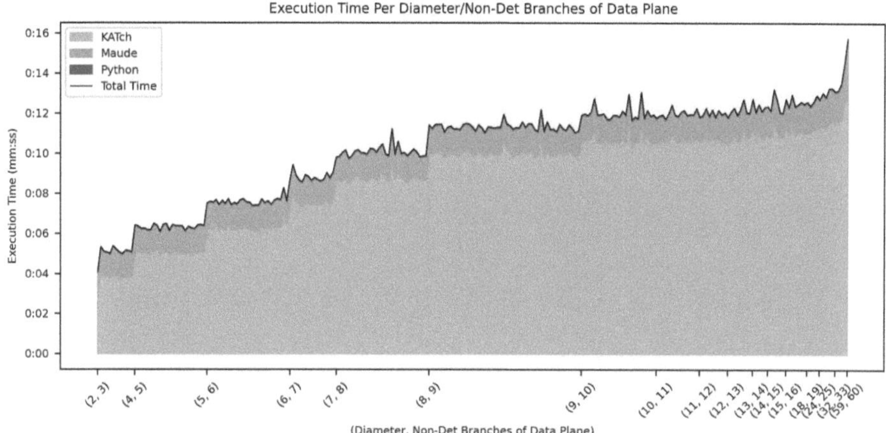

Fig. 8. Scenario 1: Performance evaluation results.

Performance Evaluation. To evaluate the performance of RaceLoom, we draw inspiration from NetKAT verification tools, such as KATch [19], and use the Topology Zoo dataset [14], which contains 261 real-world network topologies ranging from 4 to 754 switches. For each connected topology in the Topology Zoo, we build our test case as follows: (i) we assign ports to all links and switches, (ii) connect two hosts using the switches on the diameter of the network, (iii) generate NetKAT policies for every switch to forward packets in one direction between the two hosts, (iv) construct the DyNetKAT expression of the data plane (as in 4) with all flow tables empty, (v) construct the DyNetKAT expression of the controller, which sequentially installs the NetKAT policies from step (iii). Note that, because we only have two hosts, we use the diameter of the network to connect them, i.e. the longest shortest switch path. In this case, we use the network diameter as a heuristic to ensure that the size of the test cases scale appropriately.

We evaluate our tool in two scenarios: (1) a single controller establishing a unidirectional connection between hosts, and (2) two controllers independently updating the data plane, each handling opposite directions of the connection. We test both scenarios with traces up to depth 10, using a non-trivial forwarding property (always false but dependent on data plane policy) to force full race condition analysis and better measure performance. The depth bound was set to 10 to reflect the fact that about 75% of Topology Zoo networks have a diameter of 10 or less. This choice also ensured a manageable state space, keeping the benchmark setup consistent across both scenarios.

Results. Performance evaluation was performed in a cloud environment running Ubuntu 22.04.3 LTS. The hardware used for the experiments involved a Dell PowerEdge R7615 processor with 64 cores at 3.675 GHz and 1TB of RAM. In Fig. 8 and Fig. 10 we report the execution time of the three main technolo-

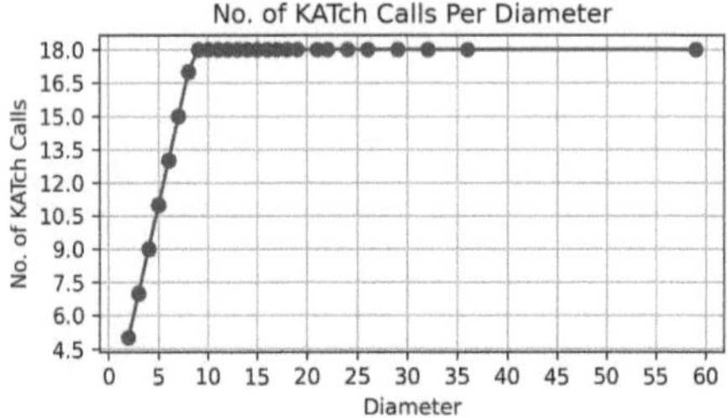

Fig. 9. Scenario 1: Number of KATch calls made per network diameter.

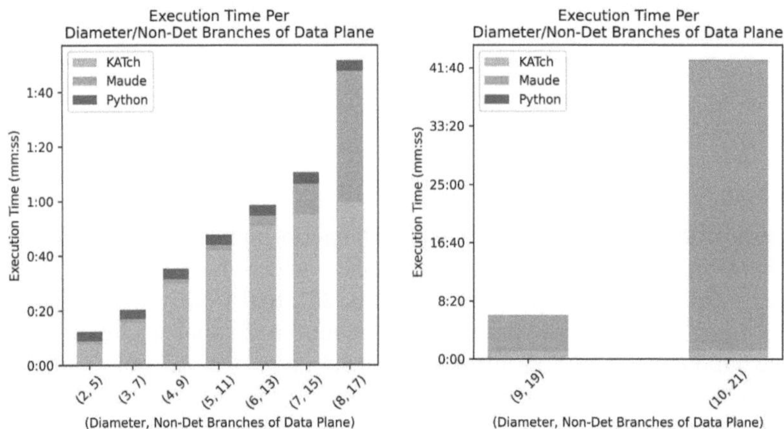

(a) Results for networks with a diameter up to 8

(b) Results for networks with diameter 9 and 10

Fig. 10. Scenario 2: Performance evaluation results.

gies employed in our tool, namely Python, Maude [8], and KATch [19]. Execution time is reported against both network diameter and the number of non-deterministic branches, which are closely correlated by our modeling approach (Fig. 2). The big switch has one branch for packet processing and an additional branch for each controller(s) update, corresponding to switch updates along the network diameter.

The results for the first scenario (Fig. 8) show that RaceLoom processes all DyNetKAT models in under 16 s. The main performance bottleneck is the repeated evaluation of the forwarding property via KATch, despite result caching. Although KATch is the fastest available NetKAT evaluation tool [19] at the time of writing, the overhead introduced by the numerous external calls to it significantly impacts the overall runtime. All other RaceLoom operations, such as model construction, trace generation, and race detection, complete in approx. 2 s, except for the largest topology with a diameter length of 59, which takes approx. 3 s.

Figure 9 shows KATch calls by network diameter. With depth 10, calls rise with diameter up to 18, then stabilize as traces end before all updates are installed. Even the smallest case (5 calls) takes 4 s - twice all other steps. A deeper bound would complete updates but explode the state space, making RaceLoom infeasible. This does not affect benchmarking, since race hazards occur with the same frequency regardless of trace length; our scalability study targets model complexity, not trace depth.

For the second scenario, the results in Fig. 10 differ significantly from the results of the first scenario. In this case, our tool fails to complete all network models within a reasonable time. The figure shows execution times for a single network per diameter up to 10 switches. For diameters below 9, analysis completes within 2 min; for diameters 9 and 10, runtime increases sharply to approx. 8 and 42 min, respectively.

NetKAT evaluation dominates for small diameters, but from diameter 8 trace generation in Maude [8] becomes the main bottleneck. We omit KATch calls here, as they are irrelevant. Maude is only used to rewrite symbolic configurations into normal form, yet its performance degrades quickly as non-deterministic branches grow: each diameter step adds two branches to the big switch, greatly increasing the number of required rewrites.

Although RaceLoom exhibits slower performance for networks with diameter >9, it has to be noted that 50% of the topologies in the Topology Zoo [14] have diameter ≤ 8, and 75% have diameter ≤ 10. Thus, RaceLoom can analyze the majority of real-world topologies in under 45 min.

9   Conclusions

We presented a new symbolic execution framework for detecting races in SDNs, extending DyNetKAT with a symbolic semantics over flow tables, rather than individual packets, for improved scalability. Unlike earlier work such as TRACER, our approach adopts the big switch abstraction and assigns a vector clock per big switch, significantly reducing the interleaving space. We formalized three types of harmful races between control and data planes, and showed that our semantics can detect all such cases. These results are implemented in RACELOOM, a tool for automated race detection, which we evaluated using the first DyNetKAT benchmark based on real-world topologies from the Topology Zoo. Our findings highlight the effectiveness of symbolic reasoning over flow tables and big switches for scalable and accurate SDN verification. Future directions include extending support for richer SDN models and improving scalability.

References

1. Anderson, C.J., Foster, N., Guha, A., Jeannin, J., Kozen, D., Schlesinger, C., Walker, D.: NetKAT: semantic foundations for networks. In: Jagannathan, S., Sewell, P. (eds.) The 41st Annual ACM SIGPLAN-SIGACT Symposium on Principles of Programming Languages, POPL '14, San Diego, CA, USA, January 20-21, 2014, pp. 113–126. ACM (2014). https://doi.org/10.1145/2535838.2535862

2. Baeten, J.C.M., Weijland, W.P.: Process algebra, Cambridge tracts in theoretical computer science, vol. 18. Cambridge University Press (1990)
3. Ball, T., et al.: VeriCon: towards verifying controller programs in software-defined networks. SIGPLAN Not. **49**(6), 282–293 (2014). https://doi.org/10.1145/2666356.2594317
4. Barrett, C., Tinelli, C.: Satisfiability Modulo Theories, pp. 305–343. Springer International Publishing, Cham (2018). https://doi.org/10.1007/978-3-319-10575-8_11
5. Caltais, G., Hojjat, H., Mousavi, M.R., Tunç, H.C.: DyNetKAT: An Algebra of Dynamic Networks. CoRR abs/2102.10035 (2021). https://arxiv.org/abs/2102.10035
6. Caltais, G., Hojjat, H., Mousavi, M.R., Tunç, H.C.: DyNetKAT: an algebra of dynamic networks. In: Bouyer, P., Schröder, L. (eds.) Foundations of Software Science and Computation Structures - 25th International Conference, FOSSACS 2022, Held as Part of the European Joint Conferences on Theory and Practice of Software, ETAPS 2022, Munich, Germany, April 2-7, 2022, Proceedings. Lecture Notes in Computer Science, vol. 13242, pp. 184–204. Springer (2022).https://doi.org/10.1007/978-3-030-99253-8_10
7. Caltais, G., Zangiabady, M., Zvirbulis, E.: Tracer: a tool for race detection in software defined network models. In: Marin, M., Leustean, L. (eds.) Proceedings Eighth Symposium on Working Formal Methods, FROM 2024, Timişoara, Romania, September 16-18. EPTCS, vol. 410, pp. 84–98 (2024). https://doi.org/10.4204/EPTCS.410.6
8. Clavel, M., et al.: The Maude system. In: Narendran, P., Rusinowitch, M. (eds.) RTA 1999. LNCS, vol. 1631, pp. 240–243. Springer, Heidelberg (1999). https://doi.org/10.1007/3-540-48685-2_18
9. Covaci, A.: RaceLoom: a tool for automated symbolic detection of race conditions in software-defined networks. https://doi.org/10.5281/zenodo.16929592 (2025). Accessed 20 June 2025
10. El-Hassany, A., Miserez, J., Bielik, P., Vanbever, L., Vechev, M.: SDNRacer: concurrency analysis for software-defined networks. ACM SIGPLAN Notices **51**, 402–415 (2016). https://doi.org/10.1145/2908080.2908124
11. Ernst, M.D.: Invited talk static and dynamic analysis: synergy and duality. In: Proceedings of the 5th ACM SIGPLAN-SIGSOFT Workshop on Program Analysis for Software Tools and Engineering, p. 35. PASTE '04, Association for Computing Machinery, New York, NY, USA (2004). https://doi.org/10.1145/996821.996823
12. Holzmann, G.: The Spin Model Checker: Primer and Reference Manual. Addison-Wesley (2004)
13. Kang, N., Liu, Z., Rexford, J., Walker, D.: Optimizing the "one big switch" abstraction in software-defined networks. In: Almeroth, K.C., Mathy, L., Papagiannaki, K., Misra, V. (eds.) Conference on emerging Networking Experiments and Technologies, CoNEXT '13, Santa Barbara, CA, USA, December 9-12, 2013, pp. 13–24. ACM (2013). https://doi.org/10.1145/2535372.2535373, https://doi.org/10.1145/2535372.2535373
14. Knight, S., Nguyen, H.X., Falkner, N., Bowden, R., Roughan, M.: The internet Topology Zoo. IEEE J. Sel. Areas Commun. **29**, 1765–1775 (2011). https://doi.org/10.1109/JSAC.2011.111002
15. Lamport, L.: Time, clocks, and the ordering of events in a distributed system. In: Malkhi, D. (ed.) Concurrency: the Works of Leslie Lamport, pp. 179–196. ACM (2019). https://doi.org/10.1145/3335772.3335934

16. Lavado, L., Panizo, L., Gallardo, M.–M., Merino, P.: A characterisation of verification tools for software defined networks. J. Reliable Intell. Environ. **3**(3), 189–207 (2017). https://doi.org/10.1007/s40860-017-0045-y
17. Lu, G., Xu, L., Yang, Y., Xu, B.: Predictive analysis for race detection in software-defined networks. Sci. China Inf. Sci. **62**(6), 1–20 (2019). https://doi.org/10.1007/s11432-018-9826-x
18. Majumdar, R., Deep Tetali, S., Wang, Z.: Kuai: a model checker for software-defined networks. In: 2014 Formal Methods in Computer-Aided Design (FMCAD), pp. 163–170 (2014). https://doi.org/10.1109/FMCAD.2014.6987609
19. Moeller, M., et al.: KATch: a fast symbolic verifier for NetKAT. In: Proceedings of the ACM on Programming Languages **8** (2024). https://doi.org/10.1145/3656454
20. Netzer, R.H.B., Miller, B.P.: What are race conditions? Some issues and formalizations. LOPLAS **1**(1), 74–88 (1992). https://doi.org/10.1145/130616.130623
21. Reitblatt, M., Foster, N., Rexford, J., Schlesinger, C., Walker, D.: Abstractions for network update. In: Eggert, L., Ott, J., Padmanabhan, V.N., Varghese, G. (eds.) ACM SIGCOMM 2012 Conference, SIGCOMM '12, Helsinki, Finland - August 13 - 17, 2012, pp. 323–334. ACM (2012). https://doi.org/10.1145/2342356.2342427
22. Scott, C., Wundsam, A., et al.: Troubleshooting blackbox SDN control software with minimal causal sequences. In: Bustamante, F.E., Hu, Y.C., Krishnamurthy, A., Ratnasamy, S. (eds.) ACM SIGCOMM 2014 Conference, SIGCOMM'14, Chicago, IL, USA, August 17-22, 2014, pp. 395–406. ACM (2014). https://doi.org/10.1145/2619239.2626304
23. Sethi, D., Narayana, S., Malik, S.: Abstractions for model checking SDN controllers. In: 2013 Formal Methods in Computer-Aided Design, pp. 145–148 (2013). https://doi.org/10.1109/FMCAD.2013.6679403
24. Vinarskii, E., López, J., Kushik, N., Yevtushenko, N., Zeghlache, D.: A model checking based approach for detecting SDN races. In: Gaston, C., Kosmatov, N., Le Gall, P. (eds.) ICTSS 2019. LNCS, vol. 11812, pp. 194–211. Springer, Cham (2019). https://doi.org/10.1007/978-3-030-31280-0_12
25. Xu, L., Huang, J., Hong, S., Zhang, J., Gu, G.: Attacking the brain: races in the SDN control plane. In: Proceedings of the 26th USENIX Conference on Security Symposium, pp. 451–468. SEC'17, USENIX Association, USA (2017)

Model-Based Testing and Synthesis

Model-Based Testing of an Intermediate Verifier Using Executable Operational Semantics

Lidia Losavio, Marco Paganoni[(✉)], and Carlo A. Furia[ID]

Software Institute, USI Università della Svizzera italiana, Lugano, Switzerland
`{losavl,marco.paganoni}@usi.ch`
`http://bugcounting.net/`

Abstract. Lightweight validation technique, such as those based on random testing, are sometimes practical alternatives to full formal verification—providing valuable benefits, such as finding bugs, without requiring a disproportionate effort. In fact, such validation techniques can be useful even for fully formally verified tools, by exercising the parts of a complex system that go beyond the reach of formal models.

In this context, this paper introduces BCC: a model-based testing technique for the Boogie intermediate verifier. BCC combines the formalization of a small, deterministic subset of the Boogie language with the generative capabilities of the PLT Redex language engineering framework. Basically, BCC uses PLT Redex to generate random Boogie programs, and to execute them according to a formal operational semantics; then, it runs the same programs through the Boogie verifier. Any inconsistency between the two executions (in PLT Redex and with Boogie) may indicate a potential bug in Boogie's implementation.

To understand whether BCC can be useful in practice, we used it to generate three million Boogie programs. These experiments found 2% of cases indicative of completeness failures (i.e., spurious verification failures) in Boogie's toolchain. These results indicate that lightweight analysis tools, such as those for model-based random testing, are also useful to test and validate formal verification tools such as Boogie.

1 Introduction

Modern verification tools are complex pieces of software; as such, they may contain defects of various kinds that can affect their soundness, precision, performance, or usability. Even if formally verifying a verifier's implementation is the ideal end goal, it usually remains a daunting challenge that requires massive amounts of expert effort [10,29]. This motivates (also) developing *lightweight* techniques [4,5,9,31,46], which do not provide absolute correctness guarantees

Work partially supported by SNF grant 200021-207919 (LastMile).

L. Losavio and M. Paganoni—These authors contributed equally; they are listed in alphabetical order.

but can still find errors or provide partial validation with a high degree of automation.

In this vein, this paper describes BCC:[1] a lightweight technique to test the implementation of the Boogie intermediate verifier [3]. BCC relies on a formalization of BPL_0—a small, deterministic subset of the Boogie language—encoded using the PLT Redex framework [11]. In a nutshell, the formal model describes the syntax of BPL_0, its typing rules, and its execution semantics by means of symbolic reduction rules. BCC first uses the formal model in PLT Redex to generate random BPL_0 programs. Then, it executes the programs according to their operational semantics, and also runs the Boogie verifier on them. The outcome of Boogie's verification run and of the execution in PLT Redex should be *consistent*; BCC reports any inconsistency as a potential *error* of Boogie.[2]

Since it is a best-effort validation technique, BCC cannot provide absolute guarantees of correctness. In particular, Boogie's verification semantics and BCC's operational semantics may be inconsistent in certain cases without implications for correctness: for example, executing a loop in BCC's semantics may time out, whereas Boogie analyzes loops symbolically without checking whether they terminate. Reconciling Boogie's verification semantics and BCC's executable operational semantics is a key challenge addressed in this work—the first, to our knowledge, to apply PLT Redex's semantic engineering techniques to a verification language (as opposed to a conventional programming language).

Our experiments demonstrate that BCC can be practically useful as a bug-finding and validation tool. We generated three million syntactically different random Boogie programs of different sizes and characteristics. BCC found 65 332 cases (2% of all generated programs) of *completeness* failures. Even though BCC only covers a small subset of the whole Boogie language (see Fig. 1), our approach shows that semantics engineering techniques, such as those made available by PLT Redex Redex, can be applied to test formal verification tools, and help improve their reliability.

In summary, the paper makes the following main contributions: *i)* An executable operational semantics of BPL_0, a deterministic subset of the Boogie intermediate verification language, built using the PLT Redex framework. *ii)* BCC: a technique to automatically generate Boogie programs with different characteristics, and test their operational semantics against Boogie's. *iii)* A large experimental evaluation of BCC, which found completeness failures in the latest Boogie version. *iv)* For reproducibility, our implementation of PLT Redex and all experimental artifacts are available [30].

2   Related Work

The implementation of a modern formal verification tool is usually a complex piece of software that integrates several independently-developed components.

---

[1] BCC stands for "Boogie consistency checker".

[2] In principle, an inconsistency may also be due to a bug in the operational semantics rules; in practice, BPL_0 and its semantics are so much simpler than Boogie that it's overwhelmingly much more likely that it's Boogie's implementation that at fault.

As such, a full end-to-end verification has remained, so far, beyond the capabilities of verification technology. The work that is perhaps closest to the ideal of a fully verified verifier are fully verified *compilers* [23,26,27,43]. Interestingly, even a fully verified compiler like CompCert still benefits from systematic testing [33].

Similarly to a compiler, a formal verification tool usually combines a front-end and a back-end. It is also increasingly common for verifiers to use an intermediate verification language—supported by tools like Boogie [3], Viper [34], and Why3 [14]—which helps bridge the semantic gap between front-end and back-end. There exist a few cases of formally verified back-end provers [2,16,39] and even intermediate verification condition generators [19]. Several works prove "once and for all" that their front-end *translation* is sound [1,13,40,45], either just on paper or with a mechanized proof. However, none of these works extend the soundness proofs to the actual software *implementations* of the front-end translation.[3] A more viable approach than "once and for all" verification is *run validation*: for any given run of a verifier, extract a checkable *certificate* that the translation is sound. This idea has been applied to validate Boogie's verification condition generation [37], Viper's front-end encoding into Boogie [36], and verifiers based on the K framework [29].

Even in the rare cases where a full formal validation of a verification tool is feasible, *lightweight* tools—usually based on testing—offer a different, appealing trade-off: while they cannot provide absolute guarantees of correctness, they are practically useful to detect bugs, and to test for properties, such as completeness/precision, robustness, or scalability, that are less amenable to formal "all or nothing" verification. In recent years, techniques based on testing have been applied to a variety of formal verification tools, including SMT solvers [4,31,46], intermediate verification languages [9], software model checkers [15,44,48], symbolic execution engines [20], and verifiers for reactive systems [42].

Effectively testing a verification tool requires generating highly structured inputs and complex "behavioral" oracles. To this end, it is common to use grammar-based generation and differential testing—two techniques mutuated from the prolific work on compiler testing [7,24,47], which presents similar challenges. The work presented in this paper also employs these techniques within the PLT Redex framework [11]: a "domain-specific language for semantic models that is embedded in the Racket programming language" [21]. To our knowledge, all applications of PLT Redex to date have been to analyze domain-specific or general-purpose programming languages—often with a functional flavor, such as JavaScript [18] and Lua [41]. One of this paper's contributions is

---

[3] In a similar vein, there has been work on formally proving the correctness of verification-condition generation algorithms [17,32,35]—often as part of developing larger verified systems [22]—in a way that a correct-by-construction implementation can be synthesized from the correctness proof. While such an approach can produce trustworthy verification components, it solves a different problem than verifying an existing implementation. For example, a correct-by-construction reimplementation of Boogie would not be a perfect replacement unless it offered the very same performance, features, and capabilities as the actual Boogie tool.

demonstrating how PLT Redex is also applicable to test the imperative features of an intermediate language for verification.

Using a combination of constraint solving and concrete enumeration, previous work targeted executing the Boogie language, with the goal of help debug failed verification attempts [28,38]. Such a goal is largely complementary to the present paper's: whereas those tools explore as efficiently as possible a subset of the (unbounded) execution space of a given (nondeterministic) Boogie program, our goal is checking the consistency of Boogie's verification semantics with a concrete execution semantics on a large number of randomly generated Boogie programs.

3   Modeling a Deterministic Subset of the Boogie Language

BCC deploys a formal model of a deterministic subset of the Boogie intermediate verification language [3], encoded using the PLT Redex framework [11]. The BPL$_0$ model consists of three components: *i)* a **grammar** defining the **syntax** of *well-formed* BPL$_0$ program terms (Sect. 3.2); *ii)* an **operational semantics** consisting of reduction rules that specify valid executions as transitions between program terms (Sect. 3.3); *iii)* **judgments** consisting of rules for name resolution and type checking (Sect. 3.4).

$$
\begin{array}{ll}
\text{Program } P ::= (\textbf{main } L\ B) & \texttt{procedure main() returns() } \{L\ B\} \\
\text{Locals } L ::= \emptyset \mid (\textbf{let } (v = \ell : t)\ L) & \epsilon \mid \textbf{var } v : t := \ell;\ L \\
\text{Type } t ::= \texttt{bool} \mid \texttt{int} & \texttt{bool} \mid \texttt{int} \\
\text{Body } B ::= \emptyset \mid (\textbf{do } s\ B) & \epsilon \mid s \\
\text{Statement } s ::= (:= v\ e) \mid (\textbf{if } e\ B\ B) \mid (\textbf{while } e\ B) & v := e \mid \textbf{if } e\ B\ \textbf{else } B \mid \textbf{while } e\ B \\
\qquad\qquad \mid (\textbf{assert } e) & \mid \textbf{assert } e \\
\text{Expression } e ::= \ell \mid v \mid (b\ e\ e) \mid (u\ e) & \ell \mid v \mid e\ b\ e \mid u\ e \\
\text{Literals } \ell ::= \mathbb{Z} \mid \textbf{true} \mid \textbf{false} & \\
\text{Binary Operator } b ::= \vee \mid \wedge \mid \Longrightarrow \mid + \mid - \mid / \mid * & \\
\text{Unary Operator } u ::= \neg \mid - &
\end{array}
$$

Fig. 1. The syntax of BPL$_0$ in PLT Redex (left), and the corresponding Boogie syntax (right).

3.1   Why a *Deterministic* Subset of Boogie?

Before delving into the details of our PLT Redex model of BPL$_0$, let's explain why we focused on this specific restricted subset of the Boogie language. Boogie combines imperative features (e.g., variables) and specification features (e.g., preconditions). Many of Boogie's features introduce nondeterminism, which is widely useful for specification, but is not readily executable. For example, the statement **assume** x > 0 is a passive statement that captures all runs where variable x is positive."Executing" the **assume** would mean either enumerating values of x up to a finite bound or defining a symbolic semantics. While this different application of PLT Redex could also be interesting, our present goal is to model Boogie's semantics in a way that is straightforward and independent of Boogie's implementation details. This increases the confidence that our execution model is accurate, which bolsters its usefulness as an oracle for differential testing of Boogie. Therefore, BPL$_0$ drops all nondeterministic constructs of Boogie.

3.2 Syntax

Figure 1 shows the grammar defining the syntax of BPL$_0$. Precisely, Boogie's actual syntax is shown on the right, but in most of the paper we will use PLT Redex's parenthesized prefix notation (since PLT Redex is implemented in Racket) shown on the left.

A program P consists of a single **main** procedure (**main** L B) with a local environment L and a body B. A *local environment* is an inductive list of **let**(**let** $(v = \ell : t)$), each binding a variable symbol v to a literal value ℓ of type t (int or bool). A *body* is an inductive list of statements s: *assignments* ($:= v$ e), *assertions* (**assert** e), *conditionals* (**if** e B_1 B_2), and *loops* (**while** e B). The rest of the grammar defines the usual Boolean and arithmetic *expressions* used in assignments and conditions.

$$E[(b\ \ell_1\ \ell_2)] \hookrightarrow E[[\![b\ \ell_1\ \ell_2]\!]] \qquad \text{Binary Evaluation}$$
$$E[(u\ \ell_1)] \hookrightarrow E[[\![u\ \ell_1]\!]] \qquad \text{Unary Evaluation}$$
$$(\textbf{main}\ L\ \emptyset) \hookrightarrow \text{success} \qquad \text{Success}$$
$$E[(\textbf{assert false})] \hookrightarrow \text{failure} \qquad \text{Failure}$$
$$E[(\textbf{do}\ (\textbf{assert true})\ B)] \hookrightarrow E[B] \qquad \text{Assert True}$$
$$(\textbf{main}\ L\ E[v]) \hookrightarrow (\textbf{main}\ L\ E[L\{v\}]) \qquad \text{Local Substitution}$$
$$(\textbf{main}\ L\ E[(\textbf{do}\ (:= v\ \ell)\ B)]) \hookrightarrow (\textbf{main}\ L\{v \leftarrow \ell\}\ E[B]) \qquad \text{Local Assignment}$$
$$E[(\textbf{do}\ (\textbf{if true}\ B_1\ B_2)\ B_3)] \hookrightarrow E[(\textbf{do}\ B_1 \cdot B_3)] \qquad \text{If-Then}$$
$$E[(\textbf{do}\ (\textbf{if false}\ B_1\ B_2)\ B_3)] \hookrightarrow E[(\textbf{do}\ B_2 \cdot B_3)] \qquad \text{If-Else}$$
$$E[(\textbf{do}\ (\textbf{while}\ e\ B_1)\ B_2)] \hookrightarrow E[(\textbf{do}\ (\textbf{if}\ e\ B_1 \cdot (\textbf{while}\ e\ B_1)\ \emptyset)\ B_2)] \qquad \text{Loop}$$

Fig. 2. Operational semantics of BPL$_0$ using evaluation contexts.

$$E ::= \text{hole} \mid (u\ E) \mid (b\ E\ e) \mid (b\ l\ E)$$
$$\mid\ (:= v\ E) \mid (\textbf{assert}\ E) \mid (\textbf{if}\ E\ B_1\ B_2)$$
$$\mid\ (\textbf{do}\ E\ B) \mid (\textbf{main}\ L\ E)$$

Fig. 3. Specification of the possible evaluation contexts for Fig. 2's rules.

Even before formally presenting its semantics, it should be clear that BPL_0 is a strictly deterministic language: *i)* each program has a single entry point to the sole **main** procedure; *ii)* before the body executes, the local environment initializes every program variable to a literal value; *iii)* the body's statements execute sequentially; *iv)* all available statements are deterministic.

3.3 Operational Semantics

Figure 2 shows BPL_0's small-step operational semantics. Each rule defines a different case of the *reduction relation* $A \hookrightarrow B$, which specifies how a program term A rewrites into another one B in a way that captures a single evaluation step.

Most of the reduction rules in Fig. 2 involve an *evaluation context E*. In a nutshell, $E[p]$ means that the program term p can only be reduced (as specified by the rule), when it is in certain parts of the whole program term. Figure 3 lists all possible evaluation contexts, defined in a way that ensures that the reduction rules can only be applied in a fixed, unambiguous order, which matches the program's sequential order. In particular, the patterns E are defined in such a way that the **hole** can only match in one position.

Figure 2's rules do not reduce the environment L directly, but use it to keep track of the current values of the program variables in each step of the reduction: $L\{v\}$ denotes a lookup of v's current value in L, whereas $L\{v \leftarrow \ell\}$ denotes an environment where v is bound to value ℓ, and all other variables are as in L.

Most of the meaning of the (other) rules should also be straightforward, as they simply capture: *i)* the evaluation of binary and unary operators, which are simply reduced to the evaluation $[\![\cdot]\!]$ of the corresponding Racket operators and literals; *ii)* successful program termination, when all statements have been "consumed" without errors; *iii)* program termination with a **failure**, when an **assert** evaluates to false; *iv)* in contrast, an **assert** that passes is equivalent to a skip; *v)* a conditional reduces to its "then" or "else" branch depending on what Boolean the condition evaluates to; *vi)* a loop recursively reduces to evaluating its body until its condition no longer holds.

$$\text{Comp.} \quad \frac{L \vdash e_1 : \texttt{int} \quad L \vdash e_2 : \texttt{int}}{L \vdash (\{<,>,=,\leq,\geq\}\ e_1\ e_2) : \texttt{bool}}$$

$$\text{Bin. int} \quad \frac{L \vdash e_1 : \texttt{int} \quad L \vdash e_2 : \texttt{int}}{L \vdash (\{+,-,*,/\}\ e_1\ e_2) : \texttt{int}}$$

$$\text{Bin. bool} \quad \frac{L \vdash e_1 : \texttt{bool} \quad L \vdash e_2 : \texttt{bool}}{L \vdash (\{\wedge,\vee,\Longrightarrow,=\}\ e_1\ e_2) : \texttt{bool}}$$

$$\text{Un. int} \quad \frac{L \vdash e : \texttt{int}}{L \vdash (-\ e) : \texttt{int}}$$

$$\text{Un. bool} \quad \frac{L \vdash e : \texttt{bool}}{L \vdash (\neg\ e) : \texttt{bool}}$$

$$\text{Vars} \quad \frac{(v : t) \in L}{L \vdash v : t}$$

$$\text{Assign} \quad \frac{L \vdash v : t \quad L \vdash e : t \quad L \vdash B}{L \vdash (\textbf{do}\ (:=\ v\ e)\ B)}$$

$$\text{Assert} \quad \frac{L \vdash e : \texttt{bool} \quad L \vdash B}{L \vdash (\textbf{do}\ (\textbf{assert}\ e)\ B)}$$

$$\text{If} \quad \frac{L \vdash e : \texttt{bool} \quad L \vdash B_1, B_2, B_3}{L \vdash (\textbf{do}\ (\textbf{if}\ e\ B_1\ B_2)\ B_3)}$$

$$\text{While} \quad \frac{L \vdash e : \texttt{bool} \quad L \vdash B_1, B_2}{L \vdash (\textbf{do}\ (\textbf{while}\ e\ B_1)\ B_2)}$$

$$\text{Empty program} \quad \frac{}{L \vdash \emptyset}$$

$$\text{Env.} \quad \frac{\emptyset \vdash \ell : t \quad v \notin L \quad \vdash L}{\vdash (\textbf{let}\ [v = \ell : t]\ L)}$$

$$\text{Main} \quad \frac{\vdash L \quad L \vdash B}{\vdash (\textbf{main}\ L\ B)}$$

Fig. 4. Inference rules for BPL$_0$'s type system in the PLT Redex model.

3.4   Judgments

BCC can generate *well-formed* BPL$_0$ programs using Fig. 1's grammar. A well-formed program may be invalid because the grammar alone does not ensure that the program is also *well-named* (variables are declared and initialized before their first usage) and *well-typed* (expression values conform to their expected `int` or `bool` type). BCC models BPL$_0$'s name resolution and typing rules using PLT Redex's judgments [12], which can be used by the generation algorithm to automatically produce BPL$_0$ programs that are well-named and/or well-typed.

Figure 4 presents BPL$_0$'s type system, where $L \vdash e : t$ denotes, as customary, that term e has type t when evaluated within local environment L, whereas $L \vdash s$ means that statement s is well-typed. Notice that rules *Vars* and *Env.* also determine whether a program is *well-named* by checking that every used variable was declared and initialized (*Vars*), and that no variable is declared twice (*Env.*). In practice, BCC includes two sets of judgments: the one in Fig. 4 checks well-typedness as well as well-namedness; and another one that *only* checks well-namedness.

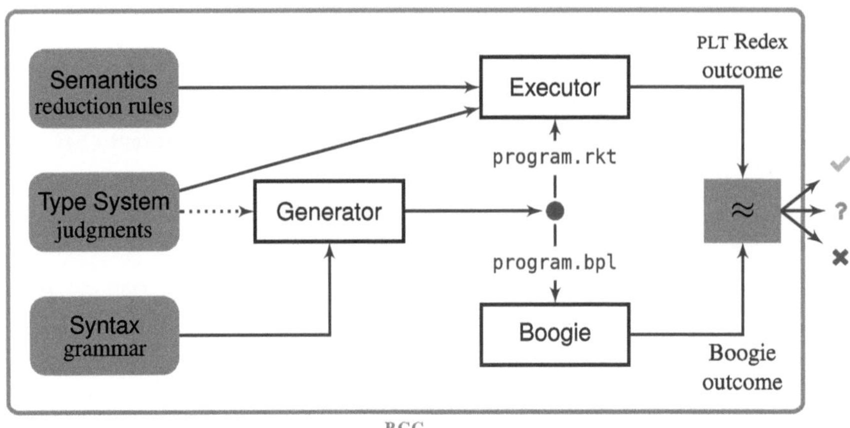

Fig. 5. An overview of how BCC works.

4 How BCC Works

Figure 5 overviews how BCC uses the PLT Redex model of BPL_0, described in Sect. 3, to: *i) Generate* a large number of BPL_0 programs; *ii) Execute* them according to their operational semantics; *iii) Verify* them using the Boogie verifier; *iv) Compare* the outcome of execution and verification, reporting any inconsistency that may be indicative of a failure. The following sections describe each step of BCC's analysis.

4.1 Generator

BCC uses PLT Redex's term generation capabilities to produce a large number of BPL_0 programs. As explained in Sect. 3.4, PLT Redex can produce three kinds of programs: *i) well-formed* programs, which conform to BPL_0's grammar; *ii) well-named* programs, which are well-formed and also free from any usage of uninitialized variables; *iii) well-typed* programs, which are well-named and also typecheck correctly. Each kind of program is suitable to test different aspects of Boogie: its verification process (well-typed), its typechecker (well-named), or its name resolver (well-formed).[4]

BCC's generator actually produces each program in two forms: one uses Racket syntax, and is used by the PLT Redex *Executor*; the other one uses Boogie's concrete syntax, and is fed to *Boogie* itself.

---

[4] In this work, we did not experiment with generating syntactically incorrect Boogie programs, which would only test Boogie's parser. To this end, there are a number of other techniques, such as fuzzing, that do not require a formal model of Boogie's type system and semantics.

Table 1. Examples of Boogie programs with various execution and verification outcomes.

```
procedure success() {          procedure failure() {         procedure name_error() {
  var x: int := 0;               var x: int := 3;              var x: int := 0;
  assert x = 0;                  assert x < 0;                 assert y = 0;
}                              }                             }


procedure type_error() {       procedure loop() {            procedure timeout() {
  var x: int := 0;               var x: int := 3;              var x: int := 0;
  assert x;                      while (true) {                while (x < 1000000) {
}                                  x := 0;                       x := x + 1;
                                 }                             }
                                 assert false;                 assert false;
                               }                             }
```

4.2   Executor

Given a BPL$_0$ program P, BCC first uses the model's *judgments* to check whether
P is well-named and well-typed. Obviously, these checks are only necessary if P
was not already generated in a well-typed form by construction. In principle, BCC
could execute P without performing these checks beforehand, so that any name
resolution or type error would result in a runtime failure. However, performing
name resolution and type checking *before* executing a program is consistent with
Boogie's behavior: it does not run P unless it typechecks. In this way, BCC's
execution of P is directly comparable to Boogie's verification run on P.

If P the judgment checks fail, BCC reports one of the following outcomes:

name-error: P is not well-named; for example, program `name_error` in Table 1
    results in a *name-error* because variable y is used but not declared.
type-error: P is not well-typed; for example, program `type_error` in Table 1
    results in a *type-error* because **int** variable x cannot be used as a **bool** asser-
    tion.

If P is well-typed, BCC *executes* it by repeatedly applying Fig. 2's reduction rules
until one of the following outcomes is reached:

success: P evaluates to an empty body $\emptyset$, which means that the program executed
    and terminated without any errors; for example, program `success` in Table 1
    clearly terminates with a *success*.
failure: P evaluates to (**assert false**), which means that the program triggered
    an assertion failure at some point during its execution; for example, program
    `failure` in Table 1 ends with an assertion *failure* because $x = 3 > 0$.
loop: P evaluates to a term T, which is identical to a term produced during
    a previous step of the evaluation; this means that the program entered an
    infinite loop. For example, program `loop` in Table 1 results in an infinite loop
    where the program state does not change. Programs that result in outcome
    loop are still (partially) correct, in that they do not trigger assertion failures:

the **assert false** in program loop never gets executed because it is effectively unreachable.

timeout: P's evaluation reaches a maximum number of steps (by default, 100 000) and is forcefully terminated; for example, program timeout in Table 1 exceeds the default maximum number of steps, and hence it would be terminated by BCC. As usual, a *timeout* is inconclusive as to whether P is correct or not: program timeout would eventually trigger an assertion failure if its loop were run to completion; but a variant of *timeout* with loop condition **true** would instead never terminate (**int** are unbounded in Boogie).

4.3 Boogie

BCC also feeds each generated program P to the Boogie verifier, which first checks whether P is well-named and well-typed; if it is, Boogie performs a deductive static verification of P by expressing its correctness conditions as logic formulas, whose validity is checked by the automated theorem prover Z3.

Thus, a Boogie verification run on P reports one of the following outcomes:

name-error: P fails name resolution; for example program name_error in Table 1.

type-error: P fails type checking; for example program type_error in Table 1.

success: P verifies correctly, which means that all possible executions of P are free from assertion failures; for example, program success in Table 1. Boogie does not check termination of loops, but only partial correctness; therefore, program loop leads to a *success* in Boogie, because it recognizes that the **assert false** is effectively unreachable.

failure: P fails verification, which means that some assertions in P may not hold; for example, program failure in Table 1.

timeout: Boogie's verification run on P is forcefully terminated after it does not return within a timeout (by default, one hour). Boogie's timeouts are quite rare on the kinds of programs generated by BCC (which usually verify in a matter of seconds), but sometimes Boogie loses control of the Z3 process it started and does not return within a reasonable amount of time. As usual, we treat a *timeout* as an inconclusive verification result.

Outcome *loop* is inapplicable to Boogie's verification: since it does not analyze termination, it won't report if a loop iterates forever. Finally, a Boogie verification run may also result in a parsing error. Since all the programs generated by BCC are (at least) syntactically correct, this outcome is irrelevant for our work.

Table 2. Consistency between PLT Redex execution and Boogie verification outcomes.

PLT **Redex outcome** p	Boogie outcome b				
	success	*failure*	*timeout*	*name-error*	*type-error*
success	✔	✘	?	✘	✘
failure	✘	✔	?	✘	✘
loop	✔	✘	?	✘	✘
timeout	?	?	?	✘	✘
name-error	✘	✘	✘	✔	✘
type-error	✘	✘	✘	✘	✔

4.4   Consistency Checking

Finally, BCC compares the outcome of PLT Redex execution according to the operational semantics and Boogie verification for the same program P, and reports any *inconsistency*. This step corresponds to box $\approx$ in Fig. 5.

Table 2 shows what BCC's consistency check reports for each combination of PLT Redex outcome p and Boogie outcome b.

✔ denotes that p and b are consistent; hence, we have successfully tested Boogie's correct behavior on a program P.

✘ denotes that p and b are inconsistent; hence, we have exposed a failure in Boogie's behavior, which is inconsistent with the expected semantics of P.

? denotes an inconclusive test: p and b are not directly comparable, and hence Boogie's behavior may or may not be correct.

As shown in Table 2, if p and b are literally the same conclusive outcome (*success* or *failure*) then the consistency check obviously results in ✔. However, also the combination $p = loop$ and $b = success$ is consistent (✔): since *loop* denotes a provably infinite loop, Boogie should also be able to verify that the program in question is (partially) correct, in that any code up to and until the loop is free from errors, whereas the code after the loop is unreachable, and hence irrelevant for correctness.

In contrast, if $p = failure$ but $b = success$, we would conclude that BCC has found a *soundness* failure ✘, since Boogie erroneously passed as correct an incorrect program (a false negative). Conversely, if $p = success$ but $b = failure$, we would conclude that BCC has found a *completeness* failure ✘, since Boogie reported a spurious verification failure for a correct program (a false positive); as explained above, the same conclusion ✘ holds if $p = loop$ but $b = failure$.

Clearly, if $p = name\text{-}error$—that is, the program is not name-correct—Boogie should report the same outcome, in which case BCC reports consistency ✔; any other Boogie outcome would result in ✘, and reveal that Boogie's name resolution pass has a bug. Similarly, if $p = type\text{-}error$—that is, the program is not type-correct—Boogie should report the same outcome, unless its type checker has a bug.

Finally, if $p = timeout$, the consistency check is inconclusive (?) regardless of whether $b = success$, $b = failure$, or $b = timeout$; similarly, if $b = timeout$, the consistency check is inconclusive (**?**) regardless of whether $p = success$, $p = failure$, or $p = loop$. For example, as discussed previously, program `timeout` in Table 1 results in $p = timeout$ and $b = failure$, which is consistent because the program is actually incorrect; however, if we removed the **assert false**, PLT Redex's outcome p would still be $timeout$ but Boogie would correctly report $b = success$ because the program would now be correct.

```
while (C)                      while (C)
   invariant J {                  invariant J {
   // ...                         assert A;
}                                 // ...
assert A;                      }
```

Fig. 6. Generic Boogie loops annotated with loop invariants.

Loop Invariants. To properly gauge the inconsistencies in our experiments that point to *completeness* failures of Boogie, we need to understand the role played by loop *invariants*. Consider Fig. 6's generic loops (annotated with an invariant J), and suppose that Boogie's outcome b is a *failure* of **assert** A , whereas PLT Redex reports $p = loop$ (program on the left) or $p = success$ (program on the right) on the same program—hence, the program is (partially) correct. For the program on the left, if $\neg C \Rightarrow A$ holds we say that it is a case of *reasoning* incompleteness of Boogie; otherwise, we call it a case of *annotation* incompleteness. Similarly, for the program on the right, if $\neg C$ holds at the loop's entrance we say that it is a case of *reasoning* incompleteness; otherwise, we call it a case of *annotation* incompleteness. In principle, annotation incompleteness merely indicates that the user should have annotated the loop with an invariant strong enough to characterize the loop's behavior: if J is indeed a correct invariant of the loop, then Boogie could use it to prove that $J \wedge \neg C \Rightarrow A$ (program on the left) or $J \Rightarrow \neg C$ (program on the right), hence establishing that the program is correct after all. Conversely, reasoning incompleteness means that A holds independent of any loop invariants, because it is a direct consequence of the loop's condition C; hence, Boogie should be able to successfully verify the program without additional annotations. These definitions generalize to cases where the assertion that spuriously fails in Boogie is not immediately after the loop (resp. at the beginning of the loop body) but follows a sequence S of statements.

Distinguishing between the two kinds of incompleteness is undecidable in general, because it requires a sound and complete loop invariant inference. This also explains why BPL$_0$ does not include loop invariant annotations: synthesizing correct (and useful) loop invariants for randomly generated loops is nontrivial, and would require to introduce different techniques. Section 5.3 describes how we tried to estimate annotation vs. reasoning incompleteness in our experiments.

5   Experiments

To evaluate BCC's capabilities, we used it to generate a large number of BPL$_0$ programs with different characteristics, and to compare the outcome of PLT Redex execution and Boogie verification on those programs.

5.1   Setup

Batches. Each *batch* of generated programs is defined by three parameters: *i)* the *number* of BPL$_0$ programs in the batch; *ii)* whether they should be well-*typed*, well-*named*, or simply well-*formed*; *iii)* the maximum *size* of each generated program.[5] In our experiments, we generated a total of 3 million syntactically different programs in 12 batches: for each kind of well-typed, well-named, and well-formed programs, *i)* 100 000 programs with maximum size 3, *ii)* 200 000 programs with maximum size 5, *iii)* 200 000 programs with maximum size 7, *iv)* 500 000 programs with maximum size 10. We chose these numbers after some informal experiments with BCC, which suggested two guidelines: first, even though a larger maximum program size should permit also small programs, using batches with different maximum sizes achieves a better program size diversity; second, batches with a smaller maximum program size should be smaller, otherwise there is a risk of inefficiently generating a lot of nearly identical programs.

System. The experiments ran on a virtual machine with 64 cores of an AMD Epyc 7713 3.7 Ghz processor with 128 GB of RAM, running Ubuntu 22.04, Racket/PLT Redex v. 8.2, Boogie v. 3.4.3 with Z3 v. 4.8.8—the latest versions of the software at the time of these experiments. To speed up the experiments, several instances of BCC ran in parallel processes, each on different BPL$_0$ programs and coordinated by a work-stealing algorithm; precisely, the generation phase used 64 parallel processes, the execution phase 128, and the verification phase 512.

Table 3. Statistics about the composition of the BPL$_0$ programs generated in the experiments. For each batch of *well-formed*, *well-named*, or *well-typed* programs of a given maximum *size*, the table reports *min*imum, *med*ian, and *max*imum number of terms of each kind in any program in the batch.

Batch	Size	Locals L			Statement s			Expr e (arith)			Expr e (bool)			Expr e (comp)			Literals l		
		min	med	max	min	med	max	min	med	max	min	med	max	min	med	max	min	med	max
formed	3	1	1	3	1	9	18	0	1	5	0	4	14	0	0	5	0	7	16
	5	1	1	5	1	20	65	0	2	14	0	10	37	0	1	11	0	15	51
	7	1	1	7	1	40	176	0	5	39	0	20	110	0	2	22	0	31	132
	10	1	2	10	1	100	637	0	16	126	0	54	379	0	8	78	0	79	517
named	3	1	1	3	1	10	18	0	0	5	0	5	17	0	0	5	0	10	20
	5	1	1	5	1	21	61	0	2	15	0	12	41	0	1	11	0	20	57
	7	1	1	7	1	41	130	0	4	31	0	23	106	0	2	19	0	38	125
	10	1	1	10	1	102	491	0	14	108	0	60	326	0	7	66	0	93	471
typed	3	1	1	3	1	10	18	0	0	4	0	7	27	0	1	6	0	8	20
	5	1	1	5	1	21	54	0	3	17	0	17	65	0	3	16	0	18	58
	7	1	1	7	1	41	139	0	9	48	0	35	187	0	7	49	0	38	170
	10	1	2	10	1	103	481	0	37	265	0	94	553	0	24	157	0	106	584

---

[5] PLT Redex's documentation is somewhat vague about how this `size-expr` parameter is used, but it's probably an upper bound on the maximum depth of the generated term tree.

5.2   Results: Generation, Execution, and Verification

Generation. In our experiments, BCC took about 30 min to generate the 3 million programs in 12 batches. Table 3 shows basic statistics about the actual size of the BPL_0 programs generated in each batch, measured in terms of the number of local variables, statements, arithmetic, Boolean and comparison operators, and literals that appear in a program. Most programs have a non-trivial size in terms of statements and expressions, whereas they tend to include few local variables (median: 1–2, maximum: 10). Well-typed programs are about as large, on average, as well-named and well-formed programs, but they tend to include larger expressions. This is an indirect effect of using typing judgments as a constraint to generate *well-typed* programs: this additional condition nudges the generation to produce more "interesting", deeply nested expressions; in contrast, the generation of well-formed programs has fewer constraints, and hence results in a more shallow enumeration of all possible literal/operator combination. Overall, BCC managed to generate a broad range of programs with different sizes and characteristics.

Table 4. Statistics about the outcome of PLT *Redex execution* (left) and *Boogie verification* (right) of the BPL_0 programs generated in the experiments. For each batch of *well-formed*, *well-named*, or *well-typed* programs of a given maximum *size*, the number of programs in the batch whose PLT Redex execution resulted in a certain outcome. Rows *all* aggregate the counts # and percentage % within each batch, and in all dataset.

Batch	Size	PLT Redex Execution Outcomes						Boogie Verification Outcomes				
		success	*failure*	*loop*	*timeout*	*name-error*	*type-error*	*success*	*failure*	*timeout*	*name-error*	*type-error*
formed	3	2	0	0	0	99 617	381	2	0	0	99 617	381
	5	2	2	0	0	199 917	79	2	2	0	199 917	79
	7	6	3	1	0	199 929	61	7	3	0	199 929	61
	10	14	5	1	0	499 838	142	15	5	0	499 838	142
all	#	24	10	2	0	999 301	663	26	10	0	999 301	663
	%	0	0	0	0	100	0	0	0	0	100	0
named	3	23	25	14	0	0	99 938	37	25	0	0	99 938
	5	21	9	1	0	0	199 969	22	9	0	0	199 969
	7	27	6	2	0	0	199 965	29	6	0	0	199 965
	10	73	18	7	0	0	499 902	80	18	0	0	499 902
all	#	144	58	24	0	0	999 774	168	58	0	0	999 774
	%	0	0	0	0	0	100	0	0	0	0	100
typed	3	3 664	64 888	31 446	2	0	0	33 960	66 040	0	0	0
	5	1 513	130 578	67 661	248	0	0	62 126	137 874	0	0	0
	7	675	130 200	68 746	379	0	0	57 021	142 978	1	0	0
	10	1 310	341 674	155 942	1 074	0	0	113 711	386 264	25	0	0
all	#	7 162	667 340	323 795	1 703	0	0	266 818	733 156	26	0	0
	%	1	67	32	0	0	0	27	73	0	0	0
all	#	7 330	667 408	323 821	1 703	999 301	1 000 437	267 012	733 224	26	999 301	1 000 437
	%	0	22	11	0	33	33	9	24	0	33	33

Execution. In our experiments, BCC took around 110 min to execute the 3 million programs according to BPL_0's operational semantics. Table 4's left half shows the number of programs in each batch whose PLT Redex execution resulted in one of five possible outcomes: *success, failure, loop, timeout, name-error,* and *type-error.* As expected, most well-formed programs resulted in a name resolution error; and most well-named programs in a type checking error (even though a few managed to pass typechecking, and even to pass execution).

As for well-typed programs, less than 1% of them timed out; thus, most executions ran to completion. Similarly, only about 1% of the programs terminated with a *success*; this indicates that it is more likely that a randomly generated assertion fails than it holds. In fact, *failure* was by far the most common outcome of executing well-typed programs: over 2/3 of them terminated with an assertion failure. Within each batch of a certain maximum size, the percentage of programs that fail is similar (around 65%) but becomes a bit higher for the batch with size 10 (around 68%), arguably because larger random expression are more likely to introduce a contradiction. Nevertheless, PLT Redex detected an infinite *loop* in nearly 1/3 of the randomly generated programs. In all, despite the simplicity of the Boogie BPL_0 subset it targets, the programs generated by BCC have a good variety of possible outcomes, and thus have the potential of exercising the verifier in different conditions.

Verification. In our experiments, BCC took around 12 h to verify the 3 million programs with Boogie; unsurprisingly, running Boogie is an order of magnitude more time consuming than running PLT Redex on relatively small programs (or generating them), since each Boogie run usually involves calls to an SMT solver. As during PLT Redex execution, Boogie reports a *name-error* (resp. *type-error*), on most well-formed (resp. well-named) programs.

The distribution of verification outcomes for well-typed programs may seem quite different from that of execution outcomes, but it is actually largely consistent. In fact, remember that both execution outcomes $p = success, loop$ correspond to the same verification outcome $b = success$—since a program with an infinite loop should be classified as correct by Boogie, which only checks partial correctness. Boogie timeouts are exceedingly rare, at least with the kinds of programs that BCC generates, which do not include complex quantified formulas that may trip up the quantifier instantiation algorithms [8,25]. However, Boogie timeouts do occasionally, and unpredictably, happen on programs that, upon inspection, do not seem to have any complex or unusual feature that stands out.

Table 5. Number and percentage of all BPL$_0$ programs generated in the experiments, for each combination of PLT Redex execution outcome p and Boogie verification outcome b as in Table 2. A red background highlights the combinations that correspond to *inconsistent* results that have been observed in the experiments.

			Boogie outcome b		
PLT Redex outcome p	*success*	*failure*	*timeout*	*name-error*	*type-error*
success	6 981 0.23%	349 0.01%			
failure		667 397 22.25%	11 0.00%		
loop	258 808 8.63%	64 998 2.17%	15 0.00%		
timeout	1 223 0.04%	480 0.02%			
name-error				999 301 33.31%	
type-error					1 000 437 33.35%

5.3   Results: Consistency Checks

Table 5 reports the number and percentage of all 3 million programs generated in the experiments that resulted in each of Table 2's possible combinations of PLT Redex execution outcome p and Boogie verification outcome b.

Correctness. In the vast majority of cases, Boogie's outcome was consistent with the result of executing according to BPL$_0$'s operational semantics. In particular, all programs with name errors or type errors were caught by Boogie's name resolution or type checking modules.

Boogie successfully verified 80% (i.e., 6 981 + 258 808)/(7 330 + 323 821)) of all (partially) correct programs according to PLT Redex execution (that is, p outcomes *success* and *loop*); it also confirmed as incorrect nearly 100% (i.e., 667 397/667 408)of all incorrect programs according to PLT Redex execution (p outcome *failure*). The cases of programs involving timeouts are inconclusive, but they are also only a tiny fraction of the total. Overall, BCC was useful to thoroughly validate Boogie, which behaved correctly in the vast majority of cases.

Table 6. How Boogie's inconsistency failures change if it uses loop invariant inference. The two rightmost columns are the same as in Table 5. A red background highlights the combinations that correspond to *incompleteness* failures.

	Boogie outcome b			
	invariant inference			
PLT Redex outcome p	*success*	*failure*	*success*	*failure*
success	7 259	71	6 981	349
loop	309 020	14 785	258 808	64 998

Soundness. BCC did not expose any soundness failure of Boogie, that is cases of incorrect programs ($p = failure$) that Boogie passes as correct ($b = success$). While it is known that SMT solvers—including Z3—do sometimes suffer from soundness bugs, exposing them requires bespoke constraints [46], which are unlikely to be generated by BCC's grammar during purely random enumeration. Furthermore, Boogie's verification condition generation algorithm adds a layer of indirection between the Boogie program and the constraints sent to the SMT solver, which may complicate triggering soundness bugs through Boogie without involving features, such as triggers, that directly interact with the underlying solver [6]. Despite these limitations, BCC's testing remains useful to increase our confidence that Boogie is generally sound.

Completeness. Our experiments found 65 347 (349 + 64 998)cases of *completeness* failure; that is, Boogie rejected as (possibly) incorrect ($b = failure$) about 20/65 347/(7 330 + 323 821))of all correct programs (PLT Redex p outcomes *success* or *loop*). These results are largely consistent with how Boogie is designed: since it aims at being a sound implementation of deductive program verification (which is undecidable in general), it will necessarily incur cases of incompleteness. Still, they also further demonstrate BCC's practical usefulness in stress-testing a verifier to better reveal its capabilities and limitations.

Section 4.4 introduced the distinction between *annotation* and *reasoning* incompleteness. How many of our experiments triggered each kind of incompleteness? To answer this question, we tried to use Boogie's support for loop invariant inference as a proxy for distinguishing between reasoning and annotation incompleteness. For each program P where $b = failure$ but $p = success$ or *loop*, we ran Boogie on P again with option /infer:j—which enables loop invariant inference. If P verifies successfully in this new run, it suggests that it is a case of annotation incompleteness; otherwise, we classify it as reasoning incompleteness. We stress that this is an imperfect proxy, which is, in general, neither sound nor precise: *i)* obviously, if P still fails verification, it may just mean that Boogie's loop invariant inference could not find the "right" loop invariant; *ii)* conversely, if P passes verification, it may still be a case of reasoning incompleteness, where adding a loop invariant J unexpectedly helps establish that A holds, even if J is subsumed by $\neg C$ or C.

With these caveats in mind, let's have a look at Table 6, which shows how the number of incompleteness inconsistencies change if Boogie uses loop invariant inference. The number of inconsistencies shrinks significantly: only 23/of spurious failures encountered in our experiments remain even if loop invariant inference is enabled. This would seem to suggest that completeness failures often denote annotation incompleteness rather than reasoning incompleteness. On the other hand, a nontrivial number of cases of actual annotation incompleteness seem to remain (those resistant to invariant inference).

In order to better understand the effect of loop invariant inference, we selected a small random sample consisting of 40 Boogie programs among those that PLT Redex execution confirmed as correct ($p = success$ or *loop*): 20

among those that Boogie without loop invariant inference flagged as incorrect ($b = \textit{failure}$), and Boogie with loop invariant inference verified successfully ($b = \textit{success}$); and 20 among those that Boogie flagged as incorrect ($b = \textit{failure}$) with or without loop invariant inference. We manually inspected these 40 Boogie programs, trying to determine whether they were cases of annotation or reasoning incompleteness. We found that 23 cases[6] out of 40 were actually instances of *reasoning* incompleteness, since they all involved unreachable code guarded by a condition that was identically false (independent of any additional annotation). Therefore, loop invariant inference should not have any effect on whether Boogie can verify these examples successfully. In practice, option `/infer:j` introduces several nontrivial changes in how Boogie generates the verification conditions of a program; therefore, it is to be expected that it can have an indirect, unpredictable effect on the kinds of programs that can be automatically verified—it is a form of brittleness, also observed in related work [9]. In all, we have reasons to believe that a larger fraction of the completeness failures encountered in BCC's experiments are actually indicative of *reasoning* incompleteness—even though it is hard to get a precise estimate without a very prohibitively time-consuming extensive manual analysis. Regardless, our experiments successfully demonstrated BCC's practical applicability to run large-scale thorough testing of the the Boogie intermediate verifier.

Examples of Reasoning Incompleteness. Figure 7 shows two programs generated by BCC in our experiments[7] that showcase *completeness* failures. For space reasons we only shows these two examples, which are, however, quite representative of numerous other similar examples that exhibit the same behavior.

The outermost loop's body in Fig. 7a's program `alwaysLoops` (which has the same general structure as Fig. 6's left program) clearly never terminates, since variable `G` is initialized to **true** and never changes value. While PLT Redex execution results in $p = \textit{loop}$, Boogie returns with $b = \textit{failure}$, flagging a violation of the **assert false** just after the outer loop. According to our classification, this is a case of annotation incompleteness, since Boogie correctly verifies the program if it is given the additional information that `G` is always true (which can be retrieved by loop invariant inference). Note that, in this case, the invariance of `G` is path and flow insensitive: in the loop, there is a single assignment to `G` of the constant **true**.

Conversely, the outermost loop's body in Fig. 7b's program `neverLoops` clearly never executes, since variable `s` is initialized to **false** and immediately checked as the loop condition. While PLT Redex execution results in $p = \textit{success}$, Boogie returns with $b = \textit{failure}$, flagging a violation of the assertion at the end of the loop body. Since the outer loop condition is obviously identically **false** when it is first evaluated, this is a case of reasoning incompleteness. However,

---

[6] Precisely, 14 cases that Boogie verifies only with `/infer:j`, and 9 cases that fail verification even with `/infer:j`.

[7] For readability, we simplified the full programs by removing parts that do not affect their behavior.

```
procedure alwaysLoops() returns () {        procedure neverLoops() returns () {
  var G : bool;                               var s: bool; var AE: bool;
  G := true;                                  s := false; AE := false;
  G := G;                                     while (s) {
  assert (0 < 1) ∧ (1 = 1);                     if ((−0 * 0 + −0) > 1) {
  while (G) {                                   } else {
    while (G) {                                   while (s) {
      assert ¬(true ⟹ false);                       AE := true;
    }                                               s := ¬(s ∧ ¬false);
    G := true;                                    }
  }                                             }
  //...                                       s := true;
  assert false;                               if (0 ≥ −3) {
}                                               if (false) {
                                                } else {
                                                  assert (¬(true ∧ s) = AE);
                                                }
                                              }
                                              /* ... */ } }
```

(a) The outer loop in this program never terminates.

(b) The outer loop in this program never executes.

Fig. 7. Two programs generated by BCC that expose incompleteness in Boogie.

Boogie returns with $b = success$ if we enable the `/infer:j` option, even though a loop invariant is not needed to determine that the loop never executes. Even more unpredictably, if we add more statements after the **assert** within the loop body, then Boogie reports a (spurious) verification failure regardless of whether loop invariant inference is or isn't enabled.

6   Conclusions

This paper presented BCC: a lightweight validation technique to test deductive verifiers such as the widely used Boogie. BCC is built atop a formal model of a small, deterministic subset of the Boogie language, consisting of a grammar, typing rules, and an executable operational semantics—encoded using the PLT Redex semantic engineering framework. In our experiments, we used BCC to thoroughly test Boogie for consistency; while we found that Boogie's output is correct and reliable in the vast majority of cases, we did find a few interesting examples that expose completeness failures.

References

1. Backes, M., Hriţcu, C., Tarrach, T.: Automatically verifying typing constraints for a data processing language. In: Jouannaud, J.-P., Shao, Z. (eds.) CPP 2011. LNCS, vol. 7086, pp. 296–313. Springer, Heidelberg (2011). https://doi.org/10.1007/978-3-642-25379-9_22

2. Baek, S.: A formally verified checker for first-order proofs. In: Cohen, L., Kaliszyk, C. (eds.) 12th International Conference on Interactive Theorem Proving, ITP 2021, June 29 to July 1, 2021, Rome, Italy (Virtual Conference). LIPIcs, vol. 193, pp. 6:1–6:13. Schloss Dagstuhl - Leibniz-Zentrum für Informatik (2021). https://doi.org/10.4230/LIPICS.ITP.2021.6

3. Barnett, M., Chang, B.-Y.E., DeLine, R., Jacobs, B., Leino, K.R.M.: Boogie: a modular reusable verifier for object-oriented programs. In: de Boer, F.S., Bonsangue, M.M., Graf, S., de Roever, W.-P. (eds.) FMCO 2005. LNCS, vol. 4111, pp. 364–387. Springer, Heidelberg (2006). https://doi.org/10.1007/11804192_17

4. Bringolf, M., Winterer, D., Su, Z.: Finding and understanding incompleteness bugs in SMT solvers. In: 37th IEEE/ACM International Conference on Automated Software Engineering, ASE 2022, Rochester, MI, USA, 10–14 October 2022, pp. 43:1–43:10. ACM (2022). https://doi.org/10.1145/3551349.3560435

5. Brummayer, R., Lonsing, F., Biere, A.: Automated testing and debugging of SAT and QBF solvers. In: Strichman, O., Szeider, S. (eds.) SAT 2010. LNCS, vol. 6175, pp. 44–57. Springer, Heidelberg (2010). https://doi.org/10.1007/978-3-642-14186-7_6

6. Bugariu, A., Ter-Gabrielyan, A., Müller, P.: Identifying overly restrictive matching patterns in SMT-based program verifiers. In: Huisman, M., Păsăreanu, C., Zhan, N. (eds.) FM 2021. LNCS, vol. 13047, pp. 273–291. Springer, Cham (2021). https://doi.org/10.1007/978-3-030-90870-6_15

7. Chen, J., et al.: A survey of compiler testing. ACM Comput. Surv. **53**(1), 4:1–4:36 (2021). https://doi.org/10.1145/3363562

8. Chen, Y.T., Furia, C.A.: Triggerless happy – intermediate verification with a first-order prover. In: Polikarpova, N., Schneider, S. (eds.) IFM 2017. LNCS, vol. 10510, pp. 295–311. Springer, Cham (2017). https://doi.org/10.1007/978-3-319-66845-1_19

9. Chen, Y.T., Furia, C.A.: Robustness testing of intermediate verifiers. In: Lahiri, S.K., Wang, C. (eds.) ATVA 2018. LNCS, vol. 11138, pp. 91–108. Springer, Cham (2018). https://doi.org/10.1007/978-3-030-01090-4_6

10. Dardinier, T., Sammler, M., Parthasarathy, G., Summers, A.J., Müller, P.: Formal foundations for translational separation logic verifiers. Proc. ACM Program. Lang. **9**(POPL), 569–599 (2025). https://doi.org/10.1145/3704856

11. Felleisen, M., Findler, R.B., Flatt, M.: Semantics Engineering with PLT Redex. MIT Press (2009). http://mitpress.mit.edu/catalog/item/default.asp?ttype=2&tid=11885

12. Fetscher, B., Claessen, K., Pałka, M., Hughes, J., Findler, R.B.: Making random judgments: automatically generating well-typed terms from the definition of a type-system. In: Vitek, J. (ed.) ESOP 2015. LNCS, vol. 9032, pp. 383–405. Springer, Heidelberg (2015). https://doi.org/10.1007/978-3-662-46669-8_16

13. Fiala, J., Itzhaky, S., Müller, P., Polikarpova, N., Sergey, I.: Leveraging rust types for program synthesis. Proc. ACM Program. Lang. **7**(PLDI), 1414–1437 (2023). https://doi.org/10.1145/3591278

14. Filliâtre, J.-C., Paskevich, A.: Why3 — where programs meet provers. In: Felleisen, M., Gardner, P. (eds.) ESOP 2013. LNCS, vol. 7792, pp. 125–128. Springer, Heidelberg (2013). https://doi.org/10.1007/978-3-642-37036-6_8

15. Fink, X., Berger, P., Katoen, J.: Configurable benchmarks for C model checkers. In: Deshmukh, J.V., Havelund, K., Perez, I. (eds.) NFM 2022. LNCS, vol. 13260, pp. 338–354. Springer, Cham (2022). https://doi.org/10.1007/978-3-031-06773-0_18

16. From, A.H., Jacobsen, F.K.: Verifying a sequent calculus prover for first-order logic with functions in Isabelle/HOL. J. Autom. Reason. $\mathbf{68}$(3), 15 (2024). https://doi.org/10.1007/s10817-024-09697-3

17. Greenaway, D., Lim, J., Andronick, J., Klein, G.: Don't sweat the small stuff: formal verification of C code without the pain. In: O'Boyle, M.F.P., Pingali, K. (eds.) ACM SIGPLAN Conference on Programming Language Design and Implementation, PLDI 2014, Edinburgh, United Kingdom - 09–11 June 2014, pp. 429–439. ACM (2014). https://doi.org/10.1145/2594291.2594296

18. Guha, A., Saftoiu, C., Krishnamurthi, S.: The essence of JavaScript. In: D'Hondt, T. (ed.) ECOOP 2010. LNCS, vol. 6183, pp. 126–150. Springer, Heidelberg (2010). https://doi.org/10.1007/978-3-642-14107-2_7

19. Herms, P., Marché, C., Monate, B.: A certified multi-prover verification condition generator. In: Joshi, R., Müller, P., Podelski, A. (eds.) VSTTE 2012. LNCS, vol. 7152, pp. 2–17. Springer, Heidelberg (2012). https://doi.org/10.1007/978-3-642-27705-4_2

20. Kapus, T., Cadar, C.: Automatic testing of symbolic execution engines via program generation and differential testing. In: Rosu, G., Penta, M.D., Nguyen, T.N. (eds.) Proceedings of the 32nd IEEE/ACM International Conference on Automated Software Engineering, ASE 2017, Urbana, IL, USA, 30 October–03 November 2017, pp. 590–600. IEEE Computer Society (2017). https://doi.org/10.1109/ASE.2017.8115669

21. Klein, C., et al.: Run your research: on the effectiveness of lightweight mechanization. In: Field, J., Hicks, M. (eds.) Proceedings of the 39th ACM SIGPLAN-SIGACT Symposium on Principles of Programming Languages, POPL 2012, Philadelphia, Pennsylvania, USA, 22–28 January 2012, pp. 285–296. ACM (2012). https://doi.org/10.1145/2103656.2103691

22. Klein, G., et al.: seL4: formal verification of an operating-system kernel. Commun. ACM $\mathbf{53}$(6), 107–115 (2010). https://doi.org/10.1145/1743546.1743574

23. Kumar, R., Myreen, M.O., Norrish, M., Owens, S.: CakeML: a verified implementation of ML. In: Jagannathan, S., Sewell, P. (eds.) The 41st Annual ACM SIGPLAN-SIGACT Symposium on Principles of Programming Languages, POPL 2014, San Diego, CA, USA, 20–21 January 2014, pp. 179–192. ACM (2014). https://doi.org/10.1145/2535838.2535841

24. Le, V., Afshari, M., Su, Z.: Compiler validation via equivalence modulo inputs. In: O'Boyle, M.F.P., Pingali, K. (eds.) ACM SIGPLAN Conference on Programming Language Design and Implementation, PLDI 2014, Edinburgh, United Kingdom - 09–11 June 2014, pp. 216–226. ACM (2014). https://doi.org/10.1145/2594291.2594334

25. Leino, K.R.M., Pit-Claudel, C.: Trigger selection strategies to stabilize program verifiers. In: Chaudhuri, S., Farzan, A. (eds.) CAV 2016. LNCS, vol. 9779, pp. 361–381. Springer, Cham (2016). https://doi.org/10.1007/978-3-319-41528-4_20

26. Leroy, X.: A formally verified compiler back-end. J. Autom. Reason. $\mathbf{43}$(4), 363–446 (2009). http://xavierleroy.org/publi/compcert-backend.pdf

27. Leroy, X., Blazy, S.: Formal verification of a C-like memory model and its uses for verifying program transformations. J. Autom. Reason. **41**(1), 1–31 (2008). http://xavierleroy.org/publi/memory-model-journal.pdf

28. Liew, D., Cadar, C., Donaldson, A.: Symbooglix: a symbolic execution engine for Boogie programs. In: IEEE International Conference on Software Testing, Verification, and Validation (ICST 2016), pp. 45–56 (2016)

29. Lin, Z., Chen, X., Trinh, M., Wang, J., Rosu, G.: Generating proof certificates for a language-agnostic deductive program verifier. Proc. ACM Program. Lang. **7**(OOPSLA1), 56–84 (2023). https://doi.org/10.1145/3586029

30. Losavio, L., Paganoni, M., Furia, C.A.: Boogie Consistency Checker: Replication package for iFM2025 (2025). https://doi.org/10.6084/m9.figshare.29338589.v2

31. Mansur, M.N., Christakis, M., Wüstholz, V., Zhang, F.: Detecting critical bugs in SMT solvers using blackbox mutational fuzzing. In: Devanbu, P., Cohen, M.B., Zimmermann, T. (eds.) ESEC/FSE 2020: 28th ACM Joint European Software Engineering Conference and Symposium on the Foundations of Software Engineering, Virtual Event, USA, 8–13 November 2020, pp. 701–712. ACM (2020). https://doi.org/10.1145/3368089.3409763

32. Marti, N., Affeldt, R.: A certified verifier for a fragment of separation logic. Inf. Media Technol. **4**(2), 304–316 (2009). https://doi.org/10.11185/IMT.4.304

33. Monniaux, D., Gourdin, L., Boulmé, S., Lebeltel, O.: Testing a formally verified compiler. In: Prevosto, V., Seceleanu, C. (eds.) TAP 2023. LNCS, vol. 14066, pp. 40–48. Springer, Cham (2023). https://doi.org/10.1007/978-3-031-38828-6_3

34. Müller, P., Schwerhoff, M., Summers, A.J.: Viper: a verification infrastructure for permission-based reasoning. In: Jobstmann, B., Leino, K.R.M. (eds.) VMCAI 2016. LNCS, vol. 9583, pp. 41–62. Springer, Heidelberg (2016). https://doi.org/10.1007/978-3-662-49122-5_2

35. Nipkow, T.: Winskel is (almost) right: towards a mechanized semantics. Formal Aspects Comput. **10**(2), 171–186 (1998). https://doi.org/10.1007/s001650050009

36. Parthasarathy, G., Dardinier, T., Bonneau, B., Müller, P., Summers, A.J.: Towards trustworthy automated program verifiers: formally validating translations into an intermediate verification language. Proc. ACM Program. Lang. **8**(PLDI), 1510–1534 (2024). https://doi.org/10.1145/3656438

37. Parthasarathy, G., Müller, P., Summers, A.J.: Formally validating a practical verification condition generator. In: Silva, A., Leino, K.R.M. (eds.) CAV 2021. LNCS, vol. 12760, pp. 704–727. Springer, Cham (2021). https://doi.org/10.1007/978-3-030-81688-9_33

38. Polikarpova, N., Furia, C.A., West, S.: To run what no one has run before: executing an intermediate verification language. In: Legay, A., Bensalem, S. (eds.) RV 2013. LNCS, vol. 8174, pp. 251–268. Springer, Heidelberg (2013). https://doi.org/10.1007/978-3-642-40787-1_15

39. Skotåm, S.H.: CreuSAT, Using Rust and Creusot to create the world's fastest deductively verified SAT solver. Master's thesis, University of Oslo (2022). https://www.duo.uio.no/handle/10852/96757

40. Smans, J., Jacobs, B., Piessens, F.: Implicit dynamic frames. ACM Trans. Program. Lang. Syst. **34**(1), 2:1–2:58 (2012). https://doi.org/10.1145/2160910.2160911

41. Soldevila, M., Ziliani, B., Silvestre, B., Fridlender, D., Mascarenhas, F.: Decoding Lua: formal semantics for the developer and the semanticist. In: Ancona, D. (ed.) Proceedings of the 13th ACM SIGPLAN International Symposium on on Dynamic Languages, Vancouver, BC, Canada, 23–27 October 2017, pp. 75–86. ACM (2017). https://doi.org/10.1145/3133841.3133848

42. Steffen, B., Isberner, M., Naujokat, S., Margaria, T., Geske, M.: Property-driven benchmark generation: synthesizing programs of realistic structure. Int. J. Softw. Tools Technol. Transfer **16**(5), 465–479 (2014). https://doi.org/10.1007/s10009-014-0336-z
43. Tan, Y.K., Myreen, M.O., Kumar, R., Fox, A.C.J., Owens, S., Norrish, M.: The verified CakeML compiler backend. J. Funct. Program. **29**, e2 (2019). https://doi.org/10.1017/S0956796818000229
44. Thoben, N., Haltermann, J., Wehrheim, H.: Timeout prediction for software analyses. In: Ferreira, C., Willemse, T.A.C. (eds.) SEFM 2023. LNCS, vol. 14323, pp. 340–358. Springer, Cham (2023). https://doi.org/10.1007/978-3-031-47115-5_19
45. Vogels, F., Jacobs, B., Piessens, F.: A machine checked soundness proof for an intermediate verification language. In: Nielsen, M., Kučera, A., Miltersen, P.B., Palamidessi, C., Tůma, P., Valencia, F. (eds.) SOFSEM 2009. LNCS, vol. 5404, pp. 570–581. Springer, Heidelberg (2009). https://doi.org/10.1007/978-3-540-95891-8_51
46. Winterer, D., Su, Z.: Validating SMT solvers for correctness and performance via grammar-based enumeration. Proc. ACM Program. Lang. **8**(OOPSLA2), 2378–2401 (2024). https://doi.org/10.1145/3689795
47. Yang, X., Chen, Y., Eide, E., Regehr, J.: Finding and understanding bugs in C compilers. In: Hall, M.W., Padua, D.A. (eds.) Proceedings of the 32nd ACM SIGPLAN Conference on Programming Language Design and Implementation, PLDI 2011, San Jose, CA, USA, 4–8 June 2011, pp. 283–294. ACM (2011). https://doi.org/10.1145/1993498.1993532
48. Zhang, C., Su, T., Yan, Y., Zhang, F., Pu, G., Su, Z.: Finding and understanding bugs in software model checkers. In: Dumas, M., Pfahl, D., Apel, S., Russo, A. (eds.) Proceedings of the ACM Joint Meeting on European Software Engineering Conference and Symposium on the Foundations of Software Engineering, ESEC/SIGSOFT FSE 2019, Tallinn, Estonia, 26–30 August 2019, pp. 763–773. ACM (2019). https://doi.org/10.1145/3338906.3338932

Quick Theory Exploration for Algebraic Data Types via Program Transformations

Gidon Ernst[1(✉)] and Grigory Fedyukovich[2]

[1] LMU Munich, Munich, Germany
gidon.ernst@lmu.de
[2] Florida State University, Tallahassee, USA
grigory@cs.fsu.edu

Abstract. We present an approach to theory exploration, i.e., a *lemma synthesis procedure* which discovers algebraic laws over recursive functions over Algebraic Data Types (ADTs). The approach, LemmaCalc, builds on, adapts and extends program calculation techniques known from optimization of functional programs (fusion and accumulator removal). Our approach avoids exponential search space of term enumeration (SyGuS) that can render state-of-the-art techniques prohibitively expensive or even useless on large theories with more than a handful of function symbols. In this paper we describe how this approach can be realized and contribute a robust implementation. The evaluation shows that different methods have complementary strengths and that each can produce lemmas not found by the other, but LemmaCalc scales much better to larger theories.

1 Introduction

Algebraic Data Types (ADTs) like applicative lists and trees enable formal modeling of programs in proof assistants like Isabelle/HOL [36] and automatic induction provers, e.g. [10,14,19,20,26,29,31,38,40,52,54]. Equational reasoning and induction are the techniques of choice when proving properties about *recursively-defined functions* over ADTs, usually relying on a set of lemmas that explain what happens if these functions interact with each other. While the libraries of proof assistants usually come with a large amount of lemmas for built-in functions, setting this up for application-specific definitions may incur a significant part of the effort of the verification. A widely-used strategy to achieve a higher-degree of automation are goal-directed proof methods [6], which derive auxiliary lemmas from stuck proofs with the help of generalization heuristics.

Theory exploration is an alternative and complementary direction, aiming to discover lemmas bottom-up from a set of given definitions. State-of-the-art methods [9,42] rely on exhaustive search over millions of candidate formulas in a combinatorial search space by enumeration akin to syntax-guided synthesis (SyGuS) [1]. In SyGuS, usually a vast majority of candidates are either wrong or redundant. Thus, significant efforts in the existing tools, including the

F. Damiani and M. Farrell (Eds.): iFM 2025, LNCS 16194, pp. 424–450, 2026.
https://doi.org/10.1007/978-3-032-10794-7_21

state-of-the-art approach THESY [42], are invested in filtering candidate lemmas using deductive, counterexample-based, or observational-equivalence-based techniques. Yet, theory exploration in general remains expensive. Furthermore, existing enumeration-based methods generate lemmas that follow no particular pattern or shape and it may be questionable how useful such lemmas are in practice in the context of interactive proofs (i.e., what constitutes progress or simplification of proof goals) and with respect to proof automation (e.g., whether lemmas fit well with proof techniques without introducing matching loops).

Contribution: The key idea behind and advantage of LEMMACALC over search-space enumeration is that it embraces *calculational techniques* based on unfold/fold transformations of recursive functions [7] to guide the search for solutions as well as the underlying induction proof at the same time. In contrast to working at the term/formula level, these approaches transform the definitions of functions themselves, by algorithmically rearranging a given computation into a new form. We emphasize that the effectiveness of LEMMACALC stems from the *combination* of two transformations which to the best of our knowledge is novel: For this work we adapt *fusion* [32] (resp. supercompilation [49], deforestation [50], Sect. 4) and *accumulator removal* by a technique similar to context shift [16] (Sect. 5) to our setting, crucially integrating deduction steps in strategic places. While we have found this combination to be effective our synthesis loop (Sect. 6) may accommodate other transformations too, such as [17, 27, 30].

Evaluation and Results: We have implemented the approach as an automated tool that takes SMT-LIB files with recursive functions over algebraic data types as input and discovers lemmas that are valid by construction. The evaluation is based on three theories within ADTs: Peano natural numbers, lists, and trees (Sect. 7). To highlight the effect of the combinatorial search space, as an example a naive enumerator would check 320K candidates over 18 list functions and 1M candidates over just 8 functions over natural numbers. When this enumerator as well as state-of-the-art tool THESY [42] would take *several hours* to cover their large but sparse search spaces, LEMMACALC consistently covers its smaller but targeted search space in a few seconds. Regarding strengths of lemmas found, there is high variability and no single approach is best. Using the method of comparison from [42] (described in Sect. 7), the proportion of lemmas generated by one method and implied by those discovered by another method ranges between ~10% to 100%.

Use and Outlook: We find that LEMMACALC is an effective and efficient method for lemma synthesis that offers a complementary alternative to enumeration-based methods. We envision that the techniques proposed here are particularly suited for larger computer formalizations, e.g. of software systems or mechanized foundations, in which user-defined theories are built on top of already-present libraries. In this scenario, enumeration may be prohibitively expensive, whereas LEMMACALC not only scales better but is well-suited to an incremental workflow.

Data Availability. The implementation of LEMMACALC, the benchmarks, the experimental setup, and instructions to repeat the evaluation are available as an artifact for Linux on Zenodo: https://doi.org/10.5281/zenodo.16932462

2   Overview

At a high-level, our approach takes a set of functions $\{f, g, \ldots\}$, performs a series of program transformations that rearrange a given computation into new synthetic functions and then relates them among each other and back to the functions originally given. The generated equational lemmas have the form

$$\textbf{fusion:} \qquad f(\overline{x}, g(\overline{y})) = fg(\overline{x}, \overline{y}) \qquad (1)$$

$$\textbf{accumulator removal:} \qquad f(\overline{x}, a) = e^?\left(f'(\overline{x}), \overline{x}', a\right) \qquad (2)$$

where f' and fg are synthetic recursive functions (i.e., fg is not just the composition of f and g), and $e^?$ is instantiated as an expression. Without loss of generality, to keep the presentation concise, we formalize fusion of g into the last parameter of f and removal of the last accumulator parameter a of f, noting that our tool of course implements the general case.

Lemmas over an original function f can be extracted by recognizing synthetic functions in three possible ways: 1) as the identity function on some argument $x_i \in \overline{x}$, 2) as being equivalent to a recursion-free expression c over a subset $\overline{x}'$ variables, $\overline{x}' \subseteq \overline{x}$, or 3) as being structurally α-equivalent to another function h after permuting its arguments (via some π). That is:

$$\textbf{replacements:} \qquad f(\overline{x}) = x_i \qquad f(\overline{x}) = c(\overline{x}') \qquad f(\overline{x}) = h(\pi(\overline{x})) \qquad (3)$$

The role of fusion and accumulator removal is thus to explore different ways to express similar computations, whereas the role of replacements is to discover correspondences that can finally be turned into lemmas.

Running Example: The list ADT is defined over [] ("nil"—base constructor) and :: ("cons"—inductive constructor). Throughout the paper, we illustrate the approach on three recursive functions over lists: ++ ("append"), and length, defined in the next two rows, respectively:

$$[] \mathbin{+\!\!+} ys := ys \qquad\qquad (x :: xs) \mathbin{+\!\!+} ys := x :: (xs \mathbin{+\!\!+} ys)$$
$$\mathsf{length}([]) := 0 \qquad\qquad \mathsf{length}(x :: xs) := \mathsf{length}(xs) + 1$$

In the rest of the section, we illustrate that it is critical to *combine* the respective transformations in LEMMACALC to leverage their full potential. Of the many lemmas discovered for this theory, we now describe how to calculate

$$\mathsf{length}(xs \mathbin{+\!\!+} ys) = \mathsf{length}(xs) + \mathsf{length}(ys) \qquad (4)$$

The first transformation, **fusion**, merges the recursive traversal in f with that of g by eliminating the intermediate data structure produced by g and consumed by f into a new synthetic function fg.

Example 1. Fusing functions $f = \mathsf{length}$ and $g = \mathbin{+\!\!+}$ e.g. by the approach of [18] or [37], calculates the following definition for synthetic function $fg = \mathsf{length}_{+\!\!+}$. Starting from the left-hand side of the desired equation, $\mathsf{length}(xs \mathbin{+\!\!+} ys)$, we discern the two cases of the definition of g,

$$\mathsf{length}_{+\!\!+}([\,],\underline{ys}) = \mathsf{length}([\,] \mathbin{+\!\!+} ys)$$
$$= \mathsf{length}(\underline{ys})$$

$$\mathsf{length}_{+\!\!+}(x :: xs, \underline{ys}) = \mathsf{length}((x :: xs) \mathbin{+\!\!+} ys) = \mathsf{length}(x :: (xs \mathbin{+\!\!+} ys))$$
$$= \mathsf{length}(xs \mathbin{+\!\!+} ys) + 1 = \mathsf{length}_{+\!\!+}(xs, \underline{ys}) + 1$$

for which $\mathsf{length}(xs \mathbin{+\!\!+} ys) = \mathsf{length}_{+\!\!+}(xs, ys)$ by construction. Note, the difference in definitions of $\mathsf{length}_{+\!\!+}$ and length is underlined: the entire base case and additional parameter ys, which is passed unchanged to the recursive call. ∎

Fusion tends to regularize the way in which computations are laid out. Complementary, **accumulator removal**, "straightens" the computations but in a different form, by relating functions with accumulators and those without them (we regard ys in Example 1 as an accumulator, too). Recall (2): removal of accumulator a in $f(\overline{x}, a)$ gives a synthetic function f' that mirrors f and an expression $e^?$ over the outputs of f', a, and $\overline{x}' \subseteq \overline{x}$. Removing accumulators is useful both for original and synthetic functions. Specifically, fused functions $fg(\_, \overline{y})$ tend to retain some of the arguments $\overline{y}$ of g as accumulators such as ys in Example 1:

Example 2. Removing accumulator ys from $\mathsf{length}_{+\!\!+}$ yields f' as $\mathsf{length}'_{+\!\!+}$

$$\mathsf{length}'_{+\!\!+}([\,]) := 0 \tag{5}$$
$$\mathsf{length}'_{+\!\!+}(x :: xs) := \mathsf{length}'_{+\!\!+}(xs) + 1$$
$$\text{so that} \quad \mathsf{length}_{+\!\!+}(xs, ys) = \mathsf{length}'_{+\!\!+}(xs) + \underline{\mathsf{length}(ys)} \tag{6}$$

where the underlined part is the base case expression from Example 1 and $e^?$ in (2) is instantiated by $+$. This solution can be found algorithmically as described in Sect. 5 by relying on neutral elements like 0 to replace base case expressions like in (5) and use the respective operator like $+$ in the solution for $e^?$. As it turns out, $\mathsf{length}'_{+\!\!+}$ is structurally equivalent to length and we can apply a corresponding **replacement** schema—here the third case in (3)—to Eq. 6 to conclude Eq. 4 as a lemma found by the approach. ∎

3   Preliminaries

In this work, we rely on a first-order, many-sorted functional specification language, which includes inductive algebraic data types (ADTs) like lists and trees. A typed n-ary function $f \colon t_1, \ldots, t_n \to t$ is presented as a

function definition $\qquad f(\overline{p}_1) := e_1 \text{ if } \varphi_1 \quad \cdots \quad f(\overline{p}_m) := e_m \text{ if } \varphi_m$

comprised of a set of m cases, each with pattern $\overline{p}_i = p_1, \ldots, p_n$, a boolean expression as guard φ_i and the right-hand side e_i, for each $0 < i \leq m$. A case is *recursive* if the right-hand side e_i or the guard φ_i contains calls to f. We call functions f and g supplied by the user *original* whereas intermediate definitions that are generated algorithmically are called *synthetic*, typically denoted with a prime (e.g. f') or pairs of names (e.g. length₊₊ used in the previous section).

Notation and Conventions. We require that all case-distinctions are expressed at the top-level using guards, i.e., explicit if-then-else and case-of expressions have been transformed away (this is always possible). This means that the grammar for expressions e and e' just consists of variables x, and the applications of function symbols f, f', and g and *constructor* symbols c and d, patterns p and q contain no defined functions, and values v are (possibly nested) constructor terms, where $\overline{v}$ can again have constructors but no variables. That is

$$\textbf{expressions} \quad e, e' := x \mid c(\overline{e}) \mid f(\overline{e}) \qquad \text{as well as}$$

$$\textbf{patterns} \quad p, q := x \mid c(\overline{p}) \quad \text{and} \qquad \textbf{values} \quad v := c(\overline{v})$$

By *free*(e) we denote the set of free variables of e. A substitution σ is a mapping from variables to expressions, writing $\sigma(e)$ for applying it to e. Oriented left-to-right, equations from the definitions as well as the lemmas discovered can be interpreted as conditional *rewrite rules*. Let Γ be a set of definitional equations and lemmas, we write $\Gamma \vdash e \rightsquigarrow e'$ if expression e can be rewritten to e' by applying a finite number of definitions and lemmas in Γ while showing that the respective side-conditions follow from Γ. Rewriting is assumed to be soundly implemented, i.e., all models of Γ validate $e = e'$.

Assumptions and Scope. We rely on the following assumptions on the original functions, which are typical for definitions in inductive theorem provers,[1] and all synthetic functions generated by our constructions will retain these properties. All functions are terminating under strict evaluation, i.e., each function f is equipped with a corresponding well-founded order $\prec_f$ that connects arguments to recursive calls, i.e., for a recursive case $f(\overline{p}) := e(\,f(\overline{e})\,)$ if φ of the definition of f satisfies $\forall \overline{x}.\ \varphi \implies \overline{e} \prec_f \overline{p}$ where $\overline{x} = \textit{free}(\overline{p})$ are the variables in scope. Constructions in this paper are justified by induction on these orders. We require that the patterns together with guards disjointly partition the entire set of possible arguments, i.e., functions are total, and the order of matching cases is irrelevant. That is, we can represent the definition as a consistent set of logical axioms and define transformations case-by-case.

The approach presented in this paper as well as our implementation assumes that there are no nested recursive calls and there are no mutually recursive definitions. We assume that there are no recursive calls in guards and that the

---

[1] Isabelle/HOL ensures these properties even if some aspects are transparent to the user, by inferring termination orders, by translating sequential pattern matches into disjoint, parallel ones, and by replacing underspecification by a constant undefined.

bodies of definitions are quantifier-free. Finally, our approach is *essentially* first-order, but we support the SMT-LIB style functional arrays as parameters to "higher-order" functions like `map`, `filter`. Lifting these limitations future is work.

Theory Exploration. The underlying idea is to generate lemmas bottom-up from a set of definitions instead of taking these from intermediate proof goals.

Definition 1 (Theory Exploration). *Given a set F of typed functions and predicates $f\colon t_1,\ldots,t_n \to t \ \in\ F$, and given a set Δ of axioms which define the functions, compute a set Λ of lemmas, so that $\Delta \models \Lambda$, i.e., each model for the F that satisfies all axioms Δ is also a model of each lemma in Λ.*

We emphasize that this definition on its own only guarantees correctness of the lemmas found, but not their utility, which may be tricky to characterize. In practice, theory exploration methods apply heuristics to filter out trivial and redundant lemmas, an aspect that becomes relevant in the evaluation.

Given function definitions, known lemmas Γ about them, and a proof oracle that semi-decides $\Gamma \vdash \varphi$, theory exploration can thus be formulated to find a valid $\varphi^?$ from a search space $\Sigma(\overline{x}, \mathtt{bool})$ of candidate formulas:

$$\textbf{theory exploration} \qquad \Gamma \vdash \varphi^? \qquad \text{where } \varphi^? \in \Sigma(\overline{x}, \mathtt{bool}) \qquad (7)$$

We can impose a certain form for $\varphi^?$ to restrict the search space. For instance, our baseline enumerator considers candidates for $f(\overline{x}, g(\overline{y})) = rhs^?$ specifically to match the shape of lemmas generated by our approach (Sect. 2) to measure its effectiveness in relation to the search space.

Baseline: Enumerative Synthesis. Given a set F of typed functions/predicates $f\colon t_1,\ldots,t_n \to t \ \in\ F$ we can define the search space $\Sigma_d(\overline{x}, t)$ of terms of type t over typed variables $\overline{x}$ up to depth d recursively. The terms of depth 0 are just the variables of matching type, whereas in the recursive case, for each function f from F we enumerate possible arguments of smaller depth.

$$\begin{aligned}
\Sigma_0(\overline{x}, t) &= \{x_i \in \overline{x} \mid x_i : t\} \\
\Sigma_d(\overline{x}, t) &= \{\, f(e_1,\ldots,e_n) \mid f\colon t_1,\ldots,t_n \to t \in F \text{ and} \\
&\qquad e_i \in \Sigma_{d_i}(\overline{x}, t_i) \text{ for } d_i < d, i = 1,\ldots,n \,\}
\end{aligned} \qquad (8)$$

Empirically, it is a good strategy to limit the number of occurrences o of each variable. For the theories considered in this paper, choosing $o = 2$ or $o = 3$ cuts down the search space significantly while still retaining all "reasonable" lemmas (i.e., those that one would use in practice, see also Sect. 7 and Apeendix C).

$$\Sigma_d^o(\overline{x}, t) = \{\, e \in \Sigma_d(\overline{x}, t) \mid \text{each } x_i \in \overline{x} \text{ occurs max. } o\text{-times in } e \,\}$$

4   Fusion

Fusion of two functions f and g aims to compute a synthetic function fg such that $f(\overline{x}, g(\overline{y})) = fg(\overline{x}, \overline{y}))$ is valid by construction. We first introduce the notion of a *fused form* that guarantees that each recursive call of f over a recursive one of g has been merged into a joint recursive call to fg. The intuition is that fused form captures when elimination of the intermediate result of g is possible.

Definition 2 (Fused Form). *An expression e is in* fused form *with respect to f and g if g does not occur nested in any argument of f anywhere in e.*

Definition 3 (Pattern Unification and Refutation). *Assuming that free variables of p are disjoint to those of e, we write $p \overset{\sigma}{\equiv} e$ when substitution σ is the most general unifier of pattern p and expression e [41, Definition 5.9]. We write $p \perp e$ when there can be no such unifier, i.e., the pattern match is "refuted".*

$$p \overset{\sigma}{\equiv} e \iff (\exists\, \sigma.\ \sigma(p) = \sigma(e)) \wedge (\forall\, \sigma'.\ \sigma'(p) = \sigma'(e) \Rightarrow \exists\, \sigma''.\ \sigma' = \sigma'' \circ \sigma)$$

$$p \perp e \iff (\forall\, \sigma.\ \sigma(p) \neq \sigma(e))$$

The fusion algorithm, Algorithm 1, is realized as an unfold/fold transformation [7]. Conceptually, it lets $fg(\overline{x}, \overline{y}) := f(\overline{x}, g(\overline{y}))$ and then transforms the right-hand side into the fused form. Algorithmically, it pairs each defining j-th case of g with each i-th case of f, by analyzing how the result returned by g via body expression e_j^g can be matched by pattern q^f of the fused argument position. The case analyses correspond to "unfolds", cf. line 3 for g and line 7 for f (we discuss the optimization in line 4 shortly). Line 9 checks whether the pairing is feasible by computing the most general unifier (cf. Definition 3) between g's result and f's pattern, and if so, adds a corresponding defining case for fg.

The main concern is that the expression e'', which is ultimately used in the definition of fg (line 11), is in the fused form wrt. f and g. To achieve this we can make use of folding that collapses joined recursive calls $f(\_, g(\_))$ into recursive fg-calls (applied in lines 4 or 11). Technically, it is realized by a *fold rule*, added to the set of known facts Γ in line 3 (we discuss its premise below).

Our presentation makes explicit the way in which fusion is intertwined with the application of definitions and facts already known by rewriting wrt. Γ. A key optimization is in line 4, which avoids unfolding f altogether when the case of g is non-recursive as in Example 1 where the base case wraps $e^g = ys$ directly by $f = \mathsf{length}$. It applies to tail-recursive cases of g, too, which are immediately folded in line 4 by the additional rule in Γ_{fg}, and when lemmas help to eliminate g altogether. In practice, this optimization crucially retains the structure needed to recognize fused functions and their derivatives in terms of original ones.

Premise $\overline{y} \prec_g p_j^g$ of the fold rule in line 3 ensures that recursive fg calls respect the termination order $\prec_g$ of g despite the rewriting steps in lines 4 and 9 (cf. Appendix B.1). In the evaluation, this premise is always satisfied.

Example 3. Algorithm 1 works analogously to the calculations in Example 1, but instead of induction on a single argument it works alongside the cases of

---

Algorithm 1: Algorithm $\textsc{Fuse}(\Gamma, f, g)$. Without loss of generality, g is fused into the last argument of f.

Input: Γ, set of definitions and known lemmas, including
$$\big\{\, f(\overline{p}_i^f, q_i^f) := e_i^f \text{ if } \varphi_i^f \,\big\}_{i=1,\ldots,m} \subseteq \Gamma \text{ and}$$
$$\big\{\, g(\overline{p}_j^g) := e_j^g \text{ if } \varphi_j^g \,\big\}_{j=1,\ldots,n} \subseteq \Gamma$$

Output: Φ with def. of fg and lemma $f(\overline{x}, g(\overline{y})) = fg(\overline{x}, \overline{y})$

$\quad$ 1 $\quad \Phi \leftarrow \{\, f(\overline{x}, g(\overline{y})) = fg(\overline{x}, \overline{y}) \,\}$

$\quad$ 2 $\quad$ **for** $j \leftarrow 1, \ldots, n$ cases in the definition of g **do** $\qquad\qquad$ <u>unfold g</u>

$\quad$ 3 $\qquad \Gamma_{fg} \leftarrow \Gamma \cup \{\, \overline{y} \prec_g p_j^g \implies f(\overline{x}, g(\overline{y})) = fg(\overline{x}, \overline{y}) \,\}$

$\quad$ 4 $\qquad$ **if** $\Gamma \vdash f(\overline{x}, e_j^g) \rightsquigarrow e'$ and e' is in fused form wrt. f and g **then** $\quad$ <u>fold fg?</u>

$\quad$ 5 $\qquad\quad \Phi \leftarrow \Phi \cup \{\, fg(\overline{x}, \overline{p}_j^g) := e' \text{ if } \varphi_j^g \,\}$

$\quad$ 6 $\qquad$ **else**

$\quad$ 7 $\qquad\quad$ **for** $i \leftarrow 1, \ldots, m$ cases of f **do** $\qquad\qquad\qquad\qquad$ <u>unfold f</u>

$\quad$ 8 $\qquad\qquad$ **assert** $\mathit{free}(\overline{p}_i^f) \cap \mathit{free}(\overline{p}_j^g) = \varnothing$ (possibly rename)

$\quad$ 9 $\qquad\qquad$ **if** $\Gamma \vdash e_j^g \rightsquigarrow e'$ and $\exists\, \sigma.\ q_i^f \overset{\sigma}{\equiv} e'$ and $\Gamma_{fg} \vdash \sigma(e_i^f) \rightsquigarrow e''$ so that e'' is

$\qquad\qquad\qquad$ in fused form wrt. f and g **then** $\qquad\qquad\qquad\qquad\qquad$ <u>fold fg?</u>

$\quad$ 10 $\qquad\qquad\quad$ **let** $\overline{p} \leftarrow \sigma(\overline{p}_i^f, \overline{p}_j^g)$ and $\varphi \leftarrow \sigma(\varphi_i^f \wedge \varphi_j^g)$

$\quad$ 11 $\qquad\qquad\quad \Phi \leftarrow \Phi \cup \{\, fg(\overline{p}) := e'' \text{ if } \varphi \,\}$

$\quad$ 12 $\qquad\qquad$ **else if** $q_i^f \perp e'$ **then**

$\quad$ 13 $\qquad\qquad\quad$ (case i of f cannot match result of case j of g)

$\quad$ 14 $\qquad\qquad\quad$ **continue**

$\quad$ 15 $\qquad\qquad$ **else**

$\quad$ 16 $\qquad\qquad\quad$ (indeterminate or blocked due to missing lemma)

$\quad$ 17 $\qquad\qquad\quad \Phi \leftarrow \varnothing$ and **fail**

---

the inner function g (here the two notions coincide). Unfolding $\mathbin{+\mkern-10mu+}$, we have one base case ($j = 1$) and one recursive case ($j = 2$), and to illustrate wrt. the above calculation we have $\overline{p}_1^g = [\,], ys$ and $\overline{p}_2^g = x :: xs, ys$.

In the base case, moreover e_1^g is ys concretely so that $f(e_1^g)$ is $\mathsf{length}(ys)$, which is already in fused form (line 4), leading to the base case of $\mathsf{length}_{+\mkern-6mu+}$ as shown above and in Example 1. Note, if we were to unfold length as well in this situation, we would instead get *two* cases, as e' being ys unifies with both patterns $[\,]$ and $x :: xs$ of length in line 9. Apart from destroying the correspondence between $\mathsf{length}_{+\mkern-6mu+}$ and length it turns that argument into a non-accumulator and thus prevents progress later on.

In the recursive case $e_2^g = x :: (xs \mathbin{+\mkern-10mu+} ys)$ and $\mathsf{length}(e_2^g) = \mathsf{length}(xs \mathbin{+\mkern-10mu+} ys) + 1$ by definition. We make use of the fold rule (line 4), which here is

$$xs \prec_{+\mkern-6mu+} (x :: xs) \implies \mathsf{length}(xs \mathbin{+\mkern-10mu+} ys) = \mathsf{length}_{+\mkern-6mu+}(xs, ys)$$

in which the premise holds so that $e'' = \mathsf{length}_{+\mkern-6mu+}(xs, ys) + 1$ in fused form becomes the right-hand side of the recursive case. $\qquad\qquad\qquad\qquad\qquad\qquad\blacksquare$

Example 7 in Appendix. A further details how Algorithm 1 relies on known lemmas from Γ to make progress in line 9 to achieve fused form.

5   Accumulator Removal

Accumulator removal aims to express $f(\overline{x}, u)$ as $e^?(f'(\overline{x}), \overline{x}', u)$ for a synthetic function f' that in comparison to f lacks accumulator u (Definition 4). Expression $e^?$ compensates for the absence of u in the computation of f', such that the definition of f' and $e^?$ must be found hand-in-hand. This $e^?$ may depend on the accumulator and the "static" subset $\overline{x}'$ of the remaining arguments (Definition 5).

To make the recursive calls in the body of a function explicit, we denote each i-th case $f(\overline{p}_i, u) := e_i$ if φ_i of f as a decomposition into a "body" expression b_i that makes k recursive calls with regular arguments e_i^j and computes the new value for the accumulator using expressions $a_i^j(u)$.

$$e_i = b_i\big(\, f\big(e_i^1, a_i^1(u)\big), \ldots, f\big(e_i^k, a_i^k(u)\big)\,\big) \tag{9}$$

Definition 4 (Accumulator). *A parameter is an accumulator of f if 1) it is matched by a variable u in each pattern, 2) it specifies the values a_i^j for the same argument position of recursive calls in recursive cases, 3) it does not occur in guards φ_i or elsewhere in any recursive body b_i (u may be used in base cases).*

Definition 5 (Static Parameter and Expressions). *A parameter is called static if it is passed by identity only, $a_i^j(u) = u$, A subexpression of a function definition is static if it depends on static parameters only.*

Static subexpressions retain their value when lifted out of the recursion to the top-level. As an example, ys of $\text{length}_{\!+\!+}$ in Sect. 2 is static.

Algorithm 2 shows our algorithm for accumulator removal. It generates f' case-by-case from the definition of f by matching its recursive structure, but by allowing different body expressions b_i'. Note patterns p_i and guards φ are kept to preserve the recursive traversal, so that arguments match the i-th case of f exactly iff they match the i-th case of f'. For that reason, the removed accumulator may not occur in guards in the first place (cf. Definition 4). The algorithm is effectively a straight-forward translation of an inductive proof of the desired lemma. Note that it is conceptually analogous to Giesl's context transformations [16], but it is formulated in a more straight-forward way.

The algorithm is presented nondeterministically here. The key first choice occurs in line 7, where a solution for critical base cases is chosen, i.e., those base cases which refer to the accumulator u, cf. $\text{length}_{\!+\!+}([\,], ys) = \text{length}(ys)$ for ys from Example 1. The heuristic we adopt is to pick b_i in $f'(p) = b_i$ to be the neutral element c of a binary function/operator $\oplus$. We shift the entire original body b_i out of the function as part of $e^?$, noting that references to static parameters xs within b_i retain their meaning over the shift. For Example 2, the correct choice is $\oplus$ as $+$ with neutral element $c = 0$ and therefore $e^?(y) =$

Algorithm 2: Algorithm $\textsc{RemoveAcc}(\Gamma, f)$, presented without loss of generality with the accumulator as the last argument of f.

Input: Γ, set of definitions and known lemmas

Input: definition of $f \colon \bar{t}, t_u \to t_r$ as $\{\, f(\bar{p}_i, u) \coloneqq e_i \text{ if } \varphi_i \,\}_{i=1,\ldots,m} \subseteq \Gamma$

Output: Φ with of the definition of f' and $f(\bar{x}, u) = e^?(f'(\bar{x}), \bar{x}', u)$

1   $\Phi \leftarrow \{\, f(\bar{x}, u) = e^?(f'(\bar{x}), \bar{x}', u) \,\}$

2   **for** $i \leftarrow 1, \ldots, n$ (cases in the definition of f) **do**

3   **let** $\bar{z} = \mathit{free}(\bar{p}_i)$ be the free variables in $\bar{p}_i$

4   **let** $\bar{x}' \colon \bar{t}'$ be the static arguments in $\bar{p}_i$

5   **let** $b_i\big(\, f(e_i^1, a_i^1(u)), \ldots, f(e_i^k, a_i^k(u)) \,\big) = e_i$ *(cf. (9))*

6   **if** $k = 0$ (base case) and $u \in \mathit{free}(b_i)$ and $\mathit{free}(b_i) \setminus u \subseteq \bar{x}'$ **then**

7   **choose** binary $\oplus$ with neutral element c from $\Gamma \vdash \forall z.\, c \oplus z = z$

8          $b_i' \leftarrow c$ and $e^?(y, \bar{x}', u) \leftarrow y \oplus b_i$

9   **else**

10   **choose** $b_i' \in \Sigma_d(\bar{z}, t_r)$ (such as b_i if $u \notin \mathit{free}(b_i)$)

11          $\mathit{lhs} \leftarrow b_i\big(\, e^?(y^1, \bar{x}', a_i^1(u)), \ldots, e^?(y^k, \bar{x}', a_i^k(u)) \,\big)$

12          $\mathit{rhs} \leftarrow e^?\big(b_i'(\, y^1, \ldots, y^k \,), \bar{x}', u\big)$

13   **if** $\mathit{not}\ \Gamma \vdash \forall\, \bar{y}, \bar{z}, u.\ \varphi_i \implies \mathit{lhs} = \mathit{rhs}$ **then**

14   **fail**

15      $\Phi \leftarrow \Phi \cup \{\, f'(p_i) \coloneqq b_i'(\, f(e_i^1), \ldots, f(e_i^k) \,) \text{ if } \varphi_i \,\}$

$y + \texttt{length}(u)$, however, our implementation tries other combinations like $\times$ and 1 and backtracks when line 14 is hit (this is the only place where we use trial and error).

The second key choice is in line 10, where we pick a body b_i' for other all other (base and recursive) cases from the search space $\Sigma_d(\bar{z}, t_r)$ of expressions of f's return type over the variable in scope $\bar{z}$ (recall its inductive definition in (8)). The condition checked in line 13 ensures that the choice is compatible with any (prior) choice of $e^?$, i.e., that $e^?$ commutes from inside recursion all the way to the top-level of the lemma to be synthesized.

Example 4. To continue Example 2 for the accumulator removal of $f = \texttt{length}_{+\!\!+}$ works with the sketch for $f' = \texttt{length}'_{+\!\!+}$

$$\texttt{length}'_{+\!\!+}([\,]) \coloneqq b_1$$

$$\texttt{length}'_{+\!\!+}(x :: xs) \coloneqq b_2(x, xs, \texttt{length}'_{+\!\!+}(xs))$$

$$\text{so that} \quad \texttt{length}_{+\!\!+}(xs, ys) = e^?(\texttt{length}'_{+\!\!+}(xs), ys)$$

and finds instances for b_1, b_2, and $e^?$ as follows.

The base-case condition $\texttt{length}(ys) = e^?(b_1', ys)$ is solved by choosing c and $\oplus$ as left-neutral element 0 of $+$, i.e., we have $\forall z.\, 0 + z = z$. For $b_i = \texttt{length}(ys)$, we therefore instantiate $b_1' = 0$ and $e^?(zs, ys) = zs + \texttt{length}(ys)$. For the recursive case, we (heuristically) preserve $b_2' = b_2 = \_ + 1$. The condition checked in line 13 is valid: $\forall m, ys.(m + \texttt{length}(ys)) + 1 = (m + 1) + \texttt{length}(ys)$.   ■

Example 5. Associativity of $+\!+$ is discovered by fusing $(xs +\!\!+ ys) +\!\!+ zs$ into a synthetic function $+\!\!+\!\!+(xs, ys, zs)$ and then by removing its last argument. The correct choices are $b_1' = c = [\,]$ as *right*-neutral element of $\oplus = +\!\!+$ and canonically $b_2' = b_2 = \_ :: \_$ as the original function body of the outer $\_ +\!\!+ zs$. ∎

Example 6 (Reversing Lists). We show how accumulator removal is key to the classic lemma $\mathsf{reverse}(\mathsf{reverse}(xs)) = xs$ in our approach

$$\mathsf{reverse}([\,]) = [\,] \qquad \mathsf{reverse}(x :: xs) = \mathsf{reverse}(xs) +\!\!+ (x :: [\,])$$

Because $\mathsf{reverse}$ has no accumulators, we start with fusion, which fails initially for $\mathsf{reverse}(\mathsf{reverse}(\_))$ as we cannot match $+\!\!+$ in the body of the inner $g = \mathsf{reverse}$ (there is no unifier nor can we refute the match). However, from fusing $+\!\!+$ into $\mathsf{reverse}$ we get:

$$\mathsf{reverse}_{+\!\!+}([\,], ys) = \mathsf{reverse}(ys)$$
$$\mathsf{reverse}_{+\!\!+}(x :: xs, ys) = \mathsf{reverse}_{+\!\!+}(xs, ys) +\!\!+ (x :: [\,])$$

This function has an accumulator that can be removed, again with $\oplus = +\!\!+$ but now with $c = [\,]$ as its *left*-neutral element, resulting in $\mathsf{reverse}(xs +\!\!+ ys) = \mathsf{reverse}(ys) +\!\!+ f'(xs)$ and it turns out that $f' \equiv \mathsf{reverse}$. This lemma unblocks fusion of $\mathsf{reverse}(\mathsf{reverse}(\_))$ via the shortcut in line 4 of Algorithm 1. The fused function $\mathsf{reverse\_reverse}$ can subsequently be recognized as the identity function after some simplifications. ∎

Another classic example is the tail-recursive function $\mathsf{qreverse}$, shown in Example 8 in Appendix A. It requires a more complex choice for b_i' in line 10 of Algorithm 2 and is not discovered by our implementation, but is in generally in reach of our approach.

6   Main Algorithm

Algorithm 3 saturates a database Γ of definitions and discovered lemmas by repeatedly applying the transformation on original as well as synthetic functions. Algorithms FUSE (cf. Section 4) and REMOVEACC (cf. Section 5) return an equation of the corresponding shape as shown above if they succeed, together with the defining equations of the respective synthetic functions.

The three steps (fusion, accumulator removal, conditional lemmas) may benefit from the accumulated set of lemmas Γ, as shown in Example 7 for fusion. Our algorithm retries failed steps as long as new information can be gained. Intermittently, the algorithm applies replacement lemmas (3) eagerly. This de-duplicates the effort and avoids vacuously fused forms (cf. Section 4). Replacement is oriented to keep original functions if possible. The final step of the algorithm is to extract useful lemmas from Γ:

$$\text{EXTRACT}(\Gamma) = \{ \; \varphi'' \mid \text{for lemma } \varphi \in \Gamma \text{ where}$$
$$\Gamma \vdash \varphi \rightsquigarrow \varphi' \text{ and } recover(\Gamma) \vdash \varphi' \rightsquigarrow \varphi''$$
$$\text{and } \varphi'' \text{ uses original functions only} \}$$

Algorithm 3: Lemma synthesis by saturation using fusion, accumulator removal, and recognition of structurally similar functions.

    Input: Set Δ of definitions of the original functions
    Output: Set Λ of lemmas discovered over Δ

1 $\Gamma \leftarrow \Delta$

2 repeat
3 $\Gamma \leftarrow \Gamma \cup \text{FUSE}(\Gamma, f, g)$ for pairs of functions f, g
4 $\Gamma \leftarrow \Gamma \cup \text{REMOVEACC}(\Gamma, f)$ for f with accumulator
5 $\Gamma \leftarrow \Gamma[f(\overline{x}) \mapsto rhs]$ for replacements $f(\overline{x}) = rhs$

6 $\Lambda \leftarrow \text{EXTRACT}(\Gamma) \setminus \Delta$

---

where $recover(\Gamma) = \{\ fg(\overline{x}, \overline{y}) = f(\overline{x}, g(\overline{y})) \mid f(\overline{x}, g(\overline{y})) = fg(\overline{x}, \overline{y}) \in \Gamma\ \}$ recovers fused functions in terms of their original sources; done in a separate step to avoid rewrite loops between the symmetric rules in Γ and $recover(\Gamma)$.

Lemma 1 (Soundness of Transformations). *Both transformations* FUSE *and* REMOVEACC *produce valid lemmas, and new synthetic functions satisfy all assumptions of Sect. 3 (the proofs are in Appendix B).*   □

Theorem 1 (Soundness of Alg *3*). *All lemmas computed are valid wrt. the original definitions* $\Delta \models \Lambda$.   □

Final Remark: As we are relying on rewriting as our main technique to apply definitions and lemmas, we briefly address the question of potentially looping rewrite rules. A general technique to detect and avoid nontermination is [11]. Alternatively, one can represent Γ as an E-graph [12,35,51], which can accommodate cyclic expressions and is therefore more robust against this issue. In our experiments, however, the only cases for rewrite loops come from lemmas produced by accumulator removal at some intermediate stages and it was sufficient to not use these lemmas as long as they still contain synthetic functions.

7   Evaluation

We implemented LEMMACALC in a fully automated tool and evaluated it on three theories within ADTs. We used the Z3 SMT solver (v4.12.4) [34] as the proof oracle to decide entailments $\Gamma \vdash \varphi$. The goal of this evaluation is to substantiate that LEMMACALC is a practical and effective procedure for theory exploration and to understand its strengths and limitations:

- **RQ1**: What is the relative explanatory strength of the sets of lemmas generated by the different methods?
- **RQ2**: What is the impact of the search space on lemma synthesis time?

Experimental Setup. We compare LemmaCalc with two alternatives:

- **Enum**: Our own enumerative generator, based on (7) in Sect. 3, which solves for $e^?$ in equational lemmas $f(\_, g(\_)) = e^?$ without preconditions
- **TheSy**, a state-of-the-art enumerative lemma generator [42] using E-graphs. TheSy in contrast to our baseline can discover conditional lemmas.

We had originally intended to compare against HipSpec [9], too, but that was not possible due to technical issues with its installation.

The baseline enumerator (Enum) is included because it provides (approximate) ground truth on the lemmas that can possibly be discovered by LemmaCalc using fusion and removal of accumulators. In our experience on the benchmarks, deeply nested lemmas are usually redundant. Thus, Enum explores a search space up to depth $d = 3$ and maximal variable occurrence $o = 2$ in (7), which is sufficient to cover all lemmas found by LemmaCalc. Solver timeout was configured to 1000ms per query for the baseline evaluator.

As the search space is huge, before proof attempts, Enum relies on a ground evaluator to exhaustively search for counterexamples to lemma candidates of a small size. It makes a large effect when false formulas are filtered out—much faster and more reliable than using Z3. To discover any non-trivial lemma, we enrich the proof oracle by an induction preprocessing step that in turn tries all potential induction variables. For example, $\forall n\colon \mathsf{nat}.\ P(n)$ is passed as $P(0) \land (\forall n\colon \mathsf{nat}.\ P(n) \implies P(n+1))$ to the proof oracle.

All methods runs multiple rounds of lemma discovery so that proofs that had failed earlier can benefit from lemmas discovered later (Examples 6 and 7).

The evaluation is based on three theories, over Peano arithmetic, and over functional lists and trees, respectively. In addition to the full theories (nat, list, and tree below), we consider eight benchmarks with a subset of functions that together make up some interesting lemmas. As shown in Table 1, a full theory gets from 5 to 18 functions, from which our baseline enumerator generates $\sim$1.5M candidates in total, of which roughly $\sim$0.01% are true lemmas only (we comment on the run times below). Some details on the benchmarks are in Appendix C. Experiments were run on a Lenovo T470 Thinkpad with 4x Intel(R) Core(TM) i5-7440HQ CPU @ 2.80GHz and 32 GB main memory.

Method of Comparison. A benchmark consists of a set of definitions Δ, from which a lemma synthesis method generates a set Λ of lemmas so that $\Delta \models \Lambda$. For **RQ1** we are interested in a comparison in terms of relative explanatory strength of these sets Λ as discussed in depth in [42].

Definition 6 (Subsumption). *For a set of lemmas Λ_A generated by one method, the subset of Λ_A that is "subsumed" by Λ_B is $\mathcal{S}(\Lambda_A, \Lambda_B) = \{\varphi \in \Lambda_A \mid \Delta, \Lambda_B \vdash \varphi\}$ where $\Gamma \vdash \varphi$ denotes that φ is provable by an oracle given facts Γ.*

The ratio $|\mathcal{S}(\Lambda_A, \Lambda_B)|/|\Lambda_A|$ can therefore be understood as a proxy for the proportion of the knowledge that can be gained from Λ_A that can also be gained from Λ_B [42]. In practice, however, the generated sets of lemmas tend to contain some trivial lemmas (e.g. that follow from Δ without induction) and some redundancies (e.g. lemmas that are implied from the others). These aspects are not adequately captured by subsumption alone. To give an example of an effect that we have observed, if method A discovers commutativity of $+$ on numbers but method B does not, then Λ_A from Definition 6 contains two equivalent lemmas $\varphi(a+b)$ and $\varphi(b+a)$ for each suitable φ, a, and b. Moreover, many of the benchmarks contain functional and predicate symbols from the background theory, e.g., $+, <, \leq, \neg$, but we do not want to count lemmas over just these as part of more complex benchmarks. Therefore, for each set of lemmas Λ generated with respect to a given Δ, where F_0 are the background functions, we define

- $\mathcal{L}(\Lambda) = \{\varphi \in \Lambda \mid F_0 \subset \mathit{funs}(\varphi)\}$ is the relevant set of lemmas generated by the tool, the remaining ones $\mathcal{B}(\Lambda) = \Lambda \setminus \mathcal{L}(\Lambda)$ are the "background" lemmas.
- $\mathcal{N}(\Lambda) = \{\varphi \in \mathcal{L}(\Lambda) \mid \Delta, \mathcal{B}(\Lambda) \nvdash \varphi\}$ is the "non-trivial" subset of the non-background lemmas. Note, we choose to exclude also those consequences that are made true by the background lemmas (such as consequences of commutativity of $+$ as discussed above).
- $\mathcal{R}(\Lambda) \subseteq \mathcal{L}(\Lambda)$ with $\Delta, \mathcal{R}(\Lambda) \vdash \mathcal{L}(\Lambda) \setminus \mathcal{R}(\Lambda)$ is a "reduced" set of lemmas after removing some redundant ones. [2]

For any benchmark, for each lemma synthesis method A, we report the cardinalities of $\mathcal{L}(\Lambda_A) \supseteq \mathcal{N}(\Lambda_A) \supseteq \mathcal{R}(\Lambda_A)$, as well as the respective subsumptions for all other methods B, namely $\mathcal{S}(\mathcal{L}(\Lambda_A), \Lambda_B) \supseteq \mathcal{S}(\mathcal{N}(\Lambda_A), \Lambda_B) \supseteq \mathcal{S}(\mathcal{R}(\Lambda_A), \Lambda_B)$. Solver timeout was configured to 100ms per query in the comparison to keep evaluation times tractable.

RQ1: What is the relative explanatory strength of the sets of lemmas generated? This comparison is shown in Fig. 1—note that the range for the y-axis varies across the benchmarks to aid readability.

As an example, on benchmark **append**, the structural method finds 9 lemmas in $\mathcal{L}$, of which 4 are redundant (i.e. just in $\mathcal{N}$ and filtered out by $\mathcal{R}$) whereas the other 5 are in the reduced set, and there are no trivial lemmas. Enumeration and THESY cover 3 of the 4 redundant and 4 resp of the 5 reduced lemmas each. Enum misses distributivity of *count* over $+\!\!+$, this lemma is part of the final "unknown" lemmas despite having a straight-forward inductive proof. We conjecture that the solver enters a matching loop due to presence of commutativity of addition and therefore times out. On the other hand, the three lemmas uniquely found by Enum are enabled due to this commutativity in the first place. Such effects are likely to be present in other benchmarks, too. THESY moreover misses associativity of $+\!\!+$ for unknown reasons.

Overall, the performance of all methods is usually in the same order of magnitude, but the specific results differ widely across the benchmarks. In absolute terms, methods based on enumeration may be seen to to outperform LEMMACALC, as represented by the relatively larger first bar in the respective column, noticeable e.g., on benchmark **length**. This is expected as they cover a much

---

[2] Note this set is not unique. In the evaluation we used a greedy incremental algorithm.

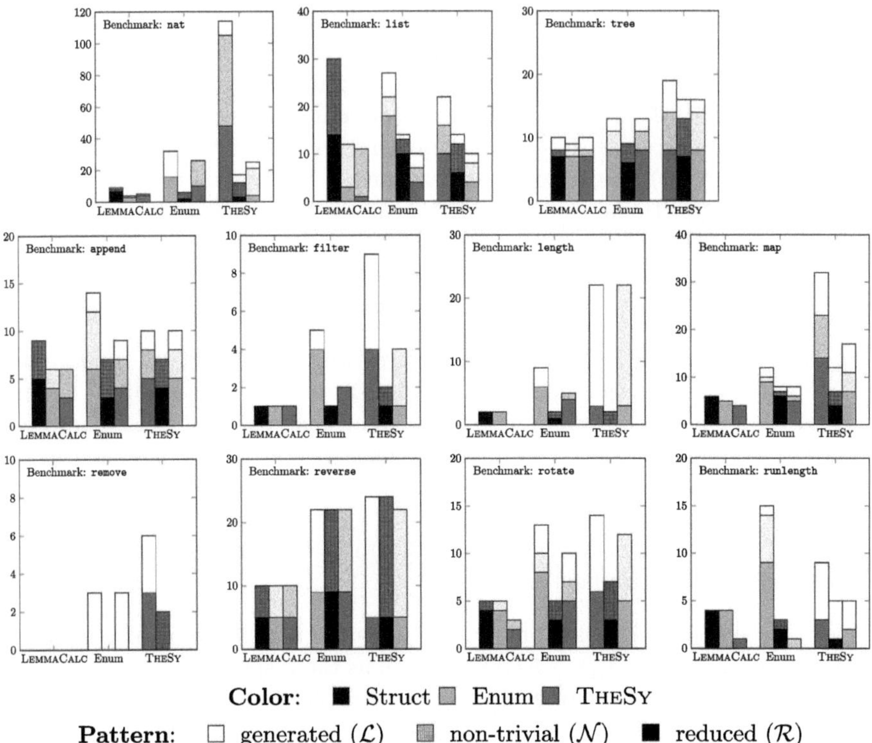

Fig. 1. Experiments for the full theories (top row) and individual benchmarks. The first bar in each group represents the number of lemmas found by the approach listed on the x-axis below (i.e., plain $\mathcal{L}$, $\mathcal{N}$, $\mathcal{R}$). The subsequent bars represent the proportion subsumed by other approaches (Definition 6), each again partitioned wrt. the classification. Four additional higher-order lemmas mentioning map(succ, _) are omitted from THESY's result in list as they were not supported by the toolchain.

larger space. However, calculational techniques can cover a significant proportion of that space, and also generate lemmas not found by the other approaches.

On benchmarks filter and remove, most resp. all interesting lemmas are conditional equations, recall that these cannot be generated by LEMMACALC and Enum. On filter, the lemmas not found by our methods are for example related to filtering twice with the same predicate (e.g., duplicate occurrence of a variable, a limitation of Algorithm 1).

On benchmarks length and reverse, our methods miss out on lemmas for the functions qlength and qreverse, which both make use of an accumulator. As described in Example 8, it requires to find a nontrivial instance for the body of the synthetic function during accumulator removal, which our current implementation does not try, but which is generally in scope of the method. On both benchmarks, THESY generates a lot of redundancy, because the functions involved can be related in many different ways (e.g., variations of Examples 1 and 2 and variants modulo properties of addition).

Regarding the full theories, benchmark `tree` is tractable for all methods, leading to similar results. Benchmark `nat` shows that the enumeration-based methods can make good use of their significantly longer running time (recall: many hours vs a few seconds for LEMMACALC). Specifically, our methods fail to produce most lemmas involving multiplication (such as distributivity wrt. addition, commutativity, associativity). Similarly, LEMMACALC does not discover commutativity of addition—the algorithmic limitation is that the critical helper lemma $m + (n + 1) = (m + n) + 1$ is not calculated (it is too specific for our fusion algorithm), and the limitation of the implementation is that it enters a rewrite loop if this lemma is assumed as an additional fact in the theory.

RQ2: What is the impact of the size of the search space? Statistics on the size of the search space are given in Table 1. It varies not only with the number of functions in the theory, but also strongly depends on how many possible combinations there are. Of the candidates generated, a few hundreds are typically valid, and about 10% of those are of interest (i.e., need induction). The relatively low number of unknowns gives an upper bound on how many results were missed—by manual inspection most of these are in fact not valid.

LEMMACALC covers these theories very quickly, taking 1 s–5 s on all benchmarks except for list, where it takes 14 s. By design, it scales more gracefully to larger theories (e.g., fusion takes square effort in the number of functions).

On the full theories, our baseline enumerator may take a significant amount of time. The exact time strongly depends on the effectiveness of the counterexample check. For example an earlier version of the implementation lacked support for conditional cases in functions, relying on the solver more heavily instead, so that run times on some benchmarks were tenfold to what is reported here. The timeout used for the solver plays an important factor, too. For example, the 1000ms per query in the experiment may be marginally better than 100ms only, and Z3 even exceeds this timeout significantly in many occasions (some queries time out after $\gg$10 s only). Therefore the numbers shown should be a rough indication only what it takes to cover the search space.

We have aborted the run of THESY after 26h resp. 21h on the `nat` and `list` benchmarks, and while THESY terminates on some benchmarks within a minute, it stalls on others, e.g., on the `remove` benchmark, it produces lemmas until 13 min and then remains unproductive for many hours without any output (similar on `map` and `runlength`). Benchmark `remove` may suggest some internal implementation issue, that may have affected THESY's performance on `list`.

Even if the run times shown are not to be taken as precise measures, it showcases that LEMMACALC in comparison to enumeration-based techniques is reliably quick, i.e., it can be incorporated into proof assistants and automated proof methods with little overhead while providing a similar benefit (cf. Figure 1).

8   Related Work

Calculational techniques for developing recursive functions go far back, notably to [7], which introduced the idea of unfold/fold transformations. An investigation of the theory of lists is provided by [2]. It already states many laws from a more general perspective. Follow-up work shows how to calculate such laws on pen and paper [3]. Program optimization using fusion-like techniques similarly have a long history [23,49] with various specialized approaches already developed, e.g., [48, 50,53]. An approach that uses known lemmas to unblock fusion is discussed as "warm-up rules" in [18]. General categorial notions that classify functions by their recursion schemes are based on a "zoo of morphisms" [24,32]. In comparison, [37] argues for a more direct approach that avoids fitting definitions into a particular shape, our algorithm in Sect. 4 is similar.

Fusion has been proposed as a building block for theorem proving before, e.g., [21,22,28]. Notably, Sonnex [45] demonstrates an effective implementation of these ideas and discusses many insights that underpin his procedure. In this work, the discovery of fold-functions—a limited form of synthesis—takes a similar role of accumulator removal in our work, in the sense that it unlocks proof steps that are out of scope of fusion. However, Sonnex does not consider theory exploration and its associated concerns in the absence of given proof goals as we do.

Accumulator transformations have been investigated in [16,27,30] with the goal of eliminating tail-recursion for ease of proof. Of these, the context manipulation techniques in [16] are very similar to our algorithm; our presentation is arguably more straight-forward and seems to encompass all four techniques mentioned. The deaccumulation technique in [17] employs a decomposition that is ultimately similar to the notion of "structured hylomorphisms" [25]. We leave it for future work to try these ideas.

Theory exploration has previously been approached by various techniques, e.g. [9,42], which utilize a conjecture generator based on testing and an induction principle enumerator. It constructs equations from a given set of functions and variables up to a certain depth, and a theorem prover is used at the backend to find the actually valid lemmas. Both approaches can be seen as instances of a more general approach called Syntax-Guided Synthesis (SyGuS) [1], that enjoys multiple applications in program verification and synthesis, [15,39,47] to name a few. A common drawback of these solutions is the exponentially-growing search space. RoughSpec [13] is an approach to overcome this problem by searching lemmas that fit particular patterns like distributivity. Another possibility to prune the search space is to rely on e-graphs [12,51], which is used by TheSy [42] and in also in Ruler [35]. FitSpec [4] represents an approach to filter redundant property-based tests, which could be applied to detect redundant conjectures.

When given a specific property to prove, theorem provers [8,26,43,46,52,54] are powered by various lemma discovery techniques that generate them by utilizing proof failures. Specifically, all of the above except [43,52] generalize a failure by replacing a common subterm by a fresh variable. AdtInd [52] instead uses syntax-guided enumeration [1] to enlarge and diversify the set of possible lemmas. Sivaraman et al. [43] uses a data-driven approach to finding lemmas: the goal itself gets an expression replaced by a hole. The synthesis specification is then formulated using input-output examples: valuations of the goal's variables are the inputs, and the valuations of the hole's original expressions are the outputs. Further data-driven approaches are [5,33] and the classic QuickCheck [44] which rely on testing only.

9   Conclusion

We have presented LEMMACALC, an approach for the synthesis of equational laws of recursive functions over algebraic data types. The approach is based on a novel combination of two program transformations. Key enabling factor is to integrate these in a procedure that chains facts discovered so far into the synthesis of subsequent lemmas. We have demonstrated that this approach to calculating lemmas is effective and efficient for many simple but non-trivial cases, and that it scales well to larger theories.

In contrast to enumeration-based methods, the lemmas generated by LEMMACALC, specifically with fusion and accumulator removal, often to match those a human engineer would specify by hand. Even though our calculations can work with intermediate synthetic functions that are not representable in the original theory, they rely on pre-existing building blocks (recursion structure, patterns, sub-expressions). This is key to taming the search space and also to limit redundancy in the discovered lemmas (cf. Section 7).

The lemmas discovered by approach in the evaluation and experiments are all good rewrite rules, i.e., we have not observed that they introduce cycles/matching loops (cf. Section 6), but we do not have a formal guarantee for this. We are not really sure yet how to define a more formal measure of utility of lemmas. Our intuition is that answering such a question leads to deep theoretical considerations such as working modulo some form of "canonicalization" (perhaps in the style of unified recursion schemes [24]), which gives a principled account of redundancy.

The approach presented is a suitable base for incorporating further transformations. While in its current form, LEMMACALC is somewhat restricted insofar that more complex lemmas than those shown in Sect. 7 are not necessarily in reach, which currently precludes us from conducting more "realistic" case studies. In the future, we want to investigate the potential of more elaborate decomposition of functions such as more principled approaches to function decomposition [17,24,25,27,30] to unlock more lemmas.

Finally, the current implementation is fairly robust but it also has some additional limitations beyond those mentioned in Sect. 3, such as not chaining on fusion with synthetic functions, not generating lemmas with duplicate variables, and not trying out more candidates during accumulator removal. Support for higher order is another feature of interest, as well as extending the approach to mutually recursive functions. Adding these involves significant additional engineering effort but it would enlarge the search space of LEMMACALC significantly, leading to larger execution times, too. As an outlook, it appears promising to combine enumeration with calculational techniques in a principled way to leverage the respective strengths.

A   Further Examples

We show two further examples, Example 7 for fusion, and Example 8 for accumulator removal.

Example 7 (Binary Trees). The data type for binary trees over type $\mathtt{Elem}$ is

$$\mathbf{data}\ \mathtt{Tree} = \mathtt{leaf} \mid \mathtt{node}(\mathtt{left} : \mathtt{Tree}, \mathtt{value} : \mathtt{Elem}, \mathtt{right} : \mathtt{Tree})$$

Function $\mathtt{elems}$ over binary trees computes a list containing its elements by pre-order traversal and function $\mathtt{size}(t)$ counts the number of nodes.

$$\mathtt{size}(\mathtt{leaf}) := 0 \qquad \mathtt{size}(\mathtt{node}(l, x, r)) := \mathtt{size}(l) + \mathtt{size}(r) + 1 \qquad (10)$$

$$\mathtt{elems}(\mathtt{leaf}) := [\,] \qquad \mathtt{elems}(\mathtt{node}(l, x, r)) := x :: (\mathtt{elems}(l) \mathbin{+\!\!+} \mathtt{elems}(r)) \qquad (11)$$

Goal is to fuse $\mathtt{length\_elems}$ with $\mathtt{length\_elems}(t) = \mathtt{length}(\mathtt{elems}(t))$, expecting that it will turn out to be equivalent to $\mathtt{size}$.

We take apart the two cases in (11) corresponding to line 2 in Alg 1. For the base case, $e_0^g = [\,]$ and $\Gamma \vdash \mathtt{length}([\,]) \rightsquigarrow 0$ in line 4 of Alg 1 by the definition of $\mathtt{length}$ that is part of Γ, so that $\mathtt{length\_elems}(\mathtt{leaf}) := 0$.

In the recursive case, $e_1^g = e' = x :: (\mathtt{elems}(l) \mathbin{+\!\!+} \mathtt{elems}(r))$. Pattern match of the base case of $\mathtt{length}$ is refuted by $[\,] \perp e'$ (line 10 of Algorithm 1). For pattern $y :: ys$ of the recursive case of $\mathtt{length}$ we get a unifier σ with $\sigma(y) = x$ and $\sigma(ys) = \mathtt{elems}(l) \mathbin{+\!\!+} \mathtt{elems}(r)$. We then look at $\sigma(\mathtt{length}(ys) + 1) = \mathtt{length}(\mathtt{elems}(l) \mathbin{+\!\!+} \mathtt{elems}(r)) + 1$. It is not possible to *immediately* apply the fold rule that collapses occurrences of $\mathtt{length}(\mathtt{elems}(\_))$ because of the intermediate occurrence of function $\mathbin{+\!\!+}$. Instead, we need lemma (4) to unblock the situation which is done by the second use of rewriting in line 9 as $\mathtt{length}(\mathtt{elems}(l) \mathbin{+\!\!+} \mathtt{elems}(r)) + 1 \rightsquigarrow e''$ with $e'' = \mathtt{length\_elems}(l)) + \mathtt{length\_elems}(r)) + 1$, which is now in fused form and can be used as the right-hand side of the case $\mathtt{length\_elems}(\mathtt{node}(l, x, r)) := \mathtt{length\_elems}(l) + \mathtt{length\_elems}(r) + 1$. This indeed gives us a definition that is equivalent to $\mathtt{size}$. From this, we can extract $\mathtt{length}(\mathtt{elems}(t)) = \mathtt{size}(t)$. $\blacksquare$

Example 8 (Reversing Lists using an Accumulator). Function $\mathtt{reverse}$ is inefficient (quadratic runtime). Function $\mathtt{qreverse}$, defined below, avoids this by introducing an accumulator us

$$\mathtt{qreverse}([\,], us) = us \qquad \mathtt{qreverse}(x :: xs, us) = \mathtt{qreverse}(xs, x :: us)$$

Algorithm REMOVEACC for the accumulator us calculates

$$\mathtt{qreverse}'([\,]) = b_1' \qquad \mathtt{qreverse}'(x :: xs) = b_2'(x, xs, \mathtt{qreverse}'(xs))$$

The solution is $b_1 = [\,]$ as right-neutral of $\mathbin{+\!\!+}$, as well as $b'_2(x, \mathit{xs}, \mathit{ys}) = \mathit{ys} \mathbin{+\!\!+} (x :: [\,])$, which produces $\mathsf{qreverse}' = \mathsf{reverse}$, i.e., removing the accomulator from $\mathsf{qreverse}$ yields again the more inefficient version so that $\mathsf{qreverse}(\mathit{xs}, \mathit{us}) = \mathsf{reverse}(\mathit{xs}) \mathbin{+\!\!+} \mathit{us}$. Note that the choice b'_2 is *not* the canonical choice, as we have $b_2(\mathit{ys}) = \mathit{ys}$ from $\mathsf{reverse}$ in line 10 of Alg 2; our implementation therefore currently misses this result. ∎

B   Soundness Proofs

We are working with typed functions $f\colon t_1, \ldots, t_n \to t$, defined by cases

$$\textbf{function definition} \qquad f(\overline{p}_1) := e_1 \text{ if } \varphi_1 \quad \cdots \quad f(\overline{p}_m) := e_m \text{ if } \varphi_m$$

Recall the assumptions placed on function definitions namely that functions terminate, and that cases match are mutually disjoint and together complete. We formalize these conditions below and prove that the synthetic functions produced by the transformations preserve these. Furthermore, we prove that all generated lemmas are valid.

Definition 7 (Termination). *A function f is terminating if and only if there is a corresponding well-founded order $\prec_f$ that connects arguments to recursive calls, i.e., for each recursive case $f(\overline{p}_i) := e_i\big(f(\overline{e})\big)$ if φ_i of the definition of f satisfies $\forall \overline{x}.\ \overline{e} \prec_f \overline{p}_i$ where $\overline{x} = \mathit{free}(\overline{p}_i)$ are the variables in scope.*

Definition 8. *Let $V_t = \{v \mid v\colon t\}$ be the carrier set of values v of type t.*

We fix a set of definitions Δ. We write $\Delta \models \varphi$ or just φ *holds* if formula φ semantically follows from Δ.

Definition 9. *Let $[\![\overline{p} \text{ if } \varphi]\!] = \{\,\overline{v} \mid \exists\, \sigma.\ \sigma(\overline{p}) = \overline{v} \wedge \Delta \models \sigma(\varphi)\,\}$ be the set of values $\overline{v}$ that match pattern $\overline{p}$ via some substitution σ so that the guard φ holds.*

Definition 10 (Pattern Disjointness). *The patterns $\overline{p}_1, \ldots, \overline{p}_m$ of function f are disjoint if $[\![\overline{p}_i \text{ if } \varphi_i]\!] \cap [\![\overline{p}_j \text{ if } \varphi_j]\!] = \varnothing$ for all $1 \le i < j < m$.*

Definition 11 (Pattern Completeness). *The patterns $\overline{p}_1, \ldots, \overline{p}_m$ of function f are complete if $V_{t_1} \times \cdots \times V_{t_n} = \bigcup_{i=1,\ldots,m} [\![\overline{p}_i \text{ if } \varphi_i]\!]$.*

We remark that the $\supseteq$ direction always holds by type-correctness, therefore it will be sufficient to demonstrate the $\subseteq$ direction.

Lemma 2. $(A_1 \cap A_2) \times (B_1 \cap B_2) = (A_1 \times B_1) \cap (A_2 \times B_2)$.

Lemma 3. *For $A_1 \subseteq A_2$ and $B_1 \subseteq B_2$ we have $A_2 \cap B_2 = \varnothing \implies A_1 \cap B_1 = \varnothing$.*

Lemma 4. *If $\mathit{free}(\varphi) \subseteq \mathit{free}(\overline{p})$ and $\mathit{free}(\psi) \subseteq \mathit{free}(\overline{q})$ then matches of p, q over disjoint variables $\mathit{free}(p) \cap \mathit{free}(q) = \varnothing$ can be split into a cross-product for the individual matches $[\![\overline{p}, \overline{q} \text{ if } \varphi \wedge \psi]\!] = [\![\overline{p} \text{ if } \varphi]\!] \times [\![\overline{q} \text{ if } \psi]\!]$.*

Lemma 5. *Substitution narrows down pattern matches* $[\![\sigma(p) \ \texttt{if} \ \sigma(\varphi)]\!] \subseteq [\![p \ \texttt{if} \ \varphi]\!]$.

Lemma 6 (f-Induction). *With a well-founded order $\prec_f$ of a terminating function $f\colon \overline{t} \to t$ that satisfies Def 11 we can prove any property $P(\overline{z})$ over $\overline{z}\colon \overline{t}$ by induction:* [3]

$$\left(\bigwedge_{i=1,\ldots,m} \forall \ \overline{x}. \ P(\overline{e}) \wedge \varphi_i \implies P(\overline{p}_i) \right) \implies \left(\forall \ \overline{z}. \ P(\overline{z}) \right)$$

B.1   Properties of FUSE (Algorithm 1 in Sect. 4)

Lemma 7 (Termination of fg). *All recursive fg calls are introduced by a fold rule $\overline{y} \prec_g p_j^g \implies f(\overline{x}, g(\overline{y})) = fg(\overline{x}, \overline{y})$ (line 3). Therefore, $\prec_{fg} = \prec_g$ witnesses termination of fg.* $\square$

Lemma 8 (Pattern Disjointness of fg). *We prove disjointness of two cases $(i,j) \neq (i',j')$ both generated by line 9, the other combinations wrt. line 4 are analogous. If $i \neq i'$, then from pattern disjointness of f*

$$[\![\overline{p}_i^f \,\texttt{if}\, \varphi_i^f]\!] \cap [\![\overline{p}_{i'}^f \,\texttt{if}\, \varphi_{i'}^f]\!] = \varnothing$$

$$\overset{\varnothing \times A = \varnothing}{\implies}$$

$$([\![\overline{p}_i^f \,\texttt{if}\, \varphi_i^f]\!] \cap [\![\overline{p}_{i'}^f \,\texttt{if}\, \varphi_{i'}^f]\!]) \times ([\![\overline{p}_j^g \,\texttt{if}\, \varphi_{j'}^g]\!] \cap [\![\overline{p}_j^g \,\texttt{if}\, \varphi_{j'}^g]\!]) = \varnothing$$

$$\overset{\text{Lemma } 2}{\iff}$$

$$([\![\overline{p}_i^f \,\texttt{if}\, \varphi_i^f]\!] \times [\![\overline{p}_j^g \,\texttt{if}\, \varphi_{j'}^g]\!]) \cap ([\![\overline{p}_{i'}^f \,\texttt{if}\, \varphi_{i'}^f]\!] \times [\![\overline{p}_j^g \,\texttt{if}\, \varphi_{j'}^g]\!]) = \varnothing$$

$$\overset{\text{Lemma } 4}{\iff}$$

$$[\![\overline{p}_i^f, \overline{p}_j^g \ \texttt{if} \ \varphi_i^f \wedge \varphi_j^g]\!] \cap [\![\overline{p}_{i'}^f, \overline{p}_{j'}^g \ \texttt{if} \ \varphi_{i'}^f \wedge \varphi_{j'}^g]\!] = \varnothing$$

$$\overset{\text{Lemmas } 3 \text{ and } 5}{\implies}$$

$$[\![\sigma(\overline{p}_i^f, \overline{p}_j^g) \ \texttt{if} \ \sigma(\varphi_i^f \wedge \varphi_j^g)]\!] \cap [\![\sigma(\overline{p}_{i'}^f, \overline{p}_{j'}^g) \ \texttt{if} \ \sigma(\varphi_{i'}^f \wedge \varphi_{j'}^g)]\!] = \varnothing$$

The argument for $i = i'$ and $j \neq j'$ is analogous via pattern disjointness of g. $\square$

Lemma 9. *If $e = e'$ and $v = \sigma(e)$ then $v = \sigma(e')$.*

Proof. Congruence of substitution with respect to semantic equality $e = e'$.

Lemma 10 (Pattern Completeness of fg). *Let $g\colon \overline{t}^g \to t$ and $f\colon \overline{t}^f, t_g \to t'$, and assume that fusion successfully computed a definition of fg. We prove pattern completeness of fg.*

---

[3] (`induction` $\overline{z}$ `rule:` f.`induct`) in Isabelle/HOL.

Proof in the light of the remark below Definition 11 it suffices that each arbitrary $\overline{v} \in V_{\overline{t}^f}$ and $\overline{w} \in V_{\overline{t}^g}$ is covered by some case in set Δ returned by Algorithm 1.

By pattern completeness of g, there is a case j of g with $\overline{w} \in [\![\overline{p}_j^g \text{ if } \varphi_j^g]\!]$, and by Definition 9 there is a substitution τ^g over $free(\overline{p}_j^g)$ with

$$\tau^g(\overline{p}_j^g) = \overline{w} \quad \text{and} \quad \tau^g(\varphi_j^g) \text{ holds} \tag{12}$$

If case j of g can be processed by line 4, we have $[\![\overline{x}, \overline{p}_j^g \text{ if } \varphi_j^g]\!] = V_{\overline{t}^f} \times [\![\overline{p}_j^g \text{ if } \varphi_j^g]\!]$. Otherwise, by pattern completeness of f, there is a case i of f that matches the result e_j^g of g instantiated with τ^g, i.e., $\overline{v}, \tau^g(e_j^g) \in [\![\overline{p}_i^f, q^f \text{ if } \varphi_i]\!]$ and by Definition 9 there is a substitution τ^f over $free(\overline{p}_j^f, q^f)$ with

$$\tau^f(\overline{p}_i^f, q_i^f) = \overline{v}, \tau^g(e_j^g) \quad \text{and} \quad \tau^f(\varphi_i^f) \text{ holds} \tag{13}$$

Note, τ^f and τ^g are over disjoint variables by the condition in line 8 of Algorithm 1. Therefore, we can freely switch between $\tau = (\tau^f \cup \tau^g)$ and the more specific substitutions for expressions over variables of either f or g exclusively. In particular both (12) and (13) hold for τ, too, and we have $\tau(q_i^f) = \tau(e_j^g)$.

At this point we have to justify that we actually satisfy the test in line 9, but it is the only possibility: Having a unifier τ contradicts the test for refutation in line 12 and having fused fg successfully in the first place rules out line 16. Therefore, there exists the consituents of line 9, in particular e' with $e' = e_j^g$ (by soundness of rewriting) and the most general unifier σ. Definition 3 splits $\tau = \tau' \circ \sigma$ for some τ', which can be partitioned into the respective sets of variables again, so that $\tau^f = \tau_f' \circ \sigma$ and so that $\tau^g = \tau_g' \circ \sigma$.

It remains to be shown that $\overline{v}, \overline{w} \in [\![\overline{p} \text{ if } \varphi]\!]$ for $\overline{p}$ and φ constructed by line 10. The substitution that witnesses Definition 9 is given as τ':

$$\begin{aligned}
\tau'(\overline{p}) &= \tau'(\sigma(\overline{p}_i^f, \overline{p}_j^g)) \\
&= \tau'(\sigma(\overline{p}_i^f)), \tau'(\sigma(\overline{p}_j^g)) \\
&= \tau_f'(\sigma(\overline{p}_i^f)), \tau_g'(\sigma(\overline{p}_j^g)) = \overline{v}, \overline{w}
\end{aligned}$$

The reasoning for the guard is analogous.

Lemma 11. *Fusion lemma $fg(\overline{x}, \overline{y}) = f(\overline{x}, g(\overline{y}))$ holds.*

Proof. By induction over $\prec_{fg}$ (cf. Lemma 6 via Lemma 7) and by taking apart the definitional cases of fg. Note that we may assume the respective guard of fg. By equational reasoning and assuming φ_j^g, for line 4 we have

$$fg(\overline{x}, \overline{p}_j^g) \overset{\text{def. } fg}{=} e' \overset{\Gamma_{fg} \text{ valid}}{=} f(\overline{x}, e_j^g) \overset{\text{def. } g}{=} f(\overline{x}, g(\overline{p}_j^g))$$

For line 9, assuming $\sigma(\varphi_i^f \wedge \varphi_j^g)$ we have

$$\begin{aligned}
fg(\sigma(\overline{p}_i^f, \overline{p}_j^g)) &\overset{\text{def. } fg}{=} e' \overset{\Gamma_{fg} \text{ valid}}{=} \sigma(e_i^f) \\
&\overset{\text{def. } f}{=} f(\sigma(\overline{p}_i^f), \sigma(q_i^f)) \overset{\text{def. } 3}{=} f(\sigma(\overline{p}_i^f), e') \\
&\overset{\Gamma \text{ valid}}{=} f(\sigma(\overline{p}_i^f), e_j^g) \overset{\text{def. } g}{=} f(\sigma(\overline{p}_i^f), g(\sigma(\overline{p}_j^g)))
\end{aligned}$$

Steps justified by validity of Γ rely on rewriting to produce valid equations because Γ contains definitions and valid lemmas only. Γ_{fg} is valid, because its additional rule is just the inductive hypothesis. The step marked Definition 3 holds because unification produces syntactically identical expressions. Steps by the respective definitions of f and g specialize the respective pattern variables, and of course one has to ensure that the respective guard follows from that of fg.

B.2   Properties of REMOVEACC (Algorithm 2 in Sect. 5)

Lemma 12 (Termination). *f' terminates by the well-founded order $\prec_{f'}$ defined as the least fixpoint of the set of implications over all i, j, where i indexes defining cases and j indexes recursive calls of that case*

$$\forall\ \overline{x}.\ \left(\forall\ u.\ \overline{e}, a_i^j(u) \prec_{f'} \overline{p}_i, u\right) \implies \overline{e} \prec_{f'} \overline{p}_i$$

Proof where $\overline{x} = \mathit{free}(\overline{p}_i)$. Since $\prec_{f'}$ is a least fixpoint, it is well-founded. It remains to show that it covers all recursive calls in f', which is apparent from the construction.

Lemma 13 (Pattern Completeness and Disjointness). *Because the accumulator $u\colon t_u$ is always matched as a variable and because it cannot occur in guards φ_i we have $[\![\overline{p}_i, u\ \text{if}\ \varphi_i]\!] = [\![\overline{p}_i\ \text{if}\ \varphi_i]\!] \times V_{t_u}$ from Lemmas 2 and 4.*   □

Lemma 14. *Lemma $f(\overline{x}, u) = e^?(f'(\overline{x}), \overline{x}', u)$ holds.*

Proof. By f-induction over $\prec_f$ (cf: Lemma 6). The base case follows from the condition in line 7. Instantiating the condition in line 13 with $\overline{y} = f(y^1), \ldots, f(y^k)$ proves the correspondence in the recursive case by the inductive hypothesis.

C   Benchmarks

The additional functions present in the respective benchmarks are listed below:

- `append`: `add, snoc, ++, length, count`
- `filter`: `not, length, filter, all, ex, countif`
- `length`: `length, length°, qlength`(tail-recursive)
- `map`: `leq, lt, length, map, take, drop`
- `remove`: `not, add, sub, length, contains, remove, count`
- `reverse`: `reverse, reverse°, qreverse`(tail-recursive)
- `rotate`: `leq, add, append, length, reverse, rotate`
- `runlength`: `add, mul, ++, sum, sumruns, decode, is_runs`

Function `not` is the logical negation. Functions/predicates `add, sub, mul, leq, lt` are structurally recursive definitions over natural numbers for $+, -, *, \leq,$ and $<$. Function `filter` keeps elements that satisfy a given predicate, `countif` counts them, and `all`/`ex` test if all/some element satisfies a given predicate. Function `rotate` reverses a prefix of a given list. Benchmark `runlength` implements the decoder for a sequence of runs, given as a pair of lists that record elements resp. the number of their occurrence in a run. [4] A critical lemma connects `sum` over the decoded sequence to `sumruns` that works on the coded one.

---

[4] https://en.wikipedia.org/wiki/Run-length_encoding.

Table 1. Statistics on benchmark theories used in the comparison. Here $|F|$ is the number of functions. The number of candidates is $\Sigma_{f(\overline{x},g(\overline{y}))}|S_3^2(\overline{x},\overline{y},t_f)|$, where t_f is the respective result type of f, i.e., potential right-hand sides to equations (7) of depth $d = 3$ and max $o = 2$ occurrences of each variable. true: proved by Z3 from axioms/prior lemmas, $|\Lambda|$: lemmas proved by induction+Z3 (i.e., including background lemmas), **?**: candidates with unknown status. Time is shown in hours:minutes:seconds. For THESY, we report the time of the last lemma found. For those benchmarks on which the tool did not terminate, we give a rough indication when it was cancelled. Note, except for nat, THESY stopped reporting lemmas long before. †: Interrupted during the second round of lemma checking when the backend solver got stuck without honoring the timeout per query. **In comparison, LEMMACALC takes 14 s on list and 1 s–5 s on all other benchmarks.**

benchmark	$|F|$	baseline enumerator statistics					THESY	
		candidates	true	$|\Lambda|$	?	time	last	killed
nat	8	1 131 799	501	32	1759	6:50:00	26:38:14	>26h
list	18	319 019	408	32	522	1:48:22	10:55:14	>21h
tree	11	123 178	130	20	38	11:25	16:47	
append	5	15 058	133	22	5	02:03	04:32	
filter	6	398	2	5	16	02:11	00:02	
length	5	7 066	558	12	1	01:59	00:00	
map	8	34 726	103	13	35	07:18	37:33	>11h
remove	7	32 302	117	14	13	22:11	13:01	>11h
reverse	4	127 926	427	22	1	03:29	00:02	
rotate	6	12 784	124	20	43	08:50	6:54:22	>11h
runlength	7	68 311	182	23	847	†1:12:12	00:40	>11h

References

1. Alur, R., et al.: Syntax-Guided Synthesis. In: FMCAD, pp. 1–17. IEEE (2013)
2. Bird, R.S.: An introduction to the theory of lists. Springer (1987)
3. Bird, R.S.: Algebraic identities for program calculation. Comput. J. **32**(2), 122–126 (1989)
4. Braquehais, R., Runciman, C.: FitSpec: refining property sets for functional testing. In: Proceedings of the 9th International Symposium on Haskell, pp. 1–12 (2016)
5. Braquehais, R., Runciman, C.: Speculate: discovering conditional equations and inequalities about black-box functions by reasoning from test results. In: Proceedings of the 10th ACM SIGPLAN International Symposium on Haskell, pp. 40–51 (2017)
6. Bundy, A., Stevens, A., van Harmelen, F., Ireland, A., Smaill, A.: Rippling: a heuristic for guiding inductive proofs. Artif. Intell. **62**(2), 185–253 (1993)
7. Burstall, R.M., Darlington, J.: A transformation system for developing recursive programs. J. ACM (JACM) **24**(1), 44–67 (1977)
8. Chamarthi, H.R., Dillinger, P., Manolios, P., Vroon, D.: The ACL2 sedan theorem proving system. In: TACAS, pp. 291–295. LNCS, Springer (2011)
9. Claessen, K., Johansson, M., Rosén, D., Smallbone, N.: Automating inductive proofs using theory exploration. In: Bonacina, M.P. (ed.) CADE 2013. LNCS

(LNAI), vol. 7898, pp. 392–406. Springer, Heidelberg (2013). https://doi.org/10.1007/978-3-642-38574-2_27

10. De Angelis, E., Fioravanti, F., Pettorossi, A., Proietti, M.: Removing algebraic data types from constrained horn clauses using difference predicates. In: Peltier, N., Sofronie-Stokkermans, V. (eds.) IJCAR 2020. LNCS (LNAI), vol. 12166, pp. 83–102. Springer, Cham (2020). https://doi.org/10.1007/978-3-030-51074-9_6

11. Dershowitz, N., Jouannaud, J.P.: Rewrite systems. In: Formal models and semantics, pp. 243–320. Elsevier (1990)

12. Detlefs, D., Nelson, G., Saxe, J.B.: Simplify: a theorem prover for program checking. J. ACM **52**(3), 365–473 (2005). https://doi.org/10.1145/1066100.1066102

13. Einarsdóttir, S.H., Smallbone, N., Johansson, M.: Template-based theory exploration: discovering properties of functional programs by testing. In: Proceedings of the 32nd Symposium on Implementation and Application of Functional Languages, pp. 67–78 (2020)

14. Fedyukovich, G., Ernst, G.: Bridging arrays and ADTs in recursive proofs. In: Groote, J.F., Larsen, K.G. (eds.) Tools and Algorithms for the Construction and Analysis of Systems - 27th International Conference, TACAS 2021, Held as Part of the European Joint Conferences on Theory and Practice of Software, ETAPS 2021, Luxembourg City, Luxembourg, March 27 - April 1, 2021, Proceedings, Part II. Lecture Notes in Computer Science, vol. 12652, pp. 24–42. Springer (2021). https://doi.org/10.1007/978-3-030-72013-1_2

15. Fedyukovich, G., Kaufman, S., Bodík, R.: Sampling invariants from frequency distributions. In: FMCAD, pp. 100–107. IEEE (2017)

16. Giesl, J.: Context-moving transformations for function verification. In: LOPSTR, pp. 293–312. Springer (1999)

17. Giesl, J., Kühnemann, A., Voigtländer, J.: Deaccumulation techniques for improving provability. J. Logic Algebraic Program. **71**(2), 79–113 (2007)

18. Gill, A., Launchbury, J., Peyton Jones, S.L.: A short cut to deforestation. In: Proceedings of the Conference on Functional Programming Languages and Computer Architecture, pp. 223–232 (1993)

19. Govind, H., Shoham, S., Gurfinkel, A.: Solving constrained horn clauses modulo algebraic data types and recursive functions. Proc. ACM Program. Lang. **6**(POPL), 1–29 (2022). https://doi.org/10.1145/3498722

20. Hajdú, M., Hozzová, P., Kovács, L., Voronkov, A.: Induction with recursive definitions in superposition. In: FMCAD, pp. 1–10. IEEE (2021)

21. Hamilton, G.W.: Poítin: distilling theorems from conjectures. Electron. Notes Theor. Comput. Sci. **151**(1), 143–160 (2006)

22. Hamilton, G.W.: Distillation: extracting the essence of programs. In: Proceedings of the 2007 ACM SIGPLAN Symposium on Partial Evaluation and Semantics-based Program Manipulation, pp. 61–70 (2007)

23. Hinze, R., Harper, T., James, D.W.: Theory and practice of fusion. In: Symposium on Implementation and Application of Functional Languages, pp. 19–37. Springer (2010)

24. Hinze, R., Wu, N., Gibbons, J.: Unifying structured recursion schemes. ACM SIGPLAN Notices **48**(9), 209–220 (2013)

25. Hu, Z., Iwasaki, H., Takeichi, M.: Deriving structural hylomorphisms from recursive definitions. ACM Sigplan Notices **31**(6), 73–82 (1996)

26. Johansson, M., Dixon, L., Bundy, A.: Case-analysis for rippling and inductive proof. In: Kaufmann, M., Paulson, L.C. (eds.) Interactive Theorem Proving, pp. 291–306. Springer, Berlin, Heidelberg (2010). https://doi.org/10.1007/978-3-642-14052-5_21

27. Kapur, D., Subramaniam, M.: Automatic generation of simple lemmas from recursive definitions using decision procedures–preliminary report. In: Advances in Computing Science–ASIAN 2003. Progamming Languages and Distributed Computation Programming Languages and Distributed Computation: 8th Asian Computing Science Conference, Mumbai, India, December 10-12, 2003. Proceedings 8, pp. 125–145. Springer (2003)

28. Klyuchnikov, I.G., Romanenko, S.A.: Proving the equivalence of higher-order terms by means of supercompilation. In: Ershov Memorial Conference, pp. 193–205. Springer (2009)

29. Kostyukov, Y., Mordvinov, D., Fedyukovich, G.: Beyond the elementary representations of program invariants over algebraic data types. In: PLDI, pp. 451–465 (2021)

30. Kühnemann, A., Glück, R., Kakehi, K.: Relating accumulative and non-accumulative functional programs. In: RTA, vol. 1, pp. 154–168. Springer (2001)

31. Leino, K.R.M.: Dafny: an automatic program verifier for functional correctness. In: Clarke, E.M., Voronkov, A. (eds.) LPAR 2010. LNCS (LNAI), vol. 6355, pp. 348–370. Springer, Heidelberg (2010). https://doi.org/10.1007/978-3-642-17511-4_20

32. Meijer, E., Fokkinga, M.M., Paterson, R.: Functional programming with bananas, lenses, envelopes and barbed wire. In: FPCA, vol. 91, pp. 124–144 (1991)

33. Miltner, A., Padhi, S., Millstein, T., Walker, D.: Data-driven inference of representation invariants. In: PLDI, pp. 1–15 (2020)

34. de Moura, L., Bjørner, N.: Z3: an efficient SMT solver. In: Ramakrishnan, C.R., Rehof, J. (eds.) TACAS 2008. LNCS, vol. 4963, pp. 337–340. Springer, Heidelberg (2008). https://doi.org/10.1007/978-3-540-78800-3_24

35. Nandi, C., et al.: Rewrite rule inference using equality saturation. In: Proceedings of the ACM on Programming Languages vol. 5(OOPSLA), pp. 1–28 (2021)

36. Nipkow, T., Paulson, L.C., Wenzel, M.: Isabelle/HOL: a proof assistant for higher-order logic. Springer (2002)

37. Ohori, A., Sasano, I.: Lightweight fusion by fixed point promotion. ACM SIGPLAN Notices **42**(1), 143–154 (2007)

38. Pham, T., Gacek, A., Whalen, M.W.: Reasoning about algebraic data types with abstractions. J. Autom. Reason. **57**(4), 281–318 (2016)

39. Reynolds, A., Barbosa, H., Nötzli, A., Barrett, C., Tinelli, C.: CVC4SY: smart and fast term enumeration for syntax-guided synthesis. In: Dillig, I., Tasiran, S. (eds.) CAV 2019. LNCS, vol. 11562, pp. 74–83. Springer, Cham (2019). https://doi.org/10.1007/978-3-030-25543-5_5

40. Reynolds, A., Kuncak, V.: Induction for SMT solvers. In: D'Souza, D., Lal, A., Larsen, K.G. (eds.) VMCAI 2015. LNCS, vol. 8931, pp. 80–98. Springer, Heidelberg (2015). https://doi.org/10.1007/978-3-662-46081-8_5

41. Robinson, J.A.: A machine-oriented logic based on the resolution principle. J. ACM (JACM) **12**(1), 23–41 (1965)

42. Singher, E., Itzhaky, S.: Theory exploration powered by deductive synthesis. In: Silva, A., Leino, K.R.M. (eds.) CAV 2021. LNCS, vol. 12760, pp. 125–148. Springer, Cham (2021). https://doi.org/10.1007/978-3-030-81688-9_6

43. Sivaraman, A., Sanchez-Stern, A., Chen, B., Lerner, S., Millstein, T.D.: Data-driven lemma synthesis for interactive proofs. Proc. ACM Program. Lang. **6**(OOPSLA2), 505–531 (2022)

44. Smallbone, N., Johansson, M., Claessen, K., Algehed, M.: Quick specifications for the busy programmer. J. Funct. Program. **27**, e18 (2017)

45. Sonnex, W.: Fixed point promotion: taking the induction out of automated induction. University of Cambridge, Computer Laboratory, Tech. rep. (2017)
46. Sonnex, W., Drossopoulou, S., Eisenbach, S.: Zeno: an automated prover for properties of recursive data structures. In: Flanagan, C., König, B. (eds.) TACAS 2012. LNCS, vol. 7214, pp. 407–421. Springer, Heidelberg (2012). https://doi.org/10.1007/978-3-642-28756-5_28
47. Srivastava, S., Gulwani, S.: Program verification using templates over predicate abstraction. In: PLDI, pp. 223–234. ACM (2009)
48. Takano, A., Meijer, E.: Shortcut deforestation in calculational form. In: Proceedings of the Seventh International Conference on Functional Programming Languages and Computer Architecture, pp. 306–313 (1995)
49. Turchin, V.F.: The concept of a supercompiler. ACM Trans. Program. Lang. Syst. (TOPLAS) **8**(3), 292–325 (1986)
50. Wadler, P.: Deforestation: transforming programs to eliminate trees. In: Ganzinger, H. (ed.) ESOP 1988. LNCS, vol. 300, pp. 344–358. Springer, Heidelberg (1988). https://doi.org/10.1007/3-540-19027-9_23
51. Willsey, M., Nandi, C., Wang, Y.R., Flatt, O., Tatlock, Z., Panchekha, P.: EGG: fast and extensible equality saturation. In: Proceedings of the ACM on Programming Languages, vol. 5(POPL), pp. 1–29 (2021)
52. Yang, W., Fedyukovich, G., Gupta, A.: Lemma synthesis for automating induction over algebraic data types. In: Schiex, T., de Givry, S. (eds.) CP 2019. LNCS, vol. 11802, pp. 600–617. Springer, Cham (2019). https://doi.org/10.1007/978-3-030-30048-7_35
53. Yokoyama, T., Hu, Z., Takeichi, M.: Calculation rules for warming-up in fusion transformation. In: the 2005 Symposium on Trends in Functional Programming, TFP 2005, Tallinn, Estonia, pp. 399–412. Citeseer (2005)
54. Zavalía, L., Chernigovskaia, L., Fedyukovich, G.: Solving constrained horn clauses over algebraic data types. In: Dragoi, C., Emmi, M., Wang, J. (eds.) Verification, Model Checking, and Abstract Interpretation - 24th International Conference, VMCAI 2023, Boston, MA, USA, January 16-17, 2023, Proceedings. Lecture Notes in Computer Science, vol. 13881, pp. 341–365. Springer (2023). https://doi.org/10.1007/978-3-031-24950-1_16

Auto-Generating Visual Editors
for Formal Logics with Blockly

Angelo Ferrando[1(✉)] [iD], Peng Lu[1], and Vadim Malvone[2] [iD]

[1] University of Modena and Reggio Emilia, Modena, Italy
angelo.ferrando@unimore.it
[2] Télécom Paris, Institut Polytechnique de Paris, Palaiseau, France
vadim.malvone@telecom-paris.fr

Abstract. Formal logics are central to the specification and verification of computational systems, yet their adoption outside highly specialised domains is hindered by steep learning curves and error-prone textual notations. Making these notations more approachable is particularly important in education and in settings where non-expert stakeholders need to engage with formal reasoning. We present a framework that automatically generates block-based visual editors for formal logics using the Blockly library. From a structured JSON specification of syntax and composition rules, our tool produces browser-based editors in which formulas are constructed by combining graphical blocks rather than writing code. This approach lowers syntactic barriers for learners and non-experts, while allowing experts to define new logics without manual interface design. Although integration with verification backends is planned, the tool already provides a reusable foundation for accessible and customisable logic editors.

Keywords: Logic Editor Generation · Block-Based Specification · Blockly

1 Introduction

Formal logics are key to specifying and verifying computational systems, particularly for modelling safety-critical properties and concurrency [19]. In highly regulated domains such as railways, avionics, and automotive, formal methods are already entrenched, supported by training pipelines that prepare domain experts to handle complex notations. However, outside of such contexts, their accessibility remains a barrier: mainstream software engineers, students, and non-expert stakeholders often struggle with precise syntax and abstract semantics [5]. This is particularly evident in educational settings, where empirical studies have shown that students may find formal notations intimidating and error-prone [12]. In these cases, visual representations and block-based metaphors can lower the entry barrier, offering a gentler on-ramp to logical reasoning without compromising formal rigor.

F. Damiani and M. Farrell (Eds.): iFM 2025, LNCS 16194, pp. 451–459, 2026.
https://doi.org/10.1007/978-3-032-10794-7_22

This gap is especially problematic in domains like software engineering and multi-agent systems, where correctness is critical but tooling is often inaccessible. Despite advances in verification backends, front-end logic specification remains mostly unchanged: users still write formulas in textual syntaxes that are error-prone and hard to learn—especially for non-experts [4].

Visual representations have been explored to improve usability [9], but existing tools are often domain-specific and not generalisable. Beyond logic-specific editors, our work connects to the broader tradition of visual programming languages, such as Scratch and Snap! [10], which demonstrate how block-based metaphors can improve accessibility and learning.

We address this challenge with a logic-agnostic framework for the automatic generation of block-based visual editors for formal logics. Built on the Blockly library [17], our system allows users to construct formulas by composing graphical blocks. Formal methods experts provide a structured JSON [3] specification of the logic's syntax; from this, the framework automatically generates a browser-based visual editor with drag-and-drop blocks, syntactic constraints, and code generation.

This approach offers three main benefits: it decouples logic definition from UI implementation, enables accessible formula construction for non-experts, and supports reuse across different logics, from standard temporal systems to domain-specific languages.

In this paper, we detail the framework's design, architecture, and implementation. We show how logic specifications are expressed in JSON, how the generation pipeline produces Blockly-compatible editors, and how the result enables constraint-aware formula construction. A case study on Alternating-time Temporal Logic (ATL) [1] demonstrates the flexibility of our approach.

Our broader vision is to lower the entry barrier to formal methods by providing customisable, accessible tools for logic specification and analysis. While this work focuses on editor generation, it sets the stage for future integration with verification pipelines—empowering a wider range of users to engage with formal techniques.

2   The Approach

Our framework generates visual editors for formal logics from structured specifications authored by experts. While the specification is expressed in JSON—which is itself a form of structured coding—it is lightweight compared to implementing a visual editor by hand, and requires no knowledge of Blockly or front-end programming. The effort resembles writing a formal grammar or BNF description rather than programming a tool, making it accessible to logic experts familiar with syntactic definitions.

Figure 1 shows the architecture: a structured logic specification feeds into a generator that produces Blockly-compatible artifacts, which power a browser-based editor where non-experts can build valid formulas interactively.

To ensure generality and logic-agnosticism, our design follows three core principles: (i) logic specifications are written in structured text, without requiring

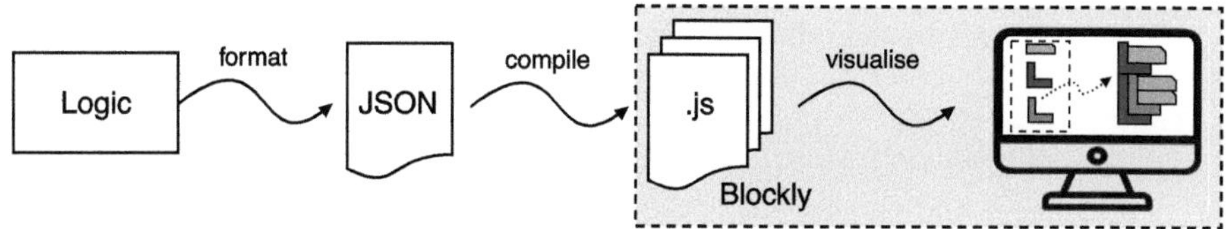

Fig. 1. Overview of the architecture highlighting the automatic translation from logic specifications to visual editors. Automatically generated artifacts are shaded.

visual programming knowledge; (ii) visual editors are generated fully automatically, with no manual or Blockly-specific steps; and (iii) the system is modular, allowing updates or new logics via specification changes alone.

We illustrate our approach using a fragment of Linear Temporal Logic (LTL) [18] as a running example. Our specification language is a structured JSON format that defines logic syntax through *constructs*. Each construct is either a *primitive* (e.g., an atomic proposition) or a *composite* (e.g., a temporal operator with arguments).

Listing 1.1. Primitive construct for atomic propositions.

```
{
"type": "primitive",
"name": "atom",
"format": "%string"
}
```

Listing 1.2. Composite construct for the LTL **F** (*eventually*) operator.

```
{
"type": "composite",
"name": "F",
"format": "F %LTL"
}
```

The `format` field is central to each construct: it defines both the block layout and the code output. Fixed symbols (e.g., `"F"`) determine block labels, while placeholders (e.g., `%string`, `%LTL`) indicate inputs and guide code generation. For example, `%string` creates a free text field, while `"F %LTL"` creates a block with label `"F"` and a subformula slot accepting elements from the **LTL** group.

To simplify constraints and promote reuse, the framework allows defining named *groups* of constructs that can be used interchangeably. This avoids redundancy and improves maintainability. For example:

Listing 1.3. Group definition for valid LTL subformulae.

```
{
"type": "group",
"name": "LTL",
"elements": ["atom", "AND", "OR", "NOT", "X", "U", "F", "G"]
}
```

Placeholders like `%LTL` refer to these groups, enforcing that composite arguments belong to predefined sets of constructs—which may include both *primitives* and *composites*. This structured use of *primitives, composites*, and *groups* enables modular, extensible, and constraint-aware specifications. The translation pipeline validates the JSON, generates blocks and toolboxes, and defines code generators—faithfully encoding the logic's structure while supporting incremental updates.

Because users build formulas via structured blocks, precedence and associativity rules are unnecessary: operation order is enforced visually, simplifying both the specification and the generated editor.

Complete documentation, sample logic definitions, and source code are available in our GitHub repository[1].

3   Case Study

To illustrate our framework's flexibility, we present a case study on ATL [1], a modal logic for verifying strategic behaviour in multi-agent systems. ATL's compositional syntax and strategic modalities make it well-suited for visual representation.

The syntax of ATL, following [1], is defined as:

$$\varphi ::= \&p \mid \neg\varphi \mid \varphi \wedge \varphi \mid \langle\!\langle A \rangle\!\rangle \, \mathsf{X}\varphi \mid \langle\!\langle A \rangle\!\rangle \, \mathsf{G}\varphi \mid \langle\!\langle A \rangle\!\rangle \, \varphi \mathsf{U}\varphi$$

where p is an atomic proposition, A represents a coalition of agents, and the remaining constructs are standard Boolean and temporal operators.

3.1   Specification of ATL Constructs

The specification of ATL in our framework begins by identifying its syntactic building blocks. These are organised into three categories: **Primitives**, such as atom (representing atomic propositions) and agent (denoting agent identifiers), which do not take subcomponents. **Composites**, representing operators such as NOT, AND, X, G, and U, which define terms composed from one or more arguments. **Groups**, which are auxiliary constructs used to define reusable collections of constructs. They help express argument constraints compactly and consistently across different composite definitions.

A group definition for ATL might appear as follows:

Listing 1.4. Group definitions for ATL constructs.

```
{
    "type": "group",
    "name": "all",
    "elements": ["atom", "NOT", "AND", "X", "G", "U", "agent"]
}
{
    "type": "group",
    "name": "all_but_agents",
    "elements": ["atom", "NOT", "AND", "X", "G", "U"]
}
```

Primitive constructs are specified in a straightforward manner as well.

---

[1] https://github.com/AngeloFerrando/Logic2Blockly.

Listing 1.5. Atomic proposition primitive.

```
{
    "type": "primitive",
    "name": "atom",
    "format": "%string"
}
```

Listing 1.6. Agent primitive with stacking.

```
{
    "type": "primitive",
    "name": "agent",
    "format": "%string",
    "connection": ["agent"]
}
```

By default, primitive blocks are atomic and not directly composable. However, some constructs—such as ATL's strategic modality $\langle\!\langle A \rangle\!\rangle$, where A is a set of agents—require collections of primitives. To support this, our specification includes an optional **connection** field, allowing compatible blocks (e.g., **agent**) to be stacked vertically, forming unordered sets as needed.

A typical composite operator in ATL, such as $\langle\!\langle A \rangle\!\rangle$ G (*globally*), can then be defined with structured placeholders that reference groups:

Listing 1.7. Composite definition for ATL G operator with agent context.

```
{
    "type": "composite",
    "name": "G",
    "format": "<<%agent>> G %all_but_agents"
}
```

This format indicates that the $\langle\!\langle \square \rangle\!\rangle$ G $\square$ operator expects two arguments (denoted as $\square$): a stackable collection of **agent** blocks and a subformula from the **all_but_agents** group. This structure enforces correct composition without manual constraint handling, and can be generalised to other strategic or nested constructs.

For brevity, we have presented only a subset of ATL constructs. Additional operators follow the same specification pattern and can be included with minimal extensions (the full ATL syntax is available on our GitHub repository).

3.2   Automatically Generated Editor

From the ATL specification described above, the framework automatically generates all the required visual artifacts. The resulting editor offers the following features: **Drag-and-drop blocks** for all ATL constructs, each with enforced input constraints derived from the specification. A **structured toolbox** organised according to the defined constructs (e.g., Boolean operators, temporal operators, agents). **Context-aware construction**: blocks accept only syntactically valid children, ensuring correctness by design.

Strategic contexts—such as the agent binding in $\langle\!\langle A \rangle\!\rangle$ G φ—are handled visually within the block structure. For instance, a user may instantiate a G block, which embeds an agent selector and a placeholder for a valid subformula. This structure enforces scoping and composition constraints interactively, preventing the creation of ill-formed expressions. Figure 2 shows a screenshot of an ATL formula constructed using the generated blocks. The expression

$\langle\!\langle Alice, Bob\rangle\!\rangle$ G (`safe_mode` $\wedge$ `no_collision`) states that the coalition of agents Alice and Bob can ensure the system always remains in a safe state with no collisions. This scenario could represent a robotic or safety-critical environment involving movement and spatial coordination. It illustrates how users can visually compose strategic temporal properties using the block-based editor[2].

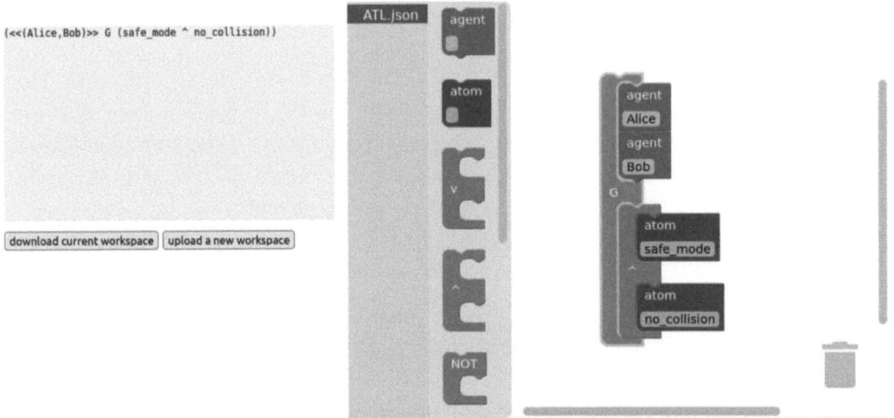

Fig. 2. Generated GUI in use: $\langle\!\langle Alice, Bob\rangle\!\rangle$ G (`safe_mode`$\wedge$`no_collision`) is composed via blocks.

4   Comparison with Related Tools

Several tools have introduced visual editors to improve the accessibility of formal specifications, especially for educational use or domain-specific applications. These tools typically provide pre-defined constructs tailored to particular logics, with interfaces designed for non-expert users. In contrast, our framework prioritises generality and extensibility: logic syntax is specified declaratively, and new visual editors are generated automatically. Table 1 compares representative systems along design and usage dimensions, highlighting their respective strengths and target contexts.

While prior tools clearly demonstrate the benefits of visual metaphors for improving accessibility, they are generally tailored to specific logics or application domains. For instance, Grobelna [9] provides a Scratch-based editor for expressing temporal logic requirements in control systems, while Nergaard et al. [14] focus on authoring XACML access control policies via a rule-building interface. Omar et al. [16] support step-by-step construction of natural deduction proofs for educational purposes. These tools are well-suited to their respective contexts but rely on fixed sets of constructs and lack general extensibility.

---

[2] Full demonstration video: https://tinyurl.com/Logic2Blockly.

Table 1. Comparison of visual tools for logic specification.

Reference	Interface	Logic	Users	Extensible	Domain
Ours	Blockly	Structured Spec.	Experts & Non-experts	Declarative	General
Grobelna [9]	Scratch-style GUI	LTL/CTL Templates	Non-experts	Fixed Operators	Control Systems
Nergaard et al. [14]	Scratch-style GUI	XACML Rules	Non-experts	Fixed Templates	Access Control
Omar et al. [16]	Structured Editor	Natural Deduction	Non-experts	Proof-based	Classical Logic

In contrast, our framework is logic-agnostic and auto-generative: experts define syntax declaratively in JSON, from which a full block-based editor is automatically produced. This enables constraint-aware visual editors for both educational and practical use, without manual interface design.

5   Conclusions and Future Work

We presented a general, extensible framework for automatically generating block-based visual editors from structured JSON logic specifications. It lets experts define new logics without coding effort and enables non-experts to construct formulas in syntax-aware visual environments.

The framework has been successfully applied to a range of logics, including CTL [2], ATL [1], NatATL [11], RB-ATL [15], and Strategy Logic [13], demonstrating both its flexibility and reusability.

While our framework enables non-experts to build formulas without worrying about syntax errors, it does not eliminate the need for a basic understanding of logical semantics. Accessibility here should be understood as syntactic support: the editor lowers barriers to entry once a user is introduced to the concepts, but it cannot replace teaching materials or domain training. Moreover, usability for non-experts depends on experts providing the initial JSON specification. This dependency is inherent to our approach, as the framework is designed to separate the tasks of logic definition (by experts) and formula composition (by end users).

Future work includes integrating with verification backends, particularly the VITAMIN framework [6–8], which supports accessible modelling for non-experts. We also plan to extend the specification language, explore educational use cases, and improve editor usability.

A limitation of the current work is that JSON specifications have so far been authored only by the tool developers. Our experience suggests that the effort is modest—similar to transcribing a logic's grammar into a structured format—but we acknowledge that non-developers may encounter difficulties or errors when writing specifications. The extent to which this overhead deters use has not yet been systematically evaluated. Addressing this requires empirical studies with external experts and user feedback on the specification process.

References

1. Alur, R., Henzinger, T.A., Kupferman, O.: Alternating-time temporal logic. J. ACM **49**(5), 672–713 (2002). https://doi.org/10.1145/585265.585270
2. Clarke, E.M., Emerson, E.A.: Design and synthesis of synchronization skeletons using branching time temporal logic. In: Kozen, D. (ed.) Logic of Programs 1981. LNCS, vol. 131, pp. 52–71. Springer, Heidelberg (1982). https://doi.org/10.1007/BFb0025774
3. Crockford, D.: The application/JSON media type for javascript object notation (json). RFC 4627 (2006). https://www.rfc-editor.org/rfc/rfc4627
4. Czepa, C., Zdun, U.: How understandable are pattern-based behavioral constraints for novice software designers? ACM Trans. Softw. Eng. Methodol. **28**(2) (2019). https://doi.org/10.1145/3306608
5. Davis, J.A., et al.: Study on the barriers to the industrial adoption of formal methods. In: Pecheur, C., Dierkes, M. (eds.) FMICS 2013. LNCS, vol. 8187, pp. 63–77. Springer, Heidelberg (2013). https://doi.org/10.1007/978-3-642-41010-9_5
6. Ferrando, A., Malvone, V.: Hands-on VITAMIN: A compositional tool for model checking of multi-agent systems. In: Alderighi, M., Baldoni, M., Baroglio, C., Micalizio, R., Tedeschi, S. (eds.) Proceedings of the 25th Workshop "From Objects to Agents", Bard (Aosta), Italy, July 8-10, 2024. CEUR Workshop Proceedings, vol. 3735, pp. 148–160. CEUR-WS.org (2024). https://ceur-ws.org/Vol-3735/paper_12.pdf
7. Ferrando, A., Malvone, V.: VITAMIN: a compositional framework for model checking of multi-agent systems. In: Rocha, A.P., Steels, L., van den Herik, H.J. (eds.) Proceedings of the 17th International Conference on Agents and Artificial Intelligence, ICAART 2025 - Volume 1, Porto, Portugal, February 23–25, 2025, pp. 648–655. SCITEPRESS (2025). https://doi.org/10.5220/0013349600003890
8. Ferrando, A., Malvone, V.: Vitamin: verification of a multi agent system. In: Proceedings of the 24th International Conference on Autonomous Agents and Multiagent Systems, AAMAS 2025, pp. 3023–3025. International Foundation for Autonomous Agents and Multiagent Systems, Richland, SC (2025)
9. Grobelna, I.: Scratch-based user-friendly requirements definition for formal verification of control systems. Informatics Educ. 19(2), 223–238 (2020). https://doi.org/10.15388/infedu.2020.11
10. Harvey, B., Mönig, J.: Snap! a visual, drag-and-drop programming language. https://snap.berkeley.edu/ (2013). Accessed Sept. 2025
11. Jamroga, W., Malvone, V., Murano, A.: Natural strategic ability. Artif. Intell. **277** (2019). https://doi.org/10.1016/j.artint.2019.103170
12. Mansoor, N., Bagheri, H., Kang, E., Sharif, B.: An empirical study assessing software modeling in alloy. In: 11th IEEE/ACM International Conference on Formal Methods in Software Engineering, FormaliSE 2023, Melbourne, Australia, May 14–15, 2023, pp. 44–54. IEEE (2023). https://doi.org/10.1109/FormaliSE58978.2023.00013
13. Mogavero, F., Murano, A., Perelli, G., Vardi, M.Y.: Reasoning about strategies: On the model-checking problem. ACM Trans. Comput. Log. **15**(4), 34:1–34:47 (2014)
14. Nergaard, H., Ulltveit-Moe, N., Gjøsæter, T.: ViSPE: a graphical policy editor for XACML. In: Camp, O., Weippl, E., Bidan, C., Aïmeur, E. (eds.) ICISSP 2015. CCIS, vol. 576, pp. 107–121. Springer, Cham (2015). https://doi.org/10.1007/978-3-319-27668-7_7

15. Nguyen, H.N., Alechina, N., Logan, B., Rakib, A.: Alternating-time temporal logic with resource bounds. J. Log. Comput. **28**(4), 631–663 (2018). https://doi.org/10.1093/logcom/exv034
16. Omar, C., Voysey, I., Chugh, R., Hammer, M.A.: Live functional programming with typed holes. Proc. ACM Program. Lang. **3**(POPL), 14:1–14:32 (2019). https://doi.org/10.1145/3290327
17. Pasternak, E., Fenichel, R., Marshall, A.N.: Tips for creating a block language with blockly. In: 2017 IEEE Blocks and Beyond Workshop (B&B), pp. 21–24 (2017). https://doi.org/10.1109/BLOCKS.2017.8120404
18. Pnueli, A.: The temporal logic of programs. In: 18th Annual Symposium on Foundations of Computer Science, Providence, Rhode Island, USA, 31 October–1 November 1977, pp. 46–57. IEEE Computer Society (1977). https://doi.org/10.1109/SFCS.1977.32
19. Woodcock, J., Larsen, P.G., Bicarregui, J., Fitzgerald, J.S.: Formal methods: practice and experience. ACM Comput. Surv. **41**(4), 19:1–19:36 (2009)https://doi.org/10.1145/1592434.1592436

Timing and Stochastic Modelling

Automata Learning – Expect Delays!⋆

Gabriel Dengler(✉), Sven Apel, and Holger Hermanns

Saarland University, Saarland Informatics Campus, Saarbrücken, Germany
`dengler@depend.uni-saarland.de`

Abstract. This paper studies active automata learning (AAL) in the presence of stochastic delays. We consider Mealy machines that have stochastic delays associated with each transition and explore how the learner can efficiently arrive at faithful estimates of those machines, the precision of which crucially relies on repetitive sampling of transition delays. While it is possible to naïvely integrate the delay sampling into AAL algorithms such as L^*, this leads to considerable oversampling near the root of the state space. We address this problem by separating conceptually the learning of behavior and delays such that the learner uses the information gained while learning the logical behavior to arrive at efficient input sequences for collecting the needed delay samples. We put emphasis on treating cases in which identical input/output behaviors might stem from distinct delay characteristics. Finally, we provide empirical evidence that our method outperforms the naïve baseline across a wide range of benchmarks and investigate its applicability in a realistic setting by studying the join order in a relational database.

1 Introduction

The goal of active automata learning (AAL) is to infer the behavioral structure of a system under learning (SUL) by executing actions upon the SUL and observing its resulting behavior [70,71]. This technique is the basis for inferring formal models of possibly large and complex systems for the sake of further analysis [53,63,67,82]. Besides the logical behavior of a system, an important aspect in real-word systems is their real-time behavior, which often comes with stochastic imprecisions due to communication delays or internal computation steps consuming time. Learning the timing behavior can become very relevant, for instance to detect bottlenecks in the implementation or to adjust to observed system performance. One of the prominent past applications of AAL is related to finding critical bugs in protocol implementations [31]. Since these implementations first and foremost are meant to provide high performance communication services, it seems natural to consider information about the delay characteristics of the various steps as additional valuable information to discover fast and slow

---

⋆ This work was partially funded by DFG grant 389792660 as part of TRR 248 CPEC, the European Union (EU) under the INTERREG North Sea project STORM_SAFE of the European Regional Development Fund, and the EU's Horizon 2020 research and innovation programme under Marie Skłodowska-Curie grant agreement 101008233 (MISSION).

F. Damiani and M. Farrell (Eds.): iFM 2025, LNCS 16194, pp. 463–486, 2026.
https://doi.org/10.1007/978-3-032-10794-7_23

steps of the system and how these could be accounted for. These delay characteristics usually need to be considered as being stochastic in nature and are representable as manifestations of continuous-time probability distributions.

There is a plethora of basic model families that come to mind as target models [32] for AAL in such a setting, including timed automata [1,21], probabilistic automata [65,72] including Markov decision processes, Markov automata [22,28], and stochastic (timed) automata [10,20]. Indeed, inspiring research work on AAL has been undertaken in many facets for timed automata [2–4,13,15,34,41,44,76, 81,83] as well as Markov decision processes (MDPs) [6,8,56,73,74]. However, to the best of our knowledge, automata models that provide explicit support for stochastic delays have not been put into the AAL research focus. At the same time, these appear as natural candidates in scenarios where the delays of activities follow continuous probability distributions over time. These can be represented directly within stochastic (timed) automata or approximated as precisely as needed within Markov automata via phase-type fitting [7].

This paper aims at exploring this topic from ground up. For this purpose, we start with the goal of performing black-box learning of a deterministic Mealy machine (MM) while collecting the time needed to traverse transitions alongside learning. While we assume determinism for the state space, the timing behavior is assumed to follow continuous probability distributions. This makes it necessary to traverse each transition multiple times to obtain statistically sound estimations. We will argue that it is theoretically justified and algorithmically beneficial to work with a global constant k of necessary transition traversals per transition to be considered. Furthermore, we consider it natural (albeit challenging) that the teacher has full knowledge of the time-abstract behavior, but that the time dependencies are entirely outside their knowledge, and thus the ground truth needs to (and can only) be inferred approximately through observations.

Related work. For models that exhibit probabilistic decisions associated to actions, e.g., MDPs or probabilistic MMs, it is—as in our scenario—essential that each input query will be asked multiple times to get statistically robust estimates of the SUL's behavior. Concepts from the literature that adapt L^* for probabilistic models either introduce queries that return the sampled results as an observation tree [56] or equip the teacher with the ability to sample the SUL and thereby obtain estimations of the transition probabilities to be used by the learner [74]. Thereby, the learner needs to reset the system frequently, which leads to considerable oversampling near the root, whereas other parts of the system are covered to a much lesser extent. Instead of actively learning the MDP, there is also the possibility to adapt passive learning approaches like ALERGIA [16] to a probabilistic setting [49]. However, experiments demonstrate an overall better performance for active learning approaches [74].

In a timed setting, delays induced by transitions are often modeled using clocks or timers in automata or MMs: This can be explicitly achieved by splitting transitions into two consecutive transitions [41,58], where time is spent in the intermediate state, i.e., by waiting for the expiration of a delay timer. While these models are (distributions aside) more general than the MM structure considered in this paper, their use in AAL research comes with other side constraints that hamper application in the real-world settings we focus on: They predominantly consider deterministic behavior for each clock/timer and sometimes assume the existence of a smart teacher [76,83] that can explicitly answer more complex queries or provide hints to the learner. We do not assume the existence of any of these helpful features. In the literature, there are also some suggestions to learn stochastic timed models passively [51,52,66], then resorting to state merging as in ALERGIA [16]. These approaches do not incorporate efficient input sequences to ensure a uniform coverage of the state space and provide no guarantees regarding the inferred logical structure.

Contributions. To the best of our knowledge, this paper is the first to establish a formal framework for the active learning of automata with stochastic delays. It starts off by extending the concept of standard MMs (Sec. 2) and introduces Mealy delay machines (MDMs) (Sec. 3) that describe the probabilistic behavior of transitions delays with continuous probability distributions. We first consider models where the learned logical structure (an MM) is the one underlying the MDM (Sec. 4). We then turn to the more intricate situation where certain sequences through the learned MM come with distinct delay characteristics albeit being indistinguishable from the perspective of the logical structure in isolation (Sec. 5). Our theoretical findings are supported by a prototypical implementation, which we empirically evaluate on publicly available benchmark models (Sec. 6) and on a database application inspired by real-world contexts (Sec. 7).

2   Preliminaries

We recall relevant notions regarding MMs and AAL, and also discuss some basics of continuous probability distributions and their estimation.

Mealy machines. An MM $\mathcal{M}$ is a 6-tuple $(S, I, O, s_0, \delta, \lambda)$, in which S is a finite set of states, I the inputs, O the outputs, $s_0 \in S$ the initial state, $\delta : S \times I \to S$ the transition function, and $\lambda : S \times I \to O$ the output function.

We denote with $|\mathcal{M}|$ the number of states of $\mathcal{M}$. A state $s \in S$ is a *sink* iff for all $i \in I$, $\delta(s, i) = s$. As usual, transition and output functions are extended to input words of length n by the functions $\delta : S \times I^n \to S$ and $\lambda : S \times I^n \to O^n$. We use w_j to identify the j-th character of the word $w \in I^*$. We use $\delta(w)$ and $\lambda(w)$ to refer to $\delta(s_0, w)$, respectively $\lambda(s_0, w)$. As common in the AAL context, we silently assume that all states in S can be reached from s_0 by some word in I^*. Furthermore, we can characterize the equivalence behavior of an MM in terms of the inputs/outputs (I/O) of its states as follows.

Definition 1. *If given a set of input sequences $W \subset I^*$ from an MM $\mathcal{M} = (S, I, O, s_0, \delta, \lambda)$, we say that two states s and t from S are W-equivalent, denoted $s \equiv^W t$, iff $\lambda(s, w) = \lambda(t, w)$ for all $w \in W$.*

They are I/O-equivalent, denoted $s \sim_{\mathrm{IO}} t$, iff $s \equiv^{I^*} t$.

The induced relation $\sim_{\mathrm{IO}} \subseteq S \times S$ is indeed an equivalence relation on the states of $\mathcal{M}$. It can be lifted to an equivalence relation on MMs: Two MMs are equivalent if their initial states are equivalent in an MM spanned by their disjoint union (whatever state is fixed as initial state in that MM).

Since we are dealing with deterministic structures, an alternative way of characterizing I/O-equivalence of two MMs harvests the notion of *bisimulation* [61].

Definition 2. *Two MMs over the same input set* I, $\mathcal{M} = (S, I, O, s_0, \delta, \lambda)$ *and* $\mathcal{M}' = (S', I, O, s_0', \delta', \lambda')$, *are said to be bisimilar, denoted* $\mathcal{M} \approx_{\mathrm{IO}} \mathcal{M}'$, *iff there is a relation* $R \subseteq S \times S'$ *(named bisimulation relation) such that* $s_0 \, R \, s_0'$, *and for each pair* $(s, s') \in S \times S'$, $s \, R \, s'$ *implies for all inputs* $i \in I$ *that* $\lambda(s, i) = \lambda'(s', i)$ *(I/O equality), and* $\delta(s, i) \, R \, \delta'(s', i)$ *(state transition correspondence).*

Lemma 1. *Two MMs are I/O-equivalent if and only if they are bisimilar.*

An MM $\mathcal{M}$ is called minimal, iff no MM bisimilar to $\mathcal{M}$ is of smaller size, i.e., $|\mathcal{M}| \leq |\mathcal{M}'|$ holds for any bisimilar $\mathcal{M}'$.

The minimal MM is unique up to permutation of states.

Active automata learning. The goal of AAL is to infer the structure of an SUL, in our case an MM $\mathcal{S} = (S, I, O, s_0, \delta_{\mathcal{S}}, \lambda_{\mathcal{S}})$, by using output queries (OQs) and equivalence queries (EQs). An OQ for an input word w returns the output word $\lambda_{\mathcal{S}}(w)$. An EQ checks whether a hypothesis MM $\mathcal{H} = (H, I, O, h_0, \delta_{\mathcal{H}}, \lambda_{\mathcal{H}})$ is bisimilar to $\mathcal{S}$, and, if not, returns a *counterexample* w so that $\lambda_{\mathcal{S}}(w) \neq \lambda_{\mathcal{H}}(w)$.

Data structure. In L^*-based algorithms [5], the learner maintains as data structure a set of access words $Q \subseteq I^*$ to reach each state in H of the current hypothesis $\mathcal{H}$ and a set of test words $T \subseteq I^*$ to distinguish each state, also called the test set. More precisely, Q and T have to satisfy the following properties:

- *Separability:* No two distinct states in $\{\delta_{\mathcal{S}}(w) \mid w \in Q\}$ are T-equivalent.
- *Closedness:* For every $q \in Q$ and $i \in I$, there is some $q' \in Q$ such that $\delta_{\mathcal{S}}(qi) \equiv^T \delta_{\mathcal{S}}(q')$.

To make statements about these properties efficiently, the learner saves the outputs of $\lambda_{\mathcal{S}}(w)$ for the words $w \in (Q \cup \{qi \mid q \in Q, i \in I\}) \times T$. By construction, the sets Q and T stay separable during L^*, but the closedness property has to be retained by extending the set Q with the state accessible by qi if no suitable counterpart q' exists in Q already. Once both separability and closedness are achieved, an EQ is issued to the teacher, leading either to the confirmation of the hypothesis $\mathcal{H}$ or an extension of the sets Q and T.

Equivalence oracles. In practice, the teacher is often unable to answer EQs by a so-called *perfect* equivalence oracle (EO). Instead, the teacher usually resorts to some *test suite* that executes a set of test words and either finds a counterexample and otherwise assumes the system's equivalence.

Under reasonable assumptions on the SUL, it is possible to construct a test suite to prove that, after successfully executing all test inputs, the learned system must be equivalent to the SUL. A prominent method to construct such a test suite practically is the W-method [17,80] which assumes a maximum number e of extra states. However, its complexity grows exponentially with the selection of e.

Therefore, practitioners often make additional real-world motivated assumptions on the SUL (e.g., some inputs always leading to a sink, multiple global phases like login or logout, sets of inputs used together, working with a known bug-free model, etc.) to reduce the size of the test suite [45,79]. Alternatively, one can also resort to randomized EOs, but they do only offer probabilistic guarantees (we refer the reader to [54,55] for an overview).

Continuous probability distributions. A continuous cumulative distribution function (CDF) F with non-negative support describes the probability that the random variable (RV) X with support $\mathbb{R}_0^+$ is smaller than x, i.e., $F(x) = \Pr(X \leq x)$. The set of all corresponding CDFs is denoted as $\mathcal{F}_0^+$.

Approximating CDFs from samples. We will later be interested in reconstructing an approximand $\widehat{F}$ from its samples $X_1, ..., X_k$. The most direct approximand is the empirical CDF $\widehat{F}_k(x) = \frac{1}{k} \sum_{i=1}^{k} \mathbf{1}_{X_i \leq x}$ ($\mathbf{1}_A$ is the indicator of event A), which counts for each value x the percentage of observed samples smaller than or equal to x. As this representation is usually unhandy, researchers have developed methods working with simpler representations instead. A common approach is to assume a distribution class, e.g., exponential distributions (for which it is enough to compute the mean of the data points), or the more general class of phase-type distributions. For deriving the best-fitting phase-type distribution given the data points, an abundant number of sophisticated phase-type fitting (or moment-matching) algorithms exist in the literature [7,12,14,29,36–38,40,42,60,75,77].

Accuracy of approximands. All approximation methods come with their accuracy analysis that invariably depends on the number of samples k. As the approach we present here is not bound to any specific approximation method, we review the question of approximation accuracy from the foundational perspective.

In full generality, the Dvoretzky–Kiefer–Wolfowitz (DKW) inequality [24, 50] provides the probability that a given maximum difference ε is overshot: $\Pr\left(\sup_{x \in \mathbb{R}_0^+} |\widehat{F}_k(x) - F(x)| > \varepsilon \right) \leq 2e^{-2k\varepsilon^2}$. If we are instead interested in bounding the approximation error of the distribution's mean, we can resort to Chebyshev's inequality [30] (adapted to the sample mean) when assuming a maximum variance or Hoeffding's inequality [35] when assuming a lower and upper bound to find an appropriate k for an absolute error bound. Furthermore, in the special case of exponential distributions, we can directly determine the number of samples k needed to achieve a relative error bound [23, Appendix C].

Checking equality of distributions. There are many established tests to decide whether two independent sets of samples are likely to come from the same distribution or not [48,64,69]. However, it is not guaranteed that such a test will retain the transitivity property, e.g. when it yields by sampling for three CDFs F_1, F_2, F_3 that $F_1 = F_2$ and $F_2 = F_3$, it may not yield $F_1 = F_3$. Therefore, researchers have adapted clustering approaches originally developed for multidimensional vectors like k-means [47] to histograms [59] and empirical CDFs [33].

3   Mealy Delay Machines

We now extend the definition of regular MMs by including for each transition a description of the stochastic delay behavior.[1] We consider the setting where every input triggers an unavoidable delay until the output arrives (in contrast to some timed models [15], where timers can be cancelled by other actions).

Definition 3. *An MDM is a 7-tuple $\mathcal{D} = (S, I, O, s_0, \delta, \lambda, D)$, where the first 6 components constitute an MM (called the* underlying *MM) and $D : S \times I \to \mathcal{F}_0^+$ represents the probabilistic delay behavior of each transition as CDF.*

As before, D can be extended to inputs of length n, resulting in $D : S \times I^n \to (\mathcal{F}_0^+)^n$. Importantly, we make the assumption that the learner will not be able to see the entire CDF upon probing the function $D(s, i)$, but, in contrast to the interaction via $\lambda(s, i)$, sees only one sampled value from the CDF upon taking the transition. Formally, the semantic interpretation of an MDM is as follows. Any given input word w induces a probability space on timed output words given by a standard cylinder set construction [9,46], detailed in [23, Appendix A].

We extend the notion of equivalence to the delay case in the obvious way:

Definition 4. *If given a set of input sequences $W \subset I^*$ from an MDM $\mathcal{D} = (S, I, O, s_0, \delta, \lambda, D)$, we say that two states s and t from S are W-equivalent, denoted $s \sim^W t$, iff $\lambda(s, w) = \lambda(t, w)$ and $D(s, w) = D(t, w)$ for all $w \in W$.*

They are delay-equivalent, denoted $s \sim_{\mathrm{IDO}} t$, iff $s \sim^{I^*} t$,

Just as for $\sim_{\mathrm{IO}}$, delay equivalence $\sim_{\mathrm{IDO}}$ can be lifted to an equivalence relation on MDMs. The size of an MDM $|\mathcal{D}|$ and its minimality are defined as for MMs. Note that in the above definition we work with perfect equivalence of CDFs (because this is the foundational yardstick), but for the practical sampling context, we will work with sampled data points obtained from the CDFs at hand, and thereby need to resort to a test to check if two distributions are the same. This, in turn, will need to work on approximands obtained from the data points (see Sec. 2).

Problem statement. So, we are facing the situation that every transition should be visited sufficiently often to obtain statistically sound estimates of the delay distributions on each transition. As discussed above, the number k of samples to collect is the decisive parameter governing the accuracy of the approximands obtained. In absence of any other information regarding the concrete SUL, we consider it natural to fix this k as a constant across the entire structure to learn. With this, we can specify the paper's challenge as follows:

> We are given an MDM $\mathcal{D} = (S, I, O, s_0, \delta, \lambda, D)$. To interact with $\mathcal{D}$, we can, for any $w \in I^*$, get the outputs from $\lambda(w)$ and one sample from each distribution $D(\delta(w_1...w_{j-1}), w_j)$ for each $j \in \{1, ..., |w|\}$. Additionally, we have an EO for the underlying MM $\mathcal{M}$. We want to learn the structure

---

[1] In this model, time advances while taking transitions, but it is easily converted into one where time advances in states (at the price of adding intermediate states).

> of $\mathcal{D}$ and find approximands of the CDFs of transitions according to D by visiting each transition $\langle s, i \rangle \in S \times I$ at least $k \in \mathbb{N}$ times.

This is the central problem we are aiming to solve. The methods we develop will equally work in settings where individual k are needed for some substructures.

Since two states might be equivalent according to $\sim_{IO}$, but not when considering delays in $\sim_{IDO}$, a peculiar observation when studying delays in an MM is:

Corollary 1. *The MM underlying a minimal MDM is not necessarily minimal.*

Though not necessarily a realistic phenomenon, a minimal MDM can in principle be to any order more complex than its corresponding minimal MM. In practical scenarios, it is assumable that either (i) the structure of the MDM indeed is equivalent to the structure of the underlying minimal MM or (ii) some deviation from the minimal MM is plausible, but only up to a certain degree. Sec. 4 and Sec. 5 will cover each case separately.

4   Methodology for Minimal Mealy Machine

As a first challenge, we assume that for an SUL MDM $\mathcal{D}$ its underlying MM $\mathcal{M}$ is indeed of minimal size. Thus, we only have to ensure that every transition is traversed at least k times.

4.1   Sampling Alongside Active Automata Learning

A straightforward approach is to repeat the sampling of any input word $w \in Q \cup \{qi \mid q \in Q, i \in I\}$ (see Sec. 2) k times and to store the resulting delay values, e.g., in an observation tree. This is very close in spirit to what is applied in the learning of probabilistic models such as MDPs [56]. Counterexamples can be handled as usual in L^*, although newly discovered test words only need to be traversed once as their delay behavior is not of interest. Additionally, we can incorporate a cache to ensure that further executions of an input word w are suppressed once the transitions of w have been sampled often enough.

Although this method can correctly infer the structure of the MDM $\mathcal{D}$, it has the fundamental problem that a high number of resets is needed, thereby causing many transitions to be traversed an excessive number of times. This problem also exists for learning regular MMs. Nonetheless, it is worsened here as each transition needs to be covered multiple times.

4.2   Efficient Coverage of Learned Mealy Machine

To address this problem, we separate the process of inferring the I/O behavior from that of sampling the delays. We start by learning the underlying minimal MM $\mathcal{M}'$ underlying $\mathcal{D}$ by some conventional AAL algorithms, e.g., L^*. While learning, we can already keep track of delay samples, yet without making any conceptual changes to the algorithmic procedure of the learning algorithm.

After that, we can assume that each transition $\langle s, i \rangle \in S \times I$ of $\mathcal{D}$ has already been traversed some $K(s, i) \in \mathbb{N}_0$ times while inferring the minimal MM $\mathcal{M}'$, and we thus know that it needs no more than further $K'(s, i) = \max(0, k - K(s, i))$ visits. With this, we will construct a sequence of input actions to cover every transition in $\mathcal{D}$ sufficiently often, with minimum total cost.

Concretely, the resulting problem can be reduced to the directed Rural Postman Problem (RPP) [27,62] with multiple edges, a variant of the Chinese Postman Problem (CPP) [25]. The goal is to find a circuit of minimal cost when some edges need to be traversed a specific number often, while other edges can be used or omitted. As we can reset the SUL at any point, we need to incorporate edges from any state to the root state in the graph. Precisely, we resort to a directed multigraph $G = (V, E, m)$, where $V = S$ and the edges E as well as their multiplicity m are defined as:

$$E = \{\langle s, \delta(s, i) \rangle \mid \forall s \in S, \forall i \in I\} \cup \{\langle s, s_0 \rangle \mid \forall s \in S, s \neq s_0\}$$

$$m(\langle s, t \rangle) = \sum_{\forall i \in I, \delta(s, i) = t} K'(s, i) \qquad \forall \langle s, t \rangle \in E$$

Mandatory edges are those where $m(\langle s, t \rangle) \neq 0$. If G is strongly connected and for each node the number of incoming edges (including its multiplicity) is equal to the number of outgoing edges, we can construct an Eulerian circuit [11] in linear time [25] and obtain the optimal strategy to cover all edges as needed. Since these conditions usually do not apply to G, we instead will have to traverse some edges from E more often than strictly required. Unfortunately, this problem is known to be NP-complete in the general case [27,62].[2] However, when G restricted to mandatory edges forms a weakly connected component (which happens frequently if the minimum number of transition visits k is large), we can compute the additional required edges with minimal cost as follows:

- For each node s, we calculate the difference of the number between outgoing and incoming edges: $d(s) = \sum_{t \in S, \langle s, t \rangle \in E} m(\langle s, t \rangle) - \sum_{t \in S, \langle t, s \rangle \in E} m(\langle t, s \rangle)$
- After that, we solve the min-cost flow problem [19,43] on the graph induced by the node flow differences as specified in $d(s)$. The solver increases the multiplicity of each edge in G such that $d(s)$ becomes zero for each node s and we obtain minimal costs: For each edge, we can specify how expensive an additional traversal of this edge will be. In our experiments, we assume a constant cost of 1, but also context-specific costs are readily supported.

In the general case, when the subgraph of G spanned by mandatory edges is not weakly connected, it can happen that G including the edges needed for

---

[2] We do not know whether the RPP limited to the case-specific graphs G we construct is NP-complete, also considering the expansion of the minimal MM $\mathcal{M}'$ in Sec. 5.2. The constructed multigraph G is not fully general, because of the multiplicity of the edges and the structure itself being dependent on the previously learned graph and the expanded MM.

additional traversals does not form a strongly connected component. Then, no Eulerian circuit can be found even if the number of incoming and outgoing edge multiplicities at each node were equal. In this case, our implementation resorts to the following: We compute the minimum spanning arborescence of minimum weight when using weight zero for edges that need to be covered and weight one elsewhere [18,26], resulting in a weakly-connected graph.

5   Expansion and State Separation

In this section, we study the case that the MDM $\mathcal{D}$ has a more complex structure than its underlying minimal MM $\mathcal{M}'$. Here, the separation of states is crucial not only to detect different delays for the same logical behavior based on the transition history, but also essential to obtain faithful estimates of distributions.

A general solution to this problem can become costly very rapidly, in case the structure of the MDM $\mathcal{D}$ differs significantly from the minimal MM $\mathcal{M}'$ or when delay distributions only differ slightly. Therefore, we first focus on practically motivated cases for which we harvest concepts from Sec. 4 to handle them efficiently. Later on, we will show that our methods do generalize beyond these cases and can indeed solve the general setting. We will discuss this as a corollary of the specific findings detailed below (Theorem 3).

The useful case. To make the analysis approachable, we propose restrictions on what the delay behavior induces compared to the I/O behavior alone. The first one states that self-loops in the underlying minimal MM indicate that no changes to the system are made. This prevents transitions between distinct states of $\mathcal{D}$ that have the same I/O behavior, which is why we use the term *stutter-free*:

Fig. 1: Minimal MM $\mathcal{M}'$

Definition 5. *An MDM* $\mathcal{D} = (S, I, O, s_0, \delta, \lambda, D)$ *is called stutter-free iff for any state* $s \in S$ *and input* $i \in I$ *with* $\delta(s, i) \sim_{\text{IO}} s$, *it holds that* $\delta(s, i) = s$.

The second restriction requires that two states which are equivalent regarding the I/O behavior also show the same delay behavior at the latest after d steps:

Definition 6. *An MDM* $\mathcal{D} = (S, I, O, s_0, \delta, \lambda, D)$ *is d-step confluent iff for all states* $s_1, s_2 \in S$ *with* $s_1 \sim_{\text{IO}} s_2$ *and all words* $w \in I^{\geq d}$ *such that* $\delta(s_1, w)$ *as well as* $\delta(s_2, w)$ *do not include a self-loop, it holds* $\delta(s_1, w) = \delta(s_2, w)$.

Example 1. Consider the minimal MM $\mathcal{M}'$ illustrated in Fig. 1 with inputs a and b. Fig. 2 shows three bisimilar MM expansions of $\mathcal{M}'$. $\mathcal{M}_1$ is an expansion satisfying the *2-step confluence* criterion as it is indeed guaranteed that from every pair of I/O equivalent states (e.g., s_{20} and s_{21}) the same state s_1 will be reached after at most $d = 2$ steps. This does not apply to the other two examples, as in both cases from s_{00} and s_{01} the same node will never be reached when repeatedly applying the input sequence aaa.

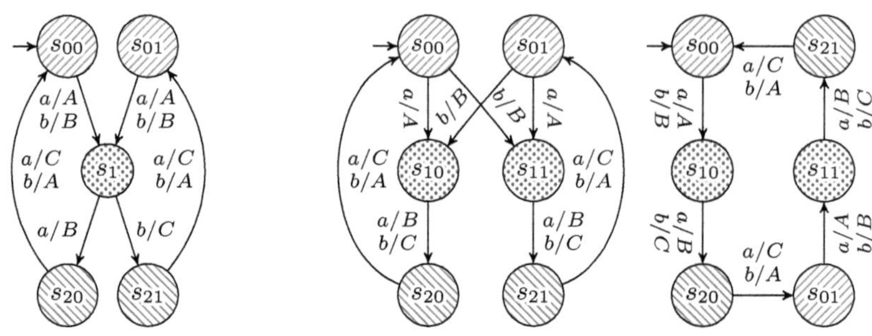

(a) 2-step confluent expansion $\mathcal{M}_1$ (b) Two non-confluent expansions

Fig. 2: Confluent and non-confluent expansions of $\mathcal{M}'$

We might impose additional constraints to further reduce the number of possible expansions. An instrumental constraint in this regard stipulates that the root state of the minimal MM has not been expanded:

Definition 7. *An MDM* $\mathcal{D} = (S, I, O, s_0, \delta, \lambda, D)$ *has a unique root iff there is no state* $s \in Q$ *different from* s_0 *such that* $s_0 \sim_{\mathrm{IO}} s$.

Another constraint disallows variations regarding delay behaviors across sink nodes, echoing that in a sink node the future behavior is considered not of interest any longer, something which we will assume across all empirical studies:

Definition 8. *We denote an MDM* $\mathcal{D} = (S, I, O, s_0, \delta, \lambda, D)$ *as sink delay-ignorant iff for each state* $s \in S$, *where* $\delta(s, i) \sim_{\mathrm{IO}} s$ *for each input* $i \in I$, *it holds* $\delta(s, i) = s$.

5.1   Sampling-Based L^* Learning

As a starting point, we modify the classical L^* algorithm such that it additionally separates states based on their delay behavior according to the d-step confluence criterion. In this criterion, we know that any two I/O-equivalent states exhibit distinguishable delay behavior for d steps at most. This behavior can be tested by test words with a maximum length of d. Thus, the easiest way to integrate the state separation into L^* is by initializing the test set T by all non-empty words $I^{\leq d}$ and sampling all queries $(Q \cup \{qi \mid q \in Q, i \in I\}) \times T$ k times. Otherwise, we can continue the general learning procedure of L^* as usual by adding any test word longer than d that arises by a counterexample (where, however, each newly added test word only needs to be queried once).

Obviously, the size of the test set T now has an exponential size regarding the parameter d, and one could argue that it is better to gradually increase T through counterexamples. However, we consider EQs to be unrealistic to pose regarding delay behavior. One possibility to implement an EO nonetheless would be by adapting the W-method [17,80] while repeating each query k times, but the size of the test suite would still grow exponentially by the maximum number of additional states of the true SUL. In the context of d-step confluence, we thus would not gain significant advantages by offloading this part to the EO.

5.2   Efficient Coverage Based on Mealy Machine Expansion

We now present how to leverage the approach in Sec. 4.2 for a procedure addressing the more general case. We perform the following steps:

1. We start by inferring the underlying minimal MM $\mathcal{M}'$ of the SUL by regular AAL algorithms, e.g., L^*.
2. Based on the assumptions on the stutter-free d-step confluence of the SUL $\mathcal{D}$, we expand $\mathcal{M}'$ into an MM $\mathcal{M}^d$, which we use to sample delays.
3. We collect sampling information for $\mathcal{M}^d$ as described in Sec. 4.2, thereby arriving at $\mathcal{D}^d$.
4. Lastly, we check for delay equivalence of states in $\mathcal{D}^d$ and merge those states that have statistically equivalent delay behavior to obtain $\mathcal{D}'$.

In the following, the second and fourth steps will be explained in detail.

Expansion of learned MM. Based on the learned minimal MM $\mathcal{M}'$, we now create an expanded MM, which we use as basis to collect delay information, under the assumption that the SUL MDM $\mathcal{D}$ satisfies the stutter-free d-step confluence criterion. We call this machine in the following $\mathcal{M}^d$. For the construction of $\mathcal{M}^d$, we need to ensure that, when two states in the actual system are different, this also needs to be the case for $\mathcal{M}^d$. We call this property *injective bisimilarity*:

Definition 9. *We say that MM $\mathcal{M} = (S, I, O, s_0, \delta, \lambda)$ is injective bisimilar to MM $\mathcal{M}' = (S', I, O, s'_0, \delta', \lambda')$ iff there exists a bisimulation relation between S and S' that is injective.*

Under the assumption that every conceivable SUL $\mathcal{D}$ satisfies the criterion of Def. 5 and Def. 6, we can construct an MM $\mathcal{M}^d$ from the learned minimal MM $\mathcal{M}' = (S', I, O, s'_0, \delta', \lambda')$ as follows: For each state $s' \in S'$, we consider how s' could be reached from any other state in d steps, or from the root s'_0 in less than d steps. More formally, we consider all pairs $\langle p', w \rangle$ with states $p' \in S'$ and loop-free input words $w \in I^*$ such that $\delta'(p', w) = s'$ with $|w| = d$ or $\delta'(s'_0, w) = s'$ with $|w| < d$. In this context, we say that a word $w \in I^*$ starting from $p \in S$ is *loop-free* iff w does not stutter on any self-loop, i.e., $\delta(p, w_1...w_j) \not\sim_{\text{IO}} \delta(p, w_1...w_{j+1})$ for each $1 \leq j < |w|$. For each pair $\langle p', w \rangle$, we create one state for the resulting MM $\mathcal{M}^d$, which we shall refer to as $s^d_{s', \langle p', w \rangle}$.

We add a transition triggered by input $i \in I$ between the two states $s^d_{s', \langle p', w \rangle}$ and $t^d_{t', \langle r', l \rangle}$ if there is a transition triggered by i from s' to t' and both states are compatible regarding their transition history. This is the case when either $\delta'(p', w_1) = r'$ and $w_2...w_{|w|}i = l$ (for $|w| = d$) or $p' = r' = s'_0$ and $wi = l$ (for $|w| < d$). For any self-loop $\delta'(s', i) = s'$ in the minimal MM $\mathcal{M}'$, we also create a self-loop in $\mathcal{M}^d$ with $\delta^d(s^d_{s', \langle p', w \rangle}, i) = s^d_{s', \langle p', w \rangle}$. We set the output to be equivalent to the minimal MM: $\lambda^d(s^d_{s', \langle p', w \rangle}, i) = \lambda'(s', i)$.

We can show that this construction of $\mathcal{M}^d$ has the required properties:

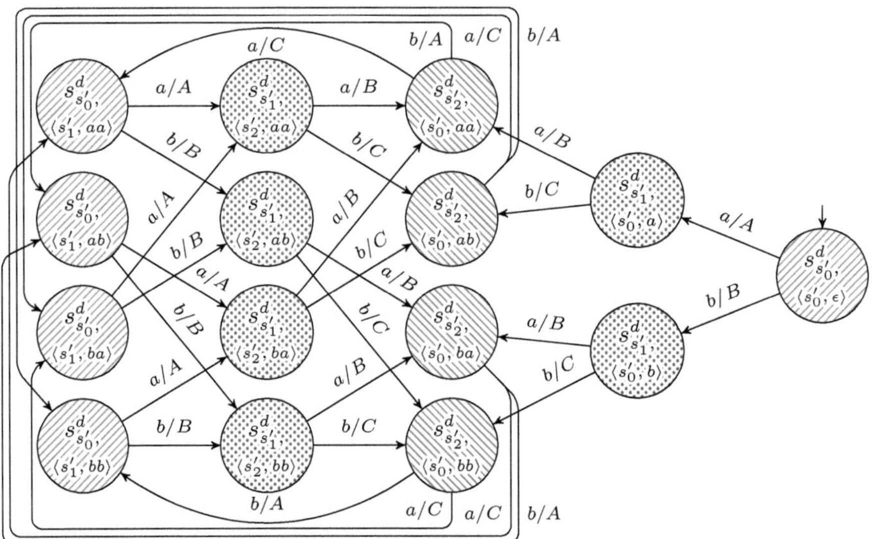

Fig. 3: Expanded $\mathcal{M}^d$ for minimal MM $\mathcal{M}'$ from Fig. 1 for depth $d = 2$

Theorem 1. *Let $\mathcal{D}$ be a stutter-free d-step confluent MDM with underlying MM $\mathcal{M}$. Then $\mathcal{M}$ is injective bisimilar to the MM $\mathcal{M}^d$ constructed as proposed above from the minimal MM $\mathcal{M}'$ of $\mathcal{M}$.*

Example 2. Let us recall the MM $\mathcal{M}'$ from Example 1. The expanded MM $\mathcal{M}^d$ for $d = 2$ is presented in Fig. 3. As we have two different inputs and are tracking two steps back, we start by creating $2 \cdot 2 = 4$ states for each state from the original automaton. In the end, we need to add three states to identify the correct state when starting from the root. It can be easily verified that the MM $\mathcal{M}_1$ from Fig. 2a is injective bisimilar to $\mathcal{M}^d$. On the other hand, when only constructing $\mathcal{M}^d$ for $d = 1$, the injective bisimulation property is no longer fulfilled for $\mathcal{M}_1$, as for identifying the state s_{00} and s_{01} by the transition history beginning with s_1, we need a horizon of at least two steps.

The resulting construction is linear in the size of the state space S' of the minimal MM $\mathcal{M}'$ and exponential only in the selection of d:

Theorem 2. $|\mathcal{M}^d| \in \mathcal{O}(|S'| \cdot |I|^d)$.

Some further restrictions can easily be applied: When assuming a unique root state (Def. 7), the additional construction to identify the proper state after d steps can be omitted, and no state splitting is necessary. Similarly, when assuming a sink delay-ignorant MDM (Def. 8), no splitting of sink states is required.

Selection of d. In general, it is unknown how large the selected d should be, but this is a general problem across AAL (shared for instance with the W-method [17,80] where the maximum additional number of states e is notoriously unknown). Furthermore, there are examples where no suitable d can be found at all, see Fig. 2b. In this case, the bisimulation relation between $\mathcal{M}$ and $\mathcal{M}^d$ is not injective, and for one state in $\mathcal{M}^d$, there can be multiple states corresponding to $\mathcal{M}$. Then, we would obtain an uncontrolled mixture of multiple CDFs (depending on how often we actually visit each corresponding transition in $\mathcal{M}$). Nevertheless, increasing d never worsens the result, as a consequence of the following lemma:

Lemma 2. *For each $d \in \mathbb{N}_0$, $\mathcal{M}^d$ is injective bisimilar to $\mathcal{M}^{d+1}$.*

So, if two states from $\mathcal{M}$ are correctly distinguished in $\mathcal{M}^d$, then also in $\mathcal{M}^{d+1}$.

Other restrictions. Note that the concept of injective bisimulations is not restricted to stutter-free d-step confluenct MDMs. By essentially using the cross-product of the MMs, as long as the number of actual state structures given a minimal MM $\mathcal{M}'$ is finite, a suitable MM $\mathcal{M}^*$ can be constructed as follows:

Theorem 3. *Given pairwise bisimilar MMs $\mathcal{M}_1, ..., \mathcal{M}_n$, one can find an MM $\mathcal{M}^*$ with, at maximum, $|\mathcal{M}_1| \cdot ... \cdot |\mathcal{M}_n|$ states such that every $\mathcal{M}_j$ with $j \in \{1, ..., n\}$ is injective bisimilar to $\mathcal{M}^*$.*

In particular, we can use this theorem on an enumeration of all MMs that are bisimilar to the learned minimal representation and at most as large as some given size b. However, the construction leads to a vast number of states in $\mathcal{M}^*$. Thus, the challenge for other restrictions as proposed in this paper lies in finding a reasonable balance between expressiveness and size of the expanded MM.

State merging. The merging step can be considered optional. It is meant to ensure the minimality of the resulting MDM. To perform the merging step, we need to check for each pair of states s and t if it holds $s \sim_{\mathrm{IDO}} t$. If $s \not\sim_{\mathrm{IO}} t$, it trivially also follows $s \not\sim_{\mathrm{IDO}} t$. Otherwise, we have to resort to a test that checks if the delay distributions are equal [48,64,69] as discussed in Sec. 2. Should the transitivity property of $\sim_{\mathrm{IDO}}$ not be justifiable statistically, the following options arise:

- Decide not to merge two state clusters if two distributions in the merged cluster are not equal according to the test for distribution equality.
- Apply a clustering method [33,59] from Sec. 2.
- Acquire more samples[3] for disambiguation of selected transitions, and retry the merging procedure subsequently.

As the construction using the expanded MM determines the size of $\mathcal{M}^d$, the sampling effort is independent of the true SUL's delay behavior. This also applies to an unstable (e.g., unreliably returning wrong outcomes) CDF equivalence test. On the other hand, an unstable test in sampling-based L^* learning can lead to a runtime explosion, when equal distributions are repeatedly reported as different.

---

[3] This takes up a remark from Sec. 3 that our method supports to work with different k for some sub-structures, here effectuated incrementally in another RPP construction.

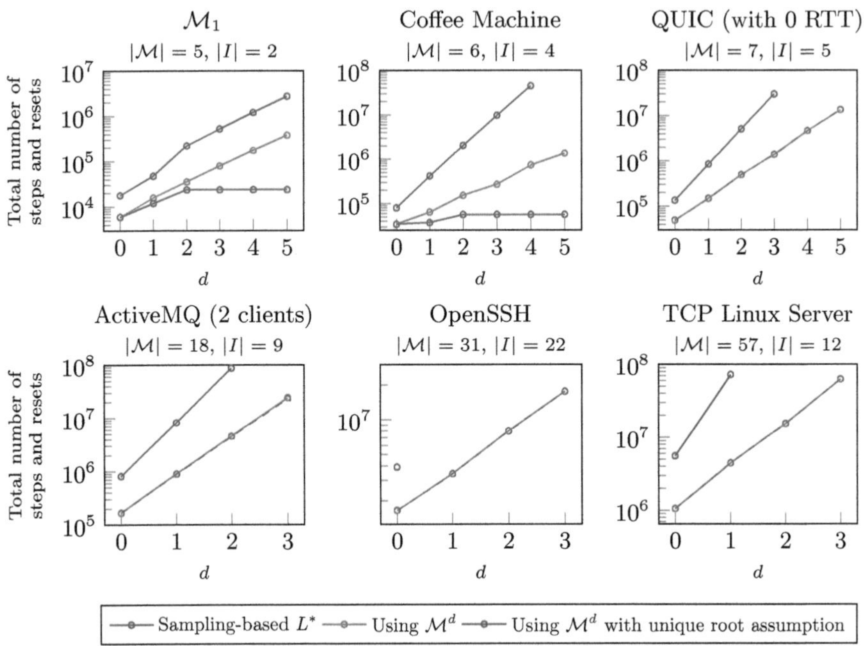

Fig. 4: Number of total actions for different models and selections of d

6　Empirical Evaluation

In this section, we evaluate the efficacy of both approaches, the baseline implementation based on the L^* algorithm (Sec. 4.1 and Sec. 5.1) as well as the improved method with additional collection of samples (Sec. 4.2 and Sec. 5.2). For the second approach, we also use L^* to learn the I/O behavior. Although we could have resorted to better-performing alternatives, e.g., TTT [39] or $L^\#$ [78], the impact on the final runtime is negligible as the majority of steps are needed for the subsequent sampling of delays. Furthermore, we do not require that self-loops are sampled k times in the expanded MM, given the assumed stutter-freeness (see Def. 5). Both approaches were implemented on top of AALpy [55]. The research questions in focus of our benchmarking studies are the following:

RQ1: How is the performance of both approaches compared to each other?
RQ2: What is the impact of d in the d-step confluence criterion on the runtime?
RQ3: How does the alphabet size $|I|$ influence the methods' scalability?
RQ4: What changes if making the assumption of a unique root (Def. 7)?

Experimental setup. We considered the MM $\mathcal{M}_1$ from Fig. 2a together with cases from a publicly available test suite for MMs [57], a selection of which is presented here. Even though the MMs from [57] are minimal regarding their I/O behavior, they can be used to assess the impact of parameter d, corresponding to an assumed need for state separation caused by the delay behavior. Ideally, the state merging step leads to a final merge back to the I/O minimal result. The delay of each transition is synthetic, based on exponential distributions with random rates. We assume two distributions to be different if the relative deviation of the sample mean is more than 20 percent and the absolute deviation is, at least, 0.01. Each transition has to be visited at least $k = 1000$ times (for parameter selection see [23, Appendix C]. As the number of performed actions per experiment can grow large rapidly, executions exceeding 10^8 actions are aborted.

Measurement data. In Fig. 4, the results for a selection of experiments are depicted, showing the number of total steps and resets depending on the selection of the parameter d. While the upper row presents studies of small examples, the lower row covers larger real-world examples. All results from the test suite [57] can be found in [23, Appendix D]. (Although we include results for $\mathcal{M}_1$ from Fig. 2a with values $d < 2$ and assuming a unique root, it should be noted that the correct structure of $\mathcal{M}_1$ can only be inferred by selecting $d \geq 2$ and allowing for non-unique roots.)

Evaluation. **RQ1:** Across all cases, the sampling-based L^* is outperformed by the approach using the expanded MM $\mathcal{M}^d$ by a large margin. Fig. 5 documents the unsurprising finding that for both methods the runtime grows linearly with k (once the effect of the initial L^* step fades out).

RQ2: For both methods, the number of actions needed increases mostly exponentially with increasing parameter d. However, the analysis still is feasible for larger values of d if using expansion $\mathcal{M}^d$ for sample collection. Exceptions to the exponential growth are due to the size of $\mathcal{M}^d$ no longer increasing for larger choices of d, rooted in acyclicity (see also the database example in Sec. 7).

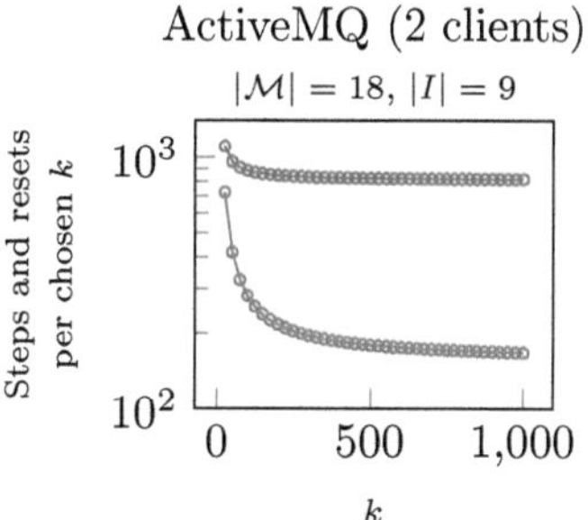

Fig. 5: Impact of k ($d = 0$)

RQ3: The size of the input alphabet can induce a massive performance hit for the sampling-based L^* approach, while the size of $\mathcal{M}^d$ remains manageable, as exemplified in the OpenSSH example. The reason is that the former approach needs to maintain a test set for the non-empty words $I^{\leq d}$ which increases significantly in size for a large $|I|$, whereas the expanded machine $\mathcal{M}^d$ eradicates many combinations, e.g., by the stutter-free restriction (see Def. 5).

RQ4: The assumption of a unique root can lead to a vast reduction in the size of $\mathcal{M}^d$, especially in small, cyclic examples, as the transition history of a state becomes irrelevant as soon as the (by assumption unique) root is visited. In some larger examples, there is also a small size difference w.r.t. $\mathcal{M}^d$ noticeable, for instance in the ActiveMQ example. However, in most cases, the presence or absence of the assumption has no impact on the number of steps needed.

7 Towards Practice: When the Order of Tasks Matters

For the benefit of full reproducibility and internal validity [68] and in line with the foundational nature of our contribution, the above empirical studies are fully synthetic. Nevertheless, to obtain a first view on ecological validity, we now complement them by reporting on experiments where real measured delays occur. Specifically, we consider a scenario where there is an intrinsic need for state separations, namely a situation where a system component may offer to perform some tasks but where the order of them being requested determines the overall time to completion, and where it is not clear a priori which orders are supported at all. So there is a need to learn the supported orders while studying the delays induced. Such situations arise in very many practical settings (e.g., in compiler technology, network management, information retrieval, or verification). For the purpose of a concrete setting, we work with a relational database, holding a set of tables of different sizes. For technical reasons, it is a priori unknown whether all such orders are supported.

Experimental setup. Experiments were carried out with PostgreSQL 10.23 on an AMD EPYC 72F3 8-Core CPU with 252 GB of RAM. The database holds four tables T_4 to T_7 with sizes ranging from 10^4 to 10^7. The database is orchestrated by a Python wrapper that first collects the order of the joins to perform before finally committing the join order but discards some orders (those starting with T_4 then T_5 and those ending in T_5 then T_7, all unknown to the learner upfront). We always join on the row index, so the joined result has the number of rows of the smaller table involved. To confirm that the logical structure alone has been inferred correctly, we apply the W-method [17,80] with $e = 1$. We again use $k = 1000$ and the distribution equality test from Sec. 6.

Results. For increasing values of d, we report the average delays until the full completion of the transaction (more details of the distributions can be obtained, of course).

- For $d = 0$, the algorithm learns the MDM as to be expected, and reports that, regardless of the order of joins, the commit will be delayed with a mean duration of 191 ms. Note that this choice of d cannot distinguish the effect of different orders, and also does not induce any meaningful averaged mean of the actual delays of the different join orders (the result depending on how often a transition is taken in the true SUL).
- For $d = 1$, the last action is decisive for the delay observed until the commit. This delay ranges from a mean 47 ms observed when T_7 is last, to 432 ms, observed when T_5 is last.
- For $d = 2$, the delays observed essentially depend on the last two joins requested, ranging from 21 ms obtained if the order ends in T_7 followed by T_6, to 442 ms obtained if the order ends in T_4 followed by T_5.
- For $d = 3$, the delays observed stay unchanged from the $d = 2$ case because the first binary join behaves the same with respect to the time it takes, regardless of the order of arguments. Still, the size of the final MDM $\mathcal{M}^d$ can differ slightly due to stochastic uncertainties in the delay sampling.

– For $d = 4$, the results are as for $d = 3$, because the SUL is 3-step confluent.

We report the total runtime, the size of the expanded MM $\mathcal{M}^d$, and the size of the resulting minimal MDM $\mathcal{D}'$ in Table 1. As one can see, increasing parameter d results in an increased runtime, in line with the findings reported in Sec. 6, together with a larger number of states, indicating that different delay behaviors caused by different join orders have been discovered successfully. A plateau is reached at $d = 3$, as the size of the MM $\mathcal{M}^d$ does not change anymore.

Table 1: Experimental results for database join orders

d	0	1	2	3	4
Runtime in seconds	≈ 192	≈ 943	≈ 1263	≈ 2469	≈ 2476
$|\mathcal{M}^d|$	18	33	49	58	58
$|\mathcal{D}'|$	18	20	29	29	29

8   Conclusion

This paper has studied the active learning of Mealy machines with stochastic transition delays. To outperform the straightforward adaptation of standard AAL algorithms, we have proposed a combination of learning just the I/O structure with an efficient way to subsequently collect samples of transition delays. When facing I/O-equivalent behavior associated with distinct delay characteristics, we have focused on cases with confluent structures of bounded depth, while indicating that the theory behind the approach extends to other settings. The empirical results reported are very encouraging.

A notable dimension of future work will be to exploit the cost model underlying the RPP, for instance to discriminate between resets and transition traversals based on the true overhead a reset induces, and/or to incorporate the delay information already gathered, thereby achieving a reduction of the overall learning duration incurred in realistic settings.

Acknowledgments. We thank Tobias Dick from Saarland University for his assistance in conducting the database case study and the fruitful discussions.

Full version. The full version of this paper (including all proofs and experiments) can be found at [23].

Data availability statement. The artifact of this paper—a reproduction package for the experiments in Sec. 6 and Sec. 7—is available at DOI `10.6084/m9.figshare.29966641`. The source code is available on `https://dgit.cs.uni-saarland.de/gabriel.dengler/al-expect-delays`.

References

1. Alur, R., Dill, D.L.: A theory of timed automata. Theor. Comput. Sci. **126**(2), 183–235 (1994). https://doi.org/10.1016/0304-3975(94)90010-8, `https://doi.org/10.1016/0304-3975(94)90010-8`

2. An, J., Chen, M., Zhan, B., Zhan, N., Zhang, M.: Learning One-Clock Timed Automata. In: Biere, A., Parker, D. (eds.) Tools and Algorithms for the Construction and Analysis of Systems. pp. 444–462. Springer International Publishing, Cham (2020)

3. An, J., Wang, L., Zhan, B., Zhan, N., Zhang, M.: Learning real-time automata. Science China Information Sciences **64**(9), 192103 (Aug 2021). https://doi.org/10.1007/s11432-019-2767-4, `https://doi.org/10.1007/s11432-019-2767-4`

4. An, J., Zhan, B., Zhan, N., Zhang, M.: Learning nondeterministic real-time automata. ACM Trans. Embed. Comput. Syst. **20**(5s) (Sep 2021). https://doi.org/10.1145/3477030, `https://doi.org/10.1145/3477030`

5. Angluin, D.: Learning regular sets from queries and counterexamples. Information and Computation **75**(2), 87–106 (1987). https://doi.org/https://doi.org/10.1016/0890-5401(87)90052-6, `https://www.sciencedirect.com/science/article/pii/0890540187900526`

6. Ashok, P., Kretínský, J., Weininger, M.: PAC Statistical Model Checking for Markov Decision Processes and Stochastic Games. In: Dillig, I., Tasiran, S. (eds.) Computer Aided Verification - 31st International Conference, CAV 2019, New York City, NY, USA, July 15-18, 2019, Proceedings, Part I. Lecture Notes in Computer Science, vol. 11561, pp. 497–519. Springer (2019). https://doi.org/10.1007/978-3-030-25540-4_29, `https://doi.org/10.1007/978-3-030-25540-4_29`

7. Asmussen, S., Nerman, O., Olsson, M.: Fitting phase-type distributions via the EM algorithm. Scandinavian Journal of Statistics **23**(4), 419–441 (1996), `http://www.jstor.org/stable/4616418`

8. Bacci, G., Ingólfsdóttir, A., Larsen, K.G., Reynouard, R.: Active Learning of Markov Decision Processes using Baum-Welch algorithm. In: Wani, M.A., Sethi, I.K., Shi, W., Qu, G., Raicu, D.S., Jin, R. (eds.) 20th IEEE International Conference on Machine Learning and Applications, ICMLA 2021, Pasadena, CA, USA, December 13-16, 2021. pp. 1203–1208. IEEE (2021). https://doi.org/10.1109/ICMLA52953.2021.00195, `https://doi.org/10.1109/ICMLA52953.2021.00195`

9. Baier, C., Haverkort, B.R., Hermanns, H., Katoen, J.: Reachability in continuous-time markov reward decision processes. In: Flum, J., Grädel, E., Wilke, T. (eds.) Logic and Automata: History and Perspectives [in Honor of Wolfgang Thomas]. Texts in Logic and Games, vol. 2, pp. 53–72. Amsterdam University Press (2008)

10. Bertrand, N., Bouyer, P., Brihaye, T., Menet, Q., Baier, C., Größer, M., Jurdzinski, M.: Stochastic Timed Automata. Log. Methods Comput. Sci. **10**(4) (2014). https://doi.org/10.2168/LMCS-10(4:6)2014, `https://doi.org/10.2168/LMCS-10(4:6)2014`

11. Biggs, N., Lloyd, E.K., Wilson, R.J.: Graph Theory, 1736-1936. Oxford University Press (1986)

12. Bobbio, A., András Horváth and Miklós Telek: Matching three moments with minimal acyclic phase type distributions. Stochastic Models **21**(2-3), 303–326 (2005). https://doi.org/10.1081/STM-200056210

13. Bruyère, V., Garhewal, B., Pérez, G.A., Staquet, G., Vaandrager, F.W.: Active Learning of Mealy Machines with Timers. CoRR **abs/2403.02019** (2024). https://doi.org/10.48550/ARXIV.2403.02019, `https://doi.org/10.48550/arXiv.2403.02019`

14. Buchholz, P., Dohndorf, I., Kriege, J.: An online approach to estimate parameters of phase-type distributions. In: 2019 49th Annual IEEE/IFIP International Conference on Dependable Systems and Networks (DSN). pp. 100–111 (June 2019). https://doi.org/10.1109/DSN.2019.00024

15. Caldwell, B., Cardell-Oliver, R., French, T.: Learning Time Delay Mealy Machines From Programmable Logic Controllers. IEEE Trans Autom. Sci. Eng. **13**(2), 1155–1164 (2016). https://doi.org/10.1109/TASE.2015.2496242, `https://doi.org/10.1109/TASE.2015.2496242`

16. Carrasco, R.C., Oncina, J.: Learning Stochastic Regular Grammars by Means of a State Merging Method. In: Carrasco, R.C., Oncina, J. (eds.) Grammatical Inference and Applications, Second International Colloquium, ICGI-94, Alicante, Spain, September 21-23, 1994, Proceedings. Lecture Notes in Computer Science, vol. 862, pp. 139–152. Springer (1994). https://doi.org/10.1007/3-540-58473-0_144, `https://doi.org/10.1007/3-540-58473-0_144`

17. Chow, T.: Testing Software Design Modeled by Finite-State Machines. IEEE Transactions on Software Engineering **SE-4**(3), 178–187 (1978). https://doi.org/10.1109/TSE.1978.231496

18. Chu, Y.J.: On the shortest arborescence of a directed graph. Scientia Sinica **14**, 1396–1400 (1965)

19. Dantzig, G.B.: Application of the simplex method to a transportation problem. Activity analysis and production and allocation (1951)

20. D'Argenio, P.R., Katoen, J.: A theory of stochastic systems part I: Stochastic automata. Inf. Comput. **203**(1), 1–38 (2005). https://doi.org/10.1016/J.IC.2005.07.001, `https://doi.org/10.1016/j.ic.2005.07.001`

21. David, A., Larsen, K.G., Legay, A., Nyman, U., Wasowski, A.: Timed I/O automata: a complete specification theory for real-time systems. In: Johansson, K.H., Yi, W. (eds.) Proceedings of the 13th ACM International Conference on Hybrid Systems: Computation and Control, HSCC 2010, Stockholm, Sweden, April 12-15, 2010. pp. 91–100. ACM (2010). https://doi.org/10.1145/1755952.1755967, `https://doi.org/10.1145/1755952.1755967`

22. Deng, Y., Hennessy, M.: On the semantics of Markov automata. Inf. Comput. **222**, 139–168 (2013). https://doi.org/10.1016/J.IC.2012.10.010, `https://doi.org/10.1016/j.ic.2012.10.010`

23. Dengler, G., Apel, S., Hermanns, H.: Automata Learning – Expect Delays! CoRR **abs/2508.16384** (2025). https://doi.org/10.48550/ARXIV.2508.16384, `https://doi.org/10.48550/arXiv.2508.16384`

24. Dvoretzky, A., Kiefer, J., Wolfowitz, J.: Asymptotic Minimax Character of the Sample Distribution Function and of the Classical Multinomial Estimator. The Annals of Mathematical Statistics **27**(3), 642 – 669 (1956). https://doi.org/10.1214/aoms/1177728174, `https://doi.org/10.1214/aoms/1177728174`

25. Edmonds, J., Johnson, E.L.: Matching, Euler tours and the Chinese postman. Mathematical Programming **5**(1), 88–124 (Dec 1973). https://doi.org/10.1007/BF01580113, `https://doi.org/10.1007/BF01580113`

26. Edmonds, J., et al.: Optimum branchings. Journal of Research of the national Bureau of Standards B **71**(4), 233–240 (1967)

27. Eiselt, H.A., Gendreau, M., Laporte, G.: Arc routing problems, part ii: The rural postman problem. Operations research **43**(3), 399–414 (1995)
28. Eisentraut, C., Hermanns, H., Zhang, L.: On Probabilistic Automata in Continuous Time. In: Proceedings of the 25th Annual IEEE Symposium on Logic in Computer Science, LICS 2010, 11-14 July 2010, Edinburgh, United Kingdom. pp. 342–351. IEEE Computer Society (2010). https://doi.org/10.1109/LICS.2010.41, `https://doi.org/10.1109/LICS.2010.41`
29. Feldmann, A., Whitt, W.: Fitting mixtures of exponentials to long-tail distributions to analyze network. Perform. Evaluation **31**(3-4), 245–279 (1998). https://doi.org/10.1016/S0166-5316(97)00003-5
30. Feller, W.: An introduction to probability theory and its applications, Volume 2, vol. 81. John Wiley & Sons (1991)
31. Ferreira, T., Brewton, H., D'Antoni, L., Silva, A.: Prognosis: closed-box analysis of network protocol implementations. In: Proceedings of the 2021 ACM SIGCOMM 2021 Conference. p. 762–774. SIGCOMM '21, Association for Computing Machinery, New York, NY, USA (2021). https://doi.org/10.1145/3452296.3472938, `https://doi.org/10.1145/3452296.3472938`
32. Hartmanns, A., Hermanns, H.: In the quantitative automata zoo. Sci. Comput. Program. **112**, 3–23 (2015). https://doi.org/10.1016/J.SCICO.2015.08.009, `https://doi.org/10.1016/j.scico.2015.08.009`
33. Henderson, K., Gallagher, B., Eliassi-Rad, T.: EP-MEANS: an efficient nonparametric clustering of empirical probability distributions. In: Wainwright, R.L., Corchado, J.M., Bechini, A., Hong, J. (eds.) Proceedings of the 30th Annual ACM Symposium on Applied Computing, Salamanca, Spain, April 13-17, 2015. pp. 893–900. ACM (2015). https://doi.org/10.1145/2695664.2695860, `https://doi.org/10.1145/2695664.2695860`
34. Henry, L., Jéron, T., Markey, N.: Active Learning of Timed Automata with Unobservable Resets. In: Bertrand, N., Jansen, N. (eds.) Formal Modeling and Analysis of Timed Systems - 18th International Conference, FORMATS 2020, Vienna, Austria, September 1-3, 2020, Proceedings. Lecture Notes in Computer Science, vol. 12288, pp. 144–160. Springer (2020). https://doi.org/10.1007/978-3-030-57628-8_9, `https://doi.org/10.1007/978-3-030-57628-8_9`
35. Hoeffding, W.: Probability inequalities for sums of bounded random variables. Journal of the American Statistical Association **58**(301), 13–30 (1963). https://doi.org/10.1080/01621459.1963.10500830, `https://www.tandfonline.com/doi/abs/10.1080/01621459.1963.10500830`
36. Horváth, A., Telek, M.: Phfit: A general phase-type fitting tool. In: Field, T., Harrison, P.G., Bradley, J.T., Harder, U. (eds.) Computer Performance Evaluation, Modelling Techniques and Tools 12th International Conference, TOOLS 2002, London, UK, April 14-17, 2002, Proceedings. Lecture Notes in Computer Science, vol. 2324, pp. 82–91. Springer (2002). https://doi.org/10.1007/3-540-46029-2_5
37. Horváth, A., Telek, M.: Matching more than three moments with acyclic phase type distributions. Stochastic Models **23**(2), 167–194 (2007). https://doi.org/10.1080/15326340701300712
38. Horváth, G.: Moment matching-based distribution fitting with generalized hyper-erlang distributions. In: Dudin, A.N., Turck, K.D. (eds.) Analytical and Stochastic Modelling Techniques and Applications - 20th International Conference, ASMTA 2013, Ghent, Belgium, July 8-10, 2013. Proceedings. Lecture Notes in Computer Science, vol. 7984, pp. 232–246. Springer (2013). https://doi.org/10.1007/978-3-642-39408-9_17

39. Isberner, M., Howar, F., Steffen, B.: The TTT algorithm: A redundancy-free approach to active automata learning. In: Bonakdarpour, B., Smolka, S.A. (eds.) Runtime Verification - 5th International Conference, RV 2014, Toronto, ON, Canada, September 22-25, 2014. Proceedings. Lecture Notes in Computer Science, vol. 8734, pp. 307–322. Springer (2014). https://doi.org/10.1007/978-3-319-11164-3_26, https://doi.org/10.1007/978-3-319-11164-3_26
40. Johnson, M.A., Taaffe, M.R.: Matching moments to phase distributions: Mixtures of erlang distributions of common order. Communications in Statistics. Stochastic Models **5**(4), 711–743 (1989). https://doi.org/10.1080/15326348908807131
41. Jonsson, B., Vaandrager, F.: Learning Mealy machines with timers. Tech. rep., Tech. rep (2018)
42. Khayari, R.E.A., Sadre, R., Haverkort, B.R.: Fitting world-wide web request traces with the em-algorithm. Perform. Evaluation **52**(2-3), 175–191 (2003). https://doi.org/10.1016/S0166-5316(02)00179-7
43. Király, Z., Kovács, P.: Efficient implementations of minimum-cost flow algorithms. arXiv preprint arXiv:1207.6381 (2012)
44. Kogel, P., Klös, V., Glesner, S.: Learning Mealy Machines with Local Timers. In: Li, Y., Tahar, S. (eds.) Formal Methods and Software Engineering - 24th International Conference on Formal Engineering Methods, ICFEM 2023, Brisbane, QLD, Australia, November 21-24, 2023, Proceedings. Lecture Notes in Computer Science, vol. 14308, pp. 47–64. Springer (2023). https://doi.org/10.1007/978-981-99-7584-6_4, https://doi.org/10.1007/978-981-99-7584-6_4
45. Kruger, L., Junges, S., Rot, J.: Small Test Suites for Active Automata Learning. In: Finkbeiner, B., Kovács, L. (eds.) Tools and Algorithms for the Construction and Analysis of Systems. pp. 109–129. Springer Nature Switzerland, Cham (2024)
46. López, G.G.I., Hermanns, H., Katoen, J.: Beyond memoryless distributions: Model checking semi-markov chains. In: de Alfaro, L., Gilmore, S. (eds.) Process Algebra and Probabilistic Methods, Performance Modeling and Verification: Joint International Workshop, PAPM-PROBMIV 2001, Aachen, Germany, September 12-14, 2001, Proceedings. Lecture Notes in Computer Science, vol. 2165, pp. 57–70. Springer (2001). https://doi.org/10.1007/3-540-44804-7_4, https://doi.org/10.1007/3-540-44804-7_4
47. MacQueen, J.: Some methods for classification and analysis of multivariate observations. In: Proceedings of 5-th Berkeley Symposium on Mathematical Statistics and Probability/University of California Press (1967)
48. Mann, H.B., Whitney, D.R.: On a Test of Whether one of Two Random Variables is Stochastically Larger than the Other. The Annals of Mathematical Statistics **18**(1), 50 – 60 (1947). https://doi.org/10.1214/aoms/1177730491, https://doi.org/10.1214/aoms/1177730491
49. Mao, H., Chen, Y., Jaeger, M., Nielsen, T.D., Larsen, K.G., Nielsen, B.: Learning Markov Decision Processes for Model Checking. In: Fahrenberg, U., Legay, A., Thrane, C.R. (eds.) Proceedings Quantities in Formal Methods, QFM 2012, Paris, France, 28 August 2012. EPTCS, vol. 103, pp. 49–63 (2012). https://doi.org/10.4204/EPTCS.103.6, https://doi.org/10.4204/EPTCS.103.6
50. Massart, P.: The Tight Constant in the Dvoretzky-Kiefer-Wolfowitz Inequality. The Annals of Probability **18**(3), 1269 – 1283 (1990). https://doi.org/10.1214/aop/1176990746, https://doi.org/10.1214/aop/1176990746
51. de Matos Pedro, A., Crocker, P.A., de Sousa, S.M.: Learning Stochastic Timed Automata from Sample Executions. In: Margaria, T., Steffen, B. (eds.) Leveraging Applications of Formal Methods, Verification and Validation. Technologies for

Mastering Change - 5th International Symposium, ISoLA 2012, Heraklion, Crete, Greece, October 15-18, 2012, Proceedings, Part I. Lecture Notes in Computer Science, vol. 7609, pp. 508–523. Springer (2012). https://doi.org/10.1007/978-3-642-34026-0_38, https://doi.org/10.1007/978-3-642-34026-0_38

52. Mediouni, B.L., Nouri, A., Bozga, M., Bensalem, S.: Improved Learning for Stochastic Timed Models by State-Merging Algorithms. In: Barrett, C.W., Davies, M.D., Kahsai, T. (eds.) NASA Formal Methods - 9th International Symposium, NFM 2017, Moffett Field, CA, USA, May 16-18, 2017, Proceedings. Lecture Notes in Computer Science, vol. 10227, pp. 178–193 (2017). https://doi.org/10.1007/978-3-319-57288-8_13, https://doi.org/10.1007/978-3-319-57288-8_13

53. Meijer, J., van de Pol, J.: Sound black-box checking in the LearnLib. Innov. Syst. Softw. Eng. **15**(3-4), 267–287 (2019). https://doi.org/10.1007/S11334-019-00342-6, https://doi.org/10.1007/s11334-019-00342-6

54. Mohri, M.: Foundations of machine learning (2018)

55. Muškardin, E., Aichernig, B.K., Pill, I., Pferscher, A., Tappler, M.: AALpy: an active automata learning library. Innovations in Systems and Software Engineering **18**(3), 417–426 (Sep 2022). https://doi.org/10.1007/s11334-022-00449-3

56. Muškardin, E., Tappler, M., Aichernig, B.K., Pill, I.: Active model learning of stochastic reactive systems (extended version). Software and Systems Modeling **23**(2), 503–524 (Apr 2024). https://doi.org/10.1007/s10270-024-01158-0

57. Neider, D., Smetsers, R., Vaandrager, F., Kuppens, H.: Benchmarks for Automata Learning and Conformance Testing, pp. 390–416. Springer International Publishing, Cham (2019). https://doi.org/10.1007/978-3-030-22348-9_23

58. Nicollin, X., Sifakis, J.: An overview and synthesis on timed process algebras. In: Larsen, K.G., Skou, A. (eds.) Computer Aided Verification, 3rd International Workshop, CAV '91, Aalborg, Denmark, July, 1-4, 1991, Proceedings. Lecture Notes in Computer Science, vol. 575, pp. 376–398. Springer (1991). https://doi.org/10.1007/3-540-55179-4_36, https://doi.org/10.1007/3-540-55179-4_36

59. Nielsen, F.: A family of statistical symmetric divergences based on jensen's inequality. CoRR **abs/1009.4004** (2010), http://arxiv.org/abs/1009.4004

60. Panchenko, A., Thümmler, A.: Efficient phase-type fitting with aggregated traffic traces. Perform. Evaluation **64**(7-8), 629–645 (2007). https://doi.org/10.1016/J.PEVA.2006.09.002, https://doi.org/10.1016/j.peva.2006.09.002

61. Park, D.M.R.: Concurrency and automata on infinite sequences. In: Deussen, P. (ed.) Theoretical Computer Science, 5th GI-Conference, Karlsruhe, Germany, March 23-25, 1981, Proceedings. Lecture Notes in Computer Science, vol. 104, pp. 167–183. Springer (1981). https://doi.org/10.1007/BFB0017309, https://doi.org/10.1007/BFb0017309

62. Pearn, W., Wu, T.: Algorithms for the rural postman problem. Computers & Operations Research **22**(8), 819–828 (1995). https://doi.org/https://doi.org/10.1016/0305-0548(94)00070-O, https://www.sciencedirect.com/science/article/pii/0305054894000700

63. Peled, D., Vardi, M.Y., Yannakakis, M.: Black Box Checking, pp. 225–240. Springer US, Boston, MA (1999). https://doi.org/10.1007/978-0-387-35578-8_13, https://doi.org/10.1007/978-0-387-35578-8_13

64. Rubner, Y., Tomasi, C., Guibas, L.J.: A metric for distributions with applications to image databases. In: Proceedings of the Sixth International Conference on Computer Vision (ICCV-98), Bombay, India, January 4-7, 1998. pp. 59–

66. IEEE Computer Society (1998). https://doi.org/10.1109/ICCV.1998.710701, https://doi.org/10.1109/ICCV.1998.710701

65. Segala, R., Lynch, N.A.: Probabilistic simulations for probabilistic processes. Nord. J. Comput. **2**(2), 250–273 (1995)

66. Sen, K., Viswanathan, M., Agha, G.: Learning Continuous Time Markov Chains from Sample Executions. In: 1st International Conference on Quantitative Evaluation of Systems (QEST 2004), 27-30 September 2004, Enschede, The Netherlands. pp. 146–155. IEEE Computer Society (2004). https://doi.org/10.1109/QEST.2004.1348029, https://doi.org/10.1109/QEST.2004.1348029

67. Shijubo, J., Waga, M., Suenaga, K.: Probabilistic black-box checking via active MDP learning. ACM Trans. Embed. Comput. Syst. **22**(5s), 148:1–148:26 (2023). https://doi.org/10.1145/3609127, https://doi.org/10.1145/3609127

68. Siegmund, J., Siegmund, N., Apel, S.: Views on internal and external validity in empirical software engineering. In: Bertolino, A., Canfora, G., Elbaum, S.G. (eds.) 37th IEEE/ACM International Conference on Software Engineering, ICSE 2015, Florence, Italy, May 16-24, 2015, Volume 1. pp. 9–19. IEEE Computer Society (2015). https://doi.org/10.1109/ICSE.2015.24, https://doi.org/10.1109/ICSE.2015.24

69. Smirnov, N.: Table for Estimating the Goodness of Fit of Empirical Distributions. The Annals of Mathematical Statistics **19**(2), 279 – 281 (1948). https://doi.org/10.1214/aoms/1177730256, https://doi.org/10.1214/aoms/1177730256

70. Steffen, B., Howar, F., Isberner, M.: Active Automata Learning: From DFAs to Interface Programs and Beyond. In: Heinz, J., de la Higuera, C., Oates, T. (eds.) Proceedings of the Eleventh International Conference on Grammatical Inference, ICGI 2012, University of Maryland, College Park, USA, September 5-8, 2012. JMLR Proceedings, vol. 21, pp. 195–209. JMLR.org (2012), http://proceedings.mlr.press/v21/steffen12a.html

71. Steffen, B., Howar, F., Merten, M.: Introduction to Active Automata Learning from a Practical Perspective, pp. 256–296. Springer Berlin Heidelberg, Berlin, Heidelberg (2011). https://doi.org/10.1007/978-3-642-21455-4_8, https://doi.org/10.1007/978-3-642-21455-4_8

72. Stoelinga, M.: An Introduction to Probabilistic Automata. Bull. EATCS **78**, 176–198 (2002)

73. Suilen, M., Simão, T.D., Parker, D., Jansen, N.: Robust anytime learning of Markov decision processes. In: Proceedings of the 36th International Conference on Neural Information Processing Systems. NIPS '22, Curran Associates Inc., Red Hook, NY, USA (2024)

74. Tappler, M., Aichernig, B.K., Bacci, G., Eichlseder, M., Larsen, K.G.: L^*-based learning of Markov decision processes (extended version). Formal Aspects of Computing **33**(4), 575–615 (Aug 2021). https://doi.org/10.1007/s00165-021-00536-5

75. Telek, M., Horváth, G.: A minimal representation of markov arrival processes and a moments matching method. Perform. Evaluation **64**(9-12), 1153–1168 (2007). https://doi.org/10.1016/j.peva.2007.06.001

76. Teng, Y., Zhang, M., An, J.: Learning Deterministic Multi-Clock Timed Automata. In: Ábrahám, E., Jr., M.M. (eds.) Proceedings of the 27th ACM International Conference on Hybrid Systems: Computation and Control, HSCC 2024, Hong Kong SAR, China, May 14-16, 2024. pp. 6:1–6:11. ACM (2024). https://doi.org/10.1145/3641513.3650124, https://doi.org/10.1145/3641513.3650124

77. Thümmler, A., Buchholz, P., Telek, M.: A novel approach for phase-type fitting with the EM algorithm. IEEE Trans. Dependable Secur. Comput. **3**(3), 245–258 (2006). https://doi.org/10.1109/TDSC.2006.27
78. Vaandrager, F., Garhewal, B., Rot, J., Wißmann, T.: A New Approach for Active Automata Learning Based on Apartness. In: Fisman, D., Rosu, G. (eds.) Tools and Algorithms for the Construction and Analysis of Systems. pp. 223–243. Springer International Publishing, Cham (2022)
79. Vaandrager, F., Melse, I.: New Fault Domains for Conformance Testing of Finite State Machines. In: Bouyer, P., van de Pol, J. (eds.) 36th International Conference on Concurrency Theory (CONCUR 2025). Leibniz International Proceedings in Informatics (LIPIcs), vol. 348, pp. 34:1–34:22. Schloss Dagstuhl – Leibniz-Zentrum für Informatik, Dagstuhl, Germany (2025). https://doi.org/10.4230/LIPIcs.CONCUR.2025.34, https://drops.dagstuhl.de/entities/document/10.4230/LIPIcs.CONCUR.2025.34
80. Vasilevskii, M.P.: Failure diagnosis of automata. Cybernetics **9**(4), 653–665 (Jul 1973). https://doi.org/10.1007/BF01068590, https://doi.org/10.1007/BF01068590
81. Verwer, S., de Weerdt, M., Witteveen, C.: Efficiently identifying deterministic real-time automata from labeled data. Mach. Learn. **86**(3), 295–333 (2012). https://doi.org/10.1007/S10994-011-5265-4, https://doi.org/10.1007/s10994-011-5265-4
82. Waga, M.: Falsification of cyber-physical systems with robustness-guided blackbox checking. In: Ames, A.D., Seshia, S.A., Deshmukh, J. (eds.) HSCC '20: 23rd ACM International Conference on Hybrid Systems: Computation and Control, Sydney, New South Wales, Australia, April 21-24, 2020. pp. 11:1–11:13. ACM (2020). https://doi.org/10.1145/3365365.3382193, https://doi.org/10.1145/3365365.3382193
83. Waga, M.: Active Learning of Deterministic Timed Automata with Myhill-Nerode Style Characterization. In: Enea, C., Lal, A. (eds.) Computer Aided Verification. pp. 3–26. Springer Nature Switzerland, Cham (2023)

Distributed Timed Scenarios

Neda Saeedloei[1(✉)] and Feliks Kluźniak[2]

[1] Towson University, Towson, USA
nsaeedloei@towson.edu
[2] Towson, USA

Abstract. We introduce the notion of a distributed timed scenario (DTS) and define the semantics of a DTS as a set of distributed behaviours. We define the notion of consistency of a DTS in terms of its semantics and develop a constructive method for determining the consistency. We define the semantic equivalence of two distributed scenarios and develop two different, but related, canonical representations for an equivalence class of distributed scenarios. Equipped with these results we tackle the problem of realisability of sets of sequential scenarios as distributed scenarios. We develop an algorithm that determines whether a set of sequential scenarios can be realised by a DTS, i.e., whether there is a DTS whose semantics is identical to the union of the behaviours allowed by the members of the set. If so, we produce such a DTS.

1 Introduction

Sequential timed scenarios [1] were developed as a formal, yet simple notation for specifying the partial behaviours of a system or a component of a system. A timed scenario is a sequence of (names of) events along with a set of constraints between the times at which these events occur (see Sect. 2 for more details). The semantics of a timed scenario is the set of all behaviours that consist of a particular sequence of events and satisfy the same set of constraints.

Real-world systems often consist of subsystems or components which operate under time constraints, while interacting with each other. Timed scenarios can be used for specifying behaviours of sequential timed systems (or their components), but they are not so useful for modeling distributed timed systems.

In the current paper we introduce distributed timed scenarios as a natural extension of our timed scenarios. The resulting formalism, with its well-defined semantics, provides a framework for specifying behaviours of distributed timed systems. Thanks to its underlying foundation (a mathematically sound and well-developed theory of timed scenarios), this framework is conducive to direct reasoning and analysis of time-related behaviours of distributed timed systems.

Intuitively, a distributed timed scenario (DTS) is a set of timed scenarios. We refer to the individual scenarios of a DTS as its *components* and assume that time advances at the same rate in all the components. The idea is that each component performs its specified actions, represented as a sequence of events, independently from other components. However, from time to time, the components communicate or synchronise with each other by performing the same

F. Damiani and M. Farrell (Eds.): iFM 2025, LNCS 16194, pp. 487–508, 2026.
https://doi.org/10.1007/978-3-032-10794-7_24

action simultaneously. In addition to the total order induced on the events of each component, these common actions, which are called synchronising events, create some ordering dependencies between events across different components. For instance, if s is a synchronising event for components ξ and η, c occurs before s in ξ and d occurs after s in η, then c must occur before d in all behaviours. In the presence of synchronising events the explicit constraints of the individual components also imply additional dependencies between events in different components. For example, if the latest time that event e in ξ can occur after a synchronising event s' is smaller than the earliest time that event f in η can occur after s', then we can conclude that e always occurs before f.

For a DTS, $\varXi$, we define the relation $\prec_\varXi^x$ to capture all the ordering dependencies between events in $\varXi$, and introduce the distance function, $\mathcal{DF}_\varXi^{sx}$, to capture the time distance between every pair of events e and e', such that $e \prec_\varXi^x e'$. We define the *(stable) extended distance relation* of $\varXi$ as the pair $(\prec_\varXi^x, \mathcal{DF}_\varXi^{sx})$ and use it to define $[\![\varXi]\!]$, i.e., the semantics of $\varXi$: the set of behaviours whose sequences of events respect $\prec_\varXi^x$ and whose events occur at times that satisfy the constraints captured by $\mathcal{DF}_\varXi^{sx}$. We develop a method for determining whether $\varXi$ is consistent, i.e., whether $[\![\varXi]\!] \neq \emptyset$. We also introduce the notion of (semantic) equivalence of two distributed scenarios and develop two different, but related, canonical representations for all the distributed scenarios that belong to the same equivalence class. Equipped with these results, we develop an algorithm for the problem of realisability of sequential scenarios as distributed scenarios. Given a set, $\mathcal{S}$, of sequential scenarios, our algorithm determines whether there exists a DTS, $\varXi$, that realises $\mathcal{S}$, i.e., $[\![\varXi]\!]$ is identical to the set of behaviours specified by $\mathcal{S}$. If so, we produce $\varXi$. To illustrate the applicability of our approach we present a DTS describing the collaborative tasks of various healthcare team members in an Emergency Department who are involved with the treatment of a patient suspected of having a stroke.

The novelty of our work is primarily the use of (stable) extended distance relations as a linchpin of simple and efficient methods for determining consistency and equivalence of distributed scenarios, as well as for using them to realize sets of sequential scenarios.

Related Work. In our earlier work we developed the notion of a "stable distance table" as a canonical representation of the set of constraints of a sequential scenario. We used stable distance tables as the foundation of various algorithms for determining the consistency and equivalence of scenarios, as well as for optimising scenarios [1,2] and synthesizing timed automata from scenarios [3,4].

The comparison of our stable distance tables with Difference Bounds Matrices is presented elsewhere [1,5].

There are similarities between how we analyze time constraints (using distance tables) and how Simple Temporal Networks (STNs) [6] are used to check satisfiability of time constraints. However, our scenarios are fundamentally different from STNs: in scenarios the order of events is not determined *only* by the constraints. The goal is also different: scenarios provide a framework for precisely *specifying* (components of) timed systems [1].

Message Sequence Charts (MSCs) [7,8] were among the earliest scenario-based formalisms for modeling communication between components of complex systems [9,10]. To provide better support for analysis of distributed time systems, various extensions of MSCs with time have been proposed [11–14]. The semantics of these formalisms are often defined indirectly, i.e., by transforming them into other formalisms, e.g., timed automata [15,16]. Moreover, checking consistency is also carried out indirectly [12,17], e.g., by checking the consistency of individual paths in their corresponding state machines, or by using model checking tools, e.g., Uppaal [18]. In contrast to these, the semantics of our distributed scenarios is defined formally (and directly), in terms of the set of behaviours allowed by them. Moreover, consistency is determined, directly, by a simple algorithm, without using transformations or other tools.

A distributed behaviour of a DTS is essentially a timed trace of Balaguer et al. [19]. While the focus of that work is on translating a 1-bounded time petri net into a network of timed automata, our goal is to develop the theoretical foundation of distributed timed scenarios, and use it to develop methods and algorithms for determining consistency, equivalence and realisability.

Our distance relations are similar to timed partial orders (TPOs) of Watanabe et al. [20]. Unlike in that work, there is no advantage in limiting the expressive power of our distance relations by making them "race-free". The focus of that work is also quite different: they are concerned mostly with mining race-free TPOs from time-stamped event sequences, hence do not even mention the fact that in principle a TPO can be inconsistent.

The problem of realisability of global models has been investigated for global session types [21–24], global labelled transition systems [25], and choreography languages [26]. Unlike in all these works the realisability of our distributed scenarios is determined by precise time analysis enabled by our distance relations.

2   Timed Scenarios

This subsection briefly recounts our earlier work [1].

Let Σ be a finite set of symbols called *events*. A *behaviour*[1] over Σ is a non-empty sequence $(e_0, t_0)(e_1, t_1)(e_2, t_2) \ldots$, such that $e_i \in \Sigma$, $t_i \in \mathbb{R}^{\geq 0}$ and $t_{i-1} \leq t_i$ for $i \in \{1, 2 \ldots\}$. For a finite behaviour $\mathcal{B} = (e_0, t_0)(e_1, t_1) \ldots (e_{n-1}, t_{n-1})$ of length n ($n \in \mathbb{N}^{>0}$), and for any $0 \leq i < j < n$, the *distance*, in time units, of event j from event i in $\mathcal{B}$ is denoted by $t_{ij}^{\mathcal{B}}$. That is, $t_{ij}^{\mathcal{B}} = t_j - t_i$.

A *sequential timed scenario* (*scenario* for short) of length $n \in \mathbb{N}$ over Σ is a pair $(\mathcal{E}, \mathcal{C})$, where $\mathcal{E} = e_0 e_1 \ldots e_{n-1}$ is a non-empty sequence of events, and $\mathcal{C} \subset \Phi(n)$ is a finite set of constraints. Each constraint in $\Phi(n)$ is of the form $b \sim a$, where b is the symbol $\tau_{i,j}$ (for some integers $0 \leq i < j < n$), $\sim \in \{\leq, \geq, =\}^2$

---

[1] The notion of "behaviour" is equivalent to that of Alur's "timed word" [27]. We found the term "behaviour" more suitable and intuitive in the context of timed scenarios.

[2] To keep the presentation compact, we do not allow strict inequalities [1].

and $a \in \mathbb{Q}$ is a constant. The interpretation is that $\tau_{i,j}$ is the time distance between the i-th and the j-th events in the behaviours described by a scenario. The constraints $\tau_{i,j} \geq 0$ and $\tau_{i,j} \leq \infty$ are called *default constraints*.

If $\xi = (\mathcal{E}, \mathcal{C})$, we use $eseq(\xi)$ to refer to the sequence of events, $\mathcal{E}$, in ξ.

A behaviour $\mathcal{B} = (e_0, t_0)(e_1, t_1) \ldots (e_{n-1}, t_{n-1})$ over Σ is *allowed* by scenario $\xi = (\mathcal{E}, \mathcal{C})$ iff $\mathcal{E} = e_0 \ldots e_{n-1}$ and every $\tau_{i,j} \sim a$ in $\mathcal{C}$ evaluates to true after $\tau_{i,j}$ is replaced by $t_{ij}^{\mathcal{B}}$. The *semantics* of scenario ξ, denoted by $[\![\xi]\!]$, is the set of behaviours that are allowed by ξ. Additionally, if $\mathcal{S} = \{\xi_1, \ldots, \xi_n\}$ is a finite set of sequential scenarios, the semantics of $\mathcal{S}$ is $[\![\mathcal{S}]\!] = \bigcup_{1 \leq i \leq n} [\![\xi_i]\!]$.

A scenario ξ is *consistent* iff $[\![\xi]\!] \neq \emptyset$. It is *inconsistent* iff $[\![\xi]\!] = \emptyset$. For example, $\xi = (abc, \{\tau_{0,1} \geq 3, \tau_{0,2} \leq 7\})$ is a consistent scenario: $[\![\xi]\!] = \{(a, t_0)(b, t_1)(c, t_2) \mid t_0 \leq t_1 \leq t_2 \wedge t_1 - t_0 \geq 3 \wedge t_2 - t_0 \leq 7\}$.

3   Distributed Timed Scenarios

Definition 1. *A sequential timed scenario ξ is in* normalized form *iff every event of $eseq(\xi)$ has only one occurrence in $eseq(\xi)$.*

An arbitrary scenario can be trivially transformed to normalized form. If there is more than one event with the same name, say a, in a scenario of length n, we will replace the kth $(1 < k \leq n - 1)$ occurrence of a with a_k. For example, if ξ_1 is such that $eseq(\xi_1) = abac$, then in the normalized form $eseq(\xi_1) = aba_1c$.

In the rest of the paper we assume all the sequential scenarios are normalized. Therefore, in a scenario each event is uniquely identified by its name. If event i in scenario ξ is a, we will use t_a (instead of t_i) to refer to the time of a in a behaviour, $\mathcal{B}$, that is allowed by ξ. If event j $(i < j)$ in ξ is b, we will use $\tau_{a,b}$ (instead of $\tau_{i,j}$) in a constraint that restricts the time distance between a and b, and $t_{ab}^{\mathcal{B}}$ (instead of $t_{ij}^{\mathcal{B}}$) to represent the time distance between a and b in $\mathcal{B}$.

For a consistent scenario $\xi = (\mathcal{E}, \mathcal{C})$ over Σ, where $\mathcal{E} = e_0 e_1 \ldots e_n$, we use $\Sigma_\xi = \{e_0, e_1, \ldots, e_n\} \subseteq \Sigma$ to denote the set of events in $\mathcal{E}$. We assume Σ_ξ includes the event '-'. We explain the motivation for this after Definition 7.

Naturally, the sequence $\mathcal{E}$ of ξ induces a total order on Σ_ξ. We use $<_\xi$ to denote this total order: for two events e_i and e_j in $\mathcal{E}$, $e_i <_\xi e_j \iff i < j$.

Definition 2. *Let Σ be a finite set of events. A distributed timed scenario (DTS or distributed scenario for short) over Σ is a finite set $\Xi = \{\xi_1, \ldots, \xi_n\}$ of sequential timed scenarios, such that (i) each $\xi \in \Xi$ is consistent and is in normalized form, and (ii) the first event in every scenario $\xi \in \Xi$ is the event '-'.*

We refer to the individual scenarios of Ξ as the *components* of Ξ. We use $\Sigma_\Xi = \Sigma_{\xi_1} \cup \cdots \cup \Sigma_{\xi_n}$ to denote the set of events in Ξ.

Definition 3. *A DTS Ξ over Σ is* well-formed *iff $\prec_\Xi \subseteq \Sigma \times \Sigma$, defined as the transitive closure of $\bigcup_{\xi \in \Xi} <_\xi$, is a strict partial order on Σ.*

Example 1. The set $\Xi = \{\xi_1, \xi_2\}$, where $\xi_1 = (\text{-}abc, \{\tau_{\text{-},a} \leq 5, \tau_{a,b} \geq 1, \tau_{a,c} \leq 8, \tau_{b,c} \geq 3\})$, $\xi_2 = (\text{-}efb, \{\tau_{e,f} \leq 3, 2 \leq \tau_{e,b} \leq 6\})$ is a well-formed DTS over the set $\Sigma = \{\text{-}, a, b, c, e, f\}$: the relation $\prec_\Xi$, the transitive closure of $<_{\xi_1} \cup <_{\xi_2}$, is a strict partial order on Σ. Observe that $f \prec_\Xi c$, but $e \not\prec_\Xi a$ and $a \not\prec_\Xi e$.

Example 2. The set $\Xi = \{\xi_1, \xi_2\}$, where $\xi_1 = (\text{-}abc, \emptyset)$, $\xi_2 = (\text{-}dcb, \emptyset)$ is not a well-formed DTS: $\prec_\Xi$ includes both (b, c) and (c, b), so it is not a partial order.

Definition 4. *Let $\mathcal{B}$ be a behaviour over Σ and ξ be a sequential scenario, such that $\Sigma_\xi \subseteq \Sigma$. The restriction of $\mathcal{B}$ to ξ, denoted by $\mathcal{B}_\xi$, is the maximal subsequence of $\mathcal{B}$ such that every event of $\mathcal{B}_\xi$ is in Σ_ξ.*

Note that a maximal subsequence need not be contiguous.

Definition 5. *Let $\Xi = \{\xi_1, \ldots, \xi_n\}$ be a well-formed DTS over Σ. Behaviour $\mathcal{B}$ over Σ_Ξ is allowed by Ξ iff, for every $\xi_i \in \Xi$ $(1 \leq i \leq n)$, $\mathcal{B}_{\xi_i} \in [\![\xi_i]\!]$.*

If behaviour $\mathcal{B}$ is allowed by Ξ, we say $\mathcal{B}$ is a distributed behaviour *of Ξ.*

Notice that, for every $\xi_i \in \Xi$, $\text{-} \in \Sigma_{\xi_i}$, so $\mathcal{B}_{\xi_i}$ is always a non-empty sequence. Notice also that the sequence of events in every behaviour $\mathcal{B}$ allowed by Ξ is a permutation of all the symbols in Σ_Ξ. Therefore, the length of $\mathcal{B}$ is $|\Sigma_\Xi|$.

Example 3. Let $\mathcal{B} = (\text{-}, 0)(e, 1)(a, 2)(f, 3)(b, 4)(c, 7)$. The restrictions of $\mathcal{B}$ to ξ_1 and ξ_2 of Example 1 are $\mathcal{B}_{\xi_1} = (\text{-}, 0)(a, 2)(b, 4)(c, 7)$ and $\mathcal{B}_{\xi_2} = (\text{-}, 0)(e, 1)(f, 3)(b, 4)$, respectively. Behaviour $\mathcal{B}$ is allowed by Ξ of Example 1: $\mathcal{B}_{\xi_1}$ is allowed by ξ_1 and $\mathcal{B}_{\xi_2}$ is allowed by ξ_2, so $\mathcal{B}$ is a distributed behaviour of Ξ.

Notice that the distributed behaviour of Example 3 consists of an interleaving of the timed events of ξ_1 and ξ_2, except that the events '-' and b occur only once. These events are special in that they are shared by both components. The intuition behind this is the following: the DTS allows a distributed behaviour $\mathcal{B}$ if $\mathcal{B}$ is composed of a behaviour from $[\![\xi_1]\!]$ and a behaviour from $[\![\xi_2]\!]$, but only if the events shared by both ξ_1 and ξ_2 occur simultaneously. This is a consequence of Definition 5: event b (just like event '-') has only one associated time in $\mathcal{B}$, so that the time must be the same in both restrictions of $\mathcal{B}$.

One can think of the behaviours of the components as taking place concurrently, but synchronising on the shared events ("rendezvous" synchronisation).

Definition 6. *Let Ξ be a DTS over Σ. The function $dstr_\Xi : \Sigma \to 2^\Xi$, called the* distribution function *of Ξ, maps event $e \in \Sigma$ to $\{\xi \in \Xi \mid e \in \Sigma_\xi\}$.*

Definition 7. *Let $e \in \Sigma$ and let $|dstr_\Xi(e)| > 1$. Then e is called a* synchronising event *for the scenarios in $dstr_\Xi(e)$.*

If $e \in \Sigma$ is a synchronising event for some scenarios in Ξ, we sometimes say e is a synchronising event of Ξ. Observe that if $dstr_\Xi(e)$ is neither the empty set nor a singleton, and $\mathcal{B}$ is a distributed behaviour of Ξ, then event e must take place simultaneously in every $\mathcal{B}_\xi$, where $\xi \in dstr_\Xi(e)$.

The event '-' is a synchronising event for all the scenarios in Ξ, that is, $dstr_\Xi(\text{-}) = \Xi$. Its presence causes the behaviours of all the components to start at the same time. This is just a technical convenience. If the system described by the DTS is such that the behaviour described by a component ξ should start only after being triggered by an event e in another component, then this is easily modeled by making e the second event of ξ and imposing no constraints (in ξ) on the time distance between '-' and e. Similarly, if a behaviour of ξ is supposed to start with a delay of t time units, one can add an appropriate constraint for the time distance between '-' and the first "real" event of ξ.

It is often convenient to assume that event '-' occurs at time 0, i.e., $t_- = 0$.

Definition 8. *The* semantics *of a well-formed DTS, Ξ, denoted by $[\![\Xi]\!]$, is the set of behaviours that are allowed by Ξ.*

Given a DTS that models a particular aspect of a distributed time system, we are interested in knowing whether the semantics of the model includes any behaviours, i.e., whether the model is *consistent*.

Definition 9. *A well-formed DTS Ξ is* consistent *iff $[\![\Xi]\!] \neq \emptyset$. A DTS is* inconsistent *if it is not consistent.*

The DTS of Example 1 is consistent (behaviour $\mathcal{B}$, shown in Example 3, is in the semantics of the DTS).

Example 4. Consider the DTS $\Xi = \{\xi_1, \xi_2\}$, where $\xi_1 = (\text{-}abc, \{\tau_{\text{-},a} = 1, \tau_{a,b} = 1, \tau_{b,c} = 2\})$, $\xi_2 = (\text{-}dbc, \{\tau_{b,c} \geq 3\})$. Both scenarios, ξ_1 and ξ_2, are consistent, but it turns out that they cannot both be components of a consistent DTS, i.e., Ξ is inconsistent. Assume that $\mathcal{B} \in [\![\Xi]\!]$ exists. Then the events named b would have to take place simultaneously in $\mathcal{B}_{\xi_1}$ and $\mathcal{B}_{\xi_2}$, as would the events named c. The constraints $\tau_{\text{-},a} = 1$ and $\tau_{a,b} = 1$ in ξ_1 imply that b must occur at time 2 in $\mathcal{B}_{\xi_1}$. The constraints of ξ_2 allow b to also occur at time 2 in $\mathcal{B}_{\xi_2}$. However, once b has occurred, event c in $\mathcal{B}_{\xi_1}$ must take place exactly 2 units of time after b, i.e., at time 4 (because of the constraint $\tau_{b,c} = 2$ in ξ_1), but the constraint $\tau_{b,c} \geq 3$ in ξ_2 forces c in $\mathcal{B}_{\xi_2}$ to take place at least 3 units of time after b's occurrence, which is at time 5 or later. This means that behaviour $\mathcal{B}$ cannot exist.

Definition 10. *Let Ξ and Ξ' be two consistent distributed scenarios over Σ. We say Ξ and Ξ' are* equivalent *(denoted by $\Xi \equiv \Xi'$) iff $[\![\Xi]\!] = [\![\Xi']\!]$.*

Example 5. Let $\Xi' = \{\xi_3, \xi_4\}$, where $\xi_3 = (\text{-}abc, \{\tau_{\text{-},a} \leq 5, \tau_{a,b} \geq 1, \tau_{\text{-},c} \geq 5, \tau_{a,c} \leq 8, \tau_{b,c} \geq 3\})$, $\xi_4 = (\text{-}efb, \tau_{\text{-},e} \leq 8, \tau_{\text{-},f} \leq 10, \tau_{e,f} \leq 3, 2 \leq \tau_{e,b} \leq 6\})$, and consider Ξ of Example 1: $eseq(\xi_1) = eseq(\xi_3)$, $eseq(\xi_2) = eseq(\xi_4)$, but $[\![\xi_1]\!] \neq [\![\xi_3]\!]$ and $[\![\xi_2]\!] \neq [\![\xi_4]\!]$. However, $\Xi \equiv \Xi'$ (see Sect. 3.1 for details).

Example 6. Let $\Xi = \{\xi_1, \xi_2\}$ and $\Xi' = \{\xi_1\}$, where $\xi_1 = (\text{-}abc, \emptyset)$ and $\xi_2 = (\text{-}ac, \emptyset)$. Then Ξ and Ξ' are equivalent.

3.1 Distance Relations

Let Ξ be a consistent DTS. For $e_1, e_2 \in \Sigma_\Xi$ and $e_1 \prec_\Xi e_2$, we define $m^\Xi_{e_1 e_2} = min\{t^\mathcal{B}_{e_1 e_2} \mid \mathcal{B} \in [\![\Xi]\!]\}$ and $M^\Xi_{e_1 e_2} = max\{t^\mathcal{B}_{e_1 e_2} \mid \mathcal{B} \in [\![\Xi]\!]\}$. The absence of an upper bound for $t_{e_1 e_2}$ will be denoted by $M^\Xi_{e_1 e_2} = \infty$. For any behaviour $\mathcal{B}$ in $[\![\Xi]\!]$, $0 \le m^\Xi_{e_1 e_2} \le t^\mathcal{B}_{e_1 e_2} \le M^\Xi_{e_1 e_2} \le \infty$. We will write just $m_{e_1 e_2}$ and $M_{e_1 e_2}$ when Ξ is understood. For $e_1 \prec_\Xi e_2 \prec_\Xi e_3$ the following inequalities hold:

$$m_{e_1 e_2} + m_{e_2 e_3} \le m_{e_1 e_3} \le \left\{ \begin{array}{c} m_{e_1 e_2} + M_{e_2 e_3} \\ M_{e_1 e_2} + m_{e_2 e_3} \end{array} \right\} \le M_{e_1 e_3} \le M_{e_1 e_2} + M_{e_2 e_3} \qquad (1)$$

Obviously, the minimum time distance between e_1 and e_3 cannot be smaller than the sum of the minimum time distances between e_1 and e_2 and between e_2 and e_3. The other inequalities arise out of similar considerations. These inequalities are a generalisation of those for sequential scenarios [1].

Definition 11. *A distance relation is a pair* $(\prec, \mathcal{DF})$, *where* $\prec$ *is a strict partial order and* $\mathcal{DF} \colon \prec \to \mathbb{Q} \times \mathbb{Q}$ *is a total function, called a* distance function, *that maps* $(e_1, e_2) \in \prec$ *to an interval* $[l, h]$. *We use* $l_{e_1 e_2}$ *and* $h_{e_1 e_2}$ *to denote* l *and* h *for* (e_1, e_2), *respectively.*

Definition 12. *A distance relation,* $(\prec, \mathcal{DF})$, *is* valid *iff* $l_{e_1 e_2} \le h_{e_1 e_2}$ *for every* $e_1 \prec e_2$. *A distance relation that is not valid is* invalid.

Definition 13. *A distance relation,* $(\prec, \mathcal{DF})$, *is* stable *iff it is valid and, for every* $e_1 \prec e_2 \prec e_3$, *the following six inequalities hold*

$$l_{e_1 e_2} + l_{e_2 e_3} \le l_{e_1 e_3} \le \left\{ \begin{array}{c} l_{e_1 e_2} + h_{e_2 e_3} \\ h_{e_1 e_2} + l_{e_2 e_3} \end{array} \right\} \le h_{e_1 e_3} \le h_{e_1 e_2} + l_{e_2 e_3} \qquad (2)$$

A distance relation can capture the underlying partial order, as well as the constraints between the ordered events in a DTS, so it can be used as a representation of the salient features of the DTS.

Let $\Xi = \{\xi_1, \ldots, \xi_n\}$, where $\xi_i = (\mathcal{E}_i, \mathcal{C}_i)$ $(1 \le i \le n)$. We use $\mathcal{C}(\Xi)$ to denote the set of constraints in all the components of Ξ, i.e., $\mathcal{C}(\Xi) = \bigcup_{1 \le i \le n} \mathcal{C}_i$.

Definition 14. *Let* Ξ *be a well-formed DTS. For* $(e_1, e_2) \in \prec_\Xi$, *let* $L_{e_1 e_2} = \{l \mid \tau_{e_1, e_2} \ge l \in \mathcal{C}(\Xi)\}$ *and* $H_{e_1 e_2} = \{h \mid \tau_{e_1, e_2} \le h \in \mathcal{C}(\Xi)\}$. *The distance relation of* Ξ, $\mathcal{DR}_\Xi$, *is the pair* $(\prec_\Xi, \mathcal{DF}_\Xi)$, *where* $\mathcal{DF}_\Xi \colon \prec_\Xi \to \mathbb{Q} \times \mathbb{Q}$ *is a total function and* $\mathcal{DF}_\Xi(e_1, e_2) = [l_{e_1 e_2}, h_{e_1 e_2}]$, *such that*

- *if* $L_{e_1 e_2} \ne \emptyset$, *then* $l_{e_1 e_2} = \max\{l \mid l \in L_{e_1 e_2}\}$, *otherwise* $l_{e_1 e_2} = 0$.
- *if* $H_{e_1 e_2} \ne \emptyset$, *then* $h_{e_1 e_2} = \min\{h \mid h \in H_{e_1 e_2}\}$, *otherwise* $h_{e_1 e_2} = \infty$.

Intuitively, $\mathcal{DF}_\Xi(e_1, e_2) = [l_{e_1 e_2}, h_{e_1 e_2}]$ corresponds to a pair of constraints: the time distance between events e_1 and e_2 in every behaviour in $[\![\Xi]\!]$ must be at least $l_{e_1 e_2}$ and at most $h_{e_1 e_2}$.

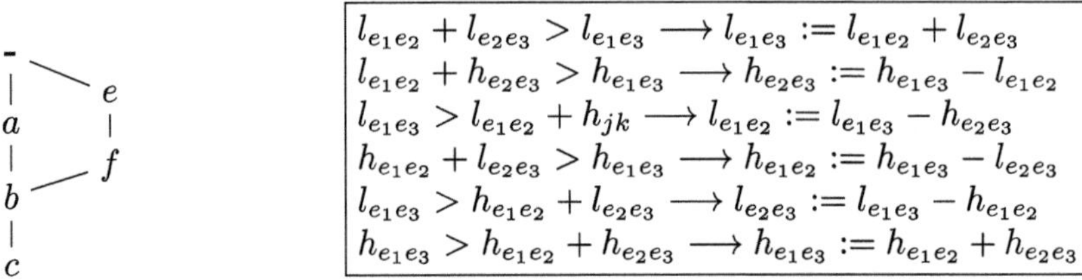

Fig. 1. Maximal chains

Fig. 2. Rules for stabilising a distance relation

Observation 1. *If $\mathcal{DR}_\Xi$ is invalid, then Ξ is inconsistent.*

In the DTS of Example 4, $L_{bc} = \{2,3\}$ (because of constraints $\tau_{b,c} = 2$ of ξ_1 and $\tau_{b,c} \geq 3$ of ξ_2), while $H_{bc} = \{2\}$ (because of the constraint $\tau_{b,c} = 2$ of ξ_1). So, $l_{bc} = \max\{2,3\} = 3$ and $h_{bc} = \min\{2\} = 2$, $l_{bc} \not\leq h_{bc}$, hence the DTS is invalid. As mentioned before, the DTS is inconsistent.

If X is a finite set partially ordered by $\prec$, the covering relation [28] of X is $\prec^c \subseteq \prec$, which includes only those pairs of elements that are immediate neighbours: $x \prec^c y$ iff $x \prec y$ and there is no element z such that $x \prec z \prec y$. The covering relation can be visually represented by a Hasse diagram, which shows the maximal chains (see Fig. 1).

In the rest of the paper we will represent a partial order by its chains and we will use a set of 4-tuples to represent a distance function. If $\mathcal{DR}_\Xi = (\prec_\Xi, \mathcal{DF}_\Xi)$ and $\mathcal{DF}_\Xi(e_1, e_2) = [l, h]$, then $\mathcal{DF}_\Xi$ contains the tuple (e_1, e_2, l, h). For brevity, tuples of the form $(e_1, e_2, 0, \infty)$ will not be included in our examples.

Example 7. For Ξ of Example 1, $H_{\text{-}a} = \{5\}$ (because of the constraint $\tau_{\text{-},a} \leq 5$ in ξ_1), so $h_{\text{-}a} = 5$. Because neither ξ_1 nor ξ_2 have constraints of the form $\tau_{\text{-},b} \geq u$ (for some u), $L_{\text{-}b} = \emptyset$, so, $l_{\text{-}b} = 0$. The distance relation is $\mathcal{DR}_\Xi = (\prec_\Xi, \mathcal{DF}_\Xi)$, where $\prec_\Xi$ is represented by the chains $- - a - b - c$ and $- - e - f - b - c$ (see Fig. 1), while $\mathcal{DF}_\Xi$ is represented by $\{(\text{-}, a, 0, 5), (a, b, 1, \infty), (a, c, 0, 8), (b, c, 3, \infty), (e, f, 0, 3), (e, b, 2, 6)\}$. This distance relation is not stable: the inequality $l_{\text{-}a} + l_{ab} \leq l_{\text{-}b} = 0 + 1 \leq 0$ does not hold, for example.

It is worth mentioning that the notion of distance relations can be applied to sequential scenarios: a scenario, ξ, is just a DTS with only one component, i.e., $\Xi = \{\xi\}$. In that case we will use $\mathcal{DR}_\xi$, instead of $\mathcal{DR}_\Xi$. Observe that if $\mathcal{DR}_\xi = (\prec_\xi, \mathcal{DF}_\xi)$, then $\prec_\xi$ is a total order. The distance relation of a sequential scenario is essentially its distance table [1].

Distance Relations and Consistency. A non-stable distance relation can be stabilised by a simple procedure that repeatedly applies the six rules shown in Fig. 2.[3] The purpose of each rule is to tighten a constraint (by increasing a

---

[3] The procedure is a generalisation of the one used for sequential scenarios [1].

lower bound or decreasing an upper bound) just enough to establish a particular inequality. If stabilisation is unsuccessful, i.e., during stabilisation the distance relation becomes invalid, then the stable distance relation does not exist, in which case the corresponding DTS is not consistent. The stabilisation procedure clearly terminates,[4] and—if successful—makes the constraints tight enough to satisfy (2), but no tighter.

We use $\mathcal{DR}^s_\Xi$ to denote the stable version of $\mathcal{DR}_\Xi$: if $\mathcal{DR}_\Xi$, obtained by Definition 14, is stable, then $\mathcal{DR}^s_\Xi = \mathcal{DR}_\Xi$, otherwise $\mathcal{DR}^s_\Xi$ is obtained by stabilising $\mathcal{DR}_\Xi$. If $\mathcal{DR}^s_\Xi = (\prec_\Xi, \mathcal{DF}^s_\Xi)$, then, for $(e_1, e_2) \in \prec_\Xi$, $\mathcal{DF}^s_\Xi(e_1, e_2) = [m_{e_1 e_2}, M_{e_1 e_2}]$. That is, all the constraints represented by $\mathcal{DF}^s_\Xi$, some of which are implied [2] by the initial set of constraints, are as tight as it is possible to make them without excluding some allowed behaviours.

Theorem 1. *Let* $\mathcal{DR}^s_\Xi$ *be a stable distance relation. Then* Ξ *is consistent.*

Proof. Let $\mathcal{DR}^s_\Xi = (\prec_\Xi, \mathcal{DF}^s_\Xi)$ and let $\mathcal{B}$ be a behaviour such that, for every $e \in \Sigma_\Xi \setminus \{\text{-}\}$, $t^{\mathcal{B}}_{\text{-}e} = m_{\text{-}e}$, where $\mathcal{DF}^s_\Xi(\text{-}, e) = [m_{\text{-}e}, M_{\text{-}e}]$. It can be easily shown that $\mathcal{B} \in [\![\Xi]\!]$. $\qquad\square$

Distance Relations and Concrete Behaviours. Given $\mathcal{DR}^s_\Xi = (\prec_\Xi, \mathcal{DF}^s_\Xi)$, any behaviour whose sequence of events respects $\prec_\Xi$ and whose event times satisfy the time constraints captured by $\mathcal{DF}^s_\Xi$ is in $[\![\Xi]\!]$.

Theorem 2. *Let* $\mathcal{DR}^s_\Xi = (\prec_\Xi, \mathcal{DF}^s_\Xi)$. *Then any value* $t_{e_1 e_2} \in \mathcal{DF}^s_\Xi(e_1, e_2)$ *can be extended to a sequence of times of a behaviour in* $[\![\Xi]\!]$.

Proof. The proof is a variant of the proof for the case of distance tables for sequential scenarios [29]. $\qquad\square$

The times of a concrete behaviour can be obtained by repeatedly choosing a concrete value in an interval and restabilising the resulting distance relation, until every interval collapses to a single value [29].

Distance Relations and Equivalence. It should be obvious that the stable distance relation of a DTS, if it exists, is unique.

Observation 2. *Let* Ξ *and* Ξ' *be two consistent distributed scenarios over* Σ. *If* $\mathcal{DR}^s_\Xi = \mathcal{DR}^s_{\Xi'}$, *then* $\Xi \equiv \Xi'$.

For Ξ of Example 1, $\mathcal{DF}^s_\Xi$ is represented by $\{(\text{-}, a, 0, 5), (\text{-}, b, 2, 10), (\text{-}, c, 5, 13), (\text{-}, e, 0, 8), (\text{-}, f, 0, 10), (a, b, 1, 5), (a, c, 4, 8), (b, c, 3, 7), (e, b, 2, 6), (e, c, 5, 13), (e, f, 0, 3), (f, b, 0, 6), (f, c, 3, 13)\}$ ($\prec_\Xi$ was shown in Example 7). The stable distance relation of Ξ' of Example 5 is the same, so, $\Xi \equiv \Xi'$.

Observation 2 provides a sufficient condition for the equivalence of distributed scenarios, but the condition is not necessary.

---

[4] The upper and lower bounds in the constraints are rational numbers. The values in all the constraints can be converted to integers by multiplying them by their smallest common denominator. At every step of stabilization a lower bound increases or an upper bound decreases. This process is repeated until no rule applies or the distance relation becomes invalid. Hence stabilisation terminates.

496   N. Saeedloei and F. Kluźniak

Example 8. Let $\Xi = \{\xi_1\}$, where $\xi_1 = (\text{-}abc, \{\tau_{\text{-},a} = 1, \tau_{\text{-},b} = 2, \tau_{\text{-},c} = 3\})$, and $\Xi' = \{\xi_2, \xi_3, \xi_4\}$, where $\xi_2 = (\text{-}a, \{\tau_{\text{-},a} = 1\})$, $\xi_3 = (\text{-}b, \{\tau_{\text{-},b} = 2\})$, and $\xi_4 = (\text{-}c, \{\tau_{\text{-},a} = 3\})$. The two distributed scenarios are equivalent: $[\![\Xi]\!] = [\![\Xi']\!] = \{(\text{-}, t_\text{-})(a, t_a)(b, t_b)(c, t_c) \mid 0 \le t_\text{-} \wedge t_a = 1 \wedge t_b = 2 \wedge t_c = 3\}$. But $\mathcal{DR}^s_\Xi \ne \mathcal{DR}^s_{\Xi'}$: $\prec_\Xi = \{(\text{-}, a), (\text{-}, b), (\text{-}, c), (a, b), (a, c), (b, c)\}$, while $\prec_{\Xi'} = \{(\text{-}, a), (\text{-}, b), (\text{-}, c)\}$, $\mathcal{DF}^s_\Xi$ is represented by $\{(\text{-}, a, 1, 1), (\text{-}, b, 2, 2), (\text{-}, c, 3, 3), (a, b, 1, 1), (a, c, 2, 2), (b, c, 1, 1)\}$, and $\mathcal{DF}^s_{\Xi'}$ is represented by $\{(\text{-}, a, 1, 1), (\text{-}, b, 2, 2), (\text{-}, c, 3, 3)\}$.

This example also shows that, given Ξ, $\mathcal{DR}^s_\Xi$ cannot be used as a canonical representation of all the distributed scenarios equivalent to Ξ. So our immediate goal is to find such a canonical representation.

3.2 Extended Distance Relations

Given Ξ, $\prec_\Xi$ captures the ordering of events within a component, as well as certain orderings between the events belonging to different components, but not orderings that are determined only by explicit constraints of different components. For example, in Ξ' of example 8, from $\prec_{\Xi'}$ one cannot infer that a occurs before b, and that b occurs before c. We can remedy that by extending $\prec_\Xi$ with (e, e') whenever e and e' belong to different components, but the timing constraints imply that e must occur before e'.

Definition 15. *Let $\mathcal{DR}^s = (\prec, \mathcal{DF}^s)$ be a stable distance relation. We define the valid extension of $\prec \subseteq \Sigma \times \Sigma$, denoted by $\prec^e$, to be the transitive closure of $\prec \cup \{(e, e') \mid \text{there exists } o \in \Sigma \text{ such that } M_{oe} < m_{oe'} \text{ or } M_{e'o} < m_{eo} \text{ in } \mathcal{DF}^s\}$. We call o a* pivot *of e and e'.*

The idea is to use Definition 15 to capture all the ordering dependencies between events in Ξ. We start with $\mathcal{DR}^s_\Xi = (\prec_\Xi, \mathcal{DF}^s_\Xi)$ and compute the valid extension of $\prec_\Xi$. If $\prec^e_\Xi \ne \prec_\Xi$, then the pair $(\prec^e_\Xi, \mathcal{DF}^s_\Xi)$ is not a distance relation, as $\mathcal{DF}^s_\Xi$ is not a total function. So we replace $\mathcal{DF}^s_\Xi$ with $\mathcal{DF}'$, which is an extension of $\mathcal{DF}^s_\Xi$ to $\prec^e_\Xi$: for every (e, e') in $\prec^e_\Xi \setminus \prec_\Xi$ we define $\mathcal{DF}'(e, e') = [0, \infty]$. Since the pair $(\prec^e_\Xi, \mathcal{DF}')$ is a distance relation, it can be stabilised. During stabilisation some of the intervals may become smaller (i.e., low values increase and high values decrease), so new opportunities for extending $\prec^e_\Xi$ might arise (see Definition 15). This process must be repeated until the partial order cannot be extended any further. We use $\prec^x_\Xi$ to denote the resulting partial order and call it the *extended partial order* of Ξ. The associated distance function, denoted by $\mathcal{DF}^{sx}_\Xi$, is the *extended distance function* of Ξ. Function $\mathcal{DF}^{sx}_\Xi$ maps (e, e') in $\prec^x_\Xi \setminus \prec_\Xi$ to an interval which is *implied* [2] by the original intervals in $\mathcal{DF}^s_\Xi$: it corresponds to the lower and upper bounds on the time distance between e and e' in all the behaviours of Ξ.

We call $\mathcal{DR}^{sx}_\Xi = (\prec^x_\Xi, \mathcal{DF}^{sx}_\Xi)$ the *(stable) extended distance relation* of Ξ.

Notice that $\prec^x_\Xi$ must be a strict partial order, because Ξ is consistent.

The interpretation is that if $e \prec^x_\Xi e'$, then e occurs before e' in every behaviour in $[\![\Xi]\!]$. The relation $\prec^x_\Xi$ is essentially Lamport's relation '$\rightarrow$' [30].

Observation 3. *If (e, e') in $\prec_\Xi^x \setminus \prec_\Xi$, then e and e' must be two events of two different components in Ξ.*

For Ξ' of Example 8, $M_{\text{-}a}^\Xi = 1 < m_{\text{-}b}^{\Xi'} = 2$ and $M_{\text{-}b}^\Xi = 2 < m_{\text{-}c}^{\Xi'} = 3$ in $\mathcal{DF}_{\Xi'}^s$: - is the pivot of a and b, and also of b and c. So $\prec_{\Xi'}$ can be extended with $(a, b), (b, c)$, and (a, c): $\prec_{\Xi'}^x = \{(-, a), (-, b), (-, c), (a, b), (a, c), (b, c)\}$. The extended distance function, $\mathcal{DF}_{\Xi'}^{sx}$, is represented by $\{(-, a, 1, 1), (-, b, 2, 2), (-, c, 3, 3), (a, b, 1, 1), (a, c, 2, 2), (b, c, 1, 1)\}$.

It is worth pointing out that for Ξ of Example 8, $\prec_\Xi^x = \prec_\Xi$. Therefore, $\mathcal{DR}_\Xi^s = \mathcal{DR}_\Xi^{sx}$, and, moreover, $\mathcal{DR}_\Xi^{sx} = \mathcal{DR}_{\Xi'}^{sx}$. As mentioned before, $\Xi \equiv \Xi'$.

$\mathcal{DR}_\Xi^{sx}$ is unique and specifies not only the underlying extended partial order of Ξ, but also all the timing dependencies between all the events of Ξ, not only the events within a component. While two equivalent distributed scenarios might have different stable distance relations, they have identical stable extended distance relations. In other words, $\mathcal{DR}_\Xi^{sx}$ is a canonical representation of the class of all distributed scenarios equivalent to Ξ.

Theorem 3. *Let Ξ and Ξ' be two consistent distributed scenarios over Σ. $\Xi \equiv \Xi'$ iff $\mathcal{DR}_\Xi^{sx} = \mathcal{DR}_{\Xi'}^{sx}$.*

Proof. If $\mathcal{DR}_\Xi^{sx} = \mathcal{DR}_{\Xi'}^{sx}$, then obviously $\Xi \equiv \Xi'$ (see Observation 2).

Assume $\Xi \equiv \Xi'$, but $\mathcal{DR}_\Xi^{sx} \neq \mathcal{DR}_{\Xi'}^{sx}$. Then there are two cases:

1. $\prec_\Xi^x = \prec_{\Xi'}^x$, but $\mathcal{DF}_\Xi^{sx} \neq \mathcal{DF}_{\Xi'}^{sx}$. Then, for some $(e, e') \in \prec_\Xi^x$, $\mathcal{DF}_\Xi^{sx}(e, e') \neq \mathcal{DF}_{\Xi'}^{sx}(e, e')$. Without loss of generality, assume there is a value $t \in \mathcal{DF}_\Xi^{sx}(e, e')$ such that $t \notin \mathcal{DF}_{\Xi'}^{sx}(e, e')$. By Theorem 2, t can be extended to a sequence of times of a behaviour, say $\mathcal{B}$, in $[\![\Xi]\!]$. But $\mathcal{B}$ cannot be in $[\![\Xi']\!]$.

2. $\prec_\Xi^x \neq \prec_{\Xi'}^x$. Without loss of generality assume that there is a pair $(e, e') \in \prec_\Xi^x$, such that $(e, e') \notin \prec_\Xi^x$. Then $[\![\Xi]\!]$ cannot include any behaviour in which e' occurs before e. But $[\![\Xi']\!]$ includes such a behaviour.

In both cases $\Xi \not\equiv \Xi'$, which is a contradiction. $\qquad\qquad\square$

Example 9. Let $\Xi = \{\xi_1\}$, where $\xi_1 = (\text{-}abc, \{3 \leq \tau_{\text{-},a} \leq 5, 4 \leq \tau_{\text{-},b} \leq 6, \tau_{a,c} = 2, \tau_{b,c} = 1\})$, and $\Xi' = \{\xi_2, \xi_3\}$, where $\xi_2 = (\text{-}ac, \{3 \leq \tau_{\text{-},a} \leq 5, \tau_{a,c} = 2\})$ and $\xi_3 = (\text{-}bc, \{4 \leq \tau_{\text{-},b} \leq 7, \tau_{b,c} = 1\})$. $\prec_{\Xi'} = \{(-, a), (-, b), (-, c), (a, c), (b, c)\}$, while $\mathcal{DF}_{\Xi'}^s$ is represented by $\{(-, a, 3, 5), (-, b, 4, 6), (-, c, 5, 7), (a, c, 2, 2), (b, c, 1, 1)\}$. Because $M_{bc}^{\Xi'} = 1 < m_{ac}^{\Xi'} = 2$, by Definition 15, $a \prec_{\Xi'}^x b$ (c is the pivot), and therefore, $\prec_{\Xi'}^x = \prec_{\Xi'} \cup \{(a, b)\}$. Moreover, $\mathcal{DF}_{\Xi'}^{sx} = \mathcal{DF}_{\Xi'}^s \cup \{(a, b, 1, 1)\}$. But $\prec_{\Xi'}^x = \prec_\Xi^x$ and $\mathcal{DF}_{\Xi'}^{sx} = \mathcal{DF}_\Xi^{sx}$, so $\mathcal{DR}_\Xi^{sx} = \mathcal{DR}_{\Xi'}^{sx}$, and therefore $\Xi \equiv \Xi'$.

As mentioned before, the notion of distance relations can be extended to sequential scenarios. For a single scenario the underlying total order between the events cannot be extended, i.e., the extended partial order is the same as the total order: the distance relation and the extended distance relation are the same.

Observation 4. *If ξ is a sequential scenario, then $\mathcal{DR}_\xi^s = \mathcal{DR}_\xi^{sx}$.*

3.3   Projections of Distributed Scenarios

Given a consistent DTS Ξ, with its stable extended distance relation $\mathcal{DR}^{sx}_{\Xi} = (\prec^x_{\Xi}, \mathcal{DF}^{sx}_{\Xi})$, our immediate goal is to identify all the behaviours of Ξ. All such behaviours must be compatible with $\mathcal{DR}^{sx}_{\Xi}$. That is, the sequences of events of the behaviours must agree with $\prec^x_{\Xi}$. Moreover, the event times of the behaviours must satisfy all the constraints captured by $\mathcal{DF}^{sx}_{\Xi}$.

We use the following simple procedure to identify all the behaviours in $[\![\Xi]\!]$. First, we generate all the possible permutations of events in Σ_{Ξ} that agree with $\prec^x_{\Xi}$: e_1 appears before e_2 in a permutation iff $e_2 \not\prec^x_{\Xi} e_1$. For each permutation, p, we create a sequential scenario $\xi_p = (p, \mathcal{C}_p)$, as follows. For every pair of events e and e' such that e appears before e' in p, if $e \prec^x_{\Xi} e'$, we add the constraints $l \leq \tau_{e,e'} \leq h$ to $\mathcal{C}_p$, where $\mathcal{DF}^{sx}_{\Xi}(e, e') = [l, h]$, otherwise we add the default constraints $0 \leq \tau_{e,e'} \leq \infty$ to $\mathcal{C}_p$. Then we stabilise the distance relation corresponding to ξ_p to obtain the final set of constraints of $\mathcal{C}_p$. What we obtain in this way is a set of consistent sequential scenarios (called the set of *projections of Ξ*), each of which allows a set of behaviours that is a subset of $[\![\Xi]\!]$.

Definition 16. *A sequential scenario ξ is a* projection *of DTS Ξ if $[\![\xi]\!] \subseteq [\![\Xi]\!]$ and, for every ξ' such that $[\![\xi]\!] \subsetneq [\![\xi']\!]$, $[\![\xi']\!] \not\subseteq [\![\Xi]\!]$.*

Given a consistent DTS Ξ, we use $\mathcal{P}_{\Xi}$ to denote its set of projections. Clearly, if Ξ is inconsistent then it has no projections.

Example 10. Scenario $\xi = (\text{-}abc, \{\tau_{\text{-},a} = 1, \tau_{\text{-},b} = 2, \tau_{\text{-},c} = 3\})$ is the only projection of Ξ and Ξ' of Example 8: $[\![\xi]\!] = \{(\text{-}, t_{\text{-}})(a, t_a)(b, t_b)(c, t_c) \mid 0 \leq t_{\text{-}} \wedge t_{\text{-}a} = 1 \wedge t_{\text{-}b} = 2 \wedge t_{\text{-}c} = 3\} = [\![\Xi]\!] = [\![\Xi']\!]$.

The semantics of projections are mutually disjoint, as each of them has a different sequence of events. Moreover, the sequences of events of the projections cover all the possible permutations of events that could form behaviours in $[\![\Xi]\!]$.

Observation 5. *Let Ξ be a consistent DTS and $\mathcal{P}_{\Xi}$ be its set of projections. Then $[\![\Xi]\!] = [\![\mathcal{P}_{\Xi}]\!]$.*

The significance of Observation 5 is that it allows us to formulate the semantics of distributed scenarios in terms of those of sequential timed scenarios.

Observation 6. *If Ξ is a consistent DTS over Σ, Σ_{Ξ} is its set of events, and $\mathcal{P}_{\Xi} = \{\xi_{p_1}, \ldots, \xi_{p_n}\}$ is its set of projections, then*

1. *each scenario ξ_{p_i} ($1 \leq i \leq n$) has a different sequence of events,*
2. *each event in Σ_{Ξ} occurs exactly once in each scenario ξ_{p_i} ($1 \leq i \leq n$), and*
3. *each scenario in $\mathcal{P}_{\Xi}$ begins with -.*

The consequence of property 2 of Observation 6 is that all the members of $\mathcal{P}_{\Xi}$ are of the same length, and of property 3 that the intersection of the total orders of events in the members of $\mathcal{P}_{\Xi}$ is a non-empty partial order (as long as $\Sigma_{\Xi} \neq \{\text{-}\}$).

Example 11. For Ξ of Example 1, $\mathcal{P}_\Xi = \{\xi_{p1}, \xi_{p2}, \xi_{p3}\}$, where
$\xi_{p1} = (\text{-}efabc, \{\tau_{e,f} \le 3, \tau_{\text{-},a} \le 5, 2 \le \tau_{e,b} \le 6, 1 \le \tau_{a,b}, \tau_{a,c} \le 8, 3 \le \tau_{b,c}\})$,
$\xi_{p2} = (\text{-}eafbc, \{\tau_{\text{-},a} \le 5, \tau_{e,f} \le 3, 2 \le \tau_{e,b} \le 6, 1 \le \tau_{a,b}, \tau_{a,c} \le 8, 3 \le \tau_{b,c}\})$,
$\xi_{p3} = (\text{-}aefbc, \{\tau_{\text{-},a} \le 5, \tau_{e,f} \le 3, 2 \le \tau_{e,b}, \tau_{a,c} \le 8, 3 \le \tau_{b,c}\})$.

Observation 7. *Let $\Xi = \{\xi\}$ be a DTS with a single component. Then $\mathcal{P}_\Xi = \Xi$.*

Since each member of $\mathcal{P}_\Xi$ has a unique sequence of events, it is not possible to replace a subset of scenarios in $\mathcal{P}_\Xi$ by their union [31]. Moreover, no member of $\mathcal{P}_\Xi$ is subsumed [31] by another member of $\mathcal{P}_\Xi$.

Observation 8. *$\mathcal{P}_\Xi$ is the smallest set of sequential scenarios such that the union of the semantics of its components equals the semantics of Ξ.*

The consequence of Observation 8 is that $\mathcal{P}_\Xi$ is a *canonical representation* of Ξ.

Theorem 4. *Let Ξ and Ξ' be two distributed scenarios. $\Xi \equiv \Xi'$ iff $\mathcal{P}_\Xi = \mathcal{P}_{\Xi'}$.*

Proof. Proof follows from Observation 5. $\qquad\qquad\qquad\qquad\qquad\qquad\qquad\qquad\square$

It is worth pointing out that we could obtain $\mathcal{P}_\Xi$ from $\mathcal{DR}^s_\Xi$, instead of $\mathcal{DR}^{sx}_\Xi$. But that would result in an inefficient algorithm. As an example consider Ξ' of example 8 once more. The set of all possible permutations that agree with $\prec_{\Xi'} = \{(\text{-}, a), (\text{-}, b), (\text{-}, c)\}$ is $\{\text{-}abc, \text{-}acb, \text{-}bac, \text{-}bca, \text{-}cab, \text{-}cba\}$. If $\mathcal{DR}^s_{\Xi'}$ were used instead of $\mathcal{DR}^{sx}_{\Xi'}$, the algorithm would consider six sequential scenarios corresponding to these six permutations. However, five of the permutations would be rejected (due to inconsistency) during the stabilisation of their distance relations: the set of constraints captured by $\mathcal{DF}^s_{\Xi'}$ implies that the only allowed permutation is *-abc*. When our algorithm uses $\prec^x_{\Xi'} = \{(\text{-}, a), (\text{-}, b), (\text{-}, c), (a, b), (a, c), (b, c)\}$, the only permutation that is considered is $\{\text{-}abc\}$, which is the only allowed permutation of events in behaviours of $[\![\Xi']\!]$.

Constructing Concrete Behaviours from Projections. In Sect. 3.1 we showed how to construct a concrete behaviour from a distance relation. Another way of doing this is to choose a projection that has the desired sequence of events, and apply a similar procedure to its distance table [29].

In Example 11 we might choose projection ξ_{p3}. Initially, $\mathcal{DF}^{sx}_{\xi_{p3}}$ includes the tuples $(e, f, 0, 3)$, $(a, b, 2, 5)$, $(f, c, 3, 8)$ and $(\text{-}, f, 0, 10)$. By setting t_{ef} to 2, stabilising, setting t_{ab} to 4, stabilising, setting t_{fc} to 6, stabilising, setting $t_{\text{-}f}$ to 6 and stabilising again we collapse all the intervals to single values, thus obtaining the behaviour $\mathcal{B} = (\text{-}, 0)(a, 4)(e, 4)(f, 6)(b, 8)(c, 12)$.

3.4   From Projections to Extended Distance Relations

Since $\mathcal{DR}^{sx}_\Xi$ and $\mathcal{P}_\Xi$ are both canonical representations of Ξ, it is natural to ask what is the relation between the two. In Sect. 3.3 we showed how the set of projections of a consistent DTS can be obtained from its stable extended distance relation. We will now show how to obtain $\mathcal{DR}^{sx}_\Xi$ from $\mathcal{P}_\Xi$.

Let $\mathcal{P}_\Xi = \{\xi_{p_1}, \xi_{p_2}, \ldots, \xi_{p_n}\}$ be a set of projections of some DTS Ξ, such that $\Sigma_\Xi \neq \{\text{-}\}$. Let $\{\mathcal{DR}^s_{\xi_{p_1}}, \ldots, \mathcal{DR}^s_{\xi_{p_n}}\}$ be the set of stable distance relations corresponding to the projections in $\mathcal{P}_\Xi$, where $\mathcal{DR}^s_{\xi_{p_i}} = (\prec_{\xi_{p_i}}, \mathcal{DF}_{\xi_{p_i}})$, for $1 \leq i \leq n$. Observe that each $\prec_{\xi_{p_i}}$ $(1 \leq i \leq n)$ is a total order. To obtain $\prec_{\mathcal{P}_\Xi}$, the underlying partial order of $\mathcal{P}_\Xi$, we take the intersection of the (strict) total orders corresponding to the projections, i.e., we compute $\prec_{\mathcal{P}_\Xi} = \bigcap_{1 \leq i \leq n} \prec_{\xi_{p_i}}$. To obtain the distance function, $\mathcal{DF}_{\mathcal{P}_\Xi}$, for every pair (e, e') in $\prec_{\mathcal{P}_\Xi}$, we define $\mathcal{DF}_{\mathcal{P}_\Xi}(e, e')$ to be the smallest interval that includes each $\mathcal{DF}_{\xi_{p_i}}(e, e')$, for $1 \leq i \leq n$. The resulting distance relation is stable, and it should be obvious that its partial order cannot be extended: $\mathcal{DR}^{sx}_\Xi = \mathcal{DR}_{\mathcal{P}_\Xi} = (\prec_{\mathcal{P}_\Xi}, \mathcal{DF}_{\mathcal{P}_\Xi})$.

Example 12. Let $\mathcal{P}_\Xi = \{\xi_{p_1}, \xi_{p_2}, \xi_{p_3}\}$ be the set of projections of some DTS Ξ, where $\xi_{p_1} = (\text{-}abdec, \{\tau_{\text{-},b} \leq 3, 4 \leq \tau_{\text{-},d}, 1 \leq \tau_{b,d}\})$, $\xi_{p_2} = (\text{-}abdce, \{\tau_{\text{-},b} \leq 3, 4 \leq \tau_{\text{-},d}, 1 \leq \tau_{b,d}\})$ and $\xi_{p_3} = (\text{-}abcde, \{\tau_{\text{-},b} \leq 3, 4 \leq \tau_{\text{-},d}, 1 \leq \tau_{b,d}\})$. The stable distance relation obtained from $\mathcal{P}_\Xi$ is $(\prec_{\mathcal{P}_\Xi}, \mathcal{DF}_{\mathcal{P}_\Xi})$, where $\prec_{\mathcal{P}_\Xi}$ is represented by the chains $\text{-} - a - b - c$ and $\text{-} - a - b - d - e$, while $\mathcal{DF}_{\mathcal{P}_\Xi}$ is represented by $\{(\text{-}, a, 0, 3), (\text{-}, b, 0, 3), (\text{-}, d, 4, \infty), (\text{-}, e, 4, \infty), (a, b, 0, 3), (a, d, 1, \infty), (a, e, 1, \infty), (b, d, 1, \infty), (b, e, 1, \infty)\}$.

4   Realisation of Sequential Scenarios as Distributed Scenarios

Given a set of sequential scenarios of equal lengths over the same set of events, our goal is to determine whether the set can be realised by a DTS, and, if so, to find such a DTS. We assume that the set of events in each potential component of the target DTS is also given.[5] More precisely:

> Given a finite set $\mathcal{S} = \{s_1, \ldots, s_n\}$ of sequential scenarios, and a finite set $\mathcal{D} = \{\Sigma_1, \ldots, \Sigma_m\}$ such that
> - members of $\mathcal{S}$ satisfy the properties of a set of projections (see Observation 6), in particular, each scenario contains all the events of the same set Σ,
> - $\bigcup_{1 \leq j \leq m} \Sigma_j = \Sigma$,
>
> we want to know whether there exists a DTS $\Xi_\mathcal{S} = \{\xi_1, \ldots, \xi_m\}$ over Σ, such that Σ_j is the set of events in component ξ_j $(1 \leq j \leq m)$ and $[\![\Xi_\mathcal{S}]\!] = [\![\mathcal{S}]\!]$. If so, we say $\mathcal{S}$ is *realisable with respect to* $\mathcal{D}$, by $\Xi_\mathcal{S}^{\mathcal{D}}$, and we produce $\Xi_\mathcal{S}^{\mathcal{D}}$. We say $\Xi_\mathcal{S}^{\mathcal{D}}$ is the *realisation* of $\mathcal{S}$ *with respect to* $\mathcal{D}$.

Example 13. Given the set of scenarios $\mathcal{S} = \{s_1\}$ over $\Sigma = \{\text{-}, a, b, c\}$, where $s_1 = (\text{-}abc, \{\tau_{a,c} = 7, \tau_{b,c} \geq 5\})$, and $\mathcal{D} = \{\{\text{-}, a, b\}, \{\text{-}, a, c\}\}$, $\mathcal{S}$ is realisable with respect to $\mathcal{D}$, by the DTS $\Xi_\mathcal{S}^{\mathcal{D}} = \{\xi_1, \xi_2\}$, where $\xi_1 = (\text{-}ab, \{\tau_{a,b} \leq 2\})$ and $\xi_2 = (\text{-}ac, \{\tau_{a,c} = 7\})$.

---

[5] In Sect. 4.1 we briefly discuss the case when this assumption does not hold.

We will now present an algorithm that solves the above problem in two steps. In the first step we assume that $\mathcal{S}$ is, in fact, a set of projections of some DTS[6] and compute the corresponding distance relation, $\mathcal{DR}_{\mathcal{S}} = (\prec_{\mathcal{S}}, \mathcal{DF}_{\mathcal{S}})$ (see Sect. 3.4). In the second step we check whether it is possible to extract (i) a total order between the events in each Σ_j $(1 \leq j \leq m)$ from $\prec_{\mathcal{S}}$, (ii) the constraints of each component from $\mathcal{DF}_{\mathcal{S}}$, in such a way that the semantics of the resulting DTS, $\Xi_{\mathcal{S}}^{\mathcal{D}}$, would be equal to that of $\mathcal{S}$. If so, we construct $\Xi_{\mathcal{S}}^{\mathcal{D}}$.

Our algorithm uses three criteria, described below, to perform these checks.

1. If the restriction of $\prec_{\mathcal{S}}$ to $\Sigma_j \in \mathcal{D}$, denoted by $\prec_{\mathcal{S}}\!\upharpoonright_{\Sigma_j}$, is a total order, then this is the order of events in the corresponding component ξ_j. If $\prec_{\mathcal{S}}\!\upharpoonright_{\Sigma_j}$ is not a total order for some j, then the events of Σ_j cannot form a component: $\prec_{\mathcal{S}}$ cannot be realised by a DTS such that one of its components is a scenario whose events include all of Σ_j.
2. If, in some chain c, there is a pair of neighbouring events e and e' such that there is no $\Sigma_k \in \mathcal{D}$ that includes both e and e', then the ordering of e and e' will not be reflected in the sequence of events of any component in the target DTS. In that case we must check that the ordering can be restored from the constraints captured by $\mathcal{DF}_{\mathcal{S}}$. That is, if $e \in \Sigma_i$ and $e' \in \Sigma_j$, then there is a pivot $o \in \Sigma_i \cap \Sigma_j$, such that $M_{oe} < m_{oe'}$ or $M_{e'o} < m_{eo}$ in $\mathcal{DF}_{\mathcal{S}}$.
3. Finally, if $e \prec_{\mathcal{S}} e'$, and there is no $\Sigma_k \in \mathcal{D}$ that includes both e and e', we must check that if $\mathcal{DF}_{\mathcal{S}}(e, e') = [u, v]$, then each of the constraints $\tau_{e,e'} \geq u$ and $\tau_{e,e'} \leq v$ is either a default constraint or is implied by the constraints of the target DTS. The reason for this is that e and e' would belong to two different components in the target DTS, so there would be no explicit time constraints between the two events. The semantics of $\mathcal{S}$ would be preserved only if all such time constraints were implied by the set of explicit constraints that would accompany the components of the target DTS.

The second step of our method is performed by Algorithm 1. We assume that $\mathcal{S}$ and $\mathcal{D}$ meet the requirements stated at the beginning of this section.

Example 14. Let $\mathcal{S} = \{s_1, s_2, s_3\}$, where $s_1 = (\text{-}abcde, \{\tau_{\text{-},b} = 3, \tau_{b,d} \geq 1\})$, $s_2 = (\text{-}abdce, \{\tau_{\text{-},b} = 3, \tau_{b,d} \geq 1\})$, and $s_3 = (\text{-}abdec, \{\tau_{\text{-},b} = 3, \tau_{b,d} \geq 1\})$. The distance relation obtained from $\mathcal{S}$ is $(\prec_{\mathcal{S}}, \mathcal{DF}_{\mathcal{S}})$, where $\prec_{\mathcal{S}}$ is represented by two chains $\text{-} - a - b - c$ and $\text{-} - a - b - d - e$, and $\mathcal{DF}_{\mathcal{S}}$ is represented by $\{(\text{-}, a, 0, 3), (\text{-}, b, 3, 3), (\text{-}, c, 3, \infty), (\text{-}, d, 4, \infty), (\text{-}, e, 4, \infty), (a, b, 0, 3), (a, d, 1, \infty),$ $(a, e, 1, \infty), (b, d, 1, \infty), (b, e, 1, \infty)\}$. It turns out that it is not possible to realise $\mathcal{S}$ by a DTS whose sets of events are given by $\mathcal{D} = \{\{\text{-}, a, c, d\}, \{\text{-}, a, b, e\}\}$. This is because the restriction of $\prec_{\mathcal{S}}$ to $\{\text{-}, a, c, d\}$ is represented by $\text{-} - a - c$ and $\text{-} - a - d$, which is not a single chain, i.e., it is not a total order, hence the events of $\{\text{-}, a, c, d\}$ cannot form a component. But if $\mathcal{D}$ is changed to $\mathcal{D}' = \{\{\text{-}, a, b, c\}, \{\text{-}, d, e\}\}$, then $\mathcal{S}$ is realisable with respect to $\mathcal{D}'$, by DTS $\Xi_{\mathcal{S}}^{\mathcal{D}'} = \{\xi_1, \xi_2\}$, where $\xi_1 = (\text{-}abc, \{\tau_{\text{-},b} = 3\})$ and $\xi_2 = (\text{-}de, \{\tau_{\text{-},d} \geq 4\})$.

---

[6] This might not be the case. See Sect. 4.2 for details.

Algorithm 1: Determining realisability of a set of sequential scenarios

Input : A set $\mathcal{S}$ of scenarios and a set $\mathcal{D}$ of sets of events.
Output: A DTS or the empty set.

$R := True$;
$components := \emptyset$;
Let $\mathcal{DR}_\mathcal{S} = (\prec_\mathcal{S}, \mathcal{DF}_\mathcal{S})$;
$\mathcal{D}' := \mathcal{D}$;
while $R \wedge \mathcal{D}' \neq \emptyset$ **do**

> Let $\Sigma_j \in \mathcal{D}'$;
> $\mathcal{D}' := \mathcal{D}' \setminus \{\Sigma_j\}$;
> $\mathcal{C} := \emptyset$;
> **if** $\prec_\mathcal{S}\!\restriction_{\Sigma_j}$ *is a total order* **then**
>
> > **foreach** $(e, e') \in \prec_\mathcal{S}\!\restriction_{\Sigma_j}$ **do**
> >
> > > $\mathcal{C} := \mathcal{C} \cup \{\tau_{e,e'} \geq u, \tau_{e,e'} \leq v\}$, where $\mathcal{DF}_\mathcal{S}(e, e') = [u, v]$;
> >
> > $\mathcal{E} := \Sigma_j$ ordered by $\prec_\mathcal{S}\!\restriction_{\Sigma_j}$;
> > $components := components \cup \{(\mathcal{E}, \mathcal{C})\}$;
>
> **else**
>
> > $R := False$;

if R **then**

> **foreach** $e \prec_\mathcal{S}^c e'$ *such that there is no $\Sigma_k \in \mathcal{D}$ that contains e and e'* **do**
>
> > **if** *there are no Σ_i and Σ_j such that $(e \in \Sigma_i \wedge e' \in \Sigma_j$ and there exists some $a \in \Sigma_i \cap \Sigma_j$ where $M_{ae} < m_{ae'}$ or $M_{e'a} < m_{ea})$* **then**
> >
> > > $R := False$;

if R **then**

> $\mathcal{DF}'_\mathcal{S} := \mathcal{DF}_\mathcal{S}$;
> **foreach** $e \prec_\mathcal{S} e'$ *such that there is no $\Sigma_k \in \mathcal{D}$ that contains e and e'* **do**
> > $\mathcal{DF}'_\mathcal{S}(e, e') = [0, \infty]$;
>
> stabilise $\mathcal{DR}'_\mathcal{S} = (\prec_\mathcal{S}, \mathcal{DF}'_\mathcal{S})$;
> **if** $\mathcal{DR}_\mathcal{S} \neq \mathcal{DR}'_\mathcal{S}$ **then**
> > $R := False$;

if $\neg R$ **then**
> $components := \emptyset$;

return $components$;

Observe that the restriction of $\prec_\mathcal{S}$ to $\{\text{-}, a, b, c\}$ is the total order $\text{-}abc$, and to $\{\text{-}, d, e\}$ is a total order, $\text{-}de$. Notice that b and d are neighbouring events in the chain $\text{-}-a-b-d-e$, but they belong to two different components (b to ξ_1 and d to ξ_2) in $\Xi_\mathcal{S}^{\mathcal{D}'}$. So our algorithm checks that the ordering between them is restored in $\Xi_\mathcal{S}^{\mathcal{D}'}$, that is, in all the behaviours of $[\![\Xi_\mathcal{S}^{\mathcal{D}'}]\!]$ b occurs before d. This is done by determining that $\mathcal{DF}_\mathcal{S}$ includes $(\text{-}, b, 3, 3)$ and $(\text{-}, d, 4, \infty)$: $M_{\text{-}b} = 3 < m_{\text{-}d} = 4$, so - is a pivot, which is included in both ξ_1 and ξ_2. The inclusion of constraints $\tau_{\text{-},b} = 3$ in ξ_1 and $\tau_{\text{-},d} \geq 4$ in ξ_2 guarantees that b always occurs before d.

Notice that the time distance between b and d in every behaviour of $[\![\mathcal{S}]\!]$ is at least 1, which is captured by the tuple $(b, d, 1, \infty)$ in $\mathcal{DF}_\mathcal{S}$. Our algorithm checks that this constraint is implied by $\tau_{-,b} = 3$ in ξ_1 and $\tau_{-,d} \geq 4$ in ξ_2 of $\Xi_\mathcal{S}^{\mathcal{D}'}$.

Example 15. Consider $\mathcal{S}$ of Example 13 and let $\mathcal{D}' = \{\{-, a, b\}, \{-, b, c\}\}$. The distance relation obtained from $\mathcal{S}$ is $(\prec_\mathcal{S}, \mathcal{DF}_\mathcal{S})$, where $\prec_\mathcal{S}$ is represented by the chain $- \, - \, a \, - \, b \, - \, c$ and $\mathcal{DF}_\mathcal{S}$ is represented by $\{(-, c, 7, \infty), (a, b, 0, 2), (a, c, 7, 7), (b, c, 5, 7)\}$. Observe that the restrictions of $\prec_\mathcal{S}$ to $\{-, a, b\}$ and to $\{-, b, c\}$ are both total orders. Notice that $a \prec_\mathcal{S} c$, but a and c must belong to different components, say ξ_1 and ξ_2. The time distance between a and c in every behaviour of $[\![\mathcal{S}]\!]$ is 7 (because of $(a, c, 7, 7)$ in $\mathcal{DF}_\mathcal{S}$), but this constraint is not implied by the remaining constraints of $\mathcal{DF}_\mathcal{S}$ that would accompany components ξ_1 and ξ_2. So, there is no DTS that realises $\mathcal{S}$ with respect to $\mathcal{D}'$.

4.1 "Uninformed" Realisation

The assumption of Algorithm 1 of Sect. 4 was that, in addition to the set of projections, we are given the set of events that should appear in each component. If only the set of projections, $\mathcal{S}$, is given, then there might be more than one DTS that realises $\mathcal{S}$. One such DTS can be trivially obtained by first building the distance relation from $\mathcal{S}$ and then using each chain of the distance relation as the sequence of events of a component of the DTS. However, obtaining all the realisations of $\mathcal{S}$ would require checking the constraints on the time distance between each pair of events, and the number of realisations could be quite large.

Example 16. Let $\mathcal{S} = \{s_1, s_2\}$, where $s_1 = (-abc, \{\tau_{-,a} \leq 2, 5 \leq \tau_{-,b}\})$ and $s_2 = (-acb, \{\tau_{-,a} \leq 2, 5 \leq \tau_{-,c}\})$. The maximal chains obtained from the distance relation of $\mathcal{S}$ are $- \, - \, a \, - \, b$ and $- \, - \, a \, - \, c$. So one DTS that realises $\mathcal{S}$ is $\Xi_1 = \{\xi_1, \xi_2\}$, where $\xi_1 = (-ab, \{\tau_{-,a} \leq 2, 5 \leq \tau_{-,b}, 3 \leq \tau_{a,b}\})$ and $\xi_2 = (-ac, \{\tau_{-,a} \leq 2, 5 \leq \tau_{-,c}, 3 \leq \tau_{a,c}\})$. However, there are three more realisations of $\mathcal{S}$:

$\Xi_2 = \{\xi_3, \xi_4\}$, where $\xi_3 = (-ac, \{\tau_{-,a} \leq 2, 5 \leq \tau_{-,c}, 3 \leq \tau_{a,c}\})$ and $\xi_4 = (-b, \{5 \leq \tau_{-,b}\})$,

$\Xi_3 = \{\xi_5, \xi_6\}$, where $\xi_5 = (-ab, \{\tau_{-,a} \leq 2, 5 \leq \tau_{-,b}, 3 \leq \tau_{a,b}\})$ and $\xi_6 = (-c, \{5 \leq \tau_{-,c}\})$,

$\Xi_4 = \{\xi_7, \xi_8, \xi_9\}$, where $\xi_7 = (-a, \{\tau_{-,a} \leq 2\})$, $\xi_8 = (-b, \{5 \leq \tau_{-,b}\})$ and $\xi_9 = (-c, \{5 \leq \tau_{-,c}\})$.

Notice that all of these four distributed scenarios would be represented by the same extended distance relation (see Sect. 3.2).

4.2 False Projections

A set of sequential scenarios might satisfy all the properties of a set of projections (see Observation 6), but not be a set of projections of any DTS.

Example 17. Let $\mathcal{P} = \{\xi_{p_1}, \xi_{p_2}\}$, where $\xi_{p_1} = (\text{-}ab, \{\tau_{\text{-},b} \leq 1\})$ and $\xi_{p_2} = (\text{-}ba, \tau_{\text{-},a} \leq 3\})$. The distance relation derived from $\mathcal{P}$, $\mathcal{DR}_\mathcal{P}$, is $(\prec_\mathcal{P}, \mathcal{DF}_\mathcal{P})$, where $\prec_\mathcal{P}$ is represented by two chains, $\text{-}-a$ and $\text{-}-b$, while $\mathcal{DF}_\mathcal{P}$ is represented by $\{(\text{-}, a, 0, 3), (\text{-}, b, 0, 3)\}$. Observe that $\mathcal{P}$ satisfies the properties of a set of projections (Observation 6), however, it turns out that $\mathcal{P}$ is not a set of projections of any DTS. This is because $\mathcal{DR}_\mathcal{P}$ allows behaviour $\mathcal{B} = (\text{-}, 0)(a, 2)(b, 3)$, for example. However, $\mathcal{B}$ is not in $[\![\xi_{p_1}]\!] \cup [\![\xi_{p_2}]\!]$: according to ξ_{p_1} event a can occur before b only when both take place within 1 unit of time since the occurrence of -, and according to ξ_{p_2} event a cannot occur before b. It is worth pointing out that if $\Xi = \{\xi_3, \xi_4\}$, where $\xi_3 = (\text{-}a, \{\tau_{\text{-},a} \leq 3\})$ and $\xi_4 = (\text{-}b, \{\tau_{\text{-},b} \leq 3\})$, then $[\![\xi_{p_1}]\!] \subseteq [\![\Xi]\!]$ and $[\![\xi_{p_2}]\!] \subseteq [\![\Xi]\!]$. So it might seem that $\mathcal{P}$ is realisable by Ξ, but the semantics of the two would not be identical: $\mathcal{P}$ is a set of false projections.

Identifying false projections is directly relevant to the problem of realisability of projections: a set of false projections cannot be realised by a DTS.

We use a simple method for identifying false projections. Given a set $\mathcal{P}$ of sequential scenarios that satisfies the properties of a set of projections (see Observation 6), first we compute the distance relation, $\mathcal{DR}_\mathcal{P}$. Then we obtain the set of projections corresponding to $\mathcal{DR}_\mathcal{P}$ (see Sect. 3.3) and compare it with $\mathcal{P}$. If they are not identical then $\mathcal{P}$ is a set of false projections.

5   An Extended Example: Timed Treatment Plans

Figure 3 shows a DTS[7] describing various steps that are taken (after triage) by healthcare team members in an Emergency Department (ED) for a patient who is suspected of having a stroke. This is a simplified example and each event in a scenario corresponds to the completion of a task.

After the initial evaluation, which occurs between 5 and 7 minutes after triage, the ER doctor (see component **ER doctor** in Fig. 3) orders a CT scan of the brain to rule out intracranial bleeding, followed by an MRI to assess the extent of ischemic stroke damage. Both of these must be performed immediately (see **Stat** in both orders). The order for CT scan, for example, takes at least 2 minutes and at most 5 minutes, after the initial evaluation. The doctor expects the reports of CT scan and MRI to be ready within 30 minutes since he places the MRI order. **CT-Stat** is a synchronising event between **ER doctor, nurse** and **CT technologist**: once the order is placed, both the nurse and the CT technologist are able to see the order. Now the nurse can prepare the patient for the CT scan, while the technologist is preparing to take the scan. Similarly, **MRI-Stat** is a synchronizing event between **ER doctor, nurse** and **MRI technologist**. The MRI technologist expects to receive the MRI checklist between 5 and 10 minutes since the MRI order is received. Since the MRI checklist is completed by the nurse with the help of the patient, **checklist** is a synchronizing event between **nurse, patient** and **MRI technologist**: it is completed at the same time for all of them. The rest of the components can be understood similarly.

---

[7] To avoid visual clutter, the constraints include the (integer) labels of events, instead of event names.

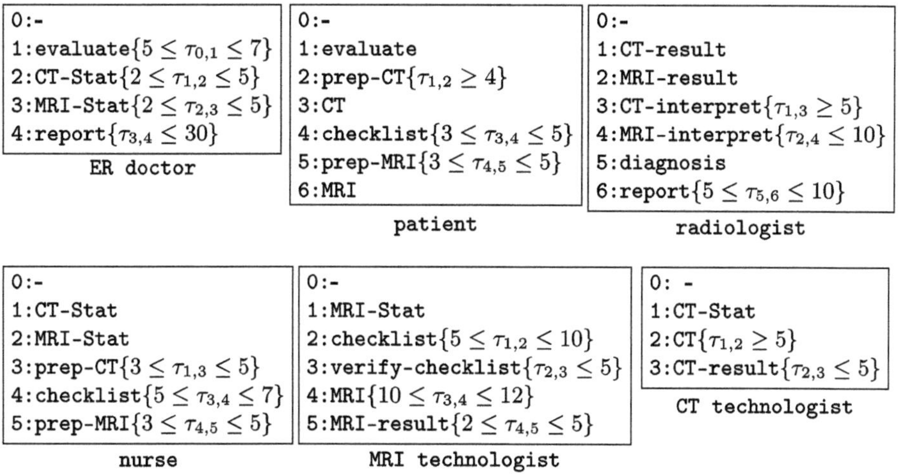

Fig. 3. A DTS describing a treatment plan for a patient suspected of having a stroke

Once the time of '-' is fixed (i.e., a treatment begins), concrete schedules for all the participants can be easily obtained from the DTS: for example, the nurse will know that `prep-CT` must end between 10 and 17 minutes after '-'. Progress in the treatment corresponds to an actual behaviour becoming more and more concrete: some time intervals become concrete time values. As a result, the remaining constraints in the DTS can be tightened (see the end of Sect. 3.3), and the schedules updated accordingly. For example, if the doctor performs `evaluate` in 5 minutes and `CT-Stat` in 3 minutes, then the nurses's schedule for `prep-CT` is updated to between 11 and 13 minutes after '-'.

6 Conclusions

We introduce the notion of distributed timed scenarios and their semantics. Given a distributed scenario (DTS), Ξ, we define its semantics, $[\![\Xi]\!]$, in terms of the set of behaviours that are allowed by Ξ. A behaviour $\mathcal{B}$ of Ξ is obtained by merging the behaviours of the individual components in Ξ in such a way that the order of events does not violate $\prec_{\Xi}^{x}$, the underlying (extended) partial order on events of Ξ. Moreover, each event that occurs in more than one component (called a synchronizing event) occurs only once.

We formally define the consistency of distributed scenarios, in terms of their semantics, and formulate a criterion (Theorem 1), as well as a practical method for determining the consistency of a DTS.

We define the notion of equivalence of two consistent distributed scenarios and identify two canonical representations for the class of distributed scenarios that are equivalent to a given one. These are the stable extended distance relation and the set of projections of a DTS (Theorem 3 and Theorem 4).

We tackle the problem of realisability of sets of sequential scenarios as distributed scenarios. We develop an algorithm that determines whether a set of sequential scenarios, $\mathcal{S}$, can be realised by a DTS, i.e., whether there exists a DTS Ξ, such that $[\![\mathcal{S}]\!] = [\![\Xi]\!]$. If so, the algorithm produces Ξ.

As a motivating example we present a DTS that specifies the collaborative tasks of healthcare team members in an Emergency Department in the course of the treatment of a patient.

The algorithms for determining consistency, equivalence and realisability are implemented and available online [32].

References

1. Saeedloei, N., Kluźniak, F.: Timed Scenarios: consistency, equivalence and optimization. In: Massoni, T., Mousavi, M.R. (eds.) SBMF 2018. LNCS, vol. 11254, pp. 215–233. Springer, Cham (2018). https://doi.org/10.1007/978-3-030-03044-5_14
2. Saeedloei, N., Kluźniak, F.: Optimization of timed scenarios. In: Carvalho, G., Stolz, V. (eds.) SBMF 2020. LNCS, vol. 12475, pp. 119–136. Springer, Cham (2020). https://doi.org/10.1007/978-3-030-63882-5_8
3. Saeedloei, N., Kluźniak, F.: Synthesizing clock-efficient timed automata. In: Dongol, B., Troubitsyna, E. (eds.) IFM 2020. LNCS, vol. 12546, pp. 276–294. Springer, Cham (2020). https://doi.org/10.1007/978-3-030-63461-2_15
4. Saeedloei, N., Kluźniak, F.: Synthesizing timed automata with minimal numbers of clocks from optimised timed scenarios. In: Castiglioni, V., Francalanza, A. (eds.), Formal Techniques for Distributed Objects, Components, and Systems - 44th IFIP WG 6.1 International Conference, FORTE 2024, Held as part of the 19th International Federated Conference on Distributed Computing Techniques, DisCoTec 2024, Groningen, The Netherlands, 17-21 June 2024, Proceedings, vol. 14678, pp. 136–154. LNCS, Springer (2024). https://doi.org/10.1007/978-3-031-62645-6_8
5. Saeedloei, N., Kluźniak, F.: From scenarios to timed automata. In: Cavalheiro, S., Fiadeiro, J. (eds.) SBMF 2017. LNCS, vol. 10623, pp. 33–51. Springer, Cham (2017). https://doi.org/10.1007/978-3-319-70848-5_4
6. Dechter, R., Meiri, I., Pearl, J.: Temporal constraint networks. Artif. Intell. **49**(1), 61–95 (1991)
7. Harel, D., Thiagarajan, P.S.: Message Sequence Charts, pp. 77–105. Springer, US, Boston, MA (2003). https://doi.org/10.1007/b105972
8. ITU-T recommendation Z.120. Message Sequence Charts (MSC 1996) (1996). ITU Telecommunication Standardization Sector
9. Alur, R., Holzmann, G.J., Peled, D.A.: An analyzer for message sequence charts. Software - Concepts and Tools **17**(2), 70–77 (1996)
10. Alur, R., Etessami, K., Yannakakis, M.: Inference of message sequence charts. IEEE Trans. Softw. Eng. **29**(7), 623–633 (2003)
11. Ben-Abdallah, H., Leue, S.: Timing constraints in message sequence chart specifications. In: Mizuno, T., Shiratori, N., Higashino, T., Togashi, A. (eds.) Formal Description Techniques and Protocol Specification, Testing and Verification. ITIFIP, pp. 91–106. Springer, Boston, MA (1997). https://doi.org/10.1007/978-0-387-35271-8_6
12. Chandrasekaran, P., Mukund, M.: Matching scenarios with timing constraints. In: Asarin, E., Bouyer, P. (eds.) Formal Modeling and Analysis of Timed Systems, pp. 98–112. Springer, Berlin, Heidelberg (2006). https://doi.org/10.1007/11867340_8

13. Akshay, S., Bollig, B., Gastin, P.: Automata and logics for timed message sequence charts. In: Arvind, V., Prasad, S. (eds.) FSTTCS 2007. LNCS, vol. 4855, pp. 290–302. Springer, Heidelberg (2007). https://doi.org/10.1007/978-3-540-77050-3_24

14. Damm, W., Harel, D.: LSC's: breathing life into message sequence charts. In: Ciancarini, P., Fantechi, A., Gorrieri, R. (eds.) Formal Methods for Open Object-Based Distributed Systems, pp. 293–311. Springer, US, Boston, MA (1999). https://doi.org/10.1023/A:1011227529550

15. Klose, J., Wittke, H.: An automata based interpretation of live sequence charts. In: Margaria, T., Yi, W. (eds.) Tools and Algorithms for the Construction and Analysis of Systems, pp. 512–527. Springer, Berlin, Heidelberg (2001). https://doi.org/10.1007/3-540-45319-9_35

16. Lucas, P.: Timed semantics of message sequence charts based on timed automata. Electron. Notes Theor. Comput. Sci. **65**(6), 160–179 (2002)

17. Sun, J., Dong, J.S.: Model checking live sequence charts. In: 10th IEEE International Conference on Engineering of Complex Computer Systems (ICECCS 2005), pp. 529–538 (2005)

18. Bengtsson, J., Larsen, K., Larsson, F., Pettersson, P., Yi, W.: UPPAAL — a tool suite for automatic verification of real-time systems. In: Alur, R., Henzinger, T.A., Sontag, E.D. (eds.) HS 1995. LNCS, vol. 1066, pp. 232–243. Springer, Heidelberg (1996). https://doi.org/10.1007/BFb0020949

19. Balaguer, S., Chatain, T., Haar, S.: A concurrency-preserving translation from Time Petri Nets to networks of timed automata. Formal Methods Syst. Des. **40**(3), 330–355 (2012)

20. Watanabe, K., Fainekos, G., Hoxha, B., Lahijanian, M., Prokhorov, D., Sankaranarayanan, S., Yamaguchi, T.: Timed partial order inference algorithm. In: Proceedings of the International Conference on Automated Planning and Scheduling, vol. 33, pp. 639–647 (2023)

21. Bejleri, A., Yoshida, N.: Synchronous multiparty session types. Electron. Notes Theor. Comput. Sci. **241**, 3–33 (2009). In: Proceedings of the First Workshop on Programming Language Approaches to Concurrency and Communication-centric Software (PLACES 2008)

22. Castagna, G., Dezani-Ciancaglini, M., Padovani, L.: On global types and multiparty sessions. In: Bruni, R., Dingel, J. (eds.) FMOODS/FORTE -2011. LNCS, vol. 6722, pp. 1–28. Springer, Heidelberg (2011). https://doi.org/10.1007/978-3-642-21461-5_1

23. Honda, K., Yoshida, N., Carbone, M.: Multiparty asynchronous session types. J. ACM **63**(1), 9:1–9:67 (2016)

24. Hüttel, H., et al.: Foundations of session types and behavioural contracts. ACM Comput. Surv. **49**(1), 3:1–3:36 (2016)

25. ter Beek, M.H., Hennicker, R., Proença, J.: Realisability of global models of interaction. In: Ábrahám, E., Dubslaff, C., Tarifa, S.L.T. (eds.) Theoretical Aspects of Computing - ICTAC 2023, pp. 236–255. Springer Nature Switzerland, Cham (2023). https://doi.org/10.1007/978-3-031-47963-2_15

26. Barbanera, F., Lanese, I., Tuosto, E.: Formal choreographic languages. In: ter Beek, M.H., Sirjani, M. (eds.) Coordination Models and Languages, pp. 121–139. Springer Nature Switzerland, Cham (2022). https://doi.org/10.1007/978-3-031-08143-9_8

27. Alur, R., Dill, D.L.: A theory of timed automata. Theor. Comput. Sci. **126**(2), 183–235 (1994)

28. https://en.wikipedia.org/wiki/Covering_relation

29. Saeedloei, N.: On the existence of unions of timed scenarios. In: Nogueira, S.C., Teodorov, C., (eds.), Formal Methods: Foundations and Applications - 27th Brazilian Symposium, SBMF 2024, Vitória, Brazil, 4-6 December 2024, Proceedings, vol. 15403, pp. 3–21. LNCS, Springer (2024)
30. Lamport, L.: Time, clocks, and the ordering of events in a distributed system. Commun. ACM **21**(7), 558–565 (1978)
31. Saeedloei, N., Kluźniak, F.: Operations on timed scenarios. In: Huisman, M., Ravara A., (eds.), Formal Techniques for Distributed Objects, Components, and Systems - 43rd IFIP WG 6.1 International Conference, FORTE 2023, Held as Part of the 18th International Federated Conference on Distributed Computing Techniques, DisCoTec 2023, Lisbon, Portugal, 19-23 June 2023, Proceedings, vol. 13910, pp. 97–114. LNCS, Springer (2023). https://doi.org/10.1007/978-3-031-35355-0
32. Kluźniak, F.: A tool-set for distributed timed scenarios. https://tigerweb.towson.edu/nsaeedloei/ (see Tools)

Author Index

F. Damiani and M. Farrell (Eds.): iFM 2025, LNCS 16194, pp. 509–510, 2026.
https://doi.org/10.1007/978-3-032-10794-7